An Invitation to
Old English
and
Anglo-Saxon England

B

For
MOLLIE
who has shared in all my work

οὐ μὲν γὰρ τοῦ γε κρεῖσσον καὶ ἄρειον
ἢ ὅθ᾽ ὁμοφρονέοντε νοήμασιν οἶκον ἔχητον
ἀνὴρ ἠδὲ γυνή.

Homer, *Odyssey* 6. 182

There is no better state than this –
A man and woman sharing like pursuits
Together keeping house.

An Invitation to
Old English
and
Anglo-Saxon England

from
Bruce Mitchell

BLACKWELL
Oxford UK & Cambridge USA

The right of Bruce Mitchell to be identified as author of this work has been
asserted in accordance with the Copyright, Designs and Patents Act 1988.

First published 1995
Reprinted 1996 (twice), 1997 (twice), 1998 (with revisions and corrections), 2000

Blackwell Publishers Ltd
108 Cowley Road
Oxford OX4 1JF, UK

Blackwell Publishers Inc.
350 Main Street
Malden, Massachusetts 02148, USA

British Library Cataloguing in Publication Data
A CIP catalogue record for this book is available from the British Library

Library of Congress Cataloging in Publication Data
Mitchell, Bruce, 1920–
An invitation to Old English and Anglo-Saxon England / from Bruce Mitchell
p.   cm.
Includes bibliographical references (p.) and indexes.
ISBN 0–631–17435–4 — ISBN 0–631–17436–2 (pbk)
1. English philology—Old English, ca. 450–1100.
2. Great Britain—History—Anglo-Saxon period, 449–1066.
3. English language—Old English, ca. 450–1100—Texts.
4. English literature—Old English, ca. 450–1100.
5. England—Civilization—To 1066. 6. Anglo-Saxons.
PE123.M58   1995   93–39658
429'.86—dc20   CIP

Typeset in 10 on 12pt. Ehrhardt
by Joshua Associates Limited, Oxford
Printed and bound in Great Britain by MPG Books Ltd,Bodmin, Cornwall

This book is printed on acid-free paper

Summary of Contents

Foreword

What is Old English? It is the vernacular Germanic language, the language of daily life, in Anglo-Saxon England before about 1100. Why bother with it? Old English is where the English language – 'the tongue that Shakespeare spake', the tongue that many millions throughout the world now speak – began: the sentence

His hand is strong and his word grim

is spelt the same in both Old English and Modern English and carries the same message. Old English is where English prose began:

God bletsode þa Noe and his suna and cwæð him to: Weahxað and beoð gemenigfilde and afyllað þa eorðan

God blessed then Noah and his sons and quoth to them: Wax and be manifold and fill the earth.

Old English is where one tributary of the great river of English poetry began:

þonne hit wæs renig weder ond ic reotogu sæt

Then it was rainy weather and I unhappy sat

is the cry of one woman separated from her lover;

þær ic sittan mot sumorlangne dæg, þær ic wepan mæg

there I must sit the summerlong day, there I may weep,

that of another. In Old English much that is still typically English finds expression. Examples include the distrust of foreigners seen in a chronicler's statement in 1052 when there was a danger of civil war:

Ac hit wes mæst eallan lað to feohtanne wið heora agenes cynnes mannum forðam þær wæs lytel elles þe aht mycel mihton butan Englisce on ægðre healfe

But it was loath to almost all to fight against their own kinsmen for there was little else of any value [*literally*, which might aught mickle] except English on either half/side

and the mood of the poetry, described by Kevin Crossley-Holland thus: 'Sometimes passionate, often sorrowful, occasionally wry, but always stoic, formal, and highly sophisticated, the voice of the Old English poets is absolutely distinctive.' To read English literature without some knowledge of, and feeling for, Old English is to cut oneself off from one of the main traditions which have nourished that literature. Hence my enthusiasm and my passionate belief that Old English should have a part in every university English syllabus and in the library of every reader of English literature.

Along with this ever-strengthening belief, I harbour an ever-growing fear that Old English is losing ground and that we are displaying 'the foule disgrace not onely of ignorance . . . but of extreme ingratitude' of which De l'isle wrote in his 1623 Preface to his treatise on the work of Ælfric from which Text 32 (§444) is taken:

> I hold the knowledge of this old English, and any good matter of humanity therein written, but diuinity above all, worthy to be preserued. . . What Englishman of vnderstanding is there, but may be delighted to see, the prety shifts our tongue made with her owne store, in all parts of learning, when they scorned to borrow words of another? Albeeit now sithence wee haue taken that liberty which our neighbours doe; and to requite them more then for need, our language is improued above all others now spoken by any nation, and became the fairest, the nimblest, the fullest; most apt to vary the phrase, most ready to receiue good composition, most adorned with sweet words and sentences, with witty quips and ouer-ruling Prouerbes: yea able to expresse any conceit whatsoeuer with great dexterity; waighty in weighty matters, merry in merry, braue in braue . . . But sure to neglect the beginnings of such an excellent tongue, will bring vpon vs the foule disgrace not onely of ignorance . . . but of extreme ingratitude towards our famous ancestors, who left vs so many, so goodly monuments in their old Dialect recorded.

There are several reasons for this: the pressure of an ever-expanding corpus of modern literature; the great attention given to critical theory, often at the expense of the literature itself; the time and effort required for learning Old English grammar (I discuss this below); active hostility from some who were nurtured in a crabbedly linguistic tradition in which the marks on the page were more important than the literary merits of what was being said and in which the Anglo-Saxons were regarded as people who made interesting scribal errors rather than as individual members of a society; and a passive indifference, on the part of some to whom the language has been entrusted, to what is in some universities its terminal illness. With these considerations in mind, I have set out to increase the popularity of Old English, to make it, in the dictionary sense of the word, both 'of or carried on by people' and 'liked or admired by people', people including university students and general readers.

Those who have tried in the past to bring Old English to the general reader have often foundered on one particular mystery – the grammar. Some methods tried have involved no grammar. But if Old English is to be understood and appreciated, grammar cannot be completely avoided. The problem is of course compounded in an age in which very few know any grammar at all. (O that our educationalists were aware of and believed Ælfric's dictum that *stæfcræft is seo cæg þe þara boca andgiet unlycþ* 'grammar is the key which unlocks the meaning of books'!) But will the reader's interest and enthusiasm evaporate before the necessary minimum of Old English grammar can be acquired? Crash courses can overcome this problem for those willing and able to attend them. However, my experience suggests to me that the bogey of grammar can be exaggerated if readers simply wish to gain a knowledge of Old English which will allow them, with some help from glossary and notes, to bring to life the dead lion which in translation is only a living dog.

I have known intelligent undergraduates who took a perverse pride in refusing to learn simple grammar. Yet the essentials of Old English are not so difficult. Indeed, H. M. Chadwick asserted that 'no language is easier to read'. Anyone who can do a crossword puzzle, cope with the competitions which appear in our more literate newspapers, or use a word-processor, should be more than capable of mastering the minimal grammar I shall set out – given the same degree of commitment. Those who wish to acquire a serious knowledge of Old English should go straight to Bruce Mitchell and Fred C. Robinson, *A Guide to Old English*, 5th edn (Oxford: Blackwell, 1992). A reader who starts with this book and finds the going too slow can transfer to the *Guide* with no harm done, apart from the need to qualify some of my generalizations. Here I am more concerned with helping those who do not know Old English than with pleasing those who do. I see no point in making things seem harder than they are; the virtues of simplicity, even of stating what may seem obvious, in expositions intended for the often hard-pressed beginner, should not need defending. I regret that the need to make cross-referencing simple has compelled me to number the sections, in textbook fashion. I have aimed at a generous layout and have decided, after some hesitation, to make use of lists and tables in the belief that their clarity and convenience will outweigh the discouraging starkness of their appearance. Nevertheless, it is my fervent hope that through this book some at any rate will catch a glimpse of the glories to be found in the cradle of modern English literature – Old English literature.

In Part III, I have tried to give some idea of how those who spoke the language and produced the literature felt and thought. The fact that the Anglo-Saxon period lasted over six hundred years (§179), coupled with limitations of space, means that I cannot give a detailed account of the variations between different parts of England or between different periods. My illustrations and quotations are selected for their relevance and interest from texts of differing periods and provenance and therefore give a general impression rather than an accurate portrayal of life and thought in one particular area or at one particular time. In justification, I can plead that the material changes which took place from the fifth to the eleventh century were far less dramatic and far less fundamental than those which have occurred since 1900.

It is a pleasant duty to render thanks for the advice and encouragement I have received. The list which follows is intended to be complete; I apologize to those whose names may have inadvertently been omitted. I am gratefully conscious of continuing stimulus derived from the work of past scholars, especially Henry Sweet, Herbert Meritt, J. R. R. Tolkien, Alistair Campbell, and the authors of the books cited in my Bibliography; of much-appreciated encouragement in the initial stages of the work from Daniel Donoghue and Tom Shippey; of invaluable help in making Parts I, II, and V, more 'user-friendly' from those who ploughed through the first drafts: Carmen Acevedo, Daniel Donoghue, Dan Friedman, Susan Irvine, Sarah Keefer, Marisa Lohr, Janet Phillips, Anne Ridler, Jane Roberts, and Renée Williams; of telling contributions to Part IIIB from John Cowdrey and Henry Mayr-Harting, to Part IIIC from Rosemary Cramp, Arthur MacGregor, and Michael Metcalf, to Part IIID from Margaret Gelling, to Parts IIIE and IV from Susan Irvine, Sarah Keefer, and Elizabeth Tyler; and of valuable suggestions from John Burrow, Carl Berkhout, and Alison Kelly, who perused the final draft. I am also grateful to the copyright holders listed separately; to Peter Hayward for the map of Anglo-Saxon England and for figure 35 in its final form; to Jennifer Speake, who edited my rough Indexes with her customary precision and understanding; to Grazyna Cooper, Marilyn Deegan, and Sara Kalim, who made me aware of the benefits of living in the twentieth century by harnessing the computer to produce the Concordance on which my Glossary is based; and to Craig Ronalds for efficient help with the proofs.

By an unjust tradition, those responsible for producing the book at Blackwell Publishers, Joshua Associates, and T. J. Press Ltd., remain anonymous. But I must make three exceptions by thanking John Davey for his wise and generous advice, Margaret Hardwidge for her informed and sensitive work as editor, and Vera Keep for setting this book with the same flair and involvement she has shown in setting four earlier books. My debt to my wife is acknowledged in the Dedication. Without all these helpers, the book would have been a poorer thing. Even with their help, it is impossible that there are no errors and no passages which might have been more felicitously phrased. Many writers hope that their book will become a bestseller. I harbour no such ambition. But if you think that this book deserves reprinting and can suggest ways of improving it, I shall be delighted to hear from you.

Let me conclude this Foreword by expressing the sincere hope that you will not think I am talking down to you. As I write, I am continually conscious that I am treading a tightrope between being patronizing on the one side and unintelligible on the other. If sometimes you think that I have fallen off (on one side or the other), please smile forgivingly and allow me to climb up again and continue my journey in your company.

St Edmund Hall, Oxford   BRUCE MITCHELL
St Swithun 1993

Acknowledgements

The author and publishers offer grateful acknowledgements to the following for permission to reproduce copyright material:

Illustrations: Harcourt Brace and Company (figure 1); British Museum (figures 2, 5, 17); Sonia Chadwick Hawkes (figures 3, 36); Eva Wilson (figures 4, 6, 7, 29); the Ashmolean Museum, Oxford (figures 8, 9, 11, 12, 28); the Board of Trustees of the National Museums and Galleries on Merseyside (Liverpool Museum) (figure 10); Royal Commission on the Ancient and Historical Monuments of Scotland and Historic Scotland (figure 13); Royal Commission on the Historical Monuments of England (figures 14, 15, 16, 19, 20, 23); the Dean and Chapter of Durham (figures 18, 30); Cambridge University Press (figures 21, 22); the Controller of Her Majesty's Stationery Office (figure 24); Professor Philip Rahtz (figure 25); University Museum of National Antiquities, Oslo, Norway (figure 27); the British Library (figures 31, 33, 34); the President and Fellows, Corpus Christi College, Oxford (figure 32); Nicholas Gould, and the British Museum (figure 35).

Quotations: British Museum Press (R. Bruce-Mitford, in §229); the British Library (M. Brown, in §292); Margaret Gelling (§§304, 323); the Wellcome Institute (W. Bonser, in §404); Fred C. Robinson (§§xx, 9, 101, 410); Random House UK Limited and Harper Collins USA (B. Bates, in §416).

The publishers apologize for any errors or omissions in the above list and would be grateful to be notified of any corrections that should be incorporated in the next edition or reprint of this book.

An acknowledgement is also due to Kevin Crossley-Holland for permission to reproduce the translations of Old English poems in §§263, 291, 295, 367, and 486. These will be found (possibly with slight variations) in *The Exeter Riddle Book* (London: The Folio Society, 1978) and/or in *The Anglo-Saxon World: Writings* (Woodbridge: The Boydell Press, 1982), both by Crossley-Holland.

The translation of the Homer passage quoted in the Dedication is taken from the English paraphrase of a Latin address by the Public Orator of Oxford University, G. W. Bond; see *Oxford University Gazette* 23 June 1989, pp. 973–4.

Contents

List of Figures

FURTHER VIEWING

The books whose short titles are listed below all contain figures and/or plates. (See Bibliography for full details.)

Archaeology	*Golden Age*
AS Art	*Jewellery*
AS 1981	*Making*
AS 1982	*Page*
Fisher	*Sutton Hoo*

Anglo-Saxon England

How to Use This Book

In the Foreword, I confessed to a passionate enthusiasm for Old English and to a desire to share this with university students and with general readers. The purpose of what follows is to answer the question you will want to ask me: 'How have you gone about this task?'

As the title of the book suggests, I have tried to tempt you by designing it so that you can learn by yourself what you will about Old English and the people who spoke it. The book differs from other introductions to Old English in tone, general approach, and contents. It may turn out to be either a splendid banquet or a cheese- and wine-tasting party, depending on how far I succeed in stimulating your appetite. For, after working through Parts I and II, you can choose what appeals to you from Part III 'An Introduction to Anglo-Saxon England' and Part IV 'The Garden of Old English Literature'.

I said 'after working through Parts I and II'. However, as my work on this book draws to a close, I am tempted to add a comment which (I fear) some critics may think should have been printed in invisible ink: Parts I and II are certainly essential for anyone who hopes to get a grip on the Old English language. But those who are primarily interested in archaeology, place-names, or Anglo-Saxon life and thought, can – initially at any rate – move straight from the Introduction to Parts IIIC, IIID, and IIIE, where all but a few passages of Old English are translated. They can also read Part IIIA before Parts I and II. So how you use this book depends on what you want from it.

What menu – for banquet or party – does it offer? I have divided it into five main courses for you to make your choice. Before I describe them, let me assure you that Old English is easier to learn than any foreign language you may have tried, partly because, as a speaker of English, you are already familiar with its basic structure and partly because you will not be called upon to display your knowledge of it by a chance meeting with someone who speaks it. If you want to read some Old English now, look at the last paragraph in §xx in the Introduction and then at the passages quoted and translated in §§130, 14, 12, and 120 (in that order). The last four passages are good, realistic examples of the language you will be learning.

The Summary of Contents has already revealed some of the aids I have provided for you: a map of Anglo-Saxon England, illustrative figures (there are thirty-six of them), a bibliography, a list of significant dates, a glossary, and two indexes.

The Introduction sets out to answer the questions 'Where did the English language come from?' and 'How did it get to England?' The history of the English people and of their ancestors can be seen in the English language, especially in its vocabulary. So I begin by analysing the vocabulary of Modern English. This study leads us back several thousand years to a time and a place – neither readily identifiable – in which a language now called Indo-European was spoken but not written. For us, it exists only in philological reconstructions. Yet from this language stem some of the Indian and many of the European languages spoken today; see figure 1. The vocabulary reveals how the speakers of Indo-European – some of whom learnt it as a foreign language – separated and migrated in various directions. (I admit that the going gets a bit tough when you encounter Grimm's Law. But the story should be interesting – perhaps even gripping – if I have told it properly.) By following the clues, we can trace roughly the movements of, and the contacts made on their way by, the people whose descendants were destined to come to what is now England in the late fourth and early fifth centuries and to bring with them a Germanic language which in the course of time developed into Modern English. The Introduction ends by discussing briefly some of the major differences between Modern English and written forms of this Old English language from the late ninth century and later.

I believe that the most difficult thing about Old English is the Germanic vocabulary. To help you with it I have translated and/or provided a key for all the passages I use in Parts I and II. I hope this will save you time as you are learning how Old English works. In Parts III and IV I have translated the shorter passages. For the longer passages – those numbered Text 1, Text 2, and so on – you will need to use both the Glossary at the end of the book and the explanations printed, where possible, on the same opening as the text.

I said in my Foreword that 'the bogey of grammar can be exaggerated'. But it has to be faced if you want to get anywhere with Old English. So I shall try to introduce you to Old English, which you do not yet know, by comparing it in Part II with Modern English, which you do know, after some preliminary remarks in Part I about how Old English was written and how it sounds; reading aloud is a valuable and enjoyable part of the fun. I hope you will find this plan helpful. The passage of Old English in §14, to which I have already referred you, demonstrates that the syntactical differences between Old English and Modern English are minimal. But if you are keen to read and savour Old English in the original, you will need to recognize as friends the most common of the inflexional endings set out in Part II. Length marks and other aids to pronunciation are provided in Parts I, II, and V. In Parts III and IV length marks are supplied in the verse texts to help you in reading aloud but not in the prose texts because they are not marked in the editions you are likely to use.

For those who have worked through Parts I and II, there is further advice about how to tackle Parts III and IV in §168. The main Contents gives full details of what is in these two Parts. In brief, Part III introduces you to the literature (IIIA), to the history of Anglo-Saxon England (IIIB, for which Parts I and II are almost essential), to its archaeology (IIIC), to its place-names (IIID), and to life in the heroic society and the impact of Christianity (IIIE). As I have already said, you can tackle Parts IIIA, C, D, and E, without the help of Parts I and II.

This is not true of Part IV 'The Garden of Old English Literature', which exemplifies all the prose genres distinguished in §177 and all the genres of poetry distinguished in §176. Each numbered text is accompanied by an introductory note and a textual commentary. You do not have to read the texts in the order in which they are printed; the choice is yours and the detailed Contents will help you to make it. The Glossary, which has an introductory note explaining how to use it, is an essential tool. I am confident you will come to feel rewarded for the hard work involved.

Words like 'paradigm' (which merely means an example or pattern) and 'inflexions' (which we have already met and means endings added to words to show their grammatical function) induce a *frisson* of horror in many. But some paradigms are useful and have been included in Part V for those who wish to consult them. I cannot avoid all technical terms but I have reduced them to a minimum, giving illustrations for those you are unlikely to have met; for references to these see the Grammatical and Lexical Index. I have not explained words like 'prefix' and 'stress'; if such words are unfamiliar, I ask you to consult a dictionary.

Now let me ask a question to which you alone can give the answer: 'Who are you and why have you come this far with me?' As I see it, you may be a student of English in a university which does not offer Old English. You may be a student who has chosen not to take the Old English course which is offered. You may be a historian who wants to make intelligent use of parallel editions of the chronicles, charters, laws, or wills. You may be interested in place-names or in archaeology or in manuscripts and illuminations. You may be the correspondent who recently wrote to a London newspaper suggesting that Old English would be a more suitable language for study in schools than Latin or Greek. You may be a general reader curious about Old English literature. You may be a member – or (dare I breathe it?) the head – of an English department which demands a limited acquaintance with Old English, or of a department which does not make Old English an essential or indeed any part of the course or programme but who will be moved by this book to decide that Old English is worth two or three hours a week for a term or semester. Or you may simply be fascinated by language or by languages. Whoever you are, I hope that you will find as much interest and pleasure as I have found in

Old English and I wish *you*, whether you are studying alone or with a teacher,

Good luck!	Success in *your* work!
Wes þū hāl!	*Wel þē þæs ġeweorces!*

Introduction

§i Where did the English language come from? How did it get to England? For the answers, we can go to the language itself. The history of the English people and of their relations with other countries is reflected in their language, through the words they use. The native vocabulary of Old English was largely of Germanic origin. More Germanic words were borrowed from the Scandinavian languages before 1100; see §25. The non-Germanic words in Old English came almost wholly from Latin; see §§23–4. But since then, words have been imported regularly from many languages. Up to *c.* 1250 the source was Anglo-Norman, whence came words such as 'dame', 'justice', 'largesse', 'noble', 'prison', and 'servant' – these indicate that the Normans were the ruling and dominant class – and ecclesiastical words, for example 'canon', 'chaplain', 'cardinal', 'miracle', and 'nativity'. Control over Normandy was lost during the reign of King John (d. 1216). There followed a period of Central French influence, *c.* 1250–1400, during which some two-fifths of the French words in English were acquired; these concern government, law, religion, defence, the feudal system, literature, art, architecture, music, education, fashion, household affairs and cooking, as well as words like 'music', 'comfort', 'ease', 'joy', 'leisure', and 'sport'. Norman influence is seen in words like 'warranty', 'war', 'cattle', and 'carite' (an obsolete form of 'charity'), Central French in words like 'guarantee', 'guerre' (now obsolete), 'chattel', and 'charity'. These two strains of French words reflect two important invasions of England: the military conquest by the Normans and a more peaceful take-over by the many Frenchmen from other areas which followed the marriage of Henry III to Eleanor of Provence in 1236. So these French words were in a sense almost compulsory loans rather than borrowings!

§ii 1400, the year of Chaucer's death, serves as a convenient but arbitrary terminus for the Middle English period (1066–1400). Since then, words have been borrowed with almost ruthless enthusiasm and the vocabulary of English has expanded in sympathy with, and as a result of, England's increasing interests and influence abroad. The Italian contribution, which began in the fourteenth century, bulks fourth after those from Latin – these reflect the continuous importance of Latin culture and literature in England – French, and Scandinavian. The earliest Italian words came through French, the first being 'florin' (1303). But during the fifteenth and sixteenth centuries galleys plied regularly between England and Venice and direct borrowings began. Like those from France, they cover many fields: commerce and trade, travel, social activities and customs, clothes, horsemanship, military matters, literature, architecture, art, and music.

§iii Germanic languages other than those of Scandinavia have also been raided. The Dutch and Flemish words which were borrowed up to the end of the fifteenth century reflect the nautical, commercial, and industrial, relations of the time; to these were later added words concerning military matters and art. The most distinctive contributions of German to English have been in the field of mineralogy; Germans were working in English mines as early as the time of Queen Elizabeth I.

§iv The French invasions, the trade between England and Venice, and the German miners already mentioned, demonstrate the fact that scholars can give a detailed and chronological account of at least some of the relationships existing between England and the countries whose words were borrowed. Other deductions which can be made concerning the languages discussed so far include the following: Old English contains words borrowed from Latin at different times (§§23–4); there were communities which contained speakers of Old English and speakers of Scandinavian languages in the ninth and tenth centuries (§xix); the French were interested in cooking; fishermen from the Grimsby area met fishermen from the Low Countries on the North Sea sometime before c. 1270; Italian horsemanship was in vogue in Elizabethan England; and in the eighteenth century there were contacts between England and Dutch South Africa. In like manner scholars can deduce the relationship with countries whose contribution to the vocabulary was smaller, including (in Europe) Spanish, Portuguese, Russian, Hungarian, Greek (both Classical and Modern), Irish, Welsh, and Scottish Gaelic; (from the East) Arabic, Persian, Turkish, Semitic dialects, Indian dialects, Chinese, and Japanese; the languages of Africa and South America; the North American Indian dialects; and Malay, Polynesian, and aboriginal Australian (no prizes for guessing that these include 'boomerang' and 'kangaroo').

§v Readers can make their own deductions from the following catalogue: 'absinthe' (from French), 'ale' (native), 'angostura' (a place-name in Venezuela), 'arrack' (from Arabic), 'beer' (native), 'brandy', earlier 'brandewine' (from Dutch), 'champagne' and 'cognac' (from France), 'chianti' (from Italy), 'curaçao' (the name of an island in the Caribbean Sea), 'gin' (from Dutch from French from Latin *juniperus* or, according to some, an abbreviation of Geneva), 'kava' (from Polynesian), 'kirsch' and 'kummel' (from German), 'lager' (from German), 'mead' (native), 'madeira' and 'port' (both from Portuguese), 'saké' (from Japanese), 'sangaree' (from West Indian), 'schnapps' (from German), 'sherry' (from a Spanish place-name), 'vermouth' (from French from German), 'whisky' (from Gaelic), and 'wine' (from Latin; the word appears in early Old English poetry). This list could be extended but I limit myself to adding 'alcohol' (from Mediaeval Latin from Arabic), 'booze' (from Dutch), 'liquor' (from French), and finally 'temperance' and 'abstinence' (both from French from Latin).

§vi For those who wish to know more about this aspect of the English language, I recommend *A History of Foreign Words in English* by Mary S. Serjeantson (London, 1935), a book to which I am indebted for much of the preceding information.

§vii But it remains for me to explain how what was to become the English language arrived in what was later called *Engla lond* 'land of the Angles, England'. Here we lack written records, unlike those interested in French, Italian, and the other Romance languages, who can go back to Latin. We therefore have to rely on the methods of comparative philology, which involve deducing (as far as is possible) the vocabulary, pronunciation, and grammar, of languages now lost from the evidence of languages which we know. Using these methods, scholars have been able to reconstruct in broad outline the story of the peoples who spoke the languages through which Old English can trace its descent. The narrative may go something like this.

§viii Several thousand years BC, perhaps on the steppes of Southern Russia or on the forested plains of Central Europe, there existed a language of which we have no written records but which we now call Indo-European. It may have been spoken by a powerful group of travelling merchants who made it the lingua franca of trading. It may have been spoken by a dominant race who made it the lingua franca of great councils and of armies of common defence. An alternative hypothesis, proposed by Professor Colin Renfrew of Cambridge University, is that the original speakers of Indo-European were peasant farmers in central Anatolia (now part of Turkey) and that their language gradually spread both west and east along with their farming economy.

§ix Many languages spoken today are descended from Indo-European. Eleven principal groups have been distinguished: Indian and Iranian (sometimes grouped as Indo-Iranian), Armenian, Hellenic, Albanian, Italic, Balto-Slavic, Germanic, Celtic, Anatolian, and Tocharian. Figure 1 (reproduced by kind permission from Pyles and Algeo, *The Origins and Development of the English Language*, 3rd edition (Harcourt Brace Jovanovich, 1982), 70–1) conveniently sets out these languages and their descendants in the form of a family tree. An examination of the vocabulary of the languages in these groups reveals certain common elements. One typical example is OE *medu* 'mead, alcoholic liquor of fermented honey and water', which appears as Sanskrit *mádhu* 'honey, sweet drink', Greek μέθυ 'wine', Lithuanian *midùs* 'mead', Old Slavonic *medŭ* 'honey, wine', and Old Irish *mid* and Welsh *medd* 'honey, wine'. From these forms, philologists reconstruct a hypothetical Indo-European word **medhu-*. Another example is OE *mōdor* 'mother' alongside Sanskrit *mātár*, Greek μήτηρ, Latin *māter*, Tocharian *mācar*, Old Slavonic *mati*, and Old Irish *māthir*. These forms are traced back to

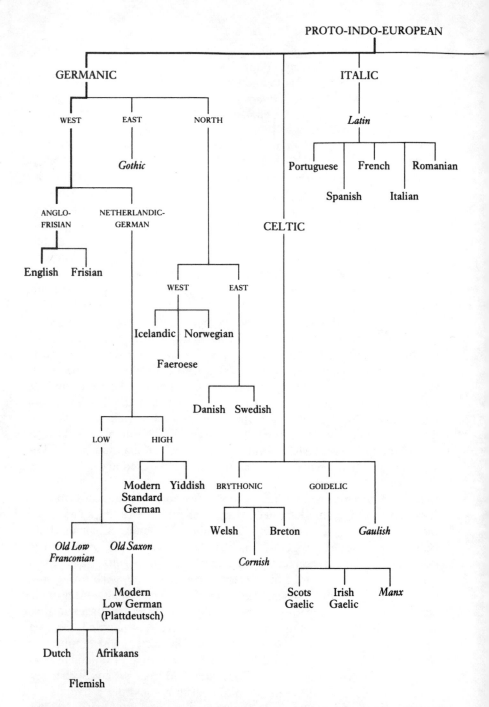

Figure 1 The Indo-European tree (from Pyles and Algeo *The Origins and Development of the English Language*, 3rd edn, 1982; copyright Harcourt Brace & Company, reproduced by permission of the publisher)

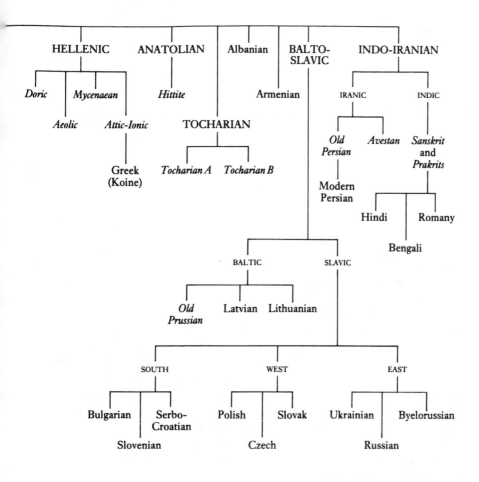

| HELLENIC | ANATOLIAN | Albanian | BALTO-SLAVIC | INDO-IRANIAN |

Doric *Mycenaean* *Hittite* Armenian IRANIC INDIC

Aeolic *Attic-Ionic* **TOCHARIAN**

Greek (Koine) *Tocharian A* *Tocharian B*

Old Persian *Avestan* *Sanskrit and Prakrits*

Modern Persian

Hindi Romany

Bengali

BALTIC SLAVIC

Old Prussian Latvian Lithuanian

SOUTH WEST EAST

Bulgarian Serbo-Croatian Polish Slovak Ukrainian Byelorussian

Slovenian Czech Russian

THE INDO-EUROPEAN TREE
MAIN BRANCHES
SUB BRANCHES
Dead languages
Living languages

Indo-European *māter. An examination of all the common elements suggests that those who spoke Indo-European built simple dwellings, domesticated animals, used horses, wheels, and a primitive plough, produced grain and wool, spun and wove, brewed liquor from honey, and were familiar with snow but not with sailing or the sea. But negative evidence is not conclusive. If it were, we should be left to believe that they had no hands.

§x   There are no written records of this language. The fact that languages can and do exist only in spoken form reminds us that language is primarily speech and that writing is only a conventional and inexact way of recording it. But even speech is not exact. Sounds are produced by the voluntary movement of the so-called 'organs of speech' and none of us regularly produces the various sounds in exactly the same way. The variations are minute and are kept in check by the need to be understood by others. So they usually pass unnoticed, for we hear what we are familiar with; here I am reminded of the apocryphal story of the Englishman who misunderstood the words 'À l'eau. C'est l'heure' as 'Hallo, sailor'. But speakers of a language can be influenced by other speakers, and variations can spread from individual to family and from there to the community or to part of it. Even if mutual intelligibility is maintained among living speakers, these variations can be significant over five or six generations. Thus Anglo-Saxon children practising the pronunciation exercise 'How now brown cow?' said '*Hū nū brūn cū?*', rhyming the sound with 'do' not 'vow', and there was a time when even people in the south of England pronounced 'grass' not with a long vowel but with the short vowel they now use in the second syllable of 'alas', a pronunciation still the norm for many in North America. Every language then is subject to change within itself.

§xi   The reconstructed Indo-European language cannot have been an exception. But there is another possible complicating factor here. Whether it was originally spoken by a group of merchants or by a dominant race or by peasant farmers, this language was probably not used only by native speakers. It may also have been spoken by people of different races and languages whose pronunciation retained some of the characteristics of their native language, just as many Welsh speakers – and sometimes even Welsh men and women who do not speak that language – to some extent echo in their pronunciation of English the vowel and consonant sounds and the intonation of Welsh. Similarly, there are differences in the pronunciation of the English spoken by many others whose native tongue is not English. But the variations from standard English will differ according to the speaker's native language, whether it be French or German or Spanish or any other.

§xii   The very great differences, the mutual incomprehensibility, between the languages descended from Indo-European, call for explanation. As long as the speakers of Indo-European were in touch with the original speakers, they would have to conform more or less to the standard; if they did not, they would not be understood. But once this contact was lost and each nomadic tribe went its own way by climbing and descending a mountain, by crossing a river, or by traversing a forest, the standard disappeared and all that mattered was that the members of each tribe could understand one another. In those tribes which did not consist of native speakers of Indo-European, the roots of change existed in an even greater degree because their members had learnt Indo-European as a foreign language and therefore (as pointed out in §xi) did not pronounce its sounds in the same way as native speakers. The resulting variations, which differed from tribe to tribe under the influence of different original languages, were gradually exaggerated as the various tribes, some of them not using exactly the same pronunciation, went off in different directions: south-east to produce speakers of Indian or Iranian; along the northern shores of the Mediterranean to produce speakers of Hellenic, Italic, or Celtic; west and north-west through the forests to produce speakers of Germanic or Balto-Slavic; and so on.

§xiii The Germanic languages, to which our attention must now turn, are usually divided into three groups: East Germanic, one of which was spoken by the Gothic conquerors of Rome in the early fifth century but none of which now survives; North Germanic, including Swedish and Danish (East Scandinavian) and Norwegian and Icelandic (West Scandinavian); and West Germanic, to which Old English belongs. It would appear that the people whose descendants were to speak these languages did not pronounce certain consonants in the same way as most speakers of Indo-European, because all the Germanic languages are distinguished by certain consonant changes which were first formulated by the German philologist Jacob Grimm (of fairy-tale fame) and are therefore known as Grimm's Law. This accounts for such variations as those between Latin (which in the examples cited retains the Indo-European consonant) and Old English (OE) seen in such pairs as

Latin	Old English	Modern English	Correspondences
piscis	*fisc*	'fish'	*p/f*
tres	*þrēo*	'three'	*t/th*
centum	*hund*	'hundred'	*k/h*
genus	*cynn*	'kin'	*g/k*
decem	*tīen*	'ten'	*d/t*

§xiv The High German branch of the West Germanic languages, from which Modern Standard German descends, is distinguished from those groups which include the ancestors of English and Frisian and of Dutch and Flemish by another consonant shift which affected the High German languages but not the members of the Anglo-Frisian or Netherlandic-German branches. The results are seen in the differences between Old

English (OE) (unchanged) and Old High German (OHG) (changed) set out here:

OE	MnE	OHG	Modern German	Correspondences
helpan	'help'	*helfan*	*helfen*	*p/f*
pīpe	'pipe'	*pfīfa*	*Pfeife*	*p/pf* or *f*
heorte	'heart'	*herza*	*Herz*	*t/z*
etan	'eat'	*ezzen*	*essen*	*t/zz*
sēcan	'seek'	*suohhen*	*suchen*	*k/hh*

§xv   The speakers of Anglo-Frisian and of Low German lived in the regions which are now the Danish peninsula and the Low Countries. To explain how some of them crossed the Channel, I quote two entries from the Parker Manuscript of the Anglo-Saxon Chronicle, on which see §§179 and 180. They are

> AN. ccccxlix. Her ... Hengest 7 Horsa from Wyrtgeorne geleaþade Bretta kyninge gesohton Bretene on þam staþe þe is genemned Ypwinesfleot ærest Brettum to fultume ac hie eft on hie fuhton.

> AN. cccclv. Her Hengest 7 Horsa fuhton wiþ Wyrtgeorne þam cyninge in þære stowe þe is gecueden Agelesþrep 7 his broþur Horsan man ofslog 7 æfter þam Hengest feng to rice.

(In the Old English, 7 is a scribal abbreviation for 'and'; þ is *th*; æ is the sound in 'hat'; the order of subject, verb, and object, is sometimes different from that of today; and the word 'invited' in the phrase 'invited by Vortigern, [the] Britons' king' seems to us to be in an unusual position.)

Literally translated, these read:

449   Here ... Hengest and Horsa by Vortigern invited, Britons' king, sought Britain in the place which is named Ebbsfleet, first to Britons as help, but they afterwards against them fought.

455   Here Hengest and Horsa fought against Vortigern the king in the place which is called Agelesthrep, and his brother Horsa [*object*] one [*subject*] slew; and after that Hengest succeeded to kingdom ...

This chronicle was compiled in the second half of the ninth century and the story of Hengest and Horsa is probably based on Bk I Ch. 15 of Bede's *Ecclesiastical History of the English People*, where (as Bede tells us the story) those who were invited came ostensibly to fight on behalf of the country, but with the real intention of conquering it. He goes on to relate that reports about the fertility of the island and the slackness of the Britons got back to the homes of the invaders and encouraged more immigrants from three very powerful Germanic tribes, the Saxons, Angles, and Jutes.

§xvi   Archaeological evidence confirms the statement that three tribes were involved (see §279) but has also been taken to suggest that invited mercenaries or settlers or invaders from the Continent began to arrive during the last years of the Roman occupation. Whether they did and, if so, in what numbers, are matters for learned dispute; see §307. However, the newcomers first settled in the south and east of the island but gradually extended their dominance to the west and the north. The accepted view has been that the migrants came in large numbers and drove out the Celtic-speaking inhabitants into Wales, where many of their descendants still speak Welsh, and into Cornwall, where Cornish was spoken until *c.* 1800. But it has recently been argued that there was no mass migration but only a seizure of power by a new ruling elite who imposed their Germanic culture and language on the Celts, many of whom remained in subjugation after their leaders had been eliminated and large numbers of their fellows had migrated to Brittany. This issue too is a matter for learned debate. However, personally I am unable to believe that a few thousand invaders could have imposed their language on a conquered people who greatly outnumbered them, as the new theory supposes, for we know that Scandinavian invaders in a similar position twice lost their language and adopted that of the people they conquered – once in Normandy and again in England after 1066. The rarity of Celtic loan-words in English (§26) and the large number of Celtic place-names in England, both of which are relevant here, are discussed in §309.

§xvii   However, whether it was brought by many or by a few, there came to England a Germanic language, a language which carried with it the differences which were to lead to the development of the four main dialects of the Old English language – Northumbrian, Mercian, Kentish, and West-Saxon (§2). One of these differences is reflected in the different spelling and pronunciation of the variant forms of the Modern English word 'deed': West-Saxon *dǣd*, non-West-Saxon *dēd*. Alfred, king of the West-Saxons from 871 to 899, called it *Englisc . . . ðæt geðiode ðe we ealle gecnawan mægen* 'English . . . the tongue we all understand can'. Under his leadership, the Scandinavian invasions were repulsed (§184), education was revived, and a policy of trans-lating important books from Latin into Old English was initiated. As a result of his influence and the work of contemporary and subsequent scholars and writers, such as the homilist Ælfric, Abbot of Eynsham 1005–*c.* 1012, the West-Saxon dialect developed into the literary standard and by the time of the Norman Conquest was far more developed for the expression of prose and poetry than any other contemporary European vernacular. I hope that, when you have read Part IV, you will agree that Old English prose writers and poets sometimes rose to great heights. My favourite examples include Text 18 (§424) and Text 11 (§467).

§xviii   A few preliminary remarks about the syntax and the vocabulary of this language are offered here in anticipation of the longer discussions in Part II. We have already seen that there are great differences between the vocabulary of the Anglo-Saxons and that of modern speakers of English. But some things have survived the centuries which separate us. Nikolaus Pevsner, in *The Englishness of English Art* (London, 1956), detects certain continuing characteristics in English art and architecture from Anglo-Saxon times until today. Wace, the twelfth-century poet who wrote a history of Britain in French verse, reports that at the battle of Hastings (§187) the Normans cried *Dex aie* 'God help [us]' and the English *Ut! Ut! Ut!* 'Out! Out! Out!' The latter cry has survived tenaciously. There is another continuity. You may be surprised but will, I hope, be relieved when I say that in my opinion one of the outstanding things about Old English syntax is its Englishness. The two Chronicle passages in §xv show two of the main differences: the frequent non-expression of what is now called the definite article, e.g. *Hengest feng to rice* (455) 'Hengest succeeded to [the] kingdom', and the use of variations of the subject (S) verb (V) object (O) order which is regular today. (On these terms, see §29.) Old English used SVO, e.g. *Hengest feng to rice* (455). But, like other Germanic languages, it also had two other orders – one in which the verb has final position, e.g. *ac hie eft on hie fuhton* (449) 'but they afterwards against them fought', and a VS order seen in this Parker Chronicle entry:

> AN. ccccxcv. Her cuomon twegen aldormen on Bretene Cerdic 7 Cynric his sunu mid v scipum in þone stede þc is gecueden Cerdicesora 7 þy ilcan dæge gefuhtun wiþ Walum

495 Here came two aldermen into Britain, Cerdic and Cynric his son, with five ships into the place which is called Cerdicesora and on the same day fought against the Welsh.

This VS order was still current in Shakespeare's day: 'Thus saith the Duke, thus hath the Duke inferred' (*King Richard III*, III. vi. 32). The absence of the definite article 'the' and these different orders will not, I imagine, worry you for long.

§xix Another point of difference is that speakers and writers of Old English sometimes changed the ending (or inflexion) of a noun or pronoun to show which word was object and which was subject; compare 'He hit him'. Examples include *7 his broþur Horsan man ofslog* (455), where the object *Horsan* has a different form from the subject *Horsa* in *Hengest 7 Horsa . . . gesohton Bretene* (449), and *He ofslog hine* 'He hit him'. Another inflexion denoted possession, e.g. the *-es* in *Ælfredes cyninges godsunu*, which is the ancestor of the *'s* in 'King Alfred's godson' but is used on both words in Old English. In addition to these three – denoting subject, object, and possession – there was a fourth inflexion (or case) which expressed a relationship now usually indicated by a preposition, e.g. *He com lytle werode* 'He came with a small troop'; cf. *þy ilcan dæge* (495) '(on) the same day', where the preposition is optional today. But quite often both a preposition and this ending were used, e.g. *mid v scipum* (495) 'with five ships'; 'Five ships came' would be *v scipu cuomon*. The gradual disappearance of most of these inflexions and their replacement as indicators of relationships by the SVO order and by prepositions is one of the most important changes in the history of the English language. In Old English itself, inflexional endings sometimes varied from dialect to dialect and (in adjectives; see §41) from one syntactical context to another. But the variations between the inflexions of Old English and those of the forms of Scandinavian spoken by the invaders and settlers were even greater. The existence of communities which contained speakers of Old English and speakers of Scandinavian languages in the ninth and tenth centuries (§iv) was a very important factor in the loss of the English inflexions. But you will find that these inflexions play a less terrifying part in Old English than the grammar books suggest. I am confident that between us we shall overcome the challenge they present.

§xx As I have already said, the Old English vocabulary is largely Germanic. You will need more help here, because many of the words are initially unrecognizable, even to those who know some German. Other words have changed their meaning, e.g. in *Englisc . . . ðæt geðiode ðe we ealle gecnawan mægen* 'English . . . the tongue which we all can understand', the transliteration 'may know' sounds closer to the Old English but gives the wrong idea; in *Her cuomon twegen aldormen* (495), *aldorman* means 'ruler, prince, chief', not a member of a town council; and in *Cerdic 7 Cynric . . . gefuhtun wiþ Walum* (495), *Walum* comes from *wealh*, which literally means 'a foreigner' or 'a stranger' (the walnut is a foreign nut!) and was dismissively used by the invading Anglo-Saxons to refer to the Britons, whose homeland they were appropriating. (This may remind you of the Chronicle passage about the English attitude to foreigners quoted in the first paragraph of my Foreword.) But the tunnel is not completely dark, as you will see by reading the following paragraph and the sentences it contains, which (along with the practice sentences in §§9 and 101) were composed by Fred C. Robinson.

Although sometimes pronounced differently from their Modern English descendants, many Old English words have the same form and the same basic meaning as their Modern English counterparts: e.g. *bliss, colt, dung, elm, finger, fox, handle, him, land, mist, nest, of, on, rest, sprang, winter, writ.* Indeed, entire sentences can have essentially the same appearance in Old English and Modern English, although it must be conceded that such sentences can be composed only through a rather artificial selection of words:

> Harold is swift. His hand is strong and his word grim. Late in
>   life he went to his wife in Rome.
> Is his inn open? His cornbin is full and his song is writen.
>   Grind his corn for him and sing me his song.
> He is dead. His bed is under him. His lamb is deaf and blind.
>   He sang for me.

He swam west in storm and wind and frost.
Bring us gold. Stand up and find wise men.

Her ealswa we sculon ofercuman 'Here also we shall overcome'!

§xxi There are, of course, more differences between Old English and Modern English than those in syntax, word (or element) order, inflexions, and vocabulary, set out above. This is inevitable because languages keep on changing; as Samuel Johnson wrote, 'It may be reasonably imagined that what is so much in the power of men as language will very often be capriciously conducted.' One of the things which make me think of Chaucer as a great modern writer, even though the language he wrote in is technically Middle English, is his recognition of the fact that languages must change. He reminded us of this, with his characteristic light touch, in this passage from *Troilus and Criseyde*. After observing that speech changes over a period of a thousand years, he goes on to say that, although words which then [*tho*] really meant something [*hadden pris*] now seem very comical and strange [*wonder nyce and straunge*] to us, yet lovers speaking them prospered [*spedde*] as well in love as we do now with the words we use:

> Ye knowe ek that in forme of speche is chaunge
> Withinne a thousand yeer, and wordes tho
> That hadden pris, now wonder nyce and straunge
> Us thinketh hem, and yet thei spake hem so,
> And spedde as wel in love as men now do;
> Ek for to wynnen love in sondry ages,
> In sondry londes, sondry ben usages.

A thousand years separate us from the time of Abbot Ælfric. I have explained in the section headed 'How to Use This Book' the ways in which I have tried to help you bridge this gap. I conclude the Introduction by again saying (this time without a translation)

Wes þū hāl! Wel þē þæs ġeweorces!

I

Spelling, Pronunciation, and Punctuation

A SPELLING

§1 The manuscript facsimiles printed as figures 31–4 show that some letters in the scripts described in §§291–300 are shaped very like those of today while others are not. The letters *v* and *z* were not much used by Old English scribes. The letter *y* is a symbol for a vowel. In this book you will meet three Old English letters (lower-case and capital) not used today: *æ Æ* (ash), *þ þ* (thorn), and *ð Ð* (eth or, as the Anglo-Saxons appear to have called it, *ðæt*). The word 'that' was written as *þæt* or *ðæt*, for *æ* represents the vowel in 'that' and *þ* or *ð* were used interchangeably for *th* in 'that' or in 'thin'. These letters appeared in different forms in the runes, an angular alphabet for carving which did not survive the Norman Conquest. We meet runes in the wood of St Cuthbert's coffin (§262), in the whalebone of the Franks Casket (§258), and in the stone of the Ruthwell Cross (§252). They were not used as a writing script by the Anglo-Saxons but occur occasionally in the prose in scientific manuscripts and from time to time in the poetry, especially in the Exeter Book riddles. The name of the poet Cynewulf/ Cynwulf appears in runes in four poems, twice in each spelling; see §176. *The Rune Poem* offers comments on the names of the various runes, e.g.

> ᚠ (feoh) byþ frofur   fira gehwylcum
> Money is a comfort to each of men

and

> ᚦ (ðorn) byþ ðearle scearp
> Thorn is very sharp.

The early texts of the Methuen Old English Library used the runic 'wynn' *ƿ* instead of *w* and the OE letter *ȝ* for *g*. In the latest volumes, these have been discarded.

§2 Differences between four major dialects – Northumbrian, Mercian, Kentish, and West-Saxon – are reflected in spelling. But even within West-Saxon, which became the basis of the standard written language, spelling was not settled. One reason for this was that early West-Saxon (the language of the time of King Alfred *c.* 900) and late West-Saxon (the language of the homilist Abbot Ælfric *c.* 1000) show significant differences. Another was that concern for uniform or 'correct' spelling is a comparatively modern phenomenon. Some Old English textbooks for beginners try to make the spelling regular. I have not done this. It is unreal and makes the transition to normal Old English texts difficult. However, I have done something unreal in marking long vowels (¯), e.g. *stān* and by putting dots on *ċ* for the sound in 'cheese' (Old English *ċēse*, *ċȳse*) and on *ġ* for the sound in 'year' (Old English *ġēar*). This will help you to recognize many words which you might not otherwise identify. But my refusal to regularize the spelling of the texts means that you must be prepared for variations such as *mē/mec* 'me', *hit/hyt* 'it', *hire/hiere* 'her', and *wǣron, wǣrun, wǣræn, wǣren*, and *wǣran* 'were'. I think you will find that you can take such anomalies in your stride.

B STRESS

§3 In English today, the stress falls on the most meaningful syllable of a word, often called the root or the stem, e.g. 'fóund-' in 'fóunded', 'fóunder', and 'fóunding'. The same is true in Old English. The root is very often the first syllable, e.g. 'híndmost', OE *híndan* 'from behínd'; 'cóming', OE *cúmende*; and 'stánding', OE *stándende*. But again as in English today, the root remains stressed in compounds even when it is not the first syllable, e.g. 'behínd', OE *behíndan*; 'overcóme', OE *ofercúman*; 'withstánd', OE *wiþ-stándan*; and in OE words beginning with the prefix *ġe-*, e.g. *ġedrífan* 'to drive'. Compounds in which both elements retain full meaning have secondary stress on the second element in both periods of English, e.g. *sǣ-wèall* 'séa-wàll' and *níht-wàco* 'níght-wàtch'.

C PRONUNCIATION

1 Introduction

§4 Obviously there are no native speakers of Old English alive today; so any attempt to reconstruct the pronunciation can be only approximate. But we can be reasonably confident of the pronunciation as a result of comparing the way words are pronounced in the various Indo-European languages, both reconstructed and existing (see Introduction §§xiii and xiv); by noting the way words borrowed into English are pronounced (see §23); and by tracing words back from Modern English through the various dialects of Middle English to Old English (see §§15 and 17–18). The pronunciations given here for those working without a teacher are in terms of the nearest equivalent in the Received Pronunciation of England today.

§5 I cannot overemphasize the value of reading aloud. It will help with the meaning and, more important, will give you some feel for the language. Use the intonation and stress of Modern English. You will make some mistakes, especially with the prefixes discussed in §§3 and 19. But that won't matter much.

2 Vowels

§6 Old English distinguished short vowels (marked ˘ only if occasion demands) and long vowels (marked ¯) by taking longer to articulate the sound. Thus MnE 'aha' contains first the sound of OE *ă* and then the sound of OE *ā*. MnE 'hat' has the sound of OE *ǽ* and MnE 'bad' the sound of OE *æ*. Approximate pronunciations are:

> *a*   as the first vowel in 'aha'
> *ā*   as the second vowel in 'aha'
> *æ*   as in 'mat'
> *ǽ*   as in 'bad'
> *e*   as in 'bet'
> *ē*   approx. as in 'hate', but a pure vowel (cf. German *See*)
> *i*   as in 'tin'
> *ī*   as in 'seen'
> *o*   as in 'cough' (lips rounded as in British pronunciation)
> *ō*   approx. as in 'so', but a pure vowel (cf. German *so*)
> *u*   as in 'pull' (NOT 'hut')
> *ū*   as in 'cool'
> *y*   as *i*, with lips in a whistling position (French *tu*)
> *ȳ*   as *ī*, with lips in a whistling position (French *ruse*)

The front vowels (pronounced in the front of the mouth) are *æ*, *e*, *i*, and *y*. The back vowels (pronounced in the back of the mouth) are *a*, *o*, and *u*.

Vowels in unstressed syllables are always short but should be pronounced clearly.

3 Diphthongs

§7 In words like 'meat' and 'field', we have one vowel sound represented by two vowel characters. But, as you will hear if you say them aloud, words such as 'find' and 'fly' contain one vowel character which represents a combination of sounds made by gliding from one vowel position to another. These sounds are called 'diphthongs'. Diphthongs also occur in words like 'boy' and 'cloud', which contain two vowel characters. Old English diphthongs are always represented by two vowel characters and can be pronounced both short and long. With approximate pronunciations, they are:

$$ea = æ + a \qquad ēo = ē + o$$
$$ēa = ǽ + a \qquad ie = i + e$$
$$eo = e + o \qquad īe = ī + e$$

Remember that, like the MnE word 'I', these sounds are diphthongs, not two distinct vowels such as we get in the *ea* of 'Leander'.

4 Consonants

§8 All consonants must be pronounced, e.g. *c* in *cniht*, *g* in *gnæt*, *h* in *hlāf*, *r* in *þǣr*, and *w* in *wrītan* and *trēow*.

Double consonants must be pronounced. Thus *biden* and *biddan* differ in much the same way as MnE 'bidden' and 'bad debt'.

Most of the consonants are pronounced in the same way as in MnE. The main exceptions are set out below.

The letters *s*, *f*, *þ*, and *ð*, are pronounced voiced (with vibration of the vocal cords), i.e. like MnE *z*, *v*, and like *th* in 'clothe', between vowels or other voiced sounds, e.g. *rīsan*, *hlāfas*, *paþas*, and *hēafdes*. In other positions, including the beginning and end of words, they are voiceless, i.e. like MnE *s*, *f*, and like *th* in 'cloth', e.g. *sittan*, *hlāf*, *pæþ*, and *oft*.

At the beginning of a word ('initially') before a vowel, *h* is pronounced as in MnE 'hound'. Elsewhere it is like German *ch* in *ich* [ç] or *ach* [x], according to the front or back quality of the neighbouring vowel. It can be pronounced like *ch* in Scots *loch*.

Before *a*, *o*, *u*, and *y*, *c* is pronounced *k* and *g* is pronounced as in MnE 'good'. Before *e* and *i*, *c* is usually pronounced like *ch* in MnE 'child' and *g* like *y* in MnE 'yet'. In Parts I, II, and V, these appear as *ċ* and *ġ* respectively.

After or between back vowels, *g* is pronounced [ɣ], like the *g* sometimes heard in dialectal German *sagen*. It can be pronounced as '*w*' in words like *dragan* and *boga*, thus anticipating its ultimate development in 'draw' and 'bow'.

The combinations *sc* and *cg* are usually pronounced like MnE *sh* and *dge* respectively. Thus *scip* 'ship' and *ecg* 'edge' are pronounced the same in both OE and MnE.

D PRACTICE SENTENCES

§9 Many OE words seem strange at first but when pronounced according to the suggestions given above they can immediately be recognized as today's words in early dress, e.g. *bæc*, *biscop*, *ċinn*, *diċ*, *disc*, *ecg*, *feðer*, *hecg*, *hwelp*, *lifer*, *piċ*, *ræfter*, *scort*, *þæċ*, *þing*, *þiðer*, *þrescold*, *wecg*, *wofen*. Among the following sentences made up by Fred C. Robinson for practice in pronunciation are a number of words which will become recognizable when pronounced correctly.

Is his þeġn hēr ġīet?
His līnen socc fēoll ofer bord in þæt wæter and scranc.
Hwǣr is his cȳþþ and cynn?

His hring is gold his disc glæs and his belt leðer.
Se fisc swam under þæt scip and ofer þone sciellfisc.
His ċicen ran from his horsweġe ofer his pæð and in his ġeard.
Se horn sang hlūde. Hlysten wē!
Se cniht is on þǣre brycge.
Sēo cwēn went fram þǣre ċiriċe.
Hē siteþ on þǣre benċe.
God is gōd.
þis trēow is æsc. Hwæt is þæt trēow?
Hē wolde dōn wiċċecræft and hē began swā tō dōnne.
Fuhton ġē manliċe?

E PUNCTUATION

§10 The punctuation found in manuscripts of Old English prose and poetry (where it is often very scarce) is different from that of Modern English and is frequently of uncertain significance. Most editors of Old English prose and poetry use modern systems of punctuation instead. But modern punctuation is misleading because the unit of both prose and poetry in Old English tends to be the equivalent of the modern paragraph. It is certainly not the sentence of today's formal English. The problem is further complicated by the fact that adverbs like *þǣr* 'there' and *þā* 'then', which can also be conjunctions meaning 'where' and 'when', are not uncommon; that the demonstrative *sē* 'that one' can also be the relative 'who'; and that in many contexts we have no means of distinguishing them today, e.g. *þā* in *The Battle of Maldon* l. 162 (§12). I believe that the heavy use of modern punctuation, especially the division of the Old English paragraph into sentences, destroys the flow of both prose and verse. As Daniel Donoghue has said, it gives a particularly misleading stereotype of Old English poetry, causing many to think that the poetry is unsophisticated, heavily end-stopped, rhythmically jerky, and somewhat primitive. By means of light stopping and a modified system of punctuation, I hope to help you to appreciate the fluidity of the syntax and to gain some interpretive control of what you read. I set this system out in §11 but suggest that you do not try to master it immediately. When the need arises, I shall refer you back to it.

§11 The new system involves the use of the following marks of punctuation, although not all of them will be needed in every passage I print:

1 the point (.) to indicate the end of a paragraph or of a major sense unit;
2 the elevated point (·) to indicate a less definite pause which might vary between today's comma and full stop. See 9 below;
3 the colon to introduce speeches;
4 the comma to mark parallel constructions where necessary;

5 dashes (– –) to mark the parentheses which play an important part in Old English, especially in the poetry;

6 the question mark;

7 the exclamation mark;

8 single inverted commas, with double inverted commas inside where necessary, to mark off quotations.

To these can be added for pedagogic purposes

9 double commas (,,) to indicate the presence of ambiguous adverb/ conjunctions such as *þær* 'there'/'where' or *þā* 'then'/'when' or of the ambiguous demonstrative/relative *sē* 'that one'/'who'. Here you can make up your own mind which it is *if you feel the need*. I doubt if you always will. I use this symbol only to make a syntactic point. Normally I use the elevated point in these contexts;

10 = = to mark off *apo koinou* elements which 'face both ways'; see §§165–7. But please don't bother with this now.

§12 I do not think that the time is ripe for me to give here a passage illustrating the use of these punctuation marks. But I do suggest that, as you read, you try to link each statement in the paragraph with what goes before and with what follows. Thus in *The Battle of Maldon* ll. 162–8a below, a relationship of time, cause, and effect, will establish itself within six separate but connected statements which in the standard editions usually appear as three or four separate sentences. To make my point about the importance of light punctuation, I shall take the risk I have already taken in the other Old English passages so far quoted and use no punctuation at all within this seven-line verse paragraph:

> þā Byrhtnōð brǣd   bill of scēðe
> brād and brūneccg   and on þā byrnan slōh
> tō raþe hine gelette   lidmanna sum
> 165 þā hē þæs eorles   earm āmyrde
> fēoll þā tō foldan   fealohilte swurd
> ne mihte hē gehealdan   heardne mēce
> wǣpnes wealdan.

Somewhat literally translated, this runs:

> Then/When Byrhtnoth drew   sword from sheath
> broad and shining-edged   and struck on the corslet
> too quickly hindered him   one of the seamen
> when he wounded   the warrior's arm
> fell then to earth   golden-hilted sword
> he could not then hold   hard sword
> wield weapon.

When and how did the seaman hinder Byrhtnoth? What happened
result of Byrhtnoth's injury? Why did it happen? Did you notice the rep
tion in l. 168a of the idea expressed in l. 167? You will find that, by asking the
right questions, you can draw from the poem more than it appears to offer.

II

Other Differences between Old English and Modern English

A INTRODUCTION

§13   Apart from spelling and pronunciation, there are three differences between Old English and Modern English which I would characterize as major: Old English statements can have one of three word-orders, all of which still appear in Modern German, whereas Modern English statements have a fixed order; Old English largely relies on inflexions (changes in, or additions at, the end of words, as in the possessive -'s in 'the ship's mast' and the plural -s in 'three ships') to indicate relationships which we tend to express today by the word-order and by prepositions; and the vocabulary of Old English is mostly native Germanic, with some borrowings from Latin and from the Scandinavian languages, which were also Germanic (§xiii), whereas Modern English has borrowed with brilliant ruthlessness from all the languages with which its speakers have made contact, thereby widening its capacity for the expression of new ideas, increasing its richness by the addition of synonyms, and replacing many Old English words with borrowings. As a result, less than 20 per cent of the words which can be used in English today come down from Old English, though to be sure these are the everyday words which occur with great frequency. Even so, it may seem a startling thing to say but I have come to believe that the factor which above all makes Old English seem a foreign language to those trying to read it today is neither its inflexions nor its word-orders nor its syntax but its vocabulary.

§14   The standard books on Old English devote much space to phonology, inflexions, and syntax, but little to vocabulary. They rarely point out, as they should, that the Old English inflexions were already much reduced and frequently reinforced by prepositions or that English syntax as we now know it has been very little influenced by contact with foreign languages. So, before we examine the differences in vocabulary between Old English and Modern English, let me demonstrate what I call the 'Englishness' of Old English syntax by quoting, first in Old English and then in a literal translation which preserves the order and lineation of the original, a passage written by Ælfric c. 1000:

Sum swȳþe ġelǣred munuc cōm sūþan ofer sǣ fram sancte
Benedictes stōwe on Æþelredes cyninges dæġe tō Dūnstāne
ærċebisceope þrim ġēarum ǣr hē forþfērde and se munuc
hātte Abbo. þā wurdon hīe æt sprǣċe oþ þæt Dūnstān rehte
be sancte Ēadmunde swā swā Ēadmundes swurdbora hit
rehte Æþelstāne cyninge þā þā Dūnstān ġeong mann wæs
and se swurdbora wæs forealdod mann. þā ġesette se munuc
ealle þā ġereċednesse on ānre bēċ and eft þā þā sēo bōc cōm
tō ūs binnan fēam ġēarum þā āwendon wē hit on Englisc
swā swā hit hēræfter stent. Se munuc þā Abbo binnan twǣm
ġēarum ġewende hām tō his mynstre and wearþ sōna tō
abbode ġesett on þǣm ylcan mynstre.

A very learned monk came from the south over [the] sea from St
Benedict's place in Æthelred's king's day to Dunstan
archbishop three years before he died and the monk
was called Abbo. Then were they in conversation until Dunstan told
about St Edmund just as Edmund's swordbearer it
told Æthelstan king then when Dunstan [a] young man was
and the swordbearer was [an] aged man. Then set the monk
all the account in a book and afterwards then when the book came
to us within [a] few years then turned we it into English
just as it hereafter stands. The monk then Abbo within two
years went home to his monastery and was soon to
abbot appointed in that same monastery.

(In both passages, I use only the point (.); see §11(1).)

The differences in syntax are minimal: tautologic 'then when' twice; one
definite article 'the' and three indefinite articles 'a/an' unexpressed; the
different pattern for what today would be 'in King Æthelred's day'; and six
or seven differences in word-order. Let us now examine wherein the
differences in vocabulary between Old English and Modern English lie.

B VOCABULARY

§15 As I have already said, the Old English language is predominantly
Germanic. We have seen in the Introduction and in §9 that some Old English
words are recognizable from their Modern English counterparts, although
the meanings may have changed, e.g. *dēor* means '(any) wild animal' not 'deer';
fugol means 'bird', as in 'the fowls of the air', not 'fowl'; *lǣwede* means 'lay, as
opposed to cleric' not 'lewd'; and *sellan* means 'to give' not 'to sell'. Other
words differ in spelling and pronunciation as a result of changes in Middle
English and Modern English. But the correspondences in the table which

follows will help you to recognize the Old English forms of some of these
words.

OE spelling	MnE spelling	Vowels	Consonants
lang	long	an : on	
fæt	vat	æ : a	f : v
rǣdan	read	ǣ : ea	
dǣd	deed	ǣ : ee	
hāliġ	holy	ā : o	
hām	home	ā : o.e	
āc	oak	ā : oa	c : k
hlāf	loaf		hl : l
ecg	edge		cg : dge
dēman	deem	ē : ee	
frēosan	freeze		s : z
ċild	child		ċ : ch
miht	might	ih : ī	h : gh
scip	ship		sc : sh
līf	life	ī : i.e	
ġiellan	yell	ie : e	ġ : y
ġiefan	give	ie : i	ġ : g
dōm	doom	ō : oo	
mūs	mouse	ū : ou.e	
nū	now	ū : ow	
synn	sin	y : i	
mȳs	mice	ȳ : i.e	

§16   Some words from the passage in §14 can perhaps be guessed, e.g.
munuc 'monk', *cyning* 'king', *swurdbora* 'swordbearer', and *ġear* 'year'. But
some are less easy to recognize. Examples from the same passage include
ġelǣred 'learned', *forþfērde* 'forth went, died', and *ġereċednesse* 'narrative'. To
these we can add *stent* which means 'stands' and which is a form of *standan* 'to
stand', a word you can recognize. Here we see the same phenomenon as in
MnE 'man' plural 'men' (not 'mans'). There are inevitably exceptions to the
correspondences given above, e.g. OE *hāt* is 'hot' and OE *fylþ* is 'filth'. I shall
try to help you with these more opaque words as you meet them.

§17   To do this, I have now to ask you to follow me for a short distance into
what Dr Johnson, the eighteenth-century lexicographer, called 'the dusty
deserts of barren philology'. I have just mentioned the variation 'man/men'.
These two forms descend directly from OE *mann/menn*. Such variations are
common in Old English. At one time the form which has changed ended with
an unstressed syllable containing the sound [*i*] (as in 'mus*i*c') or [*j*] (which is
the symbol for the initial sound in 'year'); for *mann* the original plural was
probably *manniz*. These sounds [*i*] and [*j*] are made with the tongue high up

in the front of the mouth and it would seem that speakers began to prepare for this high front sound before they had finished the vowel of the stressed syllable. As a result they pronounced the stressed syllable higher and/or further forward than they should have done. The unstressed syllable then disappeared, as in *menn*, or was changed in form, as we shall see later. Grammarians call this change '*i*-mutation'.

§18 'But why should I bother about it?' The answer to this natural question is that an understanding of *i*-mutation will help you to recognize many more Old English words. If you consider the following pairs of words, you will notice that some pairs display the singular/plural variation seen in *mann/menn* but that in others the mutated form is a new word based on the non-mutated form, as in MnE 'strong/strength'.

Non-mutated		*Mutated*	
lang	'long'	*lengþ*	'length'
brād	'broad'	*brǣdan*	'to spread'
hāl	'whole'	*hǣlan*	'to heal'
fōt	'foot'	*fēt*	'feet'
dōm	'doom'	*dēman*	'to deem'
cuss	'kiss'	*cyssan*	'to kiss'
full	'full'	*fyllan*	'to fill'
mūs	'mouse'	*mȳs*	'mice'
fūl	'foul'	*fylþ*	'filth'
heorte	'heart'	*hiertan*	'to hearten'

The variation *standan/stent* above shows the same vowel relationship as *lang/lengþ* above but must await further explanation in §520.

§19 Our detour has demonstrated that some Old English words were formed from others by the addition of a suffix which caused *i*-mutation, e.g. *lang/lengþ* and *fūl/fylþ* (in these two, the suffix was -*iþ(u)*) and *cuss/cyssan* and *full/fyllan* (in which the suffix was -*jan*). Other suffixes, which do not affect the vowel of the stressed syllable or stem, include -*hād*, as in *cildhād* 'childhood'; -*iġ* (originally -*æġ*, so no *i*-mutation), as in *hāliġ* 'holy'; -*liċ*, as in *heofonliċ* 'heavenly'; and -*sum*, as in *hier-sum* 'hear-some, obedient'. Words containing these suffixes present no problems to present-day speakers of English. Nor do words formed by the addition of prefixes, e.g. *bēodan* 'to command', *forbēodan* 'to forbid, prohibit'; *bindan* 'to bind', *onbindan* 'to unbind'; and *drīfan* 'to drive', *tōdrīfan* 'to drive apart, scatter'.

§20 The formation of words by the addition of affixes (prefixes or suffixes) was one of three main ways in which the Old English language formed new words. A second was by making compounds of two (or more) words already existing in the language. A third was by borrowing from other languages. Modern English shows a strong preference for borrowing rather than for making compounds, although we can still make compounds today, e.g. 'no-go area', 'space shuttle', 'drop-out', 'guesstimate', 'do-gooder', 'non-starter', and 'skyscraper', a word which has been used of sails, horses, and men, as well as of buildings; whoever coined it had the imagination of a Shakespeare. But the Germanic habit of compounding was much more common in Old English.

§21 Ordinary everyday compounds like *niht-waco* 'night-watch', *hēah-clif* 'high-cliff', *folc-lagu* 'folk-law', *ǣr-dæg* 'early-day', and *wīn-druncen* 'wine-drunk', present no problem. Compounds with an inflected first element include *Engla-lond* 'land of the Angles'. But the Anglo-Saxons were often faced with the problem of expressing new ideas, especially when translating from Latin texts. In such situations, they either borrowed words (see below) or made new compounds. Sometimes the elements of a foreign word were represented by Old English equivalents, e.g. *wel-willend-ness* for *bene-volent-ia* 'benevolence', *fore-set-ness* for *prae-posit-io* 'preposition', and *þrī-ness* for *Tri-nitas* 'Trinity'. But sometimes the elements of a compound were based on a meaning of a Latin word. Thus the Pharisees were seen as men professing, and rigidly bound by, the law (Matthew 23: 13–29) – hence *ǣ-lārēowas* 'law-teachers' – or as men who stood apart and thought themselves holier than other men (Luke 18: 10–14) – hence *sundor-hālgan* 'apart-holies'. That these processes are now less natural for speakers of English can be seen in various ways. First, the language now tends to prefer borrowed words rather than compounds, e.g. 'benevolence' and 'preposition' above. Second, many native compounds such as *tungol-cræft* 'star-craft' for 'astronomy' and *lār-hūs* 'lore-house' for 'school' have disappeared from the language. Third, proposed native replacements like the sixteenth-century 'hundreder' for 'centurion' or the nineteenth-century 'folk-wain' for 'bus' seem to us ridiculous, whereas to Germans *Fernsprecher* 'far-speaker' for our Greek-derived 'telephone' is not unnatural, though they do, of course, use *Telephon*.

§22 The compounds used by Anglo-Saxon poets form a fascinating topic which is pursued in §§456–7.

§23 We turn now to borrowed words in Old English. The largest foreign element is the contribution from Latin; over one hundred survive today. It is not always possible to know exactly when a word was borrowed. But some decisions can be made. Early borrowings include words such as *camp*, Latin *campus*, 'field, open space, battle', from which were derived *campian* 'to fight' and *cempa* 'a warrior'; *mīl* 'mile' from Latin *mille passum* 'a thousand paces'; *wīn* 'wine' from Latin *vinum*; and *mangere* '(fish)monger' from Latin *mango* 'a dealer in slaves and other wares'. These have corresponding forms in other Germanic languages. Other early borrowings include *strǣt* 'street' from Latin *strata via* and *butere* 'butter' from Latin *butyrum*. These were borrowed before *t* became *d* between vowels in Vulgar Latin between *c.* 400 and 700; compare Italian *strada* 'street, road'. A third group of early borrowings comprises words which show Germanic or early

Old English sound changes that did not take place in words with the same sound which were borrowed later, e.g. *nǣp* 'neep, turnip', Latin *napus* (compare the later borrowing *pāpa* 'pope', Latin *papa*), and *munt* 'mount(ain)', Latin *montem* (compare the later borrowing *font* 'font', Latin *fontem*).

§24 The coming of Christianity naturally led to many ecclesiastical borrowings, including the Old English equivalents of 'altar', 'deacon', 'dean', 'epistle', 'litany', 'mass', 'prior', 'stole', and 'tunic'. We find *Pharisei* 'Pharisees' and *Fariseisc* 'of or belonging to the Pharisees'. More general borrowings include *cantere* 'cantor, singer', *plaster* '(medical) plaster', *paper* 'papyrus', and *comēta* 'comet'.

§25 Most of the Scandinavian borrowings (or loans) are found in the Anglo-Saxon Chronicle or in the Laws. About thirty appear in writing before *c.* 1016, the date of the accession of King Cnut. Examples which still survive today are: *feolaga* 'fellow, colleague', *hūsbonda* 'householder', *hūsting* 'court, assembly, tribunal' (MnE 'hustings'), *lagu* 'law', *ūtlaga* 'outlaw', and *þrǣl* 'servant, slave'. Another group of thirty-three recorded after 1016 includes twelve words which are very common today: 'crooked', 'die', 'knife', 'haven', 'hit', 'root', 'sale', 'score', 'skin', 'snare', 'take', and 'they'. These everyday borrowings reflect the existence of mixed communities of Anglo-Saxons and Scandinavians. But it is very probable that most of them were in the spoken language in the tenth century. Scandinavian loans continued into the Middle English period and (more spasmodically) thereafter.

§26 Borrowings from other languages are rare. A few words such as *engel* 'angel', *ciriċe* 'church', and *deofol* 'devil', may have reached the Germanic languages directly from Greek. Celtic elements occur mostly in place names, e.g. *torr* 'rock, rocky peak'. An early borrowing appears in Old English as *rīċe* 'kingdom'. It is parallel with Modern German *Reich* and survives as the second element in 'bishopric'. Other possible Celtic words include *assa* 'ass', *bannoc* 'piece (of cake or loaf)', *binn* 'bin, manger', and *brocc* 'badger'. The most interesting is undoubtedly OE *ambeht, ombeht*, which means both 'office, service' and 'servant' and was borrowed into Germanic probably direct from Celtic but possibly through Latin *ambactus*, the ultimate source of MnE 'ambassador'. It is recorded in Middle English but ultimately disappeared – only to be reborrowed in the twentieth century from Swedish as 'ombudsman'.

§27 There are a few words which might be derived from either Latin or French, e.g. *capun* and *castel*. But we are told by Alistair Campbell that 'in OE no loan-words which can certainly be regarded as French occur in manuscripts older than 1066, except *prūd, prūt* "proud", whence are derived *prȳte, prȳt* "pride"'. This may well reflect the impression made by the visiting Normans on their Anglo-Saxon hosts.

§28 I hope that these observations on the Old English vocabulary will be of interest and of some help. But, as I have said, there remain a large

number of Germanic words whose meaning I shall have to explain, either in
the Glossary or as we read the texts together.

C THE EXPRESSION OF RELATIONSHIPS: INFLEXIONS
OR ELEMENT ORDER AND PREPOSITIONS?

§29 George Bernard Shaw based his play *Androcles and the Lion* on the
story of the runaway slave who had the good fortune to encounter as his
opponent in the Roman arena the very lion from whose paw he had removed a
thorn while he was at liberty. The lion recognized him and embraced him
instead of tearing him to pieces. Readers of today's newspapers will not find it
difficult to imagine the sensation-seeking headline LIONESS KISSES
MAN over the story and to interpret it as meaning 'The lioness kissed the
man'. This sentence can be described in different ways. It is a statement, not a
question or a command. It contains five words – 'the' (definite article) twice,
'lioness' and 'man' (nouns), and 'kissed' (verb). But it can also be analysed into
three elements – the performer of the action ('the lioness'), the word expressing the action ('kissed'), and the sufferer or experiencer of the action ('the
man'). These elements are known respectively as the subject (S), the verb (V),
and the object (O), and the sentence can therefore be described as having SVO
order. If we now write 'The man kissed the lioness', the order is still SVO but
the meaning has changed because the man is now the subject and the lioness
the object. This change demonstrates the vital role played in Modern English
by what I have so far called word-order but will from now on call element
order, a role which can be further demonstrated by some more hypothetical
headlines: MAN FLEES DOG, DOG FLEES MAN, FLEAS DOG MAN,
and FLEAS MAN DOG.

§30 The sentences 'The boy gave the girl the book' and 'The boy gave the
book to the girl' contain a fourth element – the person for whom the action
takes place ('the girl'/'to the girl'). This is usually known as the indirect object,
in contrast to the direct object 'the book'. As the examples will remind you, it
can appear today in one of two positions – alone before the direct object ('the
book') or after the direct object but preceded by the word 'to', which is known
as a preposition because it is usually before (in pre-position to) the word it
governs ('the girl').

§31 So far we have seen examples of the typical roles played by S, V, and
both O elements, in English sentences. Different roles can be seen in
sentences like 'A stone killed the man', where the subject is inanimate and not
a person, and 'The parents gave the hospital £500' or 'The parents gave £500
to the hospital', where the indirect object is not a person. Other sentences
have a subject and a verb but no object, e.g. 'The boy laughed but the girl
cried', where we have two SV sentences joined by the conjunction 'but'.

§32 Sentences which have a direct object can frequently be reversed so that the sufferer or experiencer of the action becomes the subject, e.g. 'The man was kissed by the lioness' and '£500 was given to the hospital by the parents'. In these, the performer of the action is expressed with the help of the preposition 'by'. Grammarians describe the verb in 'The lioness kissed the man' as having active voice – the subject performs an action – and the verb in 'The man was kissed by the lioness' as passive – the subject is passive (in a grammatical sense, at any rate).

§33   In all these Modern English sentences, the form of the noun remains the same whether it is the subject, the direct object, or the indirect object. The differences in relationship are expressed either by changes in the element order or by the use of prepositions. No noun in Modern English changes its form when it changes its function from subject to direct object or to indirect object.

§34   But in the sentence 'She kissed him', where 'she' and 'him' are used in place of the noun phrases 'the lioness' and 'the man' – hence they are called pronouns – the subject and the object change in form if their roles are reversed: 'He kissed her'. The element order is still SVO. But the subject pronouns are 'she' and 'he' and the direct object pronouns are 'him' and 'her'. Similar changes occur in 'He gave her the book', 'He gave the book to her', 'She gave him the book', and 'She gave the book to him', in which the pronouns 'him' and 'her' appear as indirect objects, either alone or with the preposition 'to'. Traditional grammarians describe the subject pronouns 'he' and 'she' as having the nominative case, the direct object pronouns 'him' and 'her' as having the accusative case, and the indirect object pronouns '(to) him' and '(to) her' as having the dative case. Indeed, they often extend these terms to Modern English nouns. Modern grammarians are right to criticize the analysis of the nouns of today in terms of case because the nouns do not change their form when they change their function. The nouns do not need to change because the element order SVO and prepositions such as 'to' or 'for' tell us what role in the sentence each noun is playing.

§35   But these grammatical terms have a place in this book. The differences in the pronouns are a survival from Old English, where both nouns and pronouns had different forms for the nominative, the accusative, and the dative. There was also another case which still exists today – the possessive or, as I shall call it, the genitive. This is seen in *Godes word* 'God's word', *his bōc* 'his book', and *hire hand* 'her hand'.

§36   Modern English then relies on element order to distinguish the subject from the object. The strength of the SVO order in statements in today's standard English is such that most speakers are likely to interpret 'Her kissed he' as meaning 'She kissed him', whereas Old English *Hīe cyste hē* can only mean 'He kissed her'; here we have order OVS, with the subject *hē* in the nominative case and the object *hīe* in the accusative case. So we see that the element order had no need to be fixed in Old English statements and that the meaning depended less on the element order than on the inflexions. Inflexions are particularly important for distinguishing the subject from the object. And although inflexions can by themselves often make the interrelationship of elements clear, prepositions are sometimes used in Old English. Thus we find *Hē sende hire stānas* and *Hē sende stānas tō hire* 'He sent her stones'. 'He was slain with a stone' could be expressed as either *Hē wæs mid stāne ofslægen* or (less often) by the dative without a preposition, *Hē wæs stāne ofslægen*. Here the stone is the means (or instrument) by which the action is done. But the performer (or agent) of the action when not the subject of the verb is usually expressed by a preposition, e.g. *Rōmeburg wæs getimbred fram twām gebroðrum, Rēmuse 7 Romuluse* 'Rome was built by two brothers, Remus and Romulus'.

§37   To recapitulate. Old English distinguished four cases, illustrated here by two pronouns which preserve a number of recognizable forms in Modern English:

nominative (nom.)	*hē* 'he'	*hēo* 'she'
accusative (acc.)	*hine* 'him'	*hīe* 'her'
genitive (gen.)	*his* 'his'	*hire* 'her'
dative (dat.)	*him* 'him'	*hire* 'her'

On the instrumental (a residual fifth case) see §51. It also distinguished singular forms from plural forms, e.g.

stān : stānas	'stone : stones'
lēo : lēon	'lioness : lionesses'
guma : guman	'man : men'
iċ : wē	'I : we'
þū : ġē	'thou : ye'

As we shall see in the next section, Old English nouns and pronouns and the case system in general have a few more complications. But if you have mastered what I have said so far, these further details will hold no real terrors for you. If you want to test what you have learnt by reading some Old English, you can use the extracts from the Anglo-Saxon Chronicle in §§181–7.

D   THE OLD ENGLISH CASES AND THEIR FUNCTIONS

1 The nominative and accusative cases

§38   As we have seen, element order in Old English is not the determining factor it is in Modern English. So the Anglo-Saxon predecessor of the hypothetical newspaper man who produced the headline LIONESS KISSES MAN could have written (using the now-archaic verbal ending *-eþ/-eth*)

LĒO CYSSEþ GUMAN or *GUMAN CYSSEþ LĒO* or *GUMAN LĒO CYSSEþ,* with the orders SVO, OVS, and OSV, respectively, because in Old English many nouns change their subject or nominative form to an accusative form when they are used as direct object. Thus MAN KISSES LIONESS could have appeared as

GUMA CYSSEþ LĒON or *LĒON CYSSEþ GUMA* or *LĒON GUMA CYSSEþ.*

The equivalents which follow, all of my own making, illustrate the point.

'This lioness kissed that man'   'This man kissed that lioness'
þēos lēo cyste þone guman   *þes guma cyste þā lēon*
þone guman cyste þēos lēo   *þā lēon cyste þes guma*
þone guman þēos lēo cyste   *þā lēon þes guma cyste*

In these examples, both the nouns and the demonstratives 'this' and 'that' change their forms or, to put it another way, are inflected.

§39 Another group of examples shows us that pronouns change their form in both Old and Modern English.

'She kissed him'   'He kissed her'
Hēo cyste hine   *Hē cyste hīe*
Hine cyste hēo   *Hīe cyste hē*
Hine hēo cyste   *Hīe hē cyste*

§40 But there are nouns which have the same form whether they are subject or object. With such nouns only the demonstrative tells us which noun is nominative and which is accusative, e.g.

'The man found the hound' but 'The hound tore the man'
Se man fand þone hund   but *Se hund tær þone man*

In these two sentences, as those of you who have dared to look at the forms of *se* in §496 will know, *se* says 'I am the subject' and *þone* says 'I am the object'.

§41 If we add adjectives like *eald* 'old' and *hwīt* 'white', we find that they too can change in form:

Se ealda man fand þone hwītan hund but
Se hwīta hund tær þone ealdan man.

If we have just an adjective and a noun, the adjective changes in a different way (don't panic; more about this in §70):

'An old man found a white hound' but 'A white hound tore an old man'
Eald man fand hwītne hund   but *Hwīt hund tær ealdne man.*

In these sentences also, you may by now hear *-ne* saying 'I am the object'.

§42 All the examples I have so far given concern one person or one animal and are therefore in the singular. But when we refer to more than one, we use the plural: *lēo : lēon*, 'lioness : lionesses'. Here the nominative singular is distinguished from the plural. Nominative plurals and accusative plurals are always the same in Old English except in the pronouns *wē : ūs* 'we : us' and *ġē : ēow* 'ye : you'. So (theoretically at any rate)

þās ealdan guman fundon þā hwītan oxan

could mean 'These old men found the white oxen' (SVO) or 'The white oxen found these old men' (OVS). Similarly, we cannot be absolutely sure whether Harold found Edward or vice versa when we read *Harold fand Eadweard*. In the spoken language, the intonation would, I believe, have revealed the order. But we lack that clue when we read Old English today. However, since SVO is the regular order today and is much more common in Old English than OVS, we tend to assume that the order is SVO in these places. We are probably right, for Old English was clearly moving towards the SVO order.

§43   The nominative, the case of the subject, is also the case of address (sometimes called the vocative case), e.g. *O lēofa cyning!* 'O dear king!' But you are not called upon to learn *stān* 'O stone' as I had to learn Latin *mensa* 'O table'; few of us ever want to engage a stone or a table in conversation.

§44   The accusative, the usual case of the direct object, is also used adverbially to express extent of space, e.g. *Wyrc þē nū ǣnne arc þrēo hund fæðma lang and fīftig fæðma wīd and þritig fæðma hēah* 'Work for yourself now an ark three hundred of fathoms [cubits] long and fifty of fathoms wide and thirty of fathoms high', and to express duration of time, e.g. *Tō hwī stande ġē hēr ealne dæg ȳdele?* 'To what/Why stand you here all day idle?' and *Hē leofode niġon hund ġēara and þrittiġ ġēara* 'He lived nine hundred of years and thirty of years'.

2 The genitive case

§45   Here it will suffice to say that the Old English genitive performs the functions performed today by the endings -*'s* and -*s* and by *of*-phrases. In the examples which follow, the ending -*es* says 'I am the genitive': *Gōdes sunu* 'the son of God', *þæs mannes dōhtor* 'the man's daughter', *twēġen sciprāpas of hwæles hȳde geworht* 'two ship-ropes wrought of whale's hide', and *ġescēad ǣġðer ġe gōdes ġe ȳfeles* 'understanding both of good and of evil'.

§46   The genitive can also be used adverbially, e.g. *Hē mētte þone cyning ānes* 'He met the king once', *Hē wæs hāmweardes* 'He was homewards/at home', *ǣġhwǣr landes* 'anywhere in the land', and *dæges ond nihtes* 'by day and night'.

§47   The so-called partitive construction seen in 'some of the warriors' and 'nine of the children', as opposed to 'some warriors' and 'nine children', appears in Old English, e.g. *ān of ēow twelfum* 'one of you twelve', where *of* is followed by the dative. But it is more usually expressed with the genitive case – hence the term 'partitive genitive' – e.g. *ān hiora* 'one of them', *wācost burga* 'weakest of cities [burgs]', and *iċ dranc þæs drinces* 'I drank [some] of the drink' compared with *iċ dranc þone drinc* 'I drank the drink'. (Modern English 'foursome', meaning 'a group of four', which is derived from *fēower sum* 'one of four', conceals the Old English partitive genitive.)

3 The dative case

§48   The dative is typically the case of the indirect object. Today we say 'He gave the monastery the book' or 'He gave the book to the monastery'. As we have already seen, these patterns descend from Old English, where *þæt mynster* 'the monastery' as indirect object has the dative case whether it is used alone or with *tō*: *Hē ġeaf þām mynstre þā bōc* or *Hē ġeaf þā bōc tō þām mynstre*. In the poetry, the dative often expresses possession in phrases like *him tō hēafdum*, literally 'to them at [the] heads' and so 'at their heads', and *him on bearme* 'on his bosom'.

§49   The most frequent ending in the dative singular is *-e*, as in *mynstre* above. Unfortunately *-e* is a very common ending which can also occur in other cases in the singular. But the dative plural ending *-um*, as in *Hē fylde þæt mynster gōdum bōcum* 'He filled the monastery with good books', where the dative expresses the instrument, is less ambiguous.

§50   Most of the adverbial functions performed today by prepositional phrases can be expressed in Old English by the dative, sometimes alone, sometimes with a preposition. Examples include *God spræc ðisum wordum* 'God spoke in these words' but *Se biscop bæd hine oft mid þām ylcum wordum* 'The bishop bade him often with the same words'; . . . *forþon iċ hine sweorde ofslēan ne wille* '. . . for that/because I do not wish to kill him with a sword' but . . . *þæt iċ mid sweorde ofslōh nigene* '. . . so that I slew nine with a sword'; *þriddan sīþe* 'on the third occasion', *fēower sīþum* 'four times', *hwīlum* 'at times, formerly, whilom' but *on þæm þriddan ġeare* 'in the third year' and *æfter ðisum* 'after this'; and *þrim ġearum ǣr hē forþferde* 'three years ere he went forth [died]' but *ymbe ġeara ymbrynum* 'after a period [circuits] of years'. Modern English 'of necessity, needs [must]' can be expressed by gen. *nēdes* and dat. *nēde* or by the phrases *mid nēde* or *of nēde*.

§51   A few relics of a Germanic fifth case – the instrumental – survive in the singular declension of demonstratives and adjectives. Thus the phrases *on þæm dæge* (dative) and *on þȳ dæge* (instrumental) both mean 'on that day'. Similarly, *on þyssum ġeare* (dative) and *on þȳs ġeare* (instrumental) both mean 'in this year'.

4 Person and gender

§52   Speakers of Modern English use pronouns in the first person ('I : we'), in the second person ('[thou] : you'), and in the third person ('he/she/

it : they'). Similar distinctions were made in Old English: *ić* : *wē*, *þū* : *ġē*, *hē/ hēo/hit* : *hīe*.

§53   Both Old English and Modern English distinguish the third person singular pronouns as masculine (*hē* : 'he'), feminine (*hēo* : 'she'), and neuter (*hit* : 'it'). In Modern English, these categories of gender refer to natural gender and distinguish animate beings – 'The boy . . . he', 'The girl . . . she' – from inanimates – 'The stone . . . it'. (I disregard here the personification seen in 'The sun . . . his rays' and 'The moon . . . her light'.) The distinction between 'he' and 'she' can be very useful but there are times when it might be more convenient if, like Finnish and some other languages, we had one pronoun to cover persons of both sexes, as we have in the plural 'they'.

§54   But in Old English, gender does not refer to natural gender and is not concerned with sex or lack of it; one word for 'woman' was *se wīfmann* (masculine), another *þæt wīf* (neuter). Old English distinguishes masculine nouns such as *se coss* 'the kiss/embrace' and *se stān* 'the stone' from feminine nouns such as *sēo ġiefu* 'the gift' and *sēo rōd* 'the rood/cross' and from neuter nouns such as *þæt scip* 'the ship' and *þæt hūs* 'the house'. Such a system is called grammatical gender. Sometimes the grammatical gender reflects sex or lack of it, e.g. *se mann* (masculine) 'the man', *sēo hlǣfdiġe* (feminine) 'the mistress (of servants), the lady = the queen', and *þæt word* (neuter) 'the word'. But this is coincidental; in fact I don't think it would matter – and it might make things easier – if we called the three Old English genders red, white, and blue. We are indeed fortunate to have got rid of grammatical gender and with it other oddities such as *þæt mæġden* 'the maiden/woman' (neuter)!

§55   However, grammatical gender is something you can learn to live with and not to worry about. The meaning rarely depends on a knowledge of the gender of a noun. The word *ār* means 'messenger' if it is masc. *se ār*; 'honour, glory' or 'oar' if it is fem. *sēo ār*; and 'ore, brass, copper' if it is neut. *þæt ār*. The word *þās* 'this' can be accusative singular or plural with feminine nouns but cannot be accusative singular with neuter nouns. The word *word* is neuter and can be accusative singular or plural. You can therefore work out for yourself that *Hē wrāt þās word* can only mean 'He wrote these words'. But things like this don't crop up very often. So don't give up. Together, we can cope with the few problems of this kind which arise in this book.

§56   Grammatical gender disappeared from English soon after the Norman Conquest. But even before the Conquest, the neuter pronoun *hit* was coming to be used with inanimates irrespective of grammatical gender, e.g. *se wīsdōm* (masc.) . . . *hit* 'wisdom . . . it' and *sēo bōc* (fem.) . . . *hit* 'the book . . . it', where grammatical gender would require *se wīsdōm* . . . *sē* and *sēo bōc* . . . *sēo*. Sequences like the latter are the norm, e.g. *Hāmtunscīr* (fem.) . . . *hē hæfde þā* (fem.) *oþ hē ofslōg þone aldormon þe him lengest wunode* 'Hampshire . . . he had her/it until he slew the *aldormon* [see Glossary] who remained with

him longest'. But these are fairly obvious. If we come across any real difficulties, I shall help you.

5 'No paradigms, please!'

Introduction

§57　Why not? The word 'paradigm' merely means a pattern or example.
The sequences 'he/his/him' and 'sing/sings/sang/sung' are paradigms in
which the pronoun 'he' is declined and the verb 'sing' is conjugated. The
Old English paradigms are more complicated than those which remain in
Modern English but, as I have already said, too much can be made of them.
When we begin a new academic year or move to a new job, we soon make
friends among the strangers who confront us. You have already made one or
two friends among the Old English paradigms, e.g. *se* subject and *þone*
object. My aim in what follows is to introduce you to a few more forms so
that they too will become friends. If you consult Part V below when you are
ready, you will meet them in their family groups. If you read some of the
extracts from the Anglo-Saxon Chronicle in §§181–7, you will meet them (as
it were) in real life.

§57a　I have deliberately not provided a separate section about numerals
because by so doing I would have had to burden you with information you
will not need when reading this book. I have explained all the numerals you
will meet in the appropriate section or (for Texts 1–51) in the Glossary.
Those especially interested should in the first instance consult *A Guide to
Old English*, §§82–6.

§58　In §§38–51 above, we have seen that Old English uses the nominative and accusative cases to distinguish between subject and object whereas
Modern English relies on the element order SVO, even in questions, e.g.
'Did the lioness kiss the man?' or 'Did the man kiss the lioness?'; here we
have an auxiliary verb (v) 'Did' before the regular SVO. We have also seen
that Old English has case forms which allow it to do without prepositions in
situations where Modern English cannot. If you wish to read Old English
with some understanding, you will find that an ability to recognize a few
common inflexional endings and a few pronouns will pay great dividends.

§59　How can I help you to achieve this ability? The easiest way, I think,
will be for me to present here a list of the most significant endings so that
you can learn to recognize them easily. I have always found that recognition,
as opposed to parrot learning, is the essential thing for those wishing to read
Old English. Frankly, I do not think that the achievement of this recognition
is a very great challenge; anyone capable of getting money from a cashpoint
machine or automatic banking unit is capable of meeting it, if the desire is
there. What follows can be read and understood as it stands without reference to the paradigms. But you will not find anything too terrifying if you

look at Part V from time to time, always remembering that recognition of the forms, not a parrot knowledge of the paradigms, is your aim, and if you do not try to absorb too much at once.

The articles

§60 There is no separate definite article in Old English: *se* means both 'the' and 'that' while *þes* means 'this'.

§61 There is no indefinite article, e.g. *Lēo cyste guman* 'A lioness kissed a man'. But you can see it beginning to develop in examples like *ān wulf wearþ āsend* 'one wolf/a wolf was sent' and *on ānre bēc* 'in one book/a book'.

Pronouns

§62 We can start by agreeing that the following sequences of nominative, accusative, genitive, and dative, forms present no difficulties of recognition if you read them aloud:

Nom.	Acc.	Gen.	Dat.		Nom.	Acc.	Gen.	Dat.
ić	*mē*	*mīn*	*mē*		*wē*	*ūs*	*ūre*	*ūs*
þū	*þē*	*þīn*	*þē*		*ġē*	*ēow*	*ēower*	*ēow*

Actually, these are paradigms. But I won't try to slip any more in here. Instead, I ask you to consider the inflexional endings which are important for the OE pronouns. (You can, if you wish, look at §§494–9 as you do so.)

§63 The inflexional endings set out below are important because they indicate the case and number of the pronoun and/or of the noun. The gender is grammatical and, as I have already said, is rarely vital. I have therefore bracketed the abbreviations for gender here. Please do not expect to absorb everything at once. Please do not try to take all this in without a rest!

-ne acc. sg. (masc.)
   Ić fand þone/þisne eorl 'I found the/this warrior'
   Wē sāwon hine/nānne/hwone 'We saw him/no one/ someone'

-s, **-es** gen. sg. (masc. and neut.)
   his drihten 'his lord'; *his līc* 'its body'
   þæs/þisses weres mōd 'that/this man's courage'
   þæt styċċe þisses clāðes 'the piece of this cloth'
   Hwæs weorc? 'Whose work?'

-m, **-um** dat. sg. (masc. and neut.)
   þǣm/þissum witan . . . hwǣm 'to the/this wise man' . . . 'for someone'
   him on hēafde 'to him on head' and so 'on his head', with the dative *him* expressing possession

-re gen. and dat. sg. (fem.)

  hire (gen.) *ġesiþ . . . tō hire* (dat.) 'her retainer' . . . 'to her'
  mid þǣre dryhte þisre / þisse hlǣfdigan 'with the retinue of this queen'

-ra gen. pl.

  hira hūs 'their house'
  þāra bearna cyninga 'of the sons of kings'
  se þanc þisra / þissa lēoda 'the plan of these princes'

-m, **-um** dat. pl.

  him . . . þissum dagum 'him' . . . 'in these days'
  mid þǣm hāligum / hālgum 'with the holy (ones)/saints'
  (This ending is ambiguous in pronouns (and adjectives), but can only
  be plural – never singular – in nouns.)

§64 A few loose ends remain to be tied up for the pronouns. You will
easily recognize the following:

  nom. *hwā* 'who?' and 'anyone, someone', acc. *hwone*, gen. *hwæs*, dat.
  hwǣm
  nom. and acc. sg. neut. *hit* 'it', *þæt* 'that', *þis* 'this', and *hwæt* 'what?' and
  'anything, something'

You will soon learn to recognize

  nom. sg. masc. *hē* 'he', *sĕ* 'the/that', and *þes* 'this'
  nom. sg. fem. *hēo* 'she', *sēo* 'the/that', and *þēos* 'this'

You will certainly meet these variants of dat. sg. masc. and neut. *þǣm*:

  þām, þan, þon, þȳ

You will have to remember

  that 'she' is *hēo*
  that 'they' is *hīe*, 'them' (acc.) is *hīe*, 'their' is *hiera*, and 'them' (dat.) is *him*
  that nom. and acc. pl. *þā* means 'the/those' and *þās* means 'these'

This is the last hurdle here:

  the three forms *hīe*, *þā*, and *þās*, are **not only** nom. and acc. pl. 'they/
  them', 'the/those', and 'these'
  but also acc. sg. fem.
  Ic̄ seah hīe 'I saw her' (as well as 'I saw them')
  God worhte þā eorðan 'God wrought the earth'
  Sēo mōdor bær þās dohtor 'The mother bore this daughter'

§65 The most frequent relative pronouns today are 'who/whose/
whom', 'which', and 'that'. Old English had a different system. There are
three possibilities:

1 *þe*, which is sometimes ambiguous because it is indeclinable and can therefore be any case, gender, or number, representing 'who', 'whom', 'whose', and 'to whom';

2 *se*, which can be declined but is sometimes ambiguous because we cannot tell whether it is a relative 'who' or a demonstrative 'that (one)';

3 combinations of *se* and *þe*, the uses of which I shall explain as they occur.

Hwā 'who?' and *hwæt* 'what?' are not used as relative pronouns.

Nouns

§66 There are several groups (or declensions) of nouns with endings which differ according to declension or gender. In §63 I stressed the value of being able to recognize the forms of the demonstratives. The possessives *mīn* 'my/mine', *þīn* 'thy/thine', *ūre* 'our', and *ēower* 'your', also have the endings

-ne, -s/-es, -m/-um, -re, and *-ra*

In the examples which follow, the form of the demonstrative or possessive tells us the case and therefore the function of the noun:

Sēo hearpe is dēore 'That harp is dear/valuable'
Hē plegode þā hearpan 'He played the harp'
Wynsum wæs se sweg þǣre hearpan 'Winsome/pleasant was the sound of the harp'
mīnne eaforan 'my son' (acc. sg.)
þīnes eaforan 'of thy/your son' (gen. sg.)
ūrum eaforan 'to/for our son' (dat. sg.)
ēowerra eaforan/eaforena 'of your sons' (gen. pl.)

§67 The ending of the noun itself is not always decisive. Thus *-an* appears in six different cases in the examples I have just cited and there is nothing useful I can say here about the nominative and accusative singular of nouns. So take all the help you can get from the demonstrative or possessive. But some noun endings do give you a clue. In the singular we find

-es

You already recognize this as genitive singular. But it is also one, but not the only, sign of the genitive singular in nouns:

mīnes fæderes 'of my father'

-e

This is the most common sign of the dative singular in nouns:

tō his hūse 'to his house'   *sweorde* 'with [a] sword'
mid giefe 'with [a] gift'   *þissum stāne* 'with this stone'

But *-e* can also be a sign of the genitive singular:

se fōt þǣre rōde 'the foot of the rood/cross'

§68   No noun has different forms for the nominative and accusative plural. But there is no one ending for these two cases.

Many nouns have *-as*, e.g. *stānas* 'stones' and *āþas* 'oaths'; hence the *-s* plural ending of today.

Some end in *-an*, e.g. *oxan* 'oxen'.

But we also find

ġiefa 'gifts', *ġiefe* 'gifts',
scipu 'ships',
and *word* 'words' (unchanged in the plural; compare Modern English 'sheep', 'deer', and 'swine').

§69   The news about the other cases in the plural is more cheerful.
The genitive plural of nouns is *-a*.
The dative plural is *-um*.
BUT

1 Everything that ends in *-a* is not a genitive plural, e.g. *se guma* nom. sg. 'the man' and *lōca!* (imperative) 'look!'
2 As we have seen, *um* can appear in the dative singular of pronouns. It also occurs in the same place in adjectives.
3 The ending *-an* can appear in:
   a noun, in almost any case;
   an infinitive, e.g. *bindan* 'to bind' and *cuman* 'to come';
   an adverb, e.g. *ēastan* 'from the east' and *westan* 'from the west'.

Adjectives

§70   If you happen to notice that adjectives sometimes have different forms for the same case, don't worry. There is a certain logic to it but it does not affect the meaning. When the adjective appears without a demonstrative, you will find what may perhaps by now be familiar endings:

gōdne wer '[a] good man' (acc. sg.), *gōdes weres* (gen. sg.)
gōdum were (dat. sg.), *gōdra wera* (gen. pl.), and
gōdum werum (dat. pl.) 'to/for good men'

The ending *-e* is common in the nom. pl., e.g. *higum unrōte* 'sad in [their] hearts', and in the acc. pl., e.g. *Hē sende gōdcunde lārēowas* 'He sent religious teachers'.

§71   When the adjective is preceded by a demonstrative or possessive, you will find

nom. *se gōda wer* (masc.) 'the good man'
     sēo gōde folde (fem.) 'the good earth'
     þæt gōde līf (neut.) 'the good life'

The ending **-an** can appear in most of the other cases, e.g.

mīnne gōdan wer 'my good man' (acc. sg.)
þære gōdan foldan 'of (or to) the good earth' (gen. or dat. sg.)
þāra gōdan/ gōdena wera (gen. pl.) 'of the good men'
ūrum gōdan/ gōdum werum (dat. pl.) 'to (or for) our good men'

Here again the form of the demonstrative or possessive usually gives an unambiguous clue to the case and so to the function of the phrase. Those of you who like puzzles can work out, with the help of §§69 and 70, which *-um* tells us that *ūrum gōdan/ gōdum werum* does not mean 'to (or for) our good man'.

From the story of Orpheus and Eurydice

§72   In relating how, after the death of Eurydice, Orpheus wandered in the woods harping so beautifully that the wild beasts were spellbound, an Anglo-Saxon teller of the story used the following words:

... ond *nān* heort ne onscunode *nænne* lēon ne *nān* hara *nænne* hund ne *nān* nēat nyste *nænne* andan ne nænne ege *tō ōðrum for ðære mergðe ðæs sōnes.*

The writer then explained that, because it seemed to Orpheus that there was nothing to please him in this world, Orpheus decided to seek the gods of Hades:

Ðā *ðæm* hearpere ðā ðūhte ðæt *hine nānes ðinges* ne lyste *on ðisse* worulde· ðā ðōhte hē ðæt hē wolde gesēcan helle godu.

(On the elevated point (·), see §11(2).)
Literally translated, the two sentences mean:

... and no hart/deer not shunned no lion nor no hare no hound nor no animal not knew no malice nor no fear to another/others for the mirth/joy of the sound.
When to the harper then seemed that him of no thing not pleased in this world, then thought he that he would seek hell's gods.

In this passage, you will find some of the main endings of which I have spoken: *-ne, -es, -um, -re*; the important pronominal forms *ðære, ðæs, ðæm,* *ðisse* (where I follow the manuscript in using *ð* instead of *þ*; see §1), and *hine*; and, if you read the passage aloud, some familiar words in unfamiliar guise or with slightly different meanings.

Other points worth noting are:

the impersonal verbs *ðūhte* '[it] seemed' and *lyste* '[it] pleased' (see §98)
the gen. sg. fem. ending *-e* in *helle* 'hell's, of hell' (see §504)
the nom. acc. pl. neut. ending *-u* in *godu* (see §503)
the multiple negation, which is emphatic (see §110).

E THE OLD ENGLISH VERB SYSTEM AND ITS MODERN COUNTERPART

1 Introduction

§73 Traditional grammars of Old English have in the past perhaps tended to concentrate on the differences between the Old English verb system and that of Modern English. I hope that by stressing the similarities I can help you to realize that there is much you already know and much that you can easily learn to recognize. Here again, I recommend a process of absorption rather than of parrot learning. Here too (as in §§37 and 57), you can use the extracts from the Anglo-Saxon Chronicle in §§181–7 if you want to test what you have absorbed.

§74 Most verbs in both Old English and Modern English fall into one of two groups which are called, respectively, strong verbs and weak verbs. Strong verbs are verbs like

> *rīdan rād riden*   'to ride, rode, ridden'
> *singan sang sungen*   'to sing, sang, sung'

These change the vowel of the stressed syllable to form the past tense 'rode' and past participle 'ridden'. Weak verbs are verbs like

> *lufian lufode lufod*   'to love, loved, loved'
> *lōcian lōcode lōcod*   'to look, looked, looked'

These keep the same stressed vowel but add *-d* or *-t* (a dental suffix) to form the past tense (sometimes known as the preterite) and past participle.

§75 The remarks which follow about the Old English verb system apply to all verbs even though I had to single out one verb – *singan* – to illustrate them. We note first about the strong verb whose infinitive is *singan* 'to sing' that it has present and past forms of the indicative mood, which is a general mood used in statements:

Present Indicative	Past Indicative
ić singe 'I sing'	*ić sang* 'I sang'
þū singest 'thou singest'	*þū sunge* 'thou sangest'
hēo singeþ 'she sings'	*hē sang* 'he sang'
hīe singaþ 'they sing'	*wē/ġē sungon* 'we/you sang'

The present endings -*est* and -*eþ* will be familiar to those who have read Chaucer or Shakespeare. Old English one-word (or synthetic) verb forms like (*hē*) *singeþ* have to do duty for the modern two-word (or analytic) forms '(he) is singing', '(he) does sing', and '(he) will sing', as well as for '(he) sings'. Similarly, *hēo sang* can mean, according to the context, 'she sang' or 'she did sing' or 'she was singing', and also 'she has sung' or 'she had sung'.

§76 We next find subjunctive forms. The subjunctive is now largely obsolete but it survives in such formulae as 'Long live the King!', 'God save the Queen!', 'Be that as it may . . .', and 'If I were you', and in such patterns as 'The committee proposed that Mrs Brown be elected', 'The President must accept this plan lest he be defeated in the Senate', and 'Even if that be true, I cannot accept it'. Such one-word (or synthetic) verb forms were much more common in Old English:

Present Subjunctive	Past Subjunctive
ić/ þū/ hēo singe	*ić/ þū/ hē sunge*
wē/ ġē/ hīe singen	*wē/ ġē/ hīe sungen*

In Modern English, we nearly always express the subjunctive mood by the two-word (or analytic) forms 'may sing' and 'might sing'.

§77 Other forms of the strong verb *singan* 'to sing' include:

imperative singular *sing* 'sing!'
imperative plural *singaþ* 'sing!'
infinitives *singan* or *tō singenne* '(to) sing'
present participle *singende* 'singing', as in 'he is singing'
past participle *sungen* or *ġesungen* 'sung', as in 'he has sung'.

§78 The range of meanings of the synthetic (or one-word) verb forms (*hē*) *singeþ* and (*hēo*) *sang* and the prevalence of the synthetic subjunctives have led to the generalization that the Old English verb system is synthetic whereas that of Modern English is analytic. There is something in this. But it neglects the fact that the beginnings of most of the analytic tenses and moods of Modern English are present in Old English in form, although the functions are different.

§79 Thus we find forms with the so-called modal verbs *Ić sceal/ wille/ mæg/ can/ moste singan*, meaning 'I am obliged/wish/am able/know how/am permitted to sing'.

§80 We find forms with the verb 'to be' and the present participle: *Se ćild is weaxende* 'The child is waxing/growing' and *Eorþliću þing sind flēondu*

'Earthly things are fleeing/fleeting', where the final -*u* on *flēondu*, like that on *eorþlicu*, is an adjectival ending. It is unlikely that these combinations were verbal unities; they probably meant something like 'The child is a grower' and 'Earthly things are fleeting things'.

§81 With the past participle, we find forms with *is*, e.g. *Hē is cumen* 'He is come'; compare 'How are the mighty fallen!' These are, of course, intransitive verbs – verbs which cannot take an object – and the perfect with 'to be' tends to emphasize the state arising from the action rather than the time of the action.

§82 The modern perfect and pluperfect with 'have' and 'had' is seen in 'They have come' (intransitive verb) and 'They had slain the king' (transitive verb – one which can take an object). The ancestor of the latter pattern appears in three forms in OE:

> 1 *Hīe hæfdon þone cyning ofslægenne* 'They had the king, slain'
>   Here the participle is inflected as an adjective, showing the familiar **-ne** of the accusative singular masculine. It agrees with *þone cyning*, the object of *hæfdon*.
> 2 *Hīe hæfdon þone cyning ofslægen* 'They had the king slain'
>   This is comparable to 'I have the job finished'.
> 3 *Hīe hæfdon ofslægen þone cyning* 'They had slain the king'
>   The last is obviously identical in pattern with MnE 'They had slain the king' but whether the verb + participle combination was felt as a verbal unity is uncertain.

§83 Like Modern English, Old English had no synthetic passive; see §§127 and 511. The ancestor of today's passive is seen in patterns like

> *Hē wæs/wearþ ofslægen* 'He was/became slain'
> *Hīe wæron/wurdon ofslægene* 'They were/became slain'

In these the verb can be *bēon/wesan* 'to be' (§528) or *weorþan* 'to become' (§§513–14) and again the participle can be inflected as an adjective. So once again the exact status of these combinations in Old English is uncertain. But the passive is frequently expressed by the pronoun *man* 'one' and an active verb, e.g. *Man ofslōg þone cyning* 'Someone slew the king/the king was slain by someone'. See §127 for another example.

§84 The Old English verb system therefore was already moving towards that of Modern English. Three steps remained to be taken. The Old English equivalent of the present participle 'being' did not appear until late. So there are, as far as I know, no examples of patterns like 'It is being made' or 'he was being kissed'. The past participle 'been' is first recorded in 1096. So, again as far as I know, there are no examples of the pattern 'It has been made' or 'He had been kissed'. I am not sure whether any speaker of Modern English has ever said 'If he had been at home last night, he might have been being kissed'. But I am pretty confident that its equivalent was never uttered in Old English.

§85   The third step still to be taken was the harnessing of 'do' as an auxiliary in questions 'Does he sing?' – OE *Singeþ hē?* – in negatives 'She does not sing' – OE *Hēo ne singeþ* – and for emphasis 'He did sing'. OE *dōn* meant 'to do', e.g. *Dō swā ic þē bidde* 'Do as I bid you'; 'to make', e.g. *Dō his paðas rihte* 'Make his paths right/straight'; 'to cause', e.g. *Hē dyde hine to singenne* 'He caused him to/made him sing'; and was used to avoid repetition of a verb, e.g. *þæt cild wēox swā swā ōþre cild dōþ* 'The child waxed/grew just as other children do'.

2 Strong verbs

§86   The strong verbs of Old English have descendants today. Some distinguish three vowels, e.g. 'sing, sang, sung', 'ride, rode, ridden' (where the two *i*'s represent different sounds), and 'swim, swam, swum'. Many distinguish only two, e.g. 'break, broke, broken', 'speak, spoke, spoken', 'bear, bore, born', 'draw, drew, drawn', 'shake, shook, shaken', 'stand, stood, stood', 'blow, blew, blown', and 'fall, fell, fallen'. A few have the same vowel throughout, e.g. 'burst' and 'slit'. These verbs, like their ancestors, change their root vowels in the past tense and past participle. But there were in Old English more strong verbs. Some have disappeared completely. Some have become weak, like 'bake' and 'leap'. Some of those which have become weak have left their strong past participle to survive as an adjective, e.g. 'melt, molten', 'seethe, sodden', and 'shave, shaven'. Some have become partly weak, e.g. 'shear, sheared, shorn/sheared' and 'sow, sowed, sown/sowed'. Strong verbs with a nasal in the root, e.g. *singan* (§74), lose the *-en* at the end of the past participle. But old forms survive as adjectives in phrases like 'our bounden duty' and 'a drunken frolic'.

§87   The strong verbs of Old English also had more patterns than those of Modern English in two ways. First, there were seven classes of them. And second, some of them had four vowels, e.g. *beran* 'to bear', *bær* '[I/he] bore', *bæron* '[we/you/they] bore', and *boren* 'born/borne'. No strong verb in Modern English has more than three vowels; see §86. I give a list of the Old English patterns in §517. I do not expect you to learn this list but you may like to look at it to get an idea of what goes on and may even wish to consult it from time to time.

§88   Some important strong verbs have only one syllable in the infinitive, e.g. *flēon* 'to flee', *fōn* 'to take', *slēan* 'to strike, slay', and *sēon* 'to see'. In these verbs *ēo* and *ēa* are diphthongs (§7). They are explained in §521. I shall help you with them when they occur.

3 Weak verbs

§89   These hold few terrors apart from the meaning of those which have disappeared from the language. The verbs *lōcian*, *lōcode*, *(ġe-)lōcod*, *lufian*, *lufode*, *(ġe-)lufod*, and *sendan*, *sende*, *(ġe-)send*, are easily recognizable as 'look, looked, looked', 'love, loved, loved', and 'send, send, sent', respectively. But OE *sendan* may have pret. sg. *sendede* and past ptc. *(ġe-)sended*, in which the *d* of the ending *-d(e)* is not absorbed into the root. Other easily recognizable verbs are *willan*, *wolde* 'will, would' and *dōn*, *dȳde*, *(ġe-)dōn* 'do, did, done'.

§90   In §§75–7 I set out the moods, tenses, and inflexional endings, of the strong verb *singan*. The weak verbs distinguish the same moods and tenses, and the inflexional endings of the two groups of verbs have much in common. So I set out the forms of the weak verbs here with a minimum of comment.

§91   The forms of *lufian* 'to love' are set out in §526. But for the time being I ask you to concentrate on a more common type of weak verb represented by *timbran* 'to timber/to build'. Its indicative forms are:

	Present Indicative	*Preterite Indicative*
Sg. 1	*timbre*	*timbrede*
2	*timbrest*	*timbredest*
3	*timbreþ*	*timbrede*
Pl.	*timbraþ*	*timbredon*

§92   The subjunctive forms are:

	Present Subjunctive	*Preterite Subjunctive*
Sg.	*timbre*	*timbrede*
Pl.	*timbren*	*timbreden*

§93   Other forms of *timbran* include

imperative singular	*timbre* 'build!'
imperative plural	*timbraþ* 'build!'
infinitives	*timbran* or *tō timbrenne* '(to) build'
present participle	*timbrende* 'building'
past participle	*timbred* or *ġetimbred* 'built'

§94   Not all verbs have these endings. Thus the modern verbs 'fill', 'hear', 'drench', and 'set', may appear without the first *e* of the ending *-ed(e)*:

fyllan, *fylde*, *(ġe-)fylled* or *(ġe-)fyld*
hīeran, *hīerde*, *(ġe-)hīered* or *(ġe-)hīerd*

and (with devoicing/unvoicing of *d* to *t*; cf. MnE 'send', 'sent')

drenċan, drenċte, (ġe-)drenċed or *(ġe-)drenċt*
settan, sette, (ġe-)seted or *(ġe-)set(t)*

The verbs *fremman* 'to do' (§524), *werian* 'to defend' (§525), *lufian* 'to love' (§526), and *habban* 'to have' (§527), also differ in some respects from *timbran*.

§95 Some common weak verbs are irregular in both Old and Modern English. Try reading these verbs aloud:

Infinitive	Preterite	Past Participle
sellan 'to give'	*hēo sealde* 'she gave'	*seald*
sēċan 'to seek'	*hē sōhte* 'he sought'	*sōht*
brenġan 'to bring'	*hēo brōhte* 'she brought'	*brōht*
þenċan 'to think'	*hē þōhte* 'he thought'	*þōht*
þynċan 'to seem'	*þūhte* 'seemed'	*þūht*
bycgan 'to buy'	*hē bohte* 'he bought'	*boht*
wyrċan 'to work'	*hēo worhte* 'she worked/wrought'	*worht*

4 Other common verbs

§96 Some forms of the following verbs may also be familiar to you from MnE:

Meaning	Inf.	Pres. Ind. Sg.	Pres. Ind. Pl.	Past Sg.
'to possess'	*āgan*	*iċ/hē āh*	*āgon*	*hēo āhte*
'can/to know how to'	*cunnan*	*iċ/hē can*	*cunnon*	*hēo cūþe*
'to dare'	*durran*	*iċ/hē dearr*	*durron*	*hēo dorste*
'to be able'	*magan*	*iċ/hē mæġ*	*magon*	*hēo mihte/meahte*
'to be allowed to/may'	*mōtan*	*iċ/hē mōt*	*mōton*	*hēo mōste*
'to remember'	*(ġe-)munan*	*iċ/hē (ġe-)man*	*(ġe-)munon*	*hēo (ġe-)munde*
'to be obliged to'	*sculan*	*iċ/hē sceal*	*sculon*	*hēo sceolde*
'to know'	*witan*	*iċ/hē wāt*	*witon*	*hēo wiste*

§97 Two common verbs meaning 'to speak' or 'to say' are *cweþan*, a strong verb of class V, and *secgan*, an irregular weak verb. They are conjugated:

Inf.	*cweþan*	*secgan*
Past Sg.	*cwæþ* 'quoth'	*sæġde, sæde* 'said'
Past Pl.	*cwǣdon*	*sæġdon, sædon*
Past Ptc.	*cweden, ġecweden*	*sæġd, ġesæġd*

5 Impersonal verbs and constructions

§98 We are all familiar with sentences like 'It rained. It hailed. It snowed.' These are often called impersonal. This term is sometimes extended to verbs like 'seem', e.g. 'It seemed that nothing pleased him'. That Old English had more of these verbs is clear from the equivalent sentence *Ðūhte ðæt hine nānes ðinges ne lyste*, lit. '[It] seemed that him of no thing [it] not pleased', and from a sentence in which Wulfstan (§446) is stressing Christ's humanity: *Hine þyrste hwȳlum and hwīlum hingrode*, lit. '[It] him thirsted at times and at times [it] hungered'.

§99   Most of these constructions have disappeared. Let me quote more of the Wulfstan passage: *Hine þyrste hwȳlum and hwīlum hingrode. Hē æt and dranc and þolode ġe ċyle ġe hǣtan* '[It] him thirsted at times and at times [it] hungered. He ate and drank and tholed/suffered both chill and heat.' If the first word had been 'Christ', OE *Crīst*, which can be nominative or accusative, and not *hine*, which (as you know by now!) is accusative, we might never have suspected that we had the impersonal constructions. We could certainly never have proved it. Such ambiguities are probably a factor in the loss of these constructions from later English. They also demonstrate how uncertain our knowledge of Old English sometimes is in the absence of native speakers. So take courage.

§100   I shall help you with any impersonal constructions we meet. But if you confuse *þenċan* 'to think' with *þynċan* 'to seem' and *þōhte* 'thought' with *þūhte* 'seemed', you will not be the first or the only one to do so.

F   AND NOW SOME PRACTICE

1 Twenty sentences

§101   I suggest that you translate the sentences composed or collected by Fred C. Robinson which follow and try to understand the grammatical relationships as far as you can before you consult the key printed in §102. Remember to read them aloud, and please do NOT forget §63!

> Iċ bræc þone stān.
> Se stān is miċel.
> Ðæs stānes miċelnes is wundorliċ.
> þes stānwyrhta ġeaf þǣm stāne hīw.
> 5 Hē slōh þone mann þȳ stāne.
> Sēo sunne is swīðe miċel.
> þǣr hēo scīnþ þǣr biþ dæġ.
> Niht is þǣre eorðan sceadu betwēonan þǣre sunnan and mancynne.
> þis līf is lǣne and þēos woruld drēoseþ and fealleþ.
> 10 Sing þisne song!
> Hīe scufon ūt hira scipu and siġldon tō þǣre sǣ.
> On þissum dæġe cwealdon wē þone fēond þisses folces.
> Iċ ġeman þā naman þāra folca and þissa folca.
> His wīfes nama wæs Elizabeþ.

15 þēos ġiefu is for ūs and hēo līcaþ ūs.
Se dēaþ is þisses līfes ende ac sēo sāwol is undēadliċ.
Hīe hine ne dorston þā þing āscian.
Hwæt þyncþ ēow be Crīste? Hwæs sunu is hē?
Hwæs sunu eart þū? And hwæs dohtor eart þū?
20 Hwȳ ġeworhte God þā yfelan nǣdran?

2 Key to the twenty sentences

§102 1 **bræc** 'broke' from *brecan* (§519); **stān**: see §15 (*ā*).

2 **miċel** 'muckle, great'.

3 **miċel** + **nes** 'size'; **wundorful** would be easier!

4 **stānwyrhta** 'stone-mason'; **ġeaf** 'gave' from *ġiefan* (§519); **hīw** 'hue, form, beauty'.

5 **slōh** 'struck' from *slēan* (§88).

6 **swīðe** 'very'.

7 **þǣr . . . þǣr** 'Where . . . there'. On the element order see §137; **scīnþ** contracted form of *scīneþ* (§512); see §15 (*ī*).

8 **betwēonan** 'between'.

9 **lǣne** 'transitory'; **drēosan** 'to perish' (§519).

11 **scufon**: you may guess the modern equivalent but it is not quite the right word (§517). Try 'pushed'; the noun *seġl* means '(a) sail'.

12 **cwealdon** 'killed' from *cwellan*; **fēond** '[fiend], enemy'.

13 **ġeman** 'remember' from *ġemunan*.

15 **ġiefu**: see §54; **līcaþ** '[likes], pleases' from *līcian*.

17 **dorston** '[durst], dared' from *durran* (§96).

18 **þyncþ**: Old English has
    þencan 'to think', past *þōhte*
    impersonal *þyncan* 'to seem', past *þūhte*
You can tell which we have here by its form (contracted from *þynceþ*) and by the case of *ēow* (§62).

20 **ġeworhte** '[wrought], made' from *ġewyrċan* (§95); if an umpire was once a numpire, an apron a naperon, and an auger a nauger, then *nǣdre* means . . . But the word used in the King James/ Authorized Version of Genesis 3 is 'serpent'. (Since *nǣdre* is feminine, I can only tell from the reference that *þā yfelan nǣdran* is singular, not plural; see §§64 and 69(3).)

3 A poet's riddle

§103 Here it is:

    Iċ þā wiht ġeseah   on weġ feran·
    hēo wæs wrǣtliċe   wundrum ġeġierwed.
    Wundor wearþ on wēġe·   wæter wearþ tō bāne.

(On the elevated point (·), see §11(2).)

§104 I give a translation of, and the answer to, this riddle below. But I hope you will work through it first with the aid of the notes which follow.

Line 1:
wiht '[wight], creature'; **ġeseah**: see §521; **weġ** 'way'; **feran** 'to go, travel'.
Line 2:
wrǣtliċe 'strangely'; **wundrum** dative plural used adverbially; **ġeġierwed** 'adorned' from **(ġe-)ġierwan**.
Line 3:
wearþ see §516; **wēġ** 'wave, water'; **bān**: see §15 (*ā*).
'I the creature saw on [her] way; she was strangely with wonders/ wondrously adorned. [A] wonder happened on [the] wave; water turned to bone.'
Answer: An Iceberg.

4 A poet's deliberate ambiguity?

§105 Genesis 22 describes how God tested Abraham by commanding him to sacrifice his only son Isaac as a burnt offering. Verse 6 reads: 'And Abraham took the wood of the burnt offering, and laid it upon Isaac his son; and he took the fire in his hand, and a knife; and they went both of them together.' In telling this story an Anglo-Saxon poet wrote:

Wudu bær sunu·   fæder fȳr and sweord.

The verb *bær* is from *beran* 'to bear, carry'. So *fæder* [*bær*] *fȳr and sweord* 'father bore fire and sword'. But what is the element order in *wudu bær sunu*? Since Isaac carried the wood, it must be OVS 'son bore wood'; see §38. But if the order were SVO, the translation would be 'wood bore son'. This happened at the Crucifixion when the Cross bore the Son of God. It is possible that the poet intended this double reference. Ælfric tells us that *sēo nīwe ġecȳþnis æfter Crīstes menniscnisse wæs ġefillednys ealra þæra þinga þe sēo ealde ġecȳðnis ġetācnode tōwearde be Crīste* 'the New Testament after Christ's Incarnation was the fulfilment of all those things which the Old Testament signified [as] to come concerning Christ'. And the sacrifice of Isaac was regarded by the Fathers as a prefiguring, a type of the sacrifice of Golgotha.

G ADVERBS, PREPOSITIONS, CONJUNCTIONS, AND INTERJECTIONS

1 Adverbs

§106 Adverbs tell us where, when, how, or why, an action takes place. Old English adverbs can end in -*e*, e.g. *hraþe* 'quickly', -*liċe*, e.g. *hrædliċe* 'quickly', -*unga*, e.g. *eallunga* 'completely', and -*an* 'from', e.g. *norþ* 'north, northwards' but *norþan* 'from the north'. The endings *-or*, *-ost*, '-er', '-est' occur in the comparison of adverbs, e.g. *oft* 'often', *oftor* 'more often', *oftost* 'most often', and (through *i*-mutation) *lange* 'long', *leng*, *lengest*, and *feorr* 'far', *fierr*, *fierrest*.

§107   The genitive and dative cases can be used adverbially, e.g. *ānes* 'once'; *dæges ond nihtes* 'by day and by night'; *yfle* 'with evil, evilly'; and *hwīlum* 'at times, formerly, whilom'.

§108   Before a verb, the negative 'not' is *ne*, e.g. *Hēo ne singeþ* 'She sings not, does not sing'. The forms *nā* and *nō* usually negate words other than verbs, e.g. *Hē wæs Godes bydel and nā God* 'He was God's beadle/messenger and not God'. Other common negatives are *næfre* 'never' and *nalles/næs* 'not (at all)'.

§109   These last two forms are contractions of the negative *ne* with *æfre* and *ealles*. Similar contractions give us *nis* 'is not' from *ne is*, *næfde* 'had not' from *ne hæfde*, and *noldon* 'would/wished not' from *ne woldon*.

§110   One negative does not cancel another, as in formal English today. So *ond nān heort ne onscunode nānne lēon* 'and no hart/deer not shunned/was afraid of no lion' is comparable to the non-standard 'I didn't do nothing to nobody'. Such multiple negation often seems to carry emphasis. It had a long history in this function in English, being found in Chaucer and Shakespeare as well as in Old English, and did not become a grammatical outlaw until after 1660.

§111   The list of common adverbs which follows is supplied for reference purposes in the hope that, sometimes with the help of the table of correspondences in §15, you will learn to recognize them. What you will not know is that all of them can also serve as conjunctions. I give both meanings here and will discuss the problems which arise from these ambiguities later. Here is the list:

	Adverbs	*Conjunctions*
ǣr	'ere, before'	'ere, before'
nū	'now'	'now that'
siþþan	'after(wards)'	'after, since'
swā	'so'	'as'
þā	'then'	'when'
þanon	'thence'	'whence'
þær	'there'	'where'
þēah	'however'	'though'
þenden	'meanwhile'	'while'
þider	'thither'	'whither'
þonne	'then'	'whenever'
þȳ	'therefore'	'because'

2 Prepositions

§112 Most of the common Old English prepositions are easily recognizable from their modern equivalents, although they do not always mean the same. Particularly noteworthy exceptions are *fram* meaning 'by' as well as 'from' and *wiþ* meaning 'against', not '(in company) with'; this sense is represented by *mid*. *Būtan* is the ancestor of 'but' and its Old English meaning 'except' lingers on in expressions like 'all but one'.

§113 This list too is for reference.

æfter	'at, after, along, according to'
ǽr	'ere, before'
æt	'at, from, by'
be	'by, along(side), about'
beforan	'before, in front of'
betweox	'between, among'
būtan	'except, outside, without'
for	'before, in front of, because of'
fram	'from, by'
ġeond	'throughout'
in, on	'in, into, on, onto'
mid	'among, with (the company of), by means of'
of	'from, of'
ofer	'above, over, on'
ongēan	'against, towards'
oþ	'up to, until'
tō	'to, as'
þurh	'through, by means of'
under	'under, beneath'
wiþ	'towards, opposite, against, along, in exchange for'
ymb(e)	'at, near' (place); 'at, after' (time); 'about, concerning'

§114 In the phrase *beneoþan þǽm cnēowe* 'beneath/below the knee', *þǽm cnēowe* is in the dative case. So the preposition *beneoþan* is said to govern the dative. Old English prepositions may also govern the accusative, e.g. *wiþer þā* 'against them', or the genitive, e.g. *andlang þæs dīces* 'along the ditch'.

§115 I have used the three uncommon prepositions *beneoþan*, *wiþer*, and *andlang*, deliberately because all the more common prepositions can govern at least two cases, e.g. *mid sweorde* 'with [a] sword' (dative) but, less often, *mid hine* 'with him' (accusative). Some can govern three, e.g. *wiþ gehwone fēonda* 'against each of enemies' (accusative), *wiþ mīn* 'against me' (genitive), and *wiþ Gode* 'against God' (dative). In practice, these variations raise few problems; the preposition tells you everything which the case ending or inflexion does, and often more. (This is one of the reasons for the disappearance of inflexions discussed in §xix.) But don't forget to distinguish singular from plural, e.g. *tō his hūse* 'to his house' but *mid hondum* 'with hands'.

§116   Words like *in* and *on* may take the accusative of motion to, and the dative of rest in, a place, e.g. *Hē fēoll on þone stān* 'He fell onto the stone' but *Hēo sæt on þæm setle* 'She sat on the seat'.

3 Conjunctions

§117   Old English, like Modern English, has two kinds of conjunctions which grammarians distinguish as coordinating and subordinating. The former join coordinate clauses, clauses of equal rank, e.g. 588 *Hēr Ælle cyning forþfērde ond Æþelrīc rīcsode æfter him v ġēar* 'Here/In this year King Ælle died and Æthelric ruled after him five years'. Other coordinating conjunctions in addition to *ond* 'and' include *ac* 'but', *ne* 'nor', and *oþþe* 'or'.

§118   Subordinating conjunctions include words such as *ġif* 'if', *hwonne* 'when', and *swā þæt* 'so that'. These words introduce subordinate or dependent clauses, clauses which complete the meaning of, or depend on, a main or principal clause, e.g. *sēc ġif þū dyrre* 'seek if thou darest' and *Hē wæs ġescoten mid ānre flā on þæm cnēowe swā þæt nān man hī of þæm bāne ātēon ne mihte* 'He was shot with an arrow in the knee so/with the result that no man not could remove it [*hī*] from the bone'.

§119   The lists which follow are also for reference. Coordinating conjunctions include

and, ond	'and'
ġe	'and'
æġþer . . . ġe	'both . . . and'
ġe . . . ġe	'both . . . and'
ac	'but'
hwæþ(e)re	'however, yet'
oþþe . . . oþþe	'either . . . or'
swā . . . swā	'either . . . or'
þe . . . þe	'either . . . or'
ne . . . ne	'neither . . . nor'
nāþor ne . . . ne	'neither . . . nor'

§120   Anglo-Saxon writers made effective use of sequences of simple sentences, sometimes with conjunctions like *and*, *ac*, and *hwæþ(e)re*, sometimes without them. Both are well exemplified in this extract from *The Dream of the Rood*, where Christ's Cross is confessing the part it played in the Crucifixion. I have printed the conjunctions in bold type in the Old English version:

37   Ealle iċ mihte
   fēondas ġefyllan   **hwæðre** iċ fæste stōd.
     . . .   . . .

42   . . .   ne dorste iċ **hwæðre** būgan tō eorðan,
feallan tō foldan scēatum   **ac** iċ sceolde fæste standan.
Rōd wæs iċ ārǣred   āhōf iċ rīċne cyning
45 heofona hlāford   hyldan mē ne dorste.

(On the comma, see §11(5).)
In my literal translation I have marked off the separate simple sentences
with full stops and have also printed the conjunctions in bold type:

All I could [the] foes destroy. **Yet** I fast stood . . . Not dared I **however**
bend to [the] earth, fall to [the] land's surface. **But** I had fast to stand.
Rood/Cross was I raised. Raised I [the] mighty king, [the] lord of [the]
heavens. [I] bow myself not dared.

This use of simple sentences with or without coordinating conjunctions is
called 'parataxis', a noun whose adjective is 'paratactic'. See *Guide* §§182–6.

§121 I have already given in §111 a list of adverbs which also serve as
subordinating conjunctions. Other subordinating conjunctions include:

būtan	'unless'
ġif	'if'
hwonne	'when, until'
nefne	'unless'
oþ	'until'
swā (. . .) *þæt*	'so (. . .) that'
þā hwīle þe	'while'
þæs (*þe*)	'when, after, since, because, as'
þæs (. . .) *þæt*	'so (. . .) that'
þæt	'that, so that'
þȳ lǣs (*þe*)	'lest'

§122 These subordinating conjunctions will not cause you much
trouble because Old English and Modern English share the same types of
subordinate clauses: noun clauses (dependent statement, command, question, and exclamation), adverb clauses of place, time, purpose, result, cause,
comparison, concession, and condition, and of course adjective clauses,
which are introduced by the relative pronouns listed in §65. They also share
the accusative and infinitive construction seen in *þā hēt hē þā eorlas*
(accusative) *forð gangan* (infinitive) 'Then he ordered the warriors to go
forth'. Sentences like this and like *Se cyning hēt þone bisceop timbran þā ċiriċean*
'The king ordered the bishop to build the church' present no difficulty. But
what about sentences like 'The king ordered his horse to be saddled', where
the doer of the action is not expressed either because everybody knows or
nobody cares who it is? You will find sentences like *Se cyning hēt his hors bēon
gesadlod* or even like *Se cyning hēt his hors gesadlod* 'The king ordered his horse
saddled'. But more common is the pattern *Se cyning hēt þā ċiriċean timbran*

'The king ordered [someone] to build the church', where the doer is not named and the infinitive is active. But it can of course be translated as passive 'The king ordered the church to be built'. Similarly, *Se cyning hēt his hors sadelian*, where the doer may be the king's groom or the nearest servant, no matter who. Verbs other than *hātan* 'to order' can introduce these patterns, e.g. *hīeran* 'to hear' (§94) and *sēon* 'to see' (§88). Try translating the following sentences, which contain only words you have already met:

Hēo seah þæt wīf forþ gangan.
Hē hīerde þone man singan.
Hēo seah þæt wīf þā hearpan plegan (§66).
Hē hīerde þone man þisne song singan.
Hēo seah þā hearpan plegan.
Hē hīerde þisne song singan.

The last two could be rendered 'She saw the harp being played' and 'He heard this song being sung'.

§123 But I must say something about conjunctions made up of two elements, e.g. *swā þæt*. These often occur with the two elements together, e.g. *and þær wæs swīðe swēte stenc swā þæt ealle slǣpon* 'and there was [a] very sweet scent so that all slept'. They also occur with the elements separated, e.g. *Swā swīþe lufode God þysne middanġeard þæt hē his āncennedan Sunu sealde for ūs* 'So greatly God loved this world that He gave His only-begotten Son for us' and (with *þæs* 'so' instead of *swā*) *Nān nis þæs weliġ þæt hē sumes ēacan ne þyrfe* 'No one is so wealthy that he does not need some addition'. These will not cause you any difficulty.

§124 Most conjunctions made up of three elements contain a preposition. Typical prepositional conjunctions include *æfter þǣm þe*, as in *þā on þǣm ilcan dæġe æfter þǣm þe hīe þis ġesprecen hæfdon· fuhton Gallie on þā burg.* I can best explain this by translating it literally: 'Then on the same day after that on which [*þe*] they had spoken this, [the] Gauls fought against the city.' But the combination *æfter þǣm þe* is also found not referring back to a named day or month or year, e.g. *þā wearþ hē hrēowlīce ond hrædlīce dēad æfter þǣm þe hē þā ċild acwealde* 'Then he became cruelly and quickly dead after that namely [*þe*] he killed the children'. In the first example, *þe* can be described as a relative pronoun. But in the second (and perhaps also, to begin with at least, in the first) it functions as a more general connecting word. The nearest modern equivalent I can suggest is 'namely'. In both sentences *æfter þǣm þe* means 'after'.

§125 I hope this explanation will help you to understand that

ǣr þǣm þe 'before that, namely' means 'before'
for þǣm þe 'for/on account of that, namely' means 'because'
tō þǣm þe 'to that [end], namely' means 'so that'.

Sometimes you will find alternatives with *þæt* instead of *þe*:

> *ǣr þǣm þæt* 'before'
> *for þǣm þæt* 'because'
> *tō þǣm þæt* 'so that'

In all these conjunctions, *þǣm* can appear in various spellings, including *þām*, *þan*, *þon*, or *þȳ*. These practice sentences, all based on the passage from Ælfric in §14, may help:

> Se munuc Abbo cōm ǣr þǣm þe Dūnstān forþfērde.
> Æfter þām þæt Dūnstān forþfērde, gewende Abbo hām.
> Wē awendon þā bōc on Englisc for þon þe hit on Lǣden gewriten wæs.
> Abbo wæs tō þan gelǣred þæt hē to abbode gesett wæs.
> Abbo wæs for þȳ tō abbode gesett þæt hē swȳþe gelǣred wæs.

To complicate things further, *þe* is sometimes omitted, so that *for þǣm* adv. 'therefore/for that (reason which follows)' can also be a conj. 'because'. Similarly *ǣr þǣm* 'before' and *æfter þǣm* 'after'.

§126 If you have coped with the last two examples, you have already mastered what I can only call divided prepositional conjunctions, e.g. *for þȳ ... þe* 'for that ... namely, because' in *þā menn cōmon for þȳ on weg þe ðāra ōðerra scipu āsǣton* 'Those men got away because the ships of the others went aground', and *tō þon ... þæt* 'to that [end] ... that' in *Herodes bebēad þæt mon ācwealde eall Dauides cynn tō þon· gif Crīst geboren nǣre þā gīet· þæt hē nā siþþan geboren ne wurde* 'Herod commanded that someone kill all the race of David to the end that/so that, if Christ had not yet been born, He would not be born later'. Such sentences can at first appear confusing. But it is not difficult to sort them out. If you meet a prepositional phrase like *for þȳ* or *tō þǣm* which you cannot fit in, read on to see if there is a *þe* (or a *þæt*) waiting to be picked up. Try your strength on *Tō þǣm fīc-trēow weaxeþ þæt hit fealle. Tō þǣm hit sprytt þæt his lēaf fealwien* 'To that [end] [a] fig-tree waxes/grows, that it may fall. To that [end] it sprouts, that its leaves may fallow/turn yellow.'

§127 The second example in §126 (*Herodes ...*) shows that the impersonal *man/mon* with an active verb is an Old English way of expressing the passive. So the natural translation is 'Herod commanded that all the race of David be slain' or 'Herod commanded all the race of David to be slain'. (Those who know Latin may be interested to notice that neither Old English nor Modern English has the equivalent of the synthetic Latin passive *amatur* 'he is loved'. In Old English this would be either *Hē is gelufod* or *Man lufaþ hine* 'One loves him'.)

4 Interjections

§128   These include:

ǣ	'alas!'
ǣlā	'alas! O!'
ēalā	'alas! O!'
efne	'behold, indeed, truly!'
ġēa	'yea!'
ġēse, ġȳse	'yes!'
haha and hehe getācniað hlehter on	'. . . betoken laughter in
lēden ond on englisc	Latin and in English'
hūru	'indeed, surely, at least'
hwæt	'ah! lo!'
nese	'no!'
nic	'no!'
ono	'behold!'
wā	'woe!'

H   THE GERMANIC ELEMENT ORDERS OF OLD ENGLISH

§129   We have seen that Modern English relies on a fixed element order SVO and on prepositions to make distinctions which in Old English were often made by inflexions. We have also seen that the basic SVO order of Old English *Lēo cysseþ guman* can therefore be varied to OVS *Guman cysseþ lēo* and OSV *Guman lēo cysseþ*. There are two other basic orders in Old English – S . . . V and VS. These three orders still occur in Modern German and their presence in Old English is probably the most obvious sign that it is a Germanic language.

§130   The Old English version of Matthew 7: 24–7 will help me to illustrate these three basic orders as they are used in direct or non-dependent statements and in subordinate clauses. Read the translation, which is from the Authorized or King James Version, and then read the passage aloud. After that, work through the Old English with the help of the translation and the notes in §131.

24   Therefore whosoever heareth these sayings of mine, and doeth them, I will liken him unto a wise man, which built his house upon a rock:

25   And the rain descended, and the floods came, and the winds blew, and beat upon that house; and it fell not: for it was founded upon a rock.

26   And every one that heareth these sayings of mine, and doeth them not, shall be likened unto a foolish man, which built his house upon the sand:

27 And the rain descended, and the floods came, and the winds blew, and beat upon that house; and it fell: and great was the fall of it.

24 Ǽlċ þāra þe ðās mīne word ġehȳrþ and þā wyrcþ byþ ġelīċ þǽm wīsan were se hys hūs ofer stān ġetimbrode.

25 þā cōm þǽr reġen and myċel flōd and þǽr blēowon windas and āhruron on þæt hūs and hyt nā ne fēoll· sōþlīċe hit wæs ofer stān ġetimbrod.

26 And ǽlċ þāra þe ġehȳrþ ðās mīne word and þā ne wyrcþ· sē byþ ġelīċ þǽm dysigan menn þe ġetimbrode hys hūs ofer sand-ċeosel.

27 þā rīnde hit and þǽr cōmon flōd and blēowon windas and āhruron on þæt hūs and þæt hūs fēoll· and hys hryre wæs miċel.

(On the elevated point (·), see §11(2).)

§131 The following comments may help:

Verse 24:
Ǽlċ 'each'; **wyrcþ**: see §95; **wer** 'man'; buildings were mostly of timber.
Verse 25:
āhruron 'rushed/fell' from *āhrēosan* (§519).
Verse 26:
dȳsiġ '[dizzy]/foolish'.
Verse 27:
hryre is from the same root as *āhruron* (through *i*-mutation).

§132 As promised, I now illustrate from Matthew 7: 24–7 the three basic element orders which occur in Old English non-dependent statements and subordinate clauses:

> SVO (with its variations OVS and OSV)
> S . . . V
> VS.

§133 The order VS appears after an adverb in verses 25 *þā cōm þǽr reġen . . . and þǽr blēowon windas* and 27 *þā rīnde hit and þǽr cōmon flōd* and without an adverb in verse 27 *and blēowon windas*.

§134 The order S . . . V occurs in verse 24 *þe ðās mīne word ġehȳrþ* 'who these my words hears' and *se hys hūs ofer stān ġetimbrode* 'who his house over stone timbered/built'. In these sentences we have SOV. In verses 24 *and þā wyrcþ* and 26 *and þā ne wyrcþ* 'and them (not) does', we have OV.

§135 All the other clauses have SV or variations. In verse 24 we have *Ǽlċ þāra . . . byþ ġelīċ þǽm wīsan were* 'Each of those . . . is like to the wise man'. The corresponding passage in verse 26 has a repetitive (or tautologic) demonstrative *sē* 'Each of those . . . that one is like to the dizzy/foolish man'. Idiomatic non-expression of the subject is seen in verses 25 and 27 in both Old English *and āhruron on þæt hūs* and in Modern English 'and beat upon that house'. A common tendency to place a participle or infinitive at the end of a clause is seen in verse 25 *sōþlīce hit wæs ofer stān ġetimbrod*.

§136 In Modern German the order SOV is associated with subordinate clauses. However, this limitation does not apply in Old English; compare the SOV clauses beginning with *þe* and *se* in verse 24 with the parallel clauses in verse 26, both of which have SVO. Conversely, we find SOV in principal clauses which are non-dependent statements, e.g. *Hī þā þæt lond forlēton* 'They then that land forsook' and *Ðā rēðan hæþenan þone hālgan stǣndon* 'The cruel heathens the holy one/saint stoned'.

§137 Element order is not completely free in Old English. But it cannot be relied upon to tell us whether a clause is principal or subordinate in either prose or poetry. There is one exception: in the prose only, words like *þǣr*, *þā*, and *þonne*, are likely to be adverbs 'there, then, then' when followed by the order VS, and conjunctions 'where, when, when' when followed by SV or S . . . V, e.g. *þǣr ðīn gold is þǣr is ðīn heorte* 'Where your gold is, there will be your heart', *Ðā hē þæt hīerde· þā ferde hē þider mid fyrde* 'When he heard that, then went he thither with the levy/(Anglo-Saxon) army', and *þonne hē gesēah þā hearpan· þonne ārās hē* 'Whenever he saw the harp, then arose he'. In the prose then, *þǣr*, *þā*, and *þonne*, are likely to be adverbs when immediately followed by the verb but conjunctions when the subject precedes the verb.

§138 In the sequences conjunction *þǣr/þā/þonne* . . . adverb *þǣr/þā/þonne* in the three examples in §137, the conjunction and adverb are said to be correlative or in correlation. So too when the sequence is adverb . . . conjunction; for examples of this see §160.

§139 As I have already said, the preceding remarks apply to non-dependent statements and subordinate clauses. Element order in non-dependent commands, e.g. 'Go into my vineyard!', and in non-dependent questions, e.g. 'Why are you here?', is discussed in §§142–8.

J OLD ENGLISH SENTENCE STRUCTURE

1 The Parable of the Vineyard: Matthew 20: 1–16

§140 I suggest that you begin by reading the translation and then the Old English aloud. Then read §142. Then reread the Old English more slowly in conjunction with the translation and the comments in §141. The translation is taken from the Authorized or King James version which is based on the Greek New Testament, not on an Old English version:

For the kingdom of heaven is like unto a man that is an householder, which went out early in the morning to hire labourers into his vineyard.

2 And when he had agreed with the labourers for a penny a day, he sent them into his vineyard.

3 And he went out about the third hour, and saw others standing idle in the marketplace.

4 And said unto them: Go ye also into the vineyard, and whatsoever is right I will give you. And they went their way.

5 Again he went out about the sixth and ninth hour, and did likewise.

6 And about the eleventh hour he went out, and found others standing idle, and saith unto them, Why stand ye here all the day idle?

7 They say unto him, Because no man hath hired us. He saith unto them, Go ye also into the vineyard; and whatsoever is right, that shall ye receive.

8 So when even was come, the lord of the vineyard saith unto his steward, Call the labourers, and give them their hire, beginning from the last unto the first.

9 And when they came that were hired about the eleventh hour, they received every man a penny.

10 But when the first came, they supposed that they should have received more; and they likewise received every man a penny.

11 And when they had received it, they murmured against the goodman of the house,

12 Saying, These last have wrought but one hour, and thou hast made them equal unto us, which have borne the burden and heat of the day.

13 But he answered one of them, and said, Friend, I do thee no wrong: didst not thou agree with me for a penny?

14 Take that thine is, and go thy way: I will give unto this last, even as unto thee.

15 Is it not lawful for me to do what I will with mine own? Is thine eye evil, because I am good?

16 So the last shall be first, and the first last: for many be called, but few chosen.

On the punctuation in the Old English, see §11.

1 Sōþlīċe heofona rīċe ys ġelīċ þām hīredes ealdre þe on ǣrne merġen ūt ēode āhȳrian wyrhtan on hys wīnġeard.

2 Ġewordenre ġecwydrǣdenne þām wyrhtum· hē sealde ǣlcum ānne penig wiþ hys dæġes worce. Hē āsende hīe on hys wīnġeard.

3 And þā hē ūt ēode ymbe underntīde hē ġeseah ōþre on strǣte īdle standan.

4 Ðā cwæþ hē: 'Gā ġē on mīnne wīnġeard and iċ sylle ēow þæt riht byþ.' And hīe þā fērdon.

5 Eft hē ūt ēode ymbe þā sixtan and nigoþan tīd and dyde þām swā ġelīċe.

6 þā ymbe þā endlyftan tīd hē ūt ēode and funde ōþre standende and þā sæġde hē: 'Hwī stande ġē hēr ealne dæġ īdle?'

7   þā cwǣdon hīe: 'For þām þe ūs nān mann ne hȳrode.' Đā cwæþ hē: 'And gā ġē on mīnne wīnġeard.'

8   Sōþlīċe þā hyt wæs ǣfen ġeworden· þā sæġde se wīnġeardes hlāford his ġerēfan: 'Clypa þā wyrhtan and āġyf him heora mēde· āġynn fram þām ȳtemestan oþ þone fyrmestan.'

9   Eornostlīċe þā ðā ġecōmon þe embe þā endlyftan tīde cōmon· þā onfēngon hīe ǣlċ his pening.

10   And þā þe þǣr ǣrest cōmon wēndon þæt hīe scolden māre onfōn· þā onfēngon hīe syndriġe penegas.

11   þā ongunnon hīe murcnian onġēan þone hīredes ealdor

12   And þus cwǣdon: 'þās ȳtemestan worhton āne tīde and þū dydest hīe ġelīċe ūs þe bǣron byrþena on þisses dæġes hǣtan.'

13   Đā cwæþ hē andswarigende hyra ānum: 'Ēalā þū frēond· ne dō iċ þē nǣnne tēonan· hū· ne cōme þū tō mē tō wyrċenne wið ānum peninge?'

14   Nim þæt þīn ys and gā· iċ wylle þysum ȳtemestan syllan eall swā myċel swā þē.

15   Oþþe ne mōt iċ dōn þæt iċ wylle? Hwæþer þīn ēage mānful ys for þām þe iċ gōd eom?

16   Swā bēoð þā fyrmestan ȳtemeste and þā ȳtemestan fyrmeste· sōþlīċe maneġe synt ġeclypede and fēawe ġecorene.'

§141 A few comments may prove helpful. I have tried to give the meanings of any words which are not immediately intelligible from the translation. You will notice many spelling variations: *hys* for *his* 'his'; *byþ* for *biþ* 'is'; *þām* for *þǣm* dat. sg. and pl. of *se*; *heora* and *hyra* for *hi(e)ra* 'their'. As I have said in §2, the Anglo-Saxon scribes did not try to make the spelling uniform.

Verse 1:
þām (dat. sg. or dat. pl.) **hīredes** (gen. sg.) **ealdre** (dat. sg.) 'to the master of [a] household'.

Verse 2:
Ġewordenre ġecwydrǣdenne þām wyrhtum 'An agreement having been made with the workers'. In Old English, such constructions are in the dative case; **wiþ** 'against, in return for'.

Verse 4:
See §143.
sylle 'I [will] give'; **þæt** 'that which, what'. Cf. John 13: 27 (Authorized or King James version) 'That thou doest, do quickly'. This is common in Old English. It occurs again in verses 14 and 15.

Verse 5:
and dyde þām swā ġelīċe 'and did the same' [literally] 'and did to that [verse 4] so like'.

Verse 6:

See §146.

Verse 7:

For þām þe 'because', literally 'for that, namely'.

Such prepositional conjunctions are common; see §§124–5.

See §143.

Verse 8:

ġeworden: see §513.

wīnġeardes gen. sg. (I am sure this is an unnecessary note!)

See §143.

Verse 9:

þā ðā ġecōmon þe . . . 'when those came who . . .'.

Verse 10:

þā þe 'those who'.

þā onfēngon hīe syndriġe penegas 'Then received they separate pennies' (or 'separately, pennies').

Verse 11:

There is no 'When' clause in this verse, as there is in the translation.

hīredes: see verse 8.

Verse 12:

byrþena (acc. sg. or pl.) **þisses dæġes** (see verse 8) **hǣtan** (dat. sg.) '[the] burden(s) in this day's heat'.

Verse 13:

This is a difficult verse. After the initial salutation **Ēalā þū frēond** 'O thou friend', the speech contains first a negated statement; see the last sentence in §148. Then we have **hū**, which is an interjection 'how now, look here!' Then we have a negated question; see the beginning of §148.

Verse 14:

eall swā myċel swā þē 'exactly as much as to thee'.

Verse 15:

This consists of two more questions; see respectively the beginning of §148 and §147. **Oþþe** means 'Or'.

2 Element order in direct commands and questions

§142   In the sections which follow, I discuss element order in direct or non-dependent commands and questions:

Positive commands usually have VS or V (§143).

Negative commands usually have *Ne* VS (§144).

Many questions have the same patterns as Modern English questions (§145).

But there are other idiomatic patterns which, if they had survived into Modern English, would have enabled us to ask these questions:

'Departs the train to Edinburgh from platform 4?' (§146)
'Whether the train to Edinburgh departs from platform 4?' (§147)
'Departs not the train to Edinburgh from platform 4?' (§148)

§143 The Parable of the Vineyard in §140 contains the following commands: verses 4 and 7 *Gā ġē on mīnne wīnġeard* 'Go ye into my vineyard' with the order VS and the subject pronoun expressed, and verse 8 *Clypa þā wyrhtan and āġyf him heora mēde· aġynn fram þām ȳtemestan* ... 'Call the workmen and give them their hire; begin from the last ...', where the subject pronoun is not expressed. The latter, which is also the norm today, is much more frequent in positive commands in Old English.

§144 But in negative commands the subject pronoun is usually expressed after the verb, e.g. *Ne bēo ðū manslaga. Ne unrihthǽme ðū. Ne stel ðū* 'Do not/(Thou shalt not) be a manslayer. Do not commit adultery. Do not steal' and *Ne bēoð ġē forhte* 'Do not be afraid'. Here we note both the expression of the subject pronoun and the fact that Old English does not use the *do* construction.

§145 Some of the interrogative patterns are the same in both Old English and Modern English, e.g. *Is hit swā hī secgað?* 'Is it as they say?'; *Is hyt ālȳfed þæt man casere gaful sylle þe nā?* 'Is it allowed that one pay tribute to Caesar or not?'; *Mæġ hē inn faran?* 'Can he go in?'; *Habbað ġē ġehȳrd?* 'Have you heard?'; *Hwǽr is hē?* 'Where is he?'; *Hwanon is hēo cumen?* 'Whence is/has she come?' and *Hwæt sceal iċ singan?* 'What must I sing?'

§146 In Shakespeare we have two forms of questions: 'Goes the king hence tonight?' and 'How goes the night, boy?' as opposed to 'Did you send to him, sir?' and 'How did you dare to trade and traffic with Macbeth?' Here again, Old English lacks the *do*-construction (or periphrasis). So we find only the first pattern: *Petrus, lufast þū mē?* 'Peter, lovest thou me?' and (Matthew 20: 6 above) *Hwī stande ġē hēr ealne dæġ īdle?* 'Why stand ye here all day idle?'

§147 There are two more difficult patterns which both occur in the Parable of the Vineyard. First, we find in verse 15 *Hwæþer þīn ēage mānful ys ...?* 'Is thine eye evil ...?', with initial *hwæþer* + S ... V; a similar example with SV is *Hwæðer ġē nū sēcan gold on trēowum?* 'Do you now seek gold on trees?' In these, S precedes V and *hwæþer* tells us that we have a question. This pattern still survives in the modern dependent question 'I ask whether thine eye is evil ...' and 'I ask whether you now seek gold on trees'.

§148 Second, we have in verse 13 *ne cōme þū tō mē tō wyrċenne wið ānum peninge?* and in verse 15 *Oþþe ne mōt iċ dōn þæt iċ wylle?* These are negated questions which begin *ne* VS, the Old English equivalent of Shakespeare's 'Know you not that he has?' and 'Dismay'd not this our captains, Macbeth and Banquo?' Here again, Old English lacks the *do*-periphrasis. But the order *ne* VS is potentially ambiguous. It occurs in the Parable of the Vineyard verse 13 *ne dō iċ þē nænne tēonan*, which is a negated statement 'I do thee no wrong', and also in negated commands, e.g. *Ne stel ðū* 'Do not steal' and the other examples in §144.

3 Negation: a summary

§149 Verbs are negated by an immediately preceding *ne*, e.g. *Hēo ne swamm* 'She swam not' and, with contraction, *hē nolde sacan* 'he was not willing to/would not fight'; see §109.

§150 When *ne* + a verb begins a sentence, the sentence can express a statement, a question, or a command, depending on the context; see §148.

§151 *Nā/nō* usually negates words other than verbs, e.g. *mid langum scipum nā manegum* 'with longships, not many' and *Godes miht þē gehǣlde, nā ic̄* 'God's power healed you, not I'; see §108.

§152 *Ne* when not immediately before a finite verb is a conjunction, e.g. (before nouns) *ne tunge ne handa ne ēagan* 'neither tongue nor hands nor eyes' and (before infinitives) *Hē mihte ne tǣcan ne leornian* 'He could neither teach nor learn'. In *Ne sāw ðū þonne ne ne rīp ne ðinne wīngeard ne wyrc* 'Do not sow then nor reap nor work your vineyard', *ne* is in succession an adverb, a conjunction, an adverb, a conjunction, and an adverb!

§153 This last sentence well illustrates the fact that multiple negatives do not cancel one another; see §110. So do the sentences *and hyt nā ne fēoll* 'and it fell not', *For þām þe ūs nān mann ne hȳrode* 'Because no man hired us', and . . . *ne byð sē mann nā crīsten ne hē furþum wyrðe ne byð þæt him ǣnig crīsten man mid ete* '. . . that man is not Christian nor is he even worthy that any Christian man eat with him'.

4 The tying together of sentences and clauses

Introduction

§154 King Alfred reigned from 871 to 899. During his reign he successfully fought off the Danish invaders, promoted an ambitious educational programme, and found time for personal authorship. A great man! The scholars he gathered around him were commanded to translate from Latin *on ðæt geðiode . . . ðe wē ealle gecnāwan mægen* 'into that language . . . which we all can understand' *sume bēc ðā ðe nīedbeðearfosta sīen eallum monnum tō wiotonne* 'some books which are most necessary for all men to know'. This was a formidable task, because up till his time English had not been regularly used for the expression of serious philosophical and theological thought. Yet by the end of the tenth century, the time of the great scholar and prose stylist Ælfric, successive generations of writers had developed English into a highly sophisticated language far in advance of any other contemporary European vernacular. These later writers successfully exploited the very devices I am about to discuss. So I intend nothing derogatory in what follows.

§155   For, as I see it, signs of the struggle are apparent in the structure of the language. To put it crudely, early authors and translators frequently did one of two things: they either expressed an idea and then summed it up, as if we were to say 'Our ancestors, **those** who previously occupied these places, they loved wisdom', or gave warning that an idea was coming and then gave it separate expression, as if we were to say 'All think about it, **how** you may betray them'. I shall call these patterns 'recapitulation' and 'anticipation' respectively. They are apparent in most types of complex sentences and often create what seem to us unnecessary repetitions (or tautologies) in written prose. But these devices must have helped struggling readers and struggling hearers (for not even all those in a monastery could read or write). Indeed, they are often effectively used by speakers today.

Recapitulation

§156   Recapitulation is common in Old English sentences containing an adjective clause, e.g. **Ure ieldran·** *ðā ðe ðās stōwa ǣr hīoldon·* **hīe** *lufodon wīsdōm* **'Our ancestors,** those who previously occupied these places, **they** loved wisdom' and **Seðe** *ġelȳfð and bi ð ġefullod* **sē** *bi ð ġehealden·* **seðe** *ne ġelȳfð* **hē** *bi ð ġenyðerod* **'Whoever** believes and is baptized, **that one** shall be saved; **whoever** believes not, **he** shall be damned'. A third example shows how recapitulation helps to clarify the sense by dividing a long and not particularly well-constructed sentence into four parts:

> Ond **þæt unstille hwēol** ðe Ixīon wæs tō ġebunden Lauita cyning for his scylde· **ðæt** oðstōd for his hearpunga· ond **Tantulus se cyning** ðe on ðisse worulde unġemetliċe ġīfre wæs ond him ðǣr ðæt ilċe yfel fylġde ðǣre ġīfernesse· **hē** gestilde

> 'And **that unstill/ever-moving wheel** to which Ixion King of the Lapithae was bound for his sin, **that** stood still for his harping and **Tantalus the king** who in this world was excessively greedy and him/ whom that same sin of greed pursued, **he** was still.'

§157   The pattern 'That he is ill is not true' does not, as far as I know, occur in Old English. Nor does the pattern 'How he keeps going is a riddle to me'. It follows that there is in Old English no opportunity for the recapitulation of a noun clause by a following pronoun, as in 'That he is ill – that is not true'.

Anticipation

§158   But anticipation – the use of a pronoun to point forward to a coming clause – is common before noun clauses, e.g. **Hit** *gedafenað* **þæt** *Alleluia sȳ gesungen on ðām lande* **'It** is fitting **that** Alleluia be sung in that land', *Hū mæġ* **þæt** *bēon* **þæt** *iċ ċild hæbbe?* 'How can **that** be **that** I shall have a child?', **þæs** *iċ ġewīsce* **þæt** *iċ āna ne belīfe æfter mīnum lēofum þeġnum* **'For that** I wish, **that** I be not left alone after my beloved thanes', and *Hycgað* **his** *ealle* **hū** *ġē hī beswīcen* 'All think about **it, how** you may betray them'.

§159 Anticipation is also found in sentences containing adjective clauses. The sentence *Fremme se þe wille* (with the third person present subjunctives *Fremme* and *wille*) means literally 'May do that one who may wish' and so 'Let whoever wishes do/act'. Here *se þe* contains both the antecedent 'that one' and the relative pronoun 'who'. But we sometimes find sentences in which *se þe* is anticipated by *se* 'that one' or *hē* 'he'. Examples include *Sȳ* **se** *awyrged* **se** *ðe hǣme mid his swustor* 'Let **that one** be accursed **that one** who sleeps with his sister' and *Ac ġif* **hē** *hire ne reċċe* **se** *ðe hīe bohte* . . . 'But if **he** does not take care of her, **that one** who bought her . . .' meaning 'But, if he who bought her . . .'.

Correlation

§160 We see these tendencies in the correlation between principal and adverb clauses which is so characteristic of Old English. I have already discussed and exemplified this in §§137–8. But two more examples may help. We have recapitulation when the subordinate clause comes before the principal clause, e.g. **Đonne** *se heretoga wācað·* **þonne** *bið eall se here swīðe ġehindred* '**Whenever** the leader is weak/cowardly, **then** the whole army is greatly hindered'. When the principal clause comes first, we have anticipation, e.g. **Đā** *gelamp* **hit þāðā** *hī on þǣre byrig Bethleem wǣron* **þæt** *hire tīma wæs ġefylled* '**Then it** happened, **when** they were in the city of Bethlehem, **that** her time was fulfilled'; in this sentence the *Đā* anticipates the *þāðā* clause and the *hit* the *þæt* clause.

A sentence by Ælfric

§161 I have spoken of Ælfric (*c.* 955–*c.* 1020) as a great prose stylist. In an attempt to show why I make this claim, I shall analyse one sentence from his account of the martyrdom of St Stephen (Acts 6–7). Here it is, with a somewhat literal translation and the two parts of the sentence printed in parallel:

þider þe Stēphanus forestōp mid Sāules stānum oftorfod·
þider folgode Pāulus ġefultumod þurh Stēphanes ġebedu

Whither Stephen forestepped with Saul's stones killed,
thither followed Paul helped by Stephen's prayers.

Here we note that
1 both the subordinate clause and the principal clause contain the same elements: introductory word (conjunction/adverb), subject, verb, prepositional phrase, past participle;

2 the order is SV in the subordinate clause but VS in the principal clause. This is regular in prose (§137);

3 the order is prepositional phrase + participle in the subordinate clause but participle + prepositional phrase in the principal clause;

4 the fact that, as we see in (2) and (3), the elements in the two parts of the subordinate clause are reversed in the principal clause means that the sentence contains two examples of the figure of speech known as chiasmus. It is given this name because, if the parallel phrases are written one below the other and lines are drawn between the corresponding elements, the lines make the Greek letter χ *chi*. Let me give you two examples. The first is from Luke 16: 3 (Authorized or King James Version):

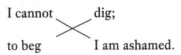

The second is from the passage from *The Dream of the Rood* discussed in §120:

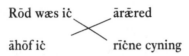

You can see for yourself that the Ælfric sentence contains two examples, first the variation SV/VS and then the variation phrase, participle/participle, phrase. So, to use the adjective which goes with chiasmus, Ælfric's sentence is doubly chiastic;

5 since Saul and Paul are the same man (Acts 7: 58–8: 4 and Acts 9: 1–22 and 13: 9), the sentence is a sermon in itself.

Ælfric was a good Latinist and it is certain that he was influenced by Latin prose style. But it is important for us to realize that this powerful and moving sentence – carefully constructed with its parallelisms, double chiasmus, and contrast between Saul and Paul – contains nothing which is not natural Old English.

5 The separation of elements

§162 Several forms of separation call for comment here. First, we may note a tendency to separate two elements joined by *and* 'and', *ac* 'but', or *ne* 'nor'. This is common with double subjects. Thus Modern English 'The King and the Queen came to Oxford' could appear in Old English either as *Se cyning and sēo hlǣfdiġe cōmon tō Oxenaford* or as *Se cyning cōm tō Oxenaford and sēo hlǣfdiġe*. Similarly we find *Hēr Cynewulf benam Sigebryht his rīċes ond Westseaxna wiotan for unryhtum dǣdum būton Hamtūnscīre* 'Here/in this year Cynewulf and the counsellors of the West Saxons deprived Sigebryht of his kingdom, apart from Hampshire, for illegal deeds'.

§163 But other double elements can be divided. I give examples, first, of

divided prepositional phrases and, second, of divided adjectives: _þā
ġegaderedon þā þe in Norþhymbrum būgeað ond on Ēastenglum sum hund scipa_
'Then those who dwell in Northumbria and in East Anglia gathered about a
hundred ships', and _Hī sǣdon þæt hī nǣfre ǣr swā clǣne gold ne swā rēad ne
gesāwon_ 'They said that they never before saw such pure, red gold'.

§164 In Modern English we nearly always put an adjective clause
immediately after its antecedent, e.g. 'He thought that the man whom he
sought would not escape'. But in Old English the two can be separated in a
way unnatural today, e.g. _ðā ongan iċ ðā bōc wendan on Englisc ðe is ġenemned on
Lǣden Pastoralis_, literally 'then began I the book to turn into English which is
called in Latin [_Cura_] _Pastoralis_'. Both patterns are seen in _Herodes ðōhte ġif hē
hī ealle ofslōge þæt se ān ne ǣtburste þe hē sōhte. Ac hē wæs unġemyndiġ þæs hālgan
ġewrites ðe cwyð: 'Nis nān wīsdōm ne nān rǣd nāht onġēan God'_ 'Herod thought, if
he slew them all, that that one would not escape whom he sought. But he
was unmindful of the holy scripture which says: "No wisdom or no counsel
is aught against God".'

6 The _apo koinou_ construction

§165 This construction is rare in Old English prose but frequent in Old
English poetry, although it is often hidden from modern readers by the
editorial use of modern punctuation; see §10. The phrase _apo koinou_ is a
transliteration of two Greek words ἀπὸ κοινοῦ and means 'in common'. It is
used to refer to that construction in which a word (or phrase or clause)
which is expressed once belongs both with what has gone before it and with
what follows after it. It is seen in its simplest form in a sentence such as 'I
like **tennis** is my favourite sport' which means 'I like tennis. Tennis is my
favourite sport'. When I wrote in §11 that I intended to use the punctuation
marks '= = to mark off _apo koinou_ elements which "face both ways"', I was
using another simple form of _apo koinou_ construction because _apo koinou_
elements are elements which face both ways. In the examples given, 'tennis'
and 'elements' are called the _koinon_, that is, the common element. My use of
the double equals sign is intended to help you to recognize a _koinon_ when
one occurs: 'I like = tennis = is my favourite sport' and '_apo koinou_ = elements = which face both ways'.

§166 A possible _koinon_ in Old English prose occurs in the passage
quoted and translated in §14: _and eft þā þā sēo bōc cōm tō ūs_ = _binnan fēam
ġēarum_ = _þā āwendon wē hit on Englisc_. Two simple examples from Old
English poetry are _Hē on mōde_ = _wearþ forht_ = _on ferhðe_ 'He in mind =
became afraid = in spirit' and _Hīe dȳgel lond_ = _warigeað_ = _wulfhleoþu_ 'They a
mysterious land = inhabit = wulf-slopes'. I shall give another example in
§167. But please allow me to postpone until §461 my attempt to justify my
claim that much of the magic and mystery of Old English poetry will be lost
to those who are insensitive to these constructions.

7 A passage from the Old English poem *Andreas*

§167 I have used some punctuation marks (§11) in this passage from the Old English poem about St Andrew:

>   Iċ wille þē
> 475 eorl unforcūð   ānre nū ġēna
>   bēne biddan   = þēah iċ þē bēaga lȳt
>   sincweorðunga   syllan mihte,
>   fǣtedsinces =   wolde iċ frēondscipe
>   þēoden þrymfæst   þīnne – ġif iċ mehte –
> 480 beġitan gōdne.

Here St Andrew is speaking to the captain of a ship in which he is a passenger, not knowing that the captain is God:

> 'And now again, renowned warrior, I wish to ask of thee a favour = though I was able to give thee little treasure, a small store of precious things, of beaten gold = I would win – if I could – thy gracious friendship, O glorious lord.'

Three points are worthy of note:

1 Here the concessive clause – the clause introduced by *þēah* 'though' and marked off by = = – stands between two principal clauses and belongs to them both: as Andrew sees it, his poverty is a bar to both the making of his request and the winning of the captain's friendship. In other words, it is used *apo koinou*. Editors and critics of the poem have wasted a lot of time in arguing whether the *þēah*-clause belongs with the preceding or the following sentence and whether to put a full stop after *biddan* or before *wolde*. There is no possible way of deciding this and no need to do so – unless we insist on using modern punctuation and thereby destroying the flow of the verse paragraph.

2 Next we may note that the existence of distinctive inflexional endings allows the separation of related elements for stylistic purposes; here the sequence *frēondscipe ... þīnne ... gōdne*, all accusative singular masculine, gives dramatic emphasis: 'friendship ... thy friendship ... thy gracious friendship'.

3 The effectiveness of this particular paragraph is heightened by another device frequently used by poets, the dramatic parenthesis '– if I could –'.

K CONCLUSION

§168 This brings us to the end of the introductory sections, in which I have tried to show you how Old English worked. Now I want to show you more of what it has to offer. From here on, you have a choice and (if I may continue the gastronomic image used in 'How to Use This Book') can select what appeals to you from the variety of menus I offer. As you make your choice, you will inevitably have to struggle. I shall be giving you some help by explaining points of interest in the numbered texts (Introduction §xxi) and by offering comments on the language with references to the sections in which the form or construction under discussion is explained. There is no need to consult these sections unless you do not understand or unless you wish to know more. But you may find it useful to try to follow the method I adopt in my literal translations. To do this, I suggest that you begin by covering the translation or the comments while you try to guess what you can. Take the following entry from the Anglo-Saxon Chronicle which appears again in §181:

> 60 BC   Ær Cristes geflæscnesse lx wintra· Gaius Iulius se casere ærest
> Romana Bretenlond gesohte 7 Brettas mid gefeohte cnysede 7 hie
> oferswiþde 7 swa þeah ne meahte þær rice gewinnan.

I wonder how much of this you can get for yourself:

> Ere Christ's fleshness sixty of winters, Gaius Julius the caesar/emperor
> ere-est of Romans Britonland sought and Britons with fight [noun] . . . . .
> and them over . . . . . and . . . . . not might there . . . . . win.

You may be able to fill in more blanks by recalling that tradition tells us that Julius Caesar won the battle (*cnysede* 'beat' and *oferswiþde* 'overcame') and by remembering 'bishopric' (§26; *rīce* 'kingdom'). I believe that you will often be pleasantly surprised at how much you can get before unveiling the commentary or consulting the Glossary. You may also find it useful to bear in mind these four 'Don'ts':

1 Don't alter the order of the words without good reason;
2 Don't leave out words that are there;
3 Don't put in words that aren't there;
4 Don't turn active constructions into the passive.

When you have really understood the sentence, you can disregard these prohibitions and, if you wish, try your hand at a more stylish translation. But there is no reason for you to feel that you must do this. After all, the object of the exercise is to think and to understand Old English. Let me conclude Part II by reminding you that there are paradigms in Part V for those who want them; by telling you that, if you want a dictionary, the best one for your purposes is J. R. Clark Hall, *A Concise Anglo-Saxon Dictionary*, fourth edition, with a Supplement by Herbert D. Meritt; by congratulating you on getting this far; by hoping that you will think it worth going on; and by wishing you well as you do so.

III

An Introduction to Anglo-Saxon England

A LITERATURE

§169 As I have already said in the Introduction (§xvii), the West-Saxon dialect, tamed to pen and paper by King Alfred and his helpers, became the standard literary language and by the time of the Norman Conquest was far more developed for the expression of prose and poetry than any other contemporary European vernacular. It is my hope that your samplings from the remainder of this book will reveal to you something of the range, the power, and the mystery, of Old English literature.

§170 Bibliographical details will be found in the relevant sections of Part IV and in the Bibliography. Here I shall content myself with a brief catalogue of the Old English literature now extant, beginning with the poetry. There are some thirty thousand lines of Old English poetry composed in the alliterative measure inherited from the Germanic ancestors of the Anglo-Saxons. This is the only system of versification used by the poets. It was originally the orally composed medium of heroic stories and sentiments and was probably first used to express Christian ideas by Cædmon between *c.* 657 and 680; see §427. The effect of this 'baptism' is discussed in §§448–50.

§171 In this system, each line consisted of two half-lines separated by a pause or caesura but linked by alliteration. The metrical unit was the half-line, each of which conformed to one of five metrical types. I give a typical passage, with the alliterating letters underlined and the stresses marked so that you can see something of the variations. The signs ´ and ` mean respectively a full and subsidiary stress, × means no stress; a modern example is 'high-crèsted'. The passage is lines 96–9 of *The Battle of Maldon*, which commemorates the defeat of the Anglo-Saxons by the Danes at Maldon, Essex, in 991.

> Wódon þá wǽlwùlfàs　　– fòr wǽtèrè nè múrnòn –
> wícìngà wéròd　　wést ófèr Pántàn
> ófèr scír wǽtèr　　scýldàs wégòn·
> lídmèn tó lándè　　líndè bǽròn.

Literally translated, this reads:

> Waded the slaughter-wolves　　– for water [they] not cared –
> Vikings' troop　　west over [river] Pante

> over gleaming water   shields carried,
> seamen to land   linden wood [shields] bore.

More is said about metre in Part IV (§§451–5).

§172   The standard edition of Old English poetry is the Anglo-Saxon Poetic Records (ASPR). This series of six volumes prints all the extant Old English poetry, with a few minor exceptions which came to light after its publication. Volume V contains metrical versions of psalms 51–150 from the Paris Psalter together with the Metres of Boethius versified from an Old English prose translation of the Latin original. Volume VI, *The Anglo-Saxon Minor Poems*, gathers together all the other poems which have been found outside the four great collections or codices of Old English poetry which I am about to describe.

§173   The Bodleian manuscript Junius 11 (ASPR I) was once owned by the Dutch scholar Franciscus Junius (1589–1677), the first editor of its four poems, all on Christian subjects – *Genesis*, *Exodus*, *Daniel*, and *Christ and Satan*. The Vercelli Book, capitolare CXVII in the chapter library of the cathedral at Vercelli in Northern Italy (ASPR II), is also a Christian collection, containing as it does *The Dream of the Rood* (§493), the lives of the saints Andreas and Elene, and three shorter poems. How it got to Vercelli is unknown; spare a moment for speculation.

§174   Next we have the Exeter Book (ASPR III). This, the largest and most miscellaneous of the poetic codices, was presented to Exeter Cathedral by its first bishop, Leofric, and is listed among his gifts to the library as *.i. mycel englisc boc be gehwilcum þingum on leoðwisan geworht* 'one large English book about various things in verse composed'. It is still there and contains some religious poems, including one of over sixteen hundred lines about Christ, two lives of saints (Guthlac and Juliana), some religious allegories, and homiletic poems; *The Wanderer* and *The Seafarer*, as they are called today (§§476–7); lyrics and elegies such as *The Ruin*, *The Wife's Lament*, and *The Husband's Message* (§§237 and 473–4); and riddles which range from the obscene to highly sensitive and Christian poems.

§175   The fourth codex (ASPR IV) is the British Library Cotton Vitellius A.xv, so-called because it was the fifteenth manuscript on the first shelf of the cabinet topped by the bust of the Roman Emperor Vitellius in the library of the antiquarian Sir Robert Cotton (1571–1631). The manuscripts were left to the nation by his grandson Sir John Cotton (1621–1701). In 1731 a fire broke out in the library, destroying some manuscripts but fortunately sparing a charred Cotton Vitellius A.xv. Thus were preserved some prose texts, a fragment of a poem on Judith, whose story is told in the Apocrypha, and (as one authority puts it), '3,182 lines of alliterative verse, beginning *Hwæt we gardena in geardagum*. Pr[inted] often, since Kemble (1833) under the title *Beowulf*.'

§176   The extant poems can be roughly classified according to subject matter.

1. Poems treating Heroic Subjects

Beowulf. Deor. The Battle of Finnsburh. Waldere. Widsith.

2. Historic Poems

The Battle of Brunanburh. The Battle of Maldon.

3. Biblical Paraphrases and Reworkings of Biblical Subjects

The Metrical Psalms. The poems of the Junius MS; note especially *Genesis B* and *Exodus. Christ. Judith.*

4. Lives of the Saints

Andreas. Elene. Guthlac. Juliana.

5. Other Religious Poems

Note especially *The Dream of the Rood* and the allegorical poems – *The Phoenix, The Panther*, and *The Whale*.

6. Short Elegies and Lyrics

The Wife's Lament. The Husband's Message. The Ruin. The Wanderer. The Seafarer. Wulf and Eadwacer. Deor might be included here as well as under 1 above.

7. Riddles and Gnomic Verse

8. Miscellaneous

Charms. The Runic Poem. The Riming Poem.

Four poems – *The Fates of the Apostles, Elene, Christ B*, and *Juliana* – contain Cynewulf's 'signature' in runes. For details of facsimile volumes, see the Bibliography.

§177 The gradual harnessing of Old English prose for the expression of serious philosophical and theological thought from the time of King Alfred has been mentioned in §§xvii and 154. But prose was of course used for the practical purposes of everyday life, for the recording of events, and for entertainment. What survives may be said to fall into the seven main divisions set out below.

1. The Anglo-Saxon Chronicle

The surviving manuscripts – lettered A to H – are discussed in *The Anglo-Saxon Chronicle*, ed. Dorothy Whitelock (Eyre and Spottiswoode, 1961), pp. xi–xviii. MS E (The Laud Chronicle) continues until the death of Stephen in 1154. This is, to all intents and purposes, the end of historical writing in English prose until the fifteenth century.

Miss Whitelock observes that 'the confident attribution of the work to Alfred's instigation cannot be upheld'.

2. The Translations of Alfred and his Circle

King Alfred explained his educational policy in his famous Preface to the *Cura Pastoralis*. This is perhaps the first of his translations. He also translated the *De Consolatione Philosophiae* of Boethius and the *Soliloquia* of St Augustine, and was responsible for a legal code.

Bishop Wærferth of Worcester translated the *Dialogues* of Gregory the Great at Alfred's request. The OE version of Bede's *Ecclesiastical History* has long been attributed to Alfred. Miss Whitelock, in her British Academy Lecture in 1962, finds no evidence for this, but says that it remains a probability that the work was undertaken at Alfred's instigation. The same is true of the OE version of the *Historia adversus Paganos* of Orosius, which incorporates the story of the voyages of Ohthere and Wulfstan.

3. Homiletic Writings

The most important of these are

(a) *The Blickling Homilies*, 971;
(b) *The Catholic Homilies*, 990–2, and *Lives of the Saints*, 993–8, of Ælfric, Abbot of Eynsham;
(c) *The Homilies* of Wulfstan, Archbishop of York, who died in 1023.

4. Other Religious Prose

This includes translations of portions of both the Old and New Testaments, and a version of the Benedictine Office.

5. Prose Fiction

Here we find the story of *Apollonius of Tyre*, *Alexander's Letter to Aristotle*, and *The Wonders of the East*. It has been said that these show that long before the Conquest the Anglo-Saxons found entertainment in the exotic romanticism of the East.

6. Scientific and Medical Writings

7. Laws, Charters, and Wills

§178 These then are the works which survived the ravages of time and the attentions of such destructive agencies as rats and mice, fire, and Christians zealous to extirpate the works of paganism. That some remain hidden in uncatalogued collections is a possibility. How many were lost we shall never know. But what remains is a remarkable legacy.

B HISTORY

1 Introduction

§179 After mentioning the sacking of Rome by the Goths (annal 409 below) and the departure of the Romans from Britain (annal 418), the Parker Manuscript (MS A) of the Anglo-Saxon Chronicle tells of the coming of Hengest and Horsa to Britain (annal 449). Archaeological evidence now suggests that the first Germanic warriors arrived from the continent at least half a century earlier; see §§xv–xvi. However, the Anglo-Saxon period can be said to end with the Norman Conquest of 1066 and so, even if it is taken as starting in 449, it lasted for 617 years. This is roughly one hundred years more than the five hundred years which separate the voyage to America by Columbus from the present day or, in literary terms, roughly the period which separates the birth of Chaucer from the deaths of Dylan Thomas and Robert Frost. In the sections which follow, I shall attempt to give a summary of the main events by means of extracts from the Anglo-Saxon Chronicle and (where necessary) brief comments. I have followed the standard editions in not normalizing the spelling or adding length marks in the (I hope justified) beliefs that their absence will not make it harder to understand the texts I print and that their presence would make it harder for those who wish to go on to those editions. You can disregard the bracketed references to paradigms in the notes explaining the text if you can follow what is being said without them. I do not regularly give references back to words after they have appeared. But all are in the Glossary.

§180 The sets of annals which make up the seven manuscripts of the Anglo-Saxon Chronicle stem from a common original compiled from various sources towards the end of the ninth century and extending from the Roman invasion of Britain until 892. These seven manuscripts were subsequently augmented by items of national and local interest, recorded more or less contemporaneously. The last annal, which appears only in the Peterborough Chronicle, tells of the death of King Stephen in 1154. The relationship between these surviving manuscripts is extremely complex and the differences in their contents are so great that we might do better to speak of the Anglo-Saxon Chronicles. Most of the entries which follow are from MS A, the Parker Manuscript, one of the treasures given to Corpus Christi College, Cambridge, by Archbishop Parker (1504–75). The rest are taken from MS E, the Laud Manuscript, which is in the Bodleian Library, Oxford, among the manuscripts of Archbishop Laud, executed in 1645, and from MS G, another Cottonian manuscript (Otho B.xi). These entries are:

MS G annals 565, 596, 604;

MS E annals 685, 793, 978 (second entry), 981, 987, 991 (second entry),
1004, 1011, 1013, 1014, 1016, 1036, 1039, 1052.

Errors and inconsistencies in the dates in the Chronicles mean that the entries which follow contain some departures from the traditional dates once known to every British schoolboy and schoolgirl which appear in the section 'Some Significant Dates'. For MSS A and G I have followed the dates given by J. M. Bately in her edition of _The Anglo-Saxon Chronicle: A Collaborative Edition 3 MS A_ (Cambridge, 1986). For MS E I have given those in _Two of the Saxon Chronicles Parallel_ edited by Charles Plummer on the basis of an edition by John Earle (Oxford, 1892). I acknowledge gratefully my debt to these authorities. The year number of the annal is usually followed by _Her_ 'Here/At this place in the annals/In this year', by _On þissum/þys geare_ 'In this year', or occasionally by both. In the early annals, these formulae sometimes introduce brief mnemonic entries which now conceal fascinating stories, such as those for 530, 607, 671, and 761, below. Others tell such stories in varying degrees of detail as the Chronicles move from merely recording events to commenting on them, judging the participants, and apportioning praise and blame; see §§183 and 185. One other source demands mention here – the _Historia gentis Anglorum ecclesiastica_ written by the Venerable Bede (_c._ 672–735). Without it, our knowledge of the history of England before the eighth century would be shadowy indeed.

2 The Romans in Britain

§181 These derivative annals record the arrival and departure of the Romans, and the fate of their gold – a topic which the Anglo-Saxons, like many others, found of absorbing interest.

Text 1

60 BC   Ær Cristes geflæscnesse lx wintra Gaius Iulius se casere ærest
Romana Bretenlond gesohte 7 Brettas mid gefeohte cnysede 7
hie oferswiþde 7 swa þeah ne meahte þær rice gewinnan.

AD 46   Her Claudius, oþer Romana cyninga, Bretenelond gesohte 7
5   þone mæstan dæl þæs ealondes on his gewald onfeng 7 eac
swelce Orcadus[1] þa ealond Romana cynedome underþeodde.

1 **ǽr** prep. §113; **gefl æscness** 'fleshness/incarnation'; **casere** Lat. _caesar_; **ǽrest** adj. 'first'.
2 **Romana** gen. pl. 'of Romans'; **mid** prep. 'with'; **cnyssan** 'to press/overcome' (wk. vb. like _fremman_ §524).
3 **oferswiþan** 'to overpower/conquer' (wk. vb. like _hieran_ §94); **swā þeah** 'however'; **rīce** 'power/kingdom'; **(ge)winnan** 'to win/gain' (st. vb. III §518).
4 **ōþer** 'second/next', with partitive gen. (§47).
5 **dæl** 'deal/part'; **gewald** 'control'; **onfōn** 'to receive' (st. contracted vb. VII(_b_) §521).
5–6 **ēac swelce** conj. 'also'.
6 **cynedom** 'kingdom'; **underþēodan** 'to make subject to' (like _oferswiþan_ l. 3).

---

[1] The Orkneys.

409   Her Gotan² abræcon Romeburg 7 næfre siþþan Romane ne
ricsodon on Bretone.

418   Her Romane gesomnodon al þa goldhord þe on Bretene wæron
10 7 sume on eorþan ahyddon þæt hie nænig mon siþþan findan ne
meahte 7 sume mid him on Gallia³ læddon.⁴

7 **ābrecan** 'to break down/destroy' (st. vb. IV §517); **siþþan** adv. 'after(wards)'.
8 **ricsian** 'to rule' (wk. vb. like *lufian* §526).
9 **(ge)somnian** 'to gather together' (like *ricsian* l. 8).
10 **āhȳdan** 'to hide' (like *oferswīþan* l. 3); **þæt** conj. 'so that'.
11 **lǣdan** 'to lead/carry' (like *oferswīþan* l. 3).

---

² The Goths.   ³ Gaul.
⁴ Some of these buried treasures of course have not yet been found. But in November 1992, a retired gardener found a rotten box in a newly ploughed field in Suffolk. Inside it was a collection of gold bracelets, silver spoons and strainers, and a large hoard of gold and silver coins dating from the reign of the last Roman emperor to rule Britain. It is thought that the box and the treasure were buried between AD 400 and 420, when the last legions were withdrawn from Britain to defend Rome. This has been described as 'one of the greatest finds of the late Roman period'.

3 The beginnings of England

§182   The annals which follow relate how the Germanic tribes who were to give their names to England (*Engla lond*) and to counties such as Essex (*East Seaxna lond*) and Sussex (*Suþ Seaxna lond*) came in response to requests from the British for protection but fought against them and took possession of the land; for further details see Introduction §§xv–xvi. The arrival of St Columba, recorded in 565, is important because it was from Iona that Aidan and his successors brought Celtic Christianity to Northern England; see §183.

Text 2

449   Her Mauricius 7 Ualentines¹ onfengon rice 7 ricsodon vii winter
7 on hiera dagum Hengest 7 Horsa, from Wyrtgeorne² geleaþade
Bretta kyninge, gesohton Bretene on þam staþe þe is genemned
Ypwinesfleot³ ærest Brettum to fultume ac hie eft on hie fuhton.

1 **onfōn** 'to receive' (st. contracted vb. VII(*b*) §521).
2 **dæg** 'day' (like *stān* §502). The letters *æ* and *a* often fluctuate; **(ge)l(e)aþian** 'to invite/ask' (wk. vb. like *lufian* §526). We have here the past ptc. with nom. pl. ending -*e* referring to Hengest and Horsa.
3 **kyninge**, with *k* for *c*; **(ge)sēcan** 'to seek' (wk. vb. §95); **stæþ** 'shore'. For *æ/a* cf. *dæg* l. 2; **nemnan** 'to name/call' (wk. vb. like *hīeran* §94).
4 **ǣrest** adv. 'first'; **Brettum tō fultume** 'for the Britons as help'. *Tō* can often be translated 'as'.

---

¹ The joint Roman emperors Martianus (so, correctly, MS E) and Valentinian. Despite this entry, Hengest and Horsa and their followers were not the first Germanic-speaking people to come to Britain; see §xvi.
² Vortigern, king of the Britons.   ³ Ebbsfleet, Thanet.

455	5 Her Hengest 7 Horsa fuhton wiþ Wyrtgeorne þam cyninge in þære stowe þe is gecueden Agælesþrep[4] 7 his broþur Horsan man ofslog 7 æfter þam Hengest feng to rice 7 Æsc his sunu.
457	Her Hengest 7 Æsc fuhton wiþ Brettas in þære stowe þe is gecueden Crecganford[5] 7 þær ofslogon iiii^m wera 7 þa Brettas þa 10 forleton Centlond 7 mid micle ege flugon to Lundenbyrg.
465	Her Hengest 7 Æsc gefuhton wiþ Walas[6] neah Wippedesfleote[4] 7 þær xii Wilisce[6] aldormenn ofslogon . . .
473	Her Hengest 7 Æsc gefuhton wiþ Walas 7 genamon unarimed- lico herereaf 7 þa Walas flugon þa Englan . . .
495	15 Her cuomon twegen aldormen on Bretene, Cerdic[7] 7 Cynric his sunu, mid v scipum in þone stede þe is gecueden Cerdicesora[4] 7 þy ilcan dæge gefuhtun wiþ Walum.
508	Her Cerdic 7 Cynric ofslogon ænne Brettisc cyning þam was nama Natanleod 7 v þusendu wera mid him.
519	20 Her Cerdic 7 Cynric Westsexena rice onfengun 7 þy ilcan geare hie fuhton wiþ Brettas þær mon nu nemneþ Cerdicesford.[8]
527	Her Cerdic 7 Cynric fuhton wiþ Brettas in þære stowe þe is gecueden Cerdicesleaga.[4]
530	Her Cerdic 7 Cynric genamon Wihte ealond . . .
534	25 Her Cerdic forþferde 7 Cynric his sunu ricsode forþ xxvi wintra . . .

5 **feohtan** 'to fight' (st. vb. III §517); **wiþ** prep. 'against'.

6 **stōw** 'place'; **cweþan** 'to say/call' (st. vb. V §97).

7 **ofslēan** 'to kill' (st. contracted vb. VI §521). See §83; **fōn tō** 'to receive' (st. contracted vb. VII(*b*) §521). For the double subject see §162.

9 **ofslōgon**. See l. 7; **iiii^m wera** '4,000 of men'.

10 **forlǣtan** 'to leave' (st. vb. VII(*b*) §517); **ege** 'fear'; **flēon** 'to flee' (st. contracted vb. II §521). Here used without an object but in l. 14 with one.

11 **gefuhton**. See l. 5.

12 The **ealdormann** was the chief officer of the Anglo-Saxon shire. But here the word is used of the British leaders.

13 **(ge)niman** 'to take' (st. vb. IV §519).

13–14 **unārīmedlic** 'innumerable'.

14 **hererēaf** 'warspoil/booty'.

15 **cuman** 'to come' (st. vb. V *cuman c(u)ōm c(u)ōmon cumen*); **twēgen** 'twain/two'.

16 **stede** 'place'; **gecueden**. See l. 6.

17 **ilc** adj. 'same'. For the construction see §xix.

19 **nama** 'name' (§501).

24 **genāmon**. See l. 13.

25 **forþfēran** 'to go forth/pass away/die' (like *nemnan* l. 3); **forþ** adv. 'forth/continuously'.

---

[4] Unidentified.

[5] Crayford, Kent, according to Earle and Plummer.

[6] The Welsh, lit. 'the foreigners' (§xx), here used interchangeably with *Brettas* 'the British' (annals 449, 457 etc.), with *Bretwalas* (annal 552), and with adjectives such as *Brettisc* (annal 508).

[7] The Anglo-Saxon and later royal families trace their ancestry back to Cerdic. See §183 annal 784.

[8] Charford, Hampshire.

552   Her Cynric gefeaht wiþ Brettas in þære stowe þe is genemned æt
           Searobyrg[9] 7 þa Bretwalas[6] gefliemde.

556   Her Cynric 7 Ceawlin fuhton wiþ Brettas æt Beranbyrg.[10]

565   Her Columba[11] mæssepreost of Scottum com in Brettas to
          30 lærenne Peohtas 7 in Hi þam ealonde mynster worhte.

568   Her Ceaulin 7 Cuþa gefuhton wiþ Æþelbryht 7 hine in Cent
           gefliemdon . . .

577   Her Cuþwine 7 Ceawlin fuhton wiþ Brettas 7 hie iii kyningas
           ofslogon . . .

584   35 Her Ceawlin 7 Cuþa fuhton wiþ Brettas . . .

27 **geflieman** 'to put to flight' (like *nemnan* l. 3).
30 **læran** 'to teach' (like *nemnan* l. 3).

---

[9] Salisbury. Here we have prep. *æt* + dat., a not unusual formula.
[10] Barbury Camp, Wiltshire. See n. 9 above.
[11] St Columba, an Irish monk who came to Iona (*Hi*) to convert the Picts, established a monastery, and became Abbot.

4 The coming of Roman and Celtic Christianity

§183   Here we read of the coming of Roman and Celtic Christianity against a background of continuing warfare between Saxons and Celts and of battles between the various kingdoms established by the invaders. That we are reading annals and not history is emphasized by the fact that there is no mention of the Synod of Whitby (664), which met to settle the differences between the Irish and Roman traditions, in particular the date of Easter, and established the supremacy of the Roman tradition.

Text 3

596   Her Gregorius papa[1] sende to Bretene Augustinum[2] mid wel
          monegum munecum þa Godes word Engla þeode godspellian.

597   Her ongon Ceolwulf ricsian on Wesseaxum 7 simle he feaht 7
          won oþþe wiþ Angelcyn oþþe uuiþ Walas oþþe wiþ Peohtas
          5 oþþe wiþ Scottas . . .

601   Her sende Gregorius papa Agustino ærcebiscepe pallium in

1 **wel** adv. 'well' or (as here) 'very'.
2 **þa** dem. pron. 'the [words of God]'. See §55; **þeod** 'people'. Here dat. sg. without a prep. Contrast l. 18 *mid his þeode*; **godspellian** 'to gospel/preach' (wk. vb. like *lufian* §526).
3 **onginnan** 'to begin' (st. vb. III §518); **simle** adv. 'always/continually'; **feohtan** 'to fight' (§182 l. 5).
4 **winnan** 'to contend' (§181 l. 3); **wiþ/uuiþ** prep. 'against'.
6 **pallium** 'pallium/cloak of office'.

---

[1] Pope Gregory I (590–604).
[2] Augustine, first Archbishop of Canterbury (annal 601), died on 26 May of an unknown year between 604 and 609.

Bretene 7 wel monige godcunde lareowas him to fultome 7 Paulinus biscep [þe] gehwerfde Edwine Norþhymbra cyning to fulwihte.[3]

604   10 Her Eastseaxe onfengon geleafan 7 fulwihtes bæð under Sæbyrhte cyninge.

607   Her Ceolwulf[4] gefeaht wiþ Suþseaxe.

625   Her Paulinus fram Iusto þam ercebiscep wæs gehadod Norþhymbrum to biscepe.[3]

626   15 Her Eanflæd, Edwines dohtor cyninges, wæs gefulwad in þone halgan æfen Pentecosten 7 Penda hæfde xxx wintra rice 7 he hæfde l wintra þa þa he to rice feng.[5]

627   Her Edwine kyning wæs gefulwad mid his þeode on Eastron.

633   Her Edwine wæs ofslægen[5] 7 Paulinus huerf eft to Cantwarum 7 20 gesæt þæt biscepsetl on Hrofesceastre.[3]

634   Her Birinus biscep bodude Westseaxum fulwuht.[6]

635   Her Cynegils wæs gefulwad from Birino þæm biscepe in Dorkeceastre . . .[7]

642   Her Oswald Norþanhymbra cyning ofslægen wæs.[8]

7 **godcunde** adj. 'religious'; **lāreōw** 'teacher'; **him tō fultome** see §182 l. 4.

8 **þe** rel. pron. 'who'. This is needed for the sense; see annal 627; **(ge)hwerfan** 'to turn/convert' (wk. vb. like *hīeran* §94).

9 **fulwiht** 'baptism/Christianity'.

10 **gelēafa** 'belief'; **bæð** 'bath/water'.

13 **fram** prep. 'from/by'; **(ge)hādian** 'to ordain/consecrate' (wk. vb. like *lufian* §526).

14 **tō** 'as'.

15 Note the two separated words with gen. sg. *-es* where we say 'King Edwin's daughter'; **(ge)fulwian** 'to baptize' (like *(ge)hādian* l. 13).

16 **æfen** 'eve/evening'.

17 **þā þā** 'then when'.

19 **hweorfan** 'to turn/return' (st. vb. III §518).

21 **bodian** 'to preach' (like *(ge)hādian* l. 13).

---

[3] Bede says that Paulinus went to Northumbria when Æthelburg, daughter of the Christian King Æthelbert of Kent, was married to the heathen King Edwin and that he was consecrated bishop at that time. There are, however, grounds for thinking that Paulinus and Æthelburg went to Northumbria in 619 and not in 625, when Paulinus was consecrated Bishop of York. Bede's account of Edwin's conversion will be found in Text 19 (§425). Paulinus returned to Canterbury on the death of Edwin and became Bishop of Rochester (annal 633), leaving a legacy of Roman Christianity in the north.

[4] See annal 597.

[5] The figures here seem confused. According to Bede, Penda became king of Mercia after he and Cadwallon, king of Gwynedd, had killed Edwin in battle (annal 633) and what is known of him suggests that he is unlikely to have been eighty – a very ripe age indeed in those days – when killed in battle (annal 655) by Oswiu (n. 10).

[6] Birinus was the first bishop of Dorchester-on-Thames (annal 635).

[7] The baptism of King Cynegils of Wessex did not mean that the whole royal house was converted. But his son Cenwalh was (annal 646, not printed here).

[8] Oswald was killed in battle by Penda (on whom see annal 626). When he was established as king, Oswald, who had lived in exile and had received Christianity from the Irish monks of Iona, sent to Iona for a bishop. As a result, Aidan came to Northumbria in 634 and established a monastery on Lindisfarne Island.

643   25 Her Cenwalh feng to Wesseaxna rice 7 heold xxxi wintra 7 se
Cenwalh het atimbran þa ciricean on Wintanceastre.[9]

651   Her Oswine kyning wæs ofslægen[10] 7 Aidan biscep forþferde.[8]

655   Her Penda forwearþ[5] 7 Mierce wurdon Cristne.

671   Her wæs þæt micle fugla wæl.

675   30 Her Wulfhere Pending[11] 7 Æscwine[12] gefuhton æt Biedan-
heafde.[13]

676   Her ... Æþered Miercna cyning[14] oferhergeada Centlond.

678   Her oþiewde cometa se steorra 7 Wilfriþ biscop[15] wæs adrifen of
his biscepdome ...

682   35 On þissum geare Centwine[16] gefliemde Bretwalas oþ sæ.

685   Her hæt Ecgferð cining[15] gehalgian Cuðberht[17] to biscope 7
Theodorus archieps̃[18] hine gehalgode on Eoforwic[19] þam forman
Eastordæge to biscope to Hagustaldes ham ...

704   Her Æþelred Pending Miercna cyning[14] onfeng munuchade 7
40 þæt rice heold xxviiii wintra ...

714   Her forþferde Guþlac se halga.[20]

---

26 **hātan** 'to order' (st. vb. VII(*b*) §517). For the construction see §122; **ātimbran** 'to build'
(wk. vb. §§91–3).

28 **forweorþan** 'to perish' (st. vb. III §518); **weorþan** 'to become' (same verb!).

29 **micel** adj. 'great'; **fug(o)l** 'fowl/bird'; **wæl** 'slaughter/slaying'.

32 **oferhergian** 'to ravage/overrun' (like (*ge*)*hādian* l. 13). The 3rd pers. sg. pret. ind. usually
ends in -*e*, not -*a*.

33 **oþiewan** 'to appear' (wk. vb. like *hīeran* §94).

35 **oþ** prep. 'up to/until'.

36 **hæt** = *hēt* l. 26; **(ge)halgian** 'to hallow/consecrate' (like (*ge*)*hādian* l. 13). For the construction see §122.

37–8 **þam forman Eastordæge** 'on the first day of Easter'.

38 **tō** means first 'as' and then 'of/for'.

39 **munuchād** 'monkhood/monastic orders'.

---

[9] This marks the establishment of the See of Winchester. As a result, Agilbert, the then
Bishop of Dorchester, went into exile.

[10] On the death of Oswald, his brother Oswiu became king of Bernicia, one division of
Northumbria. Oswine, who had become king of Deira, declined to engage in battle and was
subsequently killed by Oswiu.   [11] Wulfhere son of Penda, king of Mercia.

[12] King of Wessex.   [13] Unidentified.

[14] Æthered or Æthelred, another son of Penda; see annal 704.

[15] St Wilfred, Bishop of Ripon, a frequent visitor to Rome and a powerful advocate of
Roman practices, alienated Ecgfrith, king of Northumbria (annal 685), and was exiled. He went
to the Continent, again visited Rome, and subsequently returned to England. There he took
refuge with Æthelwalh, the Christian king of the heathen South Saxons, and converted his
people. He was later restored to his churches in Ripon and Hexham and died in 709.

[16] King of Wessex, son of Cynegils (annal 635).

[17] Cuthbert was a young shepherd who had a vision on the night of Aidan's death (annal 651)
and as a result entered the monastery of Melrose, where he became Prior. From there he went
to Lindisfarne as Prior and was subsequently consecrated Bishop of Hexham (*Hagustaldes ham*)
and then of Lindisfarne. He died in 687.

[18] A native of Tarsus and a monk of the Eastern Church, Theodore was consecrated Archbishop of Canterbury by Pope Vitalian in 668.

[19] York.

[20] A member of the Mercian royal house and founder of Crowland Abbey.

729   Her cometa se steorra hiene oþiewde 7 Sanctus Ecgbryht[21] forþferde.

734   Her wæs se mona swelce he wære mid blode begoten 7 ferdon
45   forþ Tatwine[22] 7 Bieda.[23]

743   Her Æþelbald[24] 7 Cuþræd[25] fuhton wiþ Walas.

750   Her Cuþred cyning gefeaht uuiþ Æþelhun þone ofermedan aldormonn.[26]

753   Her Cuþred feaht wiþ Walas.

755   50 Her Cynewulf benam Sigebryht his rices 7 Westseaxna wiotan
for unryhtum dædum[27] buton Hamtunscire[28] 7 he hæfde þa oþ
he ofslog þone aldormon þe him lengest wunode[29] 7 hiene þa
Cynewulf on Andred[30] adræfde 7 he þær wunade oþ þæt hiene an
swan ofstang æt Pryfetesflodan[31] 7 he wræc þone aldormon
55 Cumbran· 7 se Cynewulf oft miclum gefeohtum feaht uuiþ Bretwalum . . .

761   Her wæs se micla winter.

773   Her oþiewde read Cristesmæl on hefenum æfter sunnan
setlgonge 7 þy geare gefuhton Mierce 7 Cantware æt Ottan-
60 forda.[32]

---

42 **oþīewde** Here, but not in l. 33, this verb has a reflexive object *hiene* = *hine* 'showed itself'.

44 **mōna** 'moon'; **swelce** conj. 'as if' with subj. *wǣre* (§528); **blōd** 'blood'; **begēotan** 'to anoint/cover' (st. vb. II §517).

44-5 **fēran forþ** 'to die' (a variant of *forþfēran* §182 l. 25).

47 **ofermēde** adj. 'proud/arrogant'.

50 **beniman** 'to deprive [someone (acc.)] of [something (gen.)]' (st. vb. IV §519); for the subject of *benam* see §162; **wi(o)ta** 'wise man/councillor'.

51 **unryht** adj. 'wrongful/unjust'; **dǣd** 'deed'; **būton** prep. 'except'; **þā** acc. sg. fem. of *se* referring to *Hamtūnscire* 'it'; **oþ** conj. 'until'. So also *oþ þæt* l. 53.

52 **wunian** 'to remain (with)' (like *(ge)hādian* l. 13); **þā** adv. 'then'.

53 **ādrǣfan** 'to drive' (like *oþīewan* l. 33).

54 **swān** 'herdsman'; **ofstingan** 'to stab' (st. vb. III §518); **wrecan** 'to avenge' (st. vb. V §517).

55 **(ge)feoht** 'battle'.

57 **micel** adj. 'great', here 'severe'.

58 **rēad** adj. 'red'; **Crīstesmǣl** 'Christ's mark/cross'; **he(o)fon** 'heaven'; **sunne** 'sun'.

59 **setlgong** 'setting'; **þȳ gēare** 'in that year'. See §xix.

---

[21] This is the Egbert who in 716 persuaded the monks of Iona to adopt the Roman tonsure and date of Easter.

[22] Archbishop of Canterbury.   [23] The Venerable Bede.
[24] King of Mercia.   [25] King of Wessex.
[26] An otherwise unknown chief officer of a shire.

[27] Whether the deposition of Sigebryht by Cynewulf, king of Wessex 755–84, and the *wiotan* 'councillors' was a legal act or a *coup d'état* is uncertain. Cynewulf was killed in 784 by Sigebryht's brother Cyneheard; see annal 784. Annal 755 continues with a lively circumstantial account of this killing, which is the only incident reported twice in the Chronicle. Perhaps a scribe who knew the story inserted it to relieve his boredom.

[28] Hampshire.
[29] Cumbra (l. 55 below), the chief officer of Hampshire.
[30] The Weald, the great forest of Kent and Sussex.
[31] The stream at Privett.   [32] Otford.

777   Her Cynewulf 7 Offa³³ gefuhton ymb Benesingtun³⁴ 7 Offa nam
     þone tuun.

784   Her Cyneheard ofslog Cynewulf cyning 7 he þær wearþ ofslægen
     7 lxxxiiii monna mid him²⁷ 7 þa onfeng Beorhtric Wesseaxna
     65 rices 7 he ricsode xvi gear 7 his lic liþ æt Werham³⁵ 7 his
     ryhtfædrencyn gæþ to Cerdice.³⁶

61 **ymb** prep. 'at/near'.
62 **tuun** = *tūn* 'town'.
64 **þā** adv. 'then'. See §137.
65 **licgan** 'to lie/rest' (st. vb. V §519). The 3rd pers. sg. pres. ind. *ligeþ* is often contracted to *liþ*.
66 **ryhtfædren cyn** 'direct paternal descent'; **gān** 'to go' (§529).

---

³³ King of Mercia 757–96.   ³⁴ Bensington.   ³⁵ Wareham.   ³⁶ See annal 495.

5 The Scandinavian incursions

§184   The first Scandinavian raiders came from Norway, landed at Portland in Dorset, and killed the reeve of Dorchester (annal 787). But thereafter the Norwegians passed round the north of Scotland and established colonies in the Shetlands and Orkneys, the Hebrides, and Ireland, whence in the tenth century they came to the west coast of England. It was the Danes who were responsible for the series of summer 'smash-and-grab' raids which continued till 851, when 'heathen men' are recorded as first staying for the winter. It was the Danes who ravaged Kent in 865. In the next few years they brought about the collapse of the kingdoms of Northumbria, Mercia, and East Anglia, and kept Wessex, the only surviving kingdom, under intense pressure.

Text 4

787   Her nom Beorhtric cyning Offan dohtor Eadburge¹ 7 on his
     dagum cuomon ærest iii scipu 7 þa se gerefa þærto rad 7 hie
     wolde drifan to þæs cyninges tune þy he nyste hwæt hie wæron 7
     hiene mon ofslog. þæt wæron þa ærestan scipu deniscra monna
     5 þe Angelcynnes lond gesohton.

793   Her wæron reðe forebecna cumene ofer Norðanhymbra land 7

1 **niman** 'to take' (st. vb. IV §519).
2 **scip** 'ship' (§503); **gerefa** 'reeve/steward'; **rīdan** 'to ride' (st. vb. I §517).
3 **drīfan** 'to drive/force' (like *rīdan*); **þȳ** conj. 'because'; **nyste** 'knew not/did not know', a contraction of *ne wyste* = *wiste*, past tense of *witan* 'to know' (§§109 and 97).
4 **þæt wæron** . . . 'Those were . . .'; **denisc** adj. 'Danish'.
6 **rēðe** adj. 'fierce/terrible'; **forebēacen** 'fore-beacon/omen'.

---

¹ Eadburg, daughter of Offa (annal 787), married Beorhtric (annal 784).

þ folc earmlice bregdon: þ wæron ormete ligræscas 7 wæron geseowene fyrene dracan on þam lyfte fleogende. þam tacnum sona fyligde mycel hunger 7 litel æfter þam þæs ilcan geares on vi
10 idus Iañr[2] earmlice heðenra manna hergung adiligode Godes cyrican in Lindisfarena ee[3] þurh reaflac 7 mansleht.

832   Her hæþne men oferhergeadon Sceapige.[4]

833   Her gefeaht Ecgbryht cyning[5] wiþ xxxv sciphlæsta æt Carrum[6] 7 þær wearþ micel wæl geslægen 7 þa Denescan ahton wælstowe
15 gewald . . .

835   Her cuom micel sciphere[7] on Westwalas 7 hie to anum gecierdon 7 wiþ Ecgbryht Westseaxna cyning winnende wæron. þa he þæt hierde 7 mid fierde[7] ferde 7 him wiþ feaht æt Hengestdune[8] 7 þær gefliemde ge þa Walas ge þa Deniscan.

837   20 Her Wulfheard aldormon[9] gefeaht æt Hamtune[10] wiþ xxxiii

---

7 þ = *þæt*; **earmlice** adv. 'miserably'; **brēgan** 'to terrify' (wk. vb. like *hīeran* §94); **ormēte** adj. 'immense'; **līgræsc** 'lightning flash'.

8 **(ge)sēon** 'to see' (st. contracted vb. V §521); **fȳren** adj. 'fiery'; **draca** 'dragon'; **lyft** 'air'; **flēogan** 'to fly' (st. vb. II §517). This is the pres. ptc.; **tācen** 'token/sign'.

9 **fyl(i)gan** 'to follow' (wk. vb. with varying forms); **hunger** 'hunger/famine'; **ilc** adj. 'same'; **þæs ilcan gēares** adv. gen. (§46).

10 **hergung** 'harrying'; **ādīligian** 'to destroy/devastate' (wk. vb. like *lufian* §526).

11 **cyrice** 'church'; **rēaflāc** 'plundering'; **mansleht** 'slaughter'.

12 **oferhergian** 'to overrun/ravage' (like *ādīligian* l. 10).

13 **sciphlæst** 'ship's crew'.

14 **wæl** 'slaughter, carnage'; **(ge)slēan** 'to strike, to slay' (st. contracted vb. VI §521); **āgan** 'to possess' (irregular vb. §96); **wælstōw** 'slaughter-place/battlefield'.

15 **gew(e)ald** 'control'.

16 **tō ānum** 'together'; **(ge)cierran** 'to turn/come' (like *brēgan* l. 7). In l. 64 *tō þām gecirdon þæt*... means 'agreed to this, that . . .'.

18 **hīeran** 'to hear' (wk. vb. §94); **fēran** 'to go' (like *hīeran*).

19 **ge . . . ge** conj. 'both . . . and'.

---

[2] 8 January, a mistake for 8 June. The Danes would not have sailed in winter.

[3] This plundering of St Cuthbert's holy island Lindisfarne (see annal 651 n. 8 and annal 685 n. 17) made a great impression.

[4] The island of Shippey; see annal 855.

[5] King of Wessex; see annal 835.   [6] Charmouth.

[7] The word *sciphere* means 'the crew of a warship' or 'a ship-borne raiding force'. For *scip*, compare *sciphlæst* 'crew of a ship' (annal 833) and for *here* compare *wiþ deniscne here* 'against a Danish band' (annals 837 and 845), *hergung* 'harrying' (annal 793), *hergodon* 'harried/plundered' (annal 910), *oferhergeadon* 'overran/ravaged' (annal 832), and *here* itself 'a Danish raiding-band/host/army' (annals 851 and 867). Other names for the Danes include *hæþne men* 'heathen men' (annal 832) and *hæþen here* 'heathen army' (annal 865). The native force is the *fierd* (annals 835 and 851); the word means both military expedition or campaign and national army or levy. Later, after Danish kings had occupied the throne of England, the distinction was blurred. Ælfric, in his life of St Edmund, king of East Anglia, speaks of the Danes coming against Edmund *mid fierde* and the annal for 1066 in MS E tells how Harold, after defeating the Norwegian invaders at Stamford Bridge in Yorkshire *mid miclum here Engliscra monna*, was then forced to do battle against William at Hastings *ær þan þe his here come eall* 'before all his army could get there'. See also §185 l. 24n.

[8] Hingston Down.

[9] The *aldormon* or *dux* was chief officer of a shire.

[10] Southampton.

sciphlæsta 7 þær micel wæl geslog 7 sige nom 7 þy geare
forþferde Wulfheard 7 þy ilcan geare gefeaht Æþelhelm dux[9]
wiþ deniscne here on Port[11] mid Dornsætum[12] 7 gode hwile þone
here gefliemde 7 þa Deniscan ahton wælstowe gewald 7 þone
25 aldormon ofslogon.

840   Her Æþelwulf cyning[13] gefeaht æt Carrum[6] wiþ xxxv sciphlæsta
7 þa Deniscan ahton wælstowe gewald.

845   Her Eanulf aldorman gefeaht mid Sumursætum[14] 7 Ealchstan
biscep 7 Osric aldorman mid Dornsætum[12] gefuhton æt
30 Pedridan muþan[15] wiþ deniscne here 7 þær micel wæl geslogon 7
sige namon.

851   Her Ceorl aldormon gefeaht wiþ hæþene men mid Defenascire[16]
æt Wicganbeorge[17] 7 þær micel wæl geslogon 7 sige namon. 7 þy
ilcan geare Æþelstan cyning[18] 7 Ealchere dux micelne here
35 ofslogon æt Sondwic[19] on Cent 7 ix scipu gefengun 7 þa oþre
gefliemdon. 7 hæþne men ærest ofer winter sæton. 7 þy ilcan
geare cuom feorðe healf hund scipa on Temese[20] muþan 7
bræcon Contwaraburg[21] 7 Lundenburg[22] 7 gefliemdon Beorht-
wulf Miercna cyning mid his fierde 7 foron þa suþ ofer Temese
40 on Suþrige[23] 7 him gefeaht wiþ Æþelwulf cyning[13] 7 Æþelbald
his sunu[24] æt Aclea[25] mid Westseaxna fierde 7 þær þæt mæste
wæl geslogon on hæþnum herige þe we secgan hierdon oþ þisne
ondweardan dæg 7 þær sige namon.

21 **7 þær micel wæl geslōg** is the active form of the passive construction in ll. 13–14; **sige**
'victory'.

23 **hwīl** 'while/time'. Here acc. of duration of time (§44).

35 **(ge)fōn** 'to take/seize/capture' (st. contracted vb. VII(*b*) §521).

36 **sittan** 'to sit/settle/remain' (st. vb. V §519).

37 **feorðe healf hund** 'the fourth a half hundred' = 350.

38 **brecan** 'to break (into)/storm' (st. vb. IV §517).

39 **mid** prep. '(in company) with'; **faran** 'to go' (st. vb. VI §517); **þā** adv. 'then'.

40 **him . . . wiþ** 'against them [the Danes]'. This order is often found in OE; **gefeaht** sg. vb.
followed in ll. 40–1 by two sg. subjects joined by 7.

41 **mǣst** adj. 'most/greatest'.

42 **geslōgon** See l. 21. The subject is *Æþelwulf cyning 7 Æþelbald his sunu* (ll. 40–1); **herige**
dat. sg. of *here*; **þe** rel. pron. 'which'; **secgan** 'to say' (wk. vb. §97). See §122 and translate 'of
which we heard [anyone] tell'; **oþ** prep. 'until'.

43 **ondweard** adj. 'present'.

---

[11] Portland.   [12] The people of Dorset.
[13] King of Wessex, father of King Alfred.
[14] The people of Somerset.   [15] The mouth of the River Parrett.
[16] [The people of] Devonshire.   [17] Unidentified.
[18] Son of Æthelwulf (annal 840) and under-king of Kent, Essex, Surrey, and Sussex.
[19] Sandwich.   [20] The River Thames.
[21] Canterbury.   [22] London.   [23] Surrey.
[24] Æthelbald succeeded his father Æthelwulf as king of Wessex but died in 860. He was
succeeded in turn by his brothers Æthelbert (d. 866), Æthered (d. 871), and Alfred.
[25] Ockley, Surrey.

853　　　Her bæd Burgred Miercna cyning 7 his wiotan Æþelwulf cyning
　45　þæt he him gefultumade þæt him Norþwalas gehiersumade. He
　　þa swa dyde 7 mid fierde for ofer Mierce on Norþwalas 7 hie him
　　alle gehiersume dydon. 7 þy ilcan geare sende Æþelwulf cyning
　　Ælfred his sunu to Rome.[26] þa was domne Leo papa on Rome 7
　　he hine to cyninge gehalgode 7 hiene him to biscepsuna nam . . .
　50 Ond þæs ofer Eastron geaf Æþelwulf cyning his dohtor[27]
　　Burgrede cyninge of Wesseaxum on Merce.

855　　　Her hæþne men ærest on Sceapige[4] ofer winter sætun.

865　　　Her sæt hæþen here on Tenet[28] 7 genamon friþ wiþ Cantwarum
　　7 Cantware him feoh geheton wiþ þam friþe 7 under þam friþe 7
　55 þam feohgehate se here hiene on niht up bestæl 7 oferhergeade
　　alle Cent eastewearde.

866　　　Her feng Æþered Æþelbryhtes broþur[24] to Wesseaxna rice. 7 þy
　　ilcan geare cuom micel here on Angelcynnes lond 7 wintersetl
　　namon on Eastenglum 7 þær gehorsude wurdon 7 hie him friþ
　60 wiþ namon.

867　　　Her for se here of Eastenglum ofer Humbre[29] muþan to
　　Eoforwicceastre[30] on Norþhymbre. 7 þær wæs micel
　　ungeþuærnes þære þeode betweox him selfum . . . 7 hie late on
　　geare to þam gecirdon þæt hie wiþ þone here winnende wærun
　65 7 hie þeah micle fierd gegadrodon 7 þone here sohton æt
　　Eoforwicceastre 7 on þa ceastre bræcon 7 hie sume inne wurdon
　　7 þær was ungemetlic wæl geslægen Norþanhymbra, sume
　　binnan, sume butan, 7 þa cyningas begen ofslægene 7 sio laf wiþ
　　þone here friþ nam.

44 **biddan** 'to ask' (st. vb. V §519) governing a *þæt* clause.

45 **(ge)fultumian** 'to help' (wk. vb. like *lufian* §526); **þæt** 'so that'; **(ge)hiersumian** 'to make obedient/conquer' (like *(ge)fultumian*). The subject *Burgred* is unexpressed.

46–7 Translate '[Burgred and Æthelwulf] made all the Danes [*hie . . . alle*] obedient to them'.

47 **sendan** 'to send' (wk. vb. §89).

48 **domne** from Lat. *dominus* 'lord'.

49 **(ge)hālgian** 'to hallow' (like *(ge)fultumian* l. 45); **biscepsunu** 'godson at confirmation'.

50 **þæs** 'after that'; **giefan** 'to give' (st. vb. V §519).

53 **friþ** 'peace'.

54 **feoh** 'money'; **(ge)hātan** 'to promise' (as well as 'to command') (st. vb. VII(*b*) §517).

55 **feohgehāt** 'promise of money'; **bestelan** 'to steal away' (st. vb. V §517), here with reflexive pron. *hine*.

58 **wintersetl** 'winter quarters'.

59 **(ge)horsian** 'to provide with horses' (like *(ge)fultumian* l. 45).

63 **ungeþuærnes** 'discord'; **betweox** prep. 'between'.

64 **tō þām . . . þæt** conj. 'so that'. See §126; **gecirdon** see l. 16.

65 **þēah** adv. 'however'; **(ge)gadrian** 'to gather/assemble' (like *(ge)fultumian* l. 45); **sēcan** 'to seek' (wk. vb. §95).

66 **ceaster** 'town/fort'; **hīe sume** 'some (of) them'.

67 **ungemetlic** 'immense'.

68 **binnan** adv. 'within'; **būtan** adv. 'outside'; **bēgen** 'both'; **lāf** 'leaving/remnant'.

---

[26] Alfred was then five years old. He visited Rome again with his father in 855.
[27] Her name was Æthelswith.　　　　[28] Thanet.　　　　[29] River Humber.　　　　[30] York.

868   70 Her for se ilca here innan Mierce to Snotengaham[31] 7 þær
wintersetl namon 7 Burgred Miercna cyning 7 his wiotan bædon
Æþered Westseaxna cyning 7 Ælfred his broþur þæt hie him
gefultumadon þæt hie wiþ þone here gefuhton 7 þa ferdon hie
mid Wesseaxna fierde innan Mierce oþ Snotengaham 7 þone
   75 here þær metton on þam geweorce 7 þær nan hefelic gefeoht ne
wearþ 7 Mierce friþ namon wiþ þone here.

869   Her for se here eft to Eoforwicceastre 7 þær sæt i gear.

870   Her rad se here ofer Mierce innan Eastengle 7 wintersetl namon
æt þeodforda.[32] 7 þy wintra Eadmund cyning him wiþ feaht 7 þa
   80 Deniscan sige namon 7 þone cyning ofslogon 7 þæt lond all
geeodon.

71 **biddan** See l. 44.
74 **innan** prep. 'within/into'.
75 **mētan** 'to meet' (like *sendan* l. 47); **geweorc** 'work/fortification'; **nān** adj. 'no'; **hefelic**
adj. 'heavy/serious'.
81 **(ge)gān** 'to overrun/conquer' (irregular vb. §529).

[31] Nottingham.   [32] Thetford.

6 The reign of King Alfred

§185 The Chronicle account of the reign of King Alfred was composed
as a whole and can be said to mark the beginning of the chroniclers' use of
the annal form to write history. The kingdom of Wessex was on the defensive against the marauding Danes when Alfred came to the throne in 871 and
was almost down and out in 878. It was saved only by Alfred's ability to plan,
lead, and inspire; see n. 26 below. From 880 there was a period of uneasy
peace in which the Danes settled and ploughed and in which the boundaries
of Danelaw were established. The arrival of another great army from France
in 892 led to more bitter fighting in which the invaders were helped by the
Danes in Northumbria and East Anglia. But, as the annal for 896 tells us,
Alfred and his men succeeded in driving off the enemy before they could
destroy Wessex. For the remaining years of his reign, Alfred was free to
devote more of his time to education, learning, and administration.

Text 5

871   Her cuom se here to Readingum[1] on Westseaxe ... þæs ymb iiii
niht Æþered cyning 7 Ælfred his broþur þær micle fierd to

1 **þæs** gen. sg. of *þæt* 'from that'; **ymb** prep. 'after' (of time). It means 'about' in phrases like
sprecan ymb(e) 'to speak about', as in ll. 52–3 below.

[1] Reading.

Readingum gelæddon 7 wiþ þone here gefuhton 7 þær wæs micel
wæl geslægen on gehwæþre hond 7 Æþelwulf aldormon wearþ
5 ofslægen 7 þa Deniscan ahton wælstowe gewald ... 7 þæs ymb
xiiii niht gefeaht Æþered cyning 7 Ælfred his broður wiþ þone
here æt Basengum[2] 7 þær þa Deniscan sige namon. 7 þæs ymb ii
monaþ gefeaht Æþered cyning 7 Ælfred his broþur wiþ þone
here æt Meretune[3] ... 7 þa Deniscan ahton wælstowe gewald ...
10 7 æfter þissum gefeohte cuom micel sumorlida. 7 þæs ofer
Eastron gefor Æþered cyning 7 he ricsode v gear 7 his lic liþ æt
Winburnan.[4] þa feng Ælfred Æþelwulfing his broþur to Wesseaxna rice ... 7 þæs geares wurdon viiii folcgefeoht gefohten
wiþ þone here on þy cynerice be suþan Temese ... 7 þy geare
15 namon Westseaxe friþ wiþ þone here.

872   Her for se here to Lundenbyrig from Readingum 7 þær winter-
      setl nam 7 þa namon Mierce friþ wiþ þone here.

873   Her for se here on Norþhymbre 7 he nam wintersetl on Lindesse
      æt Turecesiege[5] 7 þa namon Mierce friþ wiþ þone here.

874   20 Her for se here from Lindesse to Hreopedune[6] 7 þær wintersetl
      nam 7 þone cyning Burgred[7] ofer sæ adræfdon ymb xxii wintra
      þæs þe he rice hæfde 7 þæt lond all geeodon ...

875   Her for se here from Hreopedune ... 7 þy sumera for Ælfred
      cyning ut on sæ mid sciphere 7 gefeaht wiþ vii sciphlæstas 7 hiera
      25 an gefeng 7 þa oþru gefliemde[8] ...

876   Her hiene bestæl se here into Werham[9] Wesseaxna fierde 7 wiþ
      þone here se cyning friþ nam ... 7 þy geare Healfdene[10] Norþan-
      hymbra lond gedælde 7 ergende wæron 7 hiera tilgende.

4 **gehwæþer** adj. 'each/either'.
8 **mōnaþ** 'month', here acc. pl.
10 **sumorlida** 'summer army', as opposed to the forces which stayed for the winter (annals
851 and 855).
11 **gefor**. See §184 l. 39. Here used as a euphemism for 'died'; cf. *forðfērde* (§182 l. 25) and
fērde forð (§183 ll. 44–5).
13 **folcgefeoht** 'general engagement/pitched battle', here pl.
14 **cynerīce** 'kingdom'.
18 **hē**, not *hit*, because it refers to *se here*.
21 **þone cyning** How do you know that this is not the subject? See §40. The subject is *se here*
(l. 20) and its verbs change from sg. *fōr* (l.20) and *nam* (l. 21) to pl. *adræfdon* (l. 21) and *geēodon*
(l. 22).
21–2 **ymb xxii wintra þæs þe** 'after 22 winters/years from that in which'.
23 **sumer** 'summer'.
24 **mid sciphere** 'in company with an English naval force'. The phrase *wiþ sciphere* would
have meant 'against a Danish naval force'. Cf. §184, ll. 38–41.
28 **(ge)dǣlan** 'to divide/distribute' (wk. vb. like *hīeran* §94); **erian** 'to plough' (wk. vb. like
werian §525). The subject of *ergende wǣron* is the unexpressed 'Healfdene's men'; **tilian** 'to till'
(wk. vb. like *lufian* §526).

---

[2] Basing.   [3] Unidentified.   [4] Wimborne.
[5] On Lindsey at Torksey.   [6] Repton.   [7] See §184 annal 853.
[8] The building of this fleet was only part of Alfred's remodelling of the national defences.
[9] Wareham.   [10] One of the Danish leaders.

878   Her hiene bestæl se here on midne winter ofer tuelftan niht to
   30 Cippanhamme[11] 7 geridon Wesseaxna lond 7 gesæton 7 micel
þæs folces ofer sæ adræfdon 7 þæs oþres þone mæstan dæl hie
geridon 7 him to gecirdon buton þam cyninge Ælfrede . . . 7 him
to coman þær ongen Sumorsæte[12] alle 7 Wilsætan[13] 7 Hamtun-
scir se dæl se hiere behinon sæ was[14] 7 his gefægene wærun. 7 he
   35 for ymb ane niht of þam wicum to Iglea[15] 7 þæs ymb ane to
Eþandune[16] 7 þær gefeaht wiþ alne þone here 7 hiene gefliemde 7
him æfter rad oþ þæt geweorc 7 þær sæt xiiii niht 7 þa salde se
here him foregislas 7 micle aþas þæt hie of his rice uuoldon 7 him
eac geheton þæt hiera kyning fulwihte onfon wolde· 7 hie þæt
   40 gelæston swa . . .

880   Her for se here of Cirenceastre[17] on Eastengle 7 gesæt þæt lond 7
gedælde.

882   Her for se here up onlong Mæse[18] feor on Fronclond[19] 7 þær sæt
an gear. 7 þy ilcan geare for Ælfred cyning mid scipum ut on sæ 7
   45 gefeaht wiþ feower sciphlæstas deniscra monna 7 þara scipa tu
genam . . .

886   Her for se here eft west þe ær east gelende 7 þa up on Sigene[20] 7
þær wintersetl namon. þy ilcan geare gesette Ælfred cyning
Lundenburg· him all Angelcyn to cirde þæt buton deniscra
   50 monna hæftniede was· 7 hie þa befæste þa burg Æþerede aldormen to haldonne.

29 **on midne winter** 'at midwinter/Christmas'.
30 **gerīdan** 'to get by riding/surprise/conquer' (st. vb. I §517); **gesittan** 'to occupy' (st. vb. V §519).
31 **dæl** 'part'.
32 **him tō** 'to them' (twice); **būton** prep. 'except'.
33 **ongē(a)n** adv. 'thither'
34 **behi(o)nan** prep. 'on this side of'; **(ge)fægen** adj. 'glad of' with gen. sg. *his* (l. 34) 'him'.
35 **wīc** 'dwelling', here plural 'fortifications/camp'; **ymb āne [niht]**.
37 **him æfter** 'after them'; **oþ** prep. 'up to'; **sellan** 'to give' (wk. vb. §95).
38 **foregīsl** 'preliminary hostage'; **āþ** 'oath'; **uuoldon** 'would [go]'.
40 **(ge)læstan** 'to fulfil/perform' (wk. vb. like *sendan* §89).
41–2 For the divided construction – here with two verbs – see §§162–3.
43 **onlong** prep. 'along'; **feor** adv. 'far'.
45 **tū** 'two'.
47 **þe** rel. pron. 'which'; **(ge)lendan** 'to land/go' (like *(ge)læstan* l. 40).
48 **(ge)settan** 'to occupy' (like *(ge)læstan* l. 40). This was an important success for Alfred.
49 **þæt** rel. pron. 'that which' referring to *all Angelcyn* (l. 49). The meaning is that all the English not subject to the Danes (*būton . . . hæftniede* 'outside the captivity') submitted to Alfred.
50 **befæstan** 'to entrust' (like *(ge)læstan* l. 40). The subject is Alfred, the object *hīe* (acc. sg. fem.) . . . *þā burg*. Or read *hē* for *hīe*?
51 **healdan** 'to hold/guard' (st. vb. VII(*a*) §517). Here we have an unusual spelling of the infinitive with *tō*.

---

[11] Chippenham.   [12] The people of Somerset.   [13] The people of Wiltshire.
[14] This means either the people of Hampshire west of Southampton Water or those men of Hampshire who had not fled abroad.
[15] Iley.   [16] Edington.   [17] Cirencester.
[18] River Meuse.   [19] The Frankish Kingdom.   [20] River Seine.

892   Her on þysum geare for se micla here þe we gefyrn ymbe
         spræcon eft of þæm eastrice westweard to Bunann[21] 7 þær
         wurdon gescipode swa þæt hie asettan him on anne siþ ofer mid
      55 horsum mid ealle 7 þa comon up on Limene muþan[22] mid ccl
         scipa ... þa sona æfter þæm com Hæsten[23] mid lxxx scipa up on
         Temese muðan 7 worhte him geweorc æt Middeltune[24] 7 se oþer
         here æt Apuldre.[25]

896   Ða þæs on sumera on ðysum gere tofor se here, sum on East-
      60 engle, sum on Norðhymbre, 7 þa þe feohlease wæron him þær
         scipu begeton 7 suð ofer sæ foron to Sigene. Næfde se here,
         Godes þonces, Angelcyn ealles forswiðe gebrocod[26] ...

900   Her gefor Ælfred Aþulfing[27] syx nihtum ær ealra haligra mæssan
         ,, se[28] wæs cyning ofer eall Ongelcyn butan ðæm dæle þe under
      65 Dena onwalde wæs 7 he heold þæt rice oþrum healfum læs þe
         xxx wintra 7 þa feng Eadweard his sunu to rice.

52 **gefyrn** adv. 'before'.
53 **sprecan** 'to speak' (st. vb. V §517). See l. 1n.; **ēastrīce** 'eastern kingdom' of *Fronclond* (l. 43).
54 **(ge)scipian** 'to embark' (like *tilian* l. 28); **āsettan** with reflexive pron. *him* and adv. *ofer* 'to cross over' (like *(ge)læstan* l. 40); **sīþ** 'journey'.
56 **sōna** adv. 'immediately/at once'.
57 **wyrcan** 'to make' (wk. vb. §95).
57–8 The verb for **se ōþer here** is *worhte him geweorc* (l. 57).
59 **tōfaran** 'to disperse/separate' (st. vb. VI §517).
60 **feohlēas** 'moneyless'.
61 **begietan** 'to get/seize' (st. vb. V like *giefan* §519); **Næfde** contraction of *Ne hæfde*.
62 **Godes þonces** 'by the grace of God'; **ealles forswiðe** adv. phrase 'utterly'; **(ge)brocian** 'to crush' (like *tilian* l. 28).
63 **ealra hāligra mæsse** 'the mass of all saints/All Saints' Day'.
64 **se** dem. or rel. pron. 'that one/he' or 'who'. See §§65 and 11(4).
64–5 **būtan ... wæs** is another way of saying what is said in ll. 49–50.
65 **onwald** 'power'.
65–6 **ōþrum ... wintra** '30 winters less the second a half', that is twenty-eight and a half years. Cf. §184 l. 37.

[21] Boulogne.   [22] The mouth of the River Lympne.
[23] One of the leaders of the Danes.   [24] Milton Royal.   [25] Appledore.
[26] The English success in the war which began in 892 was due to various factors, including the great mobility and wide-ranging movements of their forces, the establishment of a chain of fortresses, and tactful handling by Alfred of his peasant levies.
[27] Son of Æthelwulf; see §184 n. 24.
[28] This is an excellent example of a context in which *se* could mean 'he' or 'who'. Hence the double commas; see §11.4.

7 The English kings

§186 Alfred was succeeded in turn by his son Edward the Elder (d. 924) and by his grandsons Æthelstan (d. 940), Edmund (d. 946), and Eadred (d. 955). This period marks the creation of the kingdom of England, a process which (Simon Keynes has argued) began with the defeat of the

Mercians by Egbert, King of Wessex (d. 839); was continued by Alfred, who used the concept of the English people for political purposes while fighting the Danes; and culminated in the acceptance of Edgar as the king of England in 958. Eadred was succeeded by his nephews Eadwig (d. 958) and Edgar (d. 975). This is the period of the Benedictine Revival in which the devout Christian Edgar worked with Dunstan, Archbishop of Canterbury (d. 988), Æthelwold, Bishop of Winchester (d. 984), and Oswald, Bishop of Worcester (d. 992), to reform the old monastic foundations and to create new ones; to establish a common form of observance for all English monks; and to train a new generation of ecclesiastical scholars and leaders. Prominent among these was Ælfric (§177). Edgar was succeeded by his son Edward, who was treacherously murdered at Corfe in 978. It seems to be fairly generally agreed that the murder was planned and committed by the household men of Edward's teenage half-brother Æthelred (§187). If so, they succeeded in their aim, for he became king. Too young to be an accomplice, he never escaped the burden of a crime committed for his sake.

Text 6

910　　　Her bræc se here on Norðhymbrum þone frið 7 forsawon ælc frið þe Eadweard cyng 7 his witan him budon· 7 hergodon ofer Mercna lond . . .[1]

924　　　Her Eadweard cing forþferde 7 Æþelstan his sunu feng to rice.

940　　　5 Her Æþelstan cyning[2] forðferde on vi kalendas Nouembris[3] ymbe xl wintra butan anre niht þæs þe Ælfred cyning forþferde· 7 Eadmund æþeling feng to rice 7 he wæs þa xviii wintre· 7 Æþelstan cyning rixade xiiii gear 7 x wucan.

946　　　Her Eadmund cyning forðferde on Sanctes Agustinus 10 mæssedæge[4] 7 he hæfde rice seofoþe healf gear· 7 þa feng Eadred æþeling his broþor to rice . . .

955　　　Her forþferde Eadred cining on Sancte Clementes mæssedæg[5] on Frome[6] 7 he rixsade teoþe healf gear· 7 þa feng Eadwig to rice, Eadmundes sunu cinges . . .

1 **forsēon** 'to overlook/despise' (st. contracted vb. V §521); **ælc** 'each/every'.
2 **bēodan** 'to offer' (st. vb. II §517).
6 **ymbe** prep. referring to time and so 'after'; **þæs þe** conj. 'after'.
7 **þā** adv. 'then'; **xviii wintre** 'eighteen years [old]'.
8 **wuce** 'week'.
10 For the construction, see §185 ll. 65–6. (Answer: six and a half years.)
13 **tēoþa** 'tenth'. See l. 10.

---

[1] Edward's response was rapid and effective. He gathered the levies of Wessex and Mercia, brought the Danes to battle, and killed many thousands of them.
[2] In 937 Æthelstan and Edmund defeated a combined army of Norsemen from Ireland, Scots, and Strathclyde Britons, in battle at Brunanburh – a feat of arms celebrated in a poem which appears as annal 937 in most of the Chronicles and is printed in Part IV as Text 36 (§469).
[3] 27 October.　　　　[4] 26 May.　　　　[5] 23 November.　　　　[6] Frome.

958   15 Her forðferde Eadwig cyng on kalendas Octobris[7] 7 Eadgar his broðor feng to rice.

961   Her gewat Odo arcebisceop[8] 7 Sancte Dunstan feng to arcebisceoprice.[9]

975[10]   Her geendode   eorðan dreamas
        20   Eadgar, Engla cyning,   ceas him oðer leoht,
                wlitig 7 wynsum,   7 þis wace forlet,
                lif þis læne.

978(A)[11]   Her wearð Eadweard cyning ofslegen. On þis ylcan geare feng Æðelred æðeling his broðor to rice.

979(E)   25 Her wæs Eadward cyng ofslagen on æfentide æt Corfes geate[12] on xv k Apr[13] 7 hine man bebyrigde æt Wærham[14] butan ælcum cynelicum wurðscipe.

17 **gewītan** 'to go/depart' (st. vb. I §517). Another euphemism for 'to die'.

19 **(ge)endian** 'to end' (wk. vb. like _lufian_ §526). Note that the ending is -_e_, not -_on_; **eorðe** 'earth'; **drēam** 'joy'. Note -_as_ acc. pl. (§68).

20 **(ge)cēosan** 'to choose' (st. vb. II §517); **ōðer leoht** '(an)other light'.

21 **wlitig** 'radiant/fair'; **wynsum** 'delightful/joyful'. These two adjs. could be masc., referring to King Edgar, or neut., referring to the heavenly light, or possibly (such is the nature of OE poetry) to both; **wāc** 'weak/poor'. This could refer to _leoht_ (l. 20) or to _līf_ (l. 22); **forlǣtan** 'to let go/leave' (st. vb. VII(_b_) §517).

22 **līf** 'life'; **lǣne** 'transitory/fleeting'.

23 **ofslegen** a variant spelling of _ofslægen_.

24 **æðeling** 'prince'.

25 **ofslagen** another variant of _ofslægen_; **ǣfentīd** 'eventide'.

26 **bebyrigan** 'to bury' (wk. vb. with various spellings); **ǣlc** adj. 'any'.

27 **cynelic** 'kingly/royal'; **wurðscipe** 'honour'.

---

[7] 1 October.

[8] Odo, who had worked hard to create the conditions in which ecclesiastical reforms could be made successfully, actually died in 958.

[9] Dunstan's immediate predecessors were in fact Ælfsige of Winchester, who died on his journey to Rome for the pallium (§183 annal 601), and Brihthelm, who was nominated to succeed Ælfsige but was replaced by Dunstan in October 959 after Edgar had become king.

[10] This annal consists of thirty-seven lines of alliterative verse. I give this first sentence here.

[11] MS A gives 978 as the year of Edward's death. The annal in MS E, which follows, dates it 979.

[12] This may be a reference to a cutting in the chalk hills at Corfe or to the gate of the residence to which Edward had gone to visit his stepmother and his half-brother Æthelred.

[13] 18 March.   [14] Wareham.

8 The Danes and the Normans

§187 So the reign of Æthelred began inauspiciously with a murder of which the Chronicle (MS E annal 979) says: _Ne wearð Angelcynne nan wærsa dæd gedon þonne þeos wæs syððon hi ærest Brytonland gesohton_ 'No worse deed than this had been done among the English since they first came to Britain.' It continued in a welter of indecision, inaction, cowardice, and treachery, and ended disastrously with the Danes, under Sweyn (d. 1014) and Cnut, in control and the Normans already exerting influence through Emma, sister of Richard II Duke of Normandy and second wife of Æthelred, who married Cnut on the death of Æthelred in 1016. The people of London chose Æthelred's son Edmund Ironside as king but many powerful men supported Cnut. Edmund met with some initial success in battle but was badly beaten by Cnut at Ashingdon in Essex and died within a month on 30 November 1016. Cnut and his two sons reigned until 1042, when Edward the Confessor, second son of Æthelred, who had lived as an exile in Normandy for twenty-five years, became king. His reign was notable for intrigue and for tension between three parties: Godwine of Wessex and his family, the earls of Northumbria and Mercia, and the Normans of Edward's court. This nearly led to civil war in 1051. The rest, as the modern cliché has it, is history: the death of Edward *on twelftan æfen* 'Twelfth Night' (MS C annal 1065), that is 5 January 1066; the succession of Harold son of Godwine; the appearance of Halley's Comet after Easter 1066; the invasion by Harold Hardrada of Norway and King Harold's brother Tostig; their defeat by King Harold at Stamford Bridge near York on 25 September; the arrival of William of Normandy on 28 September; King Harold's forced march; and the heroic but unsuccessful resistance by his weakened and wearied force at Hastings on 14 October 1066. And, as the Chronicle (MS E annal 1066) puts it in what is in effect the obituary notice of Anglo-Saxon England, . . . *7 Willelm . . . com to Westmynstre 7 Eadred arceƀ hine to cynge gehalgode* '. . . and William . . . came to Westminster and Archbishop Eadred consecrated him as king'.

Text 7

981   Her comon ærest þa vii scipu and gehergoden Hamtun.[1]

987   Her Wecedport[2] wes gehergod.

991(A)   Her on ðissum geare com Unlaf[3] mid þrim 7 hund nigontigon
         scipum to Stane[4] 7 forhergedon þæt onytan 7 for ða ðanon to
       5 Sandwic[5] 7 swa ðanon to Gipeswic[6] 7 þæt eall ofereode 7 swa to
         Mældune[7]· 7 him ðær com togeanes Byrhtnoð ealdorman[8] mid
         his fyrde 7 him wið gefeaht 7 hy þone ealdorman þær ofslogon 7
         wælstowe geweald ahtan· 7 him man nam syððan frið wið . . .

3 *þrie* 'three'; **hund nigontig** 'ninety'.

4 **forhergian** 'to ravage' (wk. vb. like *lufian* §526); **þæt onytan** = *onūtan* 'around it'; **ðanon** adv. 'thence'.

5 **ofergān** 'to over-go/conquer' (irregular vb. §529).

6 **him . . . tōgēanes** 'against them'. Here, as in l. 4 *þæt onȳtan*, l. 7 *him wið*, and l. 8 *him . . . wið*, we have a pronoun followed by a preposition or (perhaps better) by a postposition.

8 **syððan** = *siþþan* adv. 'after(wards)'.

[1] Southampton.   [2] Watchet.   [3] Olaf Tryggvason, King of Norway.
[4] Folkestone.   [5] Sandwich.   [6] Ipswich.   [7] Maldon.
[8] Byrhtnoth was *ealdorman* of Essex.

991(E)   Her wæs Gypeswic⁶ gehergod· 7 æfter þam swiðe raðe wæs
        10 Brihtnoð ealdorman ofslægen æt Mældune. 7 on þam geare man
            gerædde þ man geald ærest gafol Deniscan mannum for þam
            mycclan brogan þe hi worhtan be þam sæ-riman· þ wæs ærest x
            þusend punda· þæne ræd gerædde Siric arceb.⁹

1001   Her on ðysum geare wæs micel unfrið on Angelcynnes londe
        15 þurh sciphere . . .

1004   Her com Swegen¹⁰ mid his flotan to Norðwic¹¹ 7 þa burh ealle
            gehergade 7 forbærndon.

1011   Her on þissum geare sende se cyng 7 his witan to ðam here 7
            georndon friðes 7 him gafol 7 metsunga behetan wið þam þe hi
        20 heora hergunga geswicon. Hi heafdon þa ofergan East Engla i¹²
            and East Seaxe ii¹³ 7 Middel Seaxe iii¹⁴ 7 Oxenafordscire iiii¹⁵ 7
            Grantabrycgescire v¹⁶ 7 Heortfordscire vi¹⁷ 7 Bucingahamscire
            vii¹⁸ 7 Bedanfordscire viii¹⁹ 7 healfe Huntadunscire²⁰ x 7 be suðan
            Temese²¹ ealle Centingas²² 7 SuðSeaxe²³ 7 Hæstingas²⁴ 7
        25 Suðrig²⁵ 7 Bearrucscire²⁶ 7 Hamtunscire²⁷ 7 micel on Wiltun-
            scire.²⁸

9 **swiðe** adv. 'very'; **raðe** adv. 'quickly'.
11 **(ge)rædan** 'to advise' (wk. vb. like *sendan* §89); **gieldan** 'to pay' (st. vb. III §518); **gafol** 'tribute'.
12 **broga** 'terror/horror'; **sæ-rima** 'sea coast'.
13 **þæne** = *þone*; **ræd** 'advice'.
14 **unfrið** 'breach of peace/strife'.
16 **flota** 'fleet'.
17 **forbærnan** 'to burn up' (wk. vb. like *hieran* §94).
19 **giernan** 'to yearn for/ask for' (like *forbærnan* l. 17). This is an unusual spelling but there is an adj. *georn* 'eager'; **metsung** 'provisions'; **behātan** 'to promise' (st. vb. VII(*b*) §517); **wið þām þe** conj. 'against that, namely' and so (§§124–5) 'on condition that'.
20 **(ge)swīcan** 'to stop' (st. vb. I §517).
23 **healf** 'half'; **be sūðan** prep. phrase 'to the south of'.

---

⁹ Sigeric, Archbishop of Canterbury. In the poem which describes the battle of Maldon, the poet puts these words in the mouth of Byrhtnoth as he defied the Danish messenger on behalf of his troops (*þis folc*):

> 'Gehȳrst þū, sǣlida,   hwæt þis folc segeð?
> Hī willað ēow tō gafole   gāras syllan . . .'
>
> 'Do you hear, seafarer, what this people says? They will give you spears as tribute . . .'

So it is especially ironical that tribute was first paid in the same year.
¹⁰ Sweyn, king of Denmark.   ¹¹ Norwich.   ¹² East Anglia.   ¹³ Essex.
¹⁴ Middlesex.   ¹⁵ Oxfordshire.   ¹⁶ Cambridgeshire.
¹⁷ Hertfordshire.   ¹⁸ Buckinghamshire.   ¹⁹ Bedfordshire.
²⁰ Huntingdonshire. This manuscript (MS E) omits here *ix 7 micel on Hamtunscire* 'ix and much in Northamptonshire'.   ²¹ River Thames.   ²² [The people of] Kent.   ²³ Sussex.
²⁴ Hastings (originally the name of a tribe).
²⁵ Surrey.   ²⁶ Berkshire.   ²⁷ Hampshire.   ²⁸ Wiltshire.

Ealle þas ungesælða us gelumpon þurh unrædes²⁹ þ mann
nolde him to timan gafol bedan³⁰ ac þonne hi mæst to yfele
gedon hæfdon þonne nam man grið 7 frið wið hi 7 naðelæs for
30 eallum þisum griðe 7 friðe 7 gafole hi ferdon æghwider folcmælum 7 hergodon 7 ure earme folc ræpton 7 slogon . . .

1013   . . . 7 seo hlafdige³¹ wende þa ofer seo to hire broðor Ricarde³² . . .
7 se cyng gewende þa fram þam flotan to ðam middan wintra to
Wiht lande³³ 7 wæs þær þa tid 7 æfter þære tide gewende þa ofer
35 sæ to Ricarde 7 wæs þær mid him oð ðone byre þe Swegen dead
wearð.

1014   Her on þissum geare Swegen geendode his dagas to candelmæssan iii Nᵒ Febr̃³⁴ 7 se flota eall gecuron Cnut to cyninge.

1016   Her on þissum geare com Cnut cyning mid his here . . . Ða
40 gelamp hit þæt se cyng Æðelred forðferde ær ða scipu comon· he
geendode his dagas on scs Georius mæssedæge³⁵ æfter mycclum
geswince 7 earfoðnissum his lifes· 7 þa æfter his ende ealle þa
witan þe on Lundene wæron 7 se burhwaru gecuron Eadmund³⁶
to cynge 7 his rice he heardlice werode þa hwile þe his tima wæs.
45 . . . Ða to scs Andreas mæssan³⁷ forðferde se cyng Eadmund.

1017   Her Cnut wearð gecoran to kinge [Engla landes].

1036   Her forðferde Cnut cyng æt Sceaftesbyrig.³⁸ . . . 7 sona æfter his
forsiðe wæs ealra witena gemot on Oxnaforda³⁹ 7 Leofric eorl 7

27 **ungesælð** 'misfortune'; **(ge)limpan** 'to happen (to)' (st. vb. III §518).
28 **nolde** = *ne wolde*; **tō tīman** 'in time'; **bēdan** = *bēodan*; **ac** conj. 'but'; **þonne** conj. 'whenever'; **tō yfele** 'to [our] evil/harm'.
28-9 **þonne . . . þonne** conj. 'whenever' . . . adv. 'then'.
29 **grið** 'truce'; **naðelæs** 'none the less'.
30 **æghwider** adv. 'every whither/in all directions'.
30-1 **folcmælum** adv. 'in troops'.
31 **earm** adj. 'miserable'; **ræpan** 'to rope/bind/capture' (like *forbærnan* l. 17).
32 **(ge)wendan** 'to go' (like *(ge)rædan* l. 11); second **sēo** = *sæ*.
33 **midde winter** 'mid-winter, Christmas'.
34 **sēo tīd** 'that season'. See §44.
35 **oð** prep. 'until'; **byre** 'event/time'. The phrase *oð ðone byre þe* is probably tautologic, like
'until such time as', for *oð* can also be a conj. 'until'.
42 **geswinc** 'labour'; **earfoðniss** 'difficulty/hardship'.
43 **wita** 'wise man/councillor'; **burhwaru** collective noun 'citizens'.
44 **heardlice** adv. 'resolutely'; **werian** 'to defend' (wk. vb. §525); **þā hwīle þe** conj. 'while';
tīma 'time'.
48 **forsīð** 'departure/death'; **witena** See l. 43 and §501; **gemot** 'meeting/assembly'.

---

²⁹ Compare *Æþelræd Unræd* 'Noble Counsel, No Counsel', a term not recorded until the
twelfth century but which may well have been on the lips of some of his despairing councillors.
³⁰ MS C emphasizes that there was no firm decision either to pay tribute or to fight by
adding here the words *oþþe wið gefeohtan* 'or to fight against [them]'.
³¹ Queen Emma. The word *hlæfdige* 'lady' is regularly used as a title of the king's wife. It may
remind some of 'the first lady' in the USA.
³² Richard II, Duke of Normandy and brother of Emma.
³³ The Isle of Wight.   ³⁴ At Candlemas on 3 February.   ³⁵ St George's Day, 23 April.
³⁶ Edmund Ironside, son of Æthelred.
³⁷ St Andrew's Day, 30 November.   ³⁸ Shaftesbury.   ³⁹ Oxford.

mæst ealle þa þegenas benorðan Temese 7 þa liðsmen on
50 Lunden gecuron Harold⁴⁰ to healdes ealles Englalandes . . .

1039 Her forðferde Harold cyng on Oxnaforda.

1042 Her forðferde Harðacnut king.⁴¹

1043 Her wæs Eduuard⁴² gehalgod to kinge.

1052 Her on ðisum geare forðferde Ælfgiue Ymma⁴³ Eadwardes
55 cynges modor 7 Hardacnutes cynges.

1066 Her forðferde Eaduuard king· 7 Harold eorl⁴⁴ feng to ðam rice 7
heold hit xl wucena 7 ænne dæg· 7 her com Willelm 7 gewann
Ængla land· 7 her on ðison geare barn Cristes cyrce⁴⁵ 7 her
atiwede cometa xiiii kalendas Mai.⁴⁶

49 **benorðan** prep. 'to the north of'; **liðsman** 'sailor'.
50 **tō healdes** An incorrect spelling of the inf. *tō healdenne* from *healdan*. The *-es* inflexions in *ealles Englalandes* are also suspect.
54–5 For the divided genitive see §§162–3.
58 **birnan** 'to burn' (st. vb. III §518).
59 **ātiwian** 'to appear' (like *forhergian* l. 4).

⁴⁰ Harold Harefoot, son of Cnut.　　　⁴¹ Harthacnut, son of Cnut.
⁴² Edward, second son of Æthelred, now known as Edward the Confessor.
⁴³ The widow of Æthelred and Cnut. MS F explains the double name: *þæt wæs Ælfgiue on Englisc and Ymma on Frencisc.*
⁴⁴ Harold, son of Godwine.
⁴⁵ Christ Church, Canterbury. In January 1993 workmen relaying the nave floor of the present cathedral uncovered what are believed to be the foundations of the building destroyed in this fire. See §301.
⁴⁶ Halley's Comet first appeared on 18 April. It is depicted in the Bayeux Tapestry, where men gaze upon it in fear and wonder. Comets were regarded as signs of disasters to come; see annals 678 and 729 above and note that annal 891 – the year before the arrival in England of *se micla here* described in annal 892 – records that *þy ilcan geare . . . æteowde se steorra þe mon on boclæden hæt cometa* 'in the same year . . . appeared the star which in Latin is called "comet"'.

9 Bibliography

§188 Those of you who wish to read more of the Chronicle are advised to begin with the editions by Bately and by Earle and Plummer cited in §180. I recommend the following books to those who would like to gain a deeper or wider understanding of Anglo-Saxon history:

F. M. Stenton *Anglo-Saxon England* (3rd edn, Oxford: Clarendon Press, 1971)
H. Mayr-Harting *The Coming of Christianity to Anglo-Saxon England* (3rd edn, London: Batsford, 1991)
P. Hunter Blair *An Introduction to Anglo-Saxon England* (2nd edn, Cambridge: Cambridge University Press, 1977)
Dorothy Whitelock (ed.) *English Historical Documents* vol. I *c.* 500–1042 (2nd edn, London: Eyre and Spottiswoode, 1979)

David C. Douglas and George W. Greenaway (eds) *English Historical Documents* vol. II 1042–1189 (2nd edn, London: Eyre and Spottiswoode, 1981)

David Hill *An Atlas of Anglo-Saxon England 700–1066* (Oxford: Basil Blackwell, 1981)

James Campbell (ed.) *The Anglo-Saxons* (Oxford: Phaidon, 1982; repr. Penguin, 1991)

C ARCHAEOLOGY, ARTS, AND CRAFTS

1 Introduction

§189   What we know about the Anglo-Saxons has increased so dramatically since 1950 that those of us who became interested in them before then can only blink with astonishment at the advances in our knowledge of their language, their literature, their history, their culture, their material circumstances, their way of life, and their attitudes to life and the mysteries which lie beyond it. These advances have come from many sources – Old English language and literature, cognate languages, manuscripts in Latin and other languages containing widely diverse material, archaeology, and place-names. But we must remember that, in the six centuries of the Anglo-Saxon period (§179), England changed in politics, society, cultural contacts, taste, and attitudes, as much as in any other period of similar length; indeed, Rosemary Cramp has argued that the ninth century was a real watershed of culture in Europe, comparable with the Renaissance. But it is impossible for me to bring out these changes in this book, which has as its starting-point the Old English language and its literature.

§190   My acquaintance with Anglo-Saxon archaeology is that of the interested amateur. I value it especially for the fascinating way in which it throws light on the life of the people. By way of illustration, let me say that for many years I have felt sympathy for the Anglo-Saxons as sufferers from toothache; indeed I have sometimes been tempted to suggest that toothache should be numbered among the causes of the haunting melancholy which marks much Old English poetry. This view was reinforced by a writer's complaint that *toðæcce me forwyrnde ælcre leornunga* 'toothache kept me from any study'. But the sympathy was misplaced and the theory wrong. For in 1991 Charlotte Roberts of Bradford University showed that tooth decay affected only a small percentage of the population of England up to the beginning of the twelfth century and has argued that the increase in dental decay thereafter is almost certainly connected with the increase in the availability of sugar.

§191   Our knowledge of Anglo-Saxon teeth comes from the skeletons exhumed during the excavations of cemeteries or found by chance elsewhere. The study of skeletons helps us to draw conclusions about the community which buried the dead and about the life-expectation, the diseases and causes of death, and perhaps the diet, of its members. The grave-goods, the objects buried with a corpse, may tell us with whom the community had traded or fought in the past and about the dead person's wealth or occupation or social position or religion. But cemeteries are not the only source of information. Other dryland sites such as settlements and villages, royal palaces and townships like Yeavering or Cheddar (§269), monasteries, defensive earthworks, and special sites like the ship-burial at Sutton Hoo (§§194–9), have also been excavated, revealing jewellery and metalwork, weapons, coins, woodwork, and other objects of significance. Work in London suggests that, to the west of the ruined Roman town, there existed a Saxon settlement which was occupied from the late seventh to the late ninth century, when the population moved inside the protection of the old Roman walls and the defences were restored. This confirms the Chronicle statement that in 886 Alfred occupied London (§185). While I was collecting the material for these sections, Kevin Leahy, Keeper of Archaeology at Scunthorpe Museum, revealed the discovery in a sand-quarry at Flixborough, South Humberside, of an important settlement; see *Making*, pp. 94–5. He described this as 'a time-capsule of Middle Saxon life during a 200-year period beginning in about 700 . . . the site is like an Anglo-Saxon Pompeii but with the remains preserved by wind-blown sand instead of ash'. It was occupied by a high-status community and the 9,000 objects found should tell us a lot about them and their life. To these sources of information must be added churches, stone crosses, sculptures and carvings, embroideries, manuscripts, and runic inscriptions.

§192 But, as John Coles has pointed out in *The Archaeology of Wetlands* (Edinburgh, 1984), 'the anaerobic conditions in bog and blanket peat preserve *organic* evidence (wood, textiles, basketry, leather and so forth) which rarely survives in dryland sites. Thus the information derived from wetlands, based largely on organic remains, both complements and extends the largely inorganic evidence in stone and metals, from dryland sites.' Such study made possible the 1981 reconstruction of an Anglo-Saxon fish weir in Nottinghamshire showing woven panels, stake uprights, and stone weights. The Tamworth water-mill provides valuable evidence of the techniques of timber construction. The excavation and reconstruction of the Viking city of Jorvik in the Coppergate area of York revealed a row of tenth-century Viking tenements separated by wattle fences, along with large supplies of waterlogged wood, leather, textile, bone, and inorganic material relating to crafts and activities. Biological evidence for diet, health, and disease, was also found. As I write, a team of mud-covered archaeologists is uncovering not only the original Anglo-Saxon causeway or *oxena ford* 'oxen's ford' which gives Oxford its name but also the foundations and timbers of Oxford's waterfront, remains of what may be the ninth-century palisade built as a defence against the Danes, and rubbish containing all kinds of remnants of

Anglo-Saxon and mediaeval Oxford. (A fortnight after I wrote the last sentence, these archaeologists announced the finding of timber from trees which, modern techniques of dating by tree rings reveal, were felled about AD 811. This find suggests that Oxford had a wooden bridge across the Thames and was an important trading link between the kingdoms of Wessex and Mercia well before the time of King Alfred and before its first mention in the Parker Manuscript of the Chronicle in 911. The excitement of the chase is not yet over, for further timber awaits dating.) To all this can be added the fascinating riddle of the eighth-century skeleton found in 1991 by archaeologists from the Museum of London on what was then the foreshore of the River Thames. Preserved and blackened by silt, it was almost complete, had a neatly cut hole about an inch and a half in diameter in the skull (probably the result of trepanning to relieve pressure or headaches or to release spirits after death), appeared to have been pegged to stop it floating away, and was sandwiched between two sheets of bark. This last feature, otherwise known only from eighth- to tenth-century sites in Finland, raises the possibility that the skeleton may be that of a sailor or visitor from Finland who died in London and was given a Finnish burial.

§193   I shall now try to relate the discoveries made by archaeologists and the knowledge we derive from such survivals as churches, sculptures, manuscripts, and embroideries, to relevant passages of Old English, translating the shorter ones and helping you with the longer. Old English poetry has most to say about weapons and jewels. But some of the prose texts, especially laws, charters, and wills, give information about the various crafts, industries, and arts, and also about villages, estates, roads, forests, and the way life was organized. Archaeological finds such as pottery and coins are of vital importance for dating sites and for assessing the contacts made by their occupiers. But here too the length of the period (§179) and the patchy nature of the evidence available means that the changes which took place (§189) and the regional and social differences which existed are obscured. As I begin my task, I acknowledge with special gratitude the help and stimulus I have received from four books and an article:

David M. Wilson (ed.) *The Archaeology of Anglo-Saxon England* (London: Methuen, 1976 and, in paperback, Cambridge: Cambridge University Press, 1981) [short title: *Archaeology*]

David Wilson *The Anglo-Saxons*, 3rd edn (London: Pelican, 1981) [short title: *AS 1981*]

James Campbell (ed.) *The Anglo-Saxons* (Oxford: Phaidon, 1982; repr. Penguin, 1991) [short title: *AS 1982*]

Leslie Webster and Janet Backhouse (eds) *The Making of England: Anglo-Saxon Art and Culture AD 600–900* (London: British Museum, 1991) [short title: *Making*]

Rosemary J. Cramp '*Beowulf* and Archaeology', *Medieval Archaeology* 1 (1957), 55–77 [short title: *BArch*].

The four books can profitably be consulted for all the topics discussed in Part IIIC (§§189–301) and contain many monochrome illustrations. The article remains a classic, despite the advances in archaeology since 1957. Coloured illustrations will be found in *AS 1982*, *Making*, and in three other books listed in the Bibliography to which I am also greatly indebted: *AS Art*, *Golden Age*, and *Jewellery*.

2 The Sutton Hoo ship-burial

§194 At Sutton Hoo near Woodbridge, Suffolk, on the tidal estuary of the River Deben, there lies a group of ancient barrows or burial mounds. In 1938 Mrs Edith May Pretty, the owner of the land on which all but one of the barrows are situated, employed a local excavator and antiquary, Mr Basil Brown, to open three of the mounds under the general supervision of the Ipswich Museum. Two of these contained cremations, the third an inhumed burial which had been placed in a small boat some twenty-five feet long. The finds from these barrows were few and fragmentary but were of sufficient interest to encourage further excavation in 1939. In that year, the largest barrow was opened to reveal a large ship and pieces of bronze, wood, and iron. The British Museum and the Office of Works were asked to advise, C. W. Phillips of Selwyn College, Cambridge, was appointed as director, and the actual excavation was completed just as war broke out in September 1939. Mrs Pretty generously presented the whole treasure to the nation.

§195 The ship had been drawn up from the estuary bow first and buried with the bow pointing inland (east) and the stern pointing west to the water, with a burial chamber of wood built on the deck. No body was found. Chemical and other evidence suggests that there may have been one. But it cannot be proved. At the east or forward end were found kitchen utensils and other everyday objects. Ceremonial objects lay to the stern end, along with the jewelled trappings and weapons of the dead man. The objects at the west end of the burial chamber include an iron standard, a sceptre, spears, an iron-bound wooden bucket, a bronze bowl with a hanging bowl inside it containing the remains of a musical instrument, ten silver bowls inscribed with equal-armed crosses, and two silver spoons engraved respectively with 'Saul' and 'Paul' in Greek. There were also a shield, helmet, and sword (all showing Swedish influence), the rusted remains of a mail coat and of an iron axe, drinking horns, thirty-seven gold coins from the continent dated early seventh century – opinions on this point vary and attempts to date them exactly to suit a particular theory about the identity of the person honoured are unjustified – and gold jewellery.

§196 The jewellery is magnificent – a purse-lid of gold elaborately jewelled with garnets (figure 2), a gold sword pommel, two gold scabbard bosses, and twenty other individual gold pieces which held together the belt,

Figure 2   The Sutton Hoo purse-lid (copyright British Museum)

baldric, and outer harness of the royal apparel, including a great gold buckle. The richness of the burial suggests that it may have been in honour of an East Anglian king. We do not know which king, or indeed whether it was a king. We do not know the exact date of the burial. Several kings who died after 625 are possibilities but the favoured candidate is Rædwald (d. 625/6) whose conversion to Christianity, subsequent relapse, and 'attempt to get the best of both worlds by scandalously setting up altars to Christ and to the devil side by side' (Bruce-Mitford (§197)), could explain the blend of pagan and Christian in the burial. Here, however, it is of interest to note Martin Carver's 1992 claim (Bibliography III C) that, because of recent changes in archaeological interests, 'the questions to be addressed became not "who was buried in these mounds?" or even "was this a royal burial ground?" but "what is the structure of Anglo-Saxon society in the seventh century and how did it change?", "what was a king?" and "did the Anglo-Saxons have them?"' Not all archaeologists agree with this but I must leave them to argue about it.

§197 As R. L. S. Bruce-Mitford rightly says in *The Sutton Hoo Ship Burial: A Handbook*, the Sutton Hoo treasure is 'the most important archaeological document yet found in Europe for the era of the migrations of the Germanic peoples (5th to 7th centuries A.D.)'. Continuing excavations under the direction of Martin Carver confirm this. They have revealed, among many other things, evidence of rituals involving human sacrifice; the body of a child of less than four buried with a tiny spear and buckle; male and female inhumations; and the remains of an Anglo-Saxon prince lying next to his horse, along with his sword, spear, shield, and other equipment. The complex is revealed as a high-status Anglo-Saxon burial site of the sixth to the eighth centuries, with both inhumations and cremations. But it can also be said that it is the most important archaeological document yet found for the study of Old English literature and of *Beowulf* in particular. It must not be thought that *Beowulf* was composed to illustrate the ship-burial or that the burial was intended to illustrate *Beowulf*. However, while, in David Wilson's words, 'what Sutton Hoo really illuminates is the general culture of the seventh century', the burial and *Beowulf* can be said to illuminate one another. Both show a mixture of cremation and inhumation. The burial affects the dating and genesis of *Beowulf*. It helps to explain why so much matter concerning the Swedes and other Scandinavian peoples should appear in an English poem and why there is a blend of pagan and Christian elements. It tells us that war-gear and treasures of gold and gems like those described by the *Beowulf* poet existed in Anglo-Saxon times and that the poet and his audience shared the pride and joy in them which he portrays. In their turn, certain passages from *Beowulf* clarify some of the features of the Sutton Hoo burial and give us some idea of the ceremonies in which the dead king was honoured on the banks of the River Deben over thirteen hundred years ago. They include the story of the funeral of Scyld (the founder of the Danish dynasty which features in the poem) whose body was committed to the sea in a ship nobly equipped with war-gear and treasures (ll. 32–52), and of the cremation of Beowulf himself on a funeral pyre along with helmets, shields, and armour; of the adding of precious treasures to the ashes of the pyre; of the building of a barrow like those at Sutton Hoo; and of the funeral rites (ll. 3137–82). Space allows me to print only two brief extracts from these stories; for the rest, I must refer you to one of the translations of *Beowulf* listed in the Bibliography.

§198   *Text 8*   **Scyld's funeral ship**

  þǣr æt hȳðe stōd hringedstefna
  īsig ond ūtfūs, æþelinges fær·
  ālēdon þā lēofne þēoden
35 bēaga bryttan on bearm scipes
  mǣrne be mǣste. þǣr wæs māðma fela
  of feorwegum, frætwa, gelǣded·
  ne hȳrde ic cȳmlicor cēol gegyrwan
  hildewǣpnum ond heaðowǣdum
40 billum ond byrnum· him on bearme læg
  māðma mænigo þā him mid scoldon
  on flōdes ǣht feor gewītan.

32 **hȳð** 'harbour' (cf. Rotherhithe); **standan** 'to stand' (st. vb. VI §520); **hringedstefna** 'ringed prow'.

33 **īsig** 'icy'; **ūtfūs** 'eager to set out'; **fær** 'vessel'.

34 **ālecgan** 'to lay down' (an irregular wk. vb.); **lēof** 'dear'; **þēoden** 'lord/king'.

35 **bēag** 'ring'; **brytta** 'distributor'; **bearm** 'bosom'.

36 **mǣre** 'famous'; **māðm** 'treasure'.

37 **feorweg** 'far way'; **frætwe** 'precious things'.

38 **hȳran** another spelling for *hīeran* (§94); **cȳmlicor** 'more nobly'; **gegyrwan** 'to equip' (an irregular wk. vb.).

39 **hildewǣpn** 'war weapon'; **heaðowǣd** 'war-dress/armour'.

40 **bill** 'sword'; **byrne** 'coat of mail'; **bearm** See l. 35 and, for the construction, §48; **licgan** 'to lie' (st. vb. V §519).

41 **māðma** See l. 36; **mænigo** 'a great many'; **þā** rel. pron. (§65).

42 **flōd** 'flood'; **ǣht** 'possession'; **feor** Cf. l. 37; **gewītan** 'to go/depart' (st. vb. I §517).

For details of an edition of this poem see §465.

§199 Text 9 illustrates the stages of Beowulf's funeral described in §197. The poem ends with the words of praise in ll. 3180–2.

    Text 9   **Beowulf's funeral**

   Him ðā gegiredan Gēata lēode
   ād on eorðan unwāclicne

3137 **gegiredan** See §198 l. 38; **lēode** 'people'.

3138 **ād** 'funeral pyre'; **unwāclic** 'not mean/splendid'.

helmum behongen   hildebordum
3140 beorhtum byrnum   swā hē bēna wæs·
ālegdon ðā tōmiddes   mǣrne þēoden
hæleð hīofende   hlāford lēofne.
Ongunnon þā on beorge   bǣlfȳra mǣst
wīgend weccan·   wudurēc āstāh
3145 sweart ofer swioðole   swōgende lēg
wōpe bewunden   ...

...   ...

Geworhton ðā   Wedra lēode
hlēo on hōe   se wæs hēah ond brād
wǣglīðendum   wīde gesȳne
ond betimbredon   on tȳn dagum
3160 beadurōfes bēcn,   bronda lāfe ...

...   ...

Hī on beorg dydon   bēg ond siglu
eall swylce hyrsta   swylce on horde ǣr
3165 nīðhēdige men   genumen hæfdon·
forlēton eorla gestrēon   eorðan healdan
gold on grēote   ...

...   ...

Swā begnornodon   Gēata lēode
hlāfordes hyre   heorðgenēatas·

3139 **helm** 'helmet'; **behōn** 'to hang about with' (st. contracted vb. VII(*b*) §521); **hildebord** 'battle-shield'.

3140 **beorht** 'bright'; **byrnum** See §198 l. 40; **bēna** 'petitioner'.

3141 **ālegdon** See §198 l. 34; **tōmiddes** 'in the midst'; **mǣrne** See §198 l. 36; **þēoden** See §198 l. 34.

3142 **hæleð** pl. 'warriors'; **hīofan** 'to lament'; **hlāford** 'lord'; **lēofne** See §198 l. 34.

3143 **onginnan** 'to begin' (st. vb. III §518); **þā** is an adv.; **beorg** 'cliff'; **bǣlfȳr** 'funeral fire'; **mǣst** 'greatest'.

3144 **wīgend** 'warrior'. Another uninflected nom. pl.; **weccan** '[wake]/kindle' (irregular wk. vb.); **wudurēc** 'wood smoke'; **āstīgan** 'to ascend' (st. vb. I §517).

3145 **sweart** 'dark'; **swioðol** 'fire/flame'; **swōgan** 'to sound' (st. vb. VII(*a*) §517); **lēg** 'flame/fire'.

3146 **wōp** 'weeping'; **bewindan** 'to mingle' (st. vb. III §518).

3156 **(ge)wyrcean** 'to make' (§95); **Weder** = *Gēat*. See l. 3137.

3157 **hlēo** 'mound'; **hōe** dat. sg. < *hōh* 'headland'; **hēah** 'high'; **brād** 'broad'.

3158 **wǣglīðend** 'seafarer'; **gesȳne** 'visible'.

3159 **betimbran** 'to build' (wk. vb. §§522–3); **tȳn** 'ten'.

3160 **beadurōf** 'battle bold'; **bēcn** 'sign/monument'; **brond** 'fire'; **lāf** 'leaving/remnant'.

3163 **dōn** 'to do/place' (§89); **bēg** = *bēag* 'ring/bracelet'; **sigle** 'jewel/necklace'.

3164 **swylce ... swylce** 'such ... as'; **hyrst** 'ornament'; **hord** 'hoard/treasure'.

3165 **nīðhēdig** 'brave'; **(ge)niman** 'to seize/take' (st. vb. IV §519).

3166 **forlǣtan** 'to take' (st. vb. VII(*b*) §517); **gestrēon** 'treasure'; **healdan** 'to hold' (st. vb. VII(*a*) §517).

3167 **grēot** 'sand/earth'.

3178 **begnornian** 'to mourn' (wk. vb. like *lufian* §526); **lēode** See l. 3137.

3179 **hlāford** See l. 3142; **hyre** 'fall/death'; **heorðgenēat** 'hearth companion'.

3180 cwǣdon þæt hē wǣre   wyruldcyninga
manna mildust   ond monðwǣrust
lēodum līðost   ond lofgeornost.

3180 **cweþan** 'to say' (§97); **wǣre** from *wesan* (§528); **wyruld** = *woruld*.
3181 **milde** 'mild'. On the ending *-ost* see §508; **monðwǣre** 'gentle'.
3182 **līþe** 'kind'; **lofgeorn** 'eager for fame'.

For details of an edition of this poem see §465.

3 Weapons

§200 These two passages from *Beowulf* lead us naturally to weapons and armour and to jewellery. Here the fact that much of my material comes from the poetry means that there tends to be an emphasis on the upper classes at the expense of all the rest; for slight antidotes, see §§224, 352–8, 359, and 369–71.

Beowulf may have been a lover of beautiful things but his life depended on his own strength and on his carefully cherished weapons and armour (*Beowulf* 671–4):

Ðā hē him of dyde   īsernbyrnan
helm of hafelan·   sealde his hyrsted sweord
īrena cyst   ombihtþegne
ond gehealdan hēt   hildegeatwe

Then he [Beowulf] took off his iron corslet and the helmet from [his] head, gave his ornamented sword, best of irons, to his attendant, and ordered him to look after his battlegear.

Then, as now, death could be due to sickness, old age, or violence:

ādl oþþe yldo   oþþe ecghete
fǣgum fromweardum   feorh oðþringeð

sickness or old age or violence will wrest life away
from the man who is doomed to depart.

The word *ecghete* used by the poet of *The Seafarer* (ll. 70–1) means literally 'edge hate' or 'sword hostility' – a sense which underlines the warlike nature of Anglo-Saxon society. This presents itself most clearly to the archaeologist in the large number of weapons or remains of weapons found in graves. Their presence may indicate a belief in some sort of martial afterlife in which they would still be needed. The frequent repetition of the formula *ahton wælstowe gew(e)ald* 'had possession of the battlefield' (§184 annal 833, 840, and so on) reflects the delight of the quartermaster as his staff collected the weapons and armour left after the battle as well as that of the victorious commander. The *franca* ('Frankish spear') and the *superne gar* ('the spear of southern make') referred to by the poet of *The Battle of Maldon* may have made their way to Maldon by way of a series of battles and skirmishes or, like Toledo blades, may have been made in a renowned workshop. As we shall see, weapons and armour figure prominently in laws and wills and in the heroic poetry; remember those placed in Scyld's funeral ship (§198 Text 8).

§201   Graves sometimes yield evidence of death by violence. Audrey Meaney, in *A Gazetteer of Early Anglo-Saxon Burial Sites* (London: George Allen and Unwin, 1964) reports two graves in Sussex containing male skeletons. The first was that of a middle-aged man with the left thigh completely severed halfway up the shaft and the dismembered femur lying at an angle to the pelvis. The second was that of a man of 40, 6 feet 4 inches in height, whose skull had suffered a sword cut nearly 5 inches long. She also reports another skeleton, that of a man of large build who had suffered a severe skull wound resulting in a hole which had half filled up before he died. Figure 3, reproduced by kind permission of Sonia Hawkes, shows the detail of the right arm of a 6 feet 6 inches warrior who died at the age of about 25 and was buried at Worthy Down, Hampshire. The thickened bone at the top of the fore-arm shows the healing of an old fracture. Below that can be seen an oblique fracture of both the radius and the ulna which was not resolved.

§202   The *Beowulf* poet warns that a dawn attack was always to be feared – *Forðon sceall gār wesan ‖ monig morgenceald mundum bewunden* 'Therefore must many a spear cold with the chill of morning be grasped by hands' (*Beowulf* 3021b–2) – and that good warriors must always be ready (*Beowulf* 1237–50):

Text 10   Warriors at rest

           Reced weardode
     unrīm eorla   swā hīe oft ǣr dydon.
     Bencþelu beredon·   hit geondbrǣded wearð
1240 beddum ond bolstrum.   . . .

     . . .   . . .
     Setton him tō hēafdon   hilderandas
     bordwudu beorhtan·   þǣr on bence wæs

1237 **reced** 'hall'; **weardian** 'to guard' (wk. vb. like *lufian* §526).
1238 **unrīm** 'countless number'; **eorl** 'warrior'. Here we have the order OVS.
1239 **bencþelu** 'bench boards/hall floor'; **berian** 'to bare/clear' (wk. vb. like *werian* §525); **geondbrǣdan** 'to over-spread' (wk. vb. like *hīeran* §94).
1242 **hēafod** 'head' with *-on* for *-um*. For the construction see §48; **hilderand** 'battle-shield'.
1243 **bordwudu** 'shield', here acc. pl.; **beorht** adj. 'bright/shining'.

Figure 3 Deformation of arm (copyright Sonia Chadwick Hawkes)

ofer æþelinge   ȳþgesēne
1245 heaþostēapa helm   hringed byrne
þrecwudu þrymlic.   Wæs þēaw hyra
þæt hīe oft wǣron   an wīg gearwe
gē æt hām gē on herge   gē gehwæþer þāra

1244 **ȳþgesēne** adj. 'easily seen'.
1245 **heaþostēap** adj. 'steep/towering in battle'; **helm** See §198 l. 40; **byrne** See §198 l. 40.
1246 **þrecwudu** 'spear'; **þrymlic** adj. 'mighty'; **þēaw** 'custom'.
1247 **an** = *on* prep., here 'for'; **wīg** 'war'; **gearu** adj. 'ready'.
1248 **gē . . . gē . . . gē** 'both . . . and . . . and'; **here** 'army'; **gehwæþer** pron. 'each/both'.

> efne swylce mǣla   swylce hira mandryhtne
> 1250 þearf gesǣlde·   wæs sēo þēod tilu.

1249 **efne** adv. 'just'; **swylc ... swylc** 'such ... as'; **mǣl** 'time'; **mandryhten** 'lord'.
1250 **þearf** 'need'; **gesǣlan** 'to befall/chance' (like *geondbrǣdan* l. 1239); **þēod** 'people'; **til** adj. 'good'.

For details of an edition of this poem see §465.

§203 This passage reflects the vital importance of loyalty to lord in a war-like military society. King Alfred decreed that it must override even the loyalty to kin so essential in a society in which many parents did not live to see their children grow to maturity:

> Eac we cweðað þæt mon mote mid his hlaforde feohtan orwige gif mon on þone hlaford feohte· swa mot se hlaford mid þy men feohtan. Æfter þære ilcan wisan mon mot feohtan mid his geborene mæge gif hine mon on woh onfeohteð· buton wið his hlaforde: þæt we ne liefað

> Also we decree that a man be permitted to fight alongside his lord without becoming liable to a charge of homicide if someone attacks the lord. Similarly the lord may fight alongside the man. In the same way a man may fight alongside his kinsman by birth if someone attacks him wrong-fully – except against his lord. That we do not allow.

It can be inferred from this that there were times when the kin loyalty was put before the lord loyalty. The latter was, however, cemented by the lord's gift of armour and horses to a man who agreed to serve under him. This was called *heregeatu* 'war-gear' or, as it is often translated, 'heriot'. If a man died before his lord, the gift was repayable unless the man had died fighting for his lord. Thus the late tenth-century will of Brihtric includes the following bequest:

> Ærest his kynehlaforde ænne beah on hundeahtotigan mancysan goldes 7 an handsacs on ealswa miclan 7 feower hors twa gerædede 7 twa sweord gefetelsode 7 twegen hafocas 7 ealle his headorhundas

> First, to his royal lord an armlet of eighty mancuses of gold and a short sword of the same [weight or value] and four horses, two with harness, and two swords with sheaths and two hawks and all his staghounds.

And Thurstan's will, made between 1043 and 1045, says

> And ic an mine kineloverd for mine hergete to marc goldes and to hors and sadelfate and helm and brinie and suerd and to scheldes and to speren

> And I grant to my royal lord as heriot two marks of gold and two horses and [their] trappings and a helmet and a coat of mail and a sword and two shields and two spears.

(The spelling in this late Old English passage illustrates the point I made in §2.)

§204 Figure 4 gives an Anglo-Saxon artist's impression of a warrior later than Beowulf. The dependence on their weapons of men living in a violent society is reflected in the high esteem in which good weaponsmiths were held. The legendary Weland the Smith appears in the poems *Deor* and *Beowulf* (§216) and on the front of the Franks Casket (§259). The Laws of Alfred list the responsibilities of the *sweordhwita* 'the sword-furbisher'. We read in *Beowulf* 2256a–7 of the *feormynd . . .* || *þā ðe beadogrīman bȳwan sceoldon* 'the polishers whose duty it was to burnish the warmasks'. Young Prince Æthelstan, who died *c.* 1015, left an inlaid sword to *Ælfnoðe minon*

Figure 4   Warrior portrayed in late Saxon manuscript (copyright Eva Wilson)

swurdhwitan 'Ælfnoth my sword-polisher'. And the Exeter Book poem now known as *The Gifts of Men* includes these among the endowments which God may bestow upon a man:

> Sum mæg wǣpenþrǣce   wīge tō nytte
> mōdcræftig smið   monige gefremman
> þonne hē gewyrceð   tō wera hilde
> helm oþþe hupseax   oððe heaþubyrnan
> scīrne mēce   oððe scyldes rond
> fæste gefēged   wið flyge gāres

One, a skilled smith, is able to prepare many a weapon-storm for use in war when he makes, for men's battle, helmet or dagger [hip-knife] or war-corslet, shining sword or shield boss firmly fixed against the flight of the spear.

§205 The riddles of the Exeter Book (ASPR III) make frequent mention of weapons and war-gear. The answer to *Riddle* 61 is a helmet, to *Riddle* 35 a coat of mail, to *Riddle* 5 a shield, to *Riddles* 20 and 71 a sword, to *Riddle* 73 a spear, and to *Riddle* 23 a bow; for references to translations see the Bibliography. The poets had a variety of words for the different items of equipment used by the warriors whose prowess they sing. These words were useful for alliteration and some at least may have survived for that purpose after the particular form of the object they denoted ceased to be made. The *Beowulf* poet, in his 3182 lines, uses seven words for sword – *bill*, *brond*, *iren*, *mece*, *seax*, *sweord*, and *heoru* (which occurs alone only twice in the poetry but is common in compounds such as *heoroblac* 'sword pale/mortally wounded' and *heorudreor* 'sword blood/battle blood'). The *Maldon* poet, in his 325 lines, uses four of these – *bill*, *iren*, *mece*, and *sweord* – but has six words for spear – *æsc*, *daroð*, *franca*, *gar*, *ord*, and *spere* – of which *franca* and *spere* are lacking in *Beowulf*. Both have the same four words for shield – *bord*, *lind*, *rand*, and *scyld*. Some of these words may be old terms which described weapons of different periods. No doubt the exact differences between these were once well known. But, not surprisingly, archaeologists are not always able to define them. Even those of my readers who are able to distinguish between a fusil, a matchlock, and a musket, or between a Bren, a Browning, and a Vickers, can imagine archaeologists of AD 3000 furrowing their brows as they try to do so.

§206 The sword was the aristocrat of weapons, used by the upper classes. Swords are sometimes found in the graves of men, sometimes by chance in rivers and elsewhere. But because of their value, they were often passed on rather than buried. Prince Æthelstan's will (§204) includes the following bequests: *þæs swurdes mid þam sylfrenan hiltan þe Wulfric worhte 7 þone gyldenan fetels* 'the sword with the silver hilt which Wulfric made and the golden belt', *þæs seolferhiltan swurdes þe Ulfcytel ahte* 'the silver-hilted sword which Ulfcytel owned', *þæs swurdes mid þam pyttedan hiltan 7 anes brandes* 'the sword with the pitted hilt and a blade', *anes seolforhiltes swurdes* 'a silver-hilted sword', *þæs malswurdes þe Wiðer ahte* 'the inlaid sword which belonged to Wither', *þæs sceardan swurdes* 'the notched sword', *anes swurdes* 'a sword', *þæs swurdes þe seo hand is on gemearcod* 'the sword on which the hand is marked', and *Æþelwine minon cnihte þæs swurdes þe he me ær sealde* 'to my servant Æthelwine the sword which he once gave me' – all these in addition to the sword he left to his sword-polisher (§204) and to the precious heirloom he left to his brother Edmund (§209).

§207 Anglo-Saxon swords were usually two-edged weapons from 30 to 33 inches in length. (The scramasax, a single-edged knife varying in length from 3 inches to 30, of which some fine examples have been found, needs only passing mention here; depending on its length, it served as dagger or sword.) The swords were either beaten out of a single piece of metal or pattern-welded: 'this method of twisting bands of iron together and beating the resulting plait into a thin blade which is then edged with hard steel adds flexibility to an otherwise comparatively intractable weapon' (D. M. Wilson). Subsequent polishing produced a marbled effect which created a play of light and shade. This process may explain the *Beowulf* poet's use of the words *brogdenmæl* and *wundenmæl*, which can be literally translated as 'woven mark' and hence 'blade with a woven pattern'. More information on swords will be found in *BArch*, pp. 63–7.

§208   The hilt is often missing; its components were probably made of perishable materials such as bone or wood bound with cloth or leather. But iron hilts and some fine silver hilts have survived, perhaps even the one owned by Ulfcytel (§206). The scabbards seem usually to have been of wood covered with leather, sometimes bound with metal, sometimes lined with fleece to prevent rusting. (Leather was also used for shields (§219) and for belts, shoes, laces, bags, cups, and other objects.)

§209   Old swords were especially valued; they had survived the shock of battle. Prince Æthelstan, who died *c.* 1015 (§204), left *Eadmunde minon breðer þæs swurdes þe Offa cyng ahte* 'to my brother Edmund the sword which King Offa owned'. Offa died in 796! King Hrothgar of Denmark gave magnificent gifts to Beowulf after he had killed Grendel but the poet picks one out as something really special:

> 1020 Forgeaf þā Bēowulfe   brand Healfdenes,
>   segen gyldenne   sigores tō lēane
>   hroden hildecumbor,   helm ond byrnan·
>   mǣre māðþumsweord   manige gesāwon
>   beforan beorn beran

[Hrothgar] gave then to Beowulf Healfdene's sword, a golden standard, a woven battle banner, as a reward of victory, a helmet, and a coat of mail. [You don't believe that the king gave away his father's sword?] Many saw the famous treasure-sword carried into the presence of the warrior.

Beowulf in his turn gave it (along with the other gifts just mentioned) to his uncle Hygelac, King of the Geats, with these words:

> 2155 'Mē ðis hildesceorp   Hrōðgār sealde
>   snotra fengel·   sume worde hēt
>   þæt ic his ǣrest ðē   ēst gesǣgde·
>   cwæð þæt hyt hæfde   Hiorogār cyning
>   lēod Scyldunga   lange hwīle . . .'

'Hrothgar gave me this war-gear, wise prince; in a short speech he ordered that I first tell you its history, said that King Hiorogar [Hrothgar's elder brother], lord of the Scyldings had it for a long time.'

§210   But even the best of swords had a limited life. Two swords so renowned that they had their own names both failed Beowulf in different hours of need. Hrunting was unequal to the task of killing Grendel's mother:

> Đā se gist onfand
> þæt se beadolēoma   bītan nolde,
> aldre sceþðan   ac sēo ecg geswāc
> 1525 ðēodne æt þearfe·   ðolode ǣr fela
> hondgemōta,   helm oft gescær,
> fǣges fyrdhrægl·   ðā wæs forma sīð
> dēorum māðme   þæt his dōm ālæg

Then the stranger [Beowulf] found that the battle-light [sword] would not bite, [would not] injure life but the edge failed the lord in his need. It had survived many hand-to-hand meetings, had often cut through the helmet, the corslet of a doomed man. That was the first time for the dear treasure that its glory was lost.

Nægling was unequal to the task of killing the dragon:

> 2680   Nægling forbærst,
> geswāc æt sæcce   sweord Bīowulfes
> gomol ond grǣgmǣl

Nægling broke! Beowulf's sword old and grey-marked failed in the fray.

So for swords, as for men, *dom alæg* 'glory perished' and life was *læne* 'transitory'.

§211   Helmets figure prominently in the poetry; see *BArch*, pp. 60–3. But they do not seem to have been common in Anglo-Saxon England until the eleventh century. Those other than chieftains or rich men wore leather caps (perhaps lined with metal) as head protection in battle. Three helmets, related by a common ancestry, survive from the Anglo-Saxon period. The earliest, the magnificent Sutton Hoo helmet (figure 5), made in Sweden or by Swedish armourers in Suffolk, is of the Roman type with a solid crown comb, with neck and cheek protection, and with a gilt boar's head at the outer edges of the eyebrow mouldings. It is the type of helmet described in *Beowulf* 303b–5a:

> Eoforlīc scionon
> ofer hlēorbergan   gehroden golde,
> 305 fāh ond fȳrheard

The boar images shone above the cheek guards adorned with gold shining and fire-hardened

and in *Beowulf* 1030–4:

> 1030 Ymb þæs helmes hrōf   hēafodbeorge
> wīrum bewunden   wala ūtan hēold

Figure 5   The Sutton Hoo helmet (copyright British Museum)

þæt him fēla lāf   frēcne ne meahte
scūrheard sceþðan   þonne scyldfreca
ongēan gramum   gangan scolde

Around the helmet's roof a comb wound about with wires kept head-
protection from outside so that no leaving of files [sword] hard in the

shower [of battle] could injure him severely when the shield warrior was obliged to advance against foes.

It also had a visor. Alliterative synonyms for a helmet used in *Beowulf* include *beadogrima* 'war mask', *heregrima* 'battle mask', and *grimhelm* 'mask helmet'.

§212 The seventh-century helmet found at Benty Grange, Derbyshire (depicted on the cover of this book), has a framework of flat iron bands, the gaps between which were filled in with horn plates which no longer survive. It was surmounted by a crest in the form of a boar (*Making*, p. 59); compare *Beowulf* 1285–7:

> 1285 þonne heoru bunden   hamere geþrūen,
> sweord swāte fāh,   swīn ofer helme
> ecgum dyhtig   andweard scireð

... when the ornamented blade, hammer forged, the sword stained with blood, trusty in its edges, shears from the helmet the opposing boar.

But in addition to the boar, the symbol of prowess in war, it carried a silver cross on the noseguard. This combination of boar and cross, heroic and Christian, is of particular interest; see §§410–11.

§213 The Coppergate helmet (*Making*, p. 61), discovered at York, is a magnificent piece of Anglo-Saxon craftsmanship in iron and brass dating from the second half of the eighth century, with a Latin inscription on the crown which reads 'In the name of our Lord Jesus, the Holy Spirit, God, and with all we pray. Amen. Oshere. Christ'; with a noseguard decorated with interlaced animals; and with a curtain of mail protecting the neck of the wearer. This confirms the possibility of interpreting *freawrasnum* 'with lordly chains' in the description of Beowulf's helmet as a reference to chain-mail protecting the neck:

> ac se hwīta helm   hafelan werede
> se þe meregrundas   mengan scolde,
> 1450 sēcan sundgebland   since geweorðad,
> befongen frēawrāsnum   swā hine fyrndagum
> worhte wǣpna smið,   wundrum tēode,
> besette swīnlicum,   þæt hine syðþan nō
> brond ne beadomēcas   bītan ne meahton

but the shining helmet guarded his head, [the helmet] whose duty it was to stir up the mere depths, to seek the surging water. [It was] adorned with gold, hung about with lordly chains just as in past days the weaponsmith had wrought it, shaped it wondrously, and set it about with boar-images so that thereafter sword or battle-blades could not cut through it.

In this passage, the helmet almost becomes a warrior whose duty it was (*scolde*) to go with his lord Beowulf as he risked his life in the bloodstained waters of the mere and to protect him like a loyal retainer.

§214 The word *helm* does not mean only 'helmet', as it does in the passages cited above and in *Beowulf* 2762b–3a *þær wæs helm monig eald and ōmig* 'many a helmet was there, old and rusty', where the poet is describing an ancient hoard of weapons and treasures – an archaeologist's dream. It also means 'lord/protector'. In *Beowulf* the Danish or Scylding king is *helm Scyldinga* 'protector of the Scyldings' and Beowulf himself is *lidmanna helm* 'protector of the seamen' and *Wedra helm* 'protector of the Geats/Weders'. These two meanings have in common the idea of protection or safety, a sense in which *helm* is used in *Beowulf* 1392 where Beowulf, speaking of his resolve to pursue the monster Grendel, boasts that *nō hē on helm losaþ* 'no way will he escape into cover'.

§215 Coats of mail are often depicted on the Bayeux Tapestry but little has survived from Anglo-Saxon times except the rusted remains of what was undoubtedly a mail coat which were found in the Sutton Hoo ship. Like swords and helmets, mail coats were the perquisite of the rich or well-born and would have been worn over the leather jerkin which gave protection to the humbler members of society. But coats of mail are mentioned more frequently in the written records. They were given as heriot (§203), and Prince Æthelstan (§204) left to his father King Æthelred *þære byrnan þe mid Morkære is* 'the coat of mail which is with Morcar'. (Morcar's comments on this bequest have not come down to us.)

§216 In *Beowulf*, we are told of the hero that

405   on him byrne scān,
    searonet seowed   smiþes orþancum

on him the corslet shone, the armour net linked by the skill of the smith

and that when Beowulf was ready to risk his life, the coat of mail (like the helmet of §213) was duty-bound to accompany him:

    scolde herebyrne   hondum gebrōden
    sīd ond searofāh   sund cunnian
1445 sēo ðe bāncofan   beorgan cūþe
    þæt him hildegrāp   hreþre ne mihte
    eorres inwitfeng   aldre gesceþðan

The battle-byrnie, woven by hand, broad and cunningly worked, was obliged to try out the water, [the byrnie] which knew how to protect his body so that the battle-grip, the malicious grasp of the angry [one], would not be able to harm his breast, his life.

It did its duty, unlike Hrunting and Nægling (§210):

Him on eaxle læg
brēostnet brōden·　　þæt gebearh fēore =
wið ord ond wið ecge =　　ingang forstōd

On his shoulder lay the woven coat of mail. That protected life = against
point and against edge = entry barred (lines 1547b–9).

Not unexpectedly, for it was (in Beowulf's own words)

beaduscrūda betst　　þæt mīne brēost wereð,
hrægla sēlest·　　þæt is Hrædlan lāf,
455 Wēlandes geweorc

the best of battle-garments that protects my breast, the most excellent of
mailcoats. It is an heirloom from Hrethel [Beowulf's grandfather], the
work of Weland.

§217 The ordinary soldier was usually equipped with a spear and shield,
though not many (I imagine) owned a spear inlaid with gold – *a goldwreken
spere* – like that bequeathed to the king by Wulfsige between 1022 and 1043.
Figure 6 shows some manuscript illustrations of shields, spearheads, and
battleaxes.

§218 No complete Anglo-Saxon spear has survived. So archaeologists'
knowledge depends on the iron tips or heads (varying from a few inches to 2
feet in length) and the iron ferrules which have been excavated. These

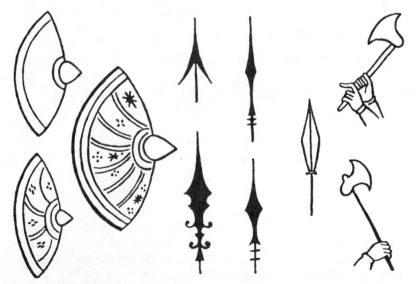

Figure 6　Shields, spearheads, and battleaxes, depicted in late Saxon manuscripts
(copyright Eva Wilson)

spearheads vary greatly in form and proportions according to region and date. The shaft to which the spearhead was riveted was often made of ash wood; the word *æsc* can mean either a spear or a ship. The spear was a weapon of the hunt as well as of warfare and both thrusting and throwing spears have survived.

§219 The main weapon of defence was the round flat shield made of wood covered with leather – not from a sheep (§243)! It had a grip behind it consisting of a bar bound with leather or cloth. Those who were richer used shields with an iron boss and sometimes with an iron rim; see figure 7. Later illustrations such as those in figure 6 show rounded shields with a pointed boss, and *mines bohscyldes* – another of Prince Æthelstan's bequests (§204) – may mean 'my curved shield'. If the Anglo-Saxons ever used the kite-shaped shields depicted on the Bayeux Tapestry, it was not until the eleventh century.

Figure 7   Reconstructed Anglo-Saxon shield (copyright Eva Wilson)

§220 The axe (*æcs, æx*) was both a tool and a weapon of war (see figure 6) for use in hand-to-hand fighting and as a throwing weapon. It also features as the instrument of the martyrdom of Archbishop Ælfheah (Alphege) of Canterbury by drunken Danes in 1012, as reported in MS C of the Anglo-Saxon Chronicle.

Ða on þæne Sæternesdæg wearð þa se here swyðe astyred angean þone bisceop forþamðe he nolde him nan feoh behaten ac he forbead þæt man nan þing wið him syllan ne moste. Wæron hi eac swyþe druncene forðam þær wæs broht win suðan. Genamon þa ðone bisceop, læddon hine to hiora hustinge on ðone Sunnanæfen octaþ Pasce (þa wæs XIII Kł Mái) and hine þær ða bysmorlice acwylmdon· oftorfedon mid banum and mid hryþera heafdum and sloh hine ða an hiora mid anre æxe yre on þæt heafod þæt mid þam dynte he nyþer asah and his halige blod on þa eorðan feol and his haligan sawle to Godes rice asende

Then, on the Saturday, the Danish army became very angry against the bishop because he was not willing to promise them any money but ordered that no one should give any ransom on his behalf. They were also very drunk because wine had been brought there from the south. Then they took the bishop, led him to their tribunal on the Sunday evening of the Octave of Easter (April 19), and then shamefully murdered him there, stoning him with bones and with heads of cattle, and one of them struck him on the head with the back of an axe so that with the blow he sank down and his holy blood fell on the earth and [he] sent his holy soul to God's kingdom.

§221 There are illustrations of archers using bows and arrows on the Franks Casket (§§258–9) and on the Bayeux Tapestry (§290). But archaeological evidence is very limited. The *Maldon* poet speaks of them (§222) and they were certainly used at the battle of Hastings. They were also weapons of the hunt.

§222 In 991, Byrhtnoth, *ealdormon* of Essex, with his levies joined battle with a force of Danes at Maldon. Byrhtnoth was killed, some cowards fled (one on Byrhtnoth's own horse), the English shield wall broke, and the Danes eventually overcame the gallant resistance of those English who fought on. The poem *The Battle of Maldon* tells the story from the English viewpoint. Space allows me to print here only a few extracts concerning weapons. But other passages appear elsewhere; see the General Index.

A resolute warrior

> Ēac him wolde Ēadrīc   his ealdre gelæstan,
> frēan tō gefeohte,   ongan þā forð beran
> gār tō gūþe.   Hē hæfde gōd geþanc
> þā hwīle þe hē mid handum   healdan mihte
> 15 bord and brād swurd·   bēot hē gelæste
> þā hē ætforan his frēan   feohtan sceolde.

Byrhtnoth's ironical reply to the Danish demand for tribute

> Byrhtnōð maþelode,   bord hafenode,
> wand wācne æsc,   wordum mælde,
> yrre and ānræd   āgēaf him andsware:
> 45 'Gehӯrst þū, sælida,   hwæt þis folc segeð?
> Hī willað ēow tō gafole   gāras syllan,
> ættrynne ord   and ealde swurd,
> þā heregeatu   þe ēow æt hilde ne dēah.'

Deaths in action

> Hī lēton þā of folman   fēolhearde speru,
> grimme gegrundene   gāras flēogan·

110 bogan wǣron bysige,   bord ord onfēng.
     Biter wæs se beadurǣs,   beornas fēollon
on gehwæðere hand,   hyssas lāgon.

Byrhtnoth at bay

     Sende ðā se særinc   sūþerne gār
135 þæt gewundod wearð   wigena hlāford·
hē scēaf þā mid ðām scylde   þæt se sceaft tōbærst
and þæt spere sprengde   þæt hit sprang ongēan.
Gegremod wearð se gūðrinc·   hē mid gāre stang
wlancne wīcing   þe him þā wunde forgeaf.
140 Frōd wæs se fyrdrinc·   hē lēt his francan wadan
þurh ðæs hysses hals,   hand wīsode
þæt hē on þām fǣrsceaðan   feorh geræhte.
Ðā hē ōþerne   ofstlice scēat
þæt sēo byrne tōbærst·   hē wæs on brēostum wund
145 þurh ðā hringlocan,   him æt heortan stōd
ætterne ord.

The battle continues

. . .   . . .
clufon cellod bord,   cēne hī weredon·
bærst bordes lærig   and sēo byrne sang
285 gryrelēoða sum.

Epitaph for a thane

294 hē læg ðegenlice   ðēodne gehende.

In addition to him, Eadric wished to help his leader, his lord, in the fight. He then advanced carrying his spear to battle. He kept his purpose strong as long as he could hold his shield and broad sword in his hands. He fulfilled his vow when he had to fight before his lord.

Byrhtnoth gave utterance, raised his shield aloft, brandished his slender spear, spoke words, angry and resolute gave him answer: 'Do you hear, seafarer, what this folk says? They will give you spears as tribute, deadly point and well-tried sword, heriot [§§203 and 215] which will not profit you in battle.'

Then they let the spears, hard as files, fly from their hands, fiercely ground spears. Bows were busy, shield parried point. Bitter was the rush of battle. Warriors fell on either side, young men lay dead.

Then a Viking sent a spear of southern make so that the lord of the warriors was wounded. Byrhtnoth then pushed with his shield so that the spearshaft broke and forced out the spear so that it sprang back from the wound. The English warrior was enraged. With his spear he stabbed the proud Viking who had given him the wound. The warrior was experienced; he caused his spear to go through the young man's neck, guiding his hand so that it took the life of his sudden attacker. Then he quickly shot down another so that his coat of mail burst apart. He was wounded in the breast through his mail, a poisoned point penetrated to his heart.

They clove the hollow shields, defending themselves boldly. The edge of the shield broke and the corselet sang a terrible song.

He lay thane-like close to his lord.

§223 As I have already hinted, individual items of war-gear are sometimes given the attributes of loyal retainers (§§213 and 216) and are shown as sharing their owner's mortality (§210). Both ideas are to be found in this moving passage from *Beowulf* (ll. 2247–66), in which the last survivor of a band of warriors addresses the earth which now must guard the war-gear in which his dead comrades once fought. (For a facsimile of the manuscript of ll. 2252b–66, see figure 34.)

Text 11   **The lament of the last survivor**

'Heald þū nū, hrūse·   nū hæleð ne mōstan·
eorla æhte!   Hwæt! hyt ǣr on ðē
gōde begēaton·   gūðdēað fornam,
2250 feorhbealo frēcne,   fȳra gehwylcne
lēoda mīnra   þāra ðe þis līf ofgeaf·
gesāwon seledrēam.   Nāh hwā sweord wege
oððe feormie   fǣted wǣge,
dryncfæt dēore·   duguð ellor sceōc.
2255 Sceal se hearda helm   hyrstedgolde,
fǣtum befeallen·   feormynd swefað
þā ðe beadogrīman   bȳwan sceoldon·

2247 **healdan** 'to hold' (st. vb. VII(*a*) §517); **hrūse** 'earth'; **hæleð** 'hero', uninflected nom. pl.
2248 **æht** 'property'; **hwæt** interj. 'lo'; **hyt** = *hit*.
2249 **begietan** 'to obtain/win' (st. vb. V §519); **gūðdēað** 'death in battle'; **forniman** 'to carry off' (st. vb. IV §519).
2250 **feorhbealo** 'violent death'; **frēcne** adj. 'terrible'; **fȳras** = *firas* 'men', here gen. pl.
2251 **lēod** 'man/member of a tribe'; **ofgiefan** 'to give up' (st. vb. V §519).
2252 **seledrēam** 'hall joy'; **Nāh hwā** 'I do not have anyone who'; **wegan** 'to carry/wear' (st. vb. V §517).
2253 **feormian** 'to polish' (wk. vb. like *lufian* §526); **fǣted** past ptc. 'ornamented'; **wǣge** 'cup'.
2254 **dryncfæt** 'drinking vessel'; **duguð** 'warrior band'; **ellor** adv. 'elsewhere'; **scacan** 'to hasten/depart' (st. vb. VI §517). The manuscript (figure 34 line 3) has **seoc**.
2255 **hyrstedgold** 'decorated gold', here dat. sg.
2256 **fǣt** 'gold plate'; **befeallen** past ptc. 'deprived of'. The inf. *bēon* '(to) be' must be understood; **feormynd** 'polisher', here uninflected plural; **swefan** 'to sleep' (st. vb. V §517).
2257 **beadogrīma** 'war-mask/helmet'; **bȳwan** 'to furbish/brighten' (wk. vb. like *hīeran* §94).

gē swylce sēo herepād   sīo æt hilde gebād
ofer borda gebræc   bite īrena
2260 brosnað æfter beorne.   Ne mæg byrnan hring
æfter wīgfruman   wīde fēran
hæleðum be healfe.   Næs hearpan wyn,
gomen glēobēames,   ne gōd hafoc
geond sæl swingeð   ne se swifta mearh
2265 burhstede bēateð.   Bealocwealm hafað
fela feorhcynna   forð onsended!'

2258 **gē swylce** conj. 'likewise'; **herepād** 'coat of mail'; **hild** 'battle'; **gebīdan** 'to live through/survive' (st. vb. I §517).

2259 **bord** 'shield'; **gebræc** 'crashing/breaking'; **bite** 'bite/cut'; **īren** 'iron (sword)'.

2260 **brosnian** 'to decay' (like *feormian* l. 2253); **beorn** 'warrior'.

2261 **wigfruma** 'war-chief'; **fēran** 'to go/journey' (like *bȳwan* l. 2257).

2262 **healf** 'side'; **Næs** = *Ne wæs*; **wyn** 'pleasure/delight'.

2263 **gomen** 'joy/mirth'; **glēobēam** 'glee-wood/harp'; **hafoc** 'hawk'.

2264 **sæl** 'hall'; **mearh** 'steed'.

2265 **burhstede** 'courtyard'; **bealocwealm** 'baleful death'.

2266 **feorhcynn** 'race of men'.

For details of an edition of this poem see §465.

4 Jewellery

§224 Ronald Jessup, in his book *Anglo-Saxon Jewellery*, writes:

Jewellery is, above all things, a mirror to life itself.

It reflects the senses and beliefs, the skill, the leisure and material comfort and the aesthetic taste of its makers and owners, and helps us to place them in their proper perspective in the general historic scene.

It is moreover an exact and particular guide to the state of trade and commerce, to the spread of ideas and the trend of fashion, a criterion even of the nature and extent of folk movement and of the survival of ancient cultures. Its distribution and use may mark, still more, the incidence of peace and war. It is, with truth, a footnote to history.

Side by side with its interest for the archaeologist and the historian, Anglo-Saxon jewellery has a foremost appeal to the artist and the craftsman of today, who find in a contemplation of its design and technique the exercise of something more than a bare academic interest. To the practising jeweller especially its excellence needs no commendation, and to him it has often yielded an inspiration far from that of unalloyed sentiment.

And much to the point, we ought certainly to mark the pleasure and delight with which the ordinary reader becomes acquainted with the jewels of his early English forefathers . . .

I hope that the sections which follow will enable you to appreciate in some small way the truth of these observations. However, the stressing of the upper classes at the expense of all the others, which I have already mentioned in §200 and elsewhere, must not lull us into believing that there were no social, regional, or generational, differences in jewellery and decoration or that Anglo-Saxon England was all gold and jewels. Thus, while elaborate brooches might fasten the garments of the wealthy, the less fortunate had to make do with the simpler of the fastenings illustrated in figure 8.

§225   New items of Anglo-Saxon jewellery continue to be found. A pouch buried beside the remains of a woman excavated in Ipswich in 1990 contained among other things gold and silver pendants and a 4-inch brooch encrusted with garnets set in tiny gold panels. In the same year a former American GI now living in Dorset found the solid gold manuscript pointer which is further discussed in §230a.

§226   Many of the jewels were of great value. Bequests in the will of Ælgar, made *c.* 950, included *tueye bege ayther of fifti mancusas goldes* 'two armlets, each of fifty mancuses of gold'. (A *mancus* was a gold coin worth thirty silver pence.) Ælfgifu, a woman of royal descent, whose will is dated *c.* 970, left (among other things) *minæn cinæhlafordæ . . . twegea bæagas æigþær ys on hundtwælftigum mancussum . . . and þæra hlæfdigan anæs swyrbeages on hund-tweltifgum mancussum* 'to my royal lord . . . two armlets each is of one hundred and twenty mancuses . . . and to the queen a necklace of one hundred and twenty mancuses'. Dorothy Whitelock calculated that, on the basis of prices assigned in the laws, this necklace would have bought 120 oxen or 300 sheep or fifteen male slaves. Alternatively, it would have purchased about 360 acres of land in East Anglia. Other bequests of jewellery include (from the will of Prince Æthelstan (§204)) *þone gyldenan fetels 7 þæne beh þe Wulfric worhte* 'the golden belt and the armlet which Wulfric wrought' and (from the will of Wulfwaru, between 984 and 1016) *Godan minre yldran dehter . . . anes bendes on ðritigum mancussum goldes and twegea preonas* 'to my elder daughter Gode . . . a band/chain of thirty mancuses of gold and two brooches'.

§227   Naturally enough, not many treasures of this value have been found in graves apart from the Sutton Hoo ship-burial (§§194–9). But many quite valuable jewels were buried with their owners. The objects most commonly found in graves are buckles and brooches. The cemetery at Buckland, Dover, produced a great variety of buckles suitable for children, youths, men, and women, mostly of bronze, some of continental origin. In a cemetery in East Kent 120 graves yielded thirty-five brooches and in Suffolk 100 graves produced seventy-five. Since, as D. M. Wilson puts it, 'brooches were integral parts of everyday dress in the days before buttons', they were of necessity used by men and women, both of whom fastened their mantles with a brooch on the right shoulder. Women sometimes used a pair of brooches to clip a tunic on each shoulder. But they were of course exploited for ornamental as well as utilitarian purposes.

§228   By experimenting, I have found that without colour plates it is

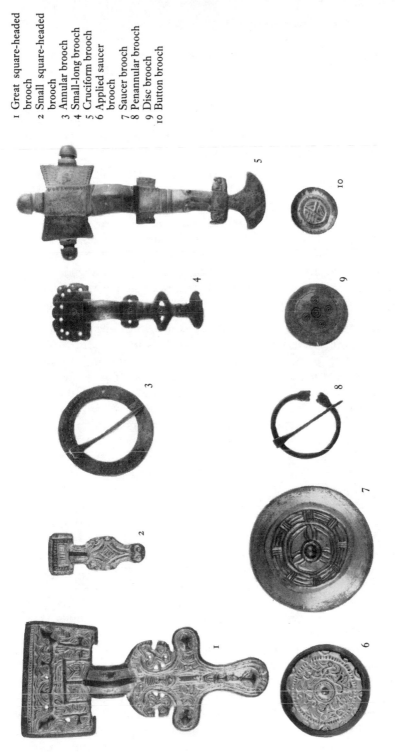

1 Great square-headed brooch
2 Small square-headed brooch
3 Annular brooch
4 Small-long brooch
5 Cruciform brooch
6 Applied saucer brooch
7 Saucer brooch
8 Penannular brooch
9 Disc brooch
10 Button brooch

Figure 8 Anglo-Saxon brooches (copyright Ashmolean Museum)

impossible to do justice to the jewellery which survives from Anglo-Saxon times. I have therefore decided to give a classified list of the more important jewels, together with details of where they can be found and of where you can find colour illustrations in the books listed in §193.

§229 Let us start with cloisonné work. According to Rupert Bruce-Mitford (Bibliography III C, first item), the native antiquities disinterred at Sutton Hoo (as distinct from the imported silver and other objects) reveal

> pagan Saxon art in its final flower, overloaded but not decadent. The gold jewellery is brimming with novel and daring ideas. It shows an overflowing exuberance and displays the highest level of craftsmanship, excelling anything known in this medium from the rest of Europe in its era ... Moreover, it is difficult to repress the feeling that the standard of perfection set by the Sutton Hoo master-goldsmith, the infinite pains taken, for instance, in the minute cloisonné work on the pair of hexagonal plaques on the purse-lid, reveal the spirit that is expressed in the work of the indefatigable and meticulous Northumbrian [manuscript] illuminators.

Cloisonné appears in jewellery of different kinds, including the Sutton Hoo purse-lid (figure 2) described in §230, which is in the British Museum (*Jewellery*, facing p. 74, and *Sutton Hoo*, facing p. 80); the Sutton Hoo shoulder clasps, also in the British Museum (*Sutton Hoo*, facing p. 65, *AS Art*, plate 7, *Making*, p. 30, and *AS 1982*, p. 77); the Kingston Brooch in the Merseyside County Museum, Liverpool (*Jewellery*, frontispiece, *Making*, p. 50, and *AS 1982*, p. 47; see §234); the Amherst Brooch in the Ashmolean Museum, Oxford (monochrome plate xxvi in *Jewellery*); the Wilton Cross in the British Museum (*AS Art*, plate 18, and *Making*, p. 27); the pectoral cross of St Cuthbert (d. 687) in the Cathedral Library, Durham (*AS Art*, plate 17, and *Making*, p. 133); the Alfred Jewel in the Ashmolean Museum, Oxford, described in §230a, and the Minster Lovell Jewel, also in the Ashmolean (both in *Jewellery*, facing p. 38, *Making*, p. 282, and *AS 1982*, p. 137; Alfred Jewel alone in *AS Art*, plate 17, and *Golden Age*, facing p. 48).

§230 Despite §228, I shall attempt a brief description of two of these items. The purse-lid, shown in monochrome in figure 2, is the most gorgeous object found. This fittingly reflects the fact that the lord was the *goldgiefa* 'goldgiver'; see §341. The gold outer-frame, 7.5 inches long, is jewelled with garnets and millefiori glass and has filigree bindings. From it four jewelled tongues protrude into the interior of the lid. The three gold hinges at the top were fastened to a belt and there is a gold sliding catch at the bottom which was attached to the mouth of the pouch, which (before its disintegration) contained thirty-seven Merovingian coins, three blanks, and two ingots. The original material of the lid, probably bone or ivory, has disappeared. In it were set four circular studs, three of which have lost their setting, and seven garnet-jewelled ornamental plaques. These consist of three pairs – two hexagonal, two representing a man between two animals and two showing a hawk seizing a duck – and one double plaque with two pairs of animals, one pair interlaced. These exhibit intricate and delicate cloisonné work, including the unusual lidded cloisons which appear in the double plaque and the man-between-animals pair.

§230a   The Alfred Jewel (figure 9), 2.45 inches (6.2 cm) long, was found in 1693 near Athelney in Somerset, where King Alfred took refuge from the Danes in 878. The inscription in the openwork gold frame reads *AELFRED MEC HEHT GEWYRCAN* 'Alfred ordered [someone] to make me'. A decorated gold plate encloses a rock crystal over a green figure on a blue background bearing in each hand a flowered sceptre. It may depict Sight but is now more commonly thought to represent Christ as Wisdom or Christ in Majesty. The terminal is an animal head whose mouth forms a socket, perhaps for the insertion of a book pointer. This possibility was highlighted in 1990 when Mr Bernard Yarosz, a former American GI, discovered a solid gold Saxon manuscript pointer in a Dorset cove, thereby

Figure 9   The Alfred Jewel (copyright Ashmolean Museum)

fuelling speculation that the two objects belonged together. The smaller Minster Lovell Jewel, 1.25 inches long (*c.* 3.2 cm), appears to have been made in the same workshop for the same purpose. A roundel of cloisonné enamel on gold, encased in a filigree setting, has on a ground of dark blue a four-petalled green flower with a white centre, a rectangular cell of white metal at each petal tip, and (between the petals) four hoop-shaped cells of light blue enamel.

§231   Belt-buckles of the type worn in Gaul by Germans in Roman military service have been found in early fifth-century graves in the River Thames area. This suggests the presence of German mercenaries in England during the Roman occupation; see §307. Buckles were, of course, in everyday use. They vary greatly in size and nature, from the purely practical to the highly ornamental. One of the former is illustrated in figure 12. Some of the latter display great craftsmanship; note especially the Sutton Hoo belt-buckle, of solid gold decorated with interlacing animal panels picked out with inlaid niello, 5.2 inches (13.2 cm) long and nearly 15 ounces (414.62 g) in weight (British Museum; *Making*, p. 31, and coloured plate facing p. 64 of *Sutton Hoo*); the gold-with-garnet Taplow buckle (British Museum; *AS 1982*, p. 39); and the silver gilt Crundale buckle (British Museum; *AS Art*, plate 16, and *Making*, p. 24).

§232   The ear-rings which survive are mostly simple rings of plain silver wire decorated with beads of coloured glass or amethyst. But a few have pendants. Two finger-rings are associated with members of the Wessex royal family, either because they wore them or because they gave them as gifts. One – a massive ring of dull reddish gold with niello enrichment – is inscribed with the name of Æthelwulf, Alfred's father, king from 839 to 858. The other is of deep yellow gold with a circular bezel containing the *Agnus Dei* and bears the name of Alfred's sister Æthelswith, wife of Burhred, king of Mercia (d. 888). Both are in the British Museum; *AS Art*, plates 117 and 118, and *Making*, p. 269.

§233   Early Anglo-Saxon brooches, which are usually made of bronze, are illustrated in figure 8 by examples from those on exhibition in the Ashmolean Museum, Oxford. They can be divided into two basic types – bow brooches and circular brooches, which continued to be made up to the Norman Conquest. Bow brooches include square-headed brooches (great and small); cruciform brooches, which had an arched bow and a foot incorporating an animal head; and small-long brooches, simple and cheap adaptations of the cruciform brooches, which had become more elaborate as time went by. These types of bow brooches are illustrated in *Jewellery*, monochrome plates XVI–XVIII, XII XIV and XV, and XIII, respectively. The circular type includes annular and penannular (broken-ring) brooches, derived from pre-Roman Celtic forms (*Jewellery*, monochrome plate XX.1); disc brooches, simple flat discs with stamped or incised decoration, some examples of which are mentioned below; saucer brooches, cast in one piece complete with decoration, and applied saucer brooches, in which a thin gilt-bronze plate with an embossed pattern was cemented to a bronze disc (*Jewellery*, monochrome plate X); and button brooches, bronze miniatures incorporating a human face (*Jewellery*, monochrome plate VI.7–8). Disc brooches of the later period, often larger in size and more commonly of silver, include the six discovered at Pentney (British Museum; *AS Art*, plate 120); the niello-inlaid silver Fuller Brooch (British Museum; *AS 1982*, p. 137); and the Strickland Brooch of silver inlaid with gold plates and niello (British Museum; *AS Art*, plate 115). These are also illustrated in *Making*; see pp. 230, 281, and 232. Openwork circular brooches include the gilt-bronze Pitney Brooch (*AS Art*, plate 272, and *Golden Age*, plate XXIV) and the niello-inlaid silver Beeston Tor Brooch (*AS Art*, plate 116), both in the British Museum.

§234 Among the richest items of early Anglo-Saxon jewellery outside the Sutton Hoo ship-burial (§§194–9) is the seventh-century circular Kingston Brooch found in a grave in Kent, listed in §229; see figure 10. It is a composite brooch 3.3 inches (8 cm) in diameter, weighing 6.25 ounces (*c.* 177 g), and consists of two plates of gold bound together by a band with beaded wire gold filigree. The interior is filled with a white clay-like substance and the whole is secured by three small clasps of gold set close

Figure 10   The Kingston Brooch (copyright The Board of Trustees of the National Museums and Galleries on Merseyside (Liverpool Museum))

together on the rim. On the back there is a bronze pin with a jewelled garnet head and a safety clasp for securing the brooch to the dress. The slightly convex front has a modified cruciform pattern and a prominent central boss. There are five concentric rings of gold cloisons enclosing garnets – step-shaped, triangular, semicircular, and square – relieved by triangular and step-shaped cells of blue glass, by cells of deeper garnet, and by a central and four smaller bosses of white shell-like material. Another fine seventh-century composite brooch from Kent is the Amherst Brooch, of gold with step, triangular, and quatrefoil, cloisons (also listed in §229). If the *Beowulf* poet had seen either of these, he might well have used two of the words with which he describes the gleaming tapestries in the Danish hall Heorot: *goldfag . . . wundorsion* 'gold decorated . . . wondrous sight'.

§235   The Old English version of Bede's *Historia ecclesiastica*, in relating the death of Æthelthryth, Abbess of Ely (St Audrey), tells us that in her lifetime she was afflicted by a tumour in the neck but was wont to rejoice in the affliction, saying

'Ic wat cuðlice þæt ic be gewyrhtum on minum sweoran bere þa byrðenne þisse aðle 7 þisse untrymnesse in þæm ic gemon mec geo beran· þa ic geong wæs· þa iidlan byrðenne gyldenra sigila. Ond ic gelyfo þætte me forðon seo uplice arfæstnis wolde mec hefigade beon mid sare mines sweoran þæt ic swa wære onlesed þære scylde þære swiðe idlan leasnisse mid þy me nu for golde 7 for gimmum of swiran forðhlifað seo readnis 7 bryne þæs swiles 7 wærces'

'I know well that I for [my] deeds/transgressions bear in my neck the burden of this illness and malady because I remember that long ago, when I was young, I bore the idle burden of a gold necklace. And I believe that the divine grace therefore wished me to be burdened with an affliction in the neck so that I might thus be released from the guilt of that very idle levity, seeing that now instead of gold and instead of gems the redness and burning of this swelling and affliction stands out on my neck.'

§236   It would seem that not all Anglo-Saxon women shared this view. Some stunning necklaces have survived: the Chessell Down polychrome beads and the amethyst necklace from Breach Down (both in the British Museum; both in *Jewellery*, facing p. 52); the gold and garnet choker necklet found at Roundway Downs (Devizes Museum; *AS 1982*, p. 35); the gold and garnet Brassington Necklace (Sheffield City Museum; *AS 1982*, p. 42); and finally the gold and garnet Desborough Necklace (British Museum; *Making*, p. 28, and *AS 1982*, p. 46), which even Æthelthryth might have tolerated, because a cross had been added to it to indicate that the owner was a Christian.

§237   It is not surprising that this beautiful jewellery gave pleasure to those who wore it and to those who saw it. The poet of *The Ruin*, describing the remains of a ruined city with large stone buildings, baths, and hot springs – identified by some with the Roman city of Bath – describes this pleasure in a typically heroic way, that is through the feelings of an Anglo-Saxon warrior. This ruin, says the poet, is

> þær iū beorn monig
> glædmōd ond goldbeorht   gleoma gefrætwed
> wlonc ond wīngāl   wīghyrstum scān·
> seah on sinc, on sylfor,   on searogimmas,
> on ēad, on æht,   on eorcanstān,
> on þās beorhtan burg   brādan rīces.
> Stānhofu stōdan·   strēam hāte wearp
> wīdan wylme·   weal eall befeng
> beorhtan bōsme   þær þā baþu wæron
> hāt on hreþre

where once many a man, glad of heart and bright with gold, splendidly arrayed, proud and flushed with wine, shone in his armour, gazed on treasure, on silver, on intricate jewels, on wealth, on possessions, on a precious stone, on this bright city with its broad domain. There stood stone buildings. The spring threw out a hot, broad stream. A wall received all of it in its bright bosom. There, in the centre, were the hot baths.

§238 These artefacts also help us to understand that the love of craftsmanship and beauty which we observe in much Old English poetry is no mere artistic pose but an accurate reflection of the society about which the poet is writing, a society whose members, like many of their descendants, could combine fierceness in battle with love of the beautiful. The *Judith* poet's account of the plunder carried back to Bethulia by Judith's warriors after the defeat of Holofernes' army illustrates these characteristics.

Text 12 **Judith's warriors bring home the plunder**

> þā sēo cnēoris eall,
> mægða mærost,   ānes mōnðes fyrst,
> 325 wlanc, wundenlocc,   wāgon ond læddon
> tō ðære beorhtan byrig,   Bēthūliam,
> helmas ond hupseax,   hāre byrnan,
> gūðsceorp gumena   golde gefrætewod,

323 **cnēoris** 'tribe'.
324 **mægð** 'race/tribe'; **fyrst** 'period/space of time'.
325 **wlanc** 'proud'; **wundenlocc** 'with braided locks'; **wāgon** = *wǣgon* (from *wegan* 'to carry' st. vb. V §517).
326 **burg** 'city/walled town'.
327 **hupseax** 'short sword'; **hār** 'gray'.
328 **gūðsceorp** 'armour'; **(ge)frætwian** 'to adorn' (wk. vb. like *lufian* §526).

> mærra mādma   þonne mon ænig
> 330 āsecgan mæge   searoþoncelra·
> eal þæt ðā ðēodguman   þrymme geēodon
> cēne under cumblum   on compwīge
> þurh Iūdithe   glēawe lāre,
> mægð mōdigre.   Hī tō mēde hyre
> 335 of ðām sīðfate   sylfre brōhton,
> eorlas æscrōfe,   Holofernes
> sweord ond swātigne helm,   swylce ēac sīde byrnan
> gerēnode rēadum golde·   ond eal þæt se rinca baldor
> swīðmōd sinces āhte   oððe sundoryrfes,
> 340 bēaga ond beorhtra māðma,   hī þæt þære beorhtan idese
> āgēafon gearoþoncolre.

329 **mærra mādma** gen. pl. 'of more glorious treasures'. It should be acc. pl. as another object of the verbs in l. 325b.

330 **searoþoncel** adj. 'wise', gen. pl. dependent on *mon ænig*.

331 **ðēodguma** 'warrior'; **þrymm** 'might'; **gegān** 'to gain/conquer' (an irregular verb §529).

332 **cēne** adj. 'bold'; **cumbol** 'banner'; **compwīg** 'battle'.

333 **glēaw** adj. 'prudent/wise'; **lār** 'counsel'.

334 **mægð** 'maiden', uninflected gen. sg. parallel with *Iūdithe* l. 333; **mōdig** adj. 'daring'.

334-5 **tō mēde hyre ... sylfre** 'as a reward for her ... the very one', Judith.

335 **sīðfæt** 'expedition'.

336 **æscrōf** adj. 'brave in battle'.

337 **swātig** adj. 'bloody'; **sīd** adj. 'wide'.

338 **gerēnod** past ptc. 'adorned'; **rinc** 'warrior', here gen. pl.; **baldor** 'lord'.

339 **swīðmōd** adj. 'stout-hearted'; **sinc** 'treasure'; **āgan** 'to have' (§96); **sundoryrfe** 'private inheritance'.

340 **ides** 'lady'.

341 **gearoþoncol** adj. 'ready-witted/wise'.

For details of an edition of this poem see §489.

5 Coins

§239 The first gold coins used in England were of foreign origin; indeed, all the coins in the Sutton Hoo ship (§195), which (on the evidence of the coins) was buried *c.* 625, were struck on mainland Europe, in the lands occupied by the Merovingian Franks. But by the mid-seventh century the Anglo-Saxons did strike their own gold coins in London, in other mints in the south-east, and in York. The hoard of one hundred coins with one forgery discovered in 1828 at Crondall in Hampshire, which was concealed (again on the evidence of the coins) *c.* 640, comprised mostly Anglo-Saxon coins, many from London, but some Merovingian. However, the gold coins became debased and were replaced by a silver coinage late in the seventh century. Silver coins have been found on monastic sites, in graves, in settlements such as royal and ecclesiastical Winchester and commercial Hamwih (Southampton), in stray caches in England and other countries, here and there where they fell from someone's pocket or purse, and (perhaps

ironically) in Scandinavia, whither large shipments of coins were taken as
Danegeld, which was first paid in 991 (§187 n. 9). Coins continued to be
struck until the Norman Conquest and after it; the men who made King
William's coins were the men who were operating the mints when Edward
the Confessor died. For a detailed discussion of the coinage, which space
does not permit here, see *Archaeology*, pp. 349–72. Figure 11 shows coins
from the time of Offa (§183), of Alfred (§185), and of Cnut (§187).

§240   Coinage was essentially a royal prerogative and the law tightened
in the later Anglo-Saxon period. One of the laws of Æthelstan (d. 940) says
that *an mynet sy ofer eall ðæs cynges onweald 7 nan mon ne mynetige buton on port* 'a
mint is to be completely under the king's jurisdiction and no man is to mint
except in a town'. Æthelred (d. 1016) decreed that *nan man ne age nænne
mynetere buton cyng* 'no man is to have a minter/coiner except the king'.
However, some kings granted the privilege to others. There are coins which
were minted by the Archbishops of Canterbury or York, and another law of
Æthelstan decrees that there be

> on Cantwarabyrig VII myneteras: IV ðæs cynges 7 II þæs biscopes 7 I þæs
> abbodes· to Hrofeceastre: II cynges 7 I þæs biscopes· to Lundenbyrig
> VIII· to Wintaceastre VI· to Læwe II· to Hæstingaceastre I· oþer to
> Cisseceastre· to Hamtune II· to Wærham II· to Execeastre II· to Sceaftes-
> byrig II· elles to þam oþrum burgum I

> in Canterbury seven coiners: four the king's and two the bishop's and one
> the abbot's; at Rochester: two [the] king's and one the bishop's; at Lon-
> don eight; at Winchester six; at Lewes two; at Hastings one; another at
> Cirencester; at Southampton two; at Wareham two; at Exeter two; at
> Shaftesbury two; otherwise in the other towns one.

In late Anglo-Saxon England, minting was done under the control of a royal
official. Penalties for illegal minting or for debasing the currency were
severe. Æthelstan's law on the subject reads: *7 gif se mynetere ful wurðe· slea
mon of þa hond . . . and sette up on ða mynet smiððan* 'if the coiner becomes
corrupt, let his hand be struck off . . . and displayed in the mint'. Æthelred
was even more severe: *And ælc mynetere þe man tihð þæt fals feoh sloge . . . gif he ful
beo slea hine man* 'And each coiner who is accused of striking false money . . .
if he is corrupt, he is to be killed.'

§241   In the words of James Campbell, 'it was in a sense a brutally
commercial society'. Every man had his *wergild* (or *wer*), his price according
to his degree or rank. Thus we read in a document dating from the first half
of the tenth century:

> Cynges wergild is . . . XXX þusend þrymsa: XV þusend ðrymsa byð þæs
> weres 7 XV þusend þæs cynedomes . . . Arcebiscopes 7 æþelinges wergild
> is XV þusend þrymsa . . . Biscopes 7 ealdormannes VIII þusend ðrymsa
> . . . Holdes 7 cyninges heahgerefan IIII þusend þrimsa . . . Mæsseþegnes

OFFA (d. 796)

Obverse
OFFA REX (X in
shape of a Cross)
PORTRAIT

Reverse
PEHTWALD. FLO-
REATED CROSS

scale 2/1

ALFRED (d. 899)

Obverse
ALFRED REX (X in
shape of a Cross)
PORTRAIT

Reverse
TILEWINE.
LONDINIUM
MONOGRAM

scale 61/19

CNUT (d. 1035)

Obverse
CNUT
(letters in shape of a
Benediction)
REX
(X in shape of a
Cross)

Reverse
CVNNETTI. TWO
SMALL CROSSES

scale 2/1

The name on each reverse is that of the coiner.

Figure 11   Anglo-Saxon pennies (copyright Ashmolean Museum)

7 worldþegnes II þusend þrimsa ... Ceorles wergild is CC 7 LXVI þrimsa ...

A king's *wergild* is ... 30,000 thrymsas: 15,000 for the man and 15,000 for the royal dignity ... An archbishop's and an ætheling's *wergild* is 15,000 thrymsas ... A bishop's and an alderman's 8,000 thrymsas ... A hold's [a Danish title] and a king's high sheriff 4,000 thrymsas ... A mass-priest's and a secular thane's 2,000 thrymsas ... A churl's *wergild* is 266 thrymsas.

[The exact value of a thrymsa, originally a gold and later a silver coin, cannot now be determined.]

A man's *wergild* was payable if he were slain unlawfully: *Gif man ofslægen weorðe· gylde hine man swa he geboren sy* 'If a man is killed, payment is to be made according to his birth'. But *gif man leud ofslea on þeofðe· licge buton wergelde* 'If a man is killed in theft, [he] is to lie without *wergild*'. Sometimes, a criminal could pay the value of his own *wergild* as a penalty:

> Gif friman wið fries mannes wif geligeþ· his wergelde abicge 7 oðer wif his agenum scætte begete 7 ðæm oðrum æt ham gebrenge

> If a freeman lies with the wife of a freeman, he is to requite with his *wergild* and to acquire another woman with his own money and to bring [her] to the other [freeman] at home.

Sometimes the payment of *wergild* was an alternative:

> Gif ðeof sie gefongen· swelte he deaðe oððe his lif be his were man aliese

> If a thief is captured, he is to suffer death or his life is to be redeemed with his *wergild*.

Under other codes, a thief was declared an outlaw (Text 27 §435).

§242   *Fæhþ* 'feud' – a state of enmity in which the relations of a man unlawfully killed sought vengeance against the killer or his relations – arose if *wergild* was not paid. Thus Edmund (d. 946) decreed that

> gif hwa heonanforð ænigne man ofslea· ðæt he wege sylf ða fæhþe butan he hy mid freonda fylste binnan twelf monðum forgylde be fullan were

> if anyone ... henceforth kill any man, [that] he bear the feud himself unless he, with the help of friends, pay the *wergild* in full within twelve months.

Such vengeance was permitted only under strictly regulated conditions. For example, Alfred (d. 899) promulgated this law:

> Eac we beodað: se man se ðe his gefan hamsittendne wite· þæt he ne feohte ær ðam he him ryhtes bidde

> Also we command: the man who knows his foe [to be] living at home, that he is not to fight before he asks him for what is due.

There were penalties for pursuit of an unjustified feud. Æthelstan (d. 940) laid down that

> se ðe þeof wrecan wille 7 æhlip gewyrce oððe on stræte to geliht· beo cxx scillinga scildig wið þone cing. Gif he þonne mann ofslea on þa wrace· beo he his feores scyldig 7 ealles þæs þe he age buton se cing him arian wille

> he who wants to punish a thief and makes an assault or comes near to [him] in the street, he is to forfeit thirty shillings to the king. If he then kills the man in retaliation, he is to forfeit his life and all that he has unless the king is willing to pardon him.

Christian kings such as Edmund (d. 946) tried to reduce the number of blood-feuds:

> Gif hwa Cristenes mannes blod ageote· ne cume he na on ðæs cyninges neawiste ær he on dædbote ga swa him biscop tæce 7 his scrift him wisige

> If anyone spills the blood of a Christian man, he is not to come into the king's presence until he makes amends as the bishop instructs and shows him his prescribed penance.

But the blood-feud remained part of the way of life until the end of the Anglo-Saxon kingdom.

§243 Each crime, too, had its price. Making counterfeit coins meant the loss of a hand in Æthelstan's time and death in Æthelred's (§240). Unlawful killing could be requited by the payment of *wergild* (§241). Some offences listed are unlikely to be committed today. Æthelstan decreed

> þæt nan scyldwyrhta ne lecge nan scepes fel on scyld 7 gif he do gilde xxx scillinga

> that no shieldmaker put any sheepskin in a shield and if he does he is to pay thirty shillings.

But goods made of inferior materials are still passed off. Other offences much in the news today attracted different penalties which do not always accord with modern thinking. Another law of Æthelstan stated

> ðæt nan cyping ne sy on Sunnandæges. Gif hit þonne hwa do· þolige ðæs ceapes 7 gesylle xxx scillinga

> that no trading be done on Sunday. If then anyone does, he is to forfeit the goods and pay thirty shillings.

One more law – from Alfred's time – must end this catalogue:

> gif hwa slea his ðone nehstan mid stane oððe mid fyste 7 he þeah utgongan mæge be stæfe· begite him læce 7 wyrce his weorc ða hwile þe he self ne mæge

if anyone strikes his neighbour with stone or fist in such a way that [*lit.* 'and'] he can still get about on a stick, [the offender] is to get a doctor for him and do his work as long as he cannot [do it] himself.

§244 Slaves were among the earliest exports from what is now England. Bede's story of how Pope Gregory sent Augustine to England as a result of a chance visit to a market in Rome where British slaves were for sale is well-known. Less so is his story of how a young Northumbrian was wounded in battle, was captured, and became the property of a Mercian. *þa he fullice getrumad wæs· þa bebohte he hine in Lundenne to sumum Frysan* 'When the prisoner was fully recovered, the Mercian then sold him in London to a Frisian'. Bede goes on to talk of his miraculous release. Few slaves were so fortunate and slavery, like vengeance, remained part of life throughout the Anglo-Saxon period. The Latin Penitential of Theodore Archbishop of Canterbury (d. 690) says that

> if he is compelled by necessity, a father has the power to sell his son of seven years age into slavery; after that he has not the right to sell him without his consent.

> A person of fourteen [years] can make himself a slave.

Slaves of both sexes are regularly mentioned in the charters, the laws, and the wills. In 963 Bishop Æthelwold owned an estate at Yaxley:

> þis is þ erfgewrit æt Geaceslea· þryttene wepmen weorce-wyrþe 7 V wimmen 7 æhta geonge men 7 XVI oxan faldreþere 7 III hund scepa 7 V scep 7 XXX swina 7 hundteongig fliccena 7 eal þa smean ðe þerto gebyriað 7 XXX forþer cornes 7 hundehtetig æcera gesawen 7 an egþwirf 7 VI bidenfate 7 II cuflas 7 þry trogas 7 lead 7 trefet 7 IX winterstellas 7 I fedelsswin

> This is the inventory of the stock at Yaxley: thirteen able-bodied men and five women and eight young men and sixteen oxen, a stalled ox and three hundred and five sheep and thirty swine and a hundred flitches of bacon and all the delicacies that belong to them and thirty fothers of corn and eighty acres sown and one harrow and six barrels and two tubs and three troughs and a cauldron and a trivet and nine year-old stallions and one fat pig.

And in 1014 Archbishop Wulfstan of York preached a sermon in which he denounced the sins and crimes of English society and claimed that the attacks of the Danes were God's vengeance on a wicked people. In the course of this sermon, he said:

> Eac we witan georne hwær seo yrmð gewearð þæt fæder gesealde bearn wið weorðe 7 bearn his moder 7 broþer sealde oþerne fremdum to gewealde

Also we know well where the crime was committed that a father sold a son for money and a child his mother and a brother gave another into the ownership of foreigners.

§245 Attitudes to money have not changed. As we have seen, the Anglo-Saxons spent it, gambled with it (§260), lost it, hid it for safety, bequeathed it, and gave it to honour dead men. They recognized *feohgitseras* 'misers', men who were *feohgeorn* 'eager for money' and who showed *feohlufu* 'love for money'. Some knew what it was to be *feohleas* 'moneyless'. Others deprecated *feohspillung* 'waste of money'. The *Beowulf* poet speaks of *feohleas gefeoht* 'a moneyless fight, a fight not to be atoned for by money' when describing the accidental killing of a king's son by his brother. And Bede, in his account of the death of the saintly princess Ercongate of Kent, tells us how a great company of angels was sent to her monastery *þæt heo sceolden þæt gyldne mynet mid him geneoman þætte þider of Cent cwom* 'charged with the duty of [*lit*. 'so that they should'] taking with them the golden coin that had come there from Kent'.

6 Other metalwork

§246 We know a little about Anglo-Saxon mining, smelting, and metal-workers' tools; see *Archaeology*, pp. 261–4 and 268. The monastery depicted in the *Colloquy* – a dialogue Ælfric concocted in Latin as an aid for novices learning that language but which (human nature being what it is) was soon provided with an Old English crib – had *smiþas, isene smiþas, goldsmiþ, seoloforsmiþ, arsmiþ* 'blacksmiths, ironsmiths, a goldsmith, a silversmith, [and] a coppersmith'. Not all smiths matched the craftsmanship of the great jewellers (§§224–38) or achieved the eminence of Weland (§204) but they were able to satisfy the demand of the times for nails, horseshoes, tools, domestic items, and agricultural equipment. The novice taking the part of the blacksmith in Ælfric's *Colloquy* asks *Hwanon sylan scear oþþe culter þe na gade hæfþ buton of cræfte minon?* 'From where [will come] ploughshare or coulter for the ploughman, who does not even have a goad except by my skill?' A late tenth- or early eleventh-century document *Be gesceadwisan gerefan* 'Concerning the wise reeve' lists his many duties and responsibilities. Among them is this: *He sceal fela tola to tune tilian 7 fela andlomena to husan habban* 'He must provide many tools for the farm and many items of equipment for the members of the household'. I have picked out some which you should be able to recognize with the help of §§4–8 and 15: (for the farm) *æcse, adsan, bil, mattuc, scear, culter, gadiren, sicol, weodhoc, spade, scofle, hlædre, horscamb*, and (for the house) *wulcamb, nædle, awel, cyrne, cuppan, candelstafas, sealtfæt*, and *sapbox*. Figure 12 shows a selection of metalwork (other than weapons, jewellery, and coins) from the Ashmolean Museum, Oxford.

§247 Many metal items are mentioned in charters and wills. Wynflæd's will (*c.* 950) bequeathed *ane hlidfæspe cuppan* 'a cup with a lid', *hyre aghene ieredan cuppan* 'her own ornamented cups', *II sylerenan cuppan* 'two silver

Figure 12   Everyday metal objects (copyright Ashmolean Museum)

cups', and *hyre goldfagan treowenan cuppan* 'her gold-adorned wooden cup'. Elsewhere we read of harrows, kettles, lathes, waggons, ploughs, and so on. There are riddles in the Exeter Book demanding the answers 'anchor', 'borer', 'churn', 'key', 'rake', and 'plough', in addition to weapons and armour (§205). Those with irritation of the skin are advised to follow this recipe: *Bæþ wið blæce: awyl tyn siþum þa wyrte on hwere* . . . 'A bath against blotch: boil the plants ten times in a basin . . .'. More sinister uses were found for cauldrons in the stories of the saints, not all of whom were as lucky as St George, who, having been put in a brass cauldron full of boiling lead,

> ahof . . . to heofonum his eagan . . . and he bletsode þæt lead and læg him onuppan and þæt lead wearð acolod þurh Godes mihte and Georius sæt gesund on ðam hwere

lifted his eyes to heaven . . . and he blessed the lead and lay upon it and the lead was cooled through God's power and George sat sound in the cauldron.

§248 The church, of course, had many uses for metal. On metal crosses and crucifixes, see §256. In addition to St Cuthbert's pectoral cross (§229), we have his portable altar, a small block of oak encased in a silver shrine. A small gilt-bronze chalice found at Hexham would have been suitable for use with a portable altar. A list of the gifts given to Peterborough by Æthelwold, Bishop of Winchester from 963 to 984, begins thus:

þis synd þa madmas þe Adeluuold bisceop sealde into þam mynstre þe is Medeshamstede gehaten· Gode to loue 7 sce PETRE his saule to alysed-nesse· þ is þonne an Cristes boc mid sylure berenod 7 III rode eac mid sylure berenode II sylurene candelsticcan 7 II ouergylde 7 I sylurene stor-cille 7 I æren 7 I sylurene waterfet 7 II sylurene bellen 7 IIII silurene calices IIII patenan 7 syluren pipe 7 VI masse hacelan 7 IIII cæppan 7 I roc 7 VIII stolan emfela handlina 7 XI subumbrale 7 II pistolclaþas 7 III cor-porale 7 III offrincsceatas 7 XVIIII albæn 7 IIII pælles 7 II linenweb to albæn 7 II blace regl cesternisce 7 VI uuahryft 7 VIIII setreil 7 X han-giende bellan VII handbellan 7 IIII bedreaf 7 VI hornas IIII gerenode 7 VIII sylfrene cuppan 7 II gegylde weofodsceatas

These are the treasures which Bishop Æthelwold gave to the monastery which is called Medeshamstede, to the praise of God and Saint Peter, for the redemption of his soul, namely a gospel book mounted with silver and three crosses also mounted with silver, two silver candlesticks and two overlaid with gold and a silver censer and one of brass and a silver water vessel and two silver bells and four silver chalices, four patens and a silver tube/wind instrument and six chasubles and four copes and one rochet and eight stoles, just as many maniples and eleven tunics and two epistle vest-ments and three linen clothes and three offering napkins and nineteen albs and four cloaks and two linen webs for albs and two black urban vestments and six wall curtains and nine seatcovers and ten hanging bells, seven hand-bells, four bedcovers and six horns, four decorated, and eight silver cups and two gilded altarcloths.

7 Sculpture

§249 An Anglo-Saxon poet, speaking of the gifts God bestows upon men, says

Ac hē missenlice   monna cynne
gielpes stȳreð   ond his giefe bryttað,
sumum on cystum,   sumum on cræftum . . .

But He variously restrains the race of men from pride and distributes His gifts, to some in virtues, to some in crafts . . .

Those he picks out for special mention include the weaponsmith (§§204 and 216) and the jeweller (§§224–38):

> . . . sum searocræftig
> goldes and gimma   þonne him gumena weard
> hāteð him tō mǣrþum   maþþum rēnian

one [is] skilled in gold and gems whenever a leader of men orders him to adorn a jewel for his glory.

But God did not fail to inspire Anglo-Saxon craftsmen in wood, in stone, in other kinds of metalwork, and in ivory, horn, and bone. I have found no evidence for modelling in clay, though it may be that the only recorded Anglo-Saxon instance of pin-sticking magic, which took place between 963 and 975, involved a clay image:

> þ land æt Ægeleswyrðe headde an wyduwe 7 hire sune ær forwyrt forþanþe hi drifon iserne stacan on Ælsie Wulfstanes feder· 7 þ werð æreafe 7 man teh þ morð forð of hire inclifan. þa nam man þ wif 7 adrencte hi æt Lundene brigce 7 hire sune ætberst 7 werð utlah 7 þ land eode þam kynge to handa 7 se kyng hit forgeaf þa Ælfsige 7 Wulfstan Uccea his sunu hit sealde eft Adeluuolde bisceope swa swa hit her bufan sægð

> The land at Ailsworth a widow and her son had forfeited because they drove an iron pin into [an image of] Ælfsige, Wulfstan's father, and it was discovered and one dragged the deadly image out of their closet. Then one took the woman and drowned her at London Bridge and her son escaped and became an outlaw and the land came into the possession of the king and the king then gave it to Ælfsige, and Wulfstan Uccea his son afterwards gave it to Bishop Æthelwold [§§186 and 262–3], as it says here above.

§250 Crosses and crucifixes embrace all the media used by the Anglo-Saxons. Wooden crosses must once have been a feature of the landscape. King Oswald of Northumbria was killed in battle by Penda in 642 (§183). Bede tells us how, on the eve of a previous battle (not recorded in the Anglo-Saxon Chronicle), Oswald raised a cross of wood on what was to be the battlefield:

> . . . 7 sona on morne· swa hit dagian ongan· þæt he for on þone here þe him togegnes gesomnad wæs 7 æfter geearnunge his geleafan þæt heo heora feond oferswiðdon 7 sige ahton. In þære gebedstowe æfter þon monig mægen 7 hælo tacen gefremed wæron to tacnunge 7 to gemynde þæs cyninges geleafan

... And in the morning, as soon as it began to dawn, [it happened] that he went against the army which was assembled against him and, in accordance with the earning/reward of his faith, [that] they overcame their enemies and won the victory. In that place of prayer after that, many miracles and signs of healing were done in token and in memory of the king's belief.

What may have been a painted wooden cross is mentioned in this extract from a description of the boundaries of a property: *to þæm gemærðornan· þ to ðære readan rode* 'to the boundary thorn-bush, then to the red cross'. (Traces of paint have also been found on stone sculptures and on many buildings, usually on a white plaster background.) Wooden crosses probably served also as meeting places and places of worship. But they were soon replaced by crosses of stone near which, in many places, churches were subsequently built; most of the nearly 1,300 Anglo-Saxon crosses which survive (complete or in fragments) in England alone, once stood in a churchyard. Many more must have been destroyed.

§251   An interesting account of stone crosses and their decorative motifs will be found in E. A. Fisher, *An Introduction to Anglo-Saxon Architecture and Sculpture*, with its monochrome plates 25–36. I acknowledge my debt for much of what follows. Types of crosses include those with straight arms; those with curved sides and ends so that they had the outline of axe-heads; and the wheel-head or Celtic crosses, either equal-arms (Greek) or with a long shaft and the head only in a circle (Latin). The shafts were usually rectangular but could be square, round, or even oval. The decorations include human figures, animals and birds, vine foliage with or without animals and birds, foliage interlace, geometrical interlace, and biblical scenes. Scandinavian influence is evident in sculpture in northern England. An outstanding example is the stone cross from Gosforth, Cumberland; see *AS Art*, pp. 142 and 150.

§252   Perhaps the most famous Anglo-Saxon cross is the stone Ruthwell Cross now preserved in the church at Ruthwell, Dumfriesshire. Over 17 feet high, carved and inscribed, probably dating from the first half of the eighth century, it was mutilated by Covenanters in the seventeenth century. What survives of the original cross-head bears on it the figure of St John with his eagle and a composition which must represent St Matthew with his man. The missing transom presumably bore the figures of St Mark with his lion and St Luke with his ox. The carvings on the north side include Christ the Judge, John the Baptist, and the Flight into Egypt. On the south can be seen Christ the Merciful healing the blind man, Christ with Mary Magdalen washing his feet, and the Annunciation (figure 13). These and the other scenes are accompanied by explanatory Latin inscriptions. The bottom panel on the north has been almost completely obliterated. It possibly represented the Nativity. The bottom panel on the south contains the Crucifixion; it too has been systematically obliterated. The narrower east and west sides of the shaft are decorated by a foliage scroll with birds and beasts pecking at or nibbling the

Figure 13   The Ruthwell Cross (Crown copyright Royal Commission on the Ancient and Historical Monuments of Scotland and Historic Scotland)

fruit (figure 13). They also contain runic passages which go back to the same original as the poem *The Dream of the Rood* or were used by the author of the poem; see §493. For monochrome plates of the Ruthwell Cross see *AS Art*, pp. 72–3, and *AS 1982*, p. 91. For the runes see ASPR VI pp. 114–15 and §493. Other important stone crosses include that which stands without its head in the churchyard at Bewcastle, Cumberland, and Acca's Cross, now in the Durham Cathedral Library. Monochrome plates of these two crosses will be found in *AS Art*, pp. 74–6, and *AS 1982*, pp. 89 and 91. The authoritative work is *The British Academy Corpus of Anglo-Saxon Stone Sculpture*, listed in the Bibliography.

§253   Turning now to stone crosses which carry the figure of Christ, I find myself most moved by the two crucifixion scenes at the church of Langford,

Figure 14   Church of St Matthew, Langford: the large rood (Crown copyright Royal Commission on the Historical Monuments of England)

Oxfordshire. These are doubly neglected in that (like many other Anglo-Saxon crosses) they stand without protection from the weather and in that they are not mentioned in many of the general works on the art of the period. They probably date from the first half of the eleventh century. The head is missing from the larger cross on the east side of the south porch (figure 14), which shows Christ Triumphant, standing as it were to attention, dressed in a clerical garment with finely carved detail on the cuffs and belt. The smaller rood above the entrance to the same porch (figure 15) portrays Christ Suffering, with head on one side and limbs contorted. The Virgin Mary and St John stand on His left and right respectively but the panels have apparently been moved and wrongly reassembled, for the two mourners are looking away from rather than towards Christ.

§254   It was Christ Triumphant, Christ in Majesty, the Warrior King of *The Dream of the Rood* (§493), who appealed to Anglo-Saxon warrior converts and continued to do so up to the tenth century. Christ Triumphant appears

Figure 15   Church of St Matthew, Langford: the small rood (Crown copyright RCHME)

in two roods in Romsey Abbey, Hampshire: in the large rood (figure 16), alone but with the *Dextra Dei* 'Right Hand of God' (§289) above His head, and in the smaller crucifixion panel, with a halo and accompanied by the Virgin Mary, St John, and two centurions. But the Benedictine reformers of the later tenth century (§186) were concerned with Christ Suffering and the

Figure 16   Romsey Abbey: the rood (Crown copyright RCHME)

first representations in manuscripts and in sculpture of the suffering and of the dead Christ date from this period. Christ Suffering, accompanied by the Virgin Mary and St John on the smaller Langford Rood (§253), is portrayed alone on a slab at Wormington, Gloucestershire. Monochrome plates 40 and 41 in *Fisher* show all these except the Wormington Slab.

§255   Among the passages which appear in both the runes of the Ruthwell Cross and in *The Dream of the Rood* are

> ... ic riicnæ kyninc
> ahof ic ricne cyning
>
> raised I [the] powerful king

and

ic wæs miþ blodæ bistemid

eall ic wæs mid blode bestemed

[all] I was with blood besteamed/made wet.

These lines in particular are alluded to in the inscription on the 18-inch high early eleventh-century reliquary cross of oak partly gilded with silver sheeting which is now in the Cathedral of St Michel in Brussels:

Rōd is mīn nama.   Gēo ic rīcne cyning

bær byfigynde,   blōde bestēmed

Rood is my name.   Once I [the] powerful king

bore trembling,   with blood besteamed.

§256 Cuthbert's magnificent gold and garnet pectoral cross is listed in §229. Other crosses or crucifixes of metal are mentioned in the wills, where bequests include *ænne sylfrene mele on fif pundon* 'a silver cross of five pounds'; *þære gyldenan rode* 'the gold cross'; *twegea gyldenra roda* 'two gold crosses'; and *ane litlene geldene rode* 'a little gold cross/crucifix'. Archbishop Ælfric (d. 1005) *becwæð Uulfstane ærcebiscope ane sweorrode 7 anne ring 7 anne psaltere 7 Alfheage biscope anne rode* 'bequeathed to Archbishop Wulfstan [§177.3] a pectoral cross and a ring and a psalter and to Bishop Ælfheah [murdered 1012; see §220] a crucifix'. Colour plates XXVI in *Golden Age* and 270 in *AS Art* show a crucifix some 7 inches high made of gold sheet and enamels on a wooden core bearing a walrus ivory figure of Christ with bent head but little distortion of the limbs.

§257 We learn of Anglo-Saxon ivories from J. G. Beckwith, *Ivory Carving in Early Medieval England*, who dates nine of the surviving ivories to before 800 (most of these are of elephant ivory) and the remaining forty or so (mostly of walrus ivory) to after 900. Surviving objects include St Cuthbert's comb (§262), seal matrices, a pen case, an oval box, a crozier head, and carvings of angels, the Nativity, the Baptism, and the Virgin Mary and St John the Evangelist. On these, see *AS 1982*, pp. 196–7, and colour plates XXIV, XXV, and XXVII, in *Golden Age* and 266–9 in *AS Art*.

§258 The Franks Casket, one of the chief treasures of Anglo-Saxon art in the British Museum, was carved of whalebone in the first half of the eighth century in northern England; see monochrome plate 56 in *AS 1981*. It measures 9 inches × 7.5 × 5.1 (22.9 cm × 18.9 × 12.9) and consists of five carved panels, one of which (the lid) is incomplete. The original of the right-hand side is in Florence. The four complete sides bear inscriptions, three in Old English carved in runes and one in Latin in mixed runes and insular script. All are concerned with the subjects of the carvings except one of the two in alliterative verse, which deals (as it were) with the medium:

Fisc flōdu ahōf   on fergenberig·
warþ gāsrīc grorn   þǣr hē on grēut giswom.
Hronæs bān

Flood/tide lifted fish onto cliffbank

OR

Fish splashed water onto cliffbank;
Whale became sad where he swam on grit/sand.
[This is] whale's bone.

One can sympathize even while reflecting that, if the whale had been able to swim away, there may not have been a Franks Casket.

§259 The incidents depicted are not all identifiable. But they show a remarkable and in a sense incongruous diversity, portraying as they do scenes from classical legend, from Germanic story, and from Jewish and Christian tradition. A selection of colour and monochrome plates will be found in *AS Art* (plates 34–7) and in *Making* (pp. 101–2). The left-hand side depicts the finding of the twins Romulus and Remus by four shepherds. The lid shows Egil the Archer defending his home against an attack by armed men. The carving on the front panel is divided into two parts; see figure 17. On the left is shown an episode from the adventures of Weland the Smith (§204). On the right, below a large star and the word MÆGI in runes, the three kings carry their gifts to the Virgin and Child. The rear panel shows the capture of Jerusalem in AD 70 by the Roman emperor Titus. The right-hand side has so far been regarded as depicting scenes from Germanic legend but these have never been satisfactorily identified. However, Heiner Eichner of Vienna has now suggested an association with the winged horse of Celtic legend. If accepted, this would mean that the Franks Casket embodied all the main influences on Anglo-Saxon art and culture – a very satisfying concept. The whole of the Casket is carved with what has been called 'barbaric abandon'. Any vacant places in the design are filled with foliage, round pellets, hammers, knots, and scrolls.

§260 In addition to the objects of ivory and the whalebone Franks Casket (§§257–9), a variety of objects made from horn and bone have survived, including sword-mounts, spearheads, buckles, bracelets, pendants, beads, combs, skates, flutes, and dice; as a poet says

Īdle hond ǣmetlan geneah tæfles monnes   þonne teoselum weorpeð

An idle hand contents the gambler when he throws the dice.

§261 By the nature of the material, few wooden objects survive from Anglo-Saxon times. Examples include the lyre and maplewood cups from Sutton Hoo – bequests in the wills include *twa treowenan gesplottude cuppan* 'two wooden cups ornamented with dots' and *hyre goldfagan treowenan cuppan* 'her gold-adorned wooden cup' – bowls and platters, combs and spoons,

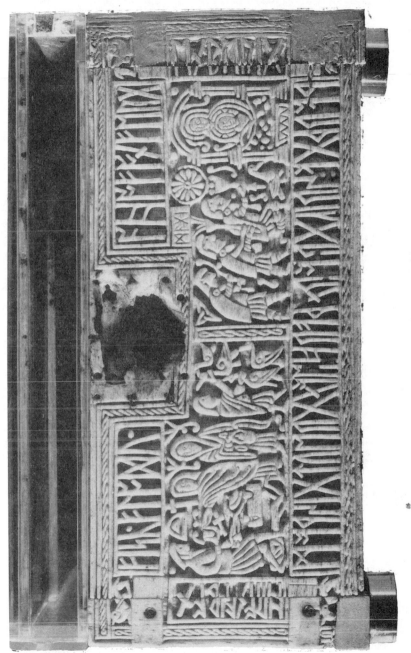

Figure 17   Franks Casket: the front panel (copyright British Museum)

and (from the Danish levels at York) a carved applewood and hawthorn flute. Buckets were made of staves bound with metal hoops. One charitable gift to a monastery includes *IIII scrinan* 'four chests'. St Cuthbert's portable altar of oak with silver plates is mentioned in §262. The gifts of Bishop Leofric to Exeter Cathedral (§174) include *I geboned altare* 'one decorated altar'.

§262 Perhaps of most interest to us is the late seventh-century oak coffin of St Cuthbert which (in David M. Wilson's words) 'is chiefly remarkable for its linear carving than for any technical details of carpentry'. The lid of the coffin has a carving of Christ haloed (figure 18) with the Evangelists' symbols above and below. One end carries the Virgin and Child, the other Michael and Gabriel. The Twelve Apostles appear on one side and five archangels on the other. The names which survive are carved mostly in Roman script but there are occasional runes. See monochrome plates 42–4 in *AS Art*. The coffin is worthy of note both as the only piece of decorated wood to survive from its period and for its contents – the skeleton of a man; a Gospel book removed from it in 1104 and now in the British Library; scissors, paten, and a chalice, recorded in 1104 but missing when the coffin was reopened in 1827; a pectoral cross (§229); an elephant ivory comb; a portable altar (§261); and textiles (§289). On these, see *AS 1982*, pp. 80–1.

§263 The coffin has an interesting history. It was probably made eleven years after Cuthbert's death, when the monks

> ontyndon his byrgenne 7 ealne his lichoman gemetton onwalhne 7 gesundne· swa swa he þa gena lifde· 7 he wæs begendlic in ðæm geðeodnessum leoða þæt he wæs myccle gelicra slæpendum menn þonne deadum
>
> opened his tomb and met/found all his body whole and sound, as if he still lived, and he was flexible in the joints of his limbs, so that he was much more like a sleeping man than a dead one.

Those of us whose limbs are not flexible eleven years before our death have cause for envy. But more adventures were in store. In *c.* 875 the Viking incursions caused the monks to leave Lindisfarne with the body of St Cuthbert in its wooden coffin protected by a hide-covered chest. In 883, having come to terms with their attackers, they settled in Chester-le-Street remaining there until 995, when they moved to Durham. In 1104 the body of St Cuthbert was translated to its final resting-place in the new Durham Cathedral. Here too is to be found Bede's tomb, with the doggerel inscription

Hac sunt in fossa	Here lie beneath the stones
Bedae venerabilis ossa	The Venerable Bede's bones.

Figure 18　St Cuthbert's coffin: the lid (copyright the Dean and Chapter of Durham)

These bones had been brought from Jarrow in the eleventh century – stolen one by one, so one story goes, by an enterprising monk alert to the attraction they would have for pilgrims. As a result tourists flocked to Durham during the Middle Ages, bringing wealth to a city whose charms were extolled in an

Anglo-Saxon poem written soon after what must have been magnificently
staged ceremonies of consecration in the newly built cathedral:

> Is ðēos burch brēome　　geond Breotenrīce,
> steppa gestaðolad,　　stānas ymbūtan
> wundrum gewæxen.　　Weor ymbeornad,
> ēa ȳðum stronge,　　and ðēr inne wunað
> 5 feola fisca kyn　　on flōda gemonge.
> And ðær gewexen is　　wudafæstern micel·
> wuniad in ðēm wȳcum　　wilda dēor monige,
> in dēope dalum　　dēora ungerīm.
> Is in ðēre bȳri ēac　　bearnum gecȳðed
> 10 ðe ārfesta　　ēadig Cudberch
> and ðes clēne　　cyninges hēafud,
> Osuualdes, Engle lēo,　　and Aidan biscop,
> Ēadberch and Ēadfrið,　　æðele gefēres.
> Is ðēr inne midd heom　　Æðelwold biscop
> 15 and brēoma bōcera Bēda　　and Boisil abbot
> ðe clēne Cudberte　　on gecheðe
> lērde lustum·　　and hē his lāra wel genom.
> Eardiæð æt ðēm ēadige　　in in ðēm minstre
> unarīmeda　　reliquia·
> 20 ðær monia wundrum gewurðað·　　ðēs ðe wrīt seggeð·
> midd ðene drihnes wer　　dōmes bīdeð.

Kevin Crossley-Holland kindly allows me to print his translation:

> All Britain knows of this noble city,
> its breathtaking site: buildings backed
> by rocky slopes peer over a precipice.
> Weirs hem and madden a headstrong river,
> diverse fish dance in the foam.
> A sprawling, tangled thicket has sprung up
> there; those deep dales are the haunt
> of many animals, countless wild beasts.
> In that city, too, as men know,
> lies the body of blessed Cuthbert,
> and the head of Oswald, innocent king,
> lion of the English; also Bishop Aidan
> and Eadberch and Eadfrith, eminent men.
> Æthelwold the Bishop sleeps beside them,
> and the great scholar Bede, and Abbot Boisil
> whose fortune it was first to teach the saint,
> then still a boy; Cuthbert excelled
> in his lessons. Innumerable relics are left

in the minster by the blessed man's tomb,
scene of many miracles, as documents say.
The man of God awaits Domesday.

§264 Stone sculptures other than crosses and the figures of Christ, the Virgin, St John, and others associated with them (§§250–5), include grave slabs; figures such as the angels in the church at Bradford-on-Avon, Wiltshire; ornamental sculptures like the friezes and figural slabs (human and animal) from Breedon on the Hill, Leicestershire, and the shrine tomb in Peterborough Cathedral known as Hedda's Stone; architectural decorations on churches; fonts of varying patterns and decoration, sometimes as at Melbury Bubb, Dorset, made from a piece of hollowed out cross-shaft; and some two dozen sundials, the best-known of which is probably that above the south porch of the church at Kirkdale, Yorkshire. Fisher provides monochrome plates of all the items mentioned (and of other examples) except the last, for which see that facing p. 192 of Hunter Blair's *An Introduction to Anglo-Saxon England* (§188).

§265 Miracles are often associated with stone objects. The sudden appearance of coffins which exactly fit the body of a dead saint awaiting burial was not uncommon. In the case of King Sebbe of East Anglia, divine intervention was required to rectify the human carelessness which made the coffin too short. In the case of Abbess Æthelthryth of Ely (§§235–6), those searching for stone from which to make a coffin were spared the labour by the discovery of a magnificent custom-made one:

þa eodon heo in scip forþon Elia lond is æghwonan mid wætrum 7 mid fennum ymbseald ne hit micele stanas hafað. þa cwomon heo to sumre ceastre gehrorenre noht feor þonon seo is on Englisc Grantacester geceged. 7 heo sona gemetton bi þære ceastre wallum þruh of hwitum stane fægere geworhte 7 seo wæs swilce eac gerisenlice gehleodad mid gelice stane

Then they set out in a boat, for the district of Ely is surrounded on all sides by waters and fens and it does not have large stones. Then they came to a ruined tower not far from there which in English is called Grant-chester. And at once they found by the walls a coffin beautifully made of white stone and it was also fitted with a suitable lid made of the same stone.

8 Stone buildings

§266 Roman remains were of course known to the Anglo-Saxons. Both *The Wanderer* and *The Ruin* speak of *enta geweorc* 'the work of giants'. Bede tells us that, when St Augustine came to Canterbury, there *wæs bi eastan þære ceastre welneah sumo cirice in are Scē Martini geo geara geworht mid þy Romani þa gyt*

Breotone beeodon 'was in the east close to the town a church built in honour of St Martin long ago when the Romans still occupied Britain'. He also relates how Augustine *edneowade 7 worhte mid cyninges fultome þa cirican þe he ær geara geo geleornade ealde Romanisce weorce geworhte beon* 'repaired and restored with the king's help the church which he learned had been constructed long ago of old Roman work'. This church has undergone many changes and it is difficult to reconstruct its history with any certainty. But it contains Roman brick and the Anglo-Saxon work in it is of two periods. The ancient Saxon church of St Peter at Bradwell-iuxta-Mare, Essex, built (according to Bede) by the Northumbrian missionary Cedd *c.* 653, contains masonry from the nearby Roman fort (monochrome plate *AS 1982*, p. 50). This and other churches in the south-east were the first stone churches built in the Anglo-Saxon period. Similar sturdy work is to be found in the stone churches built in the north in the late seventh century, though it was to masons and glaziers from Gaul that Benedict Biscop entrusted the building of churches when he founded the monasteries of Monkwearmouth in 674 and of Jarrow in 681. The late seventh- or early eighth-century church at Escomb, County Durham, is illustrated in figure 19.

§267 Some of these early churches were developed to meet new needs. One example is Winchester, on which see §186 and figures 21 and 22. For the later Anglo-Saxon churches, I refer you initially to Fisher, who classifies the architectural periods, with lists of churches which exemplify them (pp. 52–4), and provides many monochrome illustrations. For greater detail, see H. M. and Joan Taylor, *Anglo-Saxon Architecture* (3 vols; Cambridge, 1965–78). The church at Earl's Barton, the west tower of which dates from *c.* 1000, and Odda's Chapel at Deerhurst (between 1050 and 1100) are shown in figures 20 and 23. The existence of the latter was unsuspected until 1885 because it had been incorporated into a private dwelling. More illustrations will be found in *AS 1982*, pp. 83–9. Colour plate XXIX in *Golden Age* shows the churches at Breamore, Hampshire, and Bradford-on-Avon, Wiltshire (late tenth or early eleventh century). The late Anglo-Saxon tower at Langford carries the carvings shown in figures 14 and 15; see §§253–4. On the newly discovered remains of the cathedral at Canterbury, see §301.

§268 Stone was used mainly for churches. But excavations in Northampton in 1981–2 revealed a rectangular stone hall *c.* 123 feet by 38 feet (37.4 metres × 11.6), with two rooms subsequently added, increasing its length by some 20 feet (6.1 metres). Tentatively dated early in the eighth century, it seems to have directly replaced a seventh-century timber hall and possibly decayed or was demolished during the Danish occupation of Northampton in the late ninth and early tenth centuries. By the end of the Anglo-Saxon period, there were royal palaces of stone at Westminster and Old Windsor.

Figure 19   Church of St John the Evangelist, Escomb (Crown copyright RCHME)

Figure 20   All Saints' Church, Earl's Barton (Crown copyright RCHME)

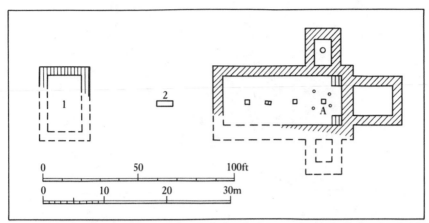

A, seating for altar in nave of four-cell church; 1, detached tower archaeologically dated to eighth century; 2, original burial place of St Swithun.

Figure 21   Winchester, Old Minster: the earliest buildings (from H. M. Taylor, *Anglo-Saxon Architecture*, vol. III, 1978; Cambridge University Press)

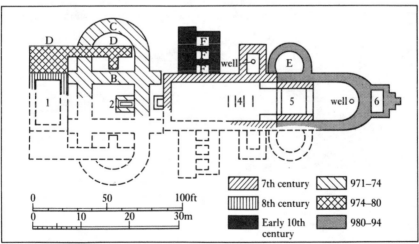

1, tower of St Martin; 2, shrine of St Swithun over original burial place; 4, steps up to high altar; 5, Alphege's new crypt; 6, exterior eastern crypt; B and C, straight and curved sides of great foundation of rammed chalk; D, later foundation for westwork; E, apsidal lateral porticus; F, family of transeptal chapels.

Figure 22   Winchester, Old Minster: the fully developed church (from H. M. Taylor, *Anglo-Saxon Architecture*, vol. III, 1978; Cambridge University Press)

Figure 23   Odda's Chapel, Deerhurst (Crown copyright RCHME)

9 Timber buildings

§269 In §130 we read of the man *se hys hus ofer stan getimbrode* 'who timbered/built his house on stone'. As a result it survived a great storm. Not surprisingly, however, few Anglo-Saxon timber buildings still stand. The church at Greenstead, Essex, where (according to tradition) the body of King Edmund of East Anglia rested in 1013 on its way from London to Bury St Edmunds, is an example but its timbers may not date back to Anglo-Saxon times. Archaeologists have given us much information; see *Archaeology*, pp. 49–98 and *Making*, pp. 68–70. Here I reproduce as figure 24 a plan

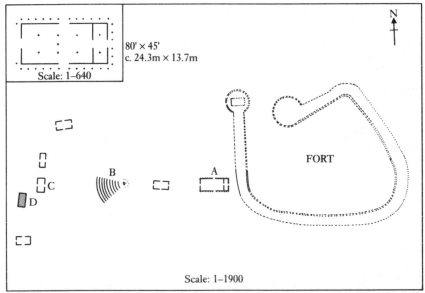

A. Hall; B. Timber 'Amphitheatre'; C. Possibly a Pagan Temple converted to Christian use; D. Building with a sunken floor. The inset shows the Timber Hall (A) to a larger scale.

Figure 24   Plan of Yeavering, Northumberland, in the time of King Edwin (616–32) (from R. Allen Brown, H. M. Colvin and A. J. Taylor, *The History of the King's Works*, vol. I *The Middle Ages*, 1963; reproduced with the permission of the Controller of Her Majesty's Stationery Office)

of the timber fort and township at Yeavering, Northumberland, in the time of King Edwin (killed in 632). Figures 25 and 26 show a plan and a reconstruction of the royal residence at Cheddar in Somerset in the time of King Alfred when it consisted of a two-storey hall and three smaller buildings, the largest of which is probably a *bur* 'sleeping chamber'. The miraculous deliverance of Dunstan related in the Laud Chronicle for 978 provides evidence for the existence of buildings with two storeys:

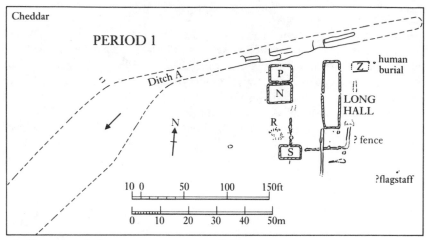

A Stormwater ditch
N Possibly a *bur*
P A building later than, and
   possibly a replacement for, N

R Entrance
S Possibly a gatehouse
Z An unidentified structure
LONG HALL probably two storeys
Isolated pits or post-holes

Figure 25   Plan of Cheddar, Somerset, Period 1: pre-*c.* 930 (copyright Philip Rahtz)

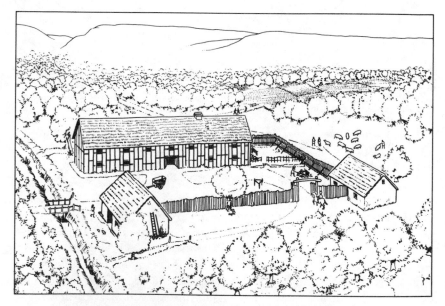

Figure 26   Reconstruction of figure 25 (after Rahtz)

978 Her on þissum geare ealle þa yldestan Angelcynnes witan gefeol-
lan æt Calne of anre upfloran butan se halga Dunstan arcebiscop ana
ætstod uppon anum beame. 7 sume þær swiðe gebrocode wæron 7 sume
hit ne gedygdan mid þam life

978 Here in this year all the most senior counsellors of England fell
from an upper room at Calne, except that the holy archbishop Dunstan
stood alone on a beam. And some were seriously injured and some did not
survive it with their life.

§270   The discoveries at Yeavering and Cheddar and the poem *Beowulf*
throw light on one another and on other recorded events; see *BArch*, pp. 68–
77. The hall at Yeavering had twice been destroyed by fire. The hall Heorot
in *Beowulf*

>   . . . þæs fæste wæs
> innan ond ūtan   īrenbendum
> 775 searoþoncum besmiþod

was made firm enough, inside and outside, by iron clamps, cunningly
forged;

> 81   sele hlīfade
> hēah ond horngēap

the hall towered, high and wide gabled;

but

> 82   heaðowylma bād
> lāðan līges

[it] awaited the hostile surges of hateful fire.

Both it and Beowulf's own hall were eventually destroyed by fire. The royal
quarters (*bur*) in Edwin's seventh-century Yeavering (§269) were attached to
the hall. Those at Cheddar and at Heorot were in a separate building. Such
separation also obtained at King Cynewulf's love-nest and had serious consequences for him, for he was surprised and killed by his enemies before his
warriors could run from the hall to rescue him; see §183 n. 27.

§271   The vast majority of monastic and almost all secular buildings
were of wood. The early churches too were built of wood. The timber nave
of St Andrew's Church, Greenstead, Essex (§269), built after *c.* 950, is the
only remaining example of an Anglo-Saxon wooden church. But see §269.
Long before this, however, stone churches were in existence; Wilfrid built
those at Ripon and Hexham in the 670s. But even when churches were
being built of stone (§§266–8), the skills of the carpenter and joiner were
still needed alongside those of the mason.

§272   Archaeologists have also excavated smaller buildings of timber
planking or wattle and daub, with floors of earth, gravel, or flint, and roofs of

thatch, turf, or (possibly) shingles. Some of these had porches and hearths and served as homes. Smaller ones, some with sunken features, were used by weavers, potters, bakers, and other craftsmen, as workshops and sometimes probably as dwellings. Others may have served for storage or as animal pens. Large planned villages with such houses have been found for example at Heslerton, Yorkshire.

10 Ships

§273 While great ship-burials like that at Sutton Hoo (§§194–9) were rare events, ships played a prominent part in Anglo-Saxon life. The early Germanic settlers made the short sea-crossings to their new home and probed their way up the rivers in rowing boats. Fishermen used small boats of wood and skin. Oar-propelled vessels were very manoeuvrable in sea fights. But sails had obvious advantages for long trading journeys. Archaeological finds and surviving documents have thrown much light on these topics. But they can receive only passing mention here.

§274 Without allowing us to distinguish them, the vocabulary of the poetry confirms the self-evident fact that there were different types of ships. Apart from poetic compounds which describe their appearance (*hringed-stefna* 'ringed prow' and *wudu wundenhals* 'curved-neck wood') or their function (*sægenga* 'sea-goer' and *yŏlida* 'wave-traverser') and words like *flota* 'floater' and *lid* 'traveller', we find *æsc, ceol, cnearr, naca, scip*, and *scrad*. Dendrochronology (tree-ring dating) has placed the clinker-built rowing boat found at Graveney, Kent, within a year or two of AD 895.

§275 The vessel buried at Sutton Hoo was a rowing boat and shows no traces of a mast, although some reconstructions show it under sail. No sailing ships survive from the seventh century in England or on the Continent; as the poet ruefully observed, *werig scealc wiþ winde roweþ* 'a weary man rows against the wind'. But by the eighth century, sailing ships were used in northern waters, with the oar secondary. P. H. Sawyer has argued that sailing ships were developed in the Baltic and Scandinavia to cope with the increasing trade with western Europe and the Mediterranean and to control the menace of piracy, and sees 'the key to the Viking age' in the development of remarkable ships like the Gokstad ship excavated on the west side of Oslo Fjord in 1880 (figure 27). This was a top-ranking sailing vessel well equipped for heavy seas; a replica crossed the Atlantic in twenty-eight days in 1893. Made of oak, it was 76 feet (23.1 metres) long and had a strong mast and sail, sixteen pairs of oars, a solid rudder on the starboard side, a shield rack, and floor boards which were movable for stowage. Without any carving or decoration, it was a sturdy vessel, serviceable for long or short trips, for trading or raiding. It was built in the middle of the ninth century, when Viking raids were beginning in grim earnest and vessels

Figure 27   The Gokstad ship (copyright University Museum of National Antiquities, Oslo, Norway)

like it brought terror, destruction, and death, to many an English community.

§276 The Anglo-Saxon Chronicle (Parker MS, annal 896) tells how King Alfred designed his own ships:

> þa het Ælfred cyng timbran langscipu ongen ða æscas. þa wæron fulneah tu swa lange swa þa oðru. Sume hæfdon lx ara, sume ma. þa wæron ægðer ge swiftran ge unwealtran ge eac hieran þonne þa oðru· næron nawðer ne on fresisc gescæpene ne on denisc bute swa him selfum ðuhte þæt hie nytwyrðoste beon meahten

> Then King Alfred ordered [his men] to build longships against Danish ships of ashwood. They were nearly twice as long as the others. Some had sixty oars, some more. They were both swifter and steadier and also higher than the others. They were neither in the Frisian shape nor in the Danish but as it seemed to him personally that they might be most serviceable.

Perhaps he would have done better to stick to the model used by the Danes or by his allies the Frisians because, as the same annal relates, his ships went aground in their first sea-battle. But this was another symptom of the enquiring mind which led Alfred to welcome new knowledge from a variety of sources, as Texts 22–4 (§§430–2) testify.

§277 Roger Smith argued in 1990 that the fact that the ships described in *Beowulf* are all sailing ships dates the poem in the ninth or tenth century because 'according to archaeologists and historians, the Scandinavians did not convert from oar power to sail power until after 700 . . . and the Anglo-Saxons until after 800'. But some archaeologists at least are unwilling to commit themselves to the proposition that sails were unknown in eighth-century England. So it remains uncertain when the *Beowulf* poet composed this picture of a sea voyage, which I analyse in §464. (For a facsimile of the manuscript of this passage, see figure 33.)

Text 13   **Beowulf's voyage**

210 Fyrst forð gewāt·   flota wæs on ȳðum,
    bāt under beorge.   Beornas gearwe
    on stefn stigon·   strēamas wundon,
    sund wið sande·   secgas bæron
    on bearm nacan   beorhte frætwe,

210 **fyrst** 'time'; **flota** 'floater/ship'; **ȳð** 'wave'.
211 **bāt** 'boat'; **beorg** 'cliff'; **beorn** 'warrior'; **gearu** adj. 'ready/eager'.
212 **stefn** 'prow'; **stigan** 'to ascend/mount' (st. vb. I §517); **windan** 'curl/eddy' (st. vb. III §518).
213 **sund** 'sea/water'; **secg** 'men'; **beran** 'to carry' (st. vb. IV §517).
214 **naca** 'ship'; **frætwe** 'decorated armour or trappings'.

215 guðsearo geatolic·   guman ūt scufon,
    weras on wilsīð   wudu bundenne.
    Gewāt þā ofer wægholm   winde gefȳsed
    flota fāmīheals   fugle gelīcost
    oð þæt ymb āntīd   ōþres dōgores
220 wundenstefna   gewaden hæfde
    þæt ðā līðende   land gesāwon,
    brimclifu blīcan,   beorgas stēape,
    sīde sænæssas·   þā wæs sund liden
    eoletes æt ende.   þanon up hraðe
225 Wedera lēode   on wang stigon·
    sæwudu sældon·   syrcan hrysedon,
    gūðgewædo·   Gode þancedon
    þæs þe him ȳþlāde   ēaðe wurdon.

215 **gūðsearo** 'armour'; **geatolic** adj. 'splendid'; **scūfan** 'to shove/push' (st. vb. II §517).
216 **wilsīð** 'wished-for journey'; **bunden** past ptc. 'bound/properly joined'.
217 **wægholm** 'sea/ocean'; **(ge)fȳsan** 'to send forth/drive' (wk. vb. like *hīeran* §94).
218 **fāmīhēals** 'foamy-necked'; **fugol** 'bird'; **gelīc** adj. 'like'.
219 **oð þæt** conj. 'until'; **āntīd** 'expected time'; **ōþer** adj. 'next'; **dōgor** 'day'.
220 **wundenstefna** 'curved prow'; **wadan** 'to go/advance' (st. vb. VI §517).
221 **līðende** 'voyagers'.
222 **brimclif** 'sea cliff'; **blīcan** 'to shine/gleam' (st. vb. I §517); **beorg** 'hill'.
223 **sænæss** 'headland'; **līðan** 'to journey (over)/traverse' (st. vb. I §517).
224 **eolet** 'voyage'; **þanon** adv. 'thence'; **hraðe** adv. 'quickly'.
225 **Wederas**, another name for Beowulf's tribe *Gēatas* 'Geats'; **lēode** 'people'; **wang** 'land'.
226 **sǣlan** 'to make fast/moor' (like *(ge)fȳsan* l. 217); **syrce** 'mail coat', here acc. pl.; **hryssan**
'to shake' (wk. vb. like *fremman* §524), here with unexpressed subject.
227 **gūðgewǣdo** 'war-dress'.
228 **þæs þe** conj. 'for that namely/because'; **ȳþlāde** 'wave-paths'; **ēaðe** adj. 'easy'.

For details of an edition of this poem see §465.

11 Pottery

§278   No Anglo-Saxon poet felt moved to address an urn as Keats did:

> Thou still unravish'd bride of quietness,
> Thou foster-child of silence and slow time,
> Sylvan historian, who canst thus express
> A flowery tale more sweetly than our rhyme.

Yet Anglo-Saxon pots have things to tell us. According to some scholars, some pots reveal that they were brought to Britain by Anglo-Saxon mercenaries before AD 449 (§182), perhaps even during the last years of the Roman occupation; on this see §307. These pots were rough hand-made wares. But J. G. Hurst (*Archaeology* p. 283) tells us that Romano-British potters supplied special Romano-Saxon pottery, made on a fast wheel and produced on an industrial scale in kilns, for the newcomers. But this art was lost with the collapse of Roman Britain. Only hand-made pottery was produced until the middle of the seventh century, when pottery made on a slow wheel was introduced into East Anglia and Northumbria. This spread slowly into other parts of England and both wheel-thrown and hand-made pottery were produced until the middle of the twelfth century. Some of it was influenced by imports from the Continent including France and Germany. Colour plates will be found in *AS Art* (plates 208–10) and *Golden Age* (plate XXII). Figure 28 shows a selection of pottery from the Ashmolean Museum, Oxford.

§279 Another striking illustration of pottery in the role of historian is the light it throws on the account of the invasions given by another historian. The translator of Bede wrote thus about the newcomers to Britain (*Historia ecclesiastica* I. 15):

> Comon hi of þrim folcum ðam strangestan Germanie· þæt of Seaxum 7 of Angle 7 of Geatum. Of Geata fruman syndon Cantware 7 Wihtsætan· þæt is seo ðeod þe Wiht þæt ealond oneardað. Of Seaxum· þæt is of ðam lande þe mon hateð Ealdseaxan· coman Eastseaxan 7 Suðseaxan 7 Westseaxan. And of Engle coman Eastengle 7 Middelengle 7 Myrce 7 eall Norðhembra cynn· is þæt land ðe Angulus is nemned· betwyh Geatum 7 Seaxum

> They came from the three strongest races of Germany, namely from Saxons and from Angles and from Jutes. Of Jutish origin are the men of Kent and the Wihtsætan, that is the tribe which dwells in the Isle of Wight. From the Saxons, that is from the land which is called Old Saxon, come the East Saxons, the South Saxons, and the West Saxons. And from Angle came the East Angles and the Middle Angles and the Mercians and the whole race of the Northumbrians; that is the land which is called Angulus, between the Jutes and the Saxons.

In 1969 J. N. L. Myres argued that his study of Anglo-Saxon pottery of the pagan period gave support to Bede's account. But subsequent research suggests that the material evidence is too complex to allow us to believe in a clear-cut theory of ethnic origins; there were, for example, Franks in Kent, Sussex, and the Upper Thames area. It now seems more likely that Bede oversimplified conditions in the fifth and sixth centuries by portraying the process as one of separate tribal settlement in well-defined areas. The Germanic tribes had been mixed on the Continent before they arrived. So there could well have been a mixed Anglian and Saxon culture in those areas described by Bede as Anglian, and pottery such as that in the Sutton Hoo find suggests the possibility of Scandinavian participation in the early settlement of England, a possibility which is supported by Bede's mention of *Dene* 'Danes' (or perhaps 'the people of southern Scandinavia') in Book V chapter 9 of his history and by other archaeological evidence. However,

1 and 3   Domestic pottery from Sutton Courtenay, Oxfordshire (in King Alfred's days Berkshire)
2   Cinerary urn with stamped decoration

Figure 28   Anglo-Saxon pottery (copyright Ashmolean Museum)

some archaeologists are perhaps too dismissive of Bede. Thus Sonia Hawkes (private communication, 1993) argues that 'Bede's informants must have meant that the ruling classes in their respective regions were Jutes, Angles and Saxons, and I see no reason whatever to reject that: the archaeology backs it up in the most satisfactory way.'

§280 The excavated pottery includes jars, bowls, beakers, pitchers, lamps, cooking and storage pots, and funerary urns. A long list of requirements which the wise reeve mentioned in §246 is advised to have available includes *hwer* 'a pot', *pannan* 'pans', *crocca* 'a crock', *hunigbinna* 'a vessel for honey', *beodas* 'bowls', *cuppan* 'cups', *candelstafas* 'candlesticks', *sealtfæt* 'a salt holder', *leohtfæt* 'a lamp', and *sapbox* 'a soap-box'. Like their modern equivalents, some of these objects could be made of either metal or pottery; see §§246–7. So we cannot be sure about the *panne* in the recipe for an eye ointment which begins *nim buteran· wyl on pannan . . .* 'take butter, boil [it] in a pan . . .' or about the *hweras* and *pannan* which played a less conventional role when they saved the three virgin sisters St Agape, St Chionia, and St Irene, from defilement by a lustful intruder:

> þær wæron inne geseted hweras ond pannan· ond he þa þurh godes miht wæs oncierred fram þæm fæmnum ond clypte þa hweras ond cyste þa pannan þæt he wæs eall sweart ond behrumig· ond þa he ut eode· þa flugon hine his agene mæn ond wendon þæt hit wære *larbo·* þæt is egesgrima

> There were pots and pans placed inside and by the power of God he was then turned away from the virgins and embraced the pots and kissed the pans so that he was all black and sooty. And when he came outside, his own men fled from him and thought that it was *larbo*, that is a ghost.

12 Glass

§281 Benedict Biscop, founder of the twin monasteries of Monkwearmouth (674) and Jarrow (681), imported glaziers from Gaul but both the plain and the coloured glass for the windows was almost certainly manufactured locally; for a conjectural reconstruction in colour, see *AS 1982*, p. 73. Glass vessels were probably made in Kent in the seventh century but not much late Anglo-Saxon glass has been found. Imports from France and the Rhineland account for much of what survives.

§282 One of the Blickling Homilies includes these words in a description of a church in which there are

> ehta eagþyrelu swiþe mycele of glæse geworht 7 æt æghwylcum anum þara hongaþ leohtfæt 7 þa beoð simle mid ele gefylde 7 æghwylce niht byrnaþ 7 to þon leohte 7 beorhte scinaþ ælce niht þurh þa eagþyrelo . . .

eight windows, very large, made of glass, and at each one there hangs a lamp and they are always filled with oil and burn all night and [they] shine very light and bright each night through the windows.

Elsewhere we read of *glæsene leohtfatu in þam gebedhuse* 'glass lamps in the chapel'.

§283   Apart from windows and lamps, glass was mainly used for tableware and containers; see figure 29. We read of *lytel ele in anum glæsenum fæte* 'a little oil in a glass vessel', *ele . . . in anre glæsenan anpollan* 'oil in a glass ampulla', and of *glæs ful wines* 'a glass full of wine'. More sinister are references to *þæt glæsfæt* 'a glass' containing *attor wið wine* 'poison with wine' and to a servant who *stod feorran mid anum glæsenum fæte on ðam wæs wines drenc mid þam cwealmbærum attre gemenged* 'stood at a distance with a glass vessel in which there was a drink of wine mixed with the deadly poison'. Medicines

Figure 29   Anglo-Saxon glassware (copyright Eva Wilson)

were often made *in glasfate* 'in a glass vessel'. Ointments were even made with glass:

> Wiþ fice . . . sealf· cnua glæs to duste· do huniges tear· onlacna þ dolg wið

> An ointment against hæmorrhoids: pound glass to dust, add a drop of honey, dress the wound with [it].

§284　Ælfric tells of a magician in Milan who had in a secret room *an wurðlic weorc on mechanisc geworht of glæse and of golde and of glitniendan cristallan* 'a valuable mechanical device made of glass and gold and shining crystal' designed to foretell the future. More conventional uses of glass for beads and other jewellery are attested by archaeological finds. The literature contains several comparisons with glass. Both the sea and ice are described as *glæshlutor* 'clear as glass'. The beak of the phoenix *lixeð swa glæs oððe gim* 'shines like glass or gem'. The body of a dead saint appeared *beorhtre þonne glæs* 'brighter than glass'. And the poet of *Christ* tells us that on the Day of Judgement

> 　　　　　　　　　　　　Bēoð þā syngan flæsc
> scandum þurhwaden　　swā þæt scīre glæs
> þæt mon ȳþæst mæg　　eall þurhwlītan

the sinful flesh shall be shamefully penetrated like bright glass which one can most easily see right through.

13　Textiles

§285　Wool, linen, silk, and dyes, were all used by the Anglo-Saxons. The merchant sailor of Ælfric's *Colloquy* (§246) includes among the things he brings back to England from Europe and beyond *pællas 7 sidan, deorwyrþe gymmas 7 gold, selcuþe reaf 7 wyrtgemangc, win 7 ele, ylpesban 7 mæstlingc, ær 7 tin, swefel 7 glæs* 'purple garments and silk, precious gems and gold, rare garments and mixtures of herbs, spices, perfumes, wine and oil, ivory and brass, copper and tin, sulphur and glass'. Wool would have been prominent among his exports if he had mentioned them. Some easily recognizable words appear in Anglo-Saxon documents concerned with *claþas* 'clothes': *bænde* 'head-band', *belt*, *brec* 'breeches', *cappa*, *cyrtel*, *glof*, *gyrdels*, *hær-nædl* 'hair-pin', *hæt*, *hosa*, *mentel* 'cloak', *scyrte* 'tunic', *scoh*, *smoc*, *socc*, *tunece*, and *wimpel*. But, as the word *scrud*, meaning not 'shroud' but 'a garment' or 'clothes for both sexes', warns us, the articles these words referred to often differed in form from those of today. Bequests include *hyre twilibrocenan cyrtel 7 oþerne linnenne* 'her gown woven of threads of two colours and another linen [gown]', *ane wellene kertel* 'a woollen gown', *anre crusnan* 'a fur robe', *on hakele* 'a cloak', and *anes wifscrudes ealles* 'a complete set of women's garments'. In the haunting *Riddle* 7 in the Exeter Book, the swan says of its wings that *hrægl min swigað* 'my dress is silent' when at rest but in flight *mec* *ahebbað . . . hyrste mine* 'my outer garment/trappings lift me up' and *frætwe mine . . . torhte singað* 'my ornaments . . . sing clearly'.

§286 The gifts of Bishop Æthelwold to Peterborough listed in §248 included ecclesiastical vestments and furnishings. Bishop Leofric (§174), who found at his accession only *I wac mæssereaf* 'one poor mass vestment', gave to Exeter Cathedral *V fulle mæssereaf 7 IIII subdiacones handlin 7 III cantercæppa 7 V pællene weofodsceatas 7 II tæppedu* 'five complete mass vestments and four sub-deacon's maniples and three cantor's copes and five altar cloths of costly material, and two carpets'. In a will dated *c.* 950 Wynflæd, who may have been a lay abbess or a widow who had taken a vow of chastity, left *Ceoldryþe hyre blacena tunecena swa þer hyre leofre beo 7 hyre betsð haliryft 7 hyre betsþan bindan* 'to Ceoldryth whichever of her black tunics is more pleasing to her and her best holy veil and her best headband'. Bishop Ælfric of East Anglia (d. 1038) left *fif pund Ælffæh min sæmestre* 'five pounds to Ælffæh my tailor'. Bishop Theodred of London (d. 951) did not remember his tailor but his will mentions *to beste messehaclen þe ic habbe . . . min wite massehakele þe ic on Pauie bouhte . . . þere gewele massehakele þe ic on Pauie bouhte . . . þer oþer gewele massehakele þat is ungerenad 7 . . . þe rede messehacle* 'the two best chasubles which I have . . . my white chasuble which I bought in Pavia . . . the yellow chasuble which I bought in Pavia . . . the other yellow chasuble which is unadorned and . . . the red chasuble'.

§287 A few scraps of wool decorated with coloured embroidery have been found in Anglo-Saxon graves and some embroideries in the ninth-century Viking ship-burial at Oseberg in Norway have been identified as Anglo-Saxon. Tapestries are mentioned in charters and wills: *an lang healwahrift 7 oþer sceort* 'a long hall tapestry and a short one', *anes beddreafes mid wahryfte 7 mid hoppscytan* 'a set of bedclothes with tapestry and curtain', *anes heallwahriftes 7 anes beddreafes* 'a hall tapestry and a set of bedclothes', and *anes heallreafes 7 anes burreafes mid beodreafe 7 mid eallum hræglum swa ðerto gebyreð* 'a tapestry for a hall and a tapestry for a chamber, with a table cover and with all the cloths which go with it'. Another bequest includes *an hræglcysð 7 an lytulu towmyderce* 'a clothes' chest and a little spinning-box'. A web and weaver's loom is the subject of *Riddle* 56 in the Exeter Book, and the *Beowulf* poet speaks of tapestries:

> Đā wæs hāten hreþe   Heort innanweard
> folmum gefrætwod·   fela þæra wæs,
> wera ond wīfa,   þe þæt wīnreced,
> gestsele gyredon.   Goldfāg scinon
> 995 web æfter wāgum,   wundorsīona fela
> secga gehwylcum   þāra þe on swylc starað

Then was quickly ordered Heorot within [to be] made beautiful by hands; many were those, men and women, who adorned the wine-building, the guest hall. Gold-ornamented, the tapestries gleamed on the walls, many wondrous sights for every man who gazes on such [things].

§288 Unfortunately, no Anglo-Saxon tapestries survive. But, against all the odds, we have three examples of needlework. The earliest are the embroideries now preserved in the church of St Catherine at Maaseik in Belgium. These form part of what is known as the *casula* (probably 'chasuble') of Sts Harlindis and Relindis. They are now roughly rectangular in shape, having been resewn several times, and measure *c.* 34.2 in × 22.6 in (87 cm × 57.5 cm), with patterns of foliate, animal, geometric, and interlace, ornament worked in gold and silk on a linen backing. Traditionally dated ninth century, they are the earliest surviving example of what became famous as *opus anglicanum*. Plates 107–9 in *AS Art* offer colour illustrations.

§289 The Maaseik embroideries are earlier by perhaps a hundred years than the stole, maniple, and girdle, which are now among the relics of St Cuthbert at Durham. These were made to the order of Queen Ælfflæd (d. 916) for Frithestan, who became Bishop of Winchester in 909, and were subsequently presented by King Æthelstan to the Community of St Cuthbert in 934. Worked with coloured silks and gold thread on a whitish silk background, they portray various prophets, deacons, popes, and saints, the Lamb of God, the *Dextra Dei* (§254; figure 30), with landscapes and animal and foliate ornament, and are, in the words of one authority, 'in the front rank of embroidery in any period'. For colour illustrations see *Golden Age* plate III, *AS Art* plates 205–7, and *AS 1982* p. 178.

§290 The so-called Bayeux Tapestry was not woven but was embroidered in coloured wools on a plain linen background by Anglo-Saxon needlewomen soon after the Norman Conquest, probably in Canterbury under the patronage of Odo, Bishop of Bayeux, half-brother to William the Conqueror. What survives – the original right-hand end has been lost – measures *c.* 231 feet × 19.5 in (70 metres × 50 cm) and depicts the events leading up to the defeat of King Harold at Hastings. The animated scenes are accompanied by explanations in Latin and are set within a border which is sometimes decorative, sometimes narrative. Several coloured reproductions are available, including *The Bayeux Tapestry* (London, 1985) by D. M. Wilson. Although produced by Anglo-Saxon needlewomen, it is (in Wilson's words) 'the most extraordinary propaganda document of Norman history', chronicling as it does the end of over six hundred years of Anglo-Saxon domination of England; as the Laud Manuscript of the Chronicle puts it:

> *7 Willelm þis land geeode*
> and William conquered this land.

Figure 30 St Cuthbert's maniple: detail, centre front (copyright the Dean and Chapter of Durham)

14 Manuscripts

§291   The answer to Exeter Book *Riddle* 51, quoted here in the original and in Kevin Crossley-Holland's translation, is Pen and Three Fingers:

> Ic seah wrætlice   wuhte fēower
> samed sīþian·   swearte wǣran lāstas,
> swaþu swīþe blacu.   Swift wæs on fōre,
> fuglum framra·   flēag on lyfte,
> dēaf under ȳþe.   Drēag unstille
> winnende wiga   se him wegas tǣcneþ
> ofer fǣted gold   fēower eallum

> I watched four curious creatures
> travelling together; their tracks were swart,
> each imprint very black. The bird's support
> moved swiftly; it flew in the air,
> dived under the wave. The toiling warrior
> worked without pause, pointing the paths
> to all four over the beaten gold.

(As gold letters on purple parchment were used for de luxe manuscripts, the phrase *ofer fæted gold* may refer to what has already been written or to gold in some form of decoration such as an elaborate capital letter. But Craig Williamson quotes a ninth-century manuscript which describes the gilding of a parchment skin. So it may mean that the scribe was writing on gilded parchment. However, no such manuscript is known. Here the riddler is still ahead of us.) We shall see in Part IV that Anglo-Saxon scribes and illuminators toiled mightily and to good effect.

§292   The ability to write was largely but not completely restricted to those in the church. Here Michelle Brown (Bibliography III C) makes a fascinating point:

> It should be recognized that, in a period when book production was a manual activity, 'literacy' might not necessarily entail the ability to write; works might be dictated to a competent scribe, even by notable scholars of the later Middle Ages. This is perhaps akin to modern computer literacy: those who can digest the written word, or even compose texts, might not personally possess the ability to use the technology for generating formal writing themselves, or might do so merely in a limited fashion.

The scripts most frequently used by Anglo-Saxon scribes were varieties of minuscule (a script in which some of the letters are taller and some longer than others; compare lower-case *a*, *b*, *f*, and *g*). Two different examples appear in the *Beowulf* manuscript; see §299. In the second half of the tenth century, scribes often used two alphabets, one for Latin and one for Old

English, in the same manuscript; see §298. Later they used different shapes of *a d e f g h r* and *s* when copying Old English. For another example of minuscule and for examples of other scripts, see §296.

§293 Almost one thousand volumes, embracing both ecclesiastical and secular writings, survive from pre-Conquest England. Most of these are in Latin. More than half the manuscripts which contain Old English are Latin manuscripts with interlinear glosses or with brief records or notes in Old English. Fewer than 150 are written entirely or mainly in Old English. Even so, what survives constitutes the most extensive vernacular literature of the early Middle Ages. For details of the literature see §§169–78 and, for the manuscripts, N. R. Ker *Catalogue of Manuscripts Containing Anglo-Saxon*. On the making of manuscripts, see Christopher de Hamel, *Medieval Craftsmen: Scribes and Illuminators* and, for the Lindisfarne Gospels, Backhouse (§296), pp. 27–32.

§294 The illuminated manuscripts produced in Ireland and England from the seventh to the eleventh centuries were unrivalled and had a power-ful influence on Continental scribes and artists. A most valuable introduc-tion is Michelle P. Brown *Anglo-Saxon Manuscripts*. The manuscripts can be studied in more detail in the first two volumes of *A Survey of Manuscripts Illuminated in the British Isles*. Volume I *Insular Manuscripts 6th to the 9th Century* by J. J. G. Alexander selects seventy-eight items, including the Book of Durrow, the Lindisfarne Gospels (§§295 and 296–7), the Codex Amiatinus (§295), and the Book of Kells. Volume II *Anglo-Saxon Manuscripts 900–1066* by Elżbieta Temple lists the important manuscripts surviving from that period. They number 106 and include Old English metrical paraphrases of biblical texts (Bodleian MS Junius 11) (§173) and Ælfric's Pentateuch and Joshua (Cotton Claudius B.iv). Colour plates will be found in the three volumes mentioned above, in *AS Art*, in *AS 1982*, and in *Making*.

§295 It is remarkable that so much has survived. Time itself is a great destroyer. The Codex Amiatinus, the oldest extant manuscript of the complete Latin Vulgate, now in Florence, is the only survivor (apart from a few odd pages which had been used as book bindings or wrappers for estate-papers) of the three bibles commissioned by Abbot Ceolfrith for the monasteries of Jarrow and Monkwearmouth and for the Pope. It was written on vellum from the skins of some 550 calves in the scriptorium of the Wearmouth-Jarrow monasteries before 716 when Bede's teacher Abbot Ceolfrith retired and set out with it for Rome, which he never reached because he died on the way. Many other manuscripts must have dis-appeared, unlike that containing the Lindisfarne Gospels (§§296–7), which, according to legend, was lost during a storm at sea and found only because St Cuthbert appeared in a dream to one of the searchers and revealed to him the place where the manuscript lay, washed up unharmed on the sand. Some were destroyed by the Viking invasions and the dissolution of the monast-eries during the reign of Henry VIII. Some were sent abroad to the missions on the Continent. But perhaps the main reason was that they were discarded because they were difficult to read and the antiquarian enthusiasm necessary for their preservation was lacking. Of those which have survived, some were very lucky. The *Beowulf* manuscript Cotton Vitellius A.xv (§299) was only just rescued from the Cottonian fire of 1731 (§175). Much of the text of the last fourteen folios of the Exeter Book has been destroyed by a long diagonal burn and the book itself has been used as a cutting board and a drinks mat. The Exeter Book *Riddle 47*, which follows with Kevin Crossley-Holland's translation, is about a bookworm but it is also a lament for what has been lost and a hint that we should carry on our traditions:

Moððe word fræt.   Mē þæt þūhte
wrǣtlicu wyrd   þā ic þæt wundor gefrægn
þæt se wyrm forswealg   wera gied sumes,
þēof in þȳstro,   þrymfæstne cwide
ond þæs strangan staþol.   Stælgiest ne wæs
wihte þȳ glēawra   þe hē þām wordum swealg

A moth devoured words. When I heard
of that wonder it struck me as a strange event
that a worm should swallow the song of some man,
a thief gorge in the darkness on fine phrases
and their firm foundation. The thievish stranger
was not a whit the wiser for swallowing words.

§296 Figure 31 (colour plate 26 in Janet Backhouse *The Lindisfarne Gospels*) shows one of the great initial or monogram pages of the Lindisfarne Gospels (British Library Cotton Nero D.iv), folio 29, at Matthew 1: 18 'Now the birth of Jesus Christ was on this wise: When as his mother Mary was espoused to Joseph ...', Latin *Christi autem generatio sic erat: Cum esset desponsata mater ejus Maria Joseph*... The first three letters of the Greek word Χριστόυ Latin *Christi* 'of Christ' are elaborated and decorated and the Latin text follows in black display script with colour filling and ornament, apart from the outline letters in the first line. Matthew 1: 18, coming as it does after seventeen verses giving the generations from Abraham to Christ, was held to mark the true beginning of the Gospel. The Latin heading is in insular half-uncial (a more formal script than minuscule), the hand in which most of the Latin text was written by Bishop Eadfrith between 698 and 721:

Incipit euangelium secundum mattheum
Begins the gospel according to Matthew.

There is a continuous gloss in Old English which was added by the priest

Figure 31   British Library MS Cotton Nero D.iv folio 29: from the Lindisfarne Gospels (reproduced by permission of the British Library)

Aldred sometime in the tenth century in Anglo-Saxon minuscule, clearly visible at the top of the page:

onginneð godspell æft matheus

and in *cristes* and *soðlice* above and below the monogram respectively.

§297   The Lindisfarne Gospels illustrate vividly the various influences in Northumbria in the time of Bede. Thus here the spiral pattern is Celtic, the birds and beasts are Germanic, and the Latin text is from the Mediterranean. These influences are not restricted to manuscripts or to the time of Bede. Some of the ornamental patterns and interlaces in the Lindisfarne Gospels show marked similarities to those in the Sutton Hoo hanging bowl (Backhouse, colour plate 48), shoulder clasps (Backhouse, colour plate 52), and gold buckle. The monogram in figure 31 invites comparison with the Tara Brooch, now in Dublin (Backhouse, colour plates 43 and 44). The *Dextra Dei*, the Right Hand of God, features not only in manuscripts of various periods but also on St Cuthbert's maniple (§289) and the Maaseik embroideries (§288), coins of Edward the Elder (d. 924) and other Saxon kings, and on the larger Romsey Rood (§254).

§298   Figure 32 – part of folio 89ᵛ of MS 197 of Corpus Christi College, Oxford, the oldest surviving copy of the bilingual Rule of St Benedict – illustrates the use of different scripts for the two languages (§292). The Latin text is in caroline minuscule, the Old English in an Anglo-Saxon square minuscule.

§299   The *Beowulf* manuscript (British Library Cotton Vitellius A.xv) was written by two different scribes, the second taking over at *moste* in *Beowulf* 1939. Figure 33, containing Text 13 (§277), shows the first hand, a smaller, more pointed and delicate version of the script. Figure 34, containing part of Text 11 (§223), is in the second hand, an Anglo-Saxon square minuscule. (The folio numbers in the Early English Text Society facsimile listed in the Bibliography Parts IIIA and IV have been superseded; hence the double folio numbers in the List of Figures.) You will note that the scribes did not write the poetry in lines as we print it today but used the full width of the page. Parchment – apparently unlike computer paper – was expensive.

§300   *Riddle* 26 of the Exeter Book describes one of the beautiful Bible books of Anglo-Saxon England, perhaps even the Lindisfarne Gospels themselves. This text, the riddles printed in §§291 and 295, and others like them, reflect (Malcolm Parkes has said) a fascination in all the processes involved in the production of manuscripts and suggest a culture in which dependency on the written word was not yet taken for granted.

uni regi militatur; Quem si etiam talē pre
spexerit abba esse liceat eū in superiori
aliquantū constituere loco. non solū autē
monachū: sed etiā desupra scriptis gradib;
sacerdotū uel clericorū stabilire potest
abba. in maiori quā ingreditur loco; Sieoz
talē prespexerit uitā esse. caueat autē abba.
ne aliquando de alio noto monasterio mona
chū ad habitandū suscipiat: sine consensu
abbatis eius. aut litteris commendatiis. quia
scriptū est; Quod tibi non uis fieri. alione
feceris;

Se man cumþia munuc þeof uncuþum
eapdū comð gif he oncuman hi þe punian
pile ⁊ mid nanþe ofþi flopednþfre· þds myn
ftþi nþge ðnþþð ac bið eað hylde ⁊ þdfie fcope
þeapū ge quitte fyhe anfangth ⁊ spa longe
punige spahim sylfū licige; Gif he gesceadlice
mið eað mod nþfe· ⁊ mið soþfie luþe hpilcu
ðing on mynfche tale odde tiðe unoðfi ro se
abboð þds mið eað mod nþfre ⁊ sineage on his ge
þance þds hine god þioþi asthoe þds seo fcop
puþh hine gegoððð ⁊ gejuho pdfie· Gif he e
tto oncemigne timan hine sylfne· tomynfquef

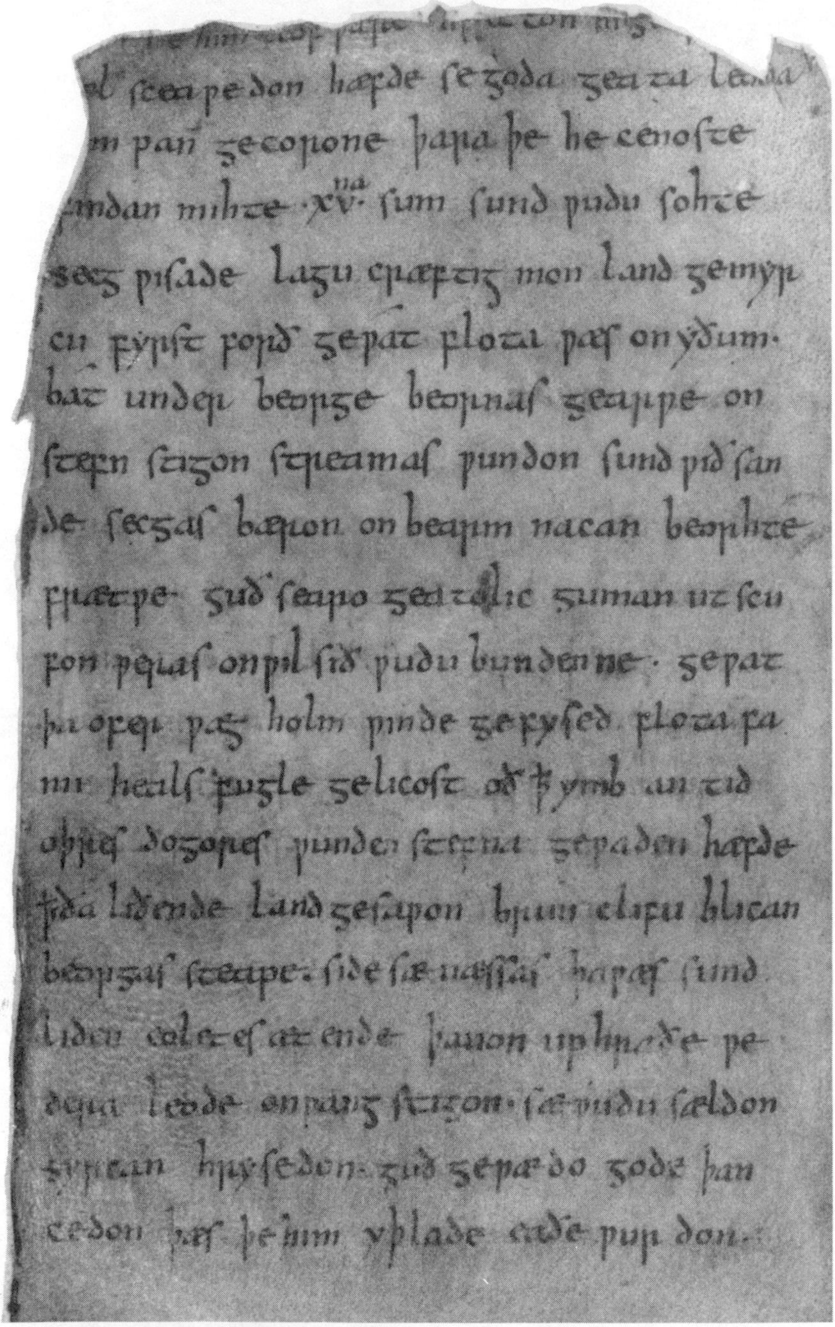
ol sceawedon hæfde se goda geata leoda
cempan gecorone þara þe he cenoste
findan mihte · xv na sum sundwudu sohte
secg wisade lagu cræftig mon land gemyr
cu fyrst forð gewat flota wæs on yðum ·
bat under beorge beornas gearwe on
stefn stigon streamas wundon sund wið san
de secgas bæron on bearm nacan beorhte
frætwe guð searo geatolic guman ut scu
fon weras on wil sið wudu bundenne · gewat
þa ofer wæg holm winde gefysed flota fa
mi heals fugle gelicost oð þæt ymb an tid
oþres dogores wunden stefna gewaden hæfde
þæt ða liðende land gesawon brim clifu blican
beorgas steape side sæ næssas þa wæs sund
liden eoletes æt ende þanon up hraðe we
dera leode on wang stigon sæ wudu sældon
syrcan hrysedon guð gewædo gode þan
cedon þæs þe him yþlade eaðe wurdon ·

Figure 33 British Library MS Cotton Vitellius A.xv folio 136ᵛ (134ᵛ): *Beowulf* (reproduced by permission of the British Library)

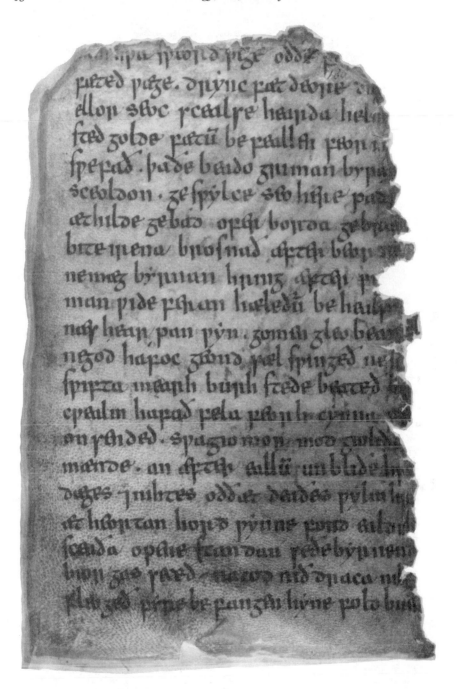

Figure 34 British Library MS Cotton Vitellius A.xv folio 183 (180ʳ): *Beowulf* (reproduced by permission of the British Library)

Text 14 **A magnificent Bible**

Mec fēonda sum   fēore besnyþede·
woruldstrenga binōm·   wǣtte siþþan·
dȳfde on wǣtre·   dyde eft þonan·
sette on sunnan   þǣr ic swīþe belēas
5 hērum þām þe ic hæfde.   Heard mec siþþan
snāð seaxses ecg,   sindrum begrunden·
fingras fēoldan   ond mec fugles wyn
geondsprengde spēddropum·   spyrede geneahhe
ofer brūnne brerd·   bēamtelge swealg,
10 strēames dǣle·   stōp eft on mec·
sīþade sweartlāst.   Mec siþþan wrāh
hæleð hlēobordum·   hȳde beþenede·
gierede mec mid golde·   forþon mē glīsedon
wrǣtlic weorc smiþa,   wīre bifongen.
15 Nū þā gerēno   ond se rēada telg
ond þā wuldorgesteald   wīde mǣre
dryhtfolca helm·   nales dol wīte.
Gif mīn bearn wera   brūcan willað,
hȳ bēoð þȳ gesundran   ond þȳ sigefǣstran,

1 **mec** = *mē*; **feorh** 'life'; **besnyþþan** 'to deprive of' (wk. vb. like *fremman* §524).

2 **woruldstrengu** 'physical strength'; **binōm** = *benam*; **wǣtan** 'to wet' (wk. vb. like *hīeran* §94).

3 **dȳfan** 'to dip' (like *wǣtan* l. 2); **dyde eft þonan** 'took [me] out again'.

4 **swīþe** adv. 'quickly'; **belēosan** 'to lose' (st. vb. II §517).

5 **hēr** 'hair'; **heard** adj. goes with *ecg* l. 6.

6 **snīðan** 'to cut' (st. vb. I §517); **seaxs** 'knife'; **sinder** 'impurity'; **begrindan** 'to grind off' (st. vb. III §518).

7 **fealdan** 'to fold' (st. vb. VII(*a*) §517); **fugles wyn** 'the bird's delight', i.e. the quill pen.

8 **geondsprengan** 'to sprinkle over' (like *wǣtan* l. 2); **spēddropa** 'useful drop'; **spyrian** 'to make a track' (wk. vb. like *werian* §525).

9 **brūn** adj. 'brown'; **brerd** 'rim [of the inkhorn]'; **bēamtelg** 'tree-dye/ink'; **swelgan** 'to swallow' (st. vb. III §518).

10 **dǣl** 'part'; **steppan** 'to step/go' (st. vb. VI §517, with present tense like *fremman* §524).

11 **sīþian** 'to journey' (wk. vb. like *lufian* §526); **sweartlāst** adj. 'leaving a black track'; **wrēon** 'to cover' (st. contracted vb. I §521).

12 **hlēobord** 'protecting board'; **hȳd** 'skin/hide'; **beþennan** 'to stretch over/cover' (like *besnyþþan* l. 1).

13 **gier(w)an** 'to adorn' (like *besnyþþan* l. 1); **forþon** adv. 'therefore'; **glīsian** 'to glisten' (like *sīþian* l. 11).

14 **wrǣtlic** adj. 'wondrous/artistic'; **weorc** '(handi)work', here nom. pl.; **bifōn** 'to surround/encircle' (st. contracted vb. VII(*b*) §521).

15 **gerēne** 'ornament'; **rēad** adj. 'red'; **telg** 'dye'.

16 **wuldorgesteald** 'glorious treasure', here nom. pl.; **mǣran** 'to make known' (like *wǣtan* l. 2), here pres. subj. pl. 'let [the three subjects in ll. 15–16a] proclaim . . .'.

17 **dryhtfolc** 'nation/people'; **helm** 'protector'; **nales** adv. 'not at all'; **dol** adj. 'foolish'; **wītan** 'to find fault' (st. vb. I §517), here 3rd pers. sg. pres. subj. 'Not at all let the fool find fault'.

18 **mīn** gen. sg. of *ic*, object of **brūcan** 'to enjoy/make use of' (st. vb. II §517).

19 **þȳ** inst. sg. neut. of *se* 'for that', meaning 'for using the bible'; **gesund** adj. 'sound/safe', here comparative; **sigefæst** adj. 'victorious', also comparative.

20 heortum þȳ hwætran   ond þȳ hygeblīþran,
   ferþe þȳ frōdran·   habbaþ frēonda þȳ mā,
   swǣsra ond gesibbra,   sōþra ond gōdra,
   tilra ond getrēowra   þā hyra tȳr ond ēad
   ēstum ȳcað   ond hȳ ārstafum
25 lissum bilecgað   ond hī lufan fæþmum
   fæste clyppað.   Frige hwæt ic hātte
   niþum tō nytte.   Nama mīn is mǣre,
   hæleþum gifre   ond hālig sylf.

20 **hwæt** adj. 'active/bold'; **hygeblīþe** adj. 'glad at heart'.
21 **ferþ** 'mind/spirit'; **frōd** 'wise/prudent'; **mā** 'more', followed by a series of gen. pls. in *-ra*.
22 **swǣs** adj. 'dear'; **gesibb** adj. 'related/familiar'; **sōþ** adj. 'true'.
23 **til** adj. 'good/brave'; **getrēowe** adj. 'faithful'; **þā** rel. pron. nom. pl. 'who'; **tȳr** 'glory'; **ēad** 'happiness'.
24 **ēst** 'favour/grace'; **ȳcan** 'to increase' (like *wǣtan* l. 2); **hȳ** pers. pron. acc. pl. 'them'; **ārstæf** 'benefit/kindness'.
25 **liss** 'kindness/joy'; **bilecgan** 'to surround' (like *besnyþþan* l. 1); **lufe** 'love', here gen. sg.; **fæðm** 'embrace'.
26 **clyppan** 'to embrace' (like *besnyþþan* l. 1); **Frige hwæt ic hātte** 'Ask what I am called', a common formula in the first-person riddles such as this.
27 **niþ(þ)as** 'men'; **tō** prep. 'as'; **nytt** 'use'.
28 **gifre** adj. 'useful'; **hālig** adj. 'holy'; **sylf** = *self*.

For details of an edition of this poem see §486.

15 Conclusion

§301   Anglo-Saxon England was no island fortress. As its extensive trade shows (§285), it had always been part of a European Economic Community. Craftsmen and scholars were frequently interchanged. Many Anglo-Saxon works of art found their way to the Continent, including the Brussels Cross (§255), the Maaseik embroideries (§288), the Franks Casket (§§258–9), illuminated manuscripts, and the Vercelli Book. This was probably left behind by one of the numerous Anglo-Saxons who made the journey to Rome – kings, archbishops, and lesser dignitaries. Danish kings and the half-Norman Edward the Confessor occupied the throne in the first half of the eleventh century. So there are good grounds for what may seem the startling claim made by R. W. Chambers in *The Continuity of English Prose* (Early English Text Society, Oxford, 1932), p. lxxvii. I have reversed the order of these quotations:

'On the day that King Edward was alive and dead,' 5 January, 1066, not two centuries had elapsed since Alfred was a fugitive at Athelney, with the whole of England harried and burnt up.

And now England possessed a civilization based upon Alfred's English prose as the national official and literary language. English jewellery, metal-work, tapestry and carving were famed throughout Western

Europe. English illumination was unrivalled, and so national that the merest novice can identify the work of the Winchester school. Even in stone-carving, those who are competent to judge speak of the superiority of the native English carver over his Norman supplanter. In building upon a large scale England was behind Normandy. But what little is left to us of Eleventh Century Anglo-Saxon architecture shows an astonishing variety. Its mark is 'greater cosmopolitanism, as compared to the more competent, but equally more restricted and traditional architecture of the Normans.'[1] ...

In the remarkable development of an official language 'England preceded the nations of Western Europe by some centuries.' From some points of view it seems as if England was making hay of the European time-table, and Eleventh-Century England was getting into the Fifteenth; as if England was escaping from the Dark Ages without passing through the later Middle Ages at all.

D PLACE-NAMES

§302 The names of English cities, towns, rivers, hills, fields, and streets, can give much information to historians and archaeologists. The title of Margaret Gelling's book *Signposts to the Past: Place-Names and the History of England*, to which the sections which follow are greatly indebted, informs or reminds us of this. Their contribution is necessarily smaller than that of the language itself (§i) because of limitations of time and space. But it is significant and we owe a great debt to the English Place-Name Society, the University, Nottingham (founded in 1923), and to the professional scholars and amateur enthusiasts who have done so much to further our knowledge.

§303 Let me cite here two illustrations of the historical interest of place-name studies. The first concerns Cornwall. To the west of Bodinnick and Bodmin lies West Penwith, the Land's End peninsula, where Cornish survived longest as a spoken language and where the highest proportion of Cornish names is to be found. Of these names, over forty begin with the word *bos* meaning 'house, dwelling'; they include Bosanketh, Bosavern, Boscarn, Boscaswell, Boscawen, Boscean, and Bosfranken 'dwelling of Frenchmen'. The first element in Bodinnick and Bodmin also means 'house, dwelling' and is an earlier form of the word which in the areas where

---

[1] The remains of the pre-Norman cathedral at Canterbury discovered in January 1993 (§187 n. 45) reveal that there was a huge cathedral on the site in the tenth century. The consultant archaeologist to Canterbury Cathedral, Martin Biddle, is quoted as saying that 'historians will no longer be able to say that the Anglo-Saxons were not builders of great churches' and that the discovery, comparable with those at Sutton Hoo (§§194–9), Cheddar (§§269–70), and St Swithun's cathedral at Winchester (§§186 and 267), 'shows that they built as mightily as they wrote prose and poetry'.

Cornish continued to be spoken developed into *bos* but remained *bod* in English-speaking areas. The distribution of Celtic names is such that it is difficult to show except on large-scale maps not possible here. But it does reflect the gradual westward expansion of the English language and the general truth that the further west one goes towards Wales and Cornwall, the higher the proportion of Celtic names which survive. For the second illustration see the discussion on the distribution of Danish and Norwegian place-names (§320).

§304 As Gelling tells us in her introduction,

the study of English place-names is a philological discipline which is based mainly on written evidence. This evidence consists of early spellings of names, and these have to be extracted from sources ranging in date from the earliest Greek and Latin texts which make reference to the British Isles to the first edition of the Ordnance Survey one-inch maps produced in the nineteenth century. The spellings are identified when possible with modern place-names, and the series of spellings for each item is presented in a manner which illustrates the development of the sounds in the spoken name, so that the philologist can study this development and reach conclusions about the original form and meaning.

Such study, she goes on, must take into consideration six languages: a non Indo-European language (§§viii–xii), assumed to have been spoken before the Celts came to Britain; the Celtic language, often called British, from which Cornish and Welsh are descended; Latin, which was both spoken and written during the Roman occupation; Old English; Old Norse, spoken in slightly different forms by Danish and Norwegian invaders; and Norman French. In the sections which follow, I discuss briefly the place-names contributed by these six languages. Here I acknowledge my debt to Gelling's book and strongly recommend that those interested should buy, beg, or borrow (but not steal), a copy.

§305 All that can be said about the non Indo-European language, or possibly languages, spoken before the Celts came to Britain, is that some unexplained river names, possibly including the Severn, and some unexplained habitation names, perhaps including London, go back to this earlier period.

§306 The place-names of Roman Britain include Latin names, e.g. *Aquae Sulis* 'the waters of Sulis (a British goddess)', the old name for Bath, and *Cataractoni*, which survives as Catterick; British names, e.g. *Brocavo* 'place of badgers' (see §26) and *Eburacum*, now York; and names which contain elements of both languages, e.g. *Lindum Colonia*, now Lincoln. In Anglo-Saxon times, English elements were sometimes added to British names, e.g. *Letoceto* + *feld* 'field' gives OE *Liccidfeld*, now Lichfield, and *Dornvaria* + *ceaster* 'Roman station' gives OE *Dornwaraceaster*, now Dorchester (Dorset).

§307 There is evidence that there were Germanic people in Britain during the Roman occupation. It has been argued that some metalwork (§231) and some pottery (§278) shows that there were substantial numbers of them serving in Roman walled towns and coastal forts in the south and east of Britain before AD 400 and that this is why Latin elements are found in Old English place-names. But other scholars think that too much weight has been placed on this archaeological evidence, that the early mercenaries were few in number, and that place-names containing Latin loan-words indicate rather that Latin speech survived in south-east Britain well into the fifth century. I dare not adjudicate on what has been described to me as a mine-field; see §§278–9. But the following words could have entered the English language direct from Latin at this time: *camp* (seen for example in the Kentish place-names Great and Little Comp, Balcombe, Swanscombe, and Maplescombe); *ceaster* (which appears alone in Caistor and Chester, as the first element in Casterton and Chesterford, and as the final element in Chichester); *port* (as in Portsmouth (see §323) and Portsdown); *strǣt* (as in Street, Streatham, and Stratford); and *wīc* (as in Wyckham and Wycomb). Two of these elements combine in the name Portchester.

§308 It is often difficult to decide whether a name which is definitely pre-English is Celtic or non Indo-European (§304). Gelling tells us that Celtic or pre-Celtic names tend to refer to important natural features which, because they were known to many people, were more likely to survive; they include the names of great rivers (Avon and Thames), large hills (Malvern and the Quantocks), and extensive forests (Arden and Wyre). Pure Celtic names include Barr, Bodmin, Crewe, Leatherhead, Neen, and Penn. Celtic and English hybrids include Breedon (Welsh *bre* + OE *dūn*, both meaning 'hill'; so Breedon on the Hill in Leicestershire is doubly tautologic), Cumberland (Welsh *cumbre* + OE *land* 'land of the Welsh'), and Pensax (Welsh *pen* + OE *Seaxna* 'hill of the Saxons').

§309 The fact that there are very few Celtic loan-words in English (§26) has been used as an argument for the view that there was little continuity between Roman Britain and Anglo-Saxon England. But this scarcity might indicate that the two peoples were at a similar stage of development and so had few objects or ideas to offer one another or, possibly, that the Anglo-Saxons had a higher form of culture than the Celts. This issue, like those discussed in §xvi and the one which follows, remains to be settled. The existence of many Celtic place-names in England could suggest that there may have been a period of co-existence between Celtic and English speakers or that these place-names were taken over from the dispossessed Celts because they were useful to the invaders. See further §313 (end).

§310 Anglo-Saxon place-names, almost unknown in the strongly Celtic regions of Wales and West Penwith (§303), occur throughout England, albeit spasmodically in the areas of strong Scandinavian influence (figure 35, p. 191). So there is little point in mapping them. Elements which contribute to their composition include words denoting habitation, the names of peoples, personal names, natural topographical features, and man-made objects, such as burial-places, prehistoric fortifications, linear earthworks, Roman remains, and sites of pagan and Christian worship. Most of these are also used in describing boundaries in the charters and many are still recognizable; for an example, see §323. But more ephemeral objects also receive mention, such as tree-stumps, bushes and trees of various kinds, including a red-leafed maple, gates, and ploughed land.

§311 A distinction can be made between habitation names, e.g. (with OE *burh* 'stronghold, enclosure') Eastbury 'east manor' and (with OE *tūn* 'town, village') Alfreton 'Ælfhere's estate' and Hunton 'settlement where hounds are kept', and topographical names, e.g. (with OE *beorg* 'hill') Farnborough 'fern hill(s)' and (with OE *ford* 'ford') Oxford 'oxen's ford'. Earlier students of place-names assumed that habitation names were likely to be earlier than topographical names but this idea has now been discarded. The existence of the elements *hām* 'village, estate' and *hamm* (variously interpreted as 'land in a river-bend', 'promontory', 'dry ground in a marsh', 'river-meadow', and 'cultivated plot in marginal land') creates problems. A decision is sometimes possible on topographical grounds or on historical or archaeological evidence of early settlement. But we shall never be certain about many names which now end in *-ham*.

§312 An area often derives its name from the people who inhabit it, e.g. East Anglia OE *Ēastengle* 'the East Angles', who were divided into two groups – the north folk and the south folk, whence Norfolk and Suffolk. The word *sǣte* 'residents, inhabitants' is found in Dorset OE *Dornsǣte* and Somerset OE *Sumorsǣte*. Canterbury is OE *Cantwaraburh* 'the fort of Kent-dwellers' and Clewer OE *clif-ware* 'dwellers on a hill-slope'. The word *burh* also occurs in Wednesbury 'Woden's fort' and Eastbury (§311). Other habitation names can be formed with *būr* 'inner chamber, small dwelling', as in Bower and Bures; with *cot* 'cottage', as in Cote and Coton; and with *tūn*, as in Alfreton (§311) and East Garston OE *Esgāres tūn* 'Esgar's settlement' (both with personal names), Hunton (§311), and Dunton OE *dūntūn* 'hill farm' (with a topographical element; §315). The first element in the common place-name Hampton may be OE *hēah* 'high' or either *hām* or *hamm* (§311). Names like Hastings and Reading are formed by the addition of *-ingas* to personal names and originally meant 'the followers of Hæsta (or Read)', while those like Gillingham and Wokingham, with the suffix *-ingahām*, meant 'the homestead of the followers of Gylla (or Wocca)'. The belief that these represent respectively the first and second stages of the Anglo-Saxon settlements has now been abandoned.

§313 Man-made objects other than settlements also provide names. Prehistoric burial grounds – which might be called habitation sites – give us Longborough and Lamborough (OE *lang* 'long' and *beorg* which meant both 'natural hill' and 'tumulus, man-made hill', MnE 'barrow' (§315)) and

Bartlow and Twemlow (OE *hlāw* 'burial-mound'). OE *burh* (§§311 and 312) and the dative form *byrig* were also used of prehistoric forts, e.g. in the names Borough Hill and Bury Hill respectively. Linear earthworks were referred to by OE *dīc* 'ditch', e.g. Grimsditch, or its Old Norse equivalent *díki*, e.g. Grimsdyke. The Latin-derived words *ceaster* and *strǣt* were used in the naming of Roman remains; see §307. Fawler, near Oxford, is OE *fāgan flōre* 'at the variegated floor', a reference to the tesselated pavement in a Roman villa, and Bath appears in the Chronicle as *æt Baðum* 'at the baths', *æt Baðum tune*, and *Baþanceaster*. Harrow (OE *hearg* 'heathen shrine') and Wye (OE *wīh* 'idol') were once places of heathen worship, as were Wednesbury 'Woden's fort' (§312) and Thundersley and Thursley, both originally OE *þunores lēah* 'the meadow of (the god) Thunder or Thor'; compare Wednesday and Thursday. Place-names with Christian associations include Southminster 'south church', Exminster 'church on the river Exe', Whitchurch 'white church' (probably 'church of white stone'), Woodchurch 'wooden church', and Christian Malford 'ford marked by a cross' from OE *cristelmæl* 'cross'. The place-name Eccles is from Latin *ecclesia*. It occurs in Norfolk, where it may be an early borrowing direct from Latin, and in Lancashire, where it was probably borrowed indirectly through the ancestor of Modern Welsh *eglwys* 'church'. Compounds with this Welsh borrowing include Eccleston in Lancashire and Cheshire, Eccleshall in Staffordshire and Yorkshire, and Exhall in Warwickshire. Gelling writes that 'this is one of our most evocative place-name elements, as it suggests that Celtic Christian churches continued to function in the post-Roman period in some areas, and that they were recognized and respected by the pagan Anglo-Saxon settlers'. This is, of course, relevant to the problem discussed in §309.

§314 Anglo-Saxon topographical names include words for hills (§315); valleys (§316); water features (§317); chalk features, e.g. Chalk in Kent and Broad Chalk in Wiltshire (OE *cealc* from Latin *calx*); and woodland and pasture, e.g. Bradfield and Swallowfield (OE *feld* 'field', sometimes 'open heathland'), Strelley and Streatley (OE *strǣt* + *lēah* 'clearing by a Roman road'), Wheatley (where *lēah* seems to mean 'arable land'), Butterley (where it seems to mean 'pasture'), and Barnwood (possibly 'Beorna's wood', with OE *wudu*). To these can be added plants and trees, e.g. Clavering (OE *clǣfre* + *-ing* 'place where clover grows'), Docking (OE *docce* + *-ing* 'place where dock grows'), Broxash ('Brocc's ash-tree', OE *æsc*) and Brimstree ('Bryni's tree', OE *trēow*). This list is far from exhaustive; it excludes, for example, OE *stān* 'stone', as in Staines and Folkestone, and *gāra* 'gore, a triangular piece of land', as in Gore, Gargrave, and Langar. But it must end with mention of some features which are perhaps not strictly natural, e.g. *pæð* 'path, road over heathland' (as in the self-explanatory Horspath and in Pateley OE *pæð* + *lēah* 'clearing by a path') and *græf* 'trench, grave' (as in Chalgrave), though it is often difficult to distinguish this element from words with OE *grāf* or *græfa* 'grove', as in Gravesend and Hargrave. Strictly speaking, some of the words discussed in §313 also belong here.

§315　It is not easy for modern lexicographers to distinguish the many OE words used to refer to hills and valleys. But place-name experts, by finding the place and studying the terrain, are beginning to understand more exactly what each word meant. Their work shows that most topographical terms have precise meanings which are the same in all parts of England and suggests that, when using topographical names, the Anglo-Saxons chose them so that they would serve strangers as substitutes for maps or signposts. Thus *beorg* meant a small, round hill; hence its use for man-made tumuli as well as for natural hills, e.g. Burford near Oxford 'ford by a hill' and Longborough (§313) respectively. OE *clif* is used in its modern sense of a promontory or cliff but it can refer to the bank of a river or to a more gentle slope. The words *dūn* and *ora* (a Latin borrowing) both refer to hills with well-marked slopes at one or both ends and both have flattish summits suitable for settlement-sites. But investigations by the geographer Ann Cole have revealed that the two have different profiles – the *dūn* has that of an upturned bowl, with a limited area of flat land, while the *ora* has that of an upturned canoe or punt, with an extensive area of flat land and sometimes with curved or steep-sloping shoulders. They are exemplified respectively by Toot Baldon and Chinnor, both in the vicinity of Oxford. Other words for a hill include *cnoll* 'knoll'; *crūc* (a Welsh borrowing), e.g. Cruckton '*tūn* by a hill'; *hlinc* 'bank, ridge, rising ground'; *hliþ* 'slope, precipitous hill'; *hōh* literally 'heel' and so 'projecting piece of land' and perhaps 'flattish hill with a sharp rise at the end'; and *scylf* 'shelf, ledge, flat area among hills'.

§316　Similar distinctions can be made for words referring to valleys. The words *cumb* and *denu* were used of different types of valley. Cole tells us that *cumb* is 'mostly used of shorter, broader valleys than *denu*, and these valleys are usually bowl- or trough-shaped with three fairly steeply rising sides'. *Denu*, which is the standard term for a main valley and which occurs in many settlement-names, is 'mostly used of long, narrow valleys with two moderately steep sides and a gentle gradient along most of their length'. Other words for a valley include *boþm*, *botm* 'bottom, a level valley'; *healh* 'corner, nook, hollow in a hill-side'; *hop* 'enclosed land in a fen, a remote valley'; and *slæd* 'dell'. OE *dæl* 'dale, gorge', as in Dawley, Middlesex, is not a common element. Many of the names in the north which end in *-dale*, e.g. Coverdale and Wensleydale, are from the ON cognate *dalr*. But the similarity between Old English and Old Norse (§xix) means that it is sometimes difficult to decide whether a name is English or Scandinavian. Gelling instances Lythe and Sneith, both in Yorkshire. The former may be OE *hlið* or ON *lið*, both meaning 'slope', and the latter could be ON *snéið* 'slice' or an adaptation of OE *snæd*, which has the same meaning.

§317　Water terms include *æwiell* 'a stream', as in Ewell; *æwielm* 'source, spring', as in Ewelme; *ēg, īeg* 'island' or 'firm land on a stream or in a fen'; *ford* 'ford'; *funta 'spring, fountain', a Latin borrowing found only in place-names, e.g. Bedfont and Fonthill; *hamm* (§311); *mere* 'lake, pool', and so 'free standing water' (occasionally used of the sea); *pōl, pyll* 'pool, tidal stream'; *rīð* 'rivulet'; and *wiell, wiella, wielle* 'stream, spring'. Gelling reports studies by Mrs Maynard which suggest that in the valley of the Avon in Warwickshire, where *mōr* is used of low-lying marsh as well as of barren upland, *mersc* is consistently employed for much more desirable land than *mōr*.

§318 Scandinavian place-name elements include (in addition to those mentioned in §§313 and 316) *bȳr* 'village' or 'homestead', as in Derby, Rugby, and Winceby; *fors* 'waterfall', as in Forcett and Fossdale; *lundr* 'grove, copse', as in Lund and Kirkland; and *vatn* 'lake', as in Wasdale and Watendlath. There are also names which consist of a Scandinavian personal name and an Old English element, e.g. Swainston and Swainswick (*Sveinn* + *tūn* or *wīc*) and names which combine a Celtic personal name with a Scandinavian element, e.g. Gatenby (*Gaithan* + *bȳr*).

§319 The presence of a large number of Scandinavian place-names in the areas shown on the map reproduced as figure 35 from Nicholas Gould's *Looking at Place Names* would seem strong evidence for the existence of large-scale Scandinavian settlements in those areas. How large is disputed by historians, who cannot agree whether the ninth-century invading Scandinavians (§§184–5) were numbered in hundreds or in thousands and so have different opinions about how many veterans actually settled in the years following 876. Some claim that these veterans and their descendants were the sole (or main) settlers. But Cameron has advanced what seems the more attractive hypothesis that the veterans were reinforced in the late eighth and ninth centuries by immigrants who founded new settlements on the less favourable sites not already occupied. More detailed work on place-names now in progress will throw more light on these unresolved problems. But the influence of these settlers on the English language was profound; see §xix.

§320 In the eastern half of England, the Scandinavian (or Norse) settlers were mostly Danes. The Norwegians were to be found west of the Pennines, though some of them moved east into Yorkshire. This is confirmed by the zones of Norwegian and Danish influence according to coin finds marked on figure 35 following R. H. M. Dolley's Map 1 in his book *The Hiberno-Norse Coins in the British Museum* (London: British Museum, 1966). However, the similarity between the dialects spoken by the Danes and by the Norwegians is such that it is often impossible to decide whether a place-name is Danish or Norwegian; hence figure 35 does not distinguish them. But the distribution of Scandinavian place-names in England is consistent with what is already known from history and archaeology, that the majority of the Scandinavians who sailed across the North Sea to the east and south coasts of England were Danes, whereas the Norwegians sailed

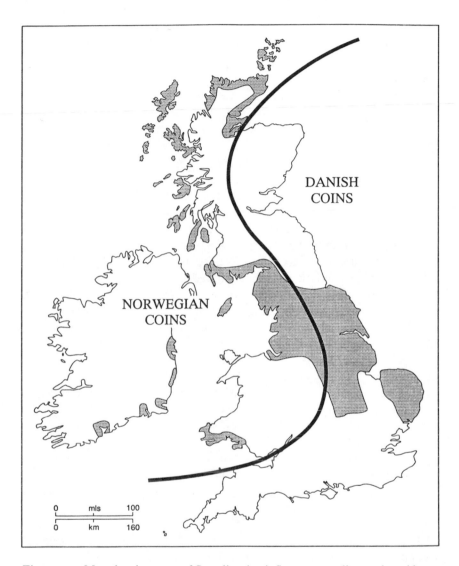

Figure 35   Map showing areas of Scandinavian influence according to the evidence of place-names (shaded areas) (from Nicholas Gould, *Looking at Place Names*; Havant: Kenneth Mason, 1978) and the very rare coin finds (dark line) (from R. H. M. Dolley, *The Hiberno-Norse Coins in the British Museum*; London: British Museum, 1966)

north about Scotland and settled in Ireland and the Isle of Man, from where they entered England from the west.

§321   Like the Romans, the Normans came as conquerors and rulers, not as immigrant settlers. And, like Latin, their language produced very few place-names in England. (It is interesting to recall here that the Normans twice subdued a land and lost their language: first when – speaking Old Norse – they invaded what became Normandy, and second when they came to England.) Many of these Norman French names contain the element *beau* or *bel* 'beautiful', e.g. Beaudesert 'beautiful wilderness', Beaulieu 'beautiful place', Belasis, Belasize, and Belsize 'beautiful seat', and Belper (earlier Beurepeir) 'beautiful retreat'. In contrast with these are a few names with *mal* 'bad', e.g. Malpas 'bad passage' (usually referring to marshy ground) and the lost Malasize in Yorkshire which, Gelling notes, 'is obviously an ironic response to Belasize'. She goes on to cite other artificial formations such as the names of the monasteries Haltemprice, *haute emprise* 'great enterprise', and Dieulacres, meaning 'May God increase it'. This is perhaps a good note on which to end this catalogue.

§322   Like every other branch of learning, the study of place-names has produced its absurdities: Barking ('where one can hear the barking of the dogs in the Isle of Dogs'), Oxshott ('where the ox was shot'), and Purfleet ('Alas, my poor fleet!', a remark attributed to Queen Elizabeth I as she watched her Armada-defeating fleet sail up the river). I am indebted to P. H. Reaney for these popular etymologies and hasten to give you those proposed by him and other scholars: Barking *OE* Berecingas, either 'the people of Berica' or 'dwellers by the birch trees'; Oxshott earlier *Okesseta* 'Ocga's piece of land'; and Purfleet earlier *Purteflyete* from OE *flēot* 'stream' perhaps combined with a personal name 'Purta's stream'.

§323   But there can be amusement in the study of place-names; consider for example the entry for 501 in the Parker MS of the Anglo-Saxon Chronicle (§180):

> 501   Her cuom Port on Bretene 7 his ii suna . . . mid ii scipum on þære stowe þe is gecweden Portes muþa . . .

> 501   In this year Port and his two sons . . . came to Britain with two ships to the place which is called Port's mouth . . .

Here the chronicler tried to do for Portsmouth 'the mouth of the harbour' what the inventor of Romulus did for Rome. There can be surprise; who, for example, would think that Chimney on the River Thames means 'Ceomma's island' (OE *Ceommenige*) or that hill-top Cricket Malherbie combines Celtic *crūc* 'hill' and the French diminutive suffix *-et* to mean 'the little place called *Cruche* (held by Robert) Malherbe (in 1228)'? There can even be something approaching romance; thus (as I write) the Vicar of St Giles, Oxford, is about to move to a parish whose boundaries are described in a charter of 953 in which King Eadred granted land in Berkshire to his servant Ælfric and his wife Eadgifu and which I now print along with Gelling's translation.

Ærest in æt þam suð geate 7 ut æt þan norþ geate on dude beorh 7 þanne on eceles beorh 7 þanne on hring pyt 7 þanne on þa andheafdu 7 þanne on þa cealc seaþas 7 þanon on þone bradan meare 7 þanon 7 lang dices on clænan mæde 7 þanne on þone bradan weg onbutan mor dune on ðyreses lace 7 þanon on læces mere norþewearde 7 þanne 7 lang mores be þan norþ stane 7 þanne þwyres ofer þone mor on bulan dic 7 swa andlang dices to æþelferðes mearce on bulen dices ende on þone þorn styb 7 þanne on talleburnan 7 þonon to þæres halgan stowe 7 sua up 7 lang broces to aþelferþes mearce weste wearde 7 swa 7 lang mearce to hremnes byrig to þan norþ geate 7 ut æt þan suþ geate on hodan hlæw 7 þanne on stan hlæwan 7 þanne to þan redan hole 7 þanne to þan dunnanhole 7 swa be þan hlide 7 þanne on domferðes hest on tættaces stan 7 þanne on hundes hlæw 7 þanne on hafoces hlæw 7 þanne on þone scortan dic 7 þanne on þa langen dic to æscesbyris eft to þan suþan geate

First in at the south gate and out at the north gate, to Dudda's tumulus, and then to ?church tumulus, and then to ring pit, and then to the headlands, and then to the chalk pits, and thence to the broad pool, and thence along the ditch to clean meadow, and then to the broad way, round marsh hill, to *thyreses* stream, and thence to the north part of bog pool, and then along the marsh by the north stone, and then crosswise over the marsh to Bula's ditch, and so along the ditch to Æthelfrith's boundary, to the end of Bula's ditch, to the thorn stump, and then to *Teale* brook, and thence to the holy place, and so up along the brook to the west part of Æthelfrith's boundary, and so along the boundary to Rams Hill to the north gate and out at the south gate, to Hod's tumulus, and then to stone tumulus, and then to the red hollow, and then to the dark hollow, and so by the slope, and then to Dunfrith's headland, to Tættuca's stone, and then to hound's tumulus, and then to hawk's tumulus, and then to the short ditch, and then to the long ditch, to Æsc's camp again to the south gate.

It might be appropriate for such a parish to observe the old custom of 'beating the bounds', in which schoolchildren accompanied by clergymen and parish officers walked around the parish boundaries once a year and the boys were beaten at the important landmarks so that they would never forget them. But I haven't consulted the boys.

E LIFE IN THE HEROIC SOCIETY AND THE IMPACT OF CHRISTIANITY

1 Introduction

§324 In what may now seem naivety, many early scholars of the Anglo-Saxon period appear to have believed that they could distil from the surviving literature and antiquities the national spirit and the beliefs of those who lived in pre-Christian times. The dangers of such a quest have been starkly exposed by E. G. Stanley in his book *The Search for Anglo-Saxon Paganism*, which includes a sub-chapter entitled 'The Search for Germanic Antiquities'. We must, for example, take care that we do not assume that the presence of the word *wyrd* (§344) in a text means that that text is pagan. Yet, if we accept that all the literature has been transmitted by Christians and if we use the evidence carefully, avoiding speculation, we can learn something. Thus a poet's observation that

> Wōden worhte wēos·   wuldor alwalda
> rūme roderas . . .
>
> Woden made idols, the glorious all-ruler
> [made] the broad heavens

suggests that the Anglo-Saxons were familiar with Germanic gods; place-names such as Wednesbury and Thursley (§313) confirm this. Yet we are not justified in imposing on the pre-Christian Anglo-Saxons the elaborate beliefs attested in Scandinavian literature.

§325   There is evidence for fertility rites, worship of natural objects, and witchcraft (§249), in the condemnation of these practices by Christian writers, and in the charms and leechdoms (medicines and remedies), in which the Christian and the pagan are often strangely mingled (§404). Thus, in the charm for unfruitful land, an invocation to a goddess *Erce, Erce, Erce eorþan modor* 'Erce, mother of earth' appears in an otherwise Christian context replete with references to Christ, the Virgin Mary, the four gospellers, and the Trinity. Again, one way of freeing someone bewitched by a heathen charm is to write in Greek letters 'alpha, omega, Jesus and [St] Veronica' and give the writing to the victim. (It may be noted here that, in the words of Mary Catherine Bodden, knowledge of Greek 'refers, essentially, to an extensive vocabulary which included words from every discipline'.)

§326   The practice of burying grave-goods with the dead suggests a belief in some sort of afterlife in which these would be needed; they include weapons, jewellery, knives, combs, and food. The skeletons of dogs and horses have been found and there are rare instances in which a female slave appears to have been buried alive to serve her dead master or mistress. The richest grave is of course that of the ship-burial at Sutton Hoo (§§194–9). This ship and the coffin of St Cuthbert (§262) demonstrate in their different ways that the burying of rich treasures with the dead did not cease with the coming of Christianity.

§327   The Church's willingness to baptize what it could not suppress is seen in the modification of the ideas implied by such words as *dom*, *lof*, and *wyrd*; see §§344 and 412–17. But we must not forget that it is both dangerous and unfruitful to seek for any expression of Anglo-Saxon genius unmodified by Christianity. The topics on which I now embark have been treated with authority and sympathy by R. I. Page in *Life in Anglo-Saxon England*, a book to which I am much indebted.

2 Town and country

§328 The length of the Anglo-Saxon period and the limited and capricious nature of the evidence – archaeological, historical, literary, and from place-names – make it impractical for me to do more than mention a few salient points about the land in which the Anglo-Saxons lived. I shall remain silent about the political boundaries; these receive some mention in §§179–88. There have been changes in the coastline. The annal for 798 in the Chronicle (MS F) tells us that *Alfhun ƀ forðferde . . . 7 he wearð bebyrged on Domuce* 'Bishop Alfhun died . . . and he was buried in Dunwich', which now lies under the sea off the coast of Suffolk. The annal for 1014 in the Laud Manuscript (MS E) concludes:

> 7 on þissum geare on sce Michæles mæsse æfan com þet mycele sæ flod geond wide þisne eard 7 ærn swa feor up swa næfre ær ne dyde 7 adrencte feala tuna 7 manncynnes unarimædlice geteall

> and in this year on Michaelmas eve the great seaflood went [far and] wide over this country and ran as far up as [it] never did before and submerged many towns and an uncountable number of people.

In his last phrase the chronicler was guilty of exaggeration; the population was in fact small. The only available evidence is provided by the Domesday surveys of 1086; it suggests that Lincoln, Norwich, and York – the three largest towns – had over 5,000 inhabitants, Oxford over 4,000, and Dunwich between 2,000 and 3,000. These and other towns, some going back to early times, some later developments, served as markets, centres for mints and administration, and as strongholds, and were usually surrounded by a wall or rampart.

§329 It was not only the absence of large cities which made the landscape markedly different. There were many marshes and fens. Bede tells us that

> Is Elia lond in Eastengla mægðe huhugu syx hund hida in ealondes gelic-nesse. Is eal· swa swa we cwædon· mid fenne 7 mid wætre ymbsald· ond mid genihtsumnesse ælo· þa ðe in þæm ilcan fennum fongne beoð· hit noman onfeng

> Ely is a district in East Anglia of about six hundred hides in the form of an island. As we have said, [it] is all surrounded by fen and by water and it got its name from the abundance of eels which are caught in those same fens.

These great East Anglian fens are mentioned in the Chronicle accounts of actions between English and Danes in 905 and 1016. In 878, when his fortunes were at their lowest, Alfred took refuge at Athelney (*Æþelinga eigge* 'the island of princes') in the fens of Somerset, whither *he lytle werede unieþelice æfter wudum for 7 on morfæstenum* 'he went with difficulty through woods and swamp[-defended] positions with a small troop'.

§330 England was more heavily wooded in Anglo-Saxon times than it is today. It was once thought that these forests (largely of oak) were damp and impassable but they were instead canopy forests through which travellers could pass and animals graze. After Alfred had taken refuge in Athelney (§329),

> on þære seofoðan wiecan ofer Eastron he gerad to Ecgbryhtes stane be eastan Sealwyda 7 him to comon þær ongen Sumorsæte alle 7 Wilsætan 7 Hamtunscir· se dæl se hiere behinon sæ was· 7 his gefægene wærun· 7 he for ymb ane niht of þam wicum to Iglea 7 þæs ymb ane to Eþandune 7 þær gefeaht wiþ alne þone here 7 hiene gefliemde

> in the seventh week after Easter he rode to Ecgbryht's stone to the east of Selwood and there all the people of Somerset and Wiltshire and [the men of] Hampshire – that part which was west of Southampton Water – flocked to him and were glad of him. And then after one night he went from those encampments to Iley and then after one [night] to Edington and there fought against the whole [Danish] army and put it to flight.

Selwood was one of the great forests. Another was the Andred or Weald in Kent and Sussex, near which the Danish armies landed in 892; *se wudu is eastlang 7 westlang hundtwelftiges mila lang oþþe lengra 7 þritiges mila brad* 'the wood is from east to west one hundred and twenty miles long or longer and thirty miles broad'. But even in Anglo-Saxon times, the forests were under threat from developers; in 825 *wæs tiolo micel sprec ymbe wuduleswe to Suþtune . . . waldon þa swangerefan þa leswe forður gedrifan 7 þone wudu geþiogan þonne hit ald geryhta weron* 'there was a very notable lawsuit about wood-pasture at Sinton . . . The reeves in charge of the swineherds wished to extend the pasture further and to take in more of the wood than the ancient rights permitted.' In this particular case, the status quo was upheld. An otherwise unknown lady called Siflæd made two wills, in both of which she left legatees the right to take two wagons into the woods to collect timber.

§331 Such fens and forests – not to mention the outlaws who infested them – made communications difficult. Rivers were used much more than they are today. Some now navigable were not. But many inland towns now inaccessible by vessels of the Anglo-Saxon or Viking pattern could then be reached by river. Thus, in 1036, Alfred, a son of King Æthelred, was brought from Guildford to captivity in Ely by ship.

§332 Some Roman roads remained passable but blocked culverts caused erosion and fallen bridges often necessitated a long detour to the nearest ford. Anglo-Saxon settlements are not obviously related to Roman roads. Some roads, like the Icknield Way from East Anglia to the west country, were of prehistoric origin. It is difficult to estimate how quickly one could travel by road. King Harold and his men covered the two hundred miles from York to London in four or five days in 1066. But they were men of military age and the emergency was dire. The roads must have been hard going for the elderly and for family groups with women and children.

§333   The absence of bridges did not help. Indeed, it had serious consequences for Sweyn's men in his campaign of 1013: *mycel his folces adranc on Temese forðam hi nanre brycge ne cepton* 'many of his army drowned in the Thames because they did not bother to find a bridge'. Bridge-building and -repairing, along with the construction of fortifications and the provision of men for military service, was one of the few obligations from which even religious communities or religious dignitaries were not exempt. In 864, King Æthelstan gave land to the monks of Winchester *on æcelcum freodomae from æghwelcum eorðlecum ðeowdomæ butan firdæ 7 festæn gewærcæ 7 brycggewæorce* 'in perpetual freedom from every worldly service except military service and the construction of fortifications and bridges'. Similarly, the land leased by Archbishop Oswald of York to the layman Æthelwold was *ælces þinges freoh buto ferdfare 7 walgeworc 7 brygcgeweorc 7 cyrcanlade* 'free from everything except military service and building of walls and bridges and carrying service for the church'. A document from Rochester Cathedral contains a list, probably drawn up in the second half of the tenth century, of those responsible for work on Rochester Bridge: the king was responsible for the fourth pier, the archbishop for the fifth and the ninth, which was the land-pier on the west, the bishop for the third and for the land-piers on the east, and various communities for the rest.

§334   However, Anglo-Saxon England was mainly an agricultural land. Numerous place-names illustrate this. Additional examples to those cited in §314 include Apperknowle (OE *apuldor-cnoll* 'apple-tree hill'), Bailey (OE *beg-leah* 'wood or clearing where berries grow'), Brilley (OE *bryne-leah* 'burnt clearing'), Butterwick (OE *butter-wic* 'butter farm, dairy farm'), Chelvey (OE *cealf-wic* 'calf farm'), Chiswick (OE *ceswican* 'cheese farm'), Shapwick (OE *sceap-wic* 'sheep farm'), and Perry (OE *pirige* 'pear-tree'; hence Waterperry and Woodperry). The importance of agriculture can be illustrated by the fact that during his campaigns against the Danes Alfred *hæfde . . . his fierd on tu tonumen swa þæt hie wæron simle healfe æt ham, healfe ute* 'had his levies divided into two so that they were always half at home, half with the army', and by the list of occupations mentioned in Ælfric's *Colloquy*, where the first answer given to the question 'Which is the most important secular occupation?' is *Eorþtilþ, forþam se yrþling us ealle fett* 'Agriculture, because the farmer feeds us all'. A good illustration is the rent set for land at Tichborne leased in 909:

ælce geare to þære edmeltide· þæt mon geselle twelf seoxtres beoras 7
twelf geswettes wilisc ealoð· 7 twentig ambra hluttor ealoð· 7 tu hund
greates hlafes 7 þridde smales· 7 tu hrieðeru oþer sealt oþer ferse· 7 six
weðeras 7 feower swin 7 feor fliccu 7 twentig cysa· gyf hit on lencten
gebyrige þ þæ þonne þære flæscun geweorð on fisce gestriene buton þ þis
forgenge sie

Every year, at festival time, shall be paid twelve sesters of beer and twelve
of sweet Welsh ale and twenty ambers of clear ale and two hundred large
loaves and a third [hundred] of small [loaves] and two oxen – one salted,
one fresh – and six wethers and four swine and four flitches [of bacon]
and twenty cheeses. If it occurs in Lent, then the value of the meat is to be
taken in fish unless this is impracticable.

§335 Closeness to fresh water supplies was an important factor in the
siting of settlements. In those areas where crops such as wheat, rye, oats,
barley, and peas, were raised, the *ceorl* – peasant, husbandman, freeman of
the lowest class – lived for protection in a village surrounded by fields which
he and his fellows farmed on the open field system whereby each man had a
series of strips. He grew his own vegetables, pears, and apples, pastured his
animals on common land, and relied on the forests for timber for building
and burning. In sheep- and cattle-raising areas, the organization was no
doubt different. The *ceorl* owed services to the lord in return for his land
and, in Page's words, 'the agricultural history of Anglo-Saxon England
shows a gradual decline in the *ceorl*'s position, and a rise in that of the lord
who could organize large-scale agricultural development'. We can perhaps
compare the decline in the number of small shops and the rise of hyper-
markets.

§336 We have already examined the royal complexes at Yeavering
(§§269–70) and at Cheddar (§§269–70), both of which in their different ways
illustrate Page's observation about the residences of Anglo-Saxon noble-
men: 'A general pattern emerges of a group of buildings incorporating some
element of defence, and a great hall, rectangular or nearly so and of timber,
multi-purpose, lit and heated by a fire placed somewhere along the main
axis.' Such a hall 'combined the characteristics of home, fortress, farm,
workshop, administrative centre and ... church'. Estates such as these
required the services of a wise reeve like the one we have already met in
§§246 and 280, and of the workers we shall meet in §§352–8. They could be in
either lay or ecclesiastical ownership; clauses like the following from the will
of Ælfgar, made *c.* 950, are not uncommon:

And ic an þat lond at Illeye mine ginger douhter hire day· and ouer hire
day Berthnoðe his day gif he leng libbe þanne heo· gif he bern habben
þanne an ic hem· gif he non ne habbeþ þanne an ic it Athelfleð mine

douhter ouer here day· and after hire day into Cristes kirke at Caunterbiri þen hirde to brice

And I grant the estate at Eleigh to my younger daughter for her life [*lit.* day] and after her death to Byrhtnoth [this is the Byrhtnoth who died at Maldon; see §187 n. 8] for his life if he lives longer than she. If they have children then I grant [it] to them. If they have none, then I grant it to my daughter Æthelflæd after their death and after her death to Christchurch at Canterbury for the use of the community.

§337 In §301 I wrote that Anglo-Saxon England was no island fortress and went on to speak of trade with Europe and beyond, of interchange of craftsmen and scholars, of foreign travel, of Scandinavian and French influence in England, and of the widening effect of Christianity. Links with the mysterious East are apparent in art and literature (§§177, 441 (Text 29), and 443 (Text 31)). But this is only one side of what Page has called 'the two faces of Anglo-Saxon England', for 'at the same time it was a solitary land, where people lived cut off from their fellows by time, distance and the difficulties and dangers of travelling'.

3 The warriors

§338 In the course of an essay urging the British Government not to fight Spain over Falkland's Islands in 1771, Dr Johnson observed that 'the life of a modern soldier is ill represented by heroick fiction'. The sections which follow walk the tightrope between reality and 'heroick fiction'; the former is illustrated by the matter-of-fact account of the battle of Maldon given by the Chronicle (§187 annal 991) and the latter by the poem of that name (§§222 and 347), where, in Johnson's words, the warriors 'die upon the bed of honour . . . and, filled with England's glory, smile in death'. The qualities admired by fighting men of all nations – bravery, loyalty, mutual trust, camaraderie, respect (and often more) for good leaders, contempt for cowardice and treachery, and disregard of life – were displayed by those who fought with Alfred and Byrhtnoth against the Danes (§§185 and 187), with King Æthelstan against a combined force of Danes, Scots, and British, at Brunanburh (Text 36 §469), and with Harold against the Normans (§187). They were displayed when British servicemen fought in the Falkland Islands in 1982. But the twentieth-century warriors were certainly not inspired by the ideals expressed in *The Battle of Maldon*. Indeed, it is more than doubtful whether *The Battle of Maldon* accurately reflects the attitude of Anglo-Saxon warriors of the historic period; such self-sacrifice would soon have resulted in the pointless destruction of any army if practised whenever any leader fell in battle, but may sometimes have been embraced by a close-knit personal bodyguard. However, the poem does portray that heroism in defeat, that triumph in disaster, which, while not restricted to the English, is a characteristic in which they have often found solace and taken pride.

§339 Anglo-Saxon heroic poetry is mainly concerned with the male aristocratic society of lord and warrior, though *The Battle of Maldon* gives us some glimpses of reality, with its references to the *unorne ceorl*, the simple yeoman Dunnere (§347), and to the *fyrd*, the common militia, and with its ironic use of the idea of heriot (§203) in Byrhtnoth's defiant reply to the Danish herald's demand for tribute quoted in §222.

§340 The life of lord and warrior was centred in the hall where the lord had his throne and he and his warriors shared its pleasures. Various aspects of this life have been mentioned elsewhere – the clearing of the hall after the feast so that the warriors, with their armour and weapons close by, could sleep (§202); the siting of the lord's sleeping quarters, sometimes attached to the hall, sometimes separated from it (§270); and the susceptibility of the hall to fire because of its timber construction (§270). The hall was an oasis of comradeship, order, warmth, and happiness, in sharp contrast to the threatening chaos of discomfort and danger outside. That this warmth was present in real life is attested by Text 19 (§425). The hall was also a symbol of the lord's authority and prestige: *līxte se lēoma ofer landa fela* 'its light shone over many lands' (*Beowulf* 311).

§341 The heroic poetry gives much detail of hall life. But we must remember that what it portrays is a literary ideal, not the social norm of Anglo-Saxon England. The poets describe a hall in which the lord protected, cherished, gave gifts; the *Beowulf* poet's praise of Hrothgar includes the words *Hē bēot ne alēh· bēagas dǣlde, ‖ sinc æt symle* 'He did not leave his promise unfulfilled, gave rings, treasure at the feast' (ll. 80–1a). The warriors paid homage, as the wanderer wistfully recalls in his solitary exile (*Wanderer* 41–4):

> þinceð him on mōde   þæt hē his mondryhten
> clyppe ond cysse   ond on cnēo lecge
> honda ond hēafod   swā hē hwīlum ǣr
> in gēardagum   giefstōlas brēac

in his mind it seems to him that he clasps and embraces his lord and lays on his knee hands and head, just as from time to time he used to make use of the throne in days of old.

They fought for their lord, as did the warriors at Finnesburh when they defended the hall against attackers – the defence of the narrow place against odds is a standard heroic situation (*Finnesburh* 14–17):

> ðā tō dura ēodon   drihtlice cempan,
> 15 Sigeferð and Ēaha,   hyra sword getugon·
> and æt ōþrum durum   Ordlāf and Gūþlāf·
> and Hengest sylf   hwearf him on lāste

then the noble warriors Sigeferth and Eaha went to the doors [and] drew their swords, and at the other [doors were] Ordlaf and Guthlaf, and Hengest himself followed in their steps.

Thus they repaid their lord's generosity (*Finnesburh* 37–40):

> Ne gefrægn ic næfre wurþlicor   æt wera hilde
> sixtig sigebeorna   sēl gebæran
> ne nēfre swānas hwītne medo   sēl forgyldan
> 40 ðonne Hnæfe guldan   his hægstealdas

Never have I heard of sixty warriors bearing themselves more worthily [or] better in battle with men or of young men repaying the shining mead better than his retainers repaid Hnæf [their dead leader].

The mutual obligation is emphasized in *Beowulf* 20–4a:

> 20 Swā sceal geong guma   gōde gewyrcean,
> fromum feohgiftum   on fæder bearme,
> þæt hine on ylde   eft gewunigen
> wilgesīþas·   þonne wīg cume·
> lēode gelæsten

So must a young man bring it about by good, by generous gifts of treasure in his father's possession, that afterwards in later years willing companions will stand by him, serve their prince when war comes.

§342   Such service, as the poets portray it, involved that loyalty unto death already mentioned, as Wiglaf's statements after the death of Beowulf testify (*Beowulf* 2890b–1 and 2650b–2): *Dēað bið sēlla ‖ eorla gehwylcum þonne edwitlīf!* 'Death is better for every warrior than a life of disgrace!' and

> 2650   God wāt on mec
> þæt mē is micle lēofre   þæt mīnne līchaman
> mid mīnne goldgyfan   glēd fæðmie

God knows of me that it is my preference by far that flame encompass my body along with my goldgiver.

The *Maldon* poet stresses the heroic loyalty to lord even as late as 991 – when a burgeoning feeling of patriotic loyalty to king and country is apparent in *The Battle of Maldon* 49–54a, another extract from Byrhtnoth's defiance of the Viking herald (§222):

> Brimmanna boda,   ābēod eft ongēan·
> 50 sege þīnum lēodum   miccle lāþre spell
> þæt hēr stynt unforcūð   eorl mid his werode
> þe wile gealgean   ēþel þysne,
> Æþelrēdes eard,   ealdres mīnes,
> folc and foldan

Messenger of the seamen, take back this reply, give thy people a much grimmer message, that here stands with his army a warrior of good reputation who will defend this land, the homeland of Æthelred my lord, the people and the earth.

But his epitaph for those who fell is not that pronounced by Horace:

> Dulce et decorum est pro patria mori
> It is sweet and fitting to die for one's native land

but (line 294)

> Hē læg ðegenlice   ðēodne gehende
> He lay thane-like   close to his lord.

§343 In such a society, the lordless man was suspect; as the poet of *The Fortunes of Men* put it, *lāð biþ æghwǣr ‖ fore his wonsceaftum winelēas hæle* 'unwelcome everywhere because of his misfortunes is the friendless man'. Had he failed his lord by disloyalty or by cowardice in battle? Had he left him dead in the field? The *Maldon* poet states the problem through Leofsunu, who *flēam forhogode* 'scorned flight', explaining why in these words:

> Ne þurfon mē embe Stūrmere   stedefæste hælæð
> 250 wordum ætwītan·   nū mīn wine gecranc·
> þæt ic hlāfordlēas   hām sīðie,
> wende fram wīge·   ac mē sceal wǣpen niman,
> ord and īren

The steadfast warriors at Sturmere will have no reason to reproach me with words now that my lord has fallen, [saying] that I return home lordless, make my way from the battle; but a weapon shall take me, point and sword.

Survivors needed to be badly wounded (like the solitary survivor on both sides in the story of Cynewulf and Cyneheard told in the annal for 755 in the Parker Chronicle). Even then they might not avoid suspicion. The wanderer was a *winelēas guma* 'a friendless man' (l. 45). We can only speculate about the circumstances of his survival and that of the warrior who uttered the lament printed as Text 11 (§223). In such a climate, Satan is easily transformed into a rebellious thane exiled by God; see Text 44 (§485).

§344 The lives of the warriors of the poetry were controlled by *wyrd* 'what happens' or 'fate'. They sought *dōm* 'glory, reputation, fame' or what the poet of *The Seafarer* calls *æftercweþendra ‖ lof lifgendra* 'the praise of men who live to speak after [them]' (ll. 72b–3a). Beowulf's vow before his encounter with Grendel's mother was *ic mē mid Hruntinge ‖ dōm gewyrce opðe* *mec dēaŏ nimeŏ!* 'I shall win glory with my sword Hrunting or death will take me!' (ll. 1490b–1), and during the course of that fight the poet praises him:

> Swā sceal man dōn
> 1535 þonne hē æt gūŏe   gegān þenceŏ
> longsumne lof: nā ymb his līf cearaŏ

So must a man do when he thinks to win enduring fame in battle: he will show no concern for his life.

These concepts of *wyrd*, *dom*, and *lof*, were modified by Christianity; see §§412–17.

§345 Kin loyalty was important in a violent society where the standard of medicine was poor; where expectation of life was short and parents did not always see their children grow to maturity; where justice was primitive; and where the blood-feud was a way of establishing such loyalty by permitting vengeance when *wergild* (§241) was not paid. The ideas of vengeance and *wergild* were codified in the Anglo-Saxon laws and to some extent softened by the influence of Christianity; see §§241–2. But kinship remained a powerful force which sometimes overrode loyalty to lord; see §203. Even as late as 991, according to the *Maldon* poet (§222), Ælfwine acknowledged a double loyalty to Byrhtnoth – *hē wæs ægŏer mīn mæg and mīn hlāford* 'he was both my kinsman and my lord' (l. 224) – and Wulfmær was Byrhtnoth's *swustersunu* 'sister's son', a particularly close relationship because there could be no doubt about its validity. Both died at Maldon. For the deaths of an uncle and his sister's son fighting on opposite sides see §362.

§346 The obligation of vengeance is a constant theme in the poetry. In *Beowulf* Grendel's mother was a *wrecend* 'avenger' seeking *suna deaŏ wrecan* 'to avenge the death of her son' whom Beowulf had killed to avenge his raids on the Danish hall Heorot. In her first attack, made while Beowulf was elsewhere, she killed Æschere, one of Hrothgar's counsellors and thereby *þā fæhŏe wræc ‖ þe þū gystran niht Grendel cwealdest* 'avenged the feud in which you [Beowulf] last night killed Grendel' because she *wolde hyre mæg wrecan* 'wished to avenge her son'. So Beowulf went in pursuit after saying to Hrothgar

> 'Ne sorga, snotor guma!   Sēlre biŏ æghwæm
> 1385 þæt hē his frēond wrece   þonne hē fela murne'

'Do not grieve, wise man! It is better for everyone to avenge his friend than to mourn much.'

In the ensuing fight, Grendel's mother was still motivated by vengeance – she *wolde hire bearn wrecan, ‖ āngan eaferan* 'wished to avenge her son, her only child' but Beowulf *fyren dæda wræc, ‖ dēaŏcwealm Denigea, swā hit gedefe wæs* 'avenged the evil deeds, the slaughter of Danes, as it was fitting', when he killed her.

§347 The *Maldon* poet made vengeance for the death of Byrhtnoth the predominating motive of the warriors who fell:

> Lēofsunu gemǣlde   and his linde āhōf,
> 245 bord tō gebeorge·   hē þām beorne oncwæð:
> 'Ic þæt gehāte   þæt ic heonon nelle
> flēon fōtes trym   ac wille furðor gān,
> wrecan on gewinne   mīnne winedrihten'

Leofsunu spoke and lifted his linden-wood shield, as protection. He replied to the man 'I promise this, that I will not flee one footstep from here but I will go forward, avenge my lord in the fight.'

> 255 Dunnere þā cwæð,   daroð ācwehte,
> unorne ceorl,   ofer eall clypode,
> bæd þæt beorna gehwylc   Byrhtnōð wrǣce:
> 'Ne mæg nā wandian   se þe wrecan þenceð
> frēan on folce   ne for fēore murnan'

Dunnere, a simple churl, then spoke, shook his spear, called over all, urged that each of the warriors avenge Byrhtnoth: 'He who thinks to avenge his lord in the press cannot flinch or show concern for his life.'

> þā gȳt on orde stōd   Eadweard se langa,
> gearo and geornful,   gylpwordum sprǣc
> 275 þæt hē nolde flēogan   fōtmǣl landes,
> ofer bæc būgan,   þā his betera leg.
> Hē brǣc þone bordweall   and wið þā beornas feaht.
> oðþæt hē his sincgyfan   on þām sǣmannum
> wurðlice wrec   ǣr hē on wæle lǣge

Then Edward the tall still stood in the vanguard, ready and eager, spoke a vow in words that he would not flee a foot's space of land [or] turn in retreat when his superior lay [dead]. He broke the [Danish] shieldwall and fought against the warriors until he fittingly avenged his treasure-giver on those seamen before he lay among the slain.

§348 But, not surprisingly, there were those who failed to meet the challenge. Of the eleven who went out with Beowulf to fight the dragon, ten fled, *tȳdre trēowlogan tȳne ætsomne* 'ten cowardly oathbreakers together'. The flight of the group of cowards after the death of Byrhtnoth at Maldon was condemned by one of those who stayed to die:

> Swā him Offa on dæg   ǣr āsǣde
> on þām meþelstede·   þā hē gemōt hæfde·
> 200 þæt þǣr mōdelice   manega sprǣcon
> þe eft æt þearfe   þolian noldon

Thus Offa had told them earlier in the day in the assembly, when he

[Byrhtnoth] held a meeting, that many spoke bravely there who afterwards would not endure in danger.

§349 Worse than flight was to accept service under the slayer of one's lord. This was rejected by the followers of the dead king Cynewulf (§343): *ond þa cuædon hie þæt him nænig mæg leofra nære þonne hiera hlaford and hie næfre his banan folgian noldon* 'and then they said that no kinsman was dearer to them than their lord and they would never follow his slayer'. Yet Hengest and his men made a truce with King Finn and his men, who had slain their king Hnæf (*Beowulf* 1102–3):

> ... hīe hira bēaggyfan   banan folgedon
> ðēodenlēase   þā him swā geþearfod wæs

lordless they followed the slayer of their lord, since it was thus forced upon them.

Necessity would not have been accepted as justification by Cynewulf's men: 'Death is better for every warrior than a life of disgrace!' (§342). But Hengest might have retorted 'Wait and see!', for in time he avenged his lord (*Beowulf* 1151b–3a):

> Ðā wæs heal roden
> fēonda fēorum·   swilce Fin slægen
> cyning on corþre

Then was the hall reddened [*or* adorned]with the corpses of foes [and] Finn the king also slain among his guard.

§350 In real life we meet the cowardly and treacherous *ealdorman* of Hampshire, Ælfric. In 992 he was entrusted with the leadership of King Æthelred's ships in an attempt to entrap the Danes. But he betrayed his trust:

Ða sende se ealdorman Ælfric 7 het warnian þone here· 7 þa on þere nihte ðe hi on ðone dæi togædere cumon sceoldon· ða sceoc he on niht fram þære fyrde him sylfum to mycclum bismore· 7 se here þa ætbærst buton an scip þær man ofsloh· 7 þa gemætte se here ða scipu of EastEnglum 7 of Lunden 7 hi ðær ofslogon mycel wæl

Then the *ealdorman* Ælfric sent and ordered [someone] to warn the Danish forces and then, on the night of the day on which they [the English] were to assemble, he absconded by night from the expedition to his own great shame and the Danish force then escaped except for one ship which was destroyed. And then the Danes met the ships from East Anglia and London and there they caused great destruction.

No doubt in revenge for this, Æthelred *het . . . ablendan Ælfgar Ælfrices sunu ealdormannes* 'ordered [someone] to blind Ælfgar, son of *ealdorman* Ælfric' in 993. We do not hear of Ælfric again until 1003 when, despite what had gone before, he was put in command of a very large force from Wiltshire and Hampshire raised to do battle against the Danes:

> Ða sceolde se ealdorman Ælfric lædan þa fyrde ac he teah forð þa his ealdan wrenceas: sona swa hi wæron swa gehende þet ægðer heora on oðer hawede· þa gebræd he hine seocne 7 ongan hine brecan to spiwenne 7 cweð þet he gesiclod wære 7 swa þ folc beswac þ he lædan sceolde· swa hit gecweðen is: Ðonne se heretoga wacað þonne bið eall se here swiðe gehindred. Ða Swegen geseah þ hi anræde næron 7 ealle tohwurfon· þa lædde he his here into Wiltune 7 hi ða burh gehergodon 7 forbærndon 7 eodon þa to Searbyrig 7 þanon eft to sæ· ferde þær he wiste his yð-hengestas

> Then it was the *ealdorman* Ælfric's duty to lead the army but he brought out his old tricks. As soon as they were so close that each of them might look on the other, he pretended to be sick and began to retch and vomit and said that he was feeling sick and so betrayed the people he should have led. As the saying is, 'When the leader is a coward then the whole force is greatly impeded.' When Sweyn saw that they were not resolute and had all separated, then he led his army into Wilton and plundered and burnt the city and then went to Salisbury and thence back to the sea, making his way to where he knew his ships [were waiting].

Ælfric was finally slain in battle against Cnut in 1016, whether in fight or in flight is not clear.

§351   In 1014 Wulfstan, Archbishop of York, denounced the crimes and sins of the English in his famous *Sermo Lupi ad Anglos*, preaching that the end of the world was near and arguing that the Danish invasions were God's punishment on a wicked people. Even if we make allowance for the exaggeration of a zealous prophet and reformer, we are left with a gloomy picture of widespread breaches of loyalty to lord and of loyalty to kin. I give a few extracts in Part IV Text 34 (§446).

4 Craftsmen, farmers, and other male members of society

§352   The heroic poetry concerned with the warrior society whose life was centred on the hall makes little mention of anyone else. Two of the three groups which can be distinguished in Anglo-Saxon England under the king – *þegnas*, *gesiþas*, or *eorlas* 'thanes, gesiths, or warriors'; *ceorlas* 'churls' (§335); and *þeowas* 'slaves' – receive mention in *Beowulf*, though the choice is some-times made for alliteration rather than for meaning. We meet many kings, in particular Hrothgar of the Danes and Hygelac of the Geats, who was succeeded by his *swustersunu* Beowulf after his own son Heardred died in battle. Æschere, who was killed by Grendel's mother, *wæs Hroþgāre hæleþa lēofost* ‖ *on gesīþes hād* 'was to Hrothgar the dearest of heroes in the rank of gesith'. Beowulf is variously described as *Higelāces þegn* 'Hygelac's thane' and *ealdor ðegna* 'leader of thanes', as *eorl* 'warrior' and *eorla sum* 'one of [the] warriors', and as *self mid gesīðum* 'himself among the gesiths'. The word *ceorl*, used in *Maldon* in the sense 'yeoman, peasant, freeman' (§339), is used of both the Danish counsellors – *snottre ceorlas* 'wise men' – and the Geatish counsellors – *snotere ceorlas* – and even of King Ongentheow of the Swedes, who is referred to (in a place where it is not needed for alliteration) as *ealdum ceorle* '[the] old churl'. But there is no certain reference to a slave in any of the heroic poems. The word *þeow* 'slave' is supplied by some editors in *Beowulf* 2223b, where the manuscript is damaged and only *þ* can be read with certainty. The reference is to the man who first plundered the dragon's hoard and so brought disaster on the Geats. But other editors read *þegn*.

§353   The poem *The Gifts of Men* speaks not only of warriors (§§338–51) and of men of religion (§§388–94) but also of men whose skills created the hall and provided the weapons and jewellery which were an integral part of its life: the architect (*sum mæg wrætlice weorc ahycgan* ‖ *hēahtimbra gehwæs* 'one [man] can devise an artistic plan for any lofty building'); the builder (*sum bið bylda til* ‖ *hām tō hebbanne* 'one is a builder good at raising a dwelling'); the goldsmith

> (. . .   sum searocræftig
> goldes ond gimma   þonne him gumena weard
> hāteð him tō mærþum   māþþum rēnian

one [is] skilful in gold and gems when a lord of men orders [him] to prepare him a jewel as an adornment for him);

and the weaponsmith (see §204).

§354   The poems treating heroic subjects are silent about workers who provide food and the necessities of life. *The Gifts of Men* mentions seamen, hunters, and fowlers. But the prose is more forthcoming.

§355   Ælfric's *Colloquy* tells us of the hardships endured by the plough-man, the shepherd, the oxherd; of the dangers braved by the hunter, the fisherman, and the seagoing merchant; and of the skills of the fowler, the shoemaker, the salter, the baker, the cook, the carpenter, and smiths of various kinds. The ploughman's complaint *ic neom frēoh* 'I am not free' reminds us that the inventory of the stock at Bishop Æthelwold's estate at Yaxley included male and female slaves (§244). Other sources – including laws and charters, place-names, illustrated manuscripts, and the Bayeux Tapestry – tell us of foresters, charcoal-burners, smelters, millers, plumbers, soapmakers, fullers, potters, and weavers, as well as granary-keepers, goatherds, and cheesemakers. The list could be continued.

§356   An eleventh-century document concerning the rights of various classes tells us that the thane held his land subject to the performance of military service, the repair of fortresses, work on bridges, and sometimes guarding the coast or equipping a guard-ship. Freemen who lived on such an estate – as opposed to those who owned their own land – had different duties according to their rank and the requirements of the estate. The *geneat* 'companion' paid rent and performed personal services for his lord – riding, carrying messages, escorting his guests, and acting as his bodyguard. The *cotsetla* 'cottage-dweller' paid no ground-rent but had to work for his lord every Monday or three days a week at harvest time. The *gebur* 'peasant' paid rent in kind, such as barley, hens, sheep, and loaves of bread, and had to work two days every week and three in harvest time and from Candlemas to Easter. In return, he was supplied with land, stock, and tools. On his death, the lord inherited what he left. The specialist workers, male and female, free or slave, were controlled by the reeve (§§246 and 280).

§357 The king had his own servants. His *ealdormenn* controlled one or more shires and sometimes the lands of one of the former kingdoms. Like their fellows (§356), the king's thanes owed military service and work on fortifications and bridges in return for their land. They also served the king at court when summoned. The *scirgerefa* 'shire-reeve' (sheriff) acted as judge and supervisor of trading, of towns, and of royal estates.

§358 And thus, as *The Fortunes of Men* puts it (ll. 64–6),

Swā missenlice meahtig dryhten
geond eorþan scēat eallum dǣleð,
scȳreþ ond scrīfeð ond gesceapo healdeð

So variously the mighty lord throughout the surface of the earth distributes, determines and ordains and controls, the destinies of all men.

See also Text 42 (§480), where the poet discusses the different fortunes which befell a woman's twin sons. On the evidence of Text 26 (§434), these twins must have been born on different days.

5 Women

§359 *Fǣmne æt hyre bordan gerīseð* 'A woman's place is at her embroidery' is an Anglo-Saxon poet's expression of a sentiment not often heard now. It might be better, albeit in Victorian terms, translated 'A lady's place is at her embroidery', for the heroic poetry is concerned only with females of high rank and makes no mention of the oven, the churn, the brew-house, the dyeing-vat, or the vegetable garden. Nor does it make much mention of happiness among women. As far as I can recall, the only woman in Anglo-Saxon poetry who laughs is Sarah. But hers was not a glad laugh of carefree joy: *þā þæt wīf āhlōh . . . ‖ nalles glædlice* (*GenesisA* 2382–3a); it was the laugh of Abraham in Genesis 17: 17 and of Sarah herself in Genesis 18: 12.

§360 The woman of high rank lived in the *bur* or *brydbur* 'women's apartment', which could be at the end of the hall, as at Yeavering (§270), or separated from it, as at Cheddar (§270). The latter was the case at Heorot where, as the *Beowulf* poet tells us,

> 920   swylce self cyning
>   of brȳdbūre   . . .
>   . . .   ond his cwēn mid him
>   medostigge mæt   mægþa hōse

the king himself too and his queen with him trod the meadpath from the women's quarters with a retinue of maidens.

On the dangers in such separation, see §270.

§361   Women do not play a large role in the heroic poetry. But those who are mentioned were not always at their embroidery. The role of the queen or the woman of high rank was to support the king or her lord. Thus we read in *Maxims i* (Exeter Book):

> Cyning sceal mid cēape   cwēne gebicgan,
> bunum ond bēagum·   bū sceolon ǣrest
> geofum gōd wesan.   Gūð sceal in eorle,
> wīg, geweaxan·   ond wīf geþēon
> 85 lēof mid hyre lēodum,   leohtmōd wesan,
> rūne healdan,   rūmheort bēon
> mēarum ond māþmum,   meodorǣdenne
> for gesīðmægen   symle ǣghwǣr
> eodor æþelinga   ǣrest gegrētan,
> 90 forman fulle   tō frēan hond
> ricene gerǣcan   ond him rǣd witan
> boldāgendum   bǣm ætsomne

A king must endow his queen with good things, with beakers and bracelets; both must from the beginning be generous with gifts. Valour and battle-power must grow in the man and the woman must prosper, loved by her people; [she must] be cheerful-minded, keep secrets, be generous with horses and treasures; at the mead-feasting [she must] always and everywhere in the presence of the warrior-band first greet the protector of nobles, at once put the first cup in her lord's hand, and give wise advice for the pair of them, the hall-rulers.

Hrothgar's queen Wealhtheow – *goldhroden . . . under gyldnum bēage . . . wīsfæst wordum* 'gold adorned . . . under a golden diadem . . . wise in words' – performed these roles to perfection in Heorot:

> Ðǣr wæs hæleþa hleahtor·   ⁻ hlyn swynsode·
> word wǣron wynsume.   Ēode Wealhþēow forð,
> cwēn Hrōðgāres   cynna gemyndig,
> grētte goldhroden   guman on healle

615 ond þā frēolic wīf   ful gesealde
   ǣrest Ēast-Dena   eþelwearde·
   bæd hine blīðne   æt þǣre bēorþege,
   lēodum lēofne·   hē on lust geþeah
   symbel ond seleful,   sigerōf kyning.
620 Ymbēode þā   ides Helminga
   duguþe ond geogoþe   dǣl ǣghwylcne,
   sincfato sealde,   oþ þæt sǣl ālamp
   þæt hīo Bēowulfe,   bēaghroden cwēn
   mōde geþungen,   medoful ætbær

There was laughter of heroes, melody was pleasing, words were cheerful. Wealhtheow, Hrothgar's queen, mindful of court etiquette, went forth, gold-adorned greeted the men in the hall and then, noble woman, first gave the cup to the land-guardian of the East Danes, urged him, beloved of his people, [to be] happy at the beer-drinking; he, the victorious king, partook of the feast and the hall-cup with joy. The queen of the Helmings then went round each group of veterans and young warriors, giving the precious cup until the time came that she, the ring-adorned queen, excellent of mind, bore the mead-cup to Beowulf.

§362   As we see in §367, the eternal triangle of today, involving two members of one sex and one of the other, was not unknown in Anglo-Saxon England; the poem *Wulf and Eadwacer* is often interpreted as an example. But it was another triangle – that involving the conflict between a man's loyalty to his lord and his loyalty to his kin – which engaged the attention of the heroic poets. The dilemma of the warrior has already been discussed in §§203 and 345. But a woman of noble birth, especially the daughter of a king, might easily find herself in a similar situation when she had been married off as a *freoðuwebbe* 'peace-weaver' into a dynasty hostile to hers, in the hope that the feud between her tribe and her husband's would thus be settled. But the *Beowulf* poet percipiently reveals the vanity of such hopes:

                          Oft seldan hwǣr
2030 æfter lēodhryre   lȳtle hwīle
    bongār būgeð   þēah sēo brȳd duge!

As a rule, it is seldom for long that the deadly spear anywhere remains idle after the fall of a prince, no matter how good the bride may be.

And he movingly portrays the stark helplessness and desolation of the Danish princess Hildeburh, sister of the Danish king Hnæf and wife of the Frisian king Finn, on the morning after the feast at Finnesburh at which the two tribes had again taken to the sword:

    Ne hūru Hildeburh   herian þorfte
    Ēotena trēowe·   unsynnum wearð

　　　　beloren lēofum　　　æt þām lindplegan
　　　　bearnum ond brōðrum·　　hīe on gebyrd hruron
1075　gāre wunde·　　þæt wæs geōmuru ides!
　　　　. . .　　　　　　. . .

　　　　Hēt ðā Hildeburh　　æt Hnæfes āde
1115　hire selfre sunu　　sweoloðe befæstan,
　　　　bānfatu bærnan,　　ond on bǣl dōn
　　　　ēame on eaxle.　　Ides gnornode,
　　　　geōmrode giddum

Hildeburh indeed had no cause to praise the good faith of the Jutes; guiltless [she] was robbed of her dear ones, son and brother, in the shield-play; they fell as was their fate wounded by the spear. She was a despairing woman . . . Then at Hnæf's pyre Hildeburh ordered her own son to be given to the flames, his body to be burnt, and to be put on the pyre by his uncle's side. The woman mourned, lamented in dirges.

§363　The prose, covering as it does a much wider canvas, demonstrates that the poet's statement 'A woman's place is at her embroidery' is even further from the reality. The dust-jacket of Christine Fell's *Women in Anglo-Saxon England* poses the question: 'A mere chattel, inferior to men, or their social equal – what was the role of the Anglo-Saxon woman?' The book 'shows how for many women Anglo-Saxon England was a golden age of power and wealth, culture and education' and concludes by showing 'the impact of the Norman Conquest and the Gregorian reform. Within a century the tide had turned: in literature the image of women lost touch with reality, and in reality women lost the status which they had so long enjoyed.'

§364　The Parker Chronicle annal for 672 reads *Her forþferde Cenwalh 7 Seaxburg an gear ricsode his cuen æfter him* 'In this year [King] Cenwalh [of Wessex] died and Seaxburg his queen ruled after him for a year'. The annal for 673 includes the sentence *Sēe Æþeldryht ongon þæt mynster æt Elige* 'Saint Æthelthryth founded the monastery at Ely'. She was the daughter of King Anna of East Anglia and the wife of King Ecgfrith of Northumbria before becoming Abbess of Ely. She was succeeded by her sister Seaxburg, wife of King Ercenberht of Kent. On the role played in the Church by such noblewomen, see §§384 and 389–92.

§365　The catalogue of remarkable noblewomen can be extended. In 722 *Æþelburg cuen towearp Tantun* 'Queen Æthelburg [of Wessex] destroyed Taunton'. Cynethryth, wife of Offa, king of Mercia 757–96, had her own coins. King Alfred's mother Osburg helped to educate him. But Æthelflæd, daughter of King Alfred, perhaps heads the list. (Most of the quotations which follow come from MS C of the Chronicle, which includes a Mercian Chronicle covering the years 902–24.) In 910 *Æðelflæd getimbrede þa burh æt Bremesbyrig* 'Æthelflæd built the fort at Bremesbyrig'. In 911 *gefor Æþered Myrcna hlaford* '[her husband] Æthered king of the Mercians died'. In 912 *com* [came] *Æþelflæd Myrcna hlæfdige* [queen] *to Scergeate* [?Shrewsbury] *7 þær ða burh getimbrede . . . 7 þa* [and that] *æt Bricge* [Bridgnorth]. In 913 she *for* [went] . . . *to Tamaweorðige* [Tamworth] *7 þa burh þær getimbrede . . . 7 þa æt Stæfforda* [Stafford]. To these she added forts at Eddisbury and Warwick (914), and at Chirbury, *Weardbyrig*, and Runcorn (915). In 916 she *sende fyrde on Wealas 7 abræc Brecenan mere 7 þær genam þæs cinges wif feower and ðritiga sume* 'sent an army into Wales and destroyed *Brecenan mere* and captured there the king's wife and thirty-three others [literally "one of thirty-four"; cf. "four-some"]'. In 917 she *begeat þa burh . . . þe ys haten Deoraby* 'took possession of the city which is called Derby'. The annal for 918 in MS E merely records her death: *Her Æðelflæd forðferde Myrcena hlæfdige*. But MS C tells us that, before she died, she *begeat on hire geweald mid Godes fultume gesybsumlice þa burh æt Ligraceastre 7 se mæsta dæl þæs herges þe ðær to hierde wearð underþeoded* 'brought under her control peacefully with the help of God the walled town of Leicester and the greater part of the [Danish] army which belonged to it was subjected [to her]'. During her eight-year reign she kept the loyalty of a formidable military household, displaying an eye for country and an ability to anticipate the enemy plans by the way she sited the forts listed above. She led her armies in person on the expeditions she had planned and cooperated with King Edward of Wessex to prevent the Welsh and the Danes joining forces. A remarkable leader indeed by any standards – and one whose existence makes it easy for us to understand why the apocryphal heroine Judith was a natural subject for an Old English poem (Text 12 §489).

§366 We have already learnt something of the valuable personal property owned by women of high rank from §§224–38 (jewellery) and §§285–90 (embroidery). Some of them owned extensive properties along with the stock appertaining thereto. Ælfflæd, wife of *ealdorman* Byrhtnoth (who fell at Maldon in 991), made a will *c.* 1000 in which she disposed of no fewer than thirty-six estates and two woodlands. Seventeen of the estates and the two woodlands had been left to various religious communities by her parents, her sister, or her husband, subject to her life-interest. She herself left seven estates to the Church, some of them subject to life-interests, and the remaining twelve to individuals. One estate deserves particular mention: *þæt is æt Rettendune þe wæs min morgengyfu* 'namely, Rettendon, which was my morning-gift'. This phrase must have brought very special memories to the widow; the *morgengyfu* was the gift made by the husband to his wife on the morning after the marriage, a gift retained by a widow provided she did not remarry within a year of her husband's death. Thus the widow Wynflæd (*c.* 950) left to Eadmær, who seems to have been her son, *þæs landes æt Faccancumbe þe hyre morgengyfu wæs* (no need to translate this) and the will of Ælfhelm (somewhere between 975 and 1016) states that *ic cyþe hwæt ic minum wive to morgengyue sealde· þæt is Beadewan 7 Burgestede 7 Strætford 7 þa þreo hyda æt Heanhelan* 'I declare what I gave to my wife as a morning-gift, namely Baddow and Burstead and Stratford and the three hides at Enhale'. Some marriage agreements survive, including two made in the early eleventh century. When Wulfric married the sister of Archbishop Wulfstan of York *c.* 1015, he promised her not only four estates but also *L mances goldes 7 xxx manna 7 xxx horsa* 'fifty mancuses of gold and thirty men and thirty horses'. A Kentish marriage agreement made a few years later reads:

Her swutelaþ on þysan gewrite þa foreward þe Godwine worhte wið Byrhtric þa he his dohter awogode: þ is ærest þ he gæf hire anes pundes gewihta goldes wið þonne þe heo his spæce underfenge 7 he geuþe hire þæs landes æt Stræte mid eallan þon þe þærto herð 7 on Burwaramersce oðer healf hund æcera 7 þærto þrittig oxna 7 twentig cuna 7 tyn hors 7 tyn ðeowmen

Here is made clear in this document the agreement which Godwine made with Brihtric when he wooed his daughter, that is, first he gave her a pound's weight of gold to persuade her to accept his suit and he granted her the estate at Street with all that belongs thereto and one hundred and fifty acres at Burmarsh and in addition thirty oxen and twenty cows and ten horses and ten slaves.

Women had the absolute right to dispose of property other than that held with a life-interest. Edwin, son of Enneawn of Herefordshire, was disinherited by his mother during the reign of Cnut. He had gone to a shire-meeting where he

spæc þær on his agene modor æfter sumon dæle landes . . . þa sæde heo þ heo nan land næfde þe him aht to gebyrede 7 gebealh heo swiðe eorlice wið hire sunu 7 gecleopode ða Leofflæde hire magan to hire . . . 7 þus cwæð: her sit Leoffled min mage þe ic geann ægðer ge mines landes ge mines goldes ge rægles ge reafes ge ealles þæs ðe ic ah æfter minon dæge . . . 7 minon agenan suna næfre nan þingc

sued there his own mother for a certain piece of land . . . Then she said that she had no land that in any way belonged to him and became exceedingly angry [*lit.* angry in a way fitting for a noble] with her son and then summoned her kinswoman Leofflæd to her . . . and spoke thus: 'Here sits my kinswoman Leofflæd to whom, after my death, I leave my land and my gold, my clothing and my raiment, and all that I possess . . . not one thing ever to my own son.'

Thirkell the White, Leofflæd's husband, assisted enthusiastically in the ratification of this bequest. Edwin's reactions to his loss are not recorded. Estates could be lost for other reasons. One in Northumbria was forfeited *c.* 970 *for unrihtan hæmede· wæron twegen gebroþra hæfdon an wif* 'for an unlawful union: there were two brothers [who] had one wife'.

§367 Conjugal love and extra-marital affairs are both attested in the poems *Maxims i* and *Maxims ii*:

> wīdgongel wīf word gespringeð·   oft hȳ mon wommum bilihð·
> 65 hæleð hȳ hospe mænað·   oft hyre hlēor abrēoþeð

... a roving woman gives rise to gossip. Often charges of vice are laid against her. Men speak of her with contempt. Her countenance continually fades;

> 100 Wīf sceal wiþ wer wǣre gehealdan·   oft hī mon wommum belihð·
> fela bið fæsthȳdigra·   fela bið fyrwetgeornra·
> frēoð hȳ fremde monnan   þonne se ōþer fēor gewīteþ

A wife must keep faith with her husband. She is often accused of vices. There are many who are constant. There are many who are curious; they love strange men when the husband goes far away;

> Ides sceal dyrne cræfte,
> fǣmne, hire frēond gesecean   gif hēo nelle on folce geþēon
> 45 þæt hī man bēagum gebicge

A lady, a woman must seek her lover with secret skill if she does not wish to prosper among her people so that a man should win her with rings [i.e. give gifts to win her hand in marriage].

(I sometimes wonder whether *nelle* 'does not wish' is a mistake for *wille* 'wishes'.)

Three pairs of star-crossed lovers are the subject of the poems from the Exeter Book which give us a glimpse of romantic love. The lovers are probably of high rank; it is unlikely that the heroic vocabulary is used conventionally. In all of them the plot is obscure but the emotions touch us all. One poem, known as *Wulf and Eadwacer* (Text 40 §475) or *Wulf*, is often interpreted as involving a woman, her husband, and her lover. But whether Wulf is one of two men or not, her love for him is passionate:

> Wulfes ic mīnes wīdlastum   wēnum dogode·
> 10 þonne hit wæs rēnig weder   ond ic rēotugu sæt·
> þonne mec se beaducafa   bogum bilegde·
> wæs mē wyn tō þon·   wæs mē hwæþre ēac lāð.
> Wulf, mīn Wulf,   wēna mē þīne
> sēoce gedydon,   þīne seldcymas,
> 15 murnende mōd,   nales metelīste.

Kevin Crossley-Holland translates this:

> How I have grieved for my Wulf's wide wanderings.
> When rain slapped the earth and I sat apart weeping,
> when the bold warrior wrapped his arms about me,

> I seethed with desire and yet with such hatred.
> Wulf, my Wulf, my yearning for you
> and your seldom coming have caused my sickness,
> my mourning heart, not mere starvation.

In *The Husband's Message* (Text 39 §474), where the lovers are separated by the machinations of kinsmen, the husband sends over the sea to his wife a messenger who urges

> þæt þū sinchroden   sylf gemunde
> 15 on gewitlocan   wordbēotunga
>   þe git on ærdagum   oft gespræcon

that thou thyself treasure-adorned recall to mind the vows which the two of you often spoke in days of yore;

affirms that his lord's greatest wish is

> 33 þæt git ætsomne   siþþan mōtan
>   secgum ond gesīþum   sinc gedælan,
>   næglede bēagas

that you two together afterwards may distribute treasure, studded bracelets, to warriors and retainers;

and conveys his lord's promise

> 51 þæt hē þā wære   ond þā winetrēowe
>   be him lifgendum   læstan wolde
>   þe git on ærdagum   oft gespræconn .

that, while he lives, he will be true to the pledge and the loving vow which both of you often uttered in days of yore.

The most passionate expression is that in *The Wife's Lament* (Text 38 §473); it can be summarized in Shakespeare's words

> How like a winter hath my absence been
> From thee . . .

§368 The Parker MS of the Chronicle gives the casualty list of a sea-battle in 897 in which King Alfred's new fleet defeated the Danes. The list includes the names of Frisians who had been acting as instructors and advisers:

þær wearð ofslægen Lucumon cynges gerefa 7 Wulfheard Friesa 7 Æbbe Friesa 7 Æðelhere Friesa 7 Æðelferð cynges geneat 7 ealra monna Fresiscra 7 Engliscra lxii 7 þara Deniscena cxx

KILLED IN ACTION
    Officers: Lucumon the king's reeve; Wulfheard the Frisian; Æbbe the

Frisian; Æthelhere the Frisian; Æthelferth the king's ADC (aide-de-camp).

Other ranks: 62 English and Frisians, 120 Danes.

This list lends poignancy to a passage from *Maxims i* which gives a rare glimpse of domestic happiness:

> lēof wilcuma
> 95 Frysan wīfe   þonne flota stondeð·
> biþ his cēol cumen   ond hyre ceorl tō hām,
> āgen ætgeofa,   ond hēo hine in laðaþ·
> wæsceð his wārig hrægl   ond him syleþ wæde nīwe·
> līþ him on londe   þæs his lufu bædeð

... welcome [is] her beloved to the Frisian wife when the ship lies at anchor. His ship has returned and her husband, her own breadwinner, is at home. She welcomes him in, washes his sea-stained garments, gives him new clothes, and grants him on his return what his love asks.

The poem *The Fortunes of Men* portrays a happy family:

> Ful oft þæt gegongeð,   mid godes meahtum,
> þætte wer ond wīf   in woruld cennað
> bearn mid gebyrdum   ond mid blēom gyrwað,
> tennaþ ond tætaþ,   oþþæt sēo tīd cymeð,
> 5 gegǣð gēarrīmum,   þæt þā geongan leomu,
> līffæstan leoþu,   geloden weorþað.
> Fergað swā ond fēþað   fæder ond modor,
> giefað ond gierwaþ.   God āna wāt
> hwæt him weaxendum   winter bringað!

Very often it happens that by God's might a man and woman bring children into the world through births, clothe [them] in colours, cheer and gladden [them] until the time comes, arrives in the course of years, that the young limbs, the living joints, become grown. Thus the father and mother carry [them] and walk [with them], give and direct. God alone knows what the winters will bring to them as they grow.

That there was another side to family life is demonstrated by the dispute between Enneawn and her son Edwin (§366) and perhaps also by the illustration of Noah's ark in the Junius Manuscript (§173), in which Mrs Noah is portrayed on a ladder refusing to enter the ark despite Noah's entreaties – a scene which forms part of several of the mediaeval miracle plays about Noah's flood.

§369 The poetry gives few glimpses of the life of women not of noble rank. These are mostly found in the riddles of the Exeter Book. In one the nightingale (or jay) is compared to a *scirenige* 'actress' or 'female jester'. Some of those with double meanings associate the vocabulary of intercourse with domestic duties. In these the joke is on both sexes. One portrays a churl's daughter peeling an onion (*Riddle* 25), another a man inserting a key in a lock (or a dagger in a sheath) (*Riddle* 44), and a third a man making butter in a churn (*Riddle* 54).

§370 Freewomen of lower rank had much the same responsibilities and rights as noble women. Some owned estates and slaves. Even those who did not were responsible for running their households; grinding, baking, brewing, preserving, spinning, and weaving, were all done at home. Women had the keys of the storeroom, the chest, and the coffer; a law of Cnut says:

> And gyf hwylc man forstolen þingc ham to his cotan bringe 7 he arasod wurðe· riht is· þæt he hæbbe þæt he æftereode. 7 butan hit under þæs wifes cæglocan gebroht wære· si heo clæne

> And if any man brings a stolen thing home to his house and he is found out, it is right that he [the owner] should receive what he went in search of. And, unless it has been brought under his [the thief's] wife's lock and key, she is to be innocent.

Space does not permit a full account of the customs and laws which affected women; these differed under different codes and rulers. But a few provisions demand mention here. The Laws of Æthelbert of Kent (d. 616) allow for a husband to return his wife to her family and to reclaim what he had paid if some relevant fact about her was not revealed at the time of a marriage, and for a woman to leave an unpleasing marriage. They also gave women a right which has only recently been restored to their descendants: *Gif mid bearnum bugan wille, healfne scæt age* 'If [a wife] wishes to depart [from her husband] with the children, she is to have half the property'. And at the end of the Anglo-Saxon period, a law of Cnut says *7 na nyde man naðer ne wif ne mæden to þam þe hyre sylfre mislicie* 'And no man is to force any woman or maiden [to marry] one whom she dislikes'.

§371 The lot of female slaves was not to be envied. Rarely, one was buried alive with her dead mistress (§326). A law of Æthelstan which survives only in Latin decreed that a slave who stole should be executed by stoning if male, by burning if female. Female slaves were included in the stock at Yaxley (§244). The theft of one of them led to a complicated lawsuit: *se fruma* [beginning of this case] *wæs þæt mon forstæl ænne wimman æt Ieceslea.* They performed the menial tasks of the household. Some masters slept with them but they were protected against rape by heavy penalties; a law of Alfred reads *Gif ðeowmon þeowne to nedhæmde genede· bete mid his eowende* 'If a slave rapes a slavewoman, he is to be castrated'. A freeman could marry a slavewoman. Some achieved freedom; in her will (*c.* 950), Wynflæd says *freoge man Wulfware· folgyge þam hyre leofost sy 7 Ættryth ealswa* 'Wulfware is to be freed [and] is to serve whom she pleases and Ættryth also'. Not all Wynflæd's slavewomen were so lucky, for the will goes on to say that *hio becwið Eadgyfe ane crencestran 7 ane semestran* 'she bequeathes to Eadgifu a woman-weaver and a sempstress'.

§372 I conclude by summarizing some passages from the Anglo-Saxon leechdoms and charms. First, a charm *wiþ wif gemæðlan· geberge on neaht nestig rædices moran· þy dæge ne mæg þe se gemæðla sceþþan* 'against a woman's chatter: eat at night, fasting, the root of a radish; that day the chatter cannot harm you'. A poor diet indeed for the man used to feasting in the hall. Cures for barrenness in a woman include boiling the herb fieldmore in a mixture of milk and water and consuming the result, or binding coriander seeds on the inside of the left thigh; for men, agrimony boiled in ale is an antaphrodisiac but boiled in milk is a remedy for impotence. The complicated description of the formation of a male foetus (Text 25 §433) includes words of interest to some modern controversialists: *On þam þriddan monþe he biþ man buton sawle* 'in the third month, he is a man without a soul'. Pregnant women are warned not to eat anything salt or sweet; to avoid swine's flesh, fat, and beer; not to ride too much on horseback; and to avoid drunkenness. Some of these prohibitions still obtain today. But the modern warning against smoking is understandably absent. The sex of an unborn child can be determined by observing the behaviour of the mother-to-be. The signs, in tabular form, are:

Boy	*Girl*
Hollow eyes	Swollen eyes
Slow walk	Brisk walk
Walks on heels	Walks on toes
Carries child high	Carries child low
Chooses lily	Chooses rose

The charm for delayed birth printed in §472 (Text 37) involves different formulae repeated at the grave of a dead man, as the woman steps over her husband as he lies in bed, and before the altar in a church. The skeletons of a mother and her undelivered babe from a sixth- or seventh-century grave at Worthy Park, Hampshire (figure 36), are a grim commentary on the efficacy of this charm.

6 Amusements and entertainments

§373 One of the epitaphs bestowed on Beowulf – *hleahtor ālegde, ‖ gamen ond glēodrēam* '[he] laid aside laughter, joy and mirth' – proves that there were lighter moments – for men at least – in this violent society where years were numbered in winters. Even the prose is silent about how women relaxed, although, as we have already seen, they took pleasure in beautiful objects – tapestries (§§287–8), jewellery (§§224–38), and dress (§285). The

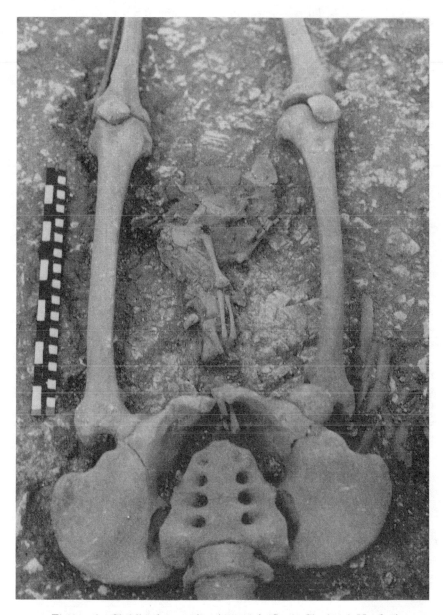

Figure 36   Childbirth mortality (copyright Sonia Chadwick Hawkes)

author of *The Riming Poem*, speaking as he was for a man of high rank, no doubt spoke for women too in these lines:

> Glæd ic wæs mid glīwum   glenged hīwum
> blissa blēoum,   blostma hīwum

I was glad with music, decorated with hues, with the colours of joy, with the hues of blossoms.

§374 The outdoor activities of the men were, not surprisingly, those which have delighted military men throughout the ages. Some are portrayed on the Bayeux Tapestry and most are mentioned in *The Gifts of Men*: hunting (*sum bið on huntoþe hrēðēadigra*, ‖ *dēora drǣfend* 'one is more famous in hunting, a pursuer of wild beasts'); hawking (*sum bið fugelbōna, hafeces crǣftig* 'one is a fowler, skilful with the hawk'); riding (*sum bið to horse hwæt* 'one is bold on horseback'); horse-racing (*Beowulf* 864–5:

> Hwīlum heaþorōfe   hlēapan lēton,
> 865   on geflit faran,   fealwe mēaras

At times the men brave in battle allowed their bay steeds to gallop, run races);

running (*sum on londe snel, fēþespēdig* 'one [is] swift on land, speedy of foot'); archery (*sum ryhtscytte* 'one [is] a dead shot'); sailing (*sum on fealone wǣg* ‖ *stefnan stēoreð, strēamrāde con* 'one steers the prow over the shining wave, is familiar with the running tides'); swimming (*sum bið syndig* 'one is skilled in swimming'); and gymnastics (*sum bið swīðsnel* 'one is very agile'). There is no mention of cricket, baseball, or tennis. But the place-name Plaistow comes from OE *plegstow* 'playing place', and the romance of *Apollonius of Tyre* (translated from a Latin version of a Greek original) tells how the shipwrecked Apollonius attracted the attention of King Arcestrates by his skill at ball play; see Text 31 (§443).

§375 After such activities, the warriors found entertainment in the hall, as described in *Beowulf* 611–24 (§361) and 491–8:

> þā wæs Gēatmæcgum   geador ætsomne
> on bēorsele   benc gerȳmed·
> þǣr swīðferhþe   sittan ēodon,
> þrȳðum dealle.   þegn nytte behēold
> 495 se þe on handa bær   hroden ealowǣge·
> scencte scīr wered.   Scop hwīlum sang
> hādor on Heorote.   þǣr wæs hæleða drēam·
> duguð unlȳtel   Dena ond Wedera

Then a bench was cleared in the hall for the men of the Geats all together. The bold ones, famous for their strength, went to sit there. The thane who carried in his hand a decorated ale-cup did his duty, poured out bright liquor. From time to time, a minstrel sang clearly in Heorot. There was revelry among the heroes – no small band of Danes and Geats.

§376 During the feast, wine, beer, or mead, was poured into cups of silver, glass, pottery, or wood (sometimes adorned with gold or silver), or into drinking-horns; in Heorot, *byrelas sealdon* ‖ *wīn of wunderfatum* 'cup-bearers poured wine from wondrous vessels'. Such things were prized, as the bequest of Ælfgifu, a woman of royal descent, testifies: *ic ann Ælfwerdæ anne sopcuppan and Æþelwerdæ anæs gerænodæs drincæhornæs* 'I grant to Ælfweard a drinking-cup and to Æthelweard an ornamented drinking-horn'. On the evidence of Ælfric's *Colloquy*, food in the monastery included *wyrta 7 ægra, fisc 7 cyse, buteran 7 beana* 'vegetables and eggs, fish and cheese, butter and beans'. There was a good choice of fish; the *Colloquy* mentions flounder, minnows, mussels, oysters, periwinkles, pike, plaice, salmon, shellfish, sprats, sturgeon, and trout. There is no doubt that other things, including bread and honey, were available. The novice says *gyt flæscmettum ic bruce forðam cild ic eom* 'I still eat meat because I am a boy'. The warriors had no such inhibitions as they consumed beef, mutton, pork, bacon, and poultry – although none of these French words was yet in the language.

§377 The hall was the place where the heroes made their *beot*, the vow in which they named their play, described in advance what they intended to do, as Beowulf did in Heorot as he waited for the monster Grendel to come:

> 636   'Ic gefremman sceal
>   eorlic ellen   oþðe endedæg
>   on þisse meoduhealle   mīnne gebīdan!'

'I shall perform a deed of heroic valour or await the end of my days in this mead-hall'.

He fulfilled his *beot*, as King Hrothgar testified:

>   'þū þē self hafast
>   dǣdum gefremed   þæt þīn dōm lyfað
> 955 āwa tō aldre'

'You yourself have brought it about by [your] deeds that your glory will live for ever'.

So too did the warriors who fell at Maldon (§347), unlike the ten cowards who deserted Beowulf and those who fled at Maldon (§348). The latter were condemned by Offa (§348), the former by Wiglaf:

>   'þæt, lā, mæg secgan   sē ðe wyle sōð specan
> 2865 þæt se mondryhten   se ēow ðā māðmas geaf,
>   ēoredgeatwe,   þe gē þǣr on standað –
>   þonne hē on ealubence   oft gesealde
>   healsittendum   helm ond byrnan,

þēoden his þegnum –   . . .
2870 þæt hē gēnunga   gūðgewǣdu
wrāðe forwurpe   ðā hyne wīg begeat'

'Indeed the man who is willing to speak the truth can say that the leader of men who gave you the treasures, the war-gear which you stand in there, when he often gave helmet and coat of mail to hall-sitters on the ale-bench, lord to his thanes, completely and grievously wasted that armour when war came upon him'.

§378   In the hall, the poet (*sum biþ wōðbora, giedda giffæst* 'one is a poet, gifted with lays'), the harper (*sum mid hondum mæg hearpan grētan· āh hē glēobēames gearobrygda list* 'one is able to play the harp, has skill in the eager pulsations of the glee-wood'), and the singer (*sum lēoða glēaw* 'one [is] skilled in songs') provided entertainment. All are described in *The Gifts of Men*. All feature in *Beowulf*:

Hwīlum cyninges þegn,
guma gilphlæden,   gidda gemyndig,
se ðe ealfela   ealdgesegena
870 worn gemunde,   word ōþer fand
sōðe gebunden

At times a thane of the prince, a man with a store of poetic phrase, mindful of many lays, who recalled innumerable old traditions, told a new story in words properly linked together,

and

þǣr wæs sang ond swēg   samod ætgædere
fore Healfdenes   hildewīsan,
1065 gomenwudu grēted,   gid oft wrecen

There was song and music together in the presence of Hrothgar's battle-captains, the joy-wood [was] played, many a song performed.

§379   There was pleasure too in riddling (see Texts 14 (§484), 45 (§486), 49 (§491), and 50 (§492), and note that *Riddle* 42 ends

Nū is undyrne
werum æt wīne   hū þā wihte mid ūs,
hēanmōde twā,   hātne sindon

Now it is clear to men at wine how you two, miserable-minded creatures, are named by us);

in speeches (*sum biþ gearuwyrdig* 'one is ready of speech'); in good company and conversation (*sum bið þegn gehweorf on meoduhealle* 'one is an active thane in the mead-hall', *sum bið lēofwende, hafað mōd ond word monnum geþwǣre* 'one is popular, has a mind and words pleasing to men', and *sum bið gewittig æt winþege, bēorhyrde gōd* 'one is witty at the wine-banquet, a good guardian of the beer'); in board games (*sumum tæfle cræft, blēobordes gebregd* 'to one [is given] skill at the game, cunning at the coloured board'); and in dice (*īdle hond æmetlan geneah tæfles monnes þonne teoselum weorpeð* 'the idle hand of the man at leisure suffices the gambling man when he throws the dice').

§380 *Word wæron wynsume* 'Words were pleasant'. But the harmony of the hall was sometimes disrupted by the attack of enemies, e.g. Grendel and then his mother at Heorot (§346); by the renewal of a blood-feud, as at Finnesburh (§362); or by the drunkenness of an individual. This last danger was recognized both by law-makers and by poets. The Laws of Hlothære and Eadric (685–6) lay down fines which are to be paid *gif man mannan on oþres flette manswara hateþ oððe hine mid bismærwordum scandlice grete* 'if someone calls a man a perjurer in another's hall or shamefully attacks him with insulting words' and *gif man wæpn abregde þær men drincen* 'if someone draws a weapon where men are drinking'. In the latter case, the penalty was more severe *gif þæt flet geblodgad wyrþe* 'if the hall becomes bloodstained'. The poet of *The Fortunes of Men* gives these grim warnings:

>   Sumum mēces ecg   on meodubence
>   yrrum ealowosan   ealdor oþþringeð,
> 50 were wīnsadum·   bið ær his worda tō hræd.
>   Sum sceal on bēore   þurh byreles hond
>   meodugāl mæcga·   þonne hē gemet ne con
>   gemearcian his mūþe   mōde sīne
>   ac sceal ful earmlice   ealdre linnan,
> 55 drēogan dryhtenbealo   drēamum biscyred,
>   ond hine tō sylfcwale   secgas nemnað,
>   mænað mid mūþe   meodugāles gedrinc

From one, an angry ale-bibber, a man satiated with wine, the edge of the sword will take life on the mead-bench; [he] has been too hasty of speech. Another shall at beer through the cupbearer's hand [become] a man flushed with drink; then he is unable to impose moderation on his mouth with his mind but shall lose his life miserably, deprived of joys, suffer the extreme evil, and men will speak of him as a self-slayer, deplore with their mouth the carousing of a drunkard.

So then, as now, *þis læne līf* 'this transitory life' was fraught with danger even in moments of relaxation. But for those who lived hard in Anglo-Saxon times, life also had its silver linings, when there was *blis in burgum, hælcða drēam*, and *ðēod on sælum* 'merriment in dwellings, rejoicing of heroes, and people in happiness'.

7 The impact of Christianity

§381 The search for Anglo-Saxon paganism (§324) has been replaced by another wild-goose chase: the search for modern Christianity in Anglo-

Saxon literature. Some critics would have us believe that not only Anglo-Saxon authors but also Anglo-Saxon audiences – often spoken of as if they were homogeneous, all responding in the same way to the same work of art – were as knowledgeable about the Bible, the Church Fathers, and the intricacies of Christian theology, as a Regius Professor of Divinity. This notion needs to be dismissed, as does that of the 'effectively converted England' envisaged by one writer on *Beowulf*. Has there ever been such a place?

§382   Christianity came to England from two sources – Rome and Ireland. As we shall see, both Roman and Celtic Christianity exercised great influence as a result of the activity of their missionaries. The main stages in the bringing of the Christian faith to England are set out in the Chronicle extracts printed in §183: the arrival of Augustine, sent from Rome by Pope Gregory in 596 (more correctly, 597); the appointment by Augustine of Paulinus as Bishop of Northumbria, his mission, and his return to Canterbury on the death of Edwin in 632; the resulting decline of Roman Christianity in the north; the arrival in 634 of Aidan, who brought Celtic Christianity to Northumbria from Iona and founded the see of Lindisfarne; and the Synod of Whitby which in 664 attempted to settle the differences between the Roman and the Celtic traditions. (The last two events are not mentioned in the Chronicle.) Other important landmarks include the formation of double monasteries (§390), the literary and educational programme formulated and carried through by King Alfred (§177), and the tenth-century monastic reform or, as it is often called, the Benedictine Revival (§186).

§383   Not unusually, the converters adopted the policy of baptizing what they could not suppress (§327) or (to put it positively) made use of what they saw as good in the customs and beliefs they were aiming to supplant. Thus Bede reports that Pope Gregory's instructions to Augustine included these sentences which do not appear in the Old English version: '. . . the idol temples of that [English] race should not be destroyed but only the idols in them. Take holy water and sprinkle it in these shrines, build altars, and place relics in them . . . Do not let them sacrifice animals to the devil but let them slaughter animals for their own food to the praise of God.' The York-educated Englishman Alcuin, who spent much of his life at Charlemagne's court, urged strict separation of pagan and Christian, addressing the monks of Lindisfarne or, Geoffrey Bullough argues, a non-monastic Mercian bishop, in 797, with these words: 'What has Ingeld to do with Christ? Narrow is the house; it will not be able to hold them both.' But it is clear that in practice the pagan (represented by Ingeld, a warrior-king who appears in *Beowulf*) and the Christian were often associated. Bede tells us that Rædwald, king of the East Angles, already mentioned in connection with the Sutton Hoo ship-burial (§196), *wæs gesewen Criste þeowian 7 eac deofolgeldum· and he in þam ilcan herige wigbed hæfde to Cristes onsægdnesse 7 oðer to deofla onsægdnisse* 'was seen to serve Christ as well as idols and in the same sanctuary he had an altar for Christ's sacrifice and a second for sacrifice to devils'. J. N. L. Myres reports evidence for the use in pagan cremations of urns bearing animal or bird stamps designed for Christian use. Rosemary Cramp notes that in the excavations at Winchester Old Minster, carvings portraying the story of Sigurd were found, reflecting the pride of the late Saxon kings in their pagan and northern origin.

§384   When Augustine landed in Kent, he found that King Æthelberht had to wife a Christian Frankish princess called Bertha. Bede writes:

> þa sealde se cyning him wunenesse 7 stowe in Cantwara byrig seo wæs ealles his rices ealdorburg ond· swa swa he geheht· him ondlifen forgeaf 7 weoruldþearfe ond eac swylce leafnesse sealde þæt heo mosten Cristes geleafan bodian 7 læran

> Then the king gave them [the monks] a dwelling-place in Canterbury, which was the capital of all his kingdom, and, as he promised, gave them provisions and their worldly needs and also gave permission that they might proclaim and teach the faith of Christ.

Before long, the king himself *gefeonde wæs gefulwad* 'rejoicing was baptized'. The Chronicle account of these early years (§183) adds to the list of the converted Edwin, king of Northumbria (601), and Sæbyrht, king of Essex (604), although Edwin was not baptized until 627, a year after his daughter Eanfled.

§385   The conversion of the king by the missionaries was vital; other conversions, their means of living, and perhaps even their very lives, depended on it. The clarion call was to join the warrior band of the King of Kings and to dwell with Him in Heaven – as one poet put it, *cēosan ūs eard in wuldre mid ealra cyninga cyninge,* ‖ *se is Crīst genemned* 'let us choose a dwelling in Heaven with the King of all kings, who is called Christ' – where, in the words of *The Dream of the Rood*, the Lord's warrior-band is set to the feast: *þǣr is Dryhtnes folc* ‖ *geseted tō symle.* This invitation was apparently hard to resist, initially at any rate, although some held out, including King Penda of Mercia, who killed in battle two Christian kings of Northumbria, Edwin (632) and Oswald (642); see §183. Those who did not resist showed their faith in different ways. Edwin and Oswald died for it. King Cenred of Mercia *for to Rome 7 þær scire onfeng 7 munuc wæs geworden . . . oð ðone ytemestan dæg* 'went to Rome and there received the tonsure and became a monk . . . up to his last day'. Sigeberht, king of the East Saxons, who *wæs ceasterwara gefremed þæs ecan rices* 'was made a citizen of the heavenly kingdom', continued to rule *his hwiilwendlices riices* 'his temporal kingdom' until he *þurh his mæga hond wæs ofslægen* 'was killed by the hand of his kinsmen'. What was their reason for slaying their kinsman and lord? *Heo yrre wære 7 þæm cyninge feond forðon he gewunode þæt he his feondum swiðe arode* 'they were angry and hostile to the king because he was wont to show great mercy to his enemies'. Another Sigeberht, king of East Anglia, gave up his kingdom and retired to a monastery. When Penda (§183) attacked East Anglia, Sigeberht was taken from the monastery against his will and put at the head of his army. Bede tells us how he chose death rather than fight.

Text 15 **A non-combatant warrior king**

Ond swa swiðe se cyning wæs geworden lufiend þæs heofonlican rices þæt he æt nyhstan forlet þæt eorðlice rice 7 his mæge Ecgberhte bebead 7 in mynster eode þæt he him seolf ær getimbrade 7 sceare onfeng 7 ma gemde for þam ecan rice to compienne.

5 þa he þæt þa longe tiid dyde· þa gelomp þætte Penda Mercna cyning teah here 7 fyrd wið Eastengle þider to gefeohte cwom. þa heo þa hie in þæm gefeohte neoþor gesegon 7 læssan weorude heora feondum· þa bædon heo Sigeberht þæt he mid him cwome to þæm gefeohte heora compweorod to trymmanne. þa ne wolde he ac wiðcwæð· þa tugon heo hine nydinga of

10 þam mynstre 7 læddon on þone here. Wendon heo þæt heora comp-weorodes mod þy unforhtre beon sceolde 7 þy læs fluge for his andweard-nesse· forðon he wæs ær se fromesta heretoga. Ac he wæs gemyndig his ondetnesse 7 his gehata þe he Gode geheht. þa he wæs mid þy unmætan weorode ymbhæfd· ne wolde he oðer wæpen nemne ane gyrde him on honda

15 habban· ond he wæs ofslegen mid Ecgrice þam cyninge 7 eall heora weorod oðþe geslegen oððe geflymed wæs.

2 **æt nyhstan** 'at last'; **forlætan** 'to give up' (st. vb. VII(*b*) §517); **mæg** 'kinsman'; **bebēodan** 'to offer/entrust' (st. vb. II §517), parallel to *forlēt*. See §§162–3.

3 **mynster** 'monastery'; **scear** 'tonsure'; **gīeman/gēman** 'to care/take heed' (wk. vb. like *hīeran* §94).

4 **compian** 'to fight' (wk. vb. like *lufian* §526).

5 **gelimpan** 'to happen' (st. vb. III §518).

6 **tēon** 'to assemble, to lead' (st. contracted vb. II §521); **cwōm** = *cōm*; **hēo** = *hīe* nom. pl. 'they'; **hīe** acc. pl. reflexive 'themselves'.

7 **neoþor** adv. 'inferior'; **gesēgon** = *gesāwon*; **weorud** 'troop/force'; here the dat. **fēondum** expresses comparison: 'with a smaller force than their enemies'; **biddan** 'to ask' (st. vb. V §519).

8 **hēo** = *hīe* nom. pl.; **compweorod** 'army'.

9 **trymman** 'to encourage' (wk. vb. like *fremman* §524); **wiðcweðan** 'to refuse' (st. vb. V §517); **tēon** 'to drag' (the same verb as in l. 6); **nȳdinga** adv. 'by force'.

10 **wēnan** 'to think' (like *gēman* l. 3).

11 **mōd** 'courage/spirit'; **þy unforhtre** 'because of that (i.e. the presence of the king) more fearless'; **þy læs** 'because of that less'; **flēon** 'to flee' (st. contracted vb. II §521), here pret. subj. pl. 'might flee'.

11–12 **andweardness** 'presence'.

12 **from** adj. 'active/bold'; **heretoga** 'army commander/general'; **gemyndig** adj. 'mindful'.

13 **ondetness** 'profession'; **gehāt** 'promise/vow'; **unmæte** 'immense/vast'.

14 **ymbhabban** 'to surround' (an irregular wk. vb. §527); **nemne** prep. 'except'; **gyrd** 'rod/staff'.

16 **oðþe ... oððe** conjs. 'either ... or'; **(ge)flȳman** 'to put to flight' (like *gēman* l. 3).

For an edition of the Anglo-Saxon translation of Bede's *Historia* see §425.

But Sighere, king of the East Saxons, unlike his predecessor Sigeberht, *forlet þa gerynu þæs Cristnan geleafan 7 to hæðenisse wæs gehwyrfed . . . Se seolfa cyning 7 his aldormen 7 monige of his folces lufodon þis deadlice lif 7 . . . ongunnon þa heargas edniwian* 'abandoned the mysteries of the Christian faith and was turned back to heathenism . . . The same king and his chief men and many of his people loved this mortal life . . . and began to restore the heathen temples'.

§386   The retainers of a converted king no doubt varied in their attitude to the new faith in the same way as the kings just mentioned, some with conviction but many with reluctance or worse. The Parker MS of the Chronicle tells us how, after King Alfred had defeated the Danes under King Guthrum at the battle of Edington in 878, *com se cyning to him Godrum þritiga sum þara monna þe in þam here weorþuste wæron . . . 7 se cyning þær onfeng æt fulwihte 7 his crismlising wæs æt Weþmor* 'the king Godrum came to him [Alfred], one of thirty of the men who were most honoured in the [Danish] army . . . and the king there received baptism and the loosing of his baptismal headband was at Wedmore'. It is not clear whether his warriors were also baptized but one can imagine the sheepish embarrassment of these blond giants coupled with the muttering of imprecations such as 'What's wrong with Woden?' and 'Thor's OK with me'. What, I wonder, was the reaction of such men to the story of the monk walking on water (Text 21 §429)?

§387   True conversion must have brought great comfort to men and women who had little, if any, belief in an afterlife and no awareness of what Richard Southern (Bibliography III E) has called 'the personal and secret tie between God and man'. But those who experienced it must have been a strange blend of pagan and Christian, combining as they did the fierce courage and pride of paganism with the new hope derived from Christianity – a blend seen in the Benty Grange helmet (§212), which bears the pagan boar image and the Christian cross; in King Alfred's actions during and after the fighting at Edington (§386); and in the literature (§§448–50).

§388   As the heroic warrior king gradually became the Christian warrior king, the power and influence of the Church in Anglo-Saxon England increased. In his book *Life in Anglo-Saxon England*, Ray Page has a chapter entitled 'God's Thanes'. In one sense, this could be used of the king and his warriors; in another, of those in religious life. The poem *The Gifts of Men* has something to say of them:

> Sum hēr geornlice   gǣstes þearfe
> mōde bewindeþ   ond him metudes ēst
> ofer eorðwelan   ealne gecēoseð.
> Sum bið dēormōd   deofles gewinnes·
> 90 bið ā wið firenum   in gefeoht gearo.
> Sum cræft hafað   circnytta fela·
> mæg on lōfsongum   līfes waldend
> hlūde hergan·   hafað hēalice

> 　　　beorhte stefne.　　Sum bið bōca glēaw,
> 95　lārum lēoþufæst.　　Sum biþ listhendig
> 　　　tō awrītanne　　wordgerȳno

One here eagerly entwines in his heart the needs of the spirit and chooses for himself the grace of Christ over all the wealth of the world. One is bold in warfare against the devil, is always ready to fight against sins. One has skill in many church services, is able to glorify loudly the ruler of life with songs of praise, has in high degree a clear voice. One is wise in books, devoted to learning. One is skilful of hand in writing down the mysteries of words.

Here we see the baptism of old values – devotion to one's lord, courage in battle, skill in music and song – and the creation of new ones – enthusiasm for learning and skill in writing and illuminating manuscripts. Alfred described the situation before the Danes came in his Preface to his translation of the *Cura Pastoralis* (Text 24 §432), where he wrote these words:

> Ða ic ða ðis eall gemunde· ða gemunde ic eac hu ic geseah· ær ðæm ðe hit eall forhergod wære ond forbærned· hu ða ciricean giond eall Angelcynn stodon maðma ond boca gefylda ond eac micel mengeo Godes ðiowa

> When I remembered all this, then I remembered also how I saw, before it was all plundered and destroyed by fire, how the churches throughout all England stood filled with treasures and books and also [there was] a great multitude of God's servants.

§389　These servants were not exclusively men. From the writings of Aldhelm, Abbot of Malmesbury and Bishop of Salisbury (died 709), it is clear that the nuns of Barking were skilled in Latin and versed in the scriptures, the laws, history, grammar, and metrics. Both monks and nuns copied and illuminated manuscripts (§§291–300). The composition of Christian poetry in the vernacular may not have been restricted to men; see §448.

§390　Double monasteries – monks and nuns living in strict seclusion from one another but sharing worship and liturgical unity – were an importation from Gaul and were, as far as we know, always ruled in England by abbesses. Women of noble birth, including queens and princesses, single or widowed, often founded monasteries for women, sometimes on their own lands, attracting women from the different classes of society, and added communities of men to say masses, administer the sacraments, and carry out the traditionally male tasks. Hild (d. 680), in whose monastery Cædmon (Text 20 §427) served and who was a kinswoman of Oswiu, king of Northumbria, was abbess of the monastery she founded at Whitby. Bede, who reports that five of her monks became bishops, tells us that

> wæs heo swa micelre snytro 7 wisdomes þætte nales þæt an þætte þa mættran men ymb heora nydþearfnisse wæron ac eac swylce cyningas 7

ealdormen oft from hire geþeaht 7 wisdom sohton 7 hine þær georne gemetton

she was of such great prudence and wisdom that not only the ordinary men were [there] about their business but even kings and councillors often sought advice and wisdom from her and readily found it there.

She was not only consulted but loved; Bede reports that *ealle þa þe hy cuþon . . . gewunedan heo modor cegean* 'all those who knew her . . . were wont to call her mother'. St Æthelthryth (Audrey), the daughter of King Anna of the East Angles, *ongon þæt mynster æt Elige* 'founded the monastery at Ely' in 673. She was followed by her sister Seaxburg, who in her turn was succeeded by her daughter and granddaughter. The two sisters were ranked by Ælfric among the great saints of England:

Nis angelcynn bedæled drihtnes halgena þonne on englalanda licgaþ swilce halgan swylce þæs halga cyning is and cuþberht se eadiga and sancte æþeldryð on elig and eac hire swustor

The English nation is not deprived of the saints of the Lord when in England lie such saints as this holy king [Edmund of East Anglia] is and Cuthbert the blessed and Saint Æthelthryth in Ely and also her sister . . .

Saints such as Æthelthryth and Seaxburg may well have been inspired by saints like Elene and Juliana, both of whom later became the subject of Old English poems; see Text 48 (§490).

§391 Like most modern institutions and organizations, monasteries were anxious to attract property, money, rights, and privileges. Ely was well-endowed by its founder Æthelthryth (§390), who had acquired the island of Ely as a morning-gift from her first husband. But, like many other monasteries, it often appears as a beneficiary in the charters and wills. Benefactors include King Edgar (d. 975), who gave land and provided for annual gifts for the monks, including clothing and 10,000 eels; Bishop Ælfric (a gift of money); Thurstan and Ælfhelm (estates); and Prince Æthelstan (§204), who bequeathed an annual gift of money for the monks and another to allow one hundred poor people to be fed on St Æthelthryth's day. Women also contributed; they included Wulfgyth (a woollen gown), Ælfflæd, wife of Byrhtnoth of Maldon (§366) (three estates), and her sister Æthelflæd, who left estates to Glastonbury, Christ Church Canterbury, Ely, and other monasteries. Byrhtnoth himself was also a benefactor of Ely and his body, without the head which was cut off by the Danes, was buried there. His widow gave Ely a wall-hanging depicting his deeds. King Cnut, converted after a pagan youth, was a generous supporter of monasteries, including Ely, of which he seems to have been particularly fond.

§392 But naturally enough perfection was not achieved. Some monasteries even went to the extent of forging charters (see Text 28 §437) and there are instances of 'tax-avoidance' pseudo-monasteries being established by wealthy landowners to avoid the taxes and dues which they owed the king. Not all professed monks and nuns were suited to a religious life and the documents contain many warnings against gossip, love of fine clothing and jewellery, greed, and other human failings. One of the more delightful is the story of the negligent nun, who, while walking in the vegetable garden, plucked a lettuce and carelessly bit into it without making the sign of the cross. In so doing, she unwittingly swallowed the Devil, who had been sitting on it. A holy man summoned to save her was addressed by the devil, who

> þus cwæð: 'Hwæt dyde ic hire? Hwæt dyde ic hire? Ic sæt me on anum leahtrice· þa com heo and bat me!' He þa, se Godes wer, mid mycelre yrsunge, him bebead þæt he fram hire gewite and þæt he nane wunung-stowe næfde on þæs ælmihtigan Godes þeowene. He þærryhte aweg gewat and na leng syððan hire æthrinan ne dorste

> spoke thus: 'What did *I* do to *her*? What did *I* do to *her*? I was sitting on a lettuce when she came and bit me.' Then the man of God, in great anger, commanded him to come out of her and never again to have any dwelling-place in the handmaid of Almighty God. He [the Devil] immediately went away and afterwards no longer dared to touch her.

But, as far as we know, scandal affected only one double monastery, that at Coldingham, in what is now Berwickshire, Scotland, which (Bede tells us) was destroyed by fire after its occupants failed to heed a warning which a man of strange appearance revealed to a virtuous brother in a dream:

> Soð ic secge· þæt ic nu eal þis mynster ðurh endebyrdnisse geondferde 7 syndrigra hus 7 bedd geseah· 7 nænigne of eallum butan þe ic gemette ymb his saule hælo abisgodne beon· ah alle ge wæpnedmenn ge wifmenn oððo hefige slæpe syndon oððe to synnum wacedon. Ond ða hus ða ðe in to gebiddenne 7 to leornienne geworhte wæron· ða syndon nu in hus gehwerfed oferæta 7 druncennesse 7 leasspellunge 7 oðerra unalefedlecra scylda. 7 eac swelce ða fæmnan ða ðe Gode gehalgode wæron· forhogdre are heara ondetnisse ond swa oft swa hio æmtan habbað· þæt hio smælo hrægel weofað 7 wyrcað mid ðæm hio oððo hio siolfe frætwað in bryda onlicnesse in frecenesse hiora stalles oððo utwæpnedmonna friondscipes him ceapiað. Forðon bi gewyrhte þysse stowe 7 hire eardiendum hefig wræc of hiofenum grimsiendum legum is gegearwad

> I tell you the truth, that I have now gone round all this monastery in order and have seen the dwellings and beds of [all] individuals and I have found none of [them] all except you to be concerned about the salvation of his soul, but all, both men and women, are either heavy with sleep or were awake for sins. And the dwellings which were made for praying and learning in, those are now turned into dwellings of gluttony and drunkenness and empty talk and other unlawful sins. And also the virgins who

were dedicated to God, despising the respect due to their profession whenever they have leisure, weave and work fine garments with which they either adorn themselves in the likeness of brides, to the risk of their position, or buy for themselves the love of men outside. Therefore deservedly for this place and its inhabitants heavy vengeance by raging flames from heaven is prepared.

§393 Not all God's thanes in the religious sense were in monasteries. There were secular priests but we know little about them. It is clear that there was no system of parishes. Clergy of lower rank were permitted to marry; Pope Gregory's instructions to Augustine included this sentence:

Gif þonne hwylce preostas 7 Godes þeowas synd· butan halgum hadum gesette· þa ðe heo from wiifum ahabban ne mæge· nimen heom wiif 7 heora ondleofone utan onfongen

If then [there] are any priests and servants of God – unless [they are] included in holy brotherhoods – who cannot live without wives, let them take to them[selves] wives and receive their maintenance outside [the community].

Marriage was not completely forbidden even after the tenth-century Benedictine Revival (§186). Æthelred's 1014 Laws imply that such marriages occurred: *ne gebirað him ne to wife ne to worldwige gif he Gode wile rihtlice hyran 7 Godes laga healdan swa swa his hade gedafenað mid rihte* 'it does not concern him [a priest] in any way either about a wife or about worldly conflict if he wishes to obey God rightly and to hold God's laws as rightly befits his vocation'. Similarly grudging acceptance appears in the later Law of the Northumbrian Priests but the line is drawn at leaving one woman for another: *Gif preost cwenan forlete 7 oðre nime· anathema sit* 'If a priest leaves a woman and takes another, let him be excommunicated'. (Provisions for the breaking-up of marriages not involving clergy are discussed in §370.)

§394 Monastic life almost completely disappeared because of the ninth-century Viking invasions (§§184–5). King Alfred made efforts to restore it. He is generally agreed to be the founder of the Benedictine nunnery at Shaftesbury and left it a generous bequest:

ÐIS is þe quide þat Alured king ian into Sceaftesburi Gode to loue and seint Marie and alre Godes halegen· mine saule to þearue· on halre tungan þ is an hund hide mid mete and mid manne al so it stant· and mine dochte Agelyue forð mid þare erie into þan menstre for þanne hie was onbroken ihadod

This is the bequest which I, King Alfred, make to Shaftesbury to the praise of God and Saint Mary and all God's saints, for the benefit of my soul, in all sincerity, namely one hundred hides with produce and men just as it stands, and my daughter Æthelgifu, along with the inheritance, to the monastery since she took the veil because of ill health.

The double monasteries were not revived by the Benedictine reformers (§186), who kept monasteries and nunneries separate. But even after this revival, the warrior was not far below the clerical surface. Like Edwin, Oswald, and Alfred (§§183 and 185), King Harold fought against his enemies. So did his priest Leofgar after his consecration as Bishop of Hereford. The tale is told in the annal for 1056 in MS D of the Chronicle:

7 man sette Lefegar to ƀ se wæs Haroldes eorles mæsse preost 7 on his preosthade he hæfde his nepas oð þ he ƀ wæs. Se forlet his crisman 7 his rode 7 his gastlican wæpnu 7 feng to his spere 7 to his swurde 7 swa for to ferde ongean Griffin þone Wyliscan cining 7 he wearð þær ofslagen 7 his preostes mid him 7 Ælfnoð scirgerefa 7 manega oðre gode men

and Leofgar was appointed bishop, he who was Earl Harold's mass-priest and who in his priesthood kept his moustaches until he became a bishop. He gave up his chrism [holy oil] and his cross and his spiritual weapons and grasped his spear and sword and so went campaigning against Griffin the Welsh king and he [Leofgar] was killed there and his priests with him and Ælfnoth the sheriff and many other good men.

§395   The harnessing of Germanic alliterative verse to Christian themes and the way in which the heroic concepts of *dom*, *lof*, and *wyrd*, were modified by Christianity will be illustrated in Part IV (§§412–17). But a consideration of the change in the response to the universal human theme *þis læne lif* 'this transitory life' will serve as an epilogue to Part III.

8 *þis læne lif* 'This transitory life'

§396   The poet of *The Seafarer* reminds us that *þreora sum* 'one of three [things]' – *adl oþþe yldo oþþe ecghete* 'sickness or old age or violence' (see §200) – will bring an end to our transitory lives *under heofenes hador* 'under the vault of heaven'. The *Beowulf* poet expands on this in Hrothgar's reminder to Beowulf, whose fate it was to die of a wound received in his fight against the dragon, that he too is mortal:

> Nū is þīnes mægnes blǣd
> āne hwīle·   eft sōna bið
> þæt þec ādl oððe ecg   eafoþes getwǣfeð
> oððe fȳres feng   oððe flōdes wylm
> 1765 oððe gripe mēces   oððe gāres fliht
> oððe atol yldo·   oððe ēagena bearhtm
> forsiteð ond forsworceð·   semninga bið
> þæt ðec, dryhtguma,   dēað oferswȳðeð

Now the fullness of your might exists for a time. Soon after it will come to pass that sickness or sword shall cut you off from strength or the embrace of fire or the surge of a flood or an attack with a knife or the flight of an arrow or grim old age; or the brightness of the eyes shall fail and become dim. At length it will happen, noble warrior, that death will overcome you.

As we have seen, the society in which the Anglo-Saxons lived was full of reminders that 'sad mortality o'ersways their power' or that, in the words of the poet of *Solomon and Saturn*,

> Lȳtle hwīle   lēaf bēoð grēne·
> 315 ðonne hīe eft fealewiað,   feallað on eorðan
> and forweorniað,   weorðað tō dūste

For a little while the leaves are green. Then they turn yellow, fall to the earth and perish, turning to dust.

The society was violent (§§200–1) and 'brutally commercial' (§241). Years were reckoned in winters (§181 annal 60 BC, §182 annal AD 449, and §183 annal 704) and expectation of life was shorter than today, as the fate of the sons of King Æthelwulf of Wessex reminds us. Æthelwulf died in 858 and was succeeded in turn by four sons, the last of whom, King Alfred, died in 899 aged 51; see §184 n. 24. On the short expectation of life, see also §203 and the sections listed under *læne* in the General Index.

§397 Natural disasters also took their toll: drought and famine (Bede IV. 13:

> ... þrym gearum ... nænig regn in þæm stowum cwom· 7 þonon se grimmesta hungor þæt folc wæs wæcende 7 heo mid arleasre cwale fylde wæron

> ... for three years ... no rain had fallen in those parts and consequently a most severe famine afflicted the people and they were struck down by a cruel death [AD 681],

ChronE 793 *mycel hunger* 'a great famine', and *ChronE* 1005 *Her on þyssum geare wæs se mycla hunger swilce nan man ær ne gemunde swa grimne* 'Here in this year was the great famine so that no man remembered one so grim before'); fire (*ChronE* 1067 ... *on scē Nicolæs mæssedæg ... forbearn Xp̄es cyrce on Cantwarabyrig* ... 'on St Nicholas' Day ... Christ Church in Canterbury was burnt down'); flood (see §328); frost and snow (*ChronA* 761 *Her wæs se mycla winter* and *ChronD* 1048 *Her wæs se stiþa winter* 'In this year occurred the great/severe winter'. The latter is more fully described in *ChronC* 1046, which is quoted in §400); and earthquake (*ChronC* 1048 *Her on þisum geare wæs mycel eorðstyrung wide on Englalande* 'Here in this year there was a great earthquake far and wide in England').

§398 Accidents of course occurred. Buildings fell down (see §269).

People were drowned (see §328); were eaten by wild animals (*Fates of Men . . . sceal hine wulf etan, hār hǣðstapa* 'The wolf, the grey heath-prowler, shall eat him'); and fell from trees (*Fates of Men Sum sceal on holte of hēan bēame ‖ fiþerleas feallan* 'One shall fall in the wood from a high tree, [being] featherless'). No doubt they were also scalded in the kitchen, run over by carts, and trampled by horses. But I have no examples to quote.

§399 The effects of violence, natural disasters, and accidents, were compounded by diets which were not always adequate, by lack of hygiene and sanitation, by epidemics and disease, and by low standards of surgery and medicine. These topics are dealt with in Wilfrid Bonser's *The Medical Background of Anglo-Saxon England*, to which I make a blanket acknowledgement here. 'During the winter months', writes Bonser, 'the lack of fresh fruit and of many vegetables must have caused a serious deficiency of vitamins A and C, and a consequent deterioration of health and a lessening of powers of resistance to disease . . . in Anglo-Saxon times a condition of mild scurvy must have afflicted the bulk of the population during the winter . . .'. A complete absence of hygiene and sanitation, ignorance of the idea of isolation, and lack of preventive medicine, together with itinerant minstrels, monks, and pedlars, and campaigning armies, provided conditions in which epidemics of smallpox, bubonic plague, and dysentery, flourished unchecked throughout the Anglo-Saxon period; note *ChronA* 664 *þy ilcan geare wæs micel mancuealm* 'In the same year [there] was a great plague', Bede IV. 7 . . . *seo hreonis þæs oftcwedenan wooles feor 7 wide all wæs forhergende* 'the storm of the oft-mentioned plague was destroying all far and wide' (AD 676), *ChronA* 897 *hie wæron . . . gebrocede . . . mid ceapes cwilde 7 monna* 'they [the people of England] were . . . afflicted . . . with a plague of cattle and men', *ChronA* 962 . . . *7 þa . . . wæs swiðe micel mancwealm* 'and then . . . [there] was a very great plague', and *ChronC* 1047 . . . *7 wæs ofer eall Englaland swyþe mycel mancwealm* 'and [there] was over all England a very great plague'.

§400 Birds, beasts, and fish, did not escape: *ChronA* 671 *Her wæs þæt micle fugla wæl* 'Here was the great destruction of birds'; *ChronA* 897 (see §399); *ChronE* 986 *And her com ærest se myccla yrfcwealm on Angelcyn* 'And in this year the great murrain first came into England'; and *ChronC* 1046:

> 7 on þis ylcan geare æfter Candelmæssan com se stranga winter mid forste 7 mid snawe 7 mid eallon ungewederon þ næs nan man þa on liue þ mihte gemunan swa strangne winter swa se wæs· ge þurh mancwealm ge þurh orfcwealm· ge fugelas 7 fixas þurh þone micelan cyle 7 hunger forwurdan

> and in this same year after Candlemass came the severe winter with frost and with snow and with all [sorts of] bad weather so that [there] was no man then alive who could remember such a severe winter as that was, both through plague and murrain, and birds and fishes perished through the great chill and famine.

§401 Surgery was both limited (see §201 and figure 3) and primitive. Amputation was practised. Here the leechdoms give sound advice about where to cut:

> Gif þu scyle aceorfan oððe asniþan unhal lim of halum lice· þonne ne ceorf þu þæt on þam gemære þæs halan lices ac micle swiþor snið oððe ceorf on þ̄ [= þæt] hale 7 þ̄ cwice lic. Swa þu hit wel 7 raþor gelacnost. þonne þu fyr sette on mannan· þonne nim þu merwes porres leaf 7 gegniden sealt· ofer lege þa stowe. þonne bið þy þe raþor þæs fyres hæto aweg atogen

> If you must carve off or cut off an unsound limb from a sound body, then do not carve it on the boundary of the sound limb but much better cut or carve on the sound and living body. So you will heal it well and more quickly. When you set fire on/cauterize a man, then take leaves of a tender leek and grated salt, lay [them] over the place. Then by that the heat of the fire will be the more quickly taken away.

For the rest, treatment of battle casualties and civilians was limited to first aid or self-help. When Beowulf was wounded in battle, his loyal retainer Wiglaf

> winedryhten his　　wætere gelafede
> hilde sædne　　ond his helm onspēon

sprinkled his lord, wearied in battle, with water and unclasped his helmet (*Beowulf* 2722–3).

When King Ongentheow fell, *ðā wǣron monige þe his mǣg wriðon* 'then [there] were many who bandaged his lord' (*Beowulf* 2982). The leechdoms offer a little more:

> Wið foredum lime: lege þas sealfe on þ̄ forode lim 7 forlege mid elmrinde· do spilc to· eft simle niwa oþ þ̄ gehalod sie ... Monegum men gescrincað his fet to his homme· wyrc baþo· do earban to 7 cersan 7 smale netelan 7 beowyrt· do on troh hate stanas wel gehætte· gebeþe þa hamma mid þam stanbaðe. þonne hie sien geswate· þonne recce he þa ban swa he swiþost mæge

> For a broken limb: lay this salve on the broken limb and cover [it] with elm bark, add to [it] a splint, afterwards continually renew [these] until it is healed ... For many a man [with a broken leg], his feet shrink to his ham: make baths, add [there]to tares and cress and small nettles and beewort, put hot stones well-heated in a trough, bathe the hams in the stone bath. When they are in a sweat, then let him [the patient] arrange the bones as best he can.

The success rate of these treatments is not recorded.

§402 Practical medical treatments were limited to hot baths (see the last example), herbs (see §§372 and 404), blood-letting, and dieting. Bonser quotes Sir Norman Moore: blood-letting was employed 'nearly always, nearly everywhere, and nearly for everything'. The word for a 'blood-letter' is *blod-lætere*. The procedure was simple enough: *læt him blod þus: set on glæs oððe horn 7 teo þ blod ut* 'let blood from him thus: put on a cupping glass or horn and draw the blood out'. Since the blood was supposed to be stationary, the site of the blood-letting was important. A remedy for violent vomiting includes these instructions: *læt him blod of þam þæm fotum byneoþan ancleowe . . . 7 seo oþru blodlæse is . . . þ þu hym scealt blod lætan under þare tuncgan* 'let blood from him from both feet below the ankles . . . the second blood-letting is that you shall let blood from him under the tongue'. But Moore's phrase 'nearly always' needs clarification:

> Blodlæse is to forganne fiftyne nihtum ær hlafmæsse 7 æfter fif 7 þritig nihtum for þon þonne ealle æterno þing fleogaþ 7 mannum swiðe deriað . . . 7 nis nan blodlæstid swa god swa on foreweardne lencten þonne þa yfelan wætan beoþ gegaderode þe on wintra gedruncene beoð 7 on kalendas aprilis ealra selest þonne treow 7 wyrta ærest up spryttað

> Blood-letting is to be avoided for fifteen nights before Lammas and after [it] for thirty-five nights because then all venomous things fly and greatly injure men . . . and [there] is no blood-letting time as good as in early Lent when the evil humours which have been drunk in winter are gathered together, and best of all on the first of April, when trees and plants first sprout up.

Certain phases of the moon also had to be avoided. During a visit to a convent, John, then Bishop of Hexham, learned that a nun who had been bled in the arm was as a result afflicted by a severe tumour. He asked when the bleeding had been done. The reply was: '*on feowernihtne monan*' 'on the fourth night of the moon'. Whereupon he rebuked the abbess and her nuns:

> 'Swiðe unwislice 7 ungelæredlice ge dedon . . . forþon . . . ðære tide blodlæs wære swiðe frecenlic þonne ðæs monan leoht 7 sæs flod in weaxnesse bið'

> 'You acted very unwisely and unskilfully . . . because . . . blood-letting at that time was very dangerous when the light of the moon and the tides of the sea are on the increase.'

He then proceeded to cure the nun by his prayers and by the sign of the cross.

§403   After blood-letting, the man with liver disease must be given *þa drincan 7 þa læcedomas þa ðe we lærdon þæt man dyde to þære ungefelan heardnesse ongunnenre on þære lifre* 'the drinks and leechdoms which we taught one should use for the insensible hardness begun in the liver', *7 him is to sellanne* *lactucas 7 superne popig* 'and to him are to be given lettuces and the southern poppy'. But dietary restrictions were severe:

> ælc broþ is to forganne . . . ægru . . . wætan metegearwa 7 cocnunga ealle . . . eal þa wætan þing 7 þa smerewigan 7 osterhlafas . . . 7 eall swete þing . . . æppla . . . win

> every broth is to be avoided . . . eggs . . . all wet meat-preparations and cookings . . . all moist and greasy things and oyster patties . . . and all sweet things . . . apples . . . wine.

§404 Such then were the practical remedies. But there were others. Survivals of paganism and magical practices are to be found in the leechdoms and charms. Bonser speaks of 'the Church as physician'. He tells us, however,

> that the nature of the 'magic' employed before and after the conversion to Christianity is to all intents and purposes one and the same. Diseases attributed to 'devils' by the Church were still attributed to elves by the common folk. When the Church became responsible for the care of the sick, pagan prescriptions had to be christianized so as to become operative against the pagan deities and spirits of evil which were thought to have caused the disease . . .

> The difference between the condemned pagan practice and the new Christian one is often very fine. The same result could be obtained from either practice: the difference consisted in the name of the deity invoked.

Thus we find prescriptions which are pagan; one such begins *wiþ ælfe 7 wiþ uncuþum sidenan· gnid myrran on win* . . . 'against an elf and against unknown influences, rub myrrh in wine . . .', another *wiþ ælcre yfelre leodrune 7 wiþ ælfsidenne· þis gewrit writ him wiþ greciscum stafum* . . . 'against each evil witch and against elvish influence, write this writing in Greek letters for him [the bewitched man] . . .'. Others display a mixture of pagan and Christian. *The Nine Herbs Charm* (ASPR VI. 119–21) refers to both Woden and Christ. The benefits of another herbal mixture, over which nine masses have been sung, are summed up thus: *þeos sealf is god wiþ ælcre feondes costunga 7 ælfsidenne 7 lenctenadle* 'This salve is good against every temptation of the devil and against elvish influence and against spring fever'. A third begins *Wyrc sealfe wiþ ælfcynne 7 nihtgengan 7 þam mannum þe deofol mid hæmþ* 'Make a salve against the elfin race and night-goers/goblins and those women with whom the devil has intercourse'. Yet others have been completely Christianized, sometimes with amusing results:

> Drenc wiþ feondseocum men of ciricbellan to drincanne: [here follows a list of twelve herbs] gewyrc þone drenc of hluttrum ealað· gesinge seofon mæssan ofer þam wyrtum· do garleac 7 halig wæter to 7 drype on ælcne drincan þone he drincan wille eft· 7 singe þone sealm Beati Immaculati 7

Exurgat 7 Saluum me fac, Deus· 7 þonne drince þone drenc of ciricbellan·
7 se mæssepreost him singe æfter þam drence þis ofer: Domine, Sancte
Pater Omnipotens

A drink for a fiend-sick man to be drunk from a church-bell: . . . Make the
drink from pure ale, sing seven masses over the herbs, add garlic and holy
water to [it] and drip the drink into every drink which he will subsequently drink, and sing the psalm . . ., and then let him drink the drink
from a church bell and let the mass-priest sing this over him after the
drink: Lord, Holy Father Almighty.

§405   Such contributions were not the only ones made by the physician
Church. Ælfric testifies to this in his life of Edmund, King and Martyr:

Nis Angelcynn bedæled Drihtnes halgena þonne on Englalande licgað
swilce halgan swylce þes halga cyning is and Cuþberht se eadiga and
Sancte Æþeldryð on Elig and eac hire swustor· ansunde on lichaman geleafan to trymminge. Synd eac fela oðre on Angelcynne halgan þe fela
wundra wyrcað· swa swa hit wide is cuð· þam Ælmihtigan to lofe þe hi on
gelyfdon

The English race is not deprived of the saints of God when in England
[there] lie such saints as this holy king and Cuthbert the blessed and Saint
Æthelthryth in Ely and also her sister, undecayed in body, as an encouragement to belief. There are also many other saints among the English
race who perform many miracles, as is widely known, in praise to the
Almighty in whom they believed.

Miracles were performed by saints and holy men in person, e.g. Bishop John
of Hexham's curing of the sick nun (§402) and of the dumb and leprous
young man (Bede V. 2), or through holy relics, e.g. Bede's story (IV. 32) of
the young man who suffered from a tumour in the eye which threatened his
eyesight:

Teoleden his læcas 7 ðone swylce mid sealfum 7 mid beþinge geðwænan
wolde· ac hie ne mehton . . . ac a dæghwæmlice wæs wyrse 7 wyrse. Ða
gelamp him semninga mid gife þære godcundan arfæstnesse þurh
reliquias ðæs halgan fæder Cuðbryhtes gehæledne beon

His doctors tried and wished to soothe it also with salves and with
bathing, but they could not . . . but ever daily [it] was worse and worse.
Then suddenly [it] happened to him, through a gift of divine grace, to be
healed through the relics of the holy father Cuthbert.

St Cuthbert's relics were a particularly potent source of cures. So too was
the cross erected by King Oswald on the site of his victory over his pagan
foes (§250) and the earth on which his body fell when he was killed in battle

by Penda, king of Mercia (§183 n. 5). A man whose horse had collapsed while riding near the spot

> þær hwile bad hwonne his horse bet wurde oðþe he hit þær dead forlete. þa wæs hit longe mid hefige sare swiðe swenced 7 in missenlice dælas hit wond 7 þræste· þa semniga becwom hit in þa stowe þær se gemyngoda cyning ofslegen wæs. Ne wæs þa elden þætte þæt saar gestilled wæs· 7 hit blonn from unhalum styrenessum þara leoma 7 þy gewunelican þeawe horsa æfter werignesse ongon wealwian 7 on æghwæðre siidan hit gelomlice oferwearp 7 sona aras þurh eall hal 7 gesund 7 ongon giferlice þæt gærs etan

> waited there for a while until his horse might get better or he might leave it there dead. Then it was for a long time very distressed with severe pain and it rolled and twisted in various directions. Then suddenly it came to the spot where the above-mentioned king was killed. There was then no delay until the pain was relieved and it ceased from unhealthy movements of its limbs and in the usual way of horses after fatigue began to roll and threw itself repeatedly from side to side and soon arose completely whole and sound and began to eat the grass eagerly.

The rider then resumed his journey. When he reached his destination, he found that his host's daughter had long been afflicted with severe paralysis. He told them of the place where his horse had been cured.

> Hwæt hy gearwodon sona wægn 7 asettan þa fæmnan inn 7 læddon to þære stowe 7 heo þær asetton. þa heo þa on þære stowe geseted wæs· ða wæs heo werig· onslep þær hwon. Sona þæs þe heo onwooc· þa gefelde heo þæt heo wæs gehæled from hire lichoman untrymnesse 7 hire wætres bæd 7 heo þwoh 7 hire feax gerædde 7 heo mid scytan bisweop 7 mid þæm monnum þe heo þider læddon· on hire fotum hal 7 gesund ham hwearf 7 eode

> So they at once got a cart ready and put the woman in [it] and took [her] to the place and set [her] down there. When she was set down in the place, then she was weary and slept there a little. As soon as she awoke, then she felt that she had been healed of her bodily ailment and she asked for water and washed herself and arranged her hair and wrapped herself in a linen cloth and, with the men who had brought her there, returned home safe and sound walking on her feet.

§406   Let us turn now to Anglo-Saxon burial customs. There is evidence for ship-burial, cremation, and inhumation. In the heroic poetry, we have the description of Scyld's funeral ship (§198 Text 8); it was pushed out to sea but not set alight, as King Haki's ship was in the Norse Ynglinga Saga. We have the funeral pyres at Finnesburh (§362) and at the end of *Beowulf* (§199

Text 9). We find the unconsidered dead left on the battlefield as prey for 'the beasts of battle' described by the *Beowulf* poet:

> Forðon sceall gār wesan
> monig morgenceald   mundum bewunden,
> hæfen on handa·   nalles hearpan swēg
> wīgend weccean   ac se wonna hrefn
> 3025 fūs ofer fǣgum   fela reordian,
> earne secgan   hū him æt ǣte spēow
> þenden hē wið wulf   wæl rēafode

Therefore shall many a spear, morning-cold, be grasped in [the] palms, lifted in [the] hand. Not at all [shall] the music of the harp wake the warriors but the dark raven busy over the dead [shall] relate many things, tell the eagle how it prospered him at the eating while he, with the wolf, plundered the slain.

In real life, we have the ship-burial at Sutton Hoo (§§194–9), which may have been a cenotaph, and other burials involving smaller ships or parts of them. The Anglo-Saxons practised both cremation and inhumation but, as Mayr-Harting tells us, 'inhumation in itself implied, of course, no acceptance of Christianity'. That there was a belief in some sort of afterlife is attested by the burial of food, weapons (§§200–23), and jewellery (§§224–38), with the dead – and by the much less common sacrifices of slaves (§326). The splendour of the Sutton Hoo ship-burial (§§194–9) and of the burial given to the self-effacing Cuthbert (§§262–3) contrast with the carrion corpses of *Beowulf* 3021b–7 above and with the unadorned graves in which the majority of Anglo-Saxons were laid to rest.

§407 *Ubi sunt qui ante nos fuerunt?* 'Where be they bifore us weren?' The transience of life is inevitably a common human concern. The Old English poems *The Wanderer* (see below) and *The Seafarer* (Text 41 §477), which appear in all Old English readers known to me, give poetic expression to the themes of loneliness and transience. Other relevant passages will be found in Part IV; see Text 9 (§468), Text 11 (§467), and Text 42 (§480). The heroic response to *þis lǣne lif* is well exemplified by this lament from *The Wanderer*:

> Hwǣr cwōm mearg? Hwǣr cwōm mago?   Hwǣr cwōm
>   māþþumgyfa?
> Hwǣr cwōm symbla gesetu?   Hwǣr sindon seledrēamas?
> Ēalā beorht bune!   Ēalā byrnwiga!
> 95 Ēalā þēodnes þrym!   Hū sēo þrāg gewāt,
> genāp under nihthelm,   swā hēo nō wǣre.
> Stondeð nū on lāste   lēofre duguþe
> weal wundrum hēah,   wyrmlīcum fāh.
> Eorlas fornōman   asca þrȳþe,
> 100 wǣpen wælgīfru,   wyrd sēo mǣre·

ond þās stānhleoþu   stormas cnyssað·
hrīð hrēosende   hrūsan bindeð,
wintres wōma   þonne won cymeð·
nīpeð nihtscūa·   norþan onsendeð
105 hrēo hæglfare   hæleþum on andan.
Eall is earfoðlic   eorþan rīce·
onwendeð wyrda gesceaft   weoruld under heofonum.
Hēr bið feoh lǣne·   hēr bið frēond lǣne·
hēr bið mon lǣne·   hēr bið mǣg lǣne·
110 eal þis eorþan gesteal   īdel weorþeð!

Where has the horse gone? Where has the young man gone? Where has the giver of treasure gone? Where have the seats for the feasts gone? Where are the hall-joys? O, the bright cup! O, the shield-warrior! O, the glory of the lord! How the time has departed, darkened under the nightshade, as if it had never been. In the track of the beloved warrior-bands stands a wall wondrous high adorned with serpent-shapes. The power of ash[spears] has carried off the warriors, the weapons slaughter-greedy, fate the famous, and storms lash these stone-slopes, the falling snowstorm binds the earth, the tumult of winter when black comes, the shadow of night grows dark, sends from the north a fierce hailstorm in anger against men. Everything is difficult in the kingdom of earth, the decree of [the] fates changes [the] world under [the] heavens. Here is money transient, here is friend transient, here is man transient, here is kinsman transient. All this foundation of earth becomes worthless.

But *The Dream of the Rood* (Text 51 §493) offers Christian assurance. The dreamer does not ask where his friends are because he knows:

                    Nāh ic rīcra feala
        frēonda on foldan   ac hīe forð heonon
    gewiton of worulde drēamum·   sōhton him wuldres Cyning·
        lifiaþ nū on heofenum   mid Hēahfædere·
135   wuniaþ on wuldre

I do not have many great friends on earth, for they have gone forth from here from the joys of the world, they have sought for themselves the King of Glory, [they] live now in [the] heavens with [the] High Father, dwell in glory.

§408   Despite all the differences between Anglo-Saxon society and ours, a common incorrigible humanity shines through. We find nicknames, some uncomplimentary, some complimentary, e.g. *Æþelstan fætta* 'Æthelstan [the] fat', *Eadweard se langa* 'Edward the tall', *Æþelred Unræd* (§187), now translated 'Ethelred the Unready', and King Edmund (§187 annal 1016), who *Irensid wæs geclypod for his snellscipe* 'was known as Ironside because of his bravery'. We find an interest in strange things, both lay (Text 29 §441) and

Christian (Text 21 §429). We find family quarrels, e.g. the disinheriting of Edwin (§366), and family harmony, e.g. this extract from Ælfheah's will:

> þonnæ an ic Ælfsiþæ minon wifæ· gyf heo leng beoð þonne ic and it swa gehylt swa ic hiræ truwan to hæbbe· ealra þara oðæra landa þæ ic læfæ. And heo þanne gæornlicæ of þam god geþæncæ and for uncre sawle geornlicæ beo

> Then I give to my wife Ælfsith, if she lives longer than I and keeps it [the property] as I have confidence in her [to do so], all the other estates which I leave. And let her then remember God eagerly [with alms] from it and let her be zealous for our souls;

thoughtful wills, e.g. that of Ælfhelm –

> ic gean minum wiue healues þæs stodes æt Trostingtune 7 minan geferan healues þe me mid ridað

> I grant to my wife half the stud at Troston and half to my companions who ride with me –

and uncharitable ones, e.g. that of Archbishop Æthelnoth, who was not alone in expressing the wish that, if anyone tried to upset a certain grant of land, *awende hine Crist fram heofenan rices myrhðe into helle wite* 'may Christ remove him from the bliss of the kingdom of Heaven into the torment of hell'; and unfaithful wives (§367) and loving ones (§368). We find that, as Sonia Chadwick Hawkes has pointed out, 'recent work on Anglo-Saxon skeletons from pagan cemeteries is making it increasingly clear that this was a society that valued its children and kept them alive even when grossly handicapped'. Its ethos was, as we have seen, primarily military. But for the handicapped of good birth who were capable of them, other careers were available. As in many pagan Indo-European societies, there were places for blind bards, lame smiths, and short-sighted jewellers such as the Sutton Hoo master (§§229–30). The coming of Christianity, she goes on, brought with it 'both a proliferation of sheltered accommodation in monasteries and a greatly increased range of quiet skills to be practised, from gardening to calligraphy and manuscript illumination'. To sum up: we have seen bravery and cowardice, loyalty and treachery, laughter and sorrow, happiness and despair, trust in magic and superstition, trust in the things of this world, and trust in God. We find the older generation criticizing the customs of the young (Text 30 §442). Clerical denunciation of sin and crime went unheeded then as now. Wulfstan, Archbishop of York (§177), preaching *c.* 1014, saw the Danish domination of England as God's vengeance on a wicked people; see Text 34 (§446). The non-committal heroic response to the riddle of life is expressed by a Christian poet in *Beowulf* 455b: *Gæð ā wyrd swā hīo scel* 'Fate always goes as it must'. But the poet of *The Gifts of Men* says otherwise:

                          hēr weoruda god,
            meotud meahtum swīð,   monnum dǣleð,
        5 syleð, sundorgiefe·   sendeð wīde
            āgne spēde·   þāra ǣghwylc mōt
            dryhtwuniendra   dǣl onfōn

... here the God of Hosts, the Creator strong in powers, deals and gives
various gifts to mortals, sends [those gifts] by his own power [far and]
wide; of them, each of dwellers among people is permitted to receive a
share.

IV

The Garden of Old English Literature

A INTRODUCTION

§409 The pleasant conceit of literature as a garden from which one can pick blossoms of different kinds at will is not a new one. We find it applied to both prose and poetry in English. In the ninth century, King Alfred began his translation of Book II of the *Soliloquies of St Augustine* with a sentence which has no parallel in the Latin: *Her onginð seo gadorung þæra blostmena þære æftran bec* 'Here begins the collection of blossoms of the second book'. And in 1944 Field-Marshal Lord Wavell printed an anthology ('flower collection') of poetry in a volume entitled *Other Men's Flowers* (London: Jonathan Cape). So I am encouraged to think of Old English literature as (to borrow a phrase from Ælfric) *swiðe smeðe feld and brad· mid blowendum wyrtum and grennysse eall afylled* 'a very smooth and broad field, all filled with growing plants and greenness'.

§410 The famous question *Quid Hinieldus cum Christo?* 'What has Ingeld to do with Christ?' (§383) is a despairing clerical attempt to reverse what is perhaps the major phenomenon of the Anglo-Saxon period and therefore one of the major themes of this book: the cross-fertilization and fusing of the heroic with the Christian which produced a tension and a very special way of looking at things. This is apparent in the literature, in the Sutton Hoo ship-burial (§196), in the Benty Grange helmet (§212), in jewellery (§236) and sculpture (§259), in society and the law (§§242 and 345), in the behaviour of the converted (§§385–7), in the charms and leechdoms (§§325 and 404), in burial customs (§406), and in the varying reactions to the knowledge that life is transient (§407); see further the General Index under the heading 'heroic or pagan and Christian, blends of or contrasts between'. On this subject, it is hard to better Fred C. Robinson's characteristically perceptive observations:

In sum, what the Anglo-Saxons brought with them was a self-sufficient culture with a stern, imaginative, and capacious mind set which later Europeans to the south of the Germanic lands have been pleased to call 'barbaric.' 'Barbaric' means simply 'not like us,' and it is precisely this *difference* that makes the Anglo-Saxon world so fascinating to those who share the modern European cultural heritage, a heritage which has been spread now throughout much of the world into such areas as North and

South America, Australia, New Zealand, and South Africa. This heritage is that of ancient Classical culture. The Germanic culture of the Anglo-Saxons offers an alternative to that heritage – a barbaric aesthetic with a barbaric sense of life.

But this barbaric perspective comes to us in a richly complicated form. Over a century after the Anglo-Saxons migrated to England a transforming experience altered their Germanic identity in a way that makes their civilization unique. That experience was conversion to Christianity.

§411 While heeding the warning (§327) that the search for Anglo-Saxon paganism is dangerous, I must now keep the promises made in §170 and elsewhere by examining the effects of the 'baptism' of the heroic in literature. The harnessing of prose to philosophical and religious thought (§§xvii, 154, 169, and 177) and of Germanic alliterative verse to Christian subjects (§§170, 395, and 448–50) were revolutionary steps – new wine in old bottles indeed. But the bottles were up to it! Here England led the way. The techniques of conversion practised by the missionaries included the Christianization of heroic ideas and ideals such as the warrior-band and the life in hall (§385), and *dom*, *lof*, and *wyrd* (§395). It is to these last three that I now turn.

§412 The heroic warriors saw themselves living under the control of *wyrd* and striving to win *dom* and *lof*; see §344. It is difficult to pin down the precise meanings these words, which are known to us only through texts transmitted by Christians, had for such men. I must confess that I do not know whether in some of their meanings *dom* and *lof* are synonymous, overlap, or differ. The poem *Widsith* ends with this epitaph suitable for any heroic warrior:

> lof se gewyrceð·
> hafað under heofonum   hēahfæstne dōm,

which may mean either 'That man achieves *dom*, has unchangeable *lof* under the heavens' or 'Who[ever] performs *dom* has/will have unchangeable *lof* under the heavens'. Klaeber, the greatest editor of the poem *Beowulf*, assigns 'glory' as one meaning of *dom* – others include 'judgement' and 'choice' – and glosses *lof* as 'praise, glory', to which the Wrenn–Bolton edition adds 'fame'. *The Dictionary of Old English* (*DOE*) now in preparation at the University of Toronto has not yet reached *L* but gives two main meanings for *dom*: first 'judgement' and second 'favourable judgement (esp. after death), glory, fame, victory (in poetry more commonly than in prose)'.

§413 What can perhaps be safely taken as typical examples of the heroic use of *dom* and *lof* are found in *Beowulf*:

> 1086   Fin Hengeste
> elne unflitme   āðum benemde
> þæt hē þā wēalāfe   weotena dōme
> ārum hēolde

Finn declared to Hengest by oaths with incontestable zeal that he would rule the unhappy remnant [of Hengest's force] honourably at the judgement of the wise men;

> Sigemunde gesprong
> 885 æfter dēaðdæge   dōm unlȳtel
> syþðan wīges heard   wyrm ācwealde,
> hordes hyrde

For Sigemund there arose great *dom* after his death-day after [the man] hard in battle killed the dragon, the guardian of the treasure;

and

> Swā sceal man dōn
> 1535 þonne hē æt gūðe   gegān þenceð
> longsumne lof·   nā ymb his līf cearað

So must a man do when he thinks to win long-lasting *lof* in battle; he will not care about his life.

But both *dom* and *lof* were taken over by Christianity. Christ has *dom*:

> *Andreas* 540 Wes ðū gebledsod·   brego mancynnes,
> dryhten hælend!   Ā þīn dōm lyfað!

Be thou blessed, Ruler of Mankind, Lord and Saviour! Thy *dom* will live for ever!

God bestows it on His followers:

> *Andreas* 1150   Gode ealles þanc,
> dryhtna dryhten,   þæs ðe hē dōm gifeð
> gumena gehwylcum   þāra þe gēoce tō him
> sēceð mid snytrum

To God the Lord of Lords [be] thanks for everything, for that [fact] that He gives *dom* to all of men who seek help from Him in wisdom.

Christ also has *lof*:

> *GuthlacA* 393   Symle Crīstes lof
> in Gūðlāces   gōdum mōde
> wēox and wunade   . . .

Always the *lof* of Christ in Guthlac's good mind grew and dwelt . . .

His followers can achieve it:

> *Fates of the Apostles* 6   Lof wīde sprang,
> miht ond mærðo,   ofer middangeard
> þēodnes þegna

Lof arose widely, power and fame, over the earth for the thanes/apostles of the Lord.

One created thing, however, failed conspicuously in his duty, for we learn of Satan in Heaven before the Fall that

GenesisB 256   Lof sceolde hē drihtnes wyrcean·
      dȳran sceolde hē his drēamas on heofonum   and sceolde
         his drihtne þancian
      þæs lēanes þe hē him on þām lēohte gescerede   . . .

he should have performed/achieved the Lord's *lof*; he should have held dear His joys in the heavens and should have thanked his Lord for the gift which He had allotted to him in that light . . .

Lof is spectacularly baptized in *The Seafarer*:

      Forþon bið eorla gehwām   æftercweþendra
      lof lifgendra   lāstworda betst
      þæt hē gewyrce· ǣr hē on weg scyle·
 75   fremum on foldan   wið fēonda nīþ,
      dēorum dǣdum   dēofle tōgēanes,
      þæt hine ælda bearn   æfter hergen
      ond his lof siþþan   lifge mid englum
      āwa tō ealdre,   ēcan līfes blǣd,
 80   drēam mid dugeþum

For the best of footprint words for each of warriors will be the praise of those who live to speak after him, [will be] that he brings it about, ere he must away, by good actions against the malice of foes, by brave deeds against the devil, that the sons of men will praise him thereafter and his *lof* will afterwards live among the angels for ever, glory of eternal life, joy with the tried warriors.

(To some, this passage will bring to mind Longfellow's words:

      Lives of great men all remind us
        We can make our lives sublime,
      And departing, leave behind us
        Footprints on the sands of time;

      Footprints that perhaps another,
        Sailing o'er life's fitful main,
      Some forlorn and shipwrecked brother
        Seeing, may take heart again.)

This dual heroic and Christian connotation of *lof* complicates the interpretation of *Beowulf*, for the last words in the lament for Beowulf with which the poem ends are

Swā begnornodon Gēata lēode
hlāfordes hyre, heorðgenēatas:
3180 cwǣdon þæt hē wǣre wyruldcyninga
manna mildust ond monðwǣrust,
lēodum līðost ond lofgeornost

Thus the people of the Geats, the hearth-companions, mourned the fall of
their lord, saying that he was of world-kings the kindest of men, the most
gentle, most generous to the people, and most eager for *lof*.

For which *lof* was Beowulf most eager – the heroic (or pagan) or the Christian? One's interpretation of *Beowulf* turns on one's answer to this question,
a question to which (I believe) there is no certain answer.

§414 In his book *The Search for Anglo-Saxon Paganism* (§324), Stanley
discusses *wyrd* and its treatment by nineteenth- and twentieth-century
scholars. He distinguishes five meanings. (I have not kept to his order.) One
of these is the etymological one 'what happens or has happened, an event,
occurrence, incident, fact'. The word *gewyrd* is also used in much the same
meanings, for both are related to the verb *weorþan* 'to become, to happen'
(§513). In the past, certain scholars saw in some uses of *wyrd* a survival of
paganism and compared it with the *Parcae* of classical mythology and with
the Scandinavian Norns; typical examples were said to be *Beowulf* 455 *Gǣð ā
wyrd swā hīo scel* 'Fate always goes as it must', *Wanderer* 5 *Wyrd bið ful ārǣd*
'Fate is completely predetermined/inexorable', and *Wanderer* 107 ...
onwendeð wyrda gesceaft weoruld under heofonum 'the ordained course of events
changes the world under the heavens'. But it is now clear that all surviving
examples of the word may have been influenced by Christianity. In Stanley's
words, 'it is difficult, lastly, to be sure that the conception of *wyrd* in Old
English literature is not primarily Christian, that *wyrd* is not derived from
Boethius's *Fortuna* rather than from one or all of the Norns'. This is clearly
apparent if we compare these two passages from *Beowulf*:

572 Wyrd oft nereð
unfǣgne eorl þonne his ellen dēah!

Wyrd often spares an undoomed man when his courage is strong!

and

2291 Swā mæg unfǣge ēaðe gedīgan
wēan ond wrǣcsīð sē ðe Waldendes
hyldo gehealdeþ!

So may an undoomed man – that one whom the grace of the Lord holds –
easily survive woe and misery.

The remaining four meanings detected by Stanley also demonstrate this.

§415 A second meaning is seen in such collocations of *wyrd* and the poetic word *fæge* as *Beowulf* 572 (§414) and *GuthlacB* 1345 *Hē þā wyrd ne māð,* ‖ *fæges forðsīð* 'He did not conceal the *wyrd*, the going forth/death of the doomed [man]', where *wyrd* means 'something like "final fate, doom, death"'. Thirdly, in some glosses – lists of Latin words with their Anglo-Saxon equivalent – *Parcae* is rendered by *wyrd/gewyrd*. Next, *wyrd/gewyrd* occurs in Christian accounts of pagan beliefs. Thus Ælfric wrote:

> Witodlice þa þe on God belyfað· hi sind þurh ðone Halgan Gast ge-wissode . . . þa ðe ne gelyfað ðurh agenne cyre· hi scoriað na ðurh gewyrd· forðan ðe gewyrd nis nan ðing buton leas wena· ne nan ðing soðlice be gewyrde ne gewyrð ac ealle ðing þurh Godes dom beoð geendebyrde

> Verily, those who believe in God, they are directed by the Holy Ghost . . . Those who do not believe by their own choice, they perish, not through *gewyrd* for *gewyrd* is nothing but a false fancy; truly, nothing happens by *gewyrd* but all things are ordered by God's *dom* . . .

And we read that Beowulf would have died in his fight against Grendel

> 1056 nefne him wītig God   wyrd forstōde –
> ond ðæs monnes mōd

unless wise God had withstood *wyrd* – and the man's/Beowulf's courage.

Fifthly, *wyrd* is sometimes synonymous with the working of God's will. Alfred's version of Boethius (§177.2) tells us that

> Sio wyrd þonne dælð eallum gesceaftum anwlitan 7 stowa 7 tida 7 gemetgunga· ac sio wyrd cymð of ðæm gewitte 7 of ðæm foreþonce þæs ælmehtigan Godes,, se wyrcð æfter his unasecgendlicum foreþonce swa hwæt swa he wile

> *Wyrd* then deals to all creatures [their] forms and places and times and thoughts but *wyrd* comes from the understanding and forethought/ providence of Almighty God. He/God, who (§11.4) works according to His ineffable providence whatever He wills.

Similarly, the Blickling homilist (§177.3), after warning that no man can repent in the grave, goes on *ac he þær on moldan gemolsnaþ 7 þær wyrde bideþ hwonne se ælmihtiga God wille þisse worlde ende gewyrcean* 'but there he will in dust become dust and there will wait for *wyrd*, [wait] until Almighty God wishes/wills to make an end to this world'.

§416 The pre-Christian meaning of *wyrd* is therefore hard to pin down. In an attempt to do so, Brian Bates, a psychologist, wrote *The Way of Wyrd: Tales of an Anglo-Saxon Sorcerer* (London: Century, 1983). In it, he tells the story of Brand, a Christian monk and scribe from Mercia, who is sent by his superior Eappa to a pagan kingdom to prepare the way for a Christian mission, a task in which he is guided by Wulf, a pagan sorcerer and mystic. This is a fascinating book in which the author uses Anglo-Saxon magical and medical manuscripts as he tries to portray what *wyrd* might have meant to pre-Christian Anglo-Saxons. He puts this definition of *wyrd* in the mouth of Wulf:

> 'Wyrd is too vast, too complex, for us to comprehend, for we are ourselves part of wyrd and cannot stand back to observe it as if it were a separate force. Just as a fisherman cannot see the full extent of the seas, so even a sorcerer cannot view the totality of wyrd. So we carve runes into wood or bone and cast them like nets on to the sea of wyrd. The messages the runes bring back are like a good catch: enough for us to feed on until the tides of life carry us back again . . . The forces of wyrd are like the winds and tides for a fisherman. If they are known, the sailor can trim his sails to adapt to them. He can be in harmony with the forces and use their power. But he cannot thereby change them.'

Brand's conclusion is in accord with the history of the attempts to Christianize Anglo-Saxon society:

> At the end of the summer, I would have to return to the Mission and tell Eappa all I knew, though there was precious little of it which I could convey in words. But I could tell him that when the Word of Almighty God was spread in this forest it would fall on fertile ground, for the kingdom of the pagans truly contained spiritual secrets that were as much a part of God's world as the land from which we came.

§417 Here I must leave *wyrd*, with the reflection that, whether operating through *wyrd* (§415) or directly, God

> gedæleð   se þe āh dōmes geweald
> missenlice   geond þisne middangeard
> lēoda leoþocræftas   londbuendum . . .
> . . .   sum biþ wōðbora,
> giedda giffæst.   Sum biþ gearuwyrdig . . .
> sum mid hondum mæg   hearpan grētan
> āh he glēobeames   gearobrygda list . . .
> sum lēoða glēaw

who has control of *dom*, deals/distributes diversely throughout this middle-earth the skills of humans to land-dwellers . . . One is a poet gifted in song. One is eloquent . . . One with his hands can greet/play the harp, has skill in the rapid movements of the glee-wood . . . One [is] skilled in songs (*The Gifts of Men* 27–9, 35b–6, 49–50, 52a).

But the fact that we cannot isolate purely Germanic notions of *wyrd*, *dom*, and *lof*, from purely Christian ones warns us that any attempts to tease apart the two elements in the poetry will unravel the tapestries to which the poems have been compared (§462). In the last sections of this book, I hope to bring you some of the riches of the literature thus inspired. From now on, I shall leave you to use the glossary for any words you do not know but shall provide notes on difficulties of allusion, interpretation, or language. As you read, you will meet manifestations of 'man's unconquerable mind' and will often find yourself agreeing with the Preacher (Ecclesiastes 1: 9) that 'there is no new thing under the sun'.

B PLANTS FROM THE PROSE

Genres illustrated

§418 Here I shall add to the numbered Texts and the longer translated passages so that this book will demonstrate the variety of effects the prose writers achieved. The genres listed in §177 are all exemplified:

1 the Anglo-Saxon Chronicle in §§423 and 439–40;
2 the translations of Alfred and his circle in §§424–32;
3 homiletic writings in §§442 and 445–6;
4 other religious prose in §§419–22 (translations of Scripture) and 444 (Text 32, in which Ælfric discusses the problems involved in translating Scripture);
5 prose fiction in §§441 and 443;
6 scientific and medical writings in §§433–4;
7 laws, charters, and wills, in §§435–8.

These texts are listed in the Contents and their sources are given in the relevant section below. The variety of contexts in which Old English prose was used is unparalleled in other vernacular languages of the period.

§419 This section contains three versions of Exodus 14: 21–31, in which the destruction of Pharaoh's army in the Red Sea is described: the Old English text from MS British Library Cotton Claudius B.iv; the Latin Vulgate version on which the Old English is based; and the rendering in the Authorized or King James Version. Text 46 (§487), a passage from *Exodus*, the second poem in the Junius Manuscript (§173), tells the same story in Old English verse. The four extracts offer scope for comparison and contrast from which the Old English prose emerges not without credit. The differences between it and the later English version reflect the fact that the translators of the latter worked from Greek and Hebrew versions rather than from the Latin.

The destruction of Pharaoh's army is mentioned in an eight-line poem in the Exeter Book concerning the number of chariots in the Egyptian army. It opens with the injunction *Saga me* 'Tell me', which suggests that it may be a fragment of a question-and-answer poem like *Solomon and Saturn* (§480). The poem goes thus:

'Saga mē hwæt þær weorudes   wære ealles
on Farones fyrde   þā hȳ folc godes
þurh fēondscipe   fylgan ongunnon.'

     'Nāt ic hit be wihte   būtan ic wēne þus,
5   þæt þær screoda wære   gescȳred rīme
siex hund ......a   searohæbbendra·
þæt eal fornam   ȳþa geblond
wrāþe wyrde   in woruldrīce.'

'Tell me what [the number] of the multitude was altogether in Pharaoh's army when, out of enmity, they began to pursue God's people.'

'I don't really know but I rather guess that, counted numerically, there were six hundred .... armed chariots. The tumult of the waves destroyed all that [force] within the world by a grim fate.'

The missing word is a problem. In view of Exodus 14: 7 'And he [Pharaoh] took six hundred chariots and all the chariots of Egypt', six hundred seems too few. But the size of the Gulf of Suez, to which the phrase 'the Red Sea' always refers in the Bible, argues against the proposal to fill the gap with the word *þusenda*; a guess of six hundred thousand chariots would be a wild one indeed.

Text 16   Egyptian army perishes in Red Sea

21 Ða Moyses aðenode his hand ofer ða sæ· ða sende Drihten micelne wind ealle ða niht 7 gewende ða sæ to drium 7 þæt wæter wearð on twa todæled 7 læg an drige stræt ðurh ða sæ.

22 7 ðæt wæter stod on twa healfa ðære stræte swylce twegen heage
5 weallas· ða for eall Ysrahela folc ðurh ða sæ on þone weg ðe Drihten him geworhte 7 ða comon hale 7 gesunde þurh ða sæ swa Drihten him behet.

23–4 Ða Pharao com to ðære sæ 7 eal his here· ða for he on þone ylcan weg æfter Israhela folce on dægred mid eallum his folce 7 mid eallum his wæpnum.

10 26 Ða cwæð Drihten to Moyse: Aðene ðine hand ofer ða sæ 7 ofer Faraon 7 ofer ealne his here.

27 7 he ahefde up his hand 7 seo sæ sloh togædere 7 ahwylfde Pharaones cratu.

28 7 adrencte hine sylfne 7 eal his folc þæt ðær ne wearð furðon an to lafe
15 þe lif gebyrede.

29 Soðlice Moyses 7 Israhela folc foron ðurh ða sæ drium fotum.

30 7 Drihten alysde on ðam dæge Israhela folc of ðæra Egyptiscra handum.

31 7 hi gesawon þa Egyptiscan deade up to lande aworpene þe heora ær
20 ehton on ðam lande þe hi ða to cumene wæron· 7 ðæt Israhelisce folc ondredon him Drihten 7 hyrdon Gode 7 Moyses his ðeowe.

---

1 **Ða Moyses ... ða sende ...** 'When ... then'. See §§137–8.

2 **tō drīum** 'to dry (land)'. The same word as *drīge* l. 3.

3 **7 læg** 'and (there) lay'. This use of 'there' OE *þær* was not fully developed in OE. But cf. l. 14.

5 **ðe** rel. pron. 'which', here acc. sg.; **him** here dat. pl.; the first *ðā* can be adv. 'then' or nom. pl. pron. 'they'.

7 For the divided subject see §162.

12 **slēan** 'to strike' (st. contracted vb. VI §521) here means 'to rush' or 'to come quickly'.

14 **hine sylfne** 'him the same'. Here *sylf* 'self' is emphatic, not reflexive; **þæt** 'so that'.

14–15 literally 'so that there was not even one as a leaving/survivor to whom life belonged'. Compare Text 46 ll. 508–12 and contrast Text 11, where the sole survivor of a warrior-band laments his fallen comrades.

19 **hī** = *Israhela folc*; **þe** rel. pron. 'who' = *þā Égyptiscan*; **heora**, gen. pl. object of *ēhton*, = *Israhela folc*. However, a similar sequence of pronouns would be acceptable today.

20 **þe ... tō** 'to which'; **ðā** adv. 'then'.

The standard edition of this text is *The Old English Version of the Heptateuch* edited by S. J. Crawford, Early English Text Society O.S. 160 (London:· Oxford University Press, 1922). The Heptateuch is a term used first in English in the seventeenth century to denote the Pentateuch (the first five books of the Old Testament) together with the books of Joshua and Judges.

King James Version

21 And Moses stretched out his hand over the sea; and the Lord caused the sea to go back by a strong east wind all that night, and made the sea dry land, and the waters were divided.

22 And the children of Israel went into the midst of the sea upon the dry ground: and the waters were a wall unto them on their right hand, and on their left.

23 And the Egyptians pursued, and went in after them to the midst of the sea, even all Pharaoh's horses, his chariots, and his horsemen.

24 And it came to pass, that in the morning watch the Lord looked unto the host of the Egyptians through the pillar of fire and of the cloud, and troubled the host of the Egyptians,

25 And took off their chariot wheels, that they drave them heavily: so that the Egyptians said, Let us flee from the face of Israel; for the Lord fighteth for them against the Egyptians.

26 And the Lord said unto Moses, Stretch out thine hand over the sea, that the waters may come again upon the Egyptians, upon their chariots, and upon their horsemen.

27 And Moses stretched forth his hand over the sea, and the sea returned to his strength when the morning appeared; and the Egyptians fled against it; and the Lord overthrew the Egyptians in the midst of the sea.

28 And the waters returned, and covered the chariots, and the horsemen, and all the host of Pharaoh that came into the sea after them; there remained not so much as one of them.

29 But the children of Israel walked upon dry land in the midst of the sea; and the waters were a wall unto them on their right hand, and on their left.

30 Thus the Lord saved Israel that day out of the hand of the Egyptians; and Israel saw the Egyptians dead upon the sea shore.

31 And Israel saw that great work which the Lord did upon the Egyptians: and the people feared the Lord, and believed the Lord, and his servant Moses.

Latin Vulgate Version

21 Cumque extendisset Moyses manum super mare, abstulit illud Dominus flante vento vehementi et urente tota nocte, et vertit in siccum; divisaque est aqua.

22 Et ingressi sunt filii Israel per medium sicci maris; erat enim aqua quasi murus a dextra eorum et læva.

23 Persequentesque Ægyptii ingressi sunt post eos, et omnis equitatus Pharaonis, currus ejus et equites, per medium maris.

24 Jamque advenerat vigilia matutina, et ecce respiciens Dominus super castra Ægyptiorum per columnam ignis et nubis, interfecit exercitum eorum;

25 Et subvertit rotas curruum, ferebanturque in profundum. Dixerunt ergo Ægyptii: Fugiamus Israelem; Dominus enim pugnat pro eis contra nos.

26 Et ait Dominus ad Moysen: Extende manum tuam super mare, ut revertantur aquæ ad Ægyptios, super currus et equites eorum.

27 Cumque extendisset Moyses manum contra mare, reversum est primo diluculo ad priorem locum; fugientibusque Ægyptiis occurrerunt aquæ, et involvit eos Dominus in mediis fluctibus.

28 Reversæque sunt aquæ, et operuerunt currus et equites cuncti exercitus Pharaonis, qui sequentes ingressi fuerant mare; nec unus quidem superfuit ex eis.

29 Filii autem Israel perrexerunt per medium sicci maris, et aquæ eis erant quasi pro muro a dextris et a sinistris.

30 Liberavitque Dominus in die illa Israel de manu Ægyptiorum.

31 Et viderunt Ægyptios mortuos super littus maris, et manum magnam quam exercuerat Dominus contra eos; timuitque populus Dominum, et crediderunt Domino, et Moysi servo ejus.

§420 Versions of the Christian Gospels survive in three Old English dialects. MS British Library Cotton Nero D.iv – the *Lindisfarne Gospels* – contains a continuous interlinear gloss in the Northumbrian dialect written above the Latin text between 883 and 995; see §§296–7. The *Rushworth Gospels* – MS Bodleian Auct. D. 2.19 – also contain a continuous gloss to the Latin, written in the tenth century. The greater part of this is in the Northumbrian dialect but the glosses to Matthew, Mark 1: 1–2: 15, and John 18: 1–3, are in Mercian. There are, in addition to fragments, half a dozen manuscripts of the Gospels in West-Saxon, the earliest of which are dated *c.* 1000. They are MS Cambridge University Library Ii. 2. 11 folios 2–173, MS Corpus Christi College Cambridge 140, MSS British Library Cotton Otho C.i and Royal I. A.xiv, and MSS Bodleian Bodley 441 and Hatton 38. The Old English text presented here is the well-known story of the Prodigal Son which is to be found in Luke 15: 11–32. It is one of a series of parables told by Christ to illustrate His saying that 'there is joy in the presence of the angels of God over one sinner that repenteth' (Luke 15: 10). The printed text is a slightly emended version of the late West-Saxon translation of the Latin to be found in MS Corpus Christi College Cambridge 140, written early in the eleventh century.

Text 17 **The Prodigal Son**

11 He cwæð: soðlice sum man hæfde twegen suna.

12 þa cwæð se gingra to his fæder: 'Fæder, sele me minne dæl minre æhte þe me to gebyreþ.' þa dælde he him his æhte.

13 Ða æfter feawum dagum eall his þing gegaderode se gingra sunu 7
5 ferde wræclice on feorlen rice 7 forspilde þær his æhta, libbende on his gælsan.

14 Ða he hie hæfde ealle amyrrede· þa wearð micel hungor on þam rice 7 he wearð wædla.

15 þa ferde he 7 folgode anum burgsittendan men þæs rices· ða sende he
10 hine to his tune þ he heolde his swin.

16 Ða gewilnode he his wambe gefyllan of þam beancoddum þe ða swin æton· 7 him man ne sealde.

17 þa beþohte he hine 7 cwæð: 'Eala, hu fela hyrlinga on mines fæder huse hlaf genohne habbað 7 ic her on hungre forweorðe.

1 **Hē** Christ.

2 **se gingra** The manuscript, following an earlier exemplar, has *se yldra* 'the elder'. Errors such as this are a reflection of human frailty and perhaps also of the difficult conditions under which the scribes must have worked.

3 **mē tō** A typical example of an OE postposition.

4 Note the order Adv.OVS.

7 **Ðā** conj. 'when' . . . **þā** adv. 'then'. From now on, I shall assume that you recognize this pattern, with the order conj.S but adv.V. The latter appears twice in ll. 9–10.

10 **þ** = **þæt** conj. 'so that' with subj. *hēolde* l. 10.

18 Ic arise 7 ic fare to minum fæder 7 ic secge him: "Eala, fæder, ic 15
syngode on heofenas 7 beforan þe·

19 nu ic neom wyrðe þ ic beo þin sunu nemned· do me swa anne of þinum
hyrlingum.'"

20 7 he aras þa 7 com to his fæder. 7 þa gyt þa he wæs feorr· his fæder he
hine geseah 7 wearð mid mildheortnesse astyrod 7 ongean hine arn 7 hine 20
beclypte 7 cyste hine.

21 Ða cwæð his sunu: 'Fæder, ic syngode on heofon 7 beforan ðe· nu ic ne
eom wyrþe þ ic þin sunu beo genemned.'

22 Ða cwæð se fæder to his þeowum: 'Bringað raðe þone selestan ge-
gyrelan 7 scrydað hine 7 sellað him hring on his hand 7 gescy to his fotum· 25

23 7 bringað an fætt styric 7 ofsleað 7 uton etan 7 gewistfullian·

24 forþam þes min sunu wæs dead 7 he geedcucode· he forwearð 7 he is
gemet.' Ða ongunnon hie gewistlæcan.

25 Soðlice his yldra sunu wæs on æcere 7 he com. 7 þa he þam huse ge-
nealæhte· he hierde þone sweg 7 þæt werod. 30

26 þa clipode he anne þeow 7 ascode hine hwæt þæt wære.

27 Ða cwæð he: 'þin broðor com· 7 þin fæder ofsloh an fæt cealf for þam
þe he hine halne onfeng.'

28 Ða bealg he hine 7 nolde in gan· þa eode his fæder ut 7 ongan hine
biddan. 35

29 Ða cwæþ he his fæder ondswarigende: 'Efne swa fela geara ic þe
þeowode 7 ic næfre þin bebod ne forgymde· 7 ne sealdest þu me næfre an
ticcen þ ic mid minum freondum gewistfullode.

30 Ac siððan þes þin sunu com þe his spede mid miltestrum amyrde· þu
ofsloge him fætt cealf.' 40

31 Ða cwæð he: 'Sunu, þu eart simble mid me 7 ealle mine þing sint þine.

32 þe gebyrede gewistfullian 7 geblissian for þam þes þin broþor wæs
dead 7 he geedcucode. He forwearð 7 he is gemet.'

15 **ārīse . . . fare . . . secge** Translate as future (§75).

16 **syngode** Translate as perfect (§75) here and in l. 22.

17 **neom** = *ne eom*. See §109 and compare ll. 22–3.

19 **his fæder hē** An example of a repeated subject.

26 An example of separation of verbs joined by *and* (§§162–3).

30 **hē hierde** Here we have the normal order SV in a principal clause which does not begin
with *þā* adv.

32 **cōm . . . ofslōh**. Cf. *syngode* l. 16.

32–3 **for þām þe** conj. 'because' (§§124–5).

42 **þē** dat. governed by gebyrian 'to behove' (wk. vb. like *werian* §525); **for þām** conj.
'because' (§§124–5).

The standard edition of the Old English Gospels is *The Holy Gospels in Anglo-Saxon, Northumbrian and Old Mercian Versions Synoptically Arranged* edited by Walter W. Skeat (Cambridge:
Cambridge University Press, 1871–1887).

§421 *Text and translation:*
'Build on the rock and not upon the sand'

Matthew 7: 24–7, another slightly emended extract from MS Corpus Christi College Cambridge 140 (§420), was used as an illustrative text in Part II above; see §§130–1.

§422 *Text and translatiom:* **The Parable of the Vineyard**

A third slightly emended extract from the same text – Matthew 20: 1–16 – was also used in Part II; see §§140–1.

§423 The Anglo-Saxon Chronicle has been discussed in §§177 and 179–80. The following extracts have already appeared:

TEXT 1   THE ROMANS IN BRITAIN (§181)

TEXT 2   THE BEGINNINGS OF ENGLAND (§182)

TEXT 3   THE COMING OF ROMAN AND CELTIC CHRISTIANITY (§183)

TEXT 4   THE SCANDINAVIAN INCURSIONS (§184)

TEXT 5   THE REIGN OF KING ALFRED (§185)

TEXT 6   THE ENGLISH KINGS (§186)

TEXT 7   THE DANES AND THE NORMANS (§187)

§424 The Old English Orosius – one of the Alfredian translations (§177), though it would be more accurate to describe it as a paraphrase – was written during the reign of Alfred and probably at his instigation. It survives in two British Library manuscripts – Additional 47967 (the Lauderdale or Tollemache MS) and Cotton Tiberius B.i – and in two fragments. There is evidence that other manuscripts have been lost. The main source is the *Historiarum adversum Paganos Libri Septem* of Paulus Orosius, which was written in the second decade of the fifth century. 'This work', says Janet Bately (see below), 'achieved very great popularity in the Middle Ages (its author appears among the blessed in Dante's heaven) and today over 250 manuscript copies of it are still in existence.' The actual Latin manuscript on which the OE is based has not been firmly identified. But the paraphraser also used material from other sources, though he was not necessarily familiar with the originals. Thus the passage printed below expands the Latin original and adds details from the works of Livy, Ovid, and Augustine, which he may have obtained second-hand. The result is a masterly piece of ironic invective which reflects the Christian writer's desire to emphasize that, bad as things are in his own times, they were worse in the pre-Christian era. The text presented here is that of the Lauderdale MS and represents the West-Saxon dialect of the early period.

Text 18 The foundation of Rome: an historian's verdict

Ymb feower hunde wintra 7 ymb feowertig þæs þe Troia, Creca burg,
awested wæs· wearð Romeburg getimbred from twam gebroðrum, Remuse 7
Romuluse· 7 raðe æfter Romulus hiora anginn geunclænsade mid his broðor
slege 7 eac siþþan mid his hiwunge 7 his geferena: hwelce bisena he ðær
stellende wæs mid þæm þe hie bædon Sabini þa burgware þætte hi him   5
geuðen hiora dohtra him to wifum to habbanne 7 hie him þara bena
forwierndon. Hi swaþeah heora unðances mid swicdome hie begeaton mid
þæm þe hie bædon þæt hie him fylstan mosten ðæt hie hiera godum þe ieð
blotan mehten. þa hie him þæs getygðedon· þa hæfdon hi him to wifum 7
heora fæderum eft agiefan noldon. Ymb þæt wearð þæt mæste gewinn 10
monig gear oð hie fornæh mid ealle forslægene 7 forwordene wæron on
ægþere healfe þæt hie mid nanum þinge ne mehton gesemede weorþan ær
þara Romana wif mid heora cildum iernende wæron gemong ðæm
gefeohtum 7 heora fæderum wæron to fotum feallende 7 biddende þæt hie
for þara cilda lufan þæs gewinnes sumne ende gedyden. Swa weorðlice 7 15
swa mildelice wæs Romeburg on fruman gehalgod: mid broðor blode 7 mid
sweora 7 mid Romuluses eames Numetores þone he eac ofslog ða he cyning
wæs 7 him self siþþan to ðæm rice feng! þuss gebletsade Romulus Romana
rice on fruman: mid his broðor blode þone weall 7 mid þara sweora blode þa
ciricean 7 mid his eames blode þæt rice. Ond siþþan his agenne sweor to 20

1 **ymb** prep. 'after' (not 'about' when expressing time); **þæs þe** literally 'from that in
which' and so conj. 'after'; **Trōia, Crēca burg** 'Troy, city of the Greeks'. Bately points out that
Troy or Ilium was in an area that formed part of Alexander the Great's empire. This could
explain what may seem to be an error.

3 **anginn** 'beginning/enterprise'; **geunclænsade** literally 'uncleansed' and so 'defiled';
brōðor here gen. sg. So again in ll. 16 and 19.

3–4 An example of a divided gen. group (§§162–3). Cf. ll. 16–17.

4 **hwelc** 'what sort of', here introducing what is an explanatory exclamation. I suggest the
translation 'these were the sort of examples which . . .'.

5 **mid þæm þe** prepositional conj. 'when'.

5–7 The Romans asked the Sabines for their daughters as wives but were refused.

6–10 The confusion caused by the ambiguity of the pers. prons. **hī/hīe**, **hiora**, and **him**,
continues and is not solved by the use of 'they', 'their', and 'them'. Here the Romans got the
women when the Romans asked the Sabines to permit the Romans to help the Sabines sacrifice
to the Sabines' gods. When the Sabines agreed, the Romans seized the women.

7 **heora unðances** 'against their (the Sabines') will'.

8 **þē ieð** lit. 'more easily than before'. In this complicated idiom, **þē** = instr. sg. neut. **þȳ**.
Translate 'more easily'.

11 **oð** conj. 'until'; **fornæh mid ealle** 'almost completely'.

12 **þæt** conj. 'so that'; **ær** conj. 'before'.

16–17 Another divided gen. group (§§162–3): **brōðor . . . swēora . . . Romuluses ēames
Nūmetōres** ('with [the blood] of Numetor, Romulus' uncle'). The meaning is clearer in ll. 19–
20, where **blōde** is repeated with each genitive.

20 **cirice** 'church'. Here used of the pagan temple.

20–2 More confusion arises here from the numerous pronouns. Romulus betrayed his own
father-in-law to death when Romulus lured his father-in-law by promising to share the kingdom with him.

deaðe beswac· þa he hiene to him aspon 7 him gehet ðæt he his rice wið hiene dælan wolde 7 hiene under ðæm ofslog.

22 **under ðǽm** 'under (cover of) that'.

The standard edition of this text is *The Old English Orosius* edited by Janet Bately, Early English Text Society S.S. 6 (London: Oxford University Press, 1980).

§425 The Old English version of *Historia gentis Anglorum ecclesiastica* by the Venerable Bede (*c.* 672–735) was certainly not the work of Alfred but it may have been instigated by him; see §177. There are four manuscripts and fragments of a fifth: Bodleian Tanner 10; Corpus Christi College Cambridge 41; Corpus Christi College Oxford 279; Cambridge University Library Kk. 3.18; and British Library Cotton Otho B.xi, which was badly damaged in the Cottonian fire of 1731 (§175). The Tanner MS, the usual basis for editions, is defective in places. So ll. 1–32 of the text which follows are from the MS Corpus Christi College Oxford 279 and the remainder from Tanner. Both are slightly emended. The extract comes from Book II and gives an account of the conversion of King Edwin and his Northumbrian people by Bishop Paulinus; see Text 3 annals 601–633 (§183). It contains the well-known comparison of life on this earth to the flight of a sparrow through a warm hall. The Old English translation accurately represents the Latin without losing any of the effect. Indeed, in one place at least, it arguably improves on the original by rendering the Latin *sed tamen paruissimo spatio serenitatis ad momentum excurso mox de hieme in hiemem regrediens tuis oculis elabitur* ('but after the briefest moment of calm, it flits from your sight, soon returning out of winter into winter') as *ac þæt bið an eagan bryhtm and þæt læsste fæc ac he sona of wintra on þone winter eft cymeð* ('but that is the twinkling of an eye and the least space of time but it soon comes from winter back to winter').

Text 19 **Northumbria converted**

þa se cyning þa þas word gehyrde· þa andswarode he him and cwæð þæt he æghwæþer ge wolde ge sceolde þam geleafan onfon þe he lærde· cwæð hwæþere þæt he wolde mid his freondum and mid his wytum gesprec and geþeaht habban þæt· gif hi mid hine þæt geþafian woldan· þæt hi ealle
5 ætsomne on lifes willan Criste gehalgade wæran. þa dyde se cyning swa swa he cwæð and se bisceop þæt geþafade.

1 **se cyning** Edwin; **þas word** here pl. (§55); **him** dat. sg. Bishop Paulinus or (perhaps less likely) dat. pl. 'to them/to these words'. The Latin has only *respondebat* 'replied'.

2 **æghwæþer ge ... ge** conj. 'both ... and'; **cwæð** 'said'. Verbs used in this way, with no subject expressed, can often be translated by a pres. ptc., here 'saying'.

4 The conj. **þæt** 'that' introducing a noun clause is here used both before and after the *gif*-clause which is part of the dependent speech.

5 **wǽran** pret. subj. pl. 'should be'.

þa hæfde he gesprec and geþeaht mid his witum and syndriglice wæs
fram him eallum frignende hwylc him þuhte and gesewen wære þeos niwe
lar and þære godcundnesse bigong þe þær læred wæs. Him þa andswarode
his ealdorbisceop, Cefi wæs haten: 'Geseoh þu, cyning, hwelc þeos lar sie þe   10
us nu bodad is. Ic þe soðlice andette þæt ic cuðlice geleornad hæbbe þæt
eallinga nawiht mægenes ne nyttnesse hafað sio æfæstnes þe we oð ðis
hæfdon and beeodon for ðon nænig þinra þegna neodlicor ne gelustfullicor
hine sylfne underþeodde to ura goda bigange þonne ic· and noht þon læs
monige syndon þa þe maran gefe and fremsumnesse æt þe onfengon þonne   15
ic· and in eallum þingum maran gesynto hæfdon. Hwæt, ic wat· gif ure godo
ænige mihte hæfdon· þonne woldan hie me ma fultumian for þon ic him
geornlicor þeodde ond hyrde. For þon me þynceð wislic· gif þu geseo þa
þing beteran and strangran þe us niwan bodad syndon· þæt we þam onfon.'
þæs wordum oþer cyninges wita and ealdormann geþafunge sealde and   20
to þære spræce feng and þus cwæð: 'þyslic me is gesewen, þu cyning, þis
andwearde lif manna on eorðan to wiðmetenesse þære tide þe us uncuð is:
swylc swa þu æt swæsendum sitte mid þinum ealdormannum and þegnum
on wintertide and sie fyr onælæd and þin heall gewyrmed and hit rine and
sniwe and styrme ute· cume an spearwa and hrædlice þæt hus þurhfleo·   25
cume þurh oþre duru in· þurh oþre ut gewite. Hwæt, he on þa tid þe he inne
bið ne bið hrinen mid þy storme þæs wintres· ac þæt bið an eagan bryhtm
and þæt læsste fæc ac he sona of wintra on þone winter eft cymeð. Swa

7–9 The king asked all his counsellors their opinion.
  8 **hwylc** interrog. 'what/of what sort'; **þuhte** See §100.
10 **ealdorbisceop** 'chief priest'. The word was later used of the archbishop.
11–13 **þæt eallinga . . .** The order in this clause is OVS.
13 **for ðon** conj. 'because' (§125).
14 **þonne** conj. 'than'; **nōht þon lǣs** conj. 'nevertheless'.
15 **þā þe** rel. pron. nom. pl. of *se þe* 'who'; **æt þē** prep. and pers. pron. (§494) 'from thee' or
'at thy hands'.
  16 **māran gesynto hæfdon** The subject *hīe* 'they' is unexpressed and the order is OV;
Hwæt, ic wāt 'Behold, I know [that] . . .'. The conj. *þæt* is unexpressed. (You can use the
superfluous *þæt* from l. 4 if you like!)
16–17 **gif** conj. 'if' . . . **þonne** adv. 'then' . . . **for þon** conj. 'because'.
18 **For þon** adv. 'for that' looking back and so 'therefore'.
18–19 Here we have another idiomatic variation on the use of *þæt* introducing dependent
speech. We had *þæt* twice in l. 4. We had no *þæt* in ll. 16–17. Here (as in MnE) we have one
þæt. But it follows the *gif* clause and its *þe* 'which' clause instead of preceding them. Translate
'Therefore it seems to me wise that, if . . .'. All these are acceptable patterns.
  20–32 The famous simile is put by Bede in the mouth of another of the king's counsellors,
who was of course then a pagan.
20 **þæs** gen. sg. of *se*; **wordum** dat. pl. 'To the words of that [man]'.
23 **swylc swā** conj. 'as if', followed by a series of verbs in the pres. subj. *sitte . . . sīe . . . rīne . . .*
Today we use the past tense 'were sitting . . . were/was . . . were/was raining . . .'.
  25–6 **cume** and the three other pres. subjs. in these lines are also governed by *swylc swā*
(l. 23) 'as if a sparrow were to come/came . . .'.
  26 **on þā tīd þe** 'in the time in which'.
26–8 In the sentence beginning with **Hwæt**, the translator uses the pres. ind.

þonne þis monna lif to medmiclum fæce ætyweð· hwæt þær foregange oððe
30 hwæt þær æfterfylige we ne cunnun. For ðon gif þeos niwe lar owiht cuðlicre
ond gerisenlicre brenge· þæs weorþe is þæt we þære fylgen.' þeossum
wordum gelicum oðre aldormen and ðæs cyninges geþeahteras spræcan.

... Ono hwæt, he þa se cyning openlice ondette þam biscope ond him
eallum þæt he wolde fæstlice þam deofolgildum wiðsacan ond Cristes
35 geleafan onfon ...

Ða onfeng Eadwine cyning mid eallum þæm æðelingum his þeode ond
mid micle folce Cristes geleafan ond fulwihte bæðe þy endlyftan geare his
rices.

29 **þis monna lif** 'this life of men'. This separation of an article and a noun by a genitive is,
as we have seen, a common idiom.
29–30 The pres. subjs. **foregange** and **æfterfylige** are in the dependent questions governed
by *cunnun* and express uncertainty about the future.
30 **For ðon**. Cf. *for þon* l. 18.
31 **þæs** 'of that' anticipating the *þæt* clause. See §158.
31–2 **þeossum wordum gelicum**. Translate 'With words like to these'.
36 **his þeode** gen. sg. 'of his people'.

The standard English edition of this text is *The Old English Version of Bede's Ecclesiastical History of
the English People* edited by Thomas Miller, Early English Text Society O.S. 95, 96, 110, 111
(London: Oxford University Press, 1890–8, reprinted Millwood, New York: Kraus). There is
also *König Alfreds Übersetzung* (but see §177) *von Bedas Kirchengeschichte* herausgegeben von Jacob
Schipper, Bibliothek der Angelsächsischen Prosa Vierter Band (Leipzig, 1899).

§426 *Text 15* A non-combatant warrior king

An extract from Book III of the Old English Bede (§425) will be found in
Part IIIE; see §385.

§427 I have elsewhere described the baptism of Germanic alliterative
verse through its use for Christian subjects and themes as new wine in old
bottles (§411) and as the Anglo-Saxon equivalent of Christian pop or 'Rave
in the Nave' (§449) and have said that, according to Bede, the union was first
accomplished by Cædmon, a laybrother in the monastery of Whitby during
the abbacy of Hild (§449). This slightly emended extract from the Tanner
MS is taken from Book IV of Bede's *History* (§425) and tells the story in the
words of the Old English translator. The list of subjects about which
Cædmon sang (ll. 29–37 below) bears such a marked resemblance to the
contents of the Junius MS (§173) that Israel Gollancz (following Junius,
whose title for the first edition (1655) began *Cædmonis Monachi Paraphrasis
Poetica Genesios ...*) entitled his facsimile edition *The Cædmon Manuscript of
Anglo-Saxon Biblical Poetry: Junius 11 in the Bodleian Library* (Oxford University
Press, 1927), in the belief that the poems it contained were the work of
Cædmon. But this is an example of the sentimental identification which
occurs elsewhere in Anglo-Saxon studies. The reason for the resemblance is
not common authorship but the fact that the topics listed by Bede are the
fundamentals of the Christian faith. J. R. R. Tolkien, however, did say in one

of his Oxford lectures that, if any poem by Cædmon still survived, it was *Exodus*. On this see §487 Text 46.

Text 20
Unmusical laybrother sings Christian song in alliterative verse

Wæs he se mon in weoruldhade geseted oð þa tide þe he wæs gelyfdre ylde ond he næfre nænig leoð geleornade. Ond he for þon oft in gebeorscipe· þonne þær wæs blisse intinga gedemed þæt heo ealle sceolden þurh endebyrdnesse be hearpan singan· þonne he geseah þa hearpan him nealecan· þonne aras he for scome from þæm symble ond ham eode to his 5 huse. þa he þæt þa sumre tide dyde þæt he forlet þæt hus þæs gebeorscipes ond ut wæs gongende to neata scipene þara heord him wæs þære neahte beboden· þa he ða þær in gelimplicre tide his leomu on reste gesette ond onslepte· þa stod him sum mon æt þurh swefn ond hine halette ond grette ond hine be his noman nemnde: 'Cedmon, sing me hwæthwugu.' þa 10 ondswarede he ond cwæð: 'Ne con ic noht singan· ond ic for þon of þeossum gebeorscipe ut eode ond hider gewat for þon ic naht singan ne cuðe.' Eft he cwæð se ðe mid hine sprecende wæs: 'Hwæðre þu meaht me singan.' þa cwæð he: 'Hwæt sceal ic singan?' Cwæð he: 'Sing me frumsceaft.' þa he ða þas andsware onfeng· þa ongon he sona singan in 15 herenesse Godes Scyppendes þa fers ond þa word þe he næfre gehyrde· þara endebyrdnes þis is:

1 **oð þā tīde þe** 'until the time at which'. Both *oð* and 'until' can be used as preps. and conjs. So this is the equivalent of 'until such time as'.

1–2 **gelȳfdre ylde** 'of advanced age'. A descriptive gen.

2–10 This passage illustrates clearly two important things. First we find both *þonne* and *þā* used as advs. meaning 'then' and conjs. meaning 'when'. But they differ. The clues are in the sequences *oft . . . þonne . . . þonne . . . þonne* but *þā . . . þā sumre tīde . . . þā . . . þā*. These tell us that *þonne* 'whenever' refers to repeated acts (*oft*) but *þā* 'when' to single acts performed on one particular occasion (*sumre tīde*) in the past. The second point is that the element order tells us when *þonne* and *þā* are advs. and when they are conjs. See §137. You will find that this difficult passage will crack open quite easily if you first decide which is which.

3 **blisse intinga** Latin *laetitiae causā* 'for the sake of happiness'. The translator mistook the ablative *causā* for the nom. *causa* and wrote *intinga* instead of *intingan*; see §501; **hēo** = *hīe* 'they'.

5 **for scome** 'for shame'. These words were added by the translator.

7 **nēata** gen. pl. 'of the cattle'; **þāra** gen. pl. of *se* used as rel. pron. 'of which'.

8 **ðā** adv. 'then'. So also in l. 15. Neither is needed in MnE.

9 **him . . . æt** 'by him'. Another use of the postposition instead of the preposition.

11–14 **Ne con ic** 'I do not know how' **. . . ic . . . ne cūðe** 'I . . . did not know how' **. . . þū meaht** 'thou canst' **. . . sceal ic** 'must/shall I'.

13 **hē . . . se ðe** 'he who'. See §164.

17 **þāra endebyrdnes þis is** 'of which this is the order/arrangement'. The Latin has *quorum iste est sensus* 'of which this is the sense' followed by a paraphrase. The Tanner MS (§425), which we follow, presents what is now called *Cædmon's Hymn* in alliterative metre but in the West-Saxon dialect, not in what must have been the original Northumbrian. Seventeen versions of the *Hymn* survive: four in Northumbrian and thirteen in West-Saxon. Of the latter, five (including ours) appear in the text of the translation, seven in the margin of Latin versions, and one in the Latin text in a fourteenth-century manuscript.

Nū [wē] sculon herigean   heofonrīces Weard,
Meotodes meahte   ond his mōdgeþanc,
20   weorc Wuldorfæder,   swā hē wundra gehwæs,
ēce Drihten,   ōr onstealde.
Hē ǣrest sceōp   eorðan bearnum
heofon tō hrōfe,   hālig Scyppend·
þā middangeard   monncynnes Weard,
25   ēce Drihten,   æfter tēode
fīrum foldan,   Frēa ælmihtig.

þa aras he from þǣm slǣpe ond eal þa þe he slǣpende song fæste in gemynde hæfde ond þǣm wordum sona monig word in þæt ilce gemet Gode wyrðes songes togeþeodde ... Song he ærest be middangeardes gesceape 30 ond bi fruman moncynnes ond eal þæt stær Genesis (þæt is seo æreste Moyses booc)· ond eft bi utgonge Israhela folces of Ægypta londe ond bi ingonge þæs gehatlandes ond bi oðrum monegum spellum þæs halgan gewrites canones boca· ond bi Cristes menniscnesse ond bi his þrowunge ond bi his upastignesse in heofonas ond bi þæs Halgan Gastes cyme ond þara 35 apostola lare· ond eft bi þǣm dæge þæs toweardan domes ond bi fyrhtu þæs tintreglican wiites ond bi swetnesse þæs heofonlecan rices he monig leoð geworhte.

18 **[wē]** The nom. pron. *wē* (or something like it) appears as the subject of the first clause in fourteen of the seventeen manuscripts of the *Hymn*: 'Now we must praise ...'. It is supported by the Latin 1st pers. pl. *Nunc laudare debemus* 'Now we must praise ...'. This idea that we human beings must praise God and His works is of course a common one. But the two oldest Northumbrian texts and our Tanner MS (which has been described as the best West-Saxon text) do not have *wē*. Good sense can be made of them by taking l. 20a *weorc Wuldorfæder* as the subject of *herigean* and ll. 18b–19 as its object: 'Now must the works of the Father of Glory praise the Guardian of heaven-kingdom, the power of the Creator and His purpose'. This idea too is a common one. The absence of *wē* from these three manuscripts is usually said to be due to scribal omission after the time of Bede. But there is the possibility that Cædmon did not sing *wē* and that *wē* was added by some excited hearers who thereby demonstrated the inherent unreliability of human testimony. There would thus have been from the beginning two versions – one with *wē*, which was known to Bede, and one without *wē*, which was known to the scribes of the two earliest Northumbrian manuscripts mentioned above.

20 **swā**. The Latin has *quomodo* 'how'. OE *swā* can be an adv. 'so/in this way' or a conj. 'because'. But it cannot mean 'how'.

22–6 I have punctuated this passage so that it presents two actions: God first *sceōp* created heaven. Then He *tēode* adorned the earth. A raised dot after *middangeard* l. 24 would give three stages: *ǣrest* first heaven, *þā* then middle-earth, *æfter* after (these) the adornment of the earth.

27 **eal þā þe** 'all those (things) which'.

28 **in þæt ilce gemet** 'in that same metre' viz. alliterative verse.

28–9 **Gode wyrðes songes** 'of song worthy of/dear to God'.

32–3 **þæs hālgan gewrites cānones bōca** 'of the books of the canon of holy Scripture'.

The standard edition of Bede's *History* is that of Thomas Miller; see §425.

§428   *Text and translation:*
Monks and Nuns. Scandal at Coldingham

Another passage from Book IV of Bede's *History* (§425) appears in Part IIIE; see §392.

§429 Gregory the Great (d. 604), the pope who sent St Augustine to England (§183), wrote his *Dialogues c.* 593. The book takes the form of a series of conversations in which Gregory relates to his deacon Peter the lives and miracles of St Benedict and other early saints. It became very popular and was translated into many European languages. The Old English version is the work of Bishop Wærferth of Worcester, one of King Alfred's helpers. It was made somewhere between *c.* 870 and *c.* 890 and survives in two closely related manuscripts, both eleventh-century – Corpus Christi College Cambridge 322 and British Library Cotton Otho C.i – and a fragment. A third eleventh-century manuscript, Bodleian Hatton 76, contains a revision made between 950 and 1050. The reviser consulted the Latin throughout and often brought the translation closer to it. But many of his changes made the language more modern. So the revision is of special interest to students of Old English syntax and style. The story printed below is taken from Book II and follows the Hatton Manuscript, with a few alterations. It exemplifies the uncritical credulity which is a hallmark of many of the mediaeval lives of saints. None the less, it almost compels a suspension of disbelief by virtue of the simple narrative, the artless (or artful) midway exclamation, and the portrayal of believable human reactions culminating in Benedict's humble refusal to accept any credit for such a remarkable event.

Text 21 **Monk walks on water**

On sumum dæge· þa þa se arwurða Benedictus wunode on his cyricean·
þa wæs ut agan þæs halgan weres se foresprecena cnapa Placidus munuc to
hladenne wæter of þære ea. He þa unwærlice nyðer alet on þæt wæter þæt
fæt þe he on handa hæfde and eac he sylf feallende wæs him æfter fyliende.
Hine þa sona seo yð gegrap and hine fram lande innor ateah nealice anre 5
flane scyte. Se Godes wer þa binnan cyrcean geseted hrædlice þæt ongeat
and ofstlice clypode Maurum and þus cwæð: 'Broðor Maurus, yrn hraðe·
forþam þe se cnapa þe ferde to hladenne wæter gefeoll on þa ea and hine
eallunga seo yð tyhð feorr aweg.' Eala· hu wundorlic þing þær gewearð· and
æfter Petre þam apostole ungewunelic! Soðlice Maurus abæd Benedictes 10
bletsunge and· hyre onfangenre· he ferde be his ealdres bebode swiðe
hrædlice to þære stowe þær se stream bær aweg þone cnapan. He arn uppon
þam wætere and wende þæt he fore on drigeum lande. He gelæhte þone

1–2 **þā þā . . . þā** Doubled *þā* 'then when/when then' is used by some writers to distinguish the conj. from the adv. But the element order still gives the clue in prose.

2 **þæs hālgan weres** gen. sg. referring to Benedict.

4 **him** dat. sg. neut. governed by the pres. ptc. *fyliende* referring back to *þæt fæt*.

5 **Hine . . . hine** Please remember *-ne* (§63); **innor** comparative of adv. *inn* 'further in [to the water]'.

8 **gefēoll** pret. tense with a perfect sense (§75).

11 **hyre onfangenre** dat. absolute referring to *bletsunge* 'it having been received'.

13 **wēnde þæt he fōre** The verb *wēnan* 'to think/suppose' is often followed by a subj. vb., here *fōre* 'was going'.

cnapan be þam feaxe and mid swiftum ryne eft gecyrde. Sona swa he þæt
15 land gehran· þa wearð he to him sylfum gecyrred and on bæc beseah. And þa
forþam þe he ongeat þæt he arn uppon þam wætere and þæt he ne mihte
gedyrstlæcan þæt hit swa gewurde gif he hit wyste· þa wearð he mid
wundrunge afyrht for þære dæde and gecyrde to his ealdre and him rehte þa
þing swa gedon. Se arwurða wer Benedictus þa ongann tellan þis wundor to
20 Maures hyrsumnysse· na to his agenum geearnungum.

16 **forþām þe** conj. 'because'.
18 **his ealdre** Benedictus.

The only edition of this text is *Bischofs Wærferth von Worcester Übersetzung der Dialoge Gregors des Grossen* herausgegeben von Hans Hecht, Bibliothek der Angelsächsischen Prosa Fünfter Band (Leipzig, 1900–7).

§430　Mention has already been made in §424 of additions by the translator or paraphraser to the Old English Orosius from the classics and patristic writings. But there are also geographical additions. Many of these are scattered throughout the work and were drawn from personal knowledge, oral reports, Latin texts, and perhaps from a map or maps. The most interesting to us are the reports of Ohthere, who was probably a Norwegian, and Wulfstan, who may have been an Anglo-Saxon from Mercia. As the first line of Text 22 below tells us, Ohthere made his reports direct to King Alfred. Wulfstan probably did the same, although it has been argued that Ohthere passed on to the king information derived from Wulfstan. If so, he gave Wulfstan the credit. The accounts given by the two men appear in the text after other additions which describe Northern Europe and are of interest both for what they say and because they say it in natural (as opposed to translated) prose. Two short extracts follow as Text 22 below, from Ohthere's statement, and Text 23, from Wulfstan's (§431). The first paragraph of Text 22 comes from the Lauderdale Manuscript (§424). But the second survives only in the Cotton Manuscript (§424) and is therefore taken from it.

Text 22　**Arctic explorer reports to king**

Ohthere sæde his hlaforde, Ælfrede cyninge, þæt he ealra Norðmonna norþmest bude. He cwæð þæt he bude on þæm lande norþweardum wiþ þa Westsæ. He sæde þeah þæt þæt land sie swiþe lang norþ þonan ac hit is eal weste buton on feawum stowum styccemælum wiciað Finnas· on huntoðe
5 on wintra 7 on sumera on fiscaþe be þære sæ ...

1–5 These lines are in dependent speech, with the subj. mood, until *is* l. 3 and *wiciað* l. 4, where the pres. ind. seems to represent Ohthere's own words.
2–3 **þā Westsæ** the sea off the west coast of Norway.
4 **būton** conj. 'except that'; **Finnas** the Lapps.

He sæde ðæt Norðmanna land wære swyþe lang 7 swyðe smæl. Eal þæt
his man aþer oððe ettan oððe erian mæg· þæt lið wið ða sæ· 7 þæt is þeah on
sumum stowum swyðe cludig· 7 licgað wilde moras wið eastan 7 wið uppon
emnlange þæm bynum lande. On þæm morum eardiað Finnas. 7 þæt byne
land is easteweard bradost 7 symle swa norðor swa smælre· eastewerd hit 10
mæg bion syxtig mila brad oþþe hwene brædre 7 middeweard þritig oððe
bradre· 7 norðeweard· he cwæð· þær hit smalost wære þæt hit mihte beon
þreora mila brad to þæm more· 7 se mor syðþan on sumum stowum swa
brad swa man mæg on twam wucum oferferan 7 on sumum stowum swa brad
swa man mæg on syx dagum oferferan. Ðonne is toemnes þæm lande 15
suðeweardum on oðre healfe þæs mores Sweoland oþ þæt land norðeweard·
7 toemnes þæm lande norðeweardum Cwena land. þa Cwenas hergiað
hwilum on ða Norðmen ofer ðone mor· hwilum þa Norðmen on hy· 7 þær
sint swiðe micle meras fersce geond þa moras· 7 berað þa Cwenas hyra
scypu ofer land on ða meras 7 þanon hergiað on ða Norðmen· hy habbað 20
swyðe lytle scypa 7 swyðe leohte.

6–21 This passage too starts in dependent speech with the pret. subj. *wǣre* l. 6, which
represents *is* in Ohthere's original statement. Then it too reverts to the pres. ind. until l. 12.
Here what was probably intended as a parenthetic *hē cwæð* – 'and northward, he said, where it
is narrowest, it may be three miles broad . . .' – produces the pret. subj. *wǣre* and a *þæt* clause
'he said that . . .' in ll. 12–13. But then it reverts to the pres. ind.
6 **smæl** This adj. does not mean 'small'!
6–7 **Eal þæt his** 'all of it that'. *His* is gen. sg. neut.
7 **āþer oððe . . . oððe** 'either . . . or'; first **þæt** a recapitulatory pronoun (§156).
8 **wið ēastan 7 wið uppon** 'to the east and above'.
10 **ēasteweard** Authorities agree that this seems to refer to the southern part of Norway.
12 **hē cwæð** See note to ll. 6–21 above.
16 **Swēoland** land occupied by the Swedes.
17 **Cwēna** gen. pl.; **þā Cwēnas** nom. pl. members of a Finnish tribe.
18 **ðā Norðmen** the inhabitants of Norway.
19 **micle meras fersce** The order adj. noun adj. is unusual.

The standard edition of the Old English *Orosius* is that by Janet Bately; see §424.

§431 This extract from the Old English Orosius (§424) contains part of
Wulfstan's report to King Alfred about his journeys in Northern Europe; see
§430. For the reasons given there, it is taken from the Cotton Manuscript.

Text 23 **A strange burial custom**

7 þær is mid Estum ðeaw· þonne þær bið man dead· þæt he lið inne
unforbærned mid his magum 7 freondum monað ge hwilum twegen· 7 þa
kyningas 7 þa oðre heahðungene men swa micle lencg swa hi maran speda

1 Wulfstan's report began in dependent speech *Wulfstān sæde þæt hē* . . . But, like Ohthere's,
it changed to non-dependent speech, with the pres. ind., as here; **mid Ēstum** 'among the Ests',
a tribe on the east coast of the Baltic; **þæt** introduces a clause explaining *ðēaw* 'custom' (l. 1).
2 **monað ge hwīlum twēgen** acc. of duration of time (§44).
3 **lencg** comparative adv. 'longer'. The sense is that the wealthier they are, the longer they
lie unburied.

habbað· hwilum healf gear þæt hi beoð unforbærned 7 licgað bufan eorðan
5 on hyra husum. 7 ealle þa hwile þe þæt lic bið inne· þær sceal beon gedrync
7 plega oð ðone dæg þe hi hine forbærnað. þonne þy ylcan dæg þe hi hine to
þæm ade beran wyllað· þonne todælað hi his feoh· þæt þær to lafe bið æfter
þæm gedrynce 7 þæm plegan· on fif oððe syx, hwylum on ma, swa swa þæs
feos andefn bið. Alecgað hit ðonne forhwæga on anre mile þone mæstan dæl
10 fram þæm tune· þonne oðerne· ðonne þæne þriddan· oþ þe hyt eall aled bið
on þære anre mile· 7 sceall beon se læsta dæl nyhst þæm tune ðe se deada
man on lið. Ðonne sceolon beon gesamnode ealle ða menn ðe swyftoste
hors habbað on þæm lande· forhwæga on fif milum oððe on syx milum fram
þæm feo. þonne ærnað hy ealle toweard þæm feo· ðonne cymeð se man se
15 þæt swiftoste hors hafað to þæm ærestan dæle 7 to þæm mæstan 7 swa ælc
æfter oðrum oþ hit bið eall genumen· 7 se nimð þone læstan dæl se nyhst
þæm tune þæt feoh geærneð. 7 þonne rideð ælc hys weges mid ðan feo 7 hyt
motan habban eall· 7 for ðy þær beoð þa swiftan hors ungefoge dyre. 7 þonne
hys gestreon beoð þus eall aspended· þonne byrð man hine ut 7 forbærneð
20 mid his wæpnum 7 hrægle· 7 swiðost ealle hys speda hy forspendað mid þan
langan legere þæs deadan mannes inne 7 þæs þe hy be þæm wegum alecgað
þe ða fremdan to ærnað 7 nimað.

5 **ealle þā hwīle þe** 'all the time in which'.
6 **þe** rel. pron. 'on which', twice in this line.
6–7 **þonne . . . þonne** This construction is explained in §427 Text 20, note to ll. 2–10.
7 **his feoh· þæt þær tō lāfe bið** 'his money, what's left there/of it'.
8–9 **þæs feos andefn** 'the amount of the money'.
9–18 The procedure for this unusual horse-race is this. The contestants assemble five or six miles from the dead man's homestead. What's left of his money is laid out in piles of decreasing value, the first and largest about one mile from the homestead and the rest appropriately spaced out, with the smallest pile nearest the homestead. The horsemen then race towards the piles of money, the fastest gaining the largest and so on in succession until all have been claimed. No wonder fast horses are *ungefōge dȳre* (l. 18).
9 **forhwæga** adv. 'about'.
10 **oþ þe** conj. 'until'.
11–12 **ðe . . . on** 'in which'.
14 **se man se** 'the man who'.
16 **oþ** Yet another form of the conj. 'until'; **se . . . se** 'that one . . . who', with antecedent and relative separated (§164).
17 **hys weges** adverbial gen. 'on his way' (§46).
17–18 **7 hyt motan habban eall** 'and [they] are permitted to have it all'. The contestants take everything left after the expenses of the lying-in; cf. ll. 20–2. What happened to the dead man's family is not revealed.
18 **for ðȳ** adv. 'therefore'.
20 **swiðost** adv. 'chiefly/especially'. Here it seems to be used to stress the fact that everything was spent; see note to ll. 17–18.
21 **þæs þe** 'with what'.
22 **þe** rel. pron. 'which'.

The standard edition of the Old English *Orosius* is that by Janet Bately; see §424.

§432 I shall risk a renewed accusation of sentimentality by repeating here my claim that King Alfred, Queen Elizabeth I, and Winston Churchill, rank among the foremost figures in England's roll of honour. I make this claim on the grounds that they were not only outstanding wartime leaders who inspired their country to rally and save itself in dire or almost hopeless situations but also distinguished literary figures. Text 24 below shows that Alfred was in addition a pioneer in spiritual and educational reform. It comes from his Preface to the first of his own translations, the Old English version of the *Cura Pastoralis* (or *Liber Regulae Pastoralis*), which was written by Pope Gregory I (§§183 and 429) *c.* 591 and which set out the principles on which bishops should, as shepherds of souls, direct their lives. Alfred, who saw its relevance to the problems faced by kings and secular leaders, ordered that a copy be sent *to ælcum biscepstole on minum rice* 'to each episcopal see in my kingdom'. His translation survives in some half-dozen manuscripts, three of which – all written during his reign – demand mention here: Bodleian Hatton 20 (see below); British Library Cotton Tiberius B.xi, which was damaged in the Cottonian fire of 1731, was copied by Junius (§173) in MS Bodleian Junius 53, and was destroyed except for a few charred fragments in a fire at a binder's in 1864; and British Library Cotton Otho B.ii, also damaged in the Cottonian fire but not before it had been collated by Junius. The manuscript from which our selection is taken (with a few minor alterations) is Bodleian Hatton 20, which was written between 890 and 897 and bears on folio 1 an inscription written in large angular capitals between two ruled lines: *ÐEOS BOC SCEAL TO WIOGORA CEASTRE* 'This book must/is to [go] to Worcester'. Since the impression of the two ruled lines appears on folios 2 and 3, this is the actual copy which was sent to Bishop Wærferth of Worcester (§429). Here is another opportunity for sentimentality: this manuscript was handled by Alfred and Wærferth; contains stylistic alterations by Archbishop Wulfstan (§446), probably made while he was Bishop of Worcester; has Latin interlinear glosses made by a scribe with a 'tremulous hand' in the thirteenth century and by John Joscelyn (1529–1603), who was Latin secretary to Archbishop Parker (§180); was acquired for the Bodleian Library from Christopher Lord Hatton in 1671; was known as Hatton 88 to the famous palaeographer Humfrey Wanley (1671–1726), who was an assistant keeper and cataloguer at the Bodleian; and, as Hatton 20, has (I venture to say) been handled by hundreds of Anglo-Saxon scholars of varying degrees of distinction from many countries.

Alfred begins his Preface by lamenting the state of learning and religious observance in England when he came to the throne in 871, which he saw as having suffered a catastrophic decline from its past glories as a result of indifference and the Scandinavian invasions. Then follows the passage printed as Text 24 below. The king goes on to say that all this led him *onge-mang oðrum mislicum ond manigfealdum bisgum ðisses kynerices* 'among the other various and manifold concerns of this kingdom' to translate into English the book which is called in Latin *Pastoralis* and in English *Hierdeboc* 'Shepherd Book' *hwilum word be worde hwilum andgit of andgiete* 'sometimes word by word, sometimes meaning for meaning'. He concludes by expressing his intention to send a copy to each bishop and his wish that the book should remain in the cathedral except when the bishop wishes to have it with him or when it is being copied.

In Alfred's carefully constructed and balanced Preface, we feel Old English prose adapting its vocabulary and style to the expression of complex ideas without completely eliminating signs of the struggle this involved. In his translations he frequently simplifies complicated Latin sentences without sacrificing the sense. I believe that Alfred succeeded magnificently in the task he laid upon himself. Indeed, his strong, vigorous, and sinewy, prose seems to me to have virtues which Ælfric's more polished but more cloistered prose does not display. But Ælfric in his turn has virtues denied to Alfred; see Text 33 (§445).

Text 24   New deal for education

Ða ic ða ðis eall gemunde· ða gemunde ic eac hu ic geseah· ær ðæm ðe hit eall forhergod wære ond forbærned· hu ða ciricean giond eall Angelcynn stodon maðma ond boca gefylda ond eac micel mengeo Godes ðiowa· ond ða swiðe lytle fiorme ðara boca wiston for ðæm ðe hie hiora nanwuht
5 ongietan ne meahton for ðæm ðe hie næron on hiora agen geðiode awritene. Swelce hie cwæden: 'Ure ieldran· ða ðe ðas stowa ær hioldon· hie lufodon wisdom ond ðurh ðone hie begeaton welan ond us læfdon. Her mon mæg giet gesion hiora swæð ac we him ne cunnon æfter spyrigean. Ond for ðæm we habbað nu ægðer forlæten ge ðone welan ge ðone wisdom for ðæm ðe we
10 noldon to ðæm spore mid ure mode onlutan.'

Ða ic ða ðis eall gemunde· ða wundrade ic swiðe swiðe ðara godena wiotena ðe giu wæron giond Angelcynn ond ða bec ealla be fullan geliornod hæfdon· ðæt hie hiora ða nænne dæl noldon on hiora agen geðiode wendan. Ac ic ða sona eft me selfum andwyrde ond cwæð: 'Hie ne wendon ðætte æfre
15 menn sceolden swæ recelease weorðan ond sio lar swæ oðfeallan· for ðære

---

3 **gefylda** This is nom. pl. with *-a*, which in *māðma* and *bōca* is gen. pl., instead of the more usual *-e*; **ond ēac** 'and also [there was]'.

4 **ðā** nom. pl. dem. 'those [servants]'.

6 **Swelce** '[It was] as if'; **hie** a recapitulatory pronoun (§156).

7 **ðone** acc. sg. masc. referring back to *wisdōm*. Cf. l. 9.

8 **him ... æfter** 'after them'.

8–9 **for ðæm ... for ðæm ðe** 'for this reason ... because'.

9 **ægðer ... ge ... ge** 'both ... and'.

11 **wundrian** 'to wonder at' takes the gen. case; **swiðe swiðe** 'very much'.

11–13 Another example of recapitulation (§156). The key elements are *ðara gōdena wiotena ...* *hīe*; cf. 'Consider *the lilies of the field*, how *they* flourish'.

13 Take care to distinguish *wendan* 'to turn/translate' (wk. vb. like *sendan* §89) in ll. 13, 19, 21, 23, and 25, from *wēnan* 'to think' (wk. vb. like *hīeran* §94) in l. 14.

15–16 **for ðære wilnunga** 'on account of that desire' ... **woldon** '[they] wished'. Alfred is saying that they were guilty of wishful thinking by assuming that so many people would know Latin and other languages that translations would be unnecessary.

wilnunga hie hit forleton ond woldon ðæt her ðy mara wisdom on londe
wære ðy we ma geðeoda cuðon.'

Ða gemunde ic hu sio æ wæs ærest on Ebriscgeðiode funden ond eft· ða
hie Creacas geliornodon· ða wendon hie hie on heora agen geðiode ealle
ond eac ealle oðre bec. Ond eft Lædenware swæ same· siððan hie hie 20
geliornodon· hie hie wendon ealla ðurh wise wealhstodas on hiora agen
geðiode. Ond eac ealla oðra Cristna ðioda sumne dæl hiora on hiora agen
geðiode wendon. Forðy me ðyncð betre· gif iow swæ ðyncð· ðæt we eac sume
bec· ða ðe niedbeðearfosta sien eallum monnum to wiotonne· ðæt we ða on
ðæt geðiode wenden ðe we ealle gecnawan mægen ond gedon· swæ we 25
swiðe eaðe magon mid Godes fultume gif we ða stilnesse habbað· ðætte eall
sio gioguð ðe nu is on Angelcynne friora monna· ðara ðe ða speda hæbben
ðæt hie ðæm befeolan mægen· sien to liornunga oðfæste ða hwile ðe hie to
nanre oðerre note ne mægen oð ðone first ðe hie wel cunnen Englisc gewrit
arædan. Lære mon siððan furður on Lædengeðiode ða ðe mon furðor læran 30
wille ond to hierran hade don wille.

16 **hit** neut. pron. referring back to the fem. *sīo lār*. See §56.

16–17 **ðȳ māra wīsdōm . . . ðȳ . . . mā geðēoda** 'by that/the more wisdom . . . by that/the
. . . more of languages'.

18 **sīo ǣ** 'the law', referring to the Old Testament or to the Pentateuch.

19 **hīe** acc. sg. fem. 'it/the law'; **hīe** nom. pl. 'they'; **hīe . . . ealle** acc. sg. fem.'it all'.

20–1 **hīe hīe . . . hīe hīe** The first *hīe* in each pair is nom. pl. 'they'. The second of these
recapitulates *Lædenware* l. 20; cf. ll. 11–13. The second *hīe* in each pair is acc. pl. 'the books'.

22 **ealla ōðra Crīstna ðīoda** nom. pl. subj. of *wendon* l. 23, despite the fact that they all end
in *-a*; **sumne dæl hiora** 'some part of them/the books'.

23 **Forðȳ** adv. 'therefore'.

23–4 **ðæt wē ēac sume bēc** is recapitulated by *ðæt wē ða.*

24 **ðā ðe** 'those which'.

25 **gedōn** 'to do/bring about' has as its object the clause beginning *ðætte eall sīo gioguð* in
ll. 26–7.

27 **frīora monna** gen. pl. dependent on *gioguð*; **ðāra ðe** 'of those who'.

28 **ðæt** conj. 'so that'; **ðǣm** dat. sg. neut. referring either to the fem. *liornung* or to the
general plan expounded by Alfred; **befēolan** 'to apply oneself'; **oðfæstan** 'to set to a task' (wk.
vb. with past ptc. *oðfæst*).

29 **mægen** 'can [be set]'; **oð ðone first ðe** 'until the time at which'.

30 **Lǣre** pres. subj. expressing a command; **mon** = *man* 'one'; **ðā ðe** 'those whom'.

31 **dōn** here 'to promote'.

The standard edition of this text is *King Alfred's West-Saxon Version of Gregory's Pastoral Care*
edited by Henry Sweet, Early English Text Society O.S. 45 and 50 (London: Oxford University
Press, 1871–2), reprinted Millwood, New York: Kraus).

§433 British Library MS Cotton Tiberius A.iii is a miscellany containing interlinear glosses to the Rule of St Benedict and to Ælfric's *Colloquy*
(§246), prayers, homilies, a collection of prognostics from dreams, the moon,
and calendars, and other items. Text 25 is taken from folios 40ᵛ–41. On folios
42ᵛ–43 will be found the passage about sex-determination during pregnancy
referred to in §372. These two items are described by Singer in his introduction to the reprint of Cockayne's edition (see below) as 'two very curious
passages reminiscent of degenerate Greek medicine'. It is not possible to say
how widely they were known or how seriously they were taken.

Text 25   **The formation of the foetus: new medical research**

Her onginneð secgan ymb mannes gecynde· hu on his moder innoþe to men gewyrðeð. Ærest þæs mannes brægen bið geworden on his moder innoþe· þonne bið þæt brægen utan mid reoman bewefen on þære syxtan wucan. On oðrum monþe þa ædran beoð geworden· on lxv 7 þreo hundred
5 scyrtran 7 lengran hi beoð todælede 7 þæt blod þonne floweð on þa fet 7 uppan þa handa· 7 he þonne bið on limum todæled 7 tosomne gearwad. On þam þriddum monþe he biþ man butan sawle. On þam feorþan monþe he biþ on limum staþolfæst. On þam fiftan monþe he biþ cwica 7 weaxeð 7 seo moder biþ witleas· 7 þonne þa ribb beoð geworden· þonne gelimpð þær
10 manigfeald sar þonne þæs byrþnes lic on hire innoþe scyppende bið. On þam syxtan monþe he biþ gehyd 7 ban beoð weaxende. On þam seofoþan monþe þa tan 7 þa fingras beoð weaxende. On þam eahtoþan monþe him beoð þa breost þing wexende 7 heorte 7 blod· 7 he bið eall staþolfæstlice geseted. On þam nigoþan monþe witodlice wifum bið cuþ hwæþer hi
15 cennan magon. On þam teoþan monþe þæt wif ne geðigð hire feore gif þæt bearn acenned ne biþ· for þam þe hit in þam magan wyrð to feorhadle· oftost on tiwes niht.

1–2 There are from our point of view two unexpressed subjects in the first sentence: *Hēr* [*man*] *onginneð secgan* 'Here one begins to tell/Here begins the explanation' and *hū* [*hē*] ... *gewyrðeð* 'how he becomes/grows'; **tō men** 'as a man'. Like the nom./acc. pl., the dat. sg. of *man* shows *i*-mutation (§17). On *man* see §434, Text 26, 1–2 note.

3 **ūtan mid rēoman bewefen** 'covered over from outside with membrane'.

4 I do not know why there should be a vein for each day of the year.

5 **on** prep. 'into'; **fēt** an *i*-mutation pl.

6 **uppan** prep. 'up to'; **gearwian** 'to make/construct'. I read the past ptc. form for MS *gearwað*, which makes no sense.

9 **þā ribb bēoð** The dem. and the verb are unambiguously pl.

9–10 **þonne ... þonne** Note the element order.

10 **scyppende** pres. ptc. of *scyppan*, here 'to form/take shape'.

11 **gehȳd** past ptc. of *gehȳdan* 'to furnish with skin'.

13 **brēost þing** 'breast organs'.

14 **wīfum** dat. pl. 'to women'; **hī** nom. pl. 'they'.

15 **geðigð** 3rd sg. pres. ind. of *geðicgan* 'to partake of' and so here 'to escape with'.

16 **feorhādl** 'life/fatal illness'.

The most accessible edition of this text is likely to be Vol. III p. 146 of *Leechdoms, Wortcunning & Starcraft of Early England* collected and edited by the Rev. Thomas Oswald Cockayne with a new introduction by Dr Charles Singer (London: The Holland Press, 1961). The three volumes of this work were originally published as part of the Rolls Series.

§434   Text 26, like Text 25 (§433), comes from British Library MS Cotton Tiberius A.iii (folio 41) and is part of a section dealing with omens and predictions based on the age of the moon. It presents no real difficulties and can be left to speak for itself. As I was born on 8 January over seventy years ago, I myself do not put much trust in it.

Text 26 **Choose your birthday carefully!**

Gif mann biÖ acenned on anre niht ealdne monan· he biÖ lang lifes 7 welig.
Gif he biÖ on twegra nihta acenned· he biÖ a seoc 7 unhal. Gif he biÖ on
þreora nihta· he leofaÖ lange. Gif he biÖ on iv nihta acenned· he biÖ a in
wordum leas. Gif he biÖ on v nihta ealdne· on geogoÖe gewiteÖ. Gif he biÖ
on vi nihta ealdne· he biÖ lang lifes 7 gesælig. Gif he biÖ on vii nihta· he biÖ a 5
weorÖ 7 lifaÖ lange. Gif he biÖ on viii nihta ealdne· he swelteÖ sona. Gif he
biÖ on ix nihta· he biÖ frecendlice acenned. Gif he biÖ on x nihta· he biÖ
þrowere. Gif he biÖ on xi nihta· he biÖ landes ofergenga. Gif he biÖ on xii
nihta ealdne· he biÖ on eallum þingum wurÖfull. Gif he biÖ on xiii oþþe on
xiv nihta· he biÖ æwfæst 7 rihtwis. Gif he biÖ on xv nihta· he biÖ sona 10
gefaren. Gif he biÖ on xvi nihta· he biÖ on eallum þingum nytwurÖe. Gif he
biÖ on xvii nihta· he biÖ sona gewiten. Gif he biÖ on xviii nihta oÖÖe on xix·
he biÖ gesælig. Gif he biÖ on xx nihta· he biÖ sona gefaren. Gif he biÖ on xxi
nihta· he biÖ on godre weorþunge. Gif he biÖ on xxii nihta· he biÖ unearg
fihtling. Gif he biÖ on xxiii nihta· he biÖ þeof 7 sceaÖa. Gif he biÖ on xxiv 15
nihta· he biÖ geswincfull in his life. Gif he biÖ on xxv nihta· he biÖ
gehealdsum his lifes. Gif he biÖ on xxvi nihta· he biÖ weorces gælsa. Gif he
biÖ on xxvii nihta· he biÖ to frecnum þingum acenned. Gif he biÖ on xxviii
nihta· he ne biÖ naÖor ne earm ne welig. Gif he biÖ on xxix oþþe on xxx nihta
ealdne monan acenned· he biÖ god 7 freondliÖe. 20

1–2 **mann ... hē ... hē ... hē** The word *mann* is used here in one of its normal senses
'human being'. But since it is masc. by grammatical gender, it is followed by the masc. pron. *hē*,
which here implies he or she.

1 Only the first and the last of the many *gif*-clauses in this extract appear in full. All the
others are abbreviated in some way; **biÖ ... biÖ** 'is/has been ... will be'; **on ānre niht** (gen.)
ealdne mōnan (acc.) 'on a moon old of/by one night'; **lifes** gen. 'of life'.

3 **leofaÖ** 'will live'. The verbs in the principal clauses all imply futurity; see §75.

4 Exceptionally *hē* is not expressed in the principal clause *on geogoÖe gewīteÖ*.

This Text, like Text 25, is most accessible in Vol. III of Cockayne's *Leechdoms, Wortcunning &
Starcraft of Early England*, described in §433. Text 26 is on pp. 156 and 158.

§435   This extract is part of a letter recording negotiations about the
ownership of land at Fonthill, Wiltshire, the original of which is to be found
in the Canterbury Cathedral Library. The person addressed as *Leof* 'Sir' or
'My Lord' (literally 'Dear One/Friend') seems to be King Edward the Elder
(d. 924), son of King Alfred; see §186. I have omitted over two-thirds of the
complicated negotiations and concentrated on Helmstan who, having put
his land in jeopardy by theft, failed to learn his lesson and stole again. That
Helmstan was born on the 23rd of the month (Text 26 l. 15, §434) will be the
conclusion of those who put more trust in that text than I do.

Text 27　Helmstan steals again

✠ Leof· ic ðe cyðe hu hit wæs ymb ðæt lond æt Funtial· ða fif hida ðe
Æðelm Higa ymb spycð. Ða Helmstan ða undæde gedyde ðæt he Æðeredes
belt forstæl· ða ongon Higa him specan sona on mid oðran onspecendan 7
wolde him oðflitan ðæt lond. Ða sohte he me 7 bæd me ðæt ic him wære
5　forespeca forðon ic his hæfde ær onfongen æt biscopes honda ær he ða
undæde gedyde. Ða spæc ic him fore 7 ðingade him to Ælfrede cinge. Ða –
God forgelde his saule – ða lyfde he ðæt he moste beon ryhtes wyrðe for
mire forspæce 7 ryhtrace wið Æðelm ymb ðæt lond . . .

　　Ða onufan ðæt ymban oðer healf gear nat ic hweðer ðe ymb tua· ða forstæl
10　he ða unlædan oxan æt Funtial ðe he mid ealle fore forwearð 7 draf to Cytlid·
7 hine mon ðæræt aparade. 7 his speremon ahredde ða sporwreclas. Ða he
fleah· ða torypte hine an breber ofer ðæt nebb· ða he ætsacan wolde ða sæde
him mon ðæt to tacne. Ða swaf Eanulf Penearding on· wæs gerefa· ða genom
eal ðæt yrfe him on ðæt he ahte to Tyssebyrig. Ða ascade ic hine hwy he swa
15　dyde· ða cwæð he ðæt he wære ðeof. 7 mon gerehte ðæt yrfe cinge forðon he

---

1 **Lēof** 'My Lord'; **ic** 'I', inidentified; **ðē** dat. sg. 2nd pers. pron.; **Funtial** Fonthill, Wiltshire.

1–2 **ðe . . . ymb** 'about which'.

2 **undǣd** 'wicked deed/crime'. The OE prefix *un-* is often negative as in MnE, e.g. *undēop*
'not deep/shallow'. But it often has a pejorative sense, as here.

3 **him specan . . . on** 'to make a claim against'.

4 **wǣre** 'should be', pret. subj. denoting that the answer to Helmstan's request is in doubt.

5 **forðon** conj. 'because'; **his** 'him' gen. sg. governed by *onfōn* 'to stand sponsor to' (st. contracted vb. VII(*b*) §521).

6 **him fore** 'for him'.

7 **forgelde** pres. subj. expressing a wish; **his . . . hē** refer to the king, . . . **hē** to Helmstan;
ryhtes wyrðe 'capable of law'. The king granted Helmstan the protection of the law.

8 **mīre** = *mīnre*; **ryhtrace** 'correct account [of the proceedings]'.

9 **onufan ðæt** 'after that' or 'on top of that [Helmstan's first theft]'; **ymban** prep. 'after'; **ōðer
healf gēar** 'the second year a half/a year and a half'; **nāt ic hweðer ðe** 'or perhaps'.

10 **ðe . . . fore** 'on account of which'; **mid ealle** 'completely'; **drāf** 'drove [them]'; **Cytlīd**
Chicklade, three miles south of Fonthill.

11 **speremon** 'spoorman/tracker'; **sporwreclas** This word appears to mean the cattle which
had been driven off and then tracked.

12 **ætsacan** 'to deny [the charge]'.

13 **him . . . tō tācne** 'as a token/evidence against him'.

13–15 **Dā swāf . . . ðā genom . . . Dā ascade . . . ðā cwæð** According to the principle
enunciated in §137, these are all examples of adv.V, with *ðā* 'then'. This is possible. But they may
be exceptions meaning 'When . . . then . . . When . . . then'.

13 **swāf . . . on** 'intervened'; **Ēanulf Penearding** presumably the shire-reeve (§357).

14 **him on** 'from him [Helmstan]'; **ðæt** rel. pron. 'which'; **tō Tyssebyrig** 'at Tisbury'; **hine
. . . hē** the reeve.

15 **ðæt hē wǣre ðēof** This means that Helmstan was a thief, not that he might be. The verb
cweðan is very often followed by a noun clause with the subjunctive even when the truth of a
statement is clear; **gerehte** 'judged' from *reccan* (irregular wk. vb.); **yrfe** 'property'. The penalty
for theft included the forfeiture of the thief's *bōcland*, land held by written title, to the king.

wæs cinges mon. 7 Ordlaf feng to his londe· forðon hit wæs his læn ðæt he on
sæt he ne meahte na his forwyrcan. 7 tu hine hete ða flyman.

16 Ordlaf received the land at Fonthill because he had leased it to Helmstan and so it was not
forfeit.
17 **tū** = *ðū* King Edward; **hine** Helmstan; **flȳma** 'outlaw'.

The full text of this document is piece XVIII in *Select English Historical Documents of the Ninth and
Tenth Centuries* edited by F. E. Harmer (Cambridge: Cambridge University Press, 1914).

§436   *Text and translation:*   **Parish boundaries defined**

A tenth-century Latin charter in British Library MS Cotton Claudius B.vi –
charter 561 in P. H. Sawyer's *Anglo-Saxon Charters: An Annotated List and Bibliography* (London: Royal Historical Society, 1968) – contains details in Old
English of the boundaries of a parish in Berkshire; see §323.

§437   This charter – the original of which is one of a collection of
Cottonian charters in the British Library – purports to be a confirmation by
King Edward the Confessor (1042–66) of a grant of the manor of Wargrave to
the Old Minster, Winchester, by his mother Queen Ælfgifu Ymma (d. 1052);
see §187 and notes 42 and 43. Robertson, in her edition (see below), writes:
'This charter has part of the tag remaining to which presumably the king's seal
was attached. In spite of this it is almost certainly spurious.' There are strong
reasons in favour of this view. First, it is doubtful whether the queen ever
owned this manor. Second, Earl Godwine died in Winchester in 1053. Ealdred did not become Archbishop of York until 1060. Yet both are supposed to
have signed the charter. Third, it has been judged doubtful on palaeographi-
cal grounds. Fourth, the overall impression given by the spelling and inflexions is that the language is later than the reign of Edward the Confessor; note,
for example, the phrase *into þam halige stowe* (l. 9), which (since *stow* 'place' is
normally fem.) would in standard OE be *into þære haligan stowe*. This is not the
only spurious charter to survive. Some of these may be statements of existing
rights never recorded in writing or recorded in lost documents. But others
seem to be fraudulent claims to privileges never granted. The latter verdict
seems inevitable here.

Text 28   **Monks forge charter**

✠ On God ælmihtiges nama 7 ealra his halgan· ic Eadward kincg luuelice an
þa elmessan þæ Elfgyuu Ymme min moder geuþe him aforeworda 7 ealla his

1 **On God . . . halgan** 'in God Almighty's name and [in the name] of all his saints'. Here *nama*
= *naman* and *halgan* = *halgena* (§501). Note that, as in English today, *God* does not have the genitive ending; contrast the OE genitive sequences in ll. 5–6 and ll. 7–8, on which see the notes
below; **luuelice** = *lufelice*. Since *f* between vowels is pronounced [v] (§8) and *u* is a frequent spelling for *v* in late MSS, *u* often represents OE *f*; **an** from *unnan* 'to grant' (like *cunnan* §96).
2 **þæ** = *þe*; **geuþe** Also from *unnan*.
2–3 **him . . . ealla his hālgan** 'to God and to all his saints'; **aforeworda** adv. 'in the first
place'.

halgan into Ealdan mynstre of þan tunæ þe hatte Weregrauæ mid saka 7 mid
socne 7 mid eallan witan· and on eallon þingon eallswa fri eallswa hit stod
5 hyre syluan fyrmest on handan· for Æþelredes kinges mines fæderes saule
an Hardacnudes mines broþer an ealra þara kinge þe tefore me wæron oþþe
æfter me cumeð to þise rice. Nu ic bidde of Godes healua an ealra his halga
and of mine· þet ealswa hi willað habban del on þære ylkan elmesse· ealswa
hi fæstlice healdan aþan þet hy seo stedefest into þam halige stowe. And
10 lochwa þis willæ awændan· awænde hine God fram him· and fram þan ecæ
life. ✠ Ego Stigandus arc̄ consensi. Ego Ealdred arc̄ consensi. Ego
Hæreman eƀs consensi. Ego Ræimballd cancell consensi. Ego Godwine
dux consensi.

3 **intō Ealdan mynstre** 'to the Old Minster'. This was where the Benedictine monk
Ælfric studied under Bishop Æthelwold (§§186 and 438) at Winchester; **of þān tūnæ** This
goes with *þā elmessan* l. 2 'the charitable gift from the manor'; **Weregrāuæ** Wargrave,
Hampshire.

3–4 **mid saka 7 mid sōcne** 'with the right of holding civil and criminal courts'.

4 **mid eallan wītan** 'with [the receipts of]all fines'; **eallswā . . . eallswā** 'just as . . . as'.

5 **hyre syluan . . . on handan** 'in her own hands/power'.

5–6 **for Æþelredes . . . kinge** For this construction with three genitive groups depending
on *sāule* and joined by *an . . . an* 'and . . . and', see note to Text 18, ll. 3–4 and 16–17.

7–8 **Godes healua** 'behalf' **. . . mīne** The same construction as in ll. 5–6.

8 **þet** 'that' introducing a request dependent on *bidde* 'pray'; **ealswā . . . ealswā** 'as . . . so'.

9 **healdan** 3rd pers. pl. pres. subj. 'may/will hold'. This is the request; **þet** 'that' introducing a clause explaining *aþan* 'oaths' with *sēo* 3rd pers. pl. pres. subj. of the verb 'to be' (§528).

10 **lōchwā** 'look who/if anyone'; **willæ** = *wille*; **āwændan** 'to change/remove'; **āwænde**
3rd pers. sg. pres. subj. expressing a wish.

11–13 This is the list of alleged witnesses.

This text is charter CXVIII in *Anglo-Saxon Charters* edited with Translation and Notes by A. J.
Robertson (Cambridge: Cambridge University Press, 2nd edn, 1956).

§438   *Text and translation:*
Bishop Æthelwold's gifts to Peterborough

An extract from another document printed by Robertson (§437) as charter
XXXIX, which is to be found in a twelfth-century collection of Peterborough charters owned by the Society of Antiquaries, has been used in Part
IIIC to illustrate the variety of Anglo-Saxon metalwork. In the annal for 963
in the Laud Manuscript of the Chronicle (§180), we find a long Peterborough insertion which describes the contributions to monastic reform by
Æthelwold, Bishop of Winchester 963–84 (§186). First, he reformed the Old
and New Minsters at Winchester by replacing the secular (non-monastic)
clergy by monks. He then re-established the monastery at Ely. His next
concern was Peterborough, of which we are told that, when he came *to þære
mynstre . . . ðe hwilon wæs fordon fra heðene folce· ne fand þær nan þing butan ealde
weallas 7 wilde wuda* 'to the monastery . . . which formerly had been destroyed
by the heathen army, [he] found nothing but old walls and wild woods'. This
insertion goes on to describe how Æthelwold rebuilt the monastery,
appointed an abbot and monks, and persuaded King Edgar to grant lands
and privileges. Robertson's charter XXXIX gives details of Æthelwold's

own benefactions to the monastery, which included books, estates, and annual tithes, in addition to the items listed in §248 above.

§439 *Text and translation:*
Malingering leader betrays his troops

In §187 the reign of King Æthelred was described as 'a welter of indecision, inaction, cowardice, and treachery'. This is well illustrated by the story of Ælfric *ealdorman* of Hampshire as related in extracts from the annals for 992 and 1003 in the Laud MS of the Chronicle (§180) printed in Part IIIE; see §350.

§440 *Text and translation:*
Danes murder Archbishop Ælfheah

Another event in Æthelred's troubled reign is described in an extract from the annal for 1012 in MS C of the Chronicle – British Library MS Cotton Tiberius B.i (the Abingdon Chronicle) – used in Part IIIC; see §220.

§441 The Baron Münchausen of Anglo-Saxon England makes his appearance in the texts known as *Alexander's Letter to Aristotle* and *The Wonders of the East* (§177.5), which are to be found in British Library MS Cotton Vitellius A.xv, the manuscript which contains the poems *Beowulf* and *Judith* (§175) and from which Text 29 below is taken. In company with a *Life of St Christopher*, they immediately precede *Beowulf*. All three prose works were written by the man who wrote lines 1–1939 of *Beowulf* (§299). The extracts which follow are taken from *The Wonders of the East*, a text which also survives in British Library MS Cotton Tiberius B.v. Both versions were copied from another manuscript now lost. But Rypins (see below) tells us that 'the remote sources of the text, however, are not hard to discover' and concludes his survey of these by remarking that 'the fabulous element in classical literature was apparently seized upon, wherever found, by the author of *Wonders of the East*, and put together by him, in no very artistic fashion, to make what is rather a compilation than a work of literary merit'. As the reader will discover, the author shows no concern for factual accuracy. His interest, and that of his audience, was in the fabulous, in *wundorsiona fela* 'many wondrous sights'.

Text 29   A traveller's tales

þeos stow hafað nædran· þa nædran habbað twa heafdu· þara eagan scinað nihtes swa leohte swa blæcern. On sumon lande eoselas beoð acende· þa habbað swa micle hornas swa oxan· þa syndon on þære mæstan westne þ

---

1 **þāra** gen. pl. of *se* dem. 'their' or rel. pron. 'whose'.

2 **sum** adj. 'a certain' (MnE 'some').

3–5 In these lines the word *þā* – nom. pl. of *se* – occurs five times preceded in my punctuation by a raised stop. Sometimes it can be translated as a rel. pron. 'which' but it is perhaps better translated as a dem. 'they/those'.

3 **þ** scribal abbreviation for *þæt*.

is on þa suð healfe from Babiloniam· þa buað to þæm readan sæ for þara
5 nædrena mænego þe in þæm stowum beoð· þa hatton corsias· þa habbað
swa micle hornas swa weðeras· gif hy hwilcne man sleað oþþe a æthrineð
þonne swylteð he sona . . .

Ðær beoð cende men· hy beoð fiftyne fota lange 7 hy habbað hwit lic 7 twa
neb on anum heafde set 7 cneowu swyðe reade 7 lange nosa 7 sweart feax.
10 þonne hy cennan willað þonne farað hy on scipum to indeum 7 þær hyra
gecynda in world bringaþ. Ciconia in gallia hatte þ land þær beoð men
acende on drys heowes· þara heafdu beoð gemane swa leona heafdu· 7 hi
beoð xx fota lange 7 hy habbað micelne muð swa fon. Gyf hwylcne monnan
on þæm landum ongitað oððe geseoþ· oððe him hwilc man folgiende bið·
15 þonne feor hi fleoð 7 blode hy swætað. þas beoð men gewende. Begeondan
Brixonte þære ea east þonon beoð men acende lange 7 micle· þa habbað fet
7 sconcan xii fota lange· sidan mid breostum seofon fota lange· hostes hy
synd nemned· cuþlice swa hwylcne man swa hy gelæccað þonne fretað hi
hyne.

20 Ðonne sindon wildeor þa hatton lertices· hy habbað eoseles earan 7
sceapes wulle 7 fugeles fet. þonne syndon oþere ealond suð from Brixonte
on þon beoð men buton heafdum· þa habbað on hyra breostum heora eagan
7 muð· hy seondon eahta fota lange 7 eahta fota brade.

Ðær beoð dracan cende þa beoð on lenge hundteontiges fotmæla lange 7
25 fiftiges· hy beoð greate swa stænene sweras micle· for þara dracena micelnesse ne mæg nan manna yþelice on þæt land gefaran . . .

Ymb þas stowe beoð wif acenned þa habbað beardas swa side oð hyra
breost· 7 horses hyda hy habbað him to hrægle gedon· þa syndan hunticgan
swiðost nemde· 7 fore hundum tigras 7 leon 7 loxas þæt hy fedað· þæt sindon

4 **tō** prep. 'at'.
6 **ā** adv. 'at all/even'.
10 **indeum** India.
11 **Ciconia** unidentified; **gallia** This word is used by Bede to refer to the kingdom of the
Gauls, France. Note the inconsistent use of capital letters.
12 **on drȳs hēowes** 'in the form of a magician'. This is the reading of our text. But prep. *on*
does not usually take the gen. and a Latin text which survives has *homines tripartito colore*. Rypins
(see below) suggests the reading *on þrym hēowum* 'in three colours/tricoloured'; **þāra** See l. 1.
13 **hwylcne** Remember *-ne* (§41).
14 **ongitað** 3rd pers. pl. pres. ind. with subject *hī* 'they' unexpressed; **him** dat. pl. 'them'.
15 **þās bēoð men gewēnde** Rypins supports the translation 'These are thought [to be]
men'; see Glossary. But we might get better sense by deriving *gewende < gewendan* 'to change'
and translating 'These are men transformed'.
16 **Brixonte** an unidentified river.
17 **hostes** an unidentified tribe! Again, no capital letter.
18 **swā hwylc . . . swā** 'whatever'.
21 **ēalond** nom. pl.
22 **on þon** 'on which'
24–5 Note the separation of the numerals (§§162–3).
28 **tō** 'as'.
29 **fore** prep. 'instead of'; **tigras 7 lēon 7 loxas** are the object of an unexpressed 'they have/
use'; **þæt** 'which'. An unusual use of *þæt* in Old English, but now common, referring to plural
antecedents; **þæt sindon** 'those are'. A regular Old English idiom.

þa cenestan deor. . . . Ðonne sindon oþere wif þa habbað eoferes tuxas 7 feax 30
oð helan 7 oxan tægl on lendunum· þa wif sindon þryttyne fota lange 7 hyra lic
bið on marmorstanes hiwnesse 7 hi habbað olfendan fet 7 eoseles teð.

The standard edition of this text is *Three Old English Prose Texts in Ms. Cotton Vitellius A.xv* edited
by Stanley Rypins, Early English Text Society O.S. 161 (London: Oxford University Press,
1924, reprinted Millwood, New York: Kraus).

§442   Text 30 is a paragraph from a fragment of a letter preserved in MS
Bodleian Hatton 115. It is addressed to Brother Edward, presumably by a
clerical superior. The theme and the tone will be familiar to most of my
readers.

Text 30   Foreign fashions condemned

Ic secge eac ðe broðor Eadweard nu ðu me þyses bæde· þæt ge doð
unrihtlice þæt ge ða engliscan þeawas forlætað þe eowre fæderas heoldon
and hæðenra manna þeawas lufiað þe eow ðæs lifes ne unnon and mid ðam
geswuteliað þæt ge forseoð eower cynn and eowre yldran mid þam
unþeawum þonne ge him on teonan tysliað eow on denisc ableredum 5
hneccan and ablendum eagum. Ne secge ic na mare embe ða sceandlican
tyslunge buton þæt us secgað bec þæt se beo amansumod þe hæðenra
manna þeawas hylt on his life and his agen cynn unwurþað mid þam.

1 **nū** conj. 'now that'; **þyses** gen. governed by *bǣde* 'about this'; **ðū ... gē** The change from
sg. to pl. shows that Edward's 'faults' were shared by his contemporaries!

2 **þæt** conj. 'in that'.

3 **ðæs lifes** gen. governed by *ne unnon* 'do not wish/begrudge'; **mid ðām** 'with those',
referring back to *þeawas* l. 3.

5 **him on tēonan** 'to their shame'; **on denisc** 'in Danish [fashion]'.

5–6 **ābleredum hneccan and āblendum ēagum** 'with bared neck and blinded eyes'. This
is generally taken to mean that he had long hair which fell over his eyes.

7 **bēo** pres. subj. after *secgan*. Translate 'is'.

8 **hylt** 3rd sg. pres. ind. of *healdan* 'to hold/observe'; **mid þām** See note on *mid ðām* l. 3.

The letter from which this text is taken was printed in full by F. Kluge, 'Fragment eines
angelsächsischen Briefes', *Englische Studien* 8 (1885), 62.

§443   Text 31 is an extract from *Apollonius of Tyre*, an example of the prose
fiction referred to in §177.5. It is preserved in the mid-eleventh-century manuscript Corpus Christi College Cambridge 201, which also contains some laws
and some Wulfstan homilies. The Old English version is a translation from a
Latin text which is based on a lost Greek original. In general, it follows its
source faithfully, though there are additions, omissions, mistranslations, and
some paraphrases. The story was very popular throughout Europe in the
Middle Ages, was retold by John Gower (?1330–1408) in *Confessio Amantis*, and
was used by Shakespeare in *Pericles, Prince of Tyre*. The Old English style is
natural, with its avoidance of Latin constructions and its clever renderings of
unfamiliar ideas such as public baths and ball games. By means of narrative
skill, character drawing, humorous touches, and sensitive portrayal of
emotions (including love, as this extract demonstrates), the author produces

a version which, in the words of Goolden (see below), 'introduce[s] us more than any other Old English document to ordinary human nature, and the people we see are not after all very different from ourselves'.

Text 31

Shipwrecked man gains king's favour: royal romance in prospect?

Æfter þisum wordum he eode on ðone weg þe him getæht wæs oð ðæt he becom to þare ceastre geate and ðar in eode. Mid þi þe he þohte hwæne he byddan mihte lifes fultum· þa geseah he ænne nacodne cnapan geond þa stræte yrnan se wæs mid ele gesmerod and mid scitan begird and bær iungra
5 manna plegan on handa to ðam bæðstede belimpende and cliopode micelre stæfne and cwæð: 'Gehyre ge ceasterwaran· gehyre ge ælðeodige, frige and þeowe, æðele and unæðele, se bæðstede is open.' Ða ða Apollonius þæt gehirde· he hine unscridde þam healfan scicilse ðe he on hæfde and eode into ðam þweale and mid þi þe he beheold heora anra gehwilcne on heora
10 weorce he sohte his gelican ac he ne mihte hine þar findan on ðam flocce. Ða færinga com Arcestrates, ealre þare þeode cyningc, mid micelre mænio his manna and in eode on þæt bæð. Ða agan se cyngc plegan wið his geferan mid þoðere and Apollonius hine gemægnde swa swa God wolde on ðæs cyninges plegan and yrnende þone ðoðor gelæhte and mid swiftre rædnesse
15 geslegene ongean gesænde to ðam plegendan cynge. Eft he agean asænde· he rædlice sloh swa he hine næfre feallan ne let. Se cyngc ða oncneow þæs iungan snelnesse þæt he wiste þæt he næfde his gelican on þam plegan· þa cwæð he to his geferan: 'Gað eow heonon. þes cniht· þæs þe me þingð· is min gelica.' Ða ða Apollonius gehyrde þæt se cyning hyne herede· he arn
20 rædlice and genealæhte to ðam cynge and mid gelæredre handa he swang þone top mid swa micelre swiftnesse þæt se cyngc wæs geþuht swilce he of ylde to iuguðe gewænd wære· and æfter þam on his cynesetle he him gecwemlice ðenode. And þa ða he ut eode of ðam bæðe· he hine lædde be þare handa and him þa siððan þanon gewænde þæs weges þe he ær com.

1 **hē** Apollonius, Prince of Tyre, who, having discovered the incestuous relationship between King Antiochus and his daughter, left Tyre to preserve his life. The ship was wrecked and Apollonius alone survived, cast ashore naked in the realms of King Arcestrates. There he was kindly treated by a fisherman, who fed him, gave him half his cloak, and showed him the way to the city where the king had his court. Our extract takes up the story here.

2 **ðār** = *ðǣr* 'there'. So also in ll. 40 and 44 *þār*; **hwǣne** = *hwone* 'whom', introducing a dependent question. Apollonius thought 'Whom can I ask . . .?'. Cf. Stop Press l. 4 and note.

5 **plega** 'play/sports equipment'.

9 **heora anra gehwilcne** 'each of them individually/in turn'.

10 **weorc** 'work/activity', meaning 'play'!; **gelīca** 'like/equal'.

15 **geslegene** The Latin shows that this should be acc. sg. masc. *geslegenne* referring back to *þone ðoðor*: Apollonius 'running caught the ball and with swift speed sent [it] having been struck/propelled back to the playing king'.

16 **swā** conj. 'in such a way that'. This is a way of saying 'without letting it fall'.

17 **þæt hē wiste** 'so that he knew'. You could translate 'and recognized'.

18 **þingð** = *þincð*.

21 **top** 'ball'; **wæs geþuht** 'was seemed'. This is a well-attested idiom. Translate 'seemed'.

21–2 **swilce** + subj. **wǣre**, 'as if', conj. See l. 27 note.

Ða cwæð se cyningc to his mannum siððan Apollonius agan wæs: 'Ic 25
swerige þurh ða gemænan hælo þæt ic me næfre bet ne baðode þonne ic
dide todæg· nat ic þurh hwilces iunges mannes þenunge.' Ða beseah he hine
to anum his manna and cwæð: 'Ga and gewite hwæt se iunga man sy þe me
todæg swa wel gehirsumode.' Se man ða eode æfter Apollonio. Mid þi þe he
geseah þæt he wæs mid horhgum scicelse bewæfed· þa wænde he ongean to 30
ðam cynge and cwæð: 'Se iunga man þe þu æfter axsodest is forliden man.'
Ða cwæð se cyng: 'þurh hwæt wast ðu þæt?' Se man him andswerode and
cwæð: 'þeah he hit silf forswige· his gegirla hine geswutelað.' Ða cwæð se
cyngc: 'Ga rædlice and sege him þæt se cyngc bit ðe þæt ðu cume to his
gereorde.' Ða Apollonius þæt gehyrde· he þam gehyrsumode and eode forð 35
mid þam men oð þæt he becom to ðæs cynges healle. Ða eode se man in
beforan to ðam cynge and cwæð: 'Se forlidena man is cumen þe ðu æfter
sændest ac he ne mæg for scame in gan buton scrude.' Ða het se cyngc hine
sona gescridan mid wurðfullan scrude and het hine in gan to ðam gereorde.
Ða eode Apollonius in and gesæt þar him getæht wæs ongean ðone cyngc 40
. . . Ða beseah Arcestrates se cyngc bliðum andwlitan to Apollonio and
cwæð: 'Ðu iunga man beo bliðe mid us and gehiht on God þæt þu mote silf
to ðam selran becuman.'

   Mid þi ðe se cyning þas word gecwæð· ða færinga þar eode in ðæs cynges
iunge dohtor Arcestrate and cyste hyre fæder and ða ymbsittendan. þa heo 45
becom to Apollonio· þa gewænde heo ongean to hire fæder and cwæð: 'Ðu
goda cyningc and min se leofesta fæder, hwæt is þes iunga man þe ongean
ðe on swa wurðlicum setle sit mid sarlicum andwlitan?'

27 **nāt ic . . . þēnunge** lit. 'know not I through which young man's service'. In the Latin
Apollonius massaged the king, who as a result felt young again.

34 **bit** < *biddan* 'to ask'; **ðē . . . ðū** 'thee . . . thou', referring to Apollonius. Strict grammar
requires *hine . . . hē* in the dependent question but the king anticipates the words his messenger
will use to Apollonius.

41 A few lines are omitted which tell how, when he saw Apollonius eating nothing and
sitting with downcast countenance at the feast, the king felt sorry for him.

47 **se** 'the', idiomatic in OE but now tautologic.

   In the passage omitted before the Stop Press, we learn that the Princess Arcestrate, having
fallen in love with Apollonius, persuaded her father Arcestrates to allow Apollonius to become
her teacher. Then, when pressed to choose one of three noble suitors, she rejected them and
confessed to her father that she chose *þone forlidenan man* 'the shipwrecked man'. As we now
see, this was just what the king wanted.

STOP PRESS   **Arcestrate to marry Apollonius**

   And Arcestrates se cyngc heold for ðon Apollonius hand and hine lædde
ham mid him· na swilce he cuma wære ac swilce he his aðum wære. Ða æt
nyxstan forlet se cyng Apollonius hand and eode ana into ðam bure þar his

1 **for ðon** adv. 'therefore/then'.
2 **swilce . . . swilce** See ll. 21–2 above.
3 **Apollonius** gen. sg.

dohtor inne wæs and þus cwæð: 'Leofe dohtor, hwæne hafast þu ðe gecoren
5 to gemæccan?' Ðæt mæden þa feol to hyre fæder fotum and cwæð: 'Ðu
arfæsta fæder, gehyr þinre dohtor willan. Ic lufige þone forlidenan man ðe
wæs þurh ungelymp beswicen ac þi læs þe þe tweonige þare spræce·
Apollonium ic wille, minne lareow, and gif þu me him ne silst· þu forlætst
ðine dohtor.' Se cyng ða soðlice ne mihte aræfnian his dohtor tearas ac
10 arærde hi up and hire to cwæð: 'Leofe dohtor, ne ondræt þu ðe æniges
þinges. þu hafast gecoren þone wer þe me wel licað.'

4 **hwæne** — *hwone* 'whom?'. Cf. Text 31 l. 2.
7 **þī læs þe** conj. 'lest'; **þē twēonige** 'lest [it] be uncertain to thee'.

The most accessible edition of this text is likely to be *The Old English 'Apollonius of Tyre'* edited
by Peter Goolden (Oxford: Oxford University Press, 1958).

§444 Ælfric was one of the ecclesiastical scholars and leaders produced
by the monastic reforms which began in the reign of King Edgar; see §§186
and 177.3. Text 32 is an extract from his Preface to his translation of the book
of Genesis, which is preserved in Bodleian MS Laud Misc. 509 (used here)
and in other manuscripts. In his Preface, Ælfric discusses the dangers of
translating the Scriptures into the vernacular and questions its wisdom.
This problem was of concern to the Church throughout the Middle Ages. In
England, John Wycliffe (d. 1384), who believed that Christians should be
free to read the Bible in English, began to translate it into English, a task
continued by Nicholas of Hereford (d. *c.* 1420) and John Purvey (d. 1428). In
1407, the Council of Oxford forbade the making of any new translations of
the whole or of any part of the Bible and forbade the use of any translation
made in the time of John Wycliffe or thereafter without diocesan or synodi-
cal permission. In spite of this, copies of the Wycliffite versions continued to
be made and used until the Reformation, when the versions of William Tyn-
dale (d. 1536) and Miles Coverdale (d. 1568) became available. No complete
Anglo-Saxon Bible exists. There are interlinear glosses of the Psalms and
the Gospels; the four Gospels in West-Saxon; Psalms 1–50 in prose and 51–
150 in verse; the Heptateuch (§419 end); and versions of some separate portions of both Testaments in other manuscripts. See §§419–22 and 488.

Text 32 **A reluctant translator of Scripture**

Ælfric munuc gret Æðelwærd ealdormann eadmodlice. þu bæde me, leof,
þæt ic sceolde ðe awendan of Lædene on Englisc þa boc Genesis. Ða þuhte
me hefigtime þe to tiðienne þæs and þu cwæde þa þæt ic ne þorfte na mare
awendan þære bec buton to Isaace, Abrahames suna, for þam þe sum oðer

1 **grēt** < *grētan* 'to greet'.
2 **ðē** 'for thee'. So also *þē* l. 5.
3 **þē** 'to thee'; **þæs** 'that', gen. after the verb *tiðian* 'to grant'.
4–5 The story of Isaac ends with Genesis 35.

man þe hæfde awend fram Isaace þa boc oþ ende. Nu þincð me, leof, þæt 5
þæt weorc is swiðe pleolic me oððe ænigum men to underbeginnenne . . .

þa ungelæredan preostas· gif hi hwæt litles understandað of þam Læden-
bocum· þonne þincð him sona þæt hi magon mære lareowas beon· ac hi ne
cunnon swa þeah þæt gastlice andgit þærto and hu seo ealde æ wæs
getacnung toweardra þinga oþþe hu seo niwe gecyþnis æfter Cristes 10
menniscnisse wæs gefillednys ealra þæra þinga þe seo ealde gecyðnis
getacnode towearde be Criste and be hys gecorenum . . .

Nu ys seo foresæde boc on manegum stowum swiðe nearolice gesett and
þeah swiðe deoplice on þam gastlicum andgite· and heo is swa geendebyrd
swa swa God self hig gedihte þam writere Moise and we durron na mare 15
awritan on Englisc þonne þæt Læden hæfð ne þa endebirdnisse awendan
buton þam anum þæt þæt Læden and þæt Englisc nabbað na ane wisan on
þære spræce fadunge. Æfre se þe awent oððe se þe tæcð of Lædene on
Englisc· æfre he sceal gefadian hit swa þæt Englisc hæbbe his agene wisan
elles hit bið swiðe gedwolsum to rædenne þam þe þæs Lædenes wisan ne 20
can . . .

Ic cweðe nu þæt ic ne dearr ne ic nelle nane boc æfter þissere of Lædene
on Englisc awendan and ic bidde þe, leof ealdorman, þæt þu me þæs na leng
ne bidde þi læs þe ic beo þe ungehirsum oððe leas gif ic do. God þe sig
milde a on ecnisse. Ic bidde nu on Godes naman· gif hwa þas boc awritan 25
wylle· þæt he hig gerihte wel be þære bysne for þan þe ic nah geweald þeah
þe hig hwa to woge bringe þurh lease writeras and hit byð þonne his pleoh
na min: mycel yfel deð se unwritere gif he nele hys woh gerihtan.

7–8 **þā ungelǣredan prēostas** nom. pl. anticipates *hī* nom. pl. and *him* dat. pl. See
§§158–9.

10–12 On these lines, see §105.

13 **nearolice** adv. 'narrowly'. This is often glossed 'briefly' or 'summarily'. But I sometimes
wonder whether 'cryptically' was what Ælfric had in mind.

14 **dēoplice** 'deeply/profoundly'.

14–18 On the use of Latin originals by the Anglo-Saxon translators see §419.

17 **būton þām ānum þæt** 'except in that one [thing] that'.

20 **þām þe** 'for that one who'.

24 **sig** = *sīe* pres. subj. expressing a wish.

26 **hig** = *hīe* acc. sg. fem. 'it' referring to *þās bōc*. So also in l. 27.

26–7 **ic nāh geweald þēah þe** . . . *lit.* 'I do not have control though . . .' and so 'It is not my
fault if . . .'.

28 **unwrītere** 'careless scribe'.

The standard edition of this text is that edited by S. J. Crawford; see §419.

§445 Text 33 – an extract from Ælfric's Homily on the Nativity of the
Innocents, one of his First Series of Catholic Homilies – is based on
Cambridge University Library MS Gg. 3. 28. The story is told in Matthew 2:
16–18, with its reference to 'Rachel weeping for her children and would not
be comforted, because they were not', which echoes Jeremiah 31: 15 'A voice
was heard in Ramah, lamentation and bitter weeping: Rahel weeping for her
children refused to be comforted for her children because they were not.'

The homily was justly commended by Henry Sweet 'as showing that command of the tender and pathetic in which he [Ælfric] excels'. The chosen passage demonstrates this command in a magnificent piece of idiomatic Old English. Yet it 'is produced by careful selection and welding together of sentences from Latin authors'. Dorothy Whitelock justifies her verdict beyond peradventure in *Sweet's Anglo-Saxon Reader in Prose and Verse*, revised edition (Oxford: Clarendon Press, 1967), p. 252, where she quotes from three Latin homilies on the Nativity of the Innocents the sentences on which the Old English is based. But the passage is more than the sum of the Latin sources.

Text 33 Herod's massacre of the Innocents: Ælfric's verdict

Ne forseah Crist his geongan cempan ðeah ðe he lichamlice on heora slege andwerd nære· ac he asende hi fram þisum wræcfullum life to his ecan rice. Gesælige hi wurdon geborene þæt hi moston for his intingan deað þrowian. Eadig is heora yld seoðe þa gyt ne mihte Crist andettan and moste
5 for Criste þrowian. Hi wæron þæs Hælendes gewitan ðeah ðe hi hine ða gyt ne cuðon. Næron hi geripode to slege ac hi gesæliglice þeah swulton to life. Gesælig wæs heora acennednys forðan ðe hi gemetton þæt ece lif on instæpe þæs andweardan lifes. Hi wurdon gegripene fram moderlicum breostum ac hi wurdon betæhte þærrihte engellicum bosmum. Ne mihte se
10 manfulla ehtere mid nanre ðenunge þam lytlingum swa micclum fremian swa micclum swa he him fremode mid ðære reðan ehtnysse hatunge. Hi sind gehatene martyra blostman forðan ðe hi wæron swa swa upaspringende blostman on middeweardan cyle ungeleaffulnysse swilce mid sumere ehtnysse forste forsodene. Eadige sind þa innoðas þe hi gebæron and ða
15 breost þe swylce gesihton. Witodlice ða moddru on heora cildra martyrdome þrowodon: þæt swurd ðe þæra cildra lima þurharn becom to ðæra moddra heortan· and neod is þæt hi beon efenhlyttan þæs ecan edleanes þonne hi wæron geferan ðære ðrowunge. Hi wæron gehwæde and ungewittige acwealde ac hi arisað on þam gemænelicum dome mid fullum
20 wæstme and heofenlicere snoternysse. Ealle we cumað to anre ylde on þam gemænelicum æriste þeah ðe we nu on myslicere ylde of þyssere worulde gewiton.

This passage and that by Wulfstan printed as Text 34 are further striking illustrations of my claim in §13 that what is most foreign about Old English is its vocabulary, not its grammar.

4 **sēoðe** = *sēo* nom. sg. fem. referring to *yld* + *ðe* 'which'.

10 **micclum** dat. pl. used adverbially, 'greatly'.

11 **mid ðære reðan ēhtnysse hatunge** 'with the cruel hatred of persecution' or 'with the hatred of fierce persecution'.

13 **middeweard** adj. 'middle'. Translate 'the middle of'; **swilce** conj. 'as it were'; **sumere** > *sum*. Translate 'a'.

It is a reproach to Old English scholarship that the standard edition of Part I (the First Series) of the Homilies of Ælfric remains that edited by Benjamin Thorpe (London, 1844). For Part II we have *Ælfric's Catholic Homilies: The Second Series Text* edited by Malcolm Godden, Early English Text Society S.S. 5 (Oxford: Oxford University Press, 1979).

§446 Wulfstan, Bishop of London 996–1002 and Bishop of Worcester and Archbishop of York (in plurality) 1002–23, was an influential cleric during the troubled reign of King Æthelred and thereafter (§187). Among his other activities, he drafted laws and was the author of many homilies. Text 34 contains extracts from his most famous sermon, *Sermo Lupi ad Anglos*, which (it is generally agreed) was composed in 1014. What he says about heathenism, traffic in slaves, treason, and the breakdown of family relationships, can be corroborated from other sources. But in his vehement insistence that the renewed Viking attacks were God's retribution on a Christian people who were not living out their faith, he follows a tradition going back to the British monk and historian Gildas (d. *c.* 570), who was one of Bede's sources and whom both quote. (This theme is not represented in Text 34 below.) Gildas attributed the Anglo-Saxon invasions of Britain in the fifth and sixth centuries to the same cause, comparing them to the Assyrian assaults on Judaea.

The *Sermo* survives in three versions. An analysis by Stephanie Hollis has shown that the longest version (represented here by extracts from British Library MS Cotton Nero A.i) is a careful balance of alternate accounts of sins and punishment with an increasing emphasis on the notion that only repentance can halt the relentless progression of events and an ultimate disaster. This supports the view of that great but often neglected scholar Henry Sweet that the three versions are the result of a process of repeated cutting. In my cutting, I have tried to represent these three strands of sin, punishment, and repentance. Wulfstan's style is marked by distinct preferences in vocabulary; by a liking for word pairs (often linked by alliteration and/or rhyme, as in paragraphs three and four of the text) and of intensifying words and phrases (e.g. *georne*, *swyþe*, and *oft ⁊ gelome*); by the regular use of set patterns or formulae (e.g. *gecnawe se þe cunne* ll. 16–17 and *swa hit þincan mæg* l. 20); by certain syntactical preferences; by rhetorical questions; and by repetitions and parallelisms. His sentences are balanced but vary in structure and rhythm. His style is strikingly oratorical, often ironical, forceful and passionate, simple and clear, without metaphors, similes, and poetic images. I do not agree with the critic who claimed that 'the *Sermo Lupi* makes its effect by sheer monotony of commination'.

Text 34   Archbishop of York calls for repentance

Leofan men, gecnawað þæt soð is: ðeos worold is on ofste 7 hit nealæcð þam ende 7 þy hit is on worolde aa swa leng swa wyrse· 7 swa hit sceal nyde for folces synnan ær Antecristes tocyme yfelian swyþe 7 huru hit wyrð þænne egeslic 7 grimlic wide on worolde. Understandað eac georne þæt deofol þas
5 þeode nu fela geara dwelode to swyþe 7 þæt lytle getreowþa wæran mid mannum þeah hy wel spæcan 7 unrihta to fela ricsode on lande . . .

Forþam hit is on us eallum swutol 7 gesene þæt we ær þysan oftor bræcan þonne we bettan 7 þy is þysse þeode fela onsæge. Ne dohte hit nu lange inne ne ute· ac wæs here 7 hunger, bryne 7 blodgyte, on gewelhwylcan ende oft 7
10 gelome . . .

Eac we witan georne hwær seo yrmð gewearð þæt fæder gesealde bearn wið weorþe 7 bearn his modor 7 broþor sealde oþerne fremdum to gewealde· 7 eal þæt syndan micle 7 egeslice dæda· understande se þe wille. And git hit is mare 7 eac mænigfealdre þæt dereð þysse þeode. Mænige synd
15 forsworene 7 swyþe forlogene 7 wed synd tobrocene oft 7 gelome 7 þæt is gesyne on þysse þeode þæt us Godes yrre hetelice onsit· gecnawe se þe cunne . . .

Nis eac nan wundor þeah us mislimpe forþam we witan ful georne þæt nu fela geara men na ne rohtan foroft hwæt hy worhtan wordes oððe dæde· ac
20 wearð þes þeodscipe· swa hit þincan mæg· swyþe forsyngod þurh mænig-fealde synna 7 þurh fela misdæda: þurh morðdæda 7 þurh mandæda, þurh gitsunga 7 þurh gifernessa, þurh stala 7 þurh strudunga, þurh mannsylena 7 þurh hæþene unsida, þurh swicdomas 7 þurh searacræftas, þurh lahbrycas 7 þurh æwswicas, þurh mægræsas 7 þurh manslyhtas, þurh hadbrycas 7 þurh
25 æwbrycas, þurh siblegeru 7 þurh mistlice forligru . . . And þy is nu geworden wide 7 side to ful yfelan gewunan þæt menn swyþor scamað nu for goddædan þonne for misdædan . . .

Her syndan þurh synleawa· swa hit þincan mæg· sare gelewede to manege

Another text which presents more difficulties in vocabulary than in grammar; see the first sentence in the Textual Commentary on Text 33 (§445).

  1 **þæt** Here 'what/that which'. So also in l. 38.

  2 **þȳ** adv. 'therefore'; **aa** = *ā* 'always'. The practice of doubling the vowel to indicate length appears in OE with other vowels, including *ī* (*liif* 'life'), but survived into MnE only in *ē* ('feet') and *ō* ('foot'); **swā leng swā wyrse** 'the longer the worse'.

  3 **wyrð** < *weorðan* 'to become'; **þænne** = *þonne*.

  12–13 **fremdum tō gewealde**. On this idiom see §48.

  13 **eal þæt** OE frequently used the sg. pron. *þæt* in constructions like these where MnE requires the plural. Translate 'all these'; **understande se þe wille** 'let that one understand who is willing'. Another such Wulfstan formula appears in ll. 16–17 *gecnāwe se þe cunne* 'let that one understand who knows how'.

  14 **māre . . . mænigfealdre** These are neut. sg. comp. forms of adjectives agreeing with *hit*.

  18 **nān wundor þēah** 'no wonder though'. MnE prefers 'that' or 'if'.

  20 **swā hit þincan mæg** Another formula: 'as it can seem'. So also in l. 28.

  26 **tō ful** 'too completely'; **yfelan gewunan** 'evil practices'. Though plural, these words are best taken as the subject of *is geworden*; **þæt** 'so that'; **menn** dat. sg. 'mankind/human beings' dependent on the impers. vb. *scamað* 'shames', which also appears in l. 33 governing *ūs*.

on earde. Her syndan mannslagan 7 mægslagan 7 mæsserbanan 7 mynster-
hatan· 7 her syndan mansworan 7 morþorwyrhtan· 7 her syndan myltestran 7   30
bearnmyrðran 7 fule forlegene horingas manege· 7 her syndan wiccan 7
wælcyrian· 7 her syndan ryperas 7 reaferas 7 woroldstruderas 7· hrædest is to
cweþenne· mana 7 misdæda ungerim ealra. And þæs us ne scamað na . . .

Ac la· on Godes naman utan don swa us neod is: beorgan us sylfum swa
we geornost magan þe læs we ætgædere ealle forweorðan . . . And þy us is   35
þearf micel þæt we us beþencan 7 wið God sylfne þingian georne. And utan
don swa us þearf is: gebugan to rihte 7 be suman dæle unriht forlætan 7
betan swyþe georne þæt we ær bræcan. And utan God lufian 7 Godes lagum
fylgean 7 gelæstan swyþe georne þæt þæt we behetan þa we fulluht under-
fengan· oððan þa þe æt fulluhte ure forespecan wæran. And utan word 7   40
weorc rihtlice fadian 7 ure ingeþanc clænsian georne 7 að 7 wed wærlice
healdan 7 sume getrywða habban us betweonan butan uncræftan. And utan
gelome understandan þone miclan dom þe we ealle to sculon 7 beorgan us
georne wið þone weallendan bryne hellewites 7 geearnian us þa mærða 7 þa
myrhða þe God hæfð gegearwod þam þe his willan on worolde gewyrcað.   45
God ure helpe· amen.

37 **be suman dæle** 'in some part/to some extent'. This phrase seems to exemplify the
Anglo-Saxon penchant for understatement rather than to suggest that Wulfstan approved of a
certain amount of sin but not too much. Compare the *tō* phrases in ll. 5, 6, 26, and 28, and *sume
getrȳwða* in l. 42.

39 **þæt þæt** 'that which'. Contrast single *þæt* in ll. 1 and 38; *þā* conj. 'when'.

39–40 **wē . . . oððan þā þe** 'we . . . or those who'. On the separated subjects see §162.

45 **þām þe** 'for those who'.

The standard edition of this text is *The Homilies of Wulfstan* edited by Dorothy Bethurum
(Oxford: Clarendon Press, 1957).

C BLOOMS FROM THE POETRY

Introduction

§447 The selections from the poetry given here combine with the
numbered Texts and the longer translated passages already printed, to illustrate the wide variety of subjects treated by the Old English poets, to make
audible their distinctive voice as characterized by Kevin Crossley-Holland
(see my Foreword), and to reveal what in §166 I called the magic and mystery
of Old English poetry. All the major manuscripts of Old English poetry as
published in the volumes of the Anglo-Saxon Poetic Records (§§172–5) are
represented:

   I *The Junius Manuscript* in §§485 ·and 487;
  II *The Vercelli Book* in §§490 and 493;
 III *The Exeter Book* in §§473–9, 482–4, 486, and 491–2;
 IV *The Beowulf Manuscript* in §§463–8 and 489;
  V *The Paris Psalter and the Metres of Boethius* in §§481 and 488;
 VI *The Anglo-Saxon Minor Poems* in §§469–72 and 480.

And the verse genres listed in §176 are all exemplified:

1 poems treating heroic subjects in §§463–8;
2 historical poems in §§469 and 470;
3 biblical paraphrases and reworking of biblical subjects in §§485, 487–8, and 489;
4 lives of the saints in §490;
5 other religious poems in §§480–1 and 493;
6 short lyrics and elegies in §§473–7 and 479;
7 riddles and gnomic verses in §§478, 482–4, 486, and 491–2;
8 miscellaneous in §§471–2.

For a list of these texts see the Contents.

§448 Originally the alliterative verse used by all Germanic tribes for legendary, historical, and encomiastic, poetry was composed and transmitted orally. We have already seen in §14 how the swordbearer's story of the death of King Edmund in 869 was passed on orally to the monk Abbo by Dunstan Archbishop of Canterbury in 985. Dunstan heard it in the presence of King Æthelstan, who died in 939. Ælfric tells us that Dunstan related the story *swa swa Eadmundes swurdbora hit rehte* ('related') *Æþelstane cyninge þa þa Dunstan geong man wæs and se swurdbora wæs forealdod* ('aged') *mann*. The words *swa swa* 'as' do not make it clear whether the story reached Abbo in exactly the same words which the swordbearer had used or in paraphrased form. Similarly, we cannot be sure whether the early orally composed poems were memorized for later performance or whether they had no fixed text and the performer expanded or contracted the poem he was reciting in accordance with the enthusiasm of the audience on the night and perhaps with the amount of wine or mead available to him. Some have argued that *Beowulf* itself is merely one version of a poem composed and transmitted orally, others that it was composed pen in hand. We shall never know for certain the exact origin of the poems which treat heroic subjects (§176.1). But we can be sure that the psalms of the Paris Psalter (Text 47 §488) were composed by a poet working from the Latin psalms but employing the techniques of the alliterative verse inherited from pre-Christian poets. Similarly, the Metres of Boethius (Text 43 §481) were based on the earlier prose translation. Both these versions have been ascribed to King Alfred. The composers of such poetry obviously needed a good knowledge of Latin – something not restricted to men; see §389. One consequence of this was overlooked until Fred C. Robinson pointed out that the fact that women wrote works in Latin casts doubt on the 'tacit assumption' that all surviving Old English poetry was composed by men (see *American Notes and Queries* 3 (1990), 59–64).

§449 The baptism of the Germanic alliterative verse through its use for Christian subjects and themes – the Anglo-Saxon equivalent of Christian pop or of 'Rave in the Nave' – is ascribed by Bede to Cædmon, a laybrother in the monastery of Whitby during the abbacy of Hild (657–680); for details of the story, see Text 20 (§427). Bede's is the only account to come down to us of something which may have happened independently in other monasteries at about the same time. But, whether or not Cædmon was the sole or indeed the first instigator of this practice, it spread rapidly and widely, as the list of poems in §176 testifies.

§450 In §365 I pointed out that Queen Æthelflæd's success as a war-leader makes it easy to understand why Judith was a natural subject for OE poetry, with its warrior vocabulary, on which see Text 12 (§489). No doubt the success of poets depended in part on their ability. But the choice of subject was also important. Thus the story of the book of Exodus was another natural subject. In the poem *Exodus*, Moses and the Children of Israel were easily transformed into a Germanic leader and his band of warriors:

155 siððan hīe gesāwon   of sūðwegum
     fyrd Faraonis   forð ongangan

    . . .   . . .

     gūðweard gumena   grimhelm gespēon,
175 cyning cinberge   – cumbol līxton –
     wīges on wēnum   wælhlencan sceōc·
     hēt his hereciste   healdan georne
     fæst fyrdgetrum

After they saw the army of Pharaoh marching forth from the regions of the south, . . . the battle-guardian of men, the king, fastened the helmet [and its] chin-guard – the banners gleamed – in expectation of battle shook his mailcoat, commanded his war-band resolutely to maintain their battle formation.

(Another extract from *Exodus* will be found in Text 46 (§487).) Similarly, the situation of Satan, the rebellious and exiled thane who (as the poet of *GenesisB* with intentional irony shows) expected loyalty from his own followers, would have found a readier response in an Anglo-Saxon warrior than the story of King Edmund of East Anglia, who threw away his weapons when confronted by his Danish foes because he *wolde geæfenlæcan Cristes gebysnungum* 'wished to imitate Christ's example'. Christian doctrine presented even more difficulty than pacifist kings (§385) or maidens ready to embrace martyrdom. The Anglo-Saxon Christian poet seems to have been in a position akin to that of the Jugoslav poets of the 1930s and the 1940s: Marxist heroes could, perhaps without too much trouble, be made to acquire the characteristics of earlier folk-heroes but Marxist dialectic – like Christian theology in Anglo-Saxon times – proved a tougher nut. Thus I personally find myself less moved by poems such as *Andreas* and *Elene* (Text 48 §490) – both from the Vercelli Book – and *Christ*, *Guthlac*, and *Juliana* – all in the Exeter Book, none represented in this book – than by the poems whose subject-matter and ethos are more easily adapted to the heroic vocabulary. However, it is only fair to say that there are those who disagree with my opinions on this point.

§451 Now, to satisfy promises made in earlier sections, I must supplement §171 by explaining the salient characteristics of this verse. A fuller description will be found in Appendix C of *A Guide to Old English* (5th edn, 1992, or later).

§452 The metrical unit is the half-line and the acceptable metrical patterns were chosen from those common in ordinary speech. There were six basic patterns and each half-line is an example or a variation of one of these. The table below shows the identification letter and the metrical pattern ($´$ = stress, $`$ = subsidiary stress, × = no stress), and then gives a characterization and a modern English example for which I am indebted to J. R. R. Tolkien.

A	$´ × ´ ×$	falling–falling	'knights in armour'
B	$× ´ × ´$	rising–rising	'the roaring sea'
C	$× ´ ´ ×$	clashing	'on high mountains'
D1	$´ ´ ` ×$	falling by stages	'bright archangels'
D2	$´ ´ × `$	broken fall	'bold brazenfaced'
E	$´ ` × ´$	fall and rise	'highcrested helms'

Some patterns found in prose were not acceptable in poetry, e.g. × × ´´ 'and a good king' and ´ × ×´ 'God is his lord'. The minimum number of syllables for each half-line is four but extra unstressed syllables can occur in some positions, including that before the first stress of types A and D. Examples will be found in this series of half-lines from Old English poetry with the correct initial letter:

A	ān æfter ānum	(*Beowulf* 2461)
B	wæs þæt beorhte bold	(*Beowulf* 997)
C	of carcerne	(*Andreas* 57)
D1	deorc dēaþscua	(*Beowulf* 160)
D2	dēop dēada wæg	(*Maxims* i. 78)
E	egsode eorl	(*Beowulf* 6)

A few half-lines will suffice to show the close relationship between verse rhythms and those of prose. *The Battle of Maldon* 27b *brimlīþendra* 'of seagoers' is the genitive plural of a present participle. The following are some of the combinations which often form a type A half-line:

adjective + noun (*lāðe gystas* 'hateful strangers')
subject + verb (*beornas fēollon* 'warriors fell')
object + verb (*gāras bǣron* 'spears [they] carried')
complement + verb (*gearwe stōdon* 'ready stood')
infinitive + verb (*wealdan mōston* 'to wield were able')
noun + adjective (*wīges georne* 'for war eager')

§453 The alliterative unit is the line, composed of two half-lines (the *a*-line and the *b*-line) linked by alliteration of stressed syllables but separated by a pause, or caesura, here marked by a space. These stressed syllables are usually long but can in certain circumstances be short. The examples from *The Battle of Maldon* already given in §171 and those from the same poem which follow here should suffice to demonstrate the main alliterative patterns. I give the line number, the pattern (*a* and *A* mean alliterating syllables, *b* and *c* non-alliterating), and then the Old English text with the alliterating letter(s) underlined:

97	a a a b	wīcinga werod	west ofer Pantan
148	a b a c	ðæs dægweorces	þe him Drihten forgeaf
65	b a a c	þær cōm flowende	flōd æfter ebban
98	a A a A	ofer scīr wæter	scyldas wēgon
159	A a a A	ēode þā gesyrwed	secg tō þām eorle

The head-stave, the first stressed syllable in the second half-line, determines the alliteration. Any vowel can alliterate with any vowel or diphthong, e.g.

Maldon 28   ǣrænde tō þām eorle   þǣr hē on ōfre stōd.

Consonants alliterate only with themselves. The same rule holds for *sc* (as in *Maldon* 98 above), *sp*, and *st*, which never alliterate with one another or with *s*. Many archaic words were preserved for their alliterative value; see §§205, 211, and 274. This gave the poetry a rich vocabulary distinct from that of the prose, a vocabulary of which many elements survived until the glorious flowering of the alliterative measure in the late fourteenth century in poems like *Sir Gawain and the Green Knight* and *Piers Plowman*.

§454 This account deliberately omits some detail. But it should suffice to help you to read Old English poetry with reasonable accuracy if you stress the alliterating syllables and remember that nouns and adjectives are more likely to carry stress and alliteration than verbs and other parts of speech; see §460. I suggest that you test yourself by going back to §171 and working out the alliterative patterns and the metrical types exemplified in the four lines printed there before looking at the answers in the footnote.[1] You will notice that the two half-lines making up an alliterative line can, but need not, be the same. Any combination of the six types is possible.

§455 All of these types were normal patterns of four or more syllables into which both Old English and Modern English words fall. But, whereas modern English poetry rearranges words to fit a special rhythm, Old

[1] Line 96: a a a b; types D1 and A;
line 97: a a a b; types A and A;
line 98: a A a A; types C and A;
line 99: a a a b; types A and A.
You will have noted that six of the eight half-lines have more than four syllables; that in line 96*b* an unstressed syllable precedes the first stress; and that in two there is an extra subsidiary stress (line 97*a wícinga* and line 99*a lídmèn*). Without such variations the poetry would have been very monotonous.

English poetry simplifies and opposes the basic rhythmic patterns of the language. Its effects are heightened by its specialized and often archaic vocabulary, well provided with words to express the activities and shibboleths of the warrior-caste which had been its main preoccupation before Cædmon.

§456 The frequent use of compounds assists this simplifying effect by giving compression and by demanding slow and dignified delivery. Some make statements, e.g. *beadu-rof* 'battle-bold', *beadu-scearp* 'battle-sharp', *lagu-cræftig* 'sea-skilled', and *nicor-hus* 'water-monster house/abode'. Others are condensed comparisons, e.g. *feower mearas . . . æppelfealuwe* 'four steeds . . . apple-fallow/yellow-brown' and *forstes bend . . . wælrapas* 'bonds of frost . . . water-ropes/fetters'. Others are kennings, compressed metaphors in which (a) is compared to (b) without (a) or the point of the comparison being made explicit; the metaphor 'The camel is the ship of the desert' would become the kenning 'The desert ship lurched on'. Thus in *The Rune Poem* a ship out-of-control and driven by the storm is described thus: *and se brimhengest | bridles ne gymeð* 'and the seahorse heeds not the bridle'. Again, the *Exodus* poet tells us that after the death of all the first-born in the land of Egypt (Exodus 12: 29)

> wōp wæs wīde,   worulddrēama lȳt·
> wǣron hleahtorsmiðum   handa belocene

[there] was weeping far and wide, little of worldly joys. The hands of the laughter-smiths were locked.

In other words, the minstrels did not recite poems and so no longer fashioned patterns with their hands on their harps in the way a blacksmith fashions a delicate piece of metalwork. An audience would require time to grasp the implications of such sophisticated 'riddling' comparisons. This is one of its features which led J. R. R. Tolkien to complain that many modern reciters rattle through Old English poems much more quickly than the *scop* 'minstrel' of Anglo-Saxon times recited them.

§457 Another characteristic of Old English poetry is the use of formulae – set metrical combinations variable according to the needs of alliteration. Many of these were inherited from the days of oral composition. But Christian poets borrowed and adapted them for use in their literary verse. Thus the phrase 'on the sea' can be expressed by *on hronrade* 'on the whale-road' or *on seglrade* 'on the sail-road'. A lord may be a *freawine* 'lord-friend' or a *goldwine* 'gold-friend'. The formulaic half-line *goldwine gumena* is used of King Hrothgar in *Beowulf*, of the Assyrian leader Holofernes in *Judith*, and of the Emperor Constantine in *Elene*, and the compound *winedryhten* (supplemented by a genitive or by another word) 'friend-lord' refers to Beowulf himself, to Byrhtnoth (the Anglo-Saxon leader at Maldon), to St Guthlac, and (in *Andreas*) to God. There are many other such formulae, some of which cluster around a particular theme. Thus the exile, the man cut off from the warrior-band of which he was once a member, became a symbol of misery and the poets worked the changes on phrases such as *wineleas guma* 'friendless man' *dreamum bedæled* 'cut off from joys'. The exiled lover of *The Wife's Lament* is a *wineleas wræcca* 'a friendless exile'. So too are Cain and the man in *Resignation* of whom it is said *is him wrað meotud* 'the Creator is angry with him'. The wanderer is a *wineleas guma*. The word *bedæled/bidæled*, like *wineleas*, is used in heroic and Christian poems. The wanderer is also *eðle bidæled* 'bereft of his native land'. The monster Grendel in *Beowulf* is *dreamum bedæled* 'cut off from joys', a situation he shares with the fallen angels, *dreamum bedælde* in Hell. *Duguðum bedæled* 'deprived of benefits' is Cain, along with *deofla cempan* 'the devils' champions'. At the Day of Judgement the sinners on God's left hand will find themselves *eallum bidæled* ‖ *dugeþum ond dreamum*, in contrast to the blessed souls in Heaven *sorgum bedælde* 'freed from sorrows' and to Christ Himself after His Baptism *fyrena bedæled* 'free from sins'. Another such theme is that of the beasts of battle – the wolf, the raven, and the eagle – who appear when a battle is imminent. Originally, they were doubtless a reality on the battlefield as they devoured the bodies of the slain. But later their appearance is conventional and sometimes, when used by a clumsy or uninspired poet, perfunctory. The *Beowulf* poet uses them in *Beowulf* 3021b–7, quoted in §406. It is a striking confirmation of his genius that his is the most brilliant handling of this theme both in the detailed treatment and in the significant place it has in the overall structure of the poem: it is spoken by Wiglaf, Beowulf's kinsman and heir-apparent at the end of a speech in which he laments the death of Beowulf and foretells a period of *fæhþo*, *feondscipe*, and *wælnið* 'battle, enmity, and deadly hate', for his people the Geats at the hands of their Swedish enemies.

§458 Unfortunately, no *Handboc Sangcræftes* 'Handbook of the Art of Poetry' has survived. But some hints about poetic techniques can be gleaned from the poetry itself. Thus we read in *The Battle of Maldon* that, in the course of the battle,

> wund wearð Wulfmær,   wælræste gecēas
> Byrhtnōðes mæg·   hē mid billum wearð,
> 115 his swustersunu,   swīðe forhēawen

wounded was Wulfmær. Byrhtnoth's kinsman chose rest among the slain. He, Byrhtnoth's sister's son, was cruelly cut down with swords.

No translation can do justice to this passage, with its technique of repetition with variation and advance. The half-line *wund wearð Wulfmær* encapsulates what follows. The remaining *a*-lines bring Wulfmær into closer relationship with Byrhtnoth – 'kinsman . . . sister's son' (§345) – and the *b*-lines expand on *wund* – 'fatally wounded . . . by swords . . . cruelly cut down'. It was passages like this which made J. R. R. Tolkien picture poets as artists filling in (half-)lines with blocks of different colours – another image inspired by the phrase *hleahtorsmiþum handa* (§456).

§459 Other devices used by the poets and seen in these passages from *Beowulf* include parallelism:

> 126 Ðā wæs on ūhtan   mid ǣrdæge
>   Grendles gūðcræft   gumum undyrne·
>   þā wæs æfter wiste   wōp up āhafen,
>   micel morgenswēg

Then/When at dawn with break of the day, Grendel's battle power was made known to men. Then /, then after feasting weeping was raised up, a mighty morning cry;

antithesis:

> 183   Wā bið þǣm ðe sceal
>   . . .   . . .
> 186 . . .   Wel bið þǣm þe mot
>   . . .   . . .

Woe/ill will be to that one who must . . . Well will be to that one who is allowed . . .;

and the 'envelope' pattern:

>   Dryhtsele dynede·   Denum eallum wearð,
>   ceasterbūendum,   cēnra gehwylcum,
>   eorlum ealuscerwen·   yrre wǣron bēgen
> 770 rēþe renweardas·   reced hlynsode

The splendid hall resounded. To all the Danes, to the town-dwellers, to each of the bold ones, to the warriors, there was terror. Angry were both the fierce hall-guardians. The hall resounded.

This 'envelope', which is sealed by first and last half-lines with the same meaning, appears in the middle of the poet's description of the fight in the hall Heorot between Beowulf and Grendel. It is a microcosm of the whole fight – the noise, the terror of all the bystanders inside and outside the hall, and the ferocity of the combatants. Both are hall-guardians, Beowulf because Hrothgar had appointed him to guard it, Grendel ironically because he had taken it over by his reign of terror.

§460 The examples and passages quoted in the last four sections will confirm my statement in §454 that nouns and adjectives are more likely to carry stress and alliteration than other parts of speech. There is no rule against verbs or pronouns doing so but there are fewer alliterating synonyms for them than there are for nouns and adjectives, and it is through such synonyms that the poets conveyed much of their meaning and achieved many of their effects. However, alliterating and/or stressed verbs can be very effective, as in the paratactic description (§120) in *Beowulf* of Grendel devouring a hapless warrior in the hall Heorot, where they give a feeling of gruesome immediacy and reality as Grendel tears, bites, drinks, and gulps:

> Ne þæt se āglǣca   yldan þōhte
> 740 ac hē gefēng hraðe   forman sīðe
> slǣpendne rinc·   slāt unwearnum·
> bāt bānlocan·   blōd ēdrum dranc·
> synsnǣdum swealh·   sōna hæfde
> unlyfigendes   eal gefeormod,
> 745 fēt ond folma.

Here, and in the next section, I translate without punctuation:

> nor did the monster intend to delay that but he seized quickly on his first sally a sleeping warrior tore greedily bit the bone-locker/body drank blood from veins in huge morsels had soon swallowed all of the dead man devoured feet and hands.

This passage follows immediately after Text 35 (§465), which is an example of parallelism on a larger scale.

§461 As we have seen, the metrical unit was the half-line and the alliterative unit the line. But the poetic unit was the verse paragraph, often obscured or destroyed today, as I have argued in §10, by the use of modern punctuation. The poet had to have a good story to tell. But he had to tell it well, constructing verse paragraphs by a contrasted and varied balance of metrical types, by a rich use of poetic vocabulary and formulae, by appropriate references to Germanic legend, by ironical allusion and understatement (§§339 and 424), by the techniques and devices I have just described, and by the *apo koinou* construction discussed in §§165–7 and seen in the use of *secga geseldan* as the object of *greteð* and *geondsceawað* and the subject of *swimmað* in the passage from *The Wanderer* printed below. The poet describes the wanderer alternating fitfully between sleep, in which he dreams that he is back in the warm hall with the lord he has lost, and wake, when he sees the seabirds on the water amidst the driving snow and sleet. He goes on:

> þonne bēoð þȳ hefigran   heortan benne
> 50 sāre æfter swǣsne   = sorg bið genīwad =
> þonne māga gemynd   mōd geondhweorfeð·
> grēteð glīwstafum   georne geondscēawað =
> secga geseldan =   = swimmað oft on weg =
> flēotendra ferð   nō þǣr fela bringeð
> 55 cūðra cwidegiedda   -- cearo bið genīwad --
> þām þe sendan sceal   swīþe geneahhe
> ofer waþema gebind   wērigne sefan

(The broken dashes in l. 55 are my attempt to show that ll. 56–7 go with both ll. 54–5a and l. 55b.)

> then the wounds of the heart are heavier grieving after the beloved [lord] sorrow is renewed whenever the memory of kinsmen passes through the mind he greets joyfully eagerly scrutinizes the companions of men often [= always] swim away the band of floating ones does not bring there much of [another ironic understatement = brings no] recognizable spoken utterances care is renewed for him who very often must send over the binding of waves a weary spirit.

So the poet conveys the wanderer's changes of focus: *secga geseldan* his former companions – one can almost hear him call in joyful recognition 'Hengest!' 'Horsa!' – or seabirds? Is he asleep? or awake? In the reverie? or out? Which are they? Birds or men or men or birds or both? I hope that as you read on you will experience more such magic and mystery.

§462   Perhaps it may help you to bear in mind two more things. First, in her study on *The Larger Rhetorical Patterns in Anglo-Saxon Poetry* (New York: Columbia University Studies in English and Comparative Literature 122, 1935), Adeline C. Bartlett compared the longer Anglo-Saxon poems to tapestries presenting a series of elaborate and leisurely narratives (often involving speeches) which are frequently halted for decorative insets not intrinsically part of the narrative. These could contain gnomic or moralistic comment, elegiac laments for the transience of worldly things and of life itself, or descriptions of stock subjects or type scenes such as sea-voyages (see Text 13 §464), battles, or storms. Second, the *Beowulf* poet described the *scop* in the Danish hall reciting a new poem to celebrate Beowulf's victory over Grendel:

> Hwīlum cyninges þegn,
> guma gilphlæden,   gidda gemyndig,
> sē ðe ealfela   ealdgesegena
> 870 worn gemunde,   word ōþer fand
> sōðe gebunden·   secg eft ongan
> sīð Bēowulfes   snyttrum styrian
> ond on spēd wrecan   spel gerāde,
> wordum wrixlan

At times a thane of the king, a poetry-laden man, a rememberer of lays, who recollected countless old traditions, found new words correctly linked together; the man in turn began to relate skilfully Beowulf's exploit and successfully to recite a well-told tale, varying his words.

A lot more can be – indeed, has been – written about Old English poetry. The time has come for *leoðcræftige men* 'those skilled in verse' to speak for themselves.

§463   *Text 8*   **Scyld's funeral ship**

This text (*Beowulf* 32–42) is the first of two passages from *Beowulf* quoted in connection with the Sutton Hoo ship-burial; see §§198 and 406. For the second see §468.

§464   *Text 13*   **Beowulf's voyage**

This description of Beowulf's voyage from Geatland to Denmark, printed in §277 and in facsimile as figure 33, is a splendid example of a successful verse paragraph. As I see it, it is noteworthy for three things. First, its use of many of the devices and techniques described in §§455–62. Why not try your hand at identifying some? Second, it presents accurately the sequence of preparation, departure, sailing, arrival; in Mr Jingle's style, ship in harbour – men load it – tide running – shove boat out – flies before wind – routine of voyage – men see land – then shining cliffs (like Dover) – then individual headlands – journey at end – men disembark – moor ship – thank God. Third, these happenings are reflected in the metre: ll. 210–11a ship rocks at anchor; ll. 211b–14, where the half-lines all have four syllables, suggesting regularity of movement; ll. 215–16 with heavier half-lines giving the effect of weight and *ūt* breaking l. 215b with a grunt of effort; and ll. 217–18, where the ship flies before the wind. If you continue this analysis for yourself, you will find that a majority of the half-lines are type A but that the number of syllables and the make-up of the lines are more important. You may agree that l. 216b is heavier than l. 218a. Why? Metrically they are almost identical in weight – types D1 and D2 respectively. But in the former the voiced stops *d b d* cause breaks whereas in the latter the continuants *f f m h l s* allow an unbroken flow. I am sure that you will find even more in these lines, especially if you read them aloud.

§465 *Beowulf* 702b–38 (Text 35) is a much analysed passage. Klaeber, in his edition, wrote: 'Some enthusiasts have found the threefold bell-like announcement of Grendel's approach a highly dramatic device.' Unlike him, I am to be numbered among them. But I see the triple *com* as having structural significance as well, with each one introducing a new section (ll. 702b–9, ll. 710–19, and ll. 720–38), each of which contains the same four elements in the same order: Grendel, the hall, a comment by the poet, and a reference to the fate in store for Grendel. This analysis helps us to see the mind of the poet in the process of creation, telling a vigorous story, using the technique of repetition with variation and advance (§458), and, as Tolkien saw it, composing his poem with repeated blocks of different colours (§458). The poet uses the verb *scriþan* four times – of hellish monsters (l. 163), of shadows (l. 650), of Grendel, who is both a hellish monster and a *sceadugenga* 'shadow-goer' (l. 703a), and of the dragon (l. 2569). The word seems to imply smooth and graceful movement (it is used elsewhere of the sun, clouds, and stars, of a ship skimming over the sea, and of darting salmon in a pool) and an element of mystery (other poets use it of the coming of May, of the beginning and ending of the day, and of the gradual passing of human life). In *Beowulf*, there is also a suggestion of menace and danger which is echoed in other poems, where the word refers to the spread through the body of a disease which could be cancer and to flames raging unchecked. Had it survived, poets would have used it as a rhyme for 'writhe' and sports writers would have turned it into a cliché applicable to footballers, cricketers and baseballers, tennis-players, and boxers. The visual imagery has evoked comparisons with the techniques of film-makers; see the note on l. 715 below. The poet tells us that Grendel will be defeated but in so doing creates a tension between our knowledge of his impending defeat and his hopes of victory; see the note on l. 730b. Space forbids further comment. But those who persevere will find that here too there is 'God's plenty'.

Text 35 Grendel's approach to Heorot

Cōm on wanre niht

scrīðan sceadugenga.   Scēotend swǣfon

þā þæt hornreced   healdan scoldon

705 ealle būton ānum.   þæt wæs yldum cūþ

þæt hīe ne mōste·   þā Metod nolde·

se scynscaþa   under sceadu bregdan

ac hē wæccende   wrāþum on andan

bād bolgenmōd   beadwa geþinges.

710   Đā cōm of mōre   under misthleoþum

Grendel gongan·   Godes yrre bær·

mynte se mānscaða   manna cynnes

sumne besyrwan   in sele þām hēan.

Wōd under wolcnum   tō þæs þe hē wīnreced,

715 goldsele gumena,   gearwost wisse

fǣttum fāhne.   Ne wæs þæt forma sīð

þæt hē Hrōþgāres   hām gesōhte·

nǣfre hē on aldordagum   ǣr ne siþðan

702–3 **Cōm . . . scrīðan** The only translation I can suggest is 'Came . . . shrithing'!
704 **þā** nom. pl. 'they/who'.
706 **hīe** acc. pl.
709 **bād** < *bīdan* governs the gen. obj. *geþinges.*

715 **gearwost** adv. 'most/very clearly'; **wisse** < *witan* 'to know', here meaning 'discern/see'. In this second *cōm* passage, the poet (as it were) brings Grendel and the hall Heorot – seen in separate shots in ll. 702b–9 – into the same picture but at either extremity of the screen. In ll. 720–38, the two come together as Grendel's violence explodes into action.

heardran hǣle,   healðegnas fand!
720   Cōm þā tō recede   rinc sīðian
drēamum bedǣled.   Duru sōna onarn
fȳrbendum fǣst   syþðan hē hire folmum æthrān·
onbrǣd þā bealohȳdig·   ðā hē gebolgen wæs·
recedes mūþan.   Raþe æfter þon
725 on fāgne flōr   fēond treddode·
ēode yrremōd·   him of ēagum stōd
ligge gelīcost   lēoht unfǣger.
Geseah hē in recede   rinca manige
swefan sibbegedriht   samod ætgædere,
730 magorinca hēap.   þā his mōd āhlōg·
mynte þæt hē gedǣlde   ǣr þon dæg cwōme
atol āglǣca   ānra gehwylces
līf wið līce   þā him ālumpen wæs
wistfylle wēn.   Ne wæs þæt wyrd þā gēn
735 þæt hē mā mōste   manna cynnes
ðicgean ofer þā niht.   þrȳðswȳð behēold
mæg Higelāces   hū se mānscaða
under fǣrgripum   gefaran wolde.

719 **hǣle** acc. sg. < *hǣlo* 'fortune'. Some editors print *hǣle* as acc. sg. or acc. pl. of *hǣle* 'warrior'. If taken as acc. sg., the word would refer to Beowulf himself, who is described as waiting for Grendel in the first *cōm* passage (*hē* l. 708) and in the third (*mæg Higelāces* l. 737).

726b–7 A dramatic picture of the dark hall illuminated by the horrible light shining from Grendel's eyes.

730b But not for long, as the poet tells us (ll. 734b–8): Beowulf was waiting and ready.

731 **ǣr þon** conj. 'before' with pret. subj. *cwōme*.

The standard edition is *Beowulf and the Fight at Finnsburg*, Third Edition with First and Second Supplements, edited by Fr. Klaeber (Boston: D. C. Heath, 1950). *Beowulf: A Student's Edition* edited by Bruce Mitchell and Fred C. Robinson, to be published by Blackwell, is in preparation.

§466   *Text 10*   **Warriors at rest**

Beowulf 1237b–50 demonstrates the need for readiness and loyalty on the part of heroic warriors. It is printed in §202.

§467   *Text 11*   **The lament of the last survivor**

On *Beowulf* 2247–66, which appears in §223, see §§343 and 407. Part of the text appears in facsimile in figure 34.

§468   *Text 9*   **Beowulf's funeral**

The second passage from *Beowulf* quoted in connection with the Sutton

Hoo ship-burial (§463) comprises the extracts from *Beowulf* 3137–82 printed in §199. See also §§406 and 407.

§469 *The Battle of Brunanburh*, the earliest and best of the poems in the Anglo-Saxon Chronicle, is – like the others – commemorative. It celebrates the victory of King Æthelstan of Wessex and his brother Edmund at Brunanburh in 937. These two – sons of Edward the Elder and grandsons of King Alfred – led a force of West Saxons and Mercians against an invading army of Norsemen (*Norðmenn*, l. 53), Britons, and Scots, who were attempting to win back control of Northumberland from King Æthelstan. The enemy leaders were Anlaf (Olaf) the Norse king of Dublin, Constantine king of the Picts and Scots, and Owen king of the Strathclyde Britons. The exact site of the battle has not been determined. Somewhere near the sea or a large river in the north of England (perhaps on the west coast between Chester and Dumfries) is all that can usefully be said here.

Metrically, the poem is conservative, representing, as Campbell put it in his edition (see below), 'an artificial preservation, or rather, perhaps, resurrection of the old style' which is 'equally distant from the doggerel of the popular poems of the *Chronicle*, and the vigorous, but often careless, verse of *The Battle of Maldon*'. The same conservatism is apparent in the vocabulary and imagery.

The heroic spirit shines through this poem as it does through *The Battle of Maldon*. The two royal leaders win everlasting glory as they exult in the hard handplay against their foes, while the doomed warriors fall in battle, leaving their bodies to be eaten by the wolf, the raven, and the eagle. Perhaps conventional here, this was originally a grim reality; a Celtic poet speaks of 'the eagle greedy for the flesh of one I love . . . on his white breast a black raven'. Although the brothers protect their land, treasures, and homes, it would be mistaken to detect a sense of patriotism here, for England was not yet united.

But, while *Maldon* tells of defeat, *Brunanburh* celebrates a victory in panegyric terms. While in *Maldon* we see the decisive incidents in detail, *Brunanburh* tells us little of the course of the battle. The tone of *Maldon* is one of grim defiance; that of *Brunanburh* is one of scorn, exultation, and grim triumph. This emerges, not only in the typical understatements that the foe had no reason to exult, to boast, or to laugh, or in the gloating accounts of the death or flight of kings, but also in the claim that it was the greatest of all English victories – a sentence which smacks of the extravagant claims of modern advertising and confirms the impression that the poem is the work of an Anglo-Saxon publicity man, whose aim was to glorify the royal family of Wessex. But in so doing, he made a poem.

The text survives in four manuscripts of the Anglo-Saxon Chronicle – A, B, C, and D; see §177.1. I follow the critical text printed by Campbell (see below), with some normalization of the spelling and with my own punctuation.

Text 36   **The Battle of Brunanburh**

Hēr Æþelstān cyning,   eorla drihten,
beorna bēahgifa,   and his brōþor ēac,
Ēadmund æþeling,   ealdorlangne tīr
geslōgon æt sæcce   sweorda ecgum
5 ymbe Brunanburh: bordweall clufon·
hēowon heaðolinde   hamora lāfum
eaforan Ēadweardes   swā him geæþele wæs
fram cnēomāgum   þæt hī æt campe oft
wið lāþra gehwæne   land ealgodon,
10 hord and hāmas.   Hettend crungon,
Scotta lēode   and scipflotan,
fǣge fēollon·   feld dunnade
secga swāte   siðþan sunne ūpp
on morgentīd,   mǣre tungol,
15 glād ofer grundas,   Godes candel beorht,
ēces Drihtnes,   oð sīo æþele gesceaft
sāh tō setle.   þǣr læg secg monig
gārum āgēted,   guma Norþerna
ofer scyld scoten,   swylce Scyttisc ēac
20 wērig wīges sǣd.   Wesseaxe forð
andlangne dæg   ēoredcystum
on lāst legdon   lāþum þēodum·
hēowon hereflȳman   hindan þearle
mēcum mylenscearpum.   Myrce ne wyrndon
25 heardes handplegan   hæleþa nānum
þāra þe mid Anlāfe   ofer ēargebland
on lides bōsme   land gesōhton
fǣge tō gefeohte.   Fīfe lāgon
on þām campstede   cyningas geonge
30 sweordum āswefede·   swylce seofone ēac
eorlas Anlāfes·   unrīm herges
flotena and Scotta.   þǣr geflȳmed wearð
Norðmanna brego   nēade gebǣded
tō lides stefne   lȳtle weorode·

---

1 **Hēr** 'Here/In this year'. A common opening to an entry in the Chronicle; see §180. Some editors omit it.

5b–7 The subject of *clufon* and *hēowon* is *eaforan Ēadweardes*, to whom *him* also refers.

6 **hamora lāfum** a kenning (§456) for 'swords'.

12 **dunnade** < *dunnian* 'to become dark'. The variant readings of the manuscripts have been much discussed.

22 Translate 'pursued the hated peoples'.

28a Translate 'doomed in battle'.

30 **swylce ... ēac** *lit.* 'likewise ... also'. So also in l. 37.

35 crēad cnear on flot·   cyning ūt gewāt
  on fealone flōd   feorh generede.
  Swylce þǣr ēac se frōda   mid flēame cōm
  on his cȳþþe norð,   Constantīnus,
  hār hilderinc·   hrēman ne þorfte
40 mēca gemānan·   hē wæs his māga sceard,
  frēonda befylled   on folcstede,
  beslægen æt sæcce,   and his sunu forlēt
  on wælstōwe   wundum forgrunden,
  geongne æt gūðe.   Gylpan ne þorfte
45 beorn blandenfeax   billgeslihtes,
  eald inwitta,   ne Anlāf þȳ mā
  mid heora herelāfum·   hlihhan ne þorfton
  þæt hī beaduweorca   beteran wurdon
  on campstede   cumbolgehnāstes,
50 gārmittinge,   gumena gemōtes,
  wǣpengewrīxles,   þæs hī on wælfelda
  wið Ēadweardes   eaforan plegodon.
  Gewiton him þā Norðmenn   nægledcnearrum,
  drēorig daroða lāf,   on Dingesmere
55 ofer dēop wæter   Dyflīn sēcan
  and eft Īraland,   ǣwiscmōde.
  Swylce þā gebrōþor   bēgen ætsomne,
  cyning and æþeling,   cȳþþe sōhton,
  Wesseaxna land,   wīges hrēmge.
60 Lēton him behindan   hrā bryttigan
  salowigpādan,   þone sweartan hræfn,
  hyrnednebban,   and þone hasopādan
  earn æftan hwīt,   ǣses brūcan,
  grǣdigne gūðhafoc,   and þæt grǣge dēor
65 wulf on wealda.   Ne wearð wæl māre
  on þȳs īglande   ǣfre gȳta
  folces gefylled   beforan þyssum
  sweordes ecgum   þæs þe ūs secgað bēc,

39b–40a Translate '[he] had no cause to exult in the fellowship of swords'. This – the reading of MSS B and C – gives a daring kenning (§456) for battle. But the readings of the other manuscripts cast doubt on the reading *mēca*. Campbell prints *mecga gemanan* 'the fellowship of men'.

44b–5 **gylpan** 'to boast' governs the gen. *billgeslihtes*.

48 **beaduweorca beteran** 'better in (respect of) warlike deeds'. The same explanation holds for the genitives in ll. 49b–51a.

51 **þæs** This could be a rel. pron. 'which' agreeing with the preceding genitives or a conj. 'because'.

54a A powerful image for a defeated and dejected band of survivors.

60–5b The beasts of battle again; see §§406 and 457.

ealde ūðwitan,   siþþan ēastan hider
70 Engle and Seaxe   ūpp becōmon
ofer brāde brimu·   Brytene sōhton
wlance wīgsmiþas·   Wēalas ofercōmon·
eorlas ārhwate   eard begēaton.

69b–73 The poet recalls with grim exultation 'battles long ago'. Unhappily this 'melancholy strain' is still heard in too many parts of the world.

The standard edition of this poem is *The Battle of Brunanburh* edited by Alistair Campbell (London: Heinemann, 1938).

§470   *Text and translation:*
The Battle of Maldon (extracts)

The battle celebrated in the poem took place in August 991, a few miles below Maldon, Essex, on the southern bank of the River Blackwater. For the Chronicle accounts, see §187. The Danes were encamped on Northey Island, and the causeway they were allowed to cross can still be seen and is still submerged at high tide. Historically, the battle was only one of a series of minor engagements between the invading Northmen and the English; it is noteworthy (like Chalgrove Field) for the death of a distinguished leader and (more important) for what the poet has made of it.

He has given us a clear idea of the stages of the battle, even though he does follow the epic convention by which it is described as a series of single combats. We see the disposition of the English forces, the fight at the causeway, the Danes crossing the river with Byrhtnoth's permission. Then the battle begins and rages. With the death of Byrhtnoth and the flight of the sons of Odda and their cowardly companions comes the turning-point, and the rest of the poem is concerned with the grim resistance of the loyal warriors in the face of inevitable defeat.

W. P. Ker wrote: 'Late as it is, [the poem] has uttered the spirit and essence of the Northern heroic literature in its reserved and simple story.' I do not quarrel with this. But, as I have said in §§338–9, I doubt whether the poem accurately reflects the attitude of Anglo-Saxon warriors of the heroic period, even though it does give us glimpses of reality. None the less it is worthy of its theme; it deals successfully with a contemporary event and, like the warriors whose praises it sings, is plain, vigorous, strong, and 'heroic'. The original manuscript was lost in the Cottonian fire of 1731 but the poem survives in an edition printed in the eighteenth century and in the earlier transcript on which this was based. Something has been lost at the beginning and the end but the 325 lines which do survive suggest that the loss was not great. While generally following tradition in vocabulary and style, the poem shows some metrical irregularities not permitted in 'classical' Old English and makes occasional use of rhyme.

I regret that I cannot print the poem in full here. But it appears as Text 12 in *A Guide to Old English*. Extracts accompanied by translations will be found in §§222, 342–3, and 347.

§471   *Text and translation:* **Durham**

This late Anglo-Saxon poem is presented with Kevin Crossley-Holland's translation in §263. Even by Anglo-Saxon standards (§2), the spelling is eccentric. For more information on the poem see ASPR VI.

§472 The charm which follows shows a typical mixture of Christian and pagan (§§325 and 404) and is among the majority of the twelve 'metrical charms' (ASPR VI, pp. 116–28) which include ceremonial instructions in prose to accompany the incantations in verse. As I have noted in §372, figure 36 gives it a special poignancy.

Text 37   **Charm for Delayed Birth**

Se wifman se hire cild afedan ne mæg· gange to gewitenes mannes birgenne and stæppe þonne þriwa ofer þa byrgenne and cweþe þonne þriwa þas word:

       þis mē tō bōte   þǣre lāþan lætbyrde·
       þis mē tō bōte   þǣre swǣran swǣrbyrde·
5   þis mē tō bōte   þǣre lāðan lambyrde.

And þonne þæt wif seo mid bearne and heo to hyre hlaforde on reste ga· þonne cweþe heo:

       Up ic gonge·   ofer þē stæppe·
       mid cwican cilde   nālæs mid cwellendum·
10   mid fulborenum   nālæs mid fægan.

And þonne seo modor gefele þæt þæt bearn si cwic· ga þonne to cyrican and þonne heo toforan þan weofode cume· cweþe þonne:

       Crīste· ic sæde·   þis gecȳþed!

Se wifmon se hyre bearn afedan ne mæge· genime heo sylf hyre agenes cildes
15 gebyrgenne dæl· wry æfter þonne on blace wulle and bebicge to cepeman-num and cweþe þonne:

  1 **āfēdan** 'to bring forth/produce/give birth to'.
  3 **þās word** See §55.
  4–6 The subj. *sīe* 'may be' expressing a wish is to be understood in these three lines.
  7 **þonne** 'whenever' is followed by the pres. subjs. *sēo* = *sīe* and *gā*.
  8 **cweþe hēo** 'let her say'.
  12 **sī** = *sīe*.
  13 **cweþe** 'let [her] say'.
  14 **Crīste** dat. sg. Again, a verb is unexpressed. It may be *is* 'To Christ this is known' or *sīe* 'May this be known to Christ'.
  15–16 **genime . . . dæl** 'let her herself take a piece of her own child's grave', i.e. of a child of hers who has died. An unintended reflection on the dangers of pregnancy and on infant mortality in those days.
  16 **bebicge** < *bebicgan* 'to sell'.

Ic hit bebicge·   gē hit bebicgan·
þās sweartan wulle   and þysse sorge corn.
Se wifman se ne mæge bearn afedan· nime þonne anes bleos cu meoluc on   20
hyre handæ and gesupe þonne mid hyre muþe and gange þonne to
yrnendum wætere and spiwe þær in þa meolc and hlade þonne mid þære
ylcan hand þæs wæteres muð fulne and forswelge. Cweþe þonne þas word:
          Gehwēr ferde ic mē þone mǣran   maga þihtan·
          mid þysse mǣran   mēte þihtan·   25
          þonne ic mē wille habban   and hām gān.
þonne heo to þan broce ga· þonne ne beseo heo no ne eft þonne heo þanan
ga· and þonne ga heo in oþer hus oþer heo ut ofeode and þær gebyrge metes.

19 **corn** n.pl. 'seeds'.
20 **ānes blēos cū meoluc** 'milk of a cow of one colour'.
23 See l. 13 note.
24–5 This is the reading of the manuscript. The word *þihtan* occurs only here and is
unexplained. None of the attempts to emend the passage carries conviction. Obviously
something is seriously wrong. The note in ASPR VI responds to this riddle thus: 'Under these
circumstances the text is left unaltered.' I am afraid that we too must 'give up'.
27–8 **þonne ... þonne ... þonne ... þonne** See §137.

On the *Metrical Charms* I suggest that you first consult ASPR VI.

§473 The tendency to what I have elsewhere described as 'sentimental
identification' – begotten of the increasing pressure on academics to
publish, whether they have something or nothing to say – has enveloped *The
Wife's Lament* (Text 38) and *The Husband's Message* (Text 39) in elaborate
theories based on the proposition that the two poems, both of which are to
be found in the Exeter Book (§174), are about the same couple and in
attempts to identify this couple with people known to the Anglo-Saxons
from other sources. There are wilder theories about their origin and
meaning, including allegorical ones. I shall pass over all these and leave the
extracts which I print to speak for themselves across the centuries,
expressing feelings which have engaged the attention of men and women –
and of poets – throughout the ages and will continue to do so *geond þas lǣnan
worold* 'throughout this fleeting world'. As I have already said in §367, *The
Wife's Lament* is for me the most passionate expression in Old English of
these feelings.

Text 38   *The Wife's Lament* (extracts)

          Ic þis giedd wrece   bī mē ful gēomorre,
          mīnre sylfre sīð.   Ic þæt secgan mæg

1–2 **giedd ... sīð** are parallel objects of *Ic... wrece* 'I recite this tale about myself very sad,
my own fortune'. There have been claims that this poem was not spoken by a woman. This
involves disregarding the fem. endings *-re* in *gēomorre* and in *mīnre sylfre*. In my opinion, these
cannot be disregarded.
2 **þæt** 'that' recapitulates *giedd* and *sīð* and anticipates the *hwæt* clause in l. 3; see §§156–9.

hwæt ic yrmþa gebād   siþþan ic ūp āwēox,
nīwes oþþe ealdes,   nō mā þonne nū.
5 Ā ic wīte wonn   mīnra wræcsīþa.

    . . .   . . .

    . . .   Ful oft wit bēotedan
þæt unc ne gedǣlde   nemne dēað āna,
ōwiht elles·   eft is þæt onhworfen·
is nū swā hit   nǣfre wǣre
25 frēondscipe uncer.   Sceal ic feor ge nēah
mīnes felalēofan   fǣhðu drēogan.
    Heht mec mon wunian   on wuda bearwe
under āctrēo   in þām eorðscræfe.
Eald is þes eorðsele·   eal ic eom oflongad·
30 sindon dena dimme,   dūna ūphēa,
bitre burgtūnas   brērum beweaxne,
wīc wynna lēas.   Ful oft mec hēr wrāþe begeat
fromsīþ frēan.   Frȳnd sind on eorþan,
lēofe lifgende,   leger weardiað
35 þonne ic on ūhtan   āna gonge
under āctrēo   geond þās eorðscrafu.
þǣr ic sittan mōt   sumorlangne dæg·
þǣr ic wēpan mæg   mīne wræcsīþas,
earfoþa fela   forþon ic ǣfre ne mæg
40 þǣre mōdceare   mīnre gerestan
ne ealles þæs longaþes   þe mec on þissum līfe begeat.

    . . .   . . .

50 on drēorsele   drēogeð se mīn wine
micle mōdceare·   hē gemon tō oft
wynlicran wīc.   Wā bið þām þe sceal
of langoþe   lēofes ābīdan.

3–4 **gebād** < *gebīdan* (st. vb. I §517) 'to experience' governs the gens. *yrmþa* and *nīwes oþþe ealdes*.

6–21a The missing lines relate how the man was forced into exile and tell of their misery at their separation.

21b **wit** 'we two'. Cf. l. 25 *uncer* 'of us two' and see §494.

23–5 **þæt** and **hit** anticipate *frēondscipe uncer*.

39 **forþon** 'because' with this punctuation. But if a raised point were placed after *fela, forþon* could be translated 'therefore'.

40 **minre** is parallel to *þǣre mōdceare* but derives special emphasis from the fact that it is separated from these words and carries alliteration and metrical stress.

42–9 These lines express the woman's reflections on the possible state of mind of her lover in his exile. These are summed up in ll. 50–2a.

52 **þām þe** 'to that one who'.

The Wife's Lament appears as Text 15 in *A Guide to Old English*.

§474   *The Husband's Message* tells of a husband and wife of high rank – or of two lovers who have exchanged vows of some sort – separated by the machinations of kinsmen. The man who is in exile across the sea sends a message which is spoken by the human messenger or, it has been suggested, by a personified rune-stave, a piece of wood on which a message has been carved in runes (§1). The extract printed below as Text 39 contains the essence of this message and conveys the quiet sincerity of the man's love and his need for his beloved. The poem ends with his promise that, if she came,

> hē þā wǣre   ond þā winetrēowe
> be him lifgendum   lǣstan wolde
> þe git on ǣrdagum   oft gesprǣconn

he throughout his life would keep the pledges and the vows of love which the two of you often exchanged in the bygone days.

Text 39   **The Husband's Message**

> Hwǣt! þec þonne biddan hēt   se þisne bēam agrōf
> þæt þū sinchroden   sylf gemunde
> 15 on gewitlocan   wordbēotunga
> þe git on ǣrdagum   oft gesprǣcon
> þenden git mōston   on meoduburgum
> eard weardigan,   ān lond būgan,
> frēondscype fremman.   Hine fǣhþo ādrāf
> 20 of sigeþēode·   heht nū sylfa þē
> lustum lǣran   þæt þū lagu drēfde
> siþþan þū gehȳrde   on hliþes ōran
> galan gēomorne   gēac on bearwe.
> Ne lǣt þū þec siþþan   sīþes getwǣfan,
> 25 lāde gelettan   lifgendne monn.
>   Ongin mere sēcan,   mǣwes ēþel,
> onsite sǣnacan   þæt þū sūð heonan
> ofer merelāde   monnan findest
> þǣr se þēoden is   þīn on wēnum.

13 The subject of *hēt* is l. 13b. The subject of the inf. *biddan* 'to ask' is unexpressed *mē* 'me' the messenger and its object is *þec* 'thee' the lady; *þisne bēam* refers to the rune-stave. If the human messenger is speaking, the *bēam* is perhaps a means of identification as well as the bearer of the carved message. If we think of the personified stave as the speaker, this is a third person reference similar to the speaking cross's remark in *The Dream of the Rood* 56b *Crīst wæs on rōde* (§493).

16 **git** 2nd pers. dual pron. 'ye/you two' (§494).

20 The subject of *heht* is [*hē*] *sylfa*.

22 **gehȳrde**, from *hȳran/hīeran* 'to hear' (§94), is to be translated here as perfect, not preterite, tense.

24–5 The subject of the inf. *getwǣfan* is l. 25b.

27 **þæt**, conj. 'so that' introducing a clause of result, here shades into a temporal conj. 'until': 'so that/until you find . . .'.

29 **þīn** gen. sg. of *þū* 'of thee'.

The Husband's Message is to be found, along with *The Wife's Lament* (Text 38) and *The Ruin* (§237), in *Three Old English Elegies* edited by R. F. Leslie (Manchester: Manchester University Press, 1961).

§475 Text 40 immediately precedes the first of the riddles of the Exeter Book and was once thought to be one. But this idea has now been abandoned in favour of the generally accepted proposition that we have a dramatic monologue spoken by a woman separated from her lover. After that, agreement ceases and we find ourselves confronted by a riddle in the more general sense of something puzzling, something to which the last sentence of *Riddle* 61 is indeed applicable:

Rǣd hwǣt ic mǣne   'Explain what I mean'

As far as I know, no attempt has been made to allegorize the poem. But even if we pass over the various attempts to link the protagonists with figures in Germanic heroic legend, we are left with fundamental ambiguities about the number of people involved (one man or two?) and about the nature of the relations between them. I have tried to make the issues clear in my notes. I have chosen the title *Wulf* rather than *Wulf and Eadwacer* to avoid committing myself to an explanation involving a second man. The situation remains obscure. There is no 'right' answer. We do not know who the woman was. But her passion shines through and her poignant cry *Wulf, mīn Wulf* touches our hearts.

Text 40   **Wulf**

Lēodum is mīnum   swylce him mon lāc gife·
willað hȳ hine āþecgan   gif hē on þrēat cymeð.

1–2 These lines are fraught with difficulty. It has been suggested that two lines have been lost at the beginning and that the poem began with the name *Wulf*, like ll. 4, 9, and 13. This would supply a referent for the otherwise problematic *hine* and *hē* in l. 2. To read *Lēode* 'man/ prince' or *Lēofum* 'dear [one]/beloved' for *Lēodum* 'people' is another way of solving this difficulty. Both these, however, merely transfer the problem to *hȳ* 'they' in l. 2. If we add the different meanings which can be assigned to individual words, we can see that the possible variations offer great scope to those who wish to give the poem 'a local habitation and a name' in Germanic heroic legend.

1 **is** '[It] is'; **swylce** + pres. subj. **gife** 'as if one is giving/will give'. The reference cannot be to the past; **him** dat. pl. if we read *Lēodum*, dat. sg. if we read *Lēode* or *Lēofum*; **lāc** can mean 'sport' or 'strife' or 'sacrifice' or 'gift' or 'booty' or, it has been suggested, 'message'.

2 **hȳ** nom. pl. referring to *Lēodum* l. 1. If we change this word, *hȳ* has to be explained by reference to ll. 6–7. Such anticipatory use of a personal pronoun is rare but, I would judge, not impossible here; **āþecgan** The meanings suggested for this word include 'to capture', 'to oppress', 'to destroy', 'to feed', and 'to protect'; **on þrēat** The suggested meanings include 'in a troop', 'in calamity', 'in oppression', or the adverbial 'in the end'. The first riddle of l. 2 then is this: is the reception friendly or hostile? The line is repeated below as l. 7. So l. 6 may help you to decide. The second question is syntactical: is the line a statement or a question? (Here, I must confess, I am beginning to wonder whether I should have included this poem. I hope you will soon see the sun breaking through the clouds.)

Ungelīc is ūs.
Wulf is on īege·   ic on ōþerre.
5 Fæst is þæt ēglond   fenne biworpen.
Sindon wælrēowe   weras þǣr on īge·
willað hȳ hine āþecgan   gif hē on þrēat cymeð.
    Ungelīce is ūs.
Wulfes ic mīnes wīdlāstum   wēnum dogode·
10 þonne hit wæs rēnig weder   ond ic rēotugu sæt·
þonne mec se beaducāfa   bōgum bilegde·
wæs mē wyn tō þon·   wæs mē hwæþre ēac lāð.
Wulf, mīn Wulf,   wēna mē þīne
sēoce gedydon,   þīne seldcymas,
15 murnende mōd,   nālēs metelīste.
Gehȳrest þū, ēadwacer?   Uncerne earne hwelp
bireð wulf tō wuda.
þæt mon ēaþe tōslīteð   þætte næfre gesomnad wæs,
uncer giedd geador.

3 The so-called refrain appears again as l. 8. (In the poem *Deor*, a refrain occurs six times.) The final *-e* on *ungelīce* in that line is unlikely to be significant. The unexpressed subject could be [*hit*] or [*hē*].

5 **Fæst** adj. may mean that the island is 'strong' and so 'fortified' or that it is on firm ground in the middle of the fen.

9 **dogode** Since *hycgan* 'to think', an irregular wk. vb. with the pret. *hogode*, is recorded with the gen., it seems reasonable to substitute it for the otherwise unrecorded *dogode*. After all, even the most zealous defender of manuscript readings draws the line at defending MS *sittam* for *sittan* in *The Wife's Lament* 37. (As A. E. Housman wrote: 'Chance and the common course of nature will not bring it to pass that the readings of a MS. are right wherever they are possible and impossible wherever they are wrong: that needs divine intervention . . .') Translate: 'I have thought of my Wulf with far-wandering hopes' or 'in [his] wide wanderings, in [his] hopings'.

12 **tō þon** 'for that, because of that'; **lāð** This word can be taken as an adjective 'unpleasant/hateful' or as a noun 'pain/grief'. Which you choose will depend on, or will influence, how you read the poem and who you decide is *se beaducāfa* l. 11.

13 **wēna . . . þīne** lit. 'your expectations', i.e. '[my] expectations of you/your coming'.

16–17 More problems. Does *ēadwacer* mean 'guardian of [my] happiness' or is it the name of a person *Ēadwacer*? Should *wulf* be capitalized?

16 **Uncerne** acc. sg. masc. of the dual poss. 'of us two'; **earne** acc. sg. masc. of an adjective which can be translated as 'cowardly' or 'wretched' or 'swift' or (by emendation to *earmne*) 'miserable'; **hwelp** 'whelp'. Who is the father – Wulf or Eadwacer? The word-play *Wulf – hwelp* may suggest the former.

18 **þæt . . . þætte** 'That . . . that which'.

19 **giedd** 'song'. The reading *gǣd* 'fellowship' has been suggested. But *giedd* could be a poetic expression of this idea. As the editor of ASPR VI says resignedly, 'improbability is no argument against the MS. record of this text'. None the less, I dismiss the proposition advanced in 1931 that the poem is the record of a dream which a female dog of romantic temperament had about an affair with a good-looking wolf.

For more information on this poem, see ASPR III.

§476   *Text and translation:* **The Wanderer** 92–110

This passage, which so movingly expresses the heroic warrior's views on the transience of life as expressed by a poet with some knowledge of

Christianity, appears in §407. For some brief comments on *The Wanderer* as a poem see §477. It is printed in full as Text 16 in *A Guide to Old English*.

§477   *The Wanderer* and *The Seafarer*, which appear in the Exeter Book separated by two poems, are printed together in almost every Old English reader which contains poetry. Both treat the problems of loneliness and transience from the viewpoint of an heroic warrior with some knowledge of the Christian faith; see §407. The temptation to treat them as companion poems is therefore very great (§473) and has sometimes proved irresistible. Expository criticism of them has therefore followed similar paths: both have been described as a Christian reworking of a pagan poem; as a unity written by a Christian poet about the experiences of a real or imagined individual; or as a Christian allegory based on the familiar conception that life on earth is a pilgrimage towards Heaven and that those who live it are exiles from Heaven, a conception expressed in Hebrews 11: 13–16:

> These all died in faith, not having received the promises, but having seen them afar off, and were persuaded of them, and embraced them, and confessed that they were strangers and pilgrims on the earth.
>
> For they that say such things declare plainly that they seek a country . . .
>
> But now they desire a better country, that is, an heavenly: wherefore God is not ashamed to be called their God: for he hath prepared them a city.

The fact that such widely divergent theories have all been plausibly argued reflects the dilemma of those who study Old English poetry: through no fault of the poem or the poet, we are often left without an adequate frame of reference. Here I must leave it to the reader to adjudicate, with the reminder that the titles of both poems are modern and with the warning that, despite a superficial similarity, there are differences in thought and emotion. The fact that these thoughts and emotions are real ones; the telling images of wind and winter, of cold and ice, of darkness, desolation, and dawn loneliness; the vivid evocation of ruined buildings, lost treasures, and dead comrades; and the poignant contrast with past joys – all these make us very aware of

> Joy, whose hand is ever at his lips
> Bidding adieu.

Yet in both poems the transience of human life is transcended by the hope brought by Christianity. In the words of the Revelation of St John the Divine 7: 15–17,

> Therefore are they before the throne of God, and serve him day and night in his temple: and he that sitteth on the throne shall dwell among them.

They shall hunger no more, neither thirst any more; neither shall the sun light on them, nor any heat.

For the Lamb which is in the midst of the throne shall feed them, and shall lead them unto living fountains of waters: and God shall wipe away all tears from their eyes.

I turn now to specific comments on Text 41, *The Seafarer* (extracts). In ll. 1–64a, not printed here, the poet is concerned with the intolerable hardships of life at sea which cause the seafarer to think with longing of the joys experienced by those who dwell on the land. Yet when he is on land, the seafarer is driven to seek the sea. By what? Lines 64b–124, in which the sea is not mentioned at all, provide the answer in Christian terms. This led Dorothy Whitelock to see the poem as a description of the life of a *peregrinus*, a man who sought eternal life by pilgrimage and permanent exile (Latin *peregrinatio* OE *elþeodigness*) from his own land in this life. (Such men were not uncommon in Anglo-Saxon times; we read in the Parker Chronicle for 891 that

> þrie Scottas comon to Ælfrede cyninge on anum bate butan ælcum gereþrum of Hibernia þonon hi hi bestælon forþon þe hi woldon for Godes lufan on elþiodignesse beon· hi ne rohton hwær . . . þus hie wæron genemnde: Dubslane 7 Maccbethu 7 Mælinmun

> Three Scots came to King Alfred in a boat without a rudder from Ireland, whence they had stolen away because they wished to be in a foreign land, they cared not where, for love of God . . . Their names were Dubslane and Macbeth and Mælinmun.)

Other Christian interpretations include those of Geoffrey Smithers, who explained the poem as an allegory of life as a journey over a rough sea towards the harbour of Heaven, an idea which is found in Anglo-Saxon homilies and poems. Ida Gordon, however, read the poem as a symbolic religious lyric. These theories are all very interesting. But without embracing any one of them, we can see that *The Seafarer* has a significance akin to that of Psalm 107, the author of which also had sailors in mind:

Then they cry unto the Lord in their trouble, and he bringeth them out of their distresses.

He maketh the storm a calm, so that the waves thereof are still.

Then are they glad because they be quiet; so he bringeth them unto their desired haven.

O that men would praise the Lord for his goodness, and for his wonderful works to the children of men!

Text 41   **The Seafarer (extracts)**

Forþon mē hātran sind
65 Dryhtnes drēamas   þonne þis dēade līf,
    lǣne on londe.   Ic gelȳfe nō
    þæt him eorðwelan   ēce stondað.
    Simle þrēora sum   þinga gehwylce
    ǣr his tīddege   tō twēon weorþeð:
70 ādl oþþe yldo   oþþe ecghete
    fǣgum fromweardum   feorh oðþringeð.
    Forþon bið eorla gehwām   æftercweþendra
    lof lifgendra   lāstworda betst
    þæt hē gewyrce·   ǣr hē on weg scyle·
75 fremum on foldan   wið fēonda nīþ,
    dēorum dǣdum   dēofle tōgēanes,
    þæt hine ælda bearn   æfter hergen
    ond his lof siþþan   lifge mid englum
    āwa tō ealdre,   ēcan līfes blǣd,
80 drēam mid dugeþum.
                     Dagas sind gewitene,
    ealle onmēdlan   eorþan rīces·
    nearon nū cyningas   ne cāseras
    ne goldgiefan   swylce iū wǣron
    þonne hī mǣst mid him   mǣrþa gefremedon
85 ond on dryhtlicestum   dōme lifdon.
    Gedroren is þēos duguð eal·   drēamas sind gewitene·
    wuniað þā wācran   ond þās woruld healdaþ,
    brūcað þurh bisgo.   Blǣd is gehnǣged·
    eorþan indryhto   ealdað ond sēarað

As explained above, the poet has been describing how, despite its hardships, he finds the call to a life at sea irresistible. He now tells us why.

64 **Forþon** conj. 'For'.

64b–6a Cf. Luke 24: 32 'Did not our hearts burn within us, while he talked with us by the way, and while he opened to us the scriptures?'

66 **lond** 'land' as opposed to 'sea' and, in terms of Hebrews 11: 13–16 above, 'earth' as opposed to 'heaven'.

68 **Simle** 'always'; **þinga gehwylce** 'in every case'.

69b 'becomes as a doubt' i.e. 'is uncertain'.

70–1 For translation and comment, see §200.

72–80a This passage is quoted and translated in §413 in the course of a discussion on the word *lof* in §§412–13.

80b–96 This lament for the past should be compared with that from *The Wanderer* (§476) and with two from *Beowulf*: the lament of the last survivor (ll. 2247–66, §467) and the father's lament (ll. 2444–59, not printed in this book).

82 **nearon** = *ne* + *earon* (an unusual form) 'are not'.

83 **swylce** 'such as'.

84 **mǣst ... mǣrþa** 'the greatest of glorious deeds'; **mid him** 'among themselves'.

87 **þā wācran** nom. pl. 'the weaker'.

90 swā nū monna gehwylc   geond middangeard.
    Yldo him on fareð·   onsȳn blācað·
    gomelfeax gnornað·   wāt his iūwine,
    æþelinga bearn,   eorþan forgiefene.
    Ne mæg him þonne se flæschoma   þonne him þæt feorg losað
95 ne swēte forswelgan   ne sār gefēlan
    ne hond onhrēran   ne mid hyge þencan.
    . . .   . . .

    Uton wē hycgan   hwǣr wē hām āgen
    ond þonne geþencan   hū wē þider cumen
    ond wē þonne ēac tilien   þæt wē tō mōten
120 in þā ēcan   ēadignesse
    þǣr is līf gelong   in lufan Dryhtnes,
    hyht in heofonum.   þæs sȳ þām Halgan þonc
    þæt hē ūsic geweorþade,   wuldres Ealdor,
    ēce Dryhten,   in ealle tīd.
                           Amen.

93 **forgiefene** '[to have been] given/committed'.
94 **him** 'for itself'.
97–116 In these lines the poet stresses that on the Day of Judgement earthly treasures are of no avail to the soul and urges the need to fear God, to live humbly and purely, and to show moderation in love for friends and in enmity for foes.
117–18 Cf. again Hebrews 11: 13–16 above.
119b 'that we may [make our way] thither'.
122 **þæs** anticipates the *þæt* clause in ll. 123–4.

The Seafarer appears in full as Text 17 in *A Guide to Old English*.

§478   *Text and translation:*   **Maxims i 82—92**

This short extract, typical of Anglo-Saxon gnomic verse, is printed in §361. Both *Maxims i* and *Maxims ii* have been edited by T. A. Shippey; see §480.

§479   *Text and translation:*   **The Fortunes of Men 1—9**

This passage, another representative of gnomic verse or, as T. A. Shippey (§480) puts it, 'poems of wisdom and learning', appears in §368.

§480   There are four surviving dialogues in Old English – two in prose, two in verse – in which Solomon debates with Saturn or is questioned by him, often in a riddling way. The two poems are the oldest of all the extant dialogue texts on this theme in Western literature.

Of the four Old English versions, only the poem known as *Solomon and Saturn* II, which is to be found in Corpus Christi College Cambridge MS 422, has any real literary merit. It is incomplete, with gaps where leaves have been lost, and ends in mid-sentence.

It is beyond the scope of this book to explain the origin of the tradition, which, according to Dobbie (ASPR VI), 'seems to lie in the Talmudic and Arabic legends of Solomon's conversations with demons, who revealed to him the mysteries of the universe', or to discuss the versions in other languages, or even to go into the background of *Solomon and Saturn* II, which presents many difficulties of interpretation. On these questions see Menner's edition cited below.

Our passage (ll. 348–93 in ASPR VI (these numbers are used here for convenience of reference), ll. 170–214 in Shippey; see below) illustrates what Shippey sees as 'one of the poem's most surprising elements . . . its repeated condemnation of *grumblers*'. Solomon says flatly 'that things are as they are, and might be worse' and in ll. 348–9 below 'he goes so far as to rebuke Saturn implicitly for mentioning deficiencies at all'. I continue with a judgement which Shippey makes concerning the 'poems of wisdom and learning' which he edited:

> The poems discussed here have two functions: they make us aware of the true state of the world, which is a sad one; having done so, they encourage us not to be overwhelmed by it, either by offering religious hope or else by calling on our innate strength of mind.

And I conclude with a poem by John K. Bangs which I learnt as a child and which, I now see, would have appealed to the author of *Solomon and Saturn* II:

A Philosopher

To take things as they be –
That's my philosophy.
　　No use to holler, mope or cuss –
　　If they was changed they might be wuss.

If rain is pourin' down,
An' lightnin' 's buzzin' roun',
　　I ain't a-fearin' we'll be hit,
　　But grin that I ain't out in it.

If some one come along,
And tried to do me wrong,
　　Why I should sort of take a whim
　　To thank the Lord I wasn't him.

I never seen a night
So dark there wasn't light
　　Somewheres about if I took care
　　To strike a match and find out where.

Perhaps you might care to try your hand at translating this into Old English.

Text 42　**Solomon and Saturn**

Saturnus cwæð:
'Ac forhwan bēoð ðā gesīðas　　somod ætgædre,
wōp and hleahtor?　　Full oft hīe weorðgeornra
350 sælða tōslītað·　　hū gesæleð ðæt?'
　　Salomon cuæð:
'Unlæde bið and ormōd　　se ðe ā wile
gēomrian on gihðe·　　se bið gode fracoðast.'
　　Saturnus cwæð:
'Forhwon ne mōton wē ðonne ealle　　mid onmedlan
gegnum gangan　　in godes rīce?'
　　Salomon cwæð:
355 'Ne mæg fȳres feng　　ne forstes cile,
snāw ne sunne,　　somod eardian,
aldor geæfnan,　　ac hira sceal ānra gehwylc
onlūtan and onliðigan　　ðe hafað læsse mægn.'
　　Saturnus cwæð:
'Ac forhwon ðonne leofað　　se wyrsa leng?
360 Se wyrsa ne wāt　　in woroldrīce
on his mægwinum　　māran āre.'
　　Salomon cwæð:
'Ne mæg mon forildan　　ænige hwīle
ðone dēoran sīð　　ac hē hine ādrēogan sceall.'
　　Saturnus cwæð:
'Ac hū gegangeð ðæt?　　Gōde oððe ȳfle·
365 ðonne hīe bēoð ðurh āne　　idese ācende,
twēgen getwinnas,　　ne bið hira tīr gelīc.
Ōðer bið unlæde on eorðan·　　ōðer bið ēadig,
swīðe lēoftæle　　mid lēoda duguðum·
ōðer leofað　　lȳtle hwīle,
370 swīceð on ðisse sīdan gesceafte　　and ðonne eft mid sorgum
　　　gewīteð.
Fricge ic ðec, hlāford Salomon,　　hwæðres bið hira folgoð betra?'
　　Salomon cuæð:
'Mōdor ne rædeð·　　ðonne hēo magan cenneð·

349 **weorðgeornra** gen. pl. of adj. used as a noun 'of high-souled people'.
351 **unlæde** 'miserable', used in ll. 367 and 393 in contrast to *ēadig* 'happy, blessed'; **ormōd** 'spiritless'.
357 **hira . . . ānra gehwylc** 'one of them' is qualified by the *ðe* 'which' clause in l. 358b.
359 **se wyrsa** 'the worse/less good [individual]', nom. sg. as representative of the class.
365 **hīe** recapitulates l. 364b: '[Whether] good or evil, when they . . .'.
368 **mid lēoda duguðum** 'among the seasoned troop/band of nobles'.
369 **ōðer** = *Ōðer* in l. 367a. Translate 'the first'; **lȳtle hwīle** echoes *Lȳtle hwīle* in l. 314 of this poem; see §396.
371 **hwæðres . . . hira** 'of which of the two of them'.

hū him weorðe geond worold   wīdsīð sceapen.
Oft hēo tō bealwe   bearn āfēdeð,
375 seolfre tō sorge,   siððan drēogeð
his earfoðu,   orlegstunde.
Hēo ðæs afran sceall   oft and gelōme
grimme grēotan   ðonne hē geong færeð·
hafað wilde mōd,   wērige heortan,
380 sefan sorgfullne·   slīðeð geneahhe,
wērig, wilna lēas,   wuldres bedæled·
hwīlum higegēomor   healle weardað,
leofað lēodum feor·   lōcað geneahhe
fram ðām unlǣdan   āgen hlāford.
385 Forðan nāh sēo mōdor geweald   ðonne hēo magan cenneð
bearnes blǣdes   ac sceall on gebyrd faran
ān æfter ānum·   ðæt is eald gesceaft.'
     Saturnus cwæð:
'Ac forhwan nele monn him on giogoðe   georne gewyrcan
dēores dryhtscipes   and dǣdfruman,
390 wādan on wīsdōm,   winnan æfter snytro?'
     Salomon cwæð:
'Hwæt! Him mæg ēadig eorl   ēaðe gecēosan
on his mōdsefan   mildne hlāford,
ānne æðeling.   Ne mæg dōn unlǣde swā.'

373 **wīdsīð** 'wide/far journey'. Modern critics have given this name to a poem in the Exeter Book which describes the wide journeyings of an heroic warrior and *scop*.
375 **seolfre** dat. sg. fem. 'for herself'; **tō** 'as'; **siððan** adv. 'afterwards' or conj. 'from the time that'; the subject of *drēogeð* 'endures' can be [*hēo*] the mother or [*hē*] the son.
377 **ðæs afran** 'for her son'.
378b–83b The subject of all the verbs is *hē* the young man.
382 **healle** acc. sg. fem. 'hall'. In view of ll. 383b–4, the reference must be to the young man's own dwelling.
383b The subject of *lōcað* is [*his*] *āgen hlāford* l. 384b.
385 **nāh . . . geweald** Ælfric used this phrase in Text 32 l. 26 (§444).
386 **gebyrd** here means 'what is determined by birth' (cf. Text 26 §434!) and so 'fate'.
387 **ān æfter ānum** 'one [thing] after another'.
388 **him** 'for himself'; **gewyrcan** 'to win/gain' takes the gen.
393 **ānne** acc. sg. masc. 'one'. It may have an intensifying function; cf. *Beowulf* 1885 *þæt wæs ān cyning*, where *ān* carries the sense 'unique' or 'peerless'.

The standard edition of this text is *The Poetical Dialogues of Solomon and Saturn* edited by Robert J. Menner (New York and London: MLA, 1941). But initially you may find it easier to use T. A. Shippey, *Poems of Wisdom and Learning in Old English* (Cambridge: D. S. Brewer, and Totowa: Rowman and Littlefield, 1976), which offers texts, translations, and comment. Shippey's representations led me to include this passage. So I dedicate §480 to him.

§481 *De Consolatione Philosophiae*, composed by the consul Boethius (*c.* 475–525) after he had been wrongly accused of treason and imprisoned by Theodoric, king of the Ostrogoths and ruler of Rome, was one of the most popular works of the Middle Ages. It was translated into English by King

Alfred – *Ælfred cyning wæs wealhstod* ('translator') *ðisse bec 7 hie of boclædene on englisc wende* – by Chaucer, and by Queen Elizabeth I. (In view of my remarks in §432, it is a pity that I cannot add Winston Churchill to this list.)

The Old English verse translation is based on King Alfred's prose version and is not directly related to the Latin Metres. Alfred is mentioned in this Text 43 as the author of the Old English metrical version; see the note below. Two editors of it – Sedgefield (1899) and Krämer (1902) – accept Alfred's authorship. But not all editors agree and there remains a slight doubt.

Text 43 **The Metres of Boethius: Proem**

　　　Ðus Ælfred ūs　　　ealdspell reahte,
　　　cyning Westsexna,　　　cræft meldode,
　　　leoðwyrhta list.　　Him wæs lust micel
　　　ðæt hē ðiossum lēodum　　　lēoð spellode,
　5　monnum myrgen, mislice cwidas,
　　　þȳ læs ælinge　　　ūt ādrīfe
　　　selflicne secg　　　þonne hē swelces lȳt
　　　gȳmð for his gilpe.　　　Ic sceal gīet sprecan,
　　　fōn on fitte,　　　folccūðne ræd
　10　hæleðum secgean.　　　Hliste se þe wille!

1 **Ælfred** This mention of King Alfred in the third person is not an argument against his authorship. The change from the third person to the first person *Ic* l. 8 can be paralleled in King Alfred's own Preface to the *Cura Pastoralis*, which he certainly did translate (Text 24 §432): *Ælfred cyning hāteð grētan Wærferð biscep . . . ond ðē cyðan hāte . . .* 'King Alfred sends Bishop Wærferth greetings . . . and [I Alfred] order [someone] to make known to you [Wærferth] . . .'; **ūs** 'us', i.e. his people.
5 **myrgen** 'joy/pleasure'.
6 **ælinge** 'weariness'.
9 **fitt** 'song/poem'. The word 'fit' is used by modern critics to mean a sub-division in a long Old English poem such as *Beowulf*.

The standard edition of the prose and verse versions is *King Alfred's Old English Version of Boethius 'De Consolatione Philosophiae'* edited by Walter John Sedgefield (Oxford: Clarendon Press, 1899).

§482   Text and translation: **Riddle 47**

For this riddle, see §295. It and the next two riddles are all concerned with manuscripts. Details of an edition of the Exeter Book riddles will be found in §486.

§483   Text and translation: **Riddle 51**

This riddle is printed in §291. Like *Riddle 47* above, it has to do with manuscripts.

§484   *Text 14*   **Riddle 26**

Text 14 (§300) describes a beautiful Bible manuscript.

§485 The poem *Genesis* occupies folios 1–142 of the Junius MS and, as printed in ASPR I, contains 2936 lines. In the main it is a versification, with some additions from exegetical sources but not without literary merit, of the first book of the Old Testament from the Creation to the sacrifice of Isaac; by coincidence, this is where Ælfric stopped translating (Text 32 §444). We do not know how much more, if any, was originally versified.

Until 1875 it was generally accepted as one poem, although as early as 1826 W. D. Conybeare had argued on literary and stylistic grounds that the passage in folios 13–40 which appears in ASPR I as ll. 235–851 was an interpolation. In 1875 Eduard Sievers, on much the same grounds, proposed that these lines were not only interpolated but were a translation of a lost poem in Old Saxon. He called the Old English version *GenesisB* as opposed to the rest of the poem, *GenesisA*. This idea did not meet universal acceptance. The article on Cædmon in the 1908 printing of volumes of *The Dictionary of National Biography*, first printed in 1886 and 1887, contains these words:

> We must remember that the continental Saxons were evangelised by English missionaries; and . . . it is highly improbable that an ancient and cultured church like that of England should have adopted into its literature a poem written by a barbarian convert of its own missions. Moreover, Professor Sievers's linguistic arguments are not of overwhelming force.

However, Sievers was triumphantly vindicated in 1894, when Karl Zangemeister, Librarian of Heidelberg University, discovered in the Vatican Library four fragments of Old Saxon verse, one of which corresponded to ll. 790–817 of *GenesisB*. (It may be noted in passing that thereafter scholars were less ready to dismiss any theory advanced by Sievers.)

Space does not permit a full discussion of the problems associated with *Genesis*. But this summary of its contents may be helpful:

GenesisA	1–111	The revolt and fall of the angels
	112–234	Genesis 1: 1–2: 14
GenesisB	235–45	Genesis 2: 16–17
	246–337	The revolt and fall of the angels
	338–441	Satan plans revenge and seeks a subordinate to tempt Adam and Eve
	442–765a	Genesis 3: 1–7
	765b–851	The repentance of Adam and Eve
GenesisA	852–2936	Genesis 3: 8–22: 13

The only verses in Genesis 1 and 2 not represented are Genesis 2: 15, which repeats 2: 8, and Genesis 2: 18–25, which tell how Adam named the animals and give a more specific account of the creation of woman already related in Genesis 1: 27.

One of the themes which runs through the Junius MS is mankind's duty of obedience to God and the perils of disobedience. This theme is expressed in *Daniel* 1–24. In *GenesisB* 244b–5 we learn that Adam and Eve *wæron leof gode* || *ðenden heo his halige word healdan woldon* 'were dear to God as long as they were willing to keep/obey His holy word'. The formulaic *wið God/ drihten/ waldend winnan/ wann/ wunnon*, 'to contend/contended against God/the lord/the ruler' appears twice in Text 44 (ll. 298 and 303), twice elsewhere in *GenesisB* (ll. 346 and 490), in *Exodus* (Text 46 l. 515), and in *Christ and Satan* 704. The result was inevitable: in the words of *GenesisB* 327 and 329 *Hie hyra gal beswac . . . hæfdon wite micel* 'Their pride betrayed them . . . [they] had great punishment'.

The situation of Satan after the Fall – all lost, only courage left, as in *The Battle of Maldon* – and his transformation into a rebellious and exiled thane who yet demanded loyalty from his own followers were natural opportunities for an Anglo-Saxon poet; see §§343 and 450. This Satan is in marked contrast to the elegiac Satan of *Christ and Satan*, who in ll. 163–88 utters a lament which is comparable in form to that of the wanderer (§476) and which contains the words *Eala þæt ic eom ealles leas ecan dreames* 'Alas that I am completely deprived of eternal joy'. The similarity of the former to the Satan of *Paradise Lost* has not escaped attention; both share the quality of pride or arrogance stressed by the Anglo-Saxon poet – *oferhygd* (l. 328), *ofermede* (l. 293), *ofermetto* (l. 351), and *ofermod* (l. 272). Indeed, it has been argued that Milton may have been indebted to *GenesisB*; he appears to have known Junius, the first editor of the manuscript which bears his name (§173). But this is possibly another case of sentimental identification (§§427 and 473).

We may note that the theme of vengeance (§§345–7) is also exploited. In *GenesisA* the fall of the angels is described before the creation of Adam and Eve. In *GenesisB* the order is reversed. This is dramatically effective: Satan's revenge is motivated not only by his own expulsion and that of his followers but also by their replacement in God's favour by Adam and Eve. The successful tempter exults thus on behalf of himself and of Satan who trusted him with the task of tempting Adam and Eve: *ealle synt uncre hearmas gewrecene* 'all the afflictions of the two of us are avenged'.

In ll. 242–71a, which immediately precede our passage, we are told of God's creation of the angels, of His hopes for them, and of Satan's growing arrogance. In Text 44, this arrogance finds expression and punishment. Lines 306b–37 tell of the fall from Heaven to Hell and of the fallen angels' first impression of their new abode.

Text 44 **Satan's defiance of God**

Feala worda gespæc
se engel ofermōdes·   þōhte þurh his ānes cræft
hū hē him strenglicran   stōl geworhte,
hēahran on heofonum·   cwæð þæt hine his hige spēone
275 þæt hē west and norð   wyrcean ongunne,
trymede getimbro·   cwæð him twēo þūhte
þæt hē gode wolde   geongra weorðan.
'Hwæt sceal ic winnan?' cwæð hē.   'Nis me wihtæ þearf
hearran tō habbanne.   Ic mæg mid handum swā fela
280 wundra gewyrcean.   Ic hæbbe geweald micel
tō gyrwanne   gōdlecran stōl,
hēarran on heofne.   Hwȳ sceal ic æfter his hyldo ðēowian,
būgan him swilces geongordōmes?   Ic mæg wesan god swā hē.
Bigstandað mē strange genēatas   þā ne willað mē æt þām strīðe
    geswīcan,
285 hæleþas heardmōde.   Hīe habbað mē tō hearran gecorene,
rōfe rincas·   mid swilcum mæg man rǣd geþencean,
fōn mid swilcum folcgesteallan.   Frȳnd synd hīe mīne georne,
holde on hyra hygesceaftum.   Ic mæg hyra hearra wesan,
rǣdan on þīs rīce.   Swā mē þæt riht ne þinceð
290 þæt ic ōleccan   āwiht þurfe
gode æfter gōde ǣnegum.   Ne wille ic leng his geongra wurþan.'
    þā hit se allwalda   eall gehȳrde
þæt his engyl ongan   ofermēde micel
āhebban wið his hearran   and spræc hēalic word
295 dollīce wið drihten sīnne·   sceolde hē þā dǣd ongyldan,

272 **ofermōdes** gen. sg. 'in his *ofermōd*'. See §485 above; **þōhte** not to be confused with *þūhte* l. 276. See §100; **þurh his ānes cræft** belongs in the *hū* clause. Such displacement is not uncommon; **his ānes** 'of him alone'.

273 **strenglicran** comp. of adj. declined weak (§508). For more examples, see ll. 274, 281, 282.

275–6 **wyrcean ongunne, trymede** The infinitive *wyrcean* is governed by the first of the two verbs, both of which are 3rd sg. pret. subj. with the sense 'should ...'. Here *ongunne* < *onginnan* 'to begin' is almost an auxiliary. Translate 'should build, should fortify'. Cf. *gan* as auxiliary verb 'did' in Chaucer.

277 **geongra** 'subordinate'; **weorðan** 'to be/remain'. So also *wurþan* l. 291.

278 **Hwæt** 'Why'. Cf. *Hwȳ* l. 282; **wihtæ** = *wihte* adv. 'at all'.

283 **swilces geongordōmes** gen. sg. Cf. *ofermōdes* l. 272.

284 **þā** dem. or rel. pron. 'they/who'.

285 **gecorene** for *gecorenne* acc. sg. masc. of past ptc. of *cēosan* 'to choose' (§515), agreeing with *mē*.

289 **þīs** = *þȳs* inst. sg. (§497).

290 **āwiht** adv. 'at all'.

292 **þā** adv. or conj. 'Then/When'; **hit ... eall** anticipates the *þæt* clause.

293 **ongan** Cf. *ongunne* l. 275.

295 **sceolde** 'had to', i.e. it was his destiny or fate; **hē** = *his engyl* l. 293.

worc þæs gewinnes gedælan,   and sceolde his wīte habban,
ealra morðra mǣst.   Swā dēð monna gehwilc
þe wið his waldend   winnan ongynneð
mid māne wið þone mǣran drihten.   þā wearð se mihtiga
      gebolgen,
300 hēhsta heofones waldend·   wearp hine of þan hēan stōle.
Hete hæfde hē æt his hearran gewunnen·   hyldo hæfde his
      ferlorene·
gram wearð him se gōda on his mōde.   Forþon hē sceolde
      grund gesēcean
heardes hellewītes   þæs þe hē wann wið heofnes waldend.
Ācwæð hine þā fram his hyldo   and hine on helle wearp,
305 on þā dēopan dala   þǣr hē tō dēofle wearð,
se fēond mid his geferum eallum.

298 **þe** 'who'; **ongynneð** Cf. *ongunne* l. 275.
299 **þā** adv. 'Then'.
300–5 The context makes it clear whether the 3rd pers. sg. masc. pronouns refer to God or *his engyl*.
304 **Ācwæð** < *ācweðan* 'to say/utter/declare' and so by extension 'to reject' or 'to banish'.
305 **tō dēofle wearð** 'became the devil'.

For an edition of *GenesisA*, see that by A. N. Doane (Madison: University of Wisconsin Press, 1978). *GenesisB* was poorly edited by B. J. Timmer (Oxford: Scrivener Press, 1948). There is a 1960 Indiana Ph.D. dissertation '"Genesis B": A New Analysis and Edition' by John Frederick Vickrey Jr. which is available through University Microfilms.

§486   If you are outwitted by the author of the following riddle, see Genesis 19: 30–8.

Text 45   **Riddle 46**

     Wer sæt æt wīne   mid his wīfum twām
     ond his twēgen suno   ond his twā dohtor,
     swāse gesweostor,   ond hyra suno twēgen,
     frēolico frumbearn·   fæder wæs þǣr inne
5   þāra æþelinga   ǣghwæðres mid·
     ēam ond nefa.   Ealra wǣron fife
     eorla ond idesa   insittendra.

5 **mid** adv. 'in the company'.
6 **eam ond nefa** '[there was also] an uncle and a nephew'. Strictly speaking, there were two of each. There was also a grandfather, but he does not get a mention!

Kevin Crossley-Holland's translation catches the spirit of this riddle so well that, contrary to my custom with annotated texts, I print it here:

         A man sat sozzled with his two wives,
         his two sons and his two daughters,
         darling sisters, and with their two sons,
         favoured firstborn; the father of that fine
         pair was in there too, and so were

an uncle and a nephew. Five people
in all sat under that same roof.

The standard edition is *The Old English Riddles of the Exeter Book* edited by Craig Williamson
(Chapel Hill: University of North Carolina Press, 1977).

§487   *Exodus* – the second poem in the Junius MS – tells the story of the
departure of the Israelites from Egypt, their journey to the Red Sea, and the
drowning of the pursuing Egyptians; see Exodus 13: 20–14: 31. I cannot
discuss here the other sources of the poem – scriptural, exegetical, liturgical
– or its allegorical dimensions. Nor can I comment in detail on the poet's
use of heroic themes and formulae exemplified in the reference to Moses as
a war-leader (§450) and in the imagery associated with storms at sea and with
battles. The fact that there were no survivors is biblical (Exodus 14: 28) but
the poet mentions it twice (ll. 456b–7a and 508ff.), thereby providing a
variation on the theme of the last survivor (§343). The tone of Text 46 may
remind some of the note of gloating in *The Battle of Brunanburh* (Text 36
§469).

Text 16 (§419) contains three prose versions – Old English, Latin, and
seventeenth-century – of Exodus 14: 21–31, which tells of the destruction of
the Egyptian army in the Red Sea. Text 46 below (*Exodus* 447–515) is
preceded in the manuscript by a lacuna from which a section of the poem
(some sixty-six lines) has been lost; it covered Exodus 14: 23–6. The actual
drowning is related in Exodus 14: 27–8 and in our extract. The rest of the
poem (ll. 516–90) comprises an expansion of Exodus 14: 29–31 by material
from other sources.

Like Text 34 (§446), this is an extract whose main difficulty for the
beginner lies in its vocabulary. But few extant Old English poems present
more difficulties than *Exodus* for modern editors or (it would seem) for the
Anglo-Saxon scribe, who appears at times not to have understood his
exemplar and consequently to have made what now seem to be obvious
errors. These problems are compounded by missing pages and by gaps in
the manuscript. I have evaded most of these difficulties in an attempt to
prevent them overwhelming the chosen extract. Those interested in
pursuing them should compare the text presented here – basically that of
ASPR I – with that provided by the editors named below.

While preparing this text, I have wondered whether I was right to include
it. It is difficult. Perhaps you should read it in translation (preferably
Tolkien's; see below) before tackling it. But I find it intensely dramatic. The
style is simple, almost exclusively paratactic. There are eight subordinate
clauses (ll. 472, 476, 479, 485, 496, 499, 510, 514); *þær* (l. 458) can mean 'there'
or 'where'. I have counted twenty-nine sentences which occupy only one
half-line and seventeen which occupy only two half-lines. This accounts for
sixty-three of the ninety-six half-lines in the extract. Such sentence
structure makes it seem as if the poet 'in fast thick pants were breathing', as
Coleridge (somewhat unhappily to modern ears) put it.

The poet clearly got over-excited. His confusion is reflected not only in the sentence structure and in the violent imagery but also in the way the following themes are introduced in this order and then repeated apparently at random: terrified people, (terrible) sea, sea-death, sea and blood, cries, military equipment, desire to escape . . . no escape, path . . . no path, storm rose to heaven, sea-walls fell, they died, doomed, sky and blood, God at work, they got their reward.

I remember Tolkien ending his lectures on *Exodus* for the term with the words 'I'm sorry we haven't got to the Red Sea yet'. But when we did, his remarks as reconstructed from my lecture notes included the following:

If we have anything left by Cædmon [§427] apart from the *Hymn*, it is *Exodus* . . . marvellous word pictures . . . too excitable . . . at the Red Sea he just foams . . . if only he'd stood back, heard it from the top of the hill, he'd have done better . . . great scene . . . he's there . . . what happens? . . . blows up like a bullfrog!

Text 46 **The destruction of the Egyptian army**

Folc wæs āfǣred·   flōdegsa becwōm
gāstas gēomre·   geofon dēaðe hwēop·
wǣron beorhhliðu   blōde bestēmed·
450 holm heolfre spāw·   hrēam wæs on ȳðum·
wæter wǣpna ful·   wælmist āstāh.
Wǣron Ēgypte   eft oncyrde·
flugon forhtigende·   fǣr ongēton·
woldon hereblēaðe   hāmas findan·
455 gylp wearð gnornra.   Him ongēn genāp
atol ȳða gewealc·   ne ðǣr ǣnig becwōm
herges to hāme   ac behindan belēac
wyrd mid wǣge·   þǣr ǣr wegas lāgon·
mere mōdgode·   mægen wæs ādrenced·
460 strēamas stōdon·   storm up gewāt
hēah to heofonum,   herewōpa mǣst·
lāðe cyrmdon·   lyft up geswearc
fǣgum stæfnum·   flōd blōd gewōd.

447 **becwōm** < *becuman* 'to come/arrive' (§519) is here used with an object 'came upon/befell'.

451 **wæter** [*wæs*] . . .

455 **gnornra** comp. of adj. *gnorn* 'sad'.

457 The object of *belēac* is [*hīe*] 'them'.

458 **þǣr** adv. 'there' or conj. 'where'. The half-line is a *koinon* (§165).

460 **storm** 'tumult' is explained by l. 461b.

462–3a Those editors for whom the image presented here is too daring punctuate l. 462b as a parenthesis and take ll. 462a and 463a together.

Randbyrig wǣron rofene·   rodor swipode
465 meredēaða mǣst·   mōdige swulton,
cyningas on corðre·   cyre swiðrode
sǣs æt ende.   Wigbord scinon
hēah ofer hæleðum·   holmweall āstāh
merestrēam mōdig·   mægen wæs on cwealme
470 fæste gefeterod·   forðganges weg
searwum ǣsǣled·   sand bāsnodon
witodre fyrde   hwonne waðema strēam,
sincalda sǣ   sealtum ȳðum,
æflāstum gewuna,   ēce staðulas,
475 nacud nȳdboda,   nēosan cōme,
fāh fēðegāst   se ðe fēondum genēop.
Wæs sēo hæwene lyft   heolfre geblanden·
brim berstende   blōdegesan hwēop
sǣmanna sīð   oðþæt sōð metod
480 þurh Moyses hand   mōdge rȳmde·
wīde wæðde·   wælfæðmum swēop·
flōd fāmgode·   fǣge crungon·
lagu land gefēol·   lyft wæs onhrēred·
wicon weallfæsten·   wǣgas burston·
485 multon meretorras   þā se mihtiga slōh
mid hālige hand,   heofonrīces weard,
on wērbēamas.   Wlance ðēode

464b–5a The element order here is OVS.

470 **weg** [*wæs*].

471 **searwum ǣsǣled** 'fettered by cunning' (Moses' magic powers) or 'fettered by wargear' (their chariots and accoutrements); **bāsnodon** < *bāsnian* 'to await' (wk. vb. like *lufian* §526) has two objects, l. 472a and the *hwonne* clause.

472 **witodre fyrde** dat. sg. 'the appointed army'. This seems to make sense in the context. But some editors read *witodre wyrde* 'the appointed fate'; **hwonne** conj. 'until' with the pret. subj. *cōme* 'should come/came' in l. 475; **strēam** 'stream' is paralleled by ll. 473, 474a, 475a, and 476. All these are subjects of l. 475b.

474 **æflāstum gewuna** 'accustomed to [its] changed course' contrasts with **ēce staðulas** '[its] eternal foundations', i.e. its original course, which is the object of l. 475b.

476 **se ðe** 'which'; **genēop** an otherwise unknown word which Tolkien translated 'hedged in'.

478 **blōdegesan** dat. sg. 'with bloody terror'.

479 **sǣmanna sīð** 'the journey of the men through the sea'. I take ll. 477–81 to mean that the sea was a threat to the Egyptians until God, through Moses, brought the waters down upon them, and so turned the threat to terrible reality.

480 **mōdge rȳmde** 'swept away the valorous ones'. *Mōdige* has already been used of the Egyptians in l. 465.

481 Syntactically, *sōð metod* = God, which is the subject of *rȳmde*, would seem to be the subject of *wæðde* 'hunted' and *swēop* 'swept [them] away'. But these verbs would seem more appropriate to *flōd* l. 482. Perhaps l. 481 is another *koinon*, reminding us that the sea is the instrument of God.

483a 'Water fell on land'.

487a As printed here the half-line means 'on the protecting barriers', paralleling *meretorras* l. 485.

ne mihton forhabban   helpendra pað,
merestrēames mōd·   ac hē manegum gescēod
490 gyllende gryre.   Gārsecg wēdde·
up ātēah· on slēap.   Egesan stōdon·
wēollon wælbenna.   Wītrod gefēol
hēah of heofonum   handweorc godes
fāmigbosma·   flōdweard geslōh
495 unhlēowan wæg   alde mēce
þæt ðȳ dēaðdrepe   drihte swæfon,
synfullra swēot·   sawlum lunnon
fæste befarene,   flōdblāc here,
siððan hīe on bugon   brūn yppinge,
500 mōdewæga mæst.   Mægen eall gedrēas
ðā gedrencte wæron   dugoð Ēgypta,
Faraon mid his folcum.   Hē onfond hraðe
siððan grund gestāh   godes andsaca
þæt wæs mihtigra   mereflōdes weard·
505 wolde heorufæðmum   hilde gescēadan,
yrre and egesfull.   Ēgyptum wearð
þæs dægweorces   dēop lēan gescēod
forðām þæs heriges   hām eft ne cōm
ealles ungrundes   ænig to lāfe
510 þætte sīð heora   secgan mōste,
bodigean æfter burgum   bealospella mæst,
hordwearda hryre,   hæleða cwēnum
ac þā mægenþrēatas   meredēað geswealh,
spelbodan ēac.   Se ðe spēd āhte,
515 āgēat gylp wera.   Hīe wið god wunnon!

488 'the path of the helping [waves]'. Tolkien preferred *wað* 'hunting/onrush' for *pað*.
489 **hē** = *merestrēam*.
490a 'yelling with horror/shrieking horribly'.
490b–1a Tolkien's translation: 'Mad was the deep. Up it climbed, on them it slithered down.'
492 **Wītrod** = *wīgtrod* 'the army path', i.e. the way between the walls of water, is the object of *gefēol* 'fell upon'; cf. l. 483a. The subject is ll. 493–4b.
493 **handweorc godes** = the sea.
494 **flōdweard** = God.
495 **unhlēowan wæg** acc. sg. 'the unprotective wave', an understatement for 'destructive'; **alde mēce** 'with the ancient sword'. Cf. Wisdom 18: 15–16.
496 **drihte** nom. pl. 'troops'.
499–500a A much discussed and emended passage. As printed here, translate 'after the dark masses, the greatest of furious waves, fell on them'.
503 **grund gestāh** 'reached the bottom [of the sea]'.
504 **mihtigra** comp. of adj. *mihtig*.
509a gen. sg. qualifying *þæs heriges* l. 508 'of all that immense army'.
514 **Se ðe** 'He who'.
515 **āgēat** < *āgēotan* (§517) 'to pour out' and so 'destroyed'; on l. 515b see §485.

The poem *Exodus* has been edited by E. B. Irving Jr. (Yale Studies in English 122, 1953), Peter J. Lucas (London: Methuen, 1977), and Joan Turville-Petre *The Old English 'Exodus': Text, Translation and Commentary by J. R. R. Tolkien* (Oxford: Clarendon Press, 1981).

§488 The Paris Psalter, printed in ASPR V, is contained in MS Fonds Latin 8824 in the Bibliothèque Nationale in Paris. It presents a Latin text and an Old English version side by side written in the same hand in the middle of the eleventh century. The Latin, which appears in the left-hand column, is not the Latin used by the translator of Psalms 1–50, which are in prose, or of Psalms 51–150, which are in alliterative verse. The translator of the metrical version shows little knowledge of, or interest in, the traditional Anglo-Saxon poetry. Dobbie (ASPR V) notes that 'the poetical word *metod*, so common in older poetry as one of the designations of the Deity occurs so rarely, perhaps only once, in the metrical parts of the Paris Psalter'. ('Once' seems to be right; see Psalm 127: 5.) Alistair Campbell characterized the translator as a 'crude worker'.

The psalm translated here is the *Jubilate Deo*, according to modern reckoning and in Longfellow's words, 'the Hundredth Psalm, that grand old Puritan anthem'. It is the basis of the sixteenth-century metrical psalm 'All people that on earth do dwell'. In the Latin and Old English versions, it is Psalm 99.

Text 47 **Psalm 100**

1 Nū gē mycle gefēan   mihtigum drihtne
eall þēos eorðe   elne hȳre
and blisse gode   bealde þēowie.

2 Gangað on ansȳne   ealle blīðe·
wītað wīslice   þæt hē is wealdend god·
hē ūs geworhte   and wē his syndon.

3 Wē his folc syndan   and his fæle scēap
ðā hē on his edisce   ealle āfēdde·
gāð nū on his doru·   god andettað
and hine weorðiað   on wīctūnum
mid lofsangum   lustum myclum.

4 Heriað naman drihtnes   forþon hē is niðum swǣs·
is þīn milde mōd   ofer manna bearn.

v. 1 ll. 1–3 The Latin has *Jubilate Deo, omnis terra; servite Domino in laetitia*. In the OE version, *gē... eall þēos eorðe* are the subjects of the subj. verbs *hȳre* and *þēowie*, both of which govern the dative case. Because of the demands of the verse form, the eight Latin words are expanded to sixteen by means of alliterating adjectives and adverbs.
    l. 3 **blisse** may be gen. sg. with *gode* 'the god of grace' or dat. sg. 'with happiness/joy'.
v. 2 l. 1 **Gangað** is the first of a series of imperatives; **ealle blīðe** nom. pl.
v. 3 l. 2 **ðā** acc. pl. 'whom' and **ealle** go together.
    l. 5 The whole line represents Latin *in hymnis*; **lustum myclum** dat. pl. 'with great joy'.
v. 4 l. 2 The change of person with reference to God – *hē* 'he' (l. 1) but *þīn* 'thy' here – is not in the Latin.

On the Paris Psalter see initially ASPR V.

§489 *Text 12* **Judith's warriors bring home the plunder**

Lines 323b–41a of *Judith*, printed in §238, tell how Judith's warriors brought the plunder home to Bethulia after the defeat of the Assyrian army under Holofernes. For the poem as a whole, see *Judith* edited by B. J. Timmer (London: Methuen, 1951).

§490 Texts 48–51 are all concerned with the Cross. The Parker MS of the Anglo-Saxon Chronicle records the death in 885 of Pope Marinus who sent to King Alfred *þære rode dæl þe Crist on þrowude* 'part of the Cross on which Christ suffered'. Two feast days were associated with it – *Inventio Crucis* 'The Finding of the Cross' (3 May) and *Exaltatio Crucis* 'The Exaltation of the Cross' or Holy Cross Day (14 September).

Text 48 is an extract from the poem *Elene*, one of six poems in the Vercelli Manuscript (ASPR II), which also includes *Andreas* and *The Dream of the Rood* (§493). *Elene* is one of the four poems which contains the poet Cynewulf's signature in runes; see §176. That it was composed by Cynewulf is universally agreed. However, little is known about Cynewulf beyond the fact that, according to Gradon (see below), 'the evidence . . . plainly suggests that Cynewulf was a West Mercian poet writing in the first half of the ninth century'. His source for *Elene* was an unidentified version of the common Latin legend concerning the *Inventio Crucis*. Evelyn Waugh retold the story in *Helena* (London: Chapman and Hall, 1950; reprinted Penguin, 1963).

The poem opens with the vision of the Emperor Constantine (AD 274–337), in which he saw the Cross and received the message *In hoc signo vinces* 'In this sign you will conquer', and goes on to tell of his victory over the Huns, his baptism, and his order to his mother Elene to find the True Cross. Elene sought help from the wise men of the Jews, among whom was Judas (*hē* l. 804 below) but they were not willing to cooperate. However, after Elene had imprisoned him in a pit for seven days without food, Judas changed his mind and prayed that God would reveal the burial place of the three crosses by allowing smoke to come out of the ground. Text 48 tells how the crosses were found and how the True Cross was identified. The remainder of the poem tells us that the rejoicing Emperor built a church to house the True Cross, that Judas was baptized and became a bishop, and that Elene found the nails which had pierced Christ's hands and feet. It ends with the institution of the Feast of the Invention and with a homiletic passage containing the runic signature.

Those who wish to do so can now compare the *Beowulf* passages in §§463–8 with this extract and judge for themselves whether or not they agree with the views I expressed at the end of §450.

Text 48 The finding of the Cross

Ðā of ðǣre stōwe   stēam up ārās
swylce rēc under radorum.   þǣr ārǣred wearð
beornes brēostsefa.   Hē mid bǣm handum,
805 ēadig ond ǣglēaw,   upweard plegade.
Iūdas maþelode,   glēaw in geþance:
'Nū ic þurh sōð hafu   seolf gecnawen
on heardum hige   þæt ðū hǣlend eart
middangeardes·   sīe ðē, mægena god,
810 þrymsittendum   þanc būtan ende
þæs ðū mē swā mēðum   ond swā mānweorcum
þurh þīn wuldor inwrīge   wyrda gerȳno.
Nū ic þē, bearn godes,   biddan wille,
weoroda willgifa·   nū ic wāt þæt ðu eart
815 gecȳðed ond acenned   allra cyninga þrym·
þæt ðū mā ne sīe   mīnra gylta
þāra þe ic gefremede   nalles fēam sīðum,
metud, gemyndig.   Lǣt mec, mihta god,
on rīmtale   rīces þīnes
820 mid hāligra   hlyte wunigan
in þǣre beorhtan byrig   þǣr is brōðor mīn
geweorðod in wuldre   þæs hē wǣre wið þec,
Stēphanus, hēold   þēah he stāngreopum
worpod wǣre.   He hafað wīgges lēan,
825 blǣd būtan blinne.   Sint in bōcum his
wundor þā he worhte   on gewrītum cȳðed.'
Ongan þā wilfægen   æfter þām wuldres trēo,

803 **swylce** conj. 'like'.
804 **Hē** = Judas l. 806.
804–5 **mid bǣm handum . . . upweard plegade** 'applauded with both hands'.
807 **Nū** adv. 'Now' or conj. 'Now that'. So also *nū* l. 814.
809 **sīe** 3rd pers. pres. subj. expressing a wish. So also *sīe* l. 816 and *Sīe* l. 892.
810 **þrymsittendum** dat. sg. with *ðē*.
811 **þæs** conj. 'because'. So also *þæs* l. 822.
812 **wyrda gerȳno** 'the mysteries of wyrds', here meaning God's Providence; see §§414–17.
813 **Nū** adv. 'Now'.
814 **willgifa** nom. sg. parallel with *bearn* l. 813; **nū** see l. 807 note.
816 The **þæt** clause is the object of *biddan* l. 813; **sīe** see l. 809 note; the word *gemyndig* l. 818 belongs after *sīe* and governs the genitives in l. 816b.
817 **þāra þe** 'those which'.
822 **þæs** see l. 811 note; **wǣre** acc. sg. < *wǣr* 'covenant'.
823 **Stēphanus** St Stephen the first martyr (Acts 7: 57–60) could not have been the brother of a Judas who lived in the reign of Constantine. This statement is the result of confusion in the sources.
826 **wundor** nom. pl. subject of *Sint* l. 825; **þā** acc. pl. 'which'.
827 **Ongan** The subject is Judas, described as *wilfægen*.

     elnes ānhȳdig,   eorðan delfan
     under turfhagan   þæt hē on XX
830 fōtmǣlum feor   funde behelede,
     under nēolum niðer   næsse gehȳdde
     in þēostorcofan.   Hē ðǣr III mētte
     in þām rēonian hofe   rōda ætsomne,
     grēote begrauene,   swā hīo gēardagum
835 ārlēasra sceolu   eorðan beþeahton,
     Iūdēa cynn.   Hīe wið godes bearne
     nīð āhofun   swā hīe nō sceoldon
     þǣr hīe leahtra fruman   lārum ne hȳrdon.
     þā wæs mōdgemynd   myclum geblissod,
840 hige onhyrded,   þurh þæt hālige trēo,
     inbryrded brēostsefa,   syððan bēacen geseh,
     hālig under hrusan.   Hē mid handum befēng
     wuldres wynbēam   ond mid weorode āhōf
     of foldgræfe.   Fēðegestas
845 ēodon, æðelingas,   in on þā ceastre.
        Āsetton þā on gesyhðe   sīgebēamas III
     eorlas ānhȳdige   fore Elenan cnēo,
     collenferhðe.   Cwēn weorces gefeah
     on ferhðsefan   ond þā frignan ongan
850 on hwylcum þāra bēama   bearn wealdendes,
     hæleða hyhtgifa,   hangen wǣre:
     'Hwæt, wē þæt hȳrdon   þurh hālige bēc
     tācnum cȳðan   þæt twēgen mid him
     geþrowedon   ond hē wæs þridda sylf
855 on rōde trēo.   Rodor eal geswearc
     on þā slīðan tīd.   Saga· gif ðū cunne·
     on hwylcre þyssa þrēora   þēoden engla
     geþrowode,   þrymmes hyrde.'
        Ne meahte hire Iūdas·   ne ful gere wiste·

829 **þæt** conj. 'so that/with the result that', shading into 'until'.
829–30 **on XX fōtmǣlum feor** 'at a depth of twenty feet'.
832–3 **III . . . rōda** 'three crosses'.
834 **swā** conj. 'as'. So also *swā* l. 837.
836b–7a Cf. *Hīe wið god wunnon!* (Text 46 l. 515) and see §485.
837 **swā** see l. 834 note; **nō sceoldon** 'should not [have done]'.
838 **þǣr** conj. 'if' introducing a rejected condition in which the implication is 'but they did'.
848 **weorces** gen. sg. object of *gefeah*.
850 **on hwylcum** interrog. pron. 'on which', introducing a dependent question. Cf. l. 857.
851 **wǣre** pret. subj. implying that she did not know.
852 **þæt** anticipates the *þæt* clause in l. 853.
856b Formulae like this are common in the riddles of the Exeter Book.
857 **on hwylcre** see l. 850 note. The verb *geþrowode*, ambiguous in form, is in effect subjunctive.

860   sweotole gecȳþan   be ðām sigebēame·
     on hwylcne se hǣlend   āhafen wǣre,
     sigebearn godes,   ǣr hē āsettan hēht
     on þone middel   þǣre mǣran byrig
     bēamas mid bearhtme   ond gebīdan þǣr
865   oððæt him gecȳðde   cyning ælmihtig
     wundor for weorodum   be ðām wuldres trēo.
     Gesǣton sigerōfe·   sang āhōfon,
     rǣdþeahtende   ymb þā rōda þrēo
     oð þā nigoðan tīd·   hæfdon nēowne gefēan
870   mǣrðum gemēted.   þā þǣr menigo cwōm,
     folc unlytel,   ond gefǣrenne man
     brōhton on bǣre   beorna þrēate
     on nēaweste   – wæs þā nigoðe tīd –
     gingne gāstlēasne.   þā ðǣr Iūdas wæs
875   on mōdsefan   miclum geblissod.
     Hēht þā āsettan   sāwllēasne,
     līfe belidenes   līc on eorðan,
     unlifgendes,   ond up āhōf
     rihtes wēmend   þāra rōda twā
880   fyrhðglēaw on fæðme   ofer þæt fǣge hūs,
     dēophycgende.   Hit wæs dēad swā ǣr,
     līc legere fæst.   Leomu colodon
     þrēanēdum beþeaht.   þā sīo þridde wæs
     āhafen hālig.   Hrā wæs on anbide
885   oððæt him uppan   æðelinges wæs
     rōd ārǣred,   rodorcyninges bēam,
     sigebēacen sōð.   Hē sōna ārās
     gāste gegearwod,   geador bū samod
     līc ond sāwl.   þǣr wæs lof hafen
890   fæger mid þȳ folce.   Fæder weorðodon
     ond þone sōðan   sunu wealdendes

860 **gecȳþan** has two objects, l. 860b and the clause in l. 861.

861 **on hwylcne** interrog. pron. as in ll. 850 and 857. But this is the sort of context in which 'which' became a rel. pron.

862 **āsettan hēht** see §122.

870 **þā þǣr** advs. 'Then there'.

871 **gefǣrenne man** remember *-ne* (§§40–1).

872 **brōhton** 3rd pl. pret. ind. The change from singular *cwōm* (l. 870) to plural is common after collective nouns like *menigo* (l. 870) and *folc* (l. 871).

876a See l. 862 note.

877a 'of [the man] deprived of life'.

879 **wēmend** 'revealer' nom. sg.

880 **hūs** Cf. the compounds *feorh-*, *gāst-*, and *sāwel-*, *hūs* and see 1 Corinthians 6: 19.

884b The body was waiting in expectation of the return of the soul. See ll. 888–9b.

885 **æðelinges** gen. sg. 'of the prince', i.e. Christ.

> wordum heredon.   Sīe him wuldor ond þanc
> ā būtan ende   eallra gesceafta!

892 **Sīe** see l. 809 note.

The most accessible edition is *Cynewulf's 'Elene'* edited by P. O. E. Gradon (London: Methuen, 1958).

§491   The riddlers of the Exeter Book had two ways of posing their riddle – the *Ic seah* 'I saw' technique and the *Ic eom* 'I am' technique. These are exemplified in §§491 and 492. Both are used in *The Dream of the Rood* (§493).

Some of the details are obscure; see ll. 12b–14a note. But the solution of *Riddle 55* is clearly some form of cross. Early Christians believed that the Cross was made of four woods, though (naturally) these were differently identified in different areas. The *wulfhēafedtrēo* 'wolfshead tree, gallows, cross' (l. 12), once destined for the execution of outlaws, is now adorned with gold, silver, and jewels. This paradox is more fully developed in *The Dream of the Rood*.

Text 49   **Riddle 55**

> Ic seah in healle   þǣr hæleð druncon
> on flet beran   fēower cynna
> wrǣtlic wudutrēow   ond wunden gold,
> sinc searobunden,   ond seolfres dǣl
> 5 ond rōde tācn   þæs ūs tō roderum ūp
> hlǣdre rǣrde   ǣr hē helwara
> burg ābrǣce.   Ic þæs bēames mæg
> ēaþe for eorlum   æþelu secgan:
> þǣr wæs hlin ond āc   ond se hearda īw
> 10 ond se fealwa holen·   frēan sindon ealle
> nyt ætgædre·   naman habbað ānne,
> wulfhēafedtrēo·   þæt oft wǣpen ābæd

2a See §122.

2b–3a **fēower cynna** gen. pl. Translate 'a wondrous forest tree of four kinds [of wood]'.

5 **þæs [þe]** 'of that one who'; **ūs** dat. 'for us'.

6b–7a This refers to the Harrowing of Hell.

7 **ābrǣce** 3rd sg. pret. subj. < *ābrecan* 'to storm/plunder'. The subj. is very common after the conj. *ǣr* 'before' and does not imply that the event described did not take place.

10 **frēan** dat. sg. 'to the lord' (the owner of the sword) and 'to the Lord' (Christ).

11 **nyt** nom. pl. 'useful'.

12 The word *wulfeshēafod* is a legal term for an outlaw, who may be killed like a wolf without penalty; **þæt** dem. nom. sg. 'that [thing]/it'; **ābæd** 3rd sg. pret. ind. < *ābiddan* (st. vb. V §519) 'to receive'. See the Glossary.

12b–14a Translate: 'That [object] has often received a weapon from its lord, a treasure in the hall, a gold-hilted sword.' Scholars have not agreed about the nature of the object which the riddler had in mind. It was made of wood and precious metals, could hold a sword, and was shaped like a cross. Suggestions include a box with a hinged lid which could be raised up and then secured; a cruciform weapon-holder; on a reliquary containing a splinter of Christ's Cross.

his mondryhtne,   māðm in healle,
goldhilted sweord.   Nū mē þisses gieddes
15 ondsware ȳwe   se hine on mēde
wordum secgan   hū se wudu hātte.

15b Translate 'he who takes it upon himself' or 'he who presumes'.

For the standard edition of the Exeter Book Riddles, see §486.

§492   *Riddle* 30 is the only riddle in the Exeter Book of which two texts survive. They are essentially the same. *Riddle* 30a appears in its proper sequence whereas *Riddle* 30b is misplaced and defective in two places because of a burn in the manuscript. Blackburn's solution that the answer is the OE word *bēam* in its various senses is generally accepted. The meaning 'tree' suits ll. 1b–2 and 3b–4a. The word could also mean 'ship' (l. 3a), 'log' (ll. 1a and 4b), and 'cup' (ll. 5–6). In ll. 7–9 the riddle anticipates *The Dream of the Rood* in so far as it shows the Cross speaking in the first person.

Text 50   **Riddle 30a**

Ic eom lēgbysig·   lāce mid winde,
bewunden mid wuldre,   wedre gesomnad·
fūs forðweges·   fȳre gebysgad·
bearu blōwende·   byrnende glēd.
5 Ful oft mec gesīþas   sendað æfter hondum
þæt mec weras ond wīf   wlonce cyssað.
þonne ic mec onhæbbe·   hī onhnīgaþ tō mē
monige mid miltse·   þær ic monnum sceal
ȳcan ūpcyme   ēadignesse.

2a Probably a reference to the leaves and/or flowers.
3a *Lit.* 'ready for death', which the log experiences when burnt.
5 **æfter hondum** 'from hand to hand'.
8 **monnum** 'for men/among men'. See Text 26 ll. 1–2 note.

For the standard edition of the Exeter Book Riddles, see §486.

§493   *The Dream of the Rood* will bear comparison with any religious poem of comparable length in the English language. I could write a book in praise of it. Here, unfortunately, I can print only about one third of the text and must limit myself to brief mention of the features which make it so powerful and remarkable.

The poem takes the form of a monologue within a monologue – a dreamer tells of a vision in which he hears Christ's Cross speak. (The alternative title *A Vision of the Cross* is to be preferred, for the Cross does not dream.) In §§252 and 255 I said that the Ruthwell Cross contains some passages in runes which go back to the same original as, or were used by the author of, *The Dream of the Rood* and quoted ll. 44b and 48b with their runic equivalents. Lines 56b–8a (not in Text 51) provide another example:

Krist wæs on rodi	Crīst wæs on rōde.
hweþræ þer fusæ fearran kwomu	Hwæðere þǣr fūse feorran cwōman
æþþilæ til anum	tō þām æðelinge.

The first three half-lines mean 'Christ was on rood. However there eager [ones] from afar came ...'. The last half-lines mean respectively 'noble [ones] together' or 'noble [ones] to the solitary [one]' and 'to the prince'. The climactic sentence *Crīst wæs on rōde* sums up in four words the essence of the Christian faith. The two-line, first person, inscription on the Brussels Cross (§255) is another succinctly powerful expression of it.

I now attempt a schematic statement of the contents, sentence structure, and heroic elements, of *The Dream of the Rood*.

The dreamer ll. 1–27

The dreamer, stained with sins, gazes upon the Cross, high in the sky, now covered with blood, now adorned with gold and jewels. He uses a narrative style with longish sentences and six subordinate clauses. The idea of Christ as the lord of angels, men, and the whole world, is expressed in ll. 11–12.

The Cross ll. 28–77

The Cross confesses its part in the Crucifixion, tells of Christ's death and burial, of the burying of the three crosses, and of the finding of *mē* 'me', i.e. the True Cross (Text 48 §490). The style is strongly paratactic, with some stressed alliterating verbs and some powerful half-line sentences. Lines 35–56 – the actual Crucifixion – contain two clauses which must be subordinate (ll. 42 and 49) and two which could be (ll. 36 and 41). We see Christ as the warrior king of heroic literature and of the mosaic in the Archiepiscopal Chapel at Ravenna, which depicts Him as a Roman soldier in armour and cloak with a cross slung weapon-like over His shoulder. His retainers are the Cross – the *bana* 'slayer' of his lord, most loyal in that most disloyal of acts – all creation, the dreamer, and Christian readers (Romans 6: 3–8 and Hebrews 6: 6). The imagery associated with defeat in battle and the death of a leader and with exile and loneliness is also present.

The Cross ll. 78–121

The Cross reveals the meaning of the Crucifixion and assures the dreamer that the Cross (*ic* 'I') has opened the way to Heaven for all believers. The style is homiletic, with more complex sentences and no heroic imagery.

The dreamer ll. 122–56

The now happy (*blīðe*) dreamer prostrates himself before the Cross and looks forward to Heaven in the company of the *wuldres Cyning* 'King of Glory', whose triumphs he describes. The style is similar to that in ll. 1–27. The themes of exile and loneliness and of the warrior king returning home triumphant from battle are exploited.

This carefully constructed poem contains familiar elements – the dream (Text 20 §427 and Text 48 §490); the rhetorical device of *purgatio* 'self-exculpation', here on the grounds of necessity; the *Ic eom* technique (Text 50 §492, the Brussels Cross §255, and the first-person Latin riddle about Christ's Cross by Tatwine, who became Archbishop of Canterbury in 731) and the *Ic seah* technique (Text 49 §491); and the riddling element associated with these two techniques.

Some Christian elements have already been mentioned: the Invention and the Veneration of the Cross; the two manifestations of the Cross; and Christ the warrior king of the Ravenna mosaic. This last idea is also present in the *Pange lingua* 'Sing [my] tongue . . .' and *Vexilla regis* 'The king's banners' of Venantius Fortunatus (*c.* 535–*c.* 600), an Italian educated at Ravenna. Other liturgical and patristic elements can be detected. Some indeed have seen a virgin cross to parallel the virgin womb and the virgin tomb.

However, as I see it, it is the poet's vision – a vision strongly akin to that of Salvador Dali in his painting 'Christ of St John of the Cross' – and not theological considerations such as the avoidance of heresy which controls the poem. He saw the Cross in position l. 33 *gefæstnodon*, l. 38 *ic fæste stod*, l. 43 *ac ic sceolde fæste standan*. So Christ had to move, *crucem ascendere*, *gestīgan* (l. 34), 'ascend the cross'. Hence the contrast between the heroic active warrior and the suffering passive Cross. But Christ's suffering is there (ll. 48–9 and elsewhere). The figure on the Cross died (l. 49 and elsewhere). He was a man (ll. 42 and 49), a warrior king (ll. 39a, 44b, and elsewhere), and God (ll. 33, 35, 39, 51, 53, 56 – the first use of the word *Crīst* – and elsewhere). Christ, here portrayed as a volunteer (ll. 34 and 41 *wolde* 'wished'), had passed through His Gethsemane: Matthew 26: 39 'nevertheless not as I will, but as thou wilt'. The Crucifixion is the Cross's Gethsemane: ll. 37b–8a *Ealle ic mihte* ‖ *fēondas gefyllan* 'I could have felled all the foes' but l. 43b *ic sceolde fæste standan* 'I had to stand fast' and ll. 35a, 42b, 45b, 47b *ne dorste ic hira ænigum sceððan* 'I dared not harm any of them'. Both Christ and the Cross can be seen as conscripted volunteers.

Other qualities deserving comment include the dramatic vividness of the first-person confession, with the third person used twice to avoid bathos (ll. 40a and 56b *Crīst wæs on rōde*); the use of contrast seen for example in ll. 13–23 and more generally in the two manifestations of Christ, the Cross, and the dreamer; and the effective use of repetition. The words *ac* 'but' (ll. 11, 43, and elsewhere) and *hwæþre* 'however/yet' (ll. 18, 24, 38, 42, and elsewhere) reinforce the sense of paradox throughout; this is present too in the repeated *wolde* and *ne dorste* already noted. Examples of repetition abound but one more must suffice – the identification of Christ, the Cross, and the dreamer, is underlined by the fact that they all perform their tasks of duty and love *elne micle* 'with great zeal' (ll. 34a, 60a, and 123a). Here I must leave *The Dream of the Rood*, with the hope that you will come to understand the reason for my claim that in it 'Christianity and the Germanic heroic code meet and are miraculously fused'.

Text 51   **The Dream of the Rood (extracts)**

Hwæt! ic swefna cyst   secgan wylle
hwæt mē gemǣtte   tō midre nihte
syðþan reordberend   reste wunedon.
þūhte mē þæt ic gesāwe   syllicre trēow
5   on lyft lǣdan   lēohte bewunden,
bēama beorhtost.   Eall þæt bēacen wæs
begoten mid golde·   gimmas stōdon
fægere æt foldan scēatum·   swylce þǣr fīfe wǣron
uppe on þām eaxlgespanne.   Behēoldon þǣr engel Dryhtnes ealle
10 fægere þurh forðgesceaft·   ne wæs ðǣr hūru fracodes gealga
ac hine þǣr behēoldon   hālige gāstas,
men ofer moldan   and eall þēos mǣre gesceaft.
Syllic wæs se sigebēam   and ic synnum fāh,
forwundod mid wommum.   Geseah ic wuldres trēow
15 wǣdum geweorðod   wynnum scīnan,
gegyred mid golde·   gimmas hæfdon
bewrigen weorðlīce   Wealdendes trēow.
Hwæðre ic þurh þæt gold   ongytan meahte
earmra ǣrgewin   þæt hit ǣrest ongan
20 swǣtan on þā swīðran healfe.   Eall ic wæs mid sorgum gedrēfed·
forht ic wæs for þǣre fǣgran gesyhðe·   geseah ic þæt fūse bēacen
wendan wǣdum and blēom: hwīlum hit wæs mid wǣtan bestēmed

---

1 **secgan wylle** has two objects, *swefna cyst* and the *hwæt* clause in l. 2.

2 **mē gemǣtte** impersonal construction 'came to me in a dream'. Cf. *þūhte mē* l. 4.

4 **syllicre** acc. sg. neut. comp. of *syllic* 'rare': 'a rarer tree [than all the others]'.

5a See §122.

8–10 Here, and in ll. 20–3, 30–4, and 39–49, the poet uses expanded or hypermetric lines, which have three rather than two accented syllables in each half-line. We do not know exactly what effect such lines had for an Anglo-Saxon audience.

8 **æt foldan scēatum** 'at the surface of the earth' (i.e. at the foot of the Cross) or 'at the corners of the earth' (i.e. the Cross extended to four points on the horizon); **swylce** conj. 'also'.

9 **engel Dryhtnes** acc. sg. + gen. sg. '[the] angel/messenger of the Lord'. This could refer to the Cross or to Christ; **ealle** 'all' goes with ll. 10a and 11b, referring to the loyal angels in Heaven.

11 **hine** acc. sg. masc. referring to *gealga* 'gallows/Cross' or (I believe, less likely) to Christ if He has already been introduced in l. 9.

15 **wǣdum** 'with garments'. In ll. 15–23 we see the Cross in two garbs – covered with blood and covered with gold and jewels. We may compare the blood-red Cross formerly carried in Good Friday processions with the jewelled Cross of Easter Sunday.

19a 'ancient hostility of wretched ones', i.e. of those who crucified Christ. This half-line is the first object of *ongytan* 'to perceive'. The second is the *þæt* clause in ll. 19b–20a.

20 **on þā swīðran healfe** 'on the right side'. Tradition had it that the spear of John 19: 34 pierced Christ's right side.

beswyled mid swātes gange,   hwīlum mid since gegyrwed.
    Hwæðre ic þær licgende   lange hwīle
25 behēold hrēowcearig   Hǣlendes trēow
    oð ðæt ic gehȳrde   þæt hit hlēoðrode·
    ongan þā word sprecan   wudu sēlesta:
        'þæt wæs gēara iū   – ic þæt gȳta geman –
    þæt ic wæs āhēawen   holtes on ende,
30 āstyred of stefne mīnum.   Genāman mē ðǣr strange fēondas·
    geworhton him þǣr tō wæfersȳne·   hēton mē heora wergas hebban·
    bǣron mē þǣr beornas on eaxlum   oð ðæt hīe mē on beorg āsetton·
    gefæstnodon mē þǣr fēondas genōge.   Geseah ic þā Frēan
    mancynnes
    efstan elne micle   þæt hē mē wolde on gestīgan.
35   þǣr ic þā ne dorste   ofer Dryhtnes word
    būgan oððe berstan·   þā ic bifian geseah
    eorðan scēatas.   Ealle ic mihte
    fēondas gefyllan·   hwæðre ic fæste stōd.
    Ongyrede hine þā geong hæleð   – þæt wæs God ælmihtig! –
40 strang and stīðmōd·   gestāh hē on gealgan hēanne
    mōdig on manigra gesyhðe·   þā hē wolde mancyn lȳsan.
    Bifode ic þā mē se beorn ymbclypte·   ne dorste ic hwæðre būgan tō
    eorðan,
    feallan tō foldan scēatum   ac ic sceolde fæste standan.
    Rōd wæs ic ārǣred·   āhōf ic rīcne cyning,
45 heofona Hlāford·   hyldan mē ne dorste.
    þurhdrifan hī mē mid deorcan næglum·   on mē syndon þā dolg
    gesīene,
    opene inwidhlemmas·   ne dorste ic hira ǣnigum sceððan.
    Bysmeredon hīe unc būtū ætgædere·   eall ic wæs mid blōde
    bestēmed,
    begoten of þæs guman sīdan   siððan hē hæfde his gāst onsended.

27 **þā word** acc. neut. pl. (§55) 'the[se] words'.
28 The first **þæt** anticipates the second and also the *þæt* clause in ll. 29–30a.
30b Here, as in l. 33a, the subject is at the end of the clause.
31a Translate 'they made [me] as a spectacle for themselves there'. This is a reference to public executions as a form of entertainment.
33a See l. 30b note.
34 **þæt** conj. 'so that' shading into 'because'. I translate 'in His wish to climb onto me'.
36 **bifian** 'to tremble'. See Matthew 27: 51.
37b–8a **ic mihte ... gefyllan** 'I could have felled'.
39 **þā** adv. 'then'.
40 **hēanne** The heading to §105 reads 'A poet's deliberate ambiguity?' It may also be appropriate here, since *hēanne* can be the acc. sg. masc. of *hēah* 'high' or of *hēan* 'dejected/wretched'.
48 **unc būtū** 1st pers. dual acc. 'us two both', i.e. the Cross and Christ.
49 **begoten** 'covered with/drenched with' qualifies *ic* l. 48, in apposition with *bestēmed* l. 48.

  . . .   . . .

  . . .   Hiht wæs genīwad

mid blēdum and mid blisse   þām þe þær bryne þolodan.

150 Se Sunu wæs sigorfæst   on þām sīðfate,

    mihtig and spēdig,   þā hē mid manigeo cōm,

    gāsta weorode,   on Godes rīce,

    Anwealda ælmihtig,   englum tō blisse

    and eallum ðām hālgum   þām þe in heofonum ær

155 wunedon on wuldre   þā heora Wealdend cwōm,

    ælmihtig God,   þær his ēðel wæs.

148b–9 A reference to the Harrowing of Hell. Cf. Text 49 ll. 6b–7a.

149 **þām þe** 'for those who'. So also in l. 154.

150–6 These lines refer to Christ's Ascension into Heaven forty days after Easter Day with the souls He had rescued from Hell.

152 **weorode** dat. sg. in apposition with *manigeo* l. 151.

153b 'to [the] delight of [the] angels', *lit.* 'as delight to angels'.

154 **þām þe** see note on l. 149.

The Dream of the Rood is edited in full in *A Guide to Old English*. I recommend these two verse translations: by Helen Gardner in *Essays and Poems presented to Lord David Cecil* edited by W. W. Robson (London: Constable, 1970) and by Kevin Crossley-Holland in *The Anglo-Saxon World: Writings* (Woodbridge: The Boydell Press, 1982).

V

Some Paradigms – For Those Who Would Like Them

These are intended for reference.

A PRONOUNS

§494 First and second person pronouns

	Singular	Dual	Plural
Nom.	iċ 'I'	wit 'we two'	wē 'we'
Acc.	mē, meċ	unc	ūs
Gen.	mīn	uncer	ūre
Dat.	mē	unc	ūs

	Singular	Dual	Plural
Nom.	þū 'thou'	ġit 'you two'	ġē 'ye, you'
Acc.	þē, þeċ	inc	ēow
Gen.	þīn	incer	ēower
Dat.	þē	inc	ēow

§495 The third person pronoun

	Singular			Plural
	Masc.	Neut.	Fem.	All genders
Nom.	hē 'he'	hit 'it'	hēo, hīo 'she'	hīe, hī 'they'
Acc.	hine	hit	hīe, hī	hīe, hī
Gen.	his	his	hire	hira, hiera, heora, hiora
Dat.	him	him	hire	him, heom

§496   *se* 'the, that'

	Singular			Plural
	Masc.	*Neut.*	*Fem.*	*All genders*
Nom.	se	þæt	sēo, sīo	þā
Acc.	þone	þæt	þā	þā
Gen.	þæs	þæs	þære	þāra, þǣra
Dat.	þǣm, þām	þǣm, þām	þære	þǣm, þām
Inst.	þȳ, þon	þȳ, þon		

§497   *þes* 'this'

	Singular			Plural
	Masc.	*Neut.*	*Fem.*	*All genders*
Nom.	þes	þis	þēos	þās
Acc.	þisne	þis	þās	þās
Gen.	þisses	þisses	þisse, þisre	þissa, þisra
Dat.	þissum	þissum	þisse, þisre	þissum
Inst.	þȳs	þȳs		

§498   *Se* serves as demonstrative 'that' and definite article 'the'. Both *se* 'that' and *þes* 'this' can be used with nouns, e.g. *se mann* 'the man', or as pronouns, e.g. *hē sorgaþ ymb þā* 'he sorrows/is concerned about those/them'. *Se* is also used as a relative pronoun 'who'; see §65.

§499   *hwā* 'who?', 'anyone, someone'

	Masc. and Fem.	Neut.
Nom.	hwā	hwæt
Acc.	hwone	hwæt
Gen.	hwæs	hwæs
Dat.	hwǣm, hwām	hwǣm, hwām
Inst.	hwȳ	hwȳ, hwon

This word is not used as a relative pronoun; see §65.

B NOUNS

§500   I give here only the most common paradigms. Grammarians call *nama* a weak noun in contrast to the five other nouns whose paradigms I give in §§502–4, which are called strong. You will notice that the endings in *nama* give rather weak evidence of sentence function. This is particularly true in later texts, where *naman* can stand for any case except the nominative singular.

§501   *nama* (masc.) 'name'

	Singular	Plural
Nom.	nama	naman
Acc.	naman	naman
Gen.	naman	namena
Dat.	naman	namum

The weak fem. nouns have -*e* in the nom. sg., e.g. *sunne* 'sun'. Like all neut. nouns, the weak neut. *ēage* 'eye' has nom. and acc. sg. the same. Otherwise, these nouns follow *nama*.

§502   *stān* (masc.) 'stone'

	Singular	Plural
Nom.	stān	stānas
Acc.	stān	stānas
Gen.	stānes	stāna
Dat.	stāne	stānum

§503   *scip* (neut.) 'ship' and *word* (neut.) 'word'

	Singular	Plural	Singular	Plural
Nom.	scip	scipu	word	word
Acc.	scip	scipu	word	word
Gen.	scipes	scipa	wordes	worda
Dat.	scipe	scipum	worde	wordum

§504   *ġiefu* (fem.) 'gift' and *lār* (fem.) 'teaching'

	Singular	Plural	Singular	Plural
Nom.	ġiefu	ġiefa, -e	lār	lāra, -e
Acc.	ġiefe	ġiefa, -e	lāre	lāra, -e
Gen.	ġiefe	ġiefa, -ena	lāre	lāra, -ena
Dat.	ġiefe	ġiefum	lāre	lārum

C   ADJECTIVES

§505   The terms 'weak' and 'strong' (§500) are also applied to adjectives. Which form of the adjective is used depends, not on the type of noun with which it is used, but on how it is used. The strong form is used when the adjective stands alone, e.g. 'The man is old' *se mann is eald*, or just with a noun, e.g. 'old men' *ealde menn*. The weak form appears when the adjective follows a demonstrative, e.g. 'that old man' *se ealda mann*, or a possessive adjective, e.g. 'my old friend' *mīn ealda frēond*. You can remember that the strong forms stand alone, while the weak forms need the support of a demonstrative or possessive pronoun. But this 'rule' is often broken in the poetry. The adjective *til* 'good' is declined below.

§506 Weak declension

	Singular			Plural
	Masc.	*Neut.*	*Fem.*	*All genders*
Nom.	tila	tile	tile	tilan
Acc.	tilan	tile	tilan	tilan
Gen.	tilan	tilan	tilan	tilra, -ena
Dat.	tilan	tilan	tilan	tilum

Compare the endings of the weak noun *nama* (§501). The remarks made there about the ending *-an* are equally applicable here.

§507 Strong declension

	Singular		
	Masc.	*Neut.*	*Fem.*
Nom.	til	til	tilu
Acc.	til*ne*	til	tile
Gen.	tiles	tiles	til*re*
Dat.	til*um*	til*um*	til*re*
Inst.	tile	tile	

	Plural		
	Masc.	*Neut.*	*Fem.*
Nom.	tile	tilu	tile, -a
Acc.	tile	tilu	tile, -a
Gen.	til*ra*	til*ra*	til*ra*
Dat.	tilum	tilum	tilum

You have already met the italicized endings! (See §497.)

§508 Comparison
The OE equivalents of

blind, blinder, blindest

are

blind, blindra (declined weak: §506), and
blindost (declined strong: §507).

Some adjectives with the endings *-ra* and *-ost* show *i*-mutation (§§17–18):

eald 'old'	ieldra	ieldest
ġeong 'young'	ġingra	ġingest
lang 'long'	lengra	lengest (so also *strang* 'strong')
hēah 'high'	hīerra	hīehst

Some irregular comparisons survive into MnE:

lȳtel 'little'	lǣssa	lǣst
micel 'great'	māra	mǣst
yfel 'evil'	wiersa	wierst
gōd 'good'	betera,	betst,
	sēlra	sēlost

D VERBS

§509 Like Modern English, Old English has two types of verbs – weak and strong. The weak verb forms its past tense and past participle by adding a dental suffix [*t*] or [*d*], the strong verb by changing its stem vowel; see §74 and compare 'laugh, laughed' and 'judge, judged' with 'sing, sang, sung'. Modern English strong verbs are nearly all survivals from Old English, like 'drive, drove, driven', or early borrowings from other Germanic languages, like 'take, took, taken'. New verbs borrowed or made up today always join the weak conjugation. Thus we conjugate the comparatively new verb 'jive' as a weak verb 'jive, jived, jived'. But when in the thirteenth century 'strive' was borrowed from the French, it followed the pattern of 'drive' because the two infinitives rhymed; hence we get 'strive, strove, striven'. Perhaps we should regret that we can't say 'We jove the whole night through' or 'They have jiven for two hours'. Perhaps not!

§510 Such patterns as 'drive, drove, driven' and 'jive, jived' are called the 'principal parts' of the verbs. I give below a list of the principal parts of the Old English verbs. Reference to this may help you to recognize some verbs which may at first seem unfamiliar. Thus, if you find *drāf* or *boren*, you may spot that *drāf* is 'drove' and *boren* is 'born' or 'borne'. If you do not, the table in §517 will direct you to the infinitives *drīfan* and *beran* respectively. I shall be offering you some help with these verbs in case you need it as you read the texts.

§511 Both weak and strong verbs in Old English distinguish

1 two tenses – present and past or preterite;
2 indicative, subjunctive, and imperative moods, in addition to two infinitives – one without *to*, and one (the inflected infinitive) with *to* – and two participles, the present and the past (or second);

3 two numbers – singular and plural;

4 three persons, but only in the singular of the present and past or preterite indicative. All plurals and the singular of the subjunctives are the same throughout;

5 one voice only – the active. One true passive form survives from an earlier stage of the language: *hātte* 'is called, was called' and its plural *hātton*.

§512 I have already set out the main details of the strong verb *singan* in §§75–7. But I give the paradigm here for ease of reference.

		Present Indicative	*Preterite Indicative*
Sg.	1	singe	sang
	2	singest, singst	sunge
	3	singeþ, singþ	sang
Pl.		singaþ	sungon

	Present Subjunctive	*Preterite Subjunctive*
Sg.	singe	sunge
Pl.	singen	sungen

Before a 1st or 2nd pers. pron., the plural endings can be reduced to *-e*, e.g. *wē singaþ* but *singe wē*.

Imp. Sg.	sing	*Pl.*	singaþ
Inf.	singan	*Infl. Inf.*	tō singenne
Pres. Ptc.	singende	*Past Ptc.*	(ġe-)sungen

§513 The same endings are found in the common strong verb *weorþan*. I now give its paradigm, partly because you will save much time if you can recognize its forms and partly so that I can explain something about Old English strong verbs in general. This is that they have four principal parts:

(1) infinitive *weorþan*

All forms of the present tense of the strong verbs – indicative, subjunctive, imperative, infinitives, and present participle – are derived from the infinitive and have its root vowel (here *eo*).

The only exceptions are the 2nd and 3rd pers. pret. ind., which have the *i*-mutated form (§§17–18) of the vowel of the inf. (here *ie*, the equivalent of *eo*).

Most strong verbs keep the same middle (or medial) consonant or consonants throughout. You will need to remember that the remaining two parts of *weorþan*, which occur very frequently, show a change from *þ* to *d*. But the endings are the same for all strong verbs.

(2) first past or preterite *wearþ*

Only two forms of the past or preterite tense of the strong verbs have the vowel of the first preterite (here *ea*). They are the 1st and 3rd pers. pret. ind. (here *iċ wearþ* and *he wearþ*).

(3) second past or preterite *wurdon*

From this are derived all the remaining forms of the pret. ind., and all the forms of the pret. subj., of the strong verbs.

(4) past participle *worden*

The vowel of this form (here *o*) appears only in the past participle.

§514 The verb *weorþan*, as you have seen, has four different vowels in these four principal parts. This is not true of all strong verbs; see §517.

§515 Other common strong verbs which, like *weorþan* (§513), change a medial consonant are:

Class	Inf.		1st Pret.	2nd Pret.	Past Ptc.
II	čēosan 'to choose'		čēas	curon	coren
V	cweþan 'to say'		cwæþ	cwǣdon	cweden

There are four other strong verbs of class II which rhyme with *čēosan* in the infinitive and in the other three parts:

drēosan 'to fall', *frēosan* 'to freeze',
hrēosan 'to fall', *lēosan* 'to lose'.

Hence we find in Milton (*Paradise Lost* II. 594–5)

> the parching Air
> Burns frore, and cold performs th'effect of Fire . . .

and in Keats (*Ode to a Nightingale*)

> Forlorn! the very word is like a bell . . .

Here 'frore' and 'forlorn' are direct descendants of OE *froren* and *forloren*.

§516 The strong verb *weorþan* 'to become' is conjugated thus:

		Present Indicative	*Preterite Indicative*
Sg.	1	weorþe	wearþ
	2	wierþest, wierþst	wurde
	3	wierþeþ, wierþ	wearþ
Pl.		weorþaþ	wurdon

	Present Subjunctive	*Preterite Subjunctive*
Sg.	weorþe	wurde
Pl.	weorþen	wurden

Before *wē/ġē*, *-aþ* and *-en* may appear as *-e*, e.g. *weorþe wē* 'we (may) become'.

Imp. Sg.	weorþ	*Pl.*	weorþaþ
Inf.	weorþan	*Infl. Inf.*	tō weorþenne
Pres. Ptc.	weorþende	*Past Ptc.*	worden

§517 There are seven classes of strong verbs in OE. Verbs characteristic of these are:

Class	Inf.	1st Pret.	2nd Pret.	Past Ptc.
I	drīfan 'to drive'	drāf	drifon	drifen
II	crēopan 'to creep'	crēap	crupon	cropen
	scūfan 'to shove"	scēaf	scufon	scofen
	brūcan 'to enjoy'	brēac	brucon	brocen
III	breġdan 'to pull'	bræġd	brugdon	brogden
IV	beran 'to bear'	bær	bæron	boren
V	tredan 'to tread'	træd	trædon	treden
VI	faran 'to go'	fōr	fōron	faren
VII	(a) healdan 'to hold'	hēold	hēoldon	healden
	(b) hātan 'to command'	hēt	hēton	hāten

§518 Class III displays several sub-classes:

Inf.	1st Pret.	2nd Pret.	Past Ptc.
breġdan 'to pull'	bræġd	brugdon	brogden
weorþan 'to become'	wearþ	wurdon	worden
feohtan 'to fight'	feaht	fuhton	fohten
helpan 'to help'	healp	hulpon	holpen
ġieldan 'to pay'	ġeald	guldon	golden
drincan 'to drink'	dranc	druncon	druncen

§519 Some strong verbs which occur quite often have forms which depart from the patterns given in §517. They include:

Class	Inf.	1st Pret.	2nd Pret.	Past Ptc.
II	drēosan 'to fall'	drēas	druron	droren
II	hrēosan 'to fall'	hrēas	hruron	hroren
IV	cuman 'to come"	cōm	cōmon	cumen
IV	niman 'to take'	nōm	nōmon	numen
		nam	nāmon	
IV	brecan 'to break'	bræc	brǣcon	brocen
V	specan 'to speak'	spæc	spǣcon	specen
V	sprecan 'to speak'	spræc	sprǣcon	sprecen
V	ġiefan 'to give'	ġeaf	ġēafon	ġiefen
V	biddan 'to ask'	bæd	bǣdon	beden
V	licgan 'to lie/rest'	læġ	lǣġon	leġen
V	sittan 'to sit'	sæt	sǣton	seten
VI	standan 'to stand'	stōd	stōdon	standen

Note *specen* 'spoken'. All the principal parts of *brecan* IV and *specan* V rhyme except the past participles. We have now rectified this anomaly. The verbs *biddan, licgan,* and *sittan,* follow the weak verb *fremman* (§524) in the present tense.

§520 The second and third person present indicative of *weorþan* appear in §516 above as *þū wierþest* or *wierþst* and *hē/hēo wierþeþ* or *wierþ*. These forms illustrate two changes which can affect these two parts of strong verbs:

(a) they can undergo *i*-mutation (§§17–18)
(b) they are often reduced.

So also

Infinitive	Present Indicative		
	1st Pers.	*2nd Pers.*	*3rd Pers.*
beran 'to bear'	iċ bere	þū bir(e)st	hēo bir(e)þ
faran 'to go'	iċ fare	þū fær(e)st	hē fær(e)þ
fealdan 'to fold'	iċ fealde	þū field(e)st	hēo field(e)þ
		þū fieltst	hē fielt
bēatan 'to beat'	iċ bēate	þū bīet(e)st	hēo bīet(e)þ
			hē bīett
bēodan 'to command'	iċ bēode	þū bīed(e)st	hēo bīed(e)þ
		þū bīetst	hē bīett
standan 'to stand'	iċ stande	þū stenst(e)st	hēo stent

§521 Contracted strong verbs (§88) originally had a medial *h* which was lost. The infinitive ending *-an* was then absorbed into the root vowel. This is called contraction. Some common contracted verbs are:

Class	Inf.	1st Pret.	2nd Pret.	Past Ptc.
I	wrēon 'to cover'	wrāh	wrigon	wrigen
II	flēon 'to flee'	flēah	flugon	flogen
V	ġefēon 'to rejoice'	ġefeah	ġefǣgon	—
	sēon 'to see'	seah	sāwon	sewen
VI	slēan 'to strike',			
	'to slay'	slōg	slōgon	slǣgen
VII(*a*)	cnāwan 'to know'	cnēow	cnēowon	cnāwen
	healdan 'to hold'	hēold	hēoldon	healden
VII(*b*)	fōn 'to take'	fēng	fēngon	fangen
	hōn 'to hang'	hēng	hēngon	hangen

§522 The endings of the weak verb *timbran* 'to timber/to build', which you have already met in §§91–3, are very similar to those of the strong verbs (§§512–13) except in the first and third person past singular. But, like most of the Old English weak verbs, it has the same root vowel throughout the conjugation. This is seen in the three principal parts – not four, like the strong verbs – of *timbran*:

(1) infinitive *timbran*

All the present forms of the weak verbs are built on the infinitive.

(2) past or preterite *timbrede*

All the preterite forms of the weak verbs are built on the preterite.

(3) past participle ((*ġe-*)*timbred*

§523 The weak verb *timbran* 'to build' is conjugated thus:

	Present Indicative	*Preterite Indicative*
Sg. 1	timbre	timbrede
2	timbrest	timbredest
3	timbreþ	timbrede
Pl.	timbraþ	timbredon
	Present Subjunctive	*Preterite Subjunctive*
Sg.	timbre	timbrede
Pl.	timbren	timbreden

Imp. Sg.	timbre	*Pl.*	timbraþ
Inf.	timbran	*Infl. Inf.*	tō timbrenne
Pres. Ptc.	timbrende	*Past Ptc.*	(ġe-)timbred

§524 *Fremman* 'to do' (§94), another regular weak verb, is conjugated thus:

	Present Indicative	*Preterite Indicative*
Sg. 1	fremme	fremede
2	fremest	fremedest
3	fremeþ	fremede
Pl.	fremmaþ	fremedon
	Present Subjunctive	*Preterite Subjunctive*
Sg.	fremme	fremede
Pl.	fremmen	fremeden

Imp. Sg.	freme	*Pl.*	fremmaþ
Inf.	fremman	*Infl. Inf.*	tō fremmenne
Pres. Ptc.	fremmende	*Past Ptc.*	(ġe-)fremed

The forms with single *-m-* are the same as those without *-i-* in §526.

§525 *Werian* 'to protect/defend' and most other verbs ending in *-rian* have the same endings as *timbran* (§523) and *fremman* (§524). But they have

Present Indicative

Sg.	1	werie
	2	werest
	3	wereþ

They have no -*i*- in those places where *fremman* has only one -*m*-. This too is the result of *i*-mutation (§§17–18).

§526 The verbs conjugated in §§522–5 are all classified as weak verbs of class 1. Typical verbs of class 2 are *lufian* 'to love' and the long-stemmed *lōcian* 'to look'. Both have -*ode* in the pret. and, to confuse things, -*aþ* in the sg. of the pres. ind. and -*iaþ* in the pl.

		Present Indicative	*Preterite Indicative*
Sg.	1	lufie	lufode
	2	lufast	lufodest
	3	lufaþ	lufode
Pl.		lufiaþ	lufodon

	Present Subjunctive	*Preterite Subjunctive*
Sg.	lufie	lufode
Pl.	lufien	lufoden

Imp. Sg.	lufa	*Pl.*	lufiaþ
Inf.	lufian	*Infl. Inf.*	tō lufienne
Pres. Ptc.	lufiende	*Past Ptc.*	(ġe-)lufod

§527 *Habban* 'to have' is a common weak verb, with some unusual forms:

		Present Indicative	*Preterite Indicative*
Sg.	1	hæbbe	hæfde
	2	hæfst	hæfdest
		hafast	
	3	hæfþ	hæfde
		hafaþ	
Pl.		habbaþ	hæfdon

	Present Subjunctive	*Preterite Subjunctive*
Sg.	hæbbe	hæfde
Pl.	hæbben	hæfden

Imp. Sg.	hafa	*Pl.*	habbaþ
Inf.	habban	*Infl. Inf.*	tō habbenne
Pres. Ptc.	hæbbende	*Past Ptc.*	(ġe-)hæfd

§528 The verb *bēon, wesan* 'to be' has forms from different roots.

Indicative	Pres.		Pres.	Pret.
Sg. 1	eom		bēo	wæs
2	eart		bist	wǣre
3	is		biþ	wæs
Pl.	sind(on), sint		bēoþ	wǣron
Imp. Sg.	bēo, wes	Pl.	bēoþ, wesaþ	
Pres. Subj. Sg.	bēo	Pl.	bēon	
	sīe		sīen	
Pret. Subj. Sg.	wǣre	Pl.	wǣren	

§529 The verb *gān* 'to go' has *i*-mutation in 2nd and 3rd pers. sg. pres. ind. (§§17–18) and a weak preterite which follows *hīeran* (§94):

Pres. Ind. Sg.	1	gā
	2	gǣst
	3	gǣþ
	Pl.	gāþ
Imp. Sg.		gā
Pret. Ind. Sg.		ēode
	Pl.	ēodon
Past Ptc.		ġegān

§530 Some irregular verbs are set out in §§95–7. They are: *sellan, sēċan, brenġan, penċan, pynċan, bycgan,* and *wyrċan* (§95); *āgan, cunnan, durran, magan, mōtan, ġemunan, sculan, witan* (§96); *cwepan* and *secgan* (§97). For *willan* and *dōn* see §89.

Abbreviations and Symbols

LANGUAGES AND DIALECTS

Gmc.	Germanic	nWS	non-West-Saxon
IE	Indo-European	OE	Old English
Lat.	Latin	OHG	Old High German
ME	Middle English	WS	West-Saxon
MnE	Modern English		

Before the name of a language or dialect

e = Early   l = Late   Pr = Primitive

GRAMMATICAL TERMS

a., acc.	accusative	irreg.	irregular
adj.	adjective	m., masc.	masculine
adv.	adverb	n., neut.	neuter
anom.	anomalous	n., nom.	nominative
art.	article	num.	numeral
aux.	auxiliary	pl.	plural
comp., compar.	comparative	part.	partitive
conj.	conjunction	pass.	passive
contr.	contracted	perf.	perfect
correl.	correlative	p., pers.	person
d., dat.	dative	poss.	possessive
decl.	declinable	prep	preposition
def.	definite	pres.	present
dem.	demonstrative	pret.	preterite
f., fem.	feminine	pret.-pres.	preterite-present
fut.	future	pron.	pronoun
g., gen.	genitive	ptc.	participle
i., inst.	instrumental	refl.	reflexive
imp.	imperative	rel.	relative
impers.	impersonal	s., sg.	singular
ind.	indicative	st.	strong
indecl.	indeclinable	subj.	subjunctive
indef.	indefinite	super.	superlative
inf.	infinitive	tr.	transitive
infl.	inflected	v., vb.	verb
interj.	interjection	w.	with
interr.	interrogative	wk.	weak
intr.	intransitive		

'S' may be added where appropriate to form a plural

SYMBOLS INVOLVING LETTERS

C   Complement
O   Object
S   Subject
V   Verb
v   Auxiliary verb
Vv Infinitive or participle + auxiliary verb
vV Auxiliary verb + infinitive or participle

OTHER SYMBOLS

>   gives, has given
<   derived from
*   a reconstructed form
|, ‖   (in verse) the medial and end caesura respectively
. . . (in quotations) word or words omitted
/   (in phrases like *burg* 'city/walled town') alternative translations
/   (in citation of forms) alternatives. Thus *mid þæm/þam/þan/þon/þi/ þy þe* means that in this formula *mid* and *þe* can be separated by any one of the six given forms
( )   (in citation of forms) optional elements
[ ]   enclose phonetic symbols

Bibliography

SHORT TITLES

Archaeology David M. Wilson (ed.) *The Archaeology of Anglo-Saxon England* (London: Methuen, 1976 and, in paperback, Cambridge: Cambridge University Press, 1981)

AS Art David M. Wilson *Anglo-Saxon Art from the Seventh Century to the Norman Conquest* (London: Thames and Hudson, 1984)

AS 1981 David Wilson *The Anglo-Saxons*, 3rd edn (London: Pelican, 1981)

AS 1982 James Campbell (ed.) *The Anglo-Saxons* (Oxford: Phaidon, 1982; repr. Penguin, 1991)

BArch Rosemary J. Cramp '*Beowulf* and Archaeology', *Medieval Archaeology* 1 (1957), 55–77

Fisher E. A. Fisher *An Introduction to Anglo-Saxon Architecture and Sculpture* (London: Faber and Faber, 1959)

Golden Age Janet Backhouse, D. H. Turner, and Leslie Webster (edd.) *The Golden Age of Anglo-Saxon Art 966–1066* (London: British Museum, 1984)

Guide Bruce Mitchell and Fred C. Robinson *A Guide to Old English*, 5th edn (Oxford: Blackwell, 1992; repr. 1992 (twice) and (with revisions and corrections) 1994)

Jewellery Ronald Jessup *Anglo-Saxon Jewellery* (London: Faber and Faber, 1950)

Making   Leslie Webster and Janet Backhouse (edd.) *The Making of*
                England: Anglo-Saxon Art and Culture AD 600–900 (London:
                British Museum, 1991)
Page   R. I. Page *Life in Anglo-Saxon England* (London: Batsford, and
                New York: Putnam, 1970)
Sutton Hoo   R. L. S. Bruce-Mitford *The Sutton Hoo Ship Burial: A Handbook*
                (British Museum, 1968; 2nd edn 1972)

SUGGESTIONS FOR FURTHER READING

Parts I, II, and V: The Language

When you wish to pursue any topic which arises from Parts I, II, and V, I
suggest that initially you consult

A Guide to Old English (short title *Guide*).

For further reading, I recommend the following books whose titles are
self-explanatory:

Mary S. Serjeantson *A History of Foreign Words in English* (London: Routledge
    and Kegan Paul, 1935, repr. 1961)
Albert C. Baugh and Thomas Cable *A History of the English Language*, 3rd edn
    (Englewood Cliffs, NJ: Prentice-Hall Inc., and London: Routledge and
    Kegan Paul, 1978, repr. often)
Thomas Pyles and John Algeo *The Origins and Development of the English
    Language*, 3rd edn (San Diego etc.: Harcourt Brace Jovanovich, 1982)
R. I. Page *An Introduction to English Runes* (London: Methuen, 1973)

A very useful dictionary is

J. R. Clark Hall *A Concise Anglo-Saxon Dictionary with a Supplement by Herbert
    D. Meritt*, 4th edn (Medieval Academy Reprints for Teaching: University
    of Toronto Press, 1984)

On *The Dictionary of Old English* see §412.

Those wishing to try their hand at composing prose or poetry in Old
English will find these books helpful:

W. W. Skeat *An English–Anglo-Saxon Vocabulary* (Cambridge: Cambridge
    University Press, 1879. Repr. in *Old English Newsletter Subsidia* vol. 1,
    CEMERS SUNY-Binghamton, 1978)
Gregory K. Jember, with others *English–Old English, Old English–English Dic-
    tionary* (Boulder: Westview Press, 1975)
Stephen A. Barney, with the assistance of others *Word-Hoard: An Introduction
    to Old English Vocabulary* (New Haven and London: Yale University Press,
    1977)
John F. Madden and Francis P. Magoun, Jr *A Grouped Frequency Word-List of
    Anglo-Saxon Poetry* (Department of English, Harvard University, 1957)

Parts IIIA and IV: The Literature

General survey

For a general survey, see

Stanley B. Greenfield and Daniel G. Calder *A New Critical History of Old English Literature with a survey of the Anglo-Latin background by Michael Lapidge* (New York and London: New York University Press, 1986)

Bibliography

For more bibliographical details than I can give here, see

Stanley B. Greenfield and Fred C. Robinson *A Bibliography of Publications on Old English Literature to the End of 1972* (Toronto: University of Toronto Press, and Manchester: Manchester University Press, 1980)
A Supplement by Carl T. Berkhout is in preparation.

Facsimiles of manuscripts

A facsimile of the *Beowulf* manuscript is readily available in

Beowulf reproduced in facsimile from the unique manuscript British Museum MS. Cotton Vitellius A. xv with a transliteration and notes by Julius Zupitza, 2nd edn, ed. Norman Davis; Early English Text Society 245 (London: Oxford University Press, 1959). See §299.

The series Early English Manuscripts in Facsimile, published in Copenhagen by Rosenkilde and Bagger, issued its twenty-fourth volume in 1992. These are available in some libraries. For details of them and of other facsimiles, see Greenfield and Robinson above.

Editions

Details of an edition of each prose work and each poem from which Texts 1–51 are taken will be found in §180 (Texts 1–7) or in §§419–46 and 463–93 (Texts 8–51). Editions of *Beowulf* apart from Klaeber (§465) are

Beowulf with the Finnesburg Fragment ed. C. L. Wrenn, fully revised by W. F. Bolton (London: Harrap, 1973)
Beowulf: A Student's Edition by Bruce Mitchell and Fred C. Robinson (Oxford: Blackwell, in preparation)

Details of the Anglo-Saxon Poetic Records, published between 1931 and 1953, will be found in §§172–6. The accuracy of the text throughout the six volumes is inhuman; one critic has 'discovered but a single transcriptional error: *is* for *ic* in *Resignation* 51'. Even this may have been a failure in proof-reading. But the notes are now hopelessly out of date. Bernard J. Muir's *The Exeter Anthology of Old English Poetry* (Exeter: Exeter University Library, 1994) is 'based on a detailed examination of the codex' and 'discusses hundreds of previously unnoticed corrections and other alterations to the texts' (private communication, 1993). Muir's recent examination of manuscript Junius 11 (§173) has revealed similar material therein; he is currently working on a comparative study of the two manuscripts. Analysis of this material, Muir argues, 'will necessitate a major reconsideration of a number of traditional assumptions'.

For other editions of prose works and poems, see Greenfield and Robinson above.

Translations

Translations of a selection of prose will be found in

Anglo-Saxon Prose edited and translated by Michael Swanton (London: Dent, and Totowa, NJ: Rowman and Littlefield, 1975)

The Anglo-Saxon World: Writings translated and edited by Kevin Crossley-Holland (Woodbridge: The Boydell Press, 1982)

For other prose texts, see Greenfield and Robinson above.

Most of the poetry was translated into prose by

R. K. Gordon *Anglo-Saxon Poetry* (London: J. M. Dent, and New York: E. P. Dutton, 1926, repr. often)

For the longer poems see

Beowulf: A New Translation by Seamus Heaney (London: Faber & Faber, 1999)

The Cædmon Poems Translated into English Prose by Charles W. Kennedy (Gloucester, MA: Peter Smith, 1965)

The Poems of Cynewulf Translated into English Prose by Charles W. Kennedy (New York: Peter Smith, 1949)

Crossley-Holland's *The Anglo-Saxon World* contains verse translations of a wide selection of shorter Old English poems and of *Beowulf*.

Prose translations of *Beowulf* include

Beowulf and the Finnesburg Fragment: A Translation into Modern English Prose by John R. Clark Hall, new edition completely revised by C. L. Wrenn with prefatory remarks by J. R. R. Tolkien (London: George Allen and Unwin, 1950)

Beowulf: A New Prose Translation by E. Talbot Donaldson (New York: Norton, 1966, and London: Longmans Green and Co., 1967)

Other translations I must recommend are J. R. R. Tolkien's version of *Exodus* (§487); Helen Gardner's of *The Dream of the Rood* (§493); and

A Feast of Creatures: Anglo-Saxon Riddle Songs translated with Introduction, Notes and Commentary by Craig Williamson (Philadelphia: University of Pennsylvania, 1982)

Part IIIB: History

A list of books recommended is given in §188. As I point out in §180, our knowledge of the history of England before the eighth century would be very limited without Bede's *Historia gentis Anglorum ecclesiastica*. The latest edition is

Bede's Ecclesiastical History of the English People edd. Bertram Colgrave and R. A. B. Mynors (Oxford: Clarendon Press, 1969).

For the Old English translation, from which many of my quotations are taken, see §§177.2 and 425.

Part IIIC: Archaeology, Arts, and Crafts

For full details of the works of reference listed in §193 see Short Titles above. The items which follow are listed without sub-headings but in the order in which the subjects appear in the Contents of Part IIIC.

R. L. S. Bruce-Mitford *The Sutton Hoo Ship Burial: A Handbook* (British Museum, 1968; 2nd edn 1972)

R. L. S. Bruce-Mitford *The Sutton Hoo Ship-Burial*, vol. I, *Excavations, Background, The Ship, Dating and Inventory* (London: British Museum, 1975)

R. L. S. Bruce-Mitford *The Sutton Hoo Ship-Burial*, vol. II, *Arms, Armour and Regalia* (London: British Museum, 1978)

R. L. S. Bruce-Mitford *The Sutton Hoo Ship-Burial*, vol. III, *Silver, Hanging-Bowls, Drinking Vessels, Containers, Musical Instruments, Textiles, Minor Objects* (London: British Museum, 1983)

The Age of Sutton Hoo ed. Martin Carver (Woodbridge: Boydell Press, 1992)

M. O. H. Carver, 'Contemporary Artefacts Illustrated in Late Saxon Manuscripts', *Archaeologia* 108 (1986), 117–45

Sutton Hoo: Fifty Years After edd. Robert Farrell and Carol Neuman de Vegvar, American Early Medieval Studies 2 (Miami University, 1992)

H. R. Ellis Davidson *The Sword in Anglo-Saxon England* (Oxford: Clarendon Press, 1962)

Ronald Jessup *Anglo-Saxon Jewellery* (London: Faber and Faber, 1950)

J. D. A. Thompson *Sylloge of Coins of the British Isles: Ashmolean Museum Oxford Anglo-Saxon Pennies* (London: The British Academy, 1967)

The British Academy Corpus of Anglo-Saxon Stone Sculpture ed. Rosemary Cramp (Oxford: Oxford University Press, 1984–)

C. R. Dodwell *Anglo-Saxon Art: A New Perspective* (Manchester: Manchester University Press, 1982)

J. G. Beckwith *Ivory Carving in Early Medieval England* (London: Harvey Miller and Medcalf, 1972)

E. A. Fisher *An Introduction to Anglo-Saxon Architecture and Sculpture* (London: Faber and Faber, 1959)

Eric Fernie *The Architecture of the Anglo-Saxons* (London: Batsford, 1982)

N. R. Ker *Catalogue of Manuscripts Containing Anglo-Saxon* (Oxford: Clarendon Press, 1957)

Michelle P. Brown *Anglo-Saxon Manuscripts* (London: British Library, 1991)

A Survey of Manuscripts Illuminated in the British Isles:

    vol. I, *Insular Manuscripts 6th to the 9th Century* by J. J. G. Alexander (London: Harvey Miller, 1978)

    vol. II, *Anglo-Saxon Manuscripts 900–1066* by Elźbieta Temple (London: Harvey Miller, 1976)

Christopher de Hamel *Medieval Craftsmen: Scribes and Illuminators* (London: British Museum, 1992)

Janet Backhouse *The Lindisfarne Gospels* (Oxford: Phaidon Press, 1981)

Part IIID: Place-Names

Margaret Gelling *Place-Names in the Landscape* (London: Dent, 1984)

Margaret Gelling *Signposts to the Past: Place-Names and the History of England*, 2nd edn (Chichester: Phillimore, 1988)

Nicholas Gough *Looking at Place Names* (Havant: Kenneth Mason, 1978)

Eilert Ekwall *The Concise Oxford Dictionary of English Place-Names*, 3rd edn (Oxford: Clarendon Press, 1947)

Part IIIE: Life in the Heroic Society and the Impact of Christianity

E. G. Stanley *The Search for Anglo-Saxon Paganism* (Cambridge: D. S. Brewer, and Totowa, NJ: Rowman and Littlefield, 1975)

Anglo-Saxon Settlements ed. Della Hooke (Oxford: Basil Blackwell, 1988)

R. I. Page *Life in Anglo-Saxon England* (London: Batsford, and New York: Putnam, 1970)

G. A. Lester *The Anglo-Saxons: How They Lived and Worked* (Newton Abbot London Vancouver: David and Charles, 1976)

Christine Fell *Women in Anglo-Saxon England and the Impact of 1066* (London: British Museum, 1984)

Gale R. Owen-Crocker *Dress in Anglo-Saxon England* (Manchester: Manchester University Press, 1986)

Wilfrid Bonser *The Medical Background of Anglo-Saxon England: A Study in History, Psychology, and Folklore* (London: The Wellcome Historical Medical Library, 1963)

J. H. G. Grattan and Charles Singer *Anglo-Saxon Magic and Medicine* (London: The Wellcome Historical Medical Library, 1952)

R. W. Southern *The Making of the Middle Ages* (London: Hutchinson, 1953; Arrow Books, 1959)

H. Mayr-Harting *The Coming of Christianity to Anglo-Saxon England*, 3rd edn (London: Batsford, 1991)

Part IV: The Garden of Old English Literature

See pp. 355–6 above.

Relevant Fiction

For a valuable supplement to my list see C. P. Biggam *Anglo-Saxon Studies: A Select Bibliography* (Worthing: *þa Engliscan Gesipas*, 1995) 108–13.

Beowulf

W. H. Canaway *The Ring-Givers* (London: Michael Joseph, 1958, repr. Penguin, 1961)

Rosemary Sutcliff *Beowulf: Dragonslayer* (London: Bodley Head, 1961, repr. Random House Children's Books, 1992)

John Gardner *Grendel* (London: André Deutsch, 1972)

The End of Roman Britain

Rosemary Sutcliff *The Lantern Bearers* (London: Oxford University Press, 1959, repr. Puffin Books, 1981)

The Celtic Resistance

Joan Terry *The Golden Clasp* (Branscombe: Seafarer Press, n.d.)

Rosemary Sutcliff *Dawn Wind* (London: Oxford University Press, 1961, repr. Puffin Books, 1982)

Rosemary Sutcliff *The Shining Company* (London: Bodley Head, 1990, repr. Random Century Children's Books, 1991)

Kathleen Herbert *The Bride of the Spear* (London: Bodley Head, 1988)

Melvyn Bragg *Credo* (London: Sceptre, 1996)

The Anglo-Saxons

Seventh Century

Moyra Caldecott *Etheldreda* (London and New York: Routledge and Kegan Paul, Arkana Paperbacks, 1987)

Kathleen Herbert *Queen of the Lightning* (London: Bodley Head, 1983)

Brian Bates *The Way of Wyrd: Tales of an Anglo-Saxon Sorcerer* (London: Century, 1983)

Eighth Century

Bede seems to exemplify perfectly Dr Johnson's observation that 'a life devoted to learning passes quietly away, undiversified by events'. The same cannot be said of Offa, king of Mercia 757–96. Yet, as far as I have been able to discover, neither has attracted the attention of writers of fiction. I should be especially pleased to be corrected on this point.

Ninth Century

W. Victor Cook *Axes against England* (London: Sampson Low, Marston, n.d.)
Alfred Duggan *The King of Athelney* (London: Faber and Faber, 1961)
Patry Williams *Alfred the King* (London: Faber and Faber, 1951)

Tenth Century

S. Fowler Wright *Elfwin* (London: Harrap, 1930)
Patry Williams *God's Warrior* (London: Faber and Faber, 1942)

Eleventh Century

Ray Bryant *Warriors of the Dragon Gold* (London: Mildmay Books and (in paperback) Headline Book Publishing Co., 1987)
Patry Williams *I am Canute* (London: Faber and Faber, 1938)
Alfred Duggan *The Cunning of the Dove* (London: Faber and Faber, 1960)
Dorothy Dunnett *King Hereafter* (London: Michael Joseph, 1982, repr. Arrow Books, 1992)
Edward Bulwer Lytton *Harold the Last of the Saxon Kings* (first published 1848, often reprinted)

Revolt against the Normans

Charles Kingsley *Hereward the Wake, 'Last of the English'* (first published 1866, often reprinted)
Rosemary Sutcliff *The Shield Ring* (London: Oxford University Press, 1956, repr. Puffin Books, 1992)

The English Conquest of Normandy: The Battle of Tinchebrai 1106

Rosemary Sutcliff *Knight's Fee* (London: Oxford University Press, 1960, repr. Random House Children's Books, 1990)

Fifth to Eleventh Centuries

Jill Paton Walsh and Kevin Crossley-Holland *Wordhoard: Anglo-Saxon Stories for Young People* (Macmillan, 1969)

Relevant Poetry

I recommend the following series of poems by Rudyard Kipling:

'The Roman Centurion's Song (Roman Occupation of Britain, A.D. 300)', 'The Pirates of England (Saxon Invasion, A.D. 400–600)', 'Harp Song of the Danish Women', 'Danegeld (A.D. 980–1016)', 'The Anvil (Norman Conquest, 1066)', and 'Norman and Saxon (A.D. 1100)'.

Readers will be challenged by Geoffrey Hill's *Mercian Hymns*, a poetic sequence concerned with Offa, first published in 1971 and now available in Geoffrey Hill *Collected Poems* (London: Penguin, 1985) at pp. 8–9, 103–34, and 201–3 and by the poems on Anglo-Saxon themes in Jorge Luis Borges *Selected Poems 1923–1967* (London: Penguin 1972 repr. 1985).

Some Significant Dates

Where possible, the dates are taken from *Handbook of British Chronology*, edd. F. M. Powicke and E. B. Fryde (London: Royal Historical Society, 2nd edn, 1961). But see §180.

Date	Lay	Religious	Literary
449	Traditional date of coming of Angles, Saxons, and Jutes.		The legend of Arthur may rest on a British leader who resisted the invaders.
560–616	Æthelbert King of Kent.		
c. 563		St Columba brings Celtic Christianity to Iona.	
597		St Augustine brings Roman Christianity to Kent.	
616–632	Edwin King of Northumbria.		
c. 625	Earliest possible date for Sutton Hoo ship-burial.		
627		Edwin converted to Christianity.	
632	Edwin killed by heathen King Penda of Mercia.		
635		Aidan settles in Lindisfarne, bringing Celtic Christianity.	
635		King Cynegils of Wessex converted.	
641	Oswald King of Northumbria killed by Penda.		
654	Penda killed by Oswy King of Northumbria.		

Date	Lay	Religious	Literary
664		Synod of Whitby establishes supremacy of Roman Christianity. St Chad becomes bishop.	
664		Hild Abbess of Whitby.	Cædmon uses Germanic alliterative verse for religious subjects during this period.
657–680			
c. 678		English missions to the continent begin.	
680			Approximate earliest date for composition of *Beowulf*.
c. 700			Date of first linguistic records.
709		Death of Aldhelm, Bishop of Sherborne.	
731			Bede completes *Historia gentis Anglorum ecclesiastica*.
735		Death of Bede.	
c. 735		Birth of Alcuin.	
757–796	Offa King of Mercia.		
782		Alcuin settles at Charlemagne's court.	*fl.* 796 Nennius, author or reviser of *Historia Britonum*.
793	Viking raids begin.	Sacking of Lindisfarne.	
800	Four great kingdoms remain – Northumbria, Mercia, East Anglia, Wessex.		
780–850			Cynewulf probably flourishes some time in this period.
804		Death of Alcuin.	
851	Danes' first winter in England.		
865	Great Danish Army lands in East Anglia.		

867	Battle of York. End of Northumbria as a political power.		
870	King Edmund of East Anglia killed by Danes. East Anglia overrun.		
871	Alfred becomes King of Wessex.		
874	Danes settle in Yorkshire.		
877	Danes settle in East Mercia.		
880	Guthrum and his men settle in East Anglia. Only Wessex remains of the four Kingdoms.		
?886	Boundaries of Danelaw agreed with Guthrum. Alfred occupies London.		The period of the Alfredian translations and the beginning of the Anglo-Saxon Chronicle.
892	Further Danish invasion.		
896	Alfred builds a fleet.		
899	Death of King Alfred.		
899–954	The creation of the English Kingdom.		
c. 909		Birth of Dunstan.	
937	Battle of Brunanburh.		Poem commemorates the battle.
954	The extinction of the Scandinavian kingdom of York.		
959–975	Edgar reigns.		
960		Dunstan Archbishop of Canterbury. The period of the Monastic Revival.	
c. 971		*The Blickling Homilies.*	
978 or 979	Murder of King Edward.		
950–1000			Approximate dates of the poetry codices – Junius MS, Vercelli Book, Exeter Book, and *Beowulf* MS.
978–1016	Ethelred reigns.		

Date	Lay	Religious	Literary
988		Death of Dunstan.	
991	Battle of Maldon.		Poem commemorates the battle.
990–992			Ælfric's *Catholic Homilies*.
993–998			Ælfric's *Lives of the Saints*.
1003–1023		Wulfstan Archbishop of York.	
c. 1014			*Sermo Lupi ad Anglos.*
1005–c. 1012		Ælfric Abbot of Eynsham.	
1013	Sweyn acknowledged as King of England.		
1014	Sweyn dies.		
1016	Edmund Ironside dies.		
1016–1042	Canute and his sons reign.		
1042–1066	Edward the Confessor.		
1066	Harold King. Battle of Stamford Bridge. Battle of Hastings. William I King.		

Glossary

Every form which occurs in Texts 1–51 is (meant to be) glossed in its proper alphabetical order. These forms are always in bold type, both at the beginning of entries and within them. Inflected forms of the same word are grouped when that order allows; thus **dǣd**, **dǣda**, and **dǣde**, comprise one entry but **dǣdum** appears alone following **dǣdfruman**. I have tried to make the Glossary as helpful, simple, and concise, as possible.

The letter **æ** follows **a**. The letters **þ** and **ð** are interchangeable and are grouped together following **t**. Words which in Texts 1–51 always have one or the other are glossed with that letter, e.g. **ge-cȳþan** but **ge-cȳðde**. When variants occur, e.g. **ge-cȳþnis/ge-cȳðnis**, the **ð**-form is subsumed under the **þ**-form.

Most glossaries disregard the prefix **ge-** in alphabetizing words and gloss **geearnian** under **e**. But I do not think that I am justified in expecting you to know instinctively that **ge-** is a prefix in **geearnian**, **geendode**, and **gegrāp**, but an integral part of the word in **gealgan**, **geongan**, and **gegnum**. I have therefore glossed all words beginning with **ge-** under **g**, with the prefix followed by a hyphen (**ge-earnian**, **ge-endode**, **ge-grāp**) and with cross-references where necessary.

Please remember that 7 is a scribal abbreviation for **and/ond** 'and'.

As I point out in §§2 and 141, Anglo-Saxon scribes did not try to make their spelling uniform. Consonants present little difficulty. The variation **þ/ð** has already been noted. Single and double consonants may alternate, e.g. **man/mann**. Spellings such as **ascode**, **axsodest**, and (not in our Texts) **acsode** and **axode**, reflect variations in pronunciation.

You will learn to take in your stride the vowel variations marked in bold type in these examples:

> mē, mec;
> hira, hiera, hiora, hyra;
> hēo, hīo;
> þām, þǣm, þan, þon, þȳ;
> hand, hond;
> wǣron, wǣran, wǣræn, wǣren, wǣrun;
> hergode, hergede, hergade, hergude.

Abbreviations are the same as those on pp. 351–2. Where alternatives exist, the shorter form is used. Thus:

> nsn = nominative singular neuter;
> gsf = genitive singular feminine;
> isn = instrumental singular neuter;
> aplm = accusative plural masculine.

The order is always case, number, gender.

Verb classes may be identified thus:

> Roman numerals I–VII refer to strong verbs (stv) (§§517–21);
> Arabic numerals 1–2 refer to weak verbs (wkv) (§§522–6).

Verb forms may be analysed by

> person (1, 2, 3),
> number (s, pl),
> and tense (pres, pret), in that order.

The mood is indicative unless 'subj' or 'imp' is added. The following abbreviations are also used:

wa	with accusative (object)	wi	with instrumental (object)
wd	with dative (object)	w refl	with reflexive (object)
wg	with genitive (object)	wo	without

The references given for weak verbs refer the reader to the section which explains the form glossed.

A solidus indicates alternatives, e.g. n/a = nominative or accusative case and 1/3 = first or third person.

I have glossed every form of every noun and adjective. But when one form can be more than one case, I have not always differentiated them. (This is due to the demands of space.) Thus **blisse** is gs in Text 20/3 but ds in Text 47 v. 1, Text 51/149, and Text 51/153. I have glossed it

> **blisse** oblique case < *bliss* f 'merriment, happiness, grace' (§504).

(An oblique case is a case other than the nominative singular.) Similarly, **beteran** is glossed

> **beteran** oblique case < *betera* comp adj 'better' (§§505–6).

In examples like these, the context, the notes, and the paradigm in the given section, will provide the necessary clues.

I have not always given grammatical details or section references for nouns which occur only in the nominative singular (or nominative/accusative singular when they are the same), for adjectives which occur only in the nominative singular, or for verbs which occur only in the infinitive.

Names of persons, places, and things, which are explained in the notes or which are self-evident are not glossed.

All forms of the personal pronouns and of **se** and **þes** are listed, with section references. But the many uses of **se** and its oblique cases are explained only under the entries **se** and/or **þæt**.

I have also glossed every form of every verb. But here too I have not always distinguished the various functions of a particular form. Thus for **bēo, bēon, bēoð,** and **bið,** I have referred you to §528, where the forms of the verb 'to be' are set out. Infinitives appear thus:

> **ābīdan** 'to wait for' wg (stv I §517),

where the section referred to gives the principal parts of a verb of the class indicated. Inflected forms appear thus:

> **ādrāf** 3s pret < *ādrīfan* 'to drive away' (stv I §517),
> **andwyrde** 1s pret < *andwyrdan* 'to answer' (wkv like *sendan* §89),

and (with the mood given because it is not indicative)

> **styrme** 3s pres subj < *styrman* 'to storm'.

Note: In both *sendan* and *andwyrdan*, the *d* of the weak preterite ending -*de* is often absorbed into the *d* of the root *send-* and *andwyrd-*, as explained in §89.

When I have discussed a difficult form in a note, I refer the reader to the relevant text and line, e.g.

> **ge-corene** See Text 44/285 note.

For unusual or irregular forms which are not explained in this book, I have where possible given a reference to the appropriate section in *A Guide to Old English*. It is not necessary for you to follow these up unless you are interested.

You will find the following references relevant for the remaining parts of speech:

adverbs	§111
prepositions	§§112–16 and 124–6
conjunctions	§§111, 119, 121–6
interjections	§128.

But I have tried in the Glossary to give you all the information you will need about these, and also about numerals (§57a).

Occurrences of words are cited by text number and line (e.g. Text 44/285) only when the same or a similar form can have different meanings, e.g. the entries under **stefn/stefne** and **stefne**, and under **swylce**, or when some special problem arises, as with **ge-corene** above.

There are some inconsistencies in the layout of entries in the Glossary. These are the result of my reacting differently to individual problems or passages in an attempt to help you. Suggestions, comments, and criticisms, will be welcomed here too. My efforts may not always have prospered.

Those seeking further information are advised to consult (on grammatical points) the Grammatical and Lexical Index and *A Guide to Old English*, and (on vocabulary) the Clark Hall–Meritt *Dictionary* recommended in §168.

Ā adv 'always'

aa adv 'always'

ābæd 3s pret < *ābiddan* 'to ask for/request' (stv V §519). In Text 49/12 I have taken it to mean 'to get by requesting' and so 'to receive'

ābīdan 'to wait for' wg (stv I §517)

ablendum see Text 30/6 note

ableredum see Text 30/5 note

Abrahames gs 'of Abraham'

ābrǣce 3s pret subj < *ābrecan* 'to capture, to destroy' (stv V §519); **ābrǣcon** 3pl pret

āc f 'oak' (§504)

ac conj 'but, however, nevertheless, moreover'

ācende npl of past ptc < *ācennan* 'to give birth to' (wkv like *fyllan* §94), meaning 'born'; **ācenned** past ptc

ācennednys f 'birth' (§504)

actrēo n 'oak tree'

ācwæð 3s pret < *ācweðan* (stv V §517) (§§97, 515). See Text 44/304 note

ācwealde npl of past ptc < *ācwellan* 'to kill' (wkv like *sellan* §95)

ād m 'fire, funeral pyre' (§502); **āde** ds

ādīligode 3s pret < *ādīligian* 'to destroy' (wkv 2 §526)

ādl f 'sickness, disease'

ādrāf 3s pret < *ādrīfan* 'to drive away' (stv I §517)

ādrǣfde 3s pret < *ādrǣfan* 'to drive away' (wkv like *hīran* §94); **ādrǣfdon, -un** 3pl pret

ādrenced past ptc < *ādrencan* 'to drown' (wkv like *settan* §94); **ādrencte** 3s pret

ādrēogan 'to endure' (stv II §517)

ādrife 3s pret subj < *ādrīfan*. See **ādrāf**; **ādrifen** past ptc

āfǣred past ptc < *āfǣran* 'to frighten' (wkv like *hieran* §94)

āfēdan 'to feed, bring up, support; to bring forth, produce' (wkv like *hieran* §94); **āfēdde** 3s pret; **āfēdeð** 3s pres

aforeworda adv 'in the first place'

afran gs < *afra* m 'son' (§§500–1)

āfyrht contr past ptc < *afyrhtan* 'to frighten, terrify' (wkv like *sendan* §89)

āgan (Text 31/12) 3s pret < *āginnan* 'to begin' (stv III §518)

āgān (Texts 21/2 and 31/25) past ptc < *āgān* 'to go' (§529)

āgēafon 3pl pret < *āgiefan*

āgean (Text 31/15) adv in combination **eft ... āgean** 'back again'

āgēat 3s pret < *āgēotan* 'to pour out' and so 'to destroy' in Text 46/515 (stv II §517)

āgen (Text 41/117) 3pl pres subj < *āgan* 'to have, possess' (§96)

agen (all occurrences) adj 'own' (§§505–7); **agene** asf; **agenes** gsn; **agenne** asm; **agenum** dpl

āgēted past ptc < *āgētan* 'to destroy' (wkv 1 §§522–3)

āgiefan 'to give' (stv V §519)

āglǣca m 'monster' (§§500–1)

āgrof 3s pret < *āgrafan* 'to inscribe' (stv VI §517)

Agustino ds 'Augustine'; **Agustinus** gs 'Augustine's'

āhafen past ptc < *āhebban*

āhēawen past ptc < *āhēawan* 'to cut down' (stv VII(*a*) §517)

āhebban 'to raise, lift up, exalt, stir up' (stv VI §517 with pres tense like *fremman* §524); **āhefde** 3s pret. This verb sometimes has weak forms in the pret and past ptc as well as in the pres

āhlōg 3s pret < *āhliehhan* 'to laugh, exult' (stv VI §517 with pres tense like *fremman* §524)

āhōf 1/3s pret < *āhebban*; **āhōfon, -un** 3pl pret

āhredde 3s pret < *āhreddan* 'to rescue, set free' (wkv like *sendan* §89)

āhtan 3pl pret < *āgan*; **āhte** 3s pret; **āhton** 3pl pret (§96)

āhwylfde 3s pret < *āhwylfan* 'to cover over, submerge' (wkv like *hieran* §94)

āhȳddon 3pl pret < *āhȳdan* 'to hide' (wkv like *hieran* §94)

al adj 'all'

alde ism < *ald* adj 'old, ancient' (§§505, 507)
aldor n 'life' (§503)
aldordagum dpl < *ealdordagas* m 'days of life' (§502)
aldorman(n), -mon(n) m also spelt **ealdorman(n), -mon(n)**, 'ruler, chief, nobleman of high rank or office, chief officer of a shire'; **aldormen(n)** ds or n/apl with *i*-mutation (§§17–18)
aldormon(n) = aldorman
ālecgað 3pl pres < *ālecgan* 'to lay, place' (irreg wkv); **ālēd** past ptc; **ālēdon** 3pl pret; **ālegdon** 3pl pret
ālēt 3s pret < *ālǣtan* 'to let' (stv VII(*b*) §517)
all adj 'all' (§§505, 507); **alle** n/apl; **allra** gpl
allwalda m 'all-ruler, God' (§§500–1)
alne asm < **all**
alumpen past ptc < *ālimpan* 'to befall, come to pass' (stv III §518)
ālȳsde 3s pret < *ālȳsan* 'to free' (wkv like *hīeran* §94)
āmansumod past ptc < *āmansian* 'to curse, excommunicate' (wkv 2 §526)
āmen 'amen'
āmyrde 3s pret < *āmyrran* 'to waste' (irreg wkv); **āmyrrede** apl of past ptc
an (Text 28/1) 1s pres < *unnan* 'to grant' (v like *cunnan* §96)
an (Text 28/6, 6, 7) = conj **and** 'and'
an (Text 10/1247) = prep **on** 'on'. Translate 'for'
ān num 'one' shading into 'a, an', 'alone'
āna num < *ān* 'one, alone'
ānbide ds < *ānbid* n 'waiting, expectation' (§503)
and conj 'and'. (This entry must be a work of supererogation.)
andan ds < *anda* m 'anger' (§§500–1)
andefn f 'amount'
andettan 'to confess, acknowledge' (wkv); **andettað** imp pl; **andette** 1s pres
andgit n 'meaning, significance' (§503); **andgite** ds
andlangne asm < *andlang* adj 'entire, whole' (§§505, 507)
andsaca m 'adversary' (§§500–1)
andsware as < *andswaru* f 'answer, reply' (§504)
andswarode 1/3s pret < *andswarian* 'to answer' (wkv 2 §526)
andswerode = andswarode
andweardan wk gs < *andweard* adj 'present' (§§505–6); **andwearde** wk ns
andweardnesse ds < *andweardness* f 'presence' (§504)
andwerd adj 'present'
andwlitan ds < *andwlita* m 'face, countenance' (§§500–1)

andwyrde 1s pret < *andwyrdan* 'to answer' (wkv like *sendan* §89)
āne asf < **ān** num 'one'; **ānes** gs. On Text 44/272 see note
Angelcyn(n) n 'the English race, England' (§503); **Angelcynne** ds; **Angelcynnes** gs
anginn n 'beginning, design, enterprise' (§503)
ānhȳdig adj 'resolute, firm, constant'; **ānhȳdige** npl (§§505, 507)
Anlāfe, -es d and gs 'Anlaf', 'Anlaf's'
ānne asm < **ān** num 'one'; **ānra** gpl; **ānre** g/dsf
ansȳne as < *ansȳn* f 'presence' (§504)
Antecrīstes gs < *Antecrīst* m 'Antichrist' (§502)
āntīd f 'appropriate/expected time' (§504)
ānum dsm/n < **ān** num 'one'; **tō ānum** 'together'
Anwealda m 'God, Ruler'
āparade 3s pret < *āparian* 'to discover, apprehend' (wkv 2 §526)
Apollonio ds 'Apollonius'; **Apollonium** as
apostola gpl < *apostol* m 'apostle' (§502); **apostole** ds
Apr scribal abbreviation 'of April'
ārās 3s pret < *ārīsan* 'to arise' (stv I §517)
ārǣdan 'to read' (wkv like *hīeran* §94)
ārǣfnian 'to endure, bear' (wkv 2 §526)
ārǣrde 3s pret < *ārǣran* 'to raise up' (wkv like *hīeran* §94); **ārǣred** past ptc
arc scribal abbreviation 'archbishop'
arceb = arc
arcebisceop m 'archbishop'
arcebisceoprīce n 'archbishopric'
archieps = arc
āre as < *ār* f 'honour, respect' (§504)
ārfæsta wk ns < *ārfæst* adj 'merciful, compassionate' (§§505–6)
ārhwate st nmpl < *ārhwæt* adj 'eager for glory' (§§505, 507)
ārīsað 3pl pres (= fut) < *ārīsan* 'to arise' (stv I §517); **ārīse** 1s pres (= fut)
ārlēasra gpl < *ārlēas* adj 'impious, wicked' (§§505–7)
arn 3s pret < *irnan* 'to run' (stv III §518)
ārstafum dpl < *ārstæf* m 'benefit, kindness' (§502)
ārwurða wk nsm < *ārwurð* adj 'pious, venerable' (§§505–6)
āsǣnde = āsende
ascade 1s pret < *ascian* 'to ask' (wkv 2 §526); **ascode** 3s pret
āsecgan 'to narrate, explain' (wkv §97)
āsende 3s pret < *āsendan* 'to send' (wkv §89)
āsettan (Text 48/862, 876) 'to set (down)' (wkv §94); **āsettan** 3pl pret. See Text 5/69 note; **āsetton** 3pl pret

āspended past ptc < *āspendan* 'to spend' (wkv I §§522–3)

āspon 3s pret < *āspanan* 'to entice' (stv VI §517)

āstāh 3s pret < *āstīgan* 'to rise, ascend' (stv I §517)

āstyred past ptc < *āstyrian* 'to move, remove' (wkv §§525–6)

āstyrod = āstyred

āswefede npl past ptc < *āswebban* 'to put to sleep, kill' (wkv I §524)

āteah 3s pret < *ātēon* 'to carry away, climb' (contr stv II §521)

ātimbran 'to build' (wkv §§522–3)

ātīwede 3s pret < *ātīwian* 'to appear' (wkv §525)

atol adj 'horrible, dire, terrible, hideous'

āþ/āð m 'oath' (§502); āþan dpl (for *āþum*); āþas apl

āþecgan See Text 40/2 note

āðene imp s < *āðenian* 'to stretch out' (wkv 2 §526); āðenode 3s pret

āþer conj 'either'. See Text 22/7 note

Aþulfing 'son of Æþelwulf'

āðum m 'son-in-law' (§502)

Augustinum as 'Augustine'

āwa adv 'always'

āwǣndan = āwendan

āwǣnde 3s pres subj < āwendan

āweg adv 'away, forth, out'

āwend past ptc < āwendan

āwendan 'to change, alter, translate' (wkv like *sendan* §89); āwent 3s pres

āwēox 1s pret < *āweaxan* 'to grow up' (stv VII(*a*) §517)

āwēsted past ptc < *āwēstan* 'to lay waste' (wkv I §§522–3)

āwiht adv 'at all, in any way'

āworpene apl past ptc < *āweorpan* 'to throw, cast' (stv III §518)

āwrītan 'to write' (stv I §517); āwritene npl past ptc

axsodest 2s pres < *axsian* 'to ask' (wkv 2 §526)

æ f 'law (human or divine)'

æcere ds < *æcer* m 'field' (§502)

ædran npl < *ædre* f 'vein, artery' (§501)

æfæstnes f 'religion' (§504)

æfen m 'eve, evening' (§502)

æfentīde ds < *æfentīd* f 'eventide' (§504)

æflāstum See Text 46/474 note

æfre adv 'ever, always, at any time'

æftan adv 'from behind, behind, in the rear'

æfter (1) adv 'after'; (2) prep wd (rarely wa) 'after, along, according to'; (3) on its uses in prep advs and conjs like *æfter þæm* (*þe*), see the textual notes and §§124–6

æftercweþendra gpl pres ptc < *æftercweþ-* *ende* 'after-speaking'. Translate 'of those who speak after him'

æfterfylige 3s pres subj < *æfterfyligan* 'to follow after' (wkv I §§522–3)

æghwæþer ge . . . ge conj 'both . . . and'

æghwæðres gs < *æghwæðer* pron 'each'

æghwider adv 'everywhere, in all directions'

æglēaw adj 'learned in the law'

ægðer . . . ge . . . ge conj 'both . . . and'

ægþere asf < *ægþer* adj 'each'

Ægypta gpl 'of the Egyptians'

æht f 'possession, control' (§504); æhta apl; æhte (1) gs as in **minre æhte**, (2) apl

ælc adj/pron 'each'; ælcum dsm

ælda gpl < *ælde* m 'men'

Ælfrede ds 'Alfred'

ælinge (gender uncertain) 'weariness'

ælmihtig adj 'almighty'; ælmihtiges gs (§§505, 507)

ælðēodige st npl < *ælðēodig* adj 'strange, foreign' (§§505, 507)

æne adv 'once'

ænegum st dsn < ænig

Ænglaland n 'Angles' land, England'

ænig adj 'any' (§§505, 507); ænige asf; æniges gs; ænigum st dsm or dpl (§§505–7)

ænne asm < ān

ær (1) adv 'before'; (2) prep wd or wa 'before'; (3) conj 'before', often with the subj; (4) on its use in prep advs and conjs like *ær þæm* (*þe*), see the textual notes and §§124–6

ærce scribal abbreviation 'archbishop'

ærdagum dpl < *ærdagas* m 'days of old/yore' (§502)

ærest (1) super adj 'first'; (2) super adv 'first'; ærestan wk ds or npl < ærest adj; æreste st nsf (§§505–7)

ærgewin n 'ancient hostility'

æriste ds < *ærist* m/n 'resurrection'

ærnað 3pl pres < *ærnan* 'to gallop'

æsæled past ptc < *æsælan* 'to fetter' (wkv like *hīeran* §94)

Æsc proper name

æscrōfe st npl < *æscrōf* adj 'brave in battle' (§§505, 507)

æses gs object of *brūcan* < *æs* n 'food, carrion' (§503)

æt prep (1) wd 'at'; (2) wa 'as far as, until'

ætgædere adv 'together, at the same time'

ætgædre = ætgædere

æthrān 3s pret < *æthrīnan* 'to touch' (stv I §517 wg or wd); æthrīneð 3s pres

æton 3pl pret < etan

ætsacan 'to deny' (stv VI §517)

ætsomne adv 'together, at once'

ætwundon 3pl pret < *ætwindan* 'to escape' (stv V §518)

ætȳweð 3s pres < *ætȳwan* 'to appear' (wkv like *hieran* §94)

Æþelbryhtes gs 'of Æthelbryht'

æðele (1) npl; (2) nsf < *æðele* adj 'noble' (§§505–7)

æðeling m 'nobleman, prince, chief' (§502); often used of Christ in poetry; chiefly in poetry 'man, hero, saint'. In pl sometimes 'men, people'; **æþelinga** gpl; **æðelingas** npl; **æþelinge** ds; **æþelinges** gs; **æðelingun** dpl

Æþelredes gs 'Ethelred's'

æþelu apl < *æþelu* npl 'origin' (§503)

Æþelwulfing 'son of Æthelwulf'

Æþerede ds 'Æthered'; **Æðeredes** gs 'Æthered's'

æwbrycas apl < *æwbryce* m 'adultery' (§502)

æwfæst adj 'upright, devout, religious'

æwiscmōde npl < *æwiscmōd* adj 'ashamed, cowed' (§§505, 507)

æwswicas apl < *æwswice* m 'violation of God's laws' (§502)

Babiloniam ds 'Babylon'

bād 3s pret < *bīdan* 'to wait for' wg (stv I §517)

baldor m 'master, lord, hero'

bān npl < *bān* n 'bone' (§503)

barn 3s pret < *birnan* 'to burn' (stv III §518)

basnodon 3pl pret < *basnian* 'to await' wg (wkv 2 §526)

bāt 3s pret < *bītan* 'to bite' (stv I §517)

baðode 3s pret < *baðian* 'to bathe' (wkv 2 §526)

bæc n 'back'. In the phrase **on bæc** 'backwards, behind'

bæd 1/3s pret < *biddan*; **bæde** 2s pret; **bædon** 3pl pret

bælfȳra gpl < *bælfȳr* n 'funeral fire' (§503)

bæm d < **bēgen**

bær 1/3s pret < **beran**

bære ds < *bær* f 'bier, litter, handcart' (§504)

bæron pret pl < **beran**

bæð n 'bath, bathing-place' (§503); **bæðe** ds

bæðstede ns/ds < *bæðstede* m 'bathing-place' (*Guide* §§45–6)

be prep wd/a/i (1) (of place) 'near, in, on, at'; (2) (of time) 'in, about, by, before, while'; (3) (other) 'about, because of, by, through, in comparison with'

bēacen n 'sign, token, banner'

beadogrīman as < *beadogrīma* m 'war-mask, helmet' (§§500–1)

beaducāfa wk ns < *beaducāf* adj 'bold in battle' used as a noun

beadurōfes gs < *beadurōf* adj 'strong/ renowned in battle' (§§505, 507)

beaduweorca gpl < *beaduweorc* n 'war-like deed/operation' (§503)

beadwa probably for *beadwe* gs < *beadu* f 'battle' (*Guide* §40)

bēaga gpl < *bēag* m 'ring, bracelet' (§502)

bēahgifa m 'ring-giver, lord' (§§500–1)

bealde adv 'boldly, with confidence'

bealg 3s pret w refl object **hine** < *belgan* 'to be(come) angry' (stv III §518)

bealocwealm m 'baleful death'

bealohȳdig adj 'meditating evil, hostile'

bealospella gpl < *bealospell* n 'baleful message' (§503)

bealwe ds < *bealu* n 'harm, evil, ruin' (*Guide* §40)

bēam m 'tree, cross' (§502). See Text 50; **bēama** gpl; **bēamas** apl; **bēames** gs

bēamtelge ds < *bēamtelg* m 'ink or dye from wood' (§502)

bēancoddum dpl < *bēancodd* m 'bean pod or husk' (§502)

beardas apl < *beard* m 'beard' (§502)

bearhtme ds < *bearhtm* m 'acclaim' (§502)

bearm m 'bosom, breast, possession' (§502); **bearme** ds

bearn n 'child, son, descendant'. This form can be n/a s/pl (see §503); **bearne** ds; **bearnes** gs

bearnmyrðran npl < *bearnmyrðra* m/*bearnmyrðre* f 'murderer/murderess of children' (§§500–1)

bearnum dpl < **bearn**

bearu m 'grove, wood' (*Guide* §40); **bearwe** ds

bēateð 3s pres < *bēatan* 'to beat, strike' (stv VII(a) §517)

bebēad 3s pret < *bebēodan* 'to commit, entrust' (stv II §517)

bebicgan 2pl pres subj < *bebicgan* 'to sell' (wkv §95); **bebicge** (1) Text 37/18 3s pres subj; (2) Text 37/19 1s pres subj

bebod as < *bebod* n 'command' (§503); **bebode** ds

beboden past ptc < *bebēodan*. See **bebēad**

bebyrigde 3s pret < *bebyrigan* 'to bury' (wkv like *hieran* §94)

bēc < **bōc**. This form shows *i*-mutation (§§17–18) and can be g/ds or n/apl

beclypte 3s pret < *beclyppan* 'to embrace' (wkv like *settan* §94)

bēcn as < *bēcn* (= **bēacen**) 'monument' (§503)

becōm 1/3s pret < **becuman**; **becōmon** 3pl pret

becuman 'to approach, come, arrive, meet with' (stv §519)

becwōm = **becōm**

bēdan = *bēodan* 'to offer' (stv II §517)

bedǣled past ptc < *bedǣlan* 'to deprive of' wg/d (wkv like *hieran* §94)

beddum dpl < *bedd* n 'bed' (§503)

beēodon 1pl pret < *begān* 'to serve, profess, worship' (§529)

befarene npl past ptc < *befaran* 'to surround' (stv VI §517)

befæste 3s pret < *befæstan* 'to entrust to' (wkv like *settan* §94)

befeallen past ptc < *befeallan* 'to deprive of' wd (stv VII(*a*) §517)

befeng 3s pret < *befōn* 'to take hold of, receive' (stv VII(*b*) §517)

befēolan 'to apply oneself to' wd (irreg stv III *Guide* §133.2)

beforan (1) adv 'before, in front of'; (2) prep wd 'before, in front of, formerly'

befylled past ptc < *befyllan* 'to deprive of' wg (wkv §94)

bēg apl < *bēg* n 'ring, bracelet' (§503)

begeat 3s pret < *begietan* 'to seize, lay hold on' (stv V §519); **begēaton** 3pl pret

bēgen num 'both'

begeondan prep wd 'beyond'

begēton = **begēaton**. See **begeat**

begird past ptc < *begirdan* 'to gird, clothe' (wkv like *hieran* §94)

begnornodon 3pl pret < *begnornian* 'to lament' (wkv 2 (§526)

begoten past ptc < *begēotan* 'to drench, cover' (stv II §517)

begrauene apl past ptc < *begrafan* 'to bury' (stv VI §517)

begrunden past ptc < *begrindan* 'to grind, sharpen' (stv III §518)

behelede apl past ptc < *behelian* 'to hide' (wkv 1 §525)

behēold 1/3s pret < *behealdan* 'to behold, watch over' (stv VII(*a*) §517); **behēoldon** 3pl pret

behēt 3s pret < *behātan* 'to promise' (stv VII(*b*) §517); **behētan** 1/3pl pret

behindan (1) adv; (2) prep wd 'behind

behinon prep wd 'on this side of'

behongen past ptc < *behōn* 'to hang about with' wd (contr stv VII(*b*) §521)

belēac 3s pret < *belūcan* 'to enclose, shut up' (stv II §517)

belēas 3s pret < *belēosan* 'to lose' wd (stv II §517)

belidenes gs past ptc < *belīðan* 'to deprive of' wd (stv I §517)

belimpende as pres ptc < *belimpan* 'to belong to' (stv III §518)

belt m 'belt' (§502)

bēna (Text 9/3140) m 'suppliant, petitioner' (§§500–1)

bēna (Text 18/6) gpl < *bēn* f 'prayer, request' (§504)

benam 3s pret < *beniman* 'to deprive of' wg (stv IV §519)

bence ds < *benc* f 'bench' (§504)

bencþelu apl < *bencþel* n 'bench-space' and so in pl 'floor on which the benches stood' (§503)

Benedictes gs 'Benedict's'

benorðan prep wd 'to the north of'

bēo < *bēon* 'to be'. See §528

bēon 'to be'. See §528

beorg m 'mountain, hill, cliff, mound, burial-place' (§502)

beorgan 'to save, defend' (stv III §518)

beorgas apl < **beorg**; **beorge** ds

beorhliþu npl < *beorhlip* n 'mountain-height, -slope' (§503)

beorht adj 'bright, shining, clear-sounding, excellent, beautiful, pure'; **beorhtan** wk form (§§505–6); **beorhte** st apl (§§505, 507); **beorhtost** super; **beorhtra** gpl; **beorhtum** dpl

beorn m 'man, warrior, noble, chief, prince' (§502); **beorna** gpl; **beornas** n/apl; **beorne** ds; **beornes** gs

beotedan 1pl pret < *bēotian* 'to vow, promise' (wkv §525)

bēoð < *bēon*. See §528

beran 'to bear, carry' (stv IV §517); **berað** 3pl pres

beredon 3pl pret < *berian* 'to bare, clear' (wkv §525)

berstan 'to burst, fall apart' (stv III §517); **berstende** pres ptc

beseah < *besēon* 'to see, look, behold (contr stv V (§521)). This verb sometimes takes a refl object; **besēo** 3s pres subj

beslægen past ptc < *beslēan* 'to deprive of' wg (contr stv VI §521)

besnyþede 3s pret < *besnyþþan* 'to deprive of' wd (wkv 1 §524)

bestæl 3s pret < *bestelan* 'to steal away' w refl object (stv IV §517)

bestēmed past ptc < *bestēman* 'to make wet, drench' (wkv like *hieran* §94)

beswāc 3s pret < *beswīcan* 'to seduce, betray' (stv I §517); **beswicen** past ptc

beswyled past ptc < *beswyllan* 'to drench' (wkv 1 §524)

besyrwan 'to ensnare, entrap'

bet comp adv 'better'

betan 'to amend, make good' (wkv like *settan* §94)

betæhte npl past ptc < *betæcan* 'to entrust, deliver to' (wkv like *hieran* §94 with -*ht*- for -*cd*-)

beteran oblique case < *betera* comp adj 'better' (§§505–6)

Bethuliam ds 'Bethulia'

betimbredon 3pl pret < *betimbran* 'to build, construct' (wkv §§522–3)

betra comp adj 'better' m (§§505–6); **betre** nsn

betst super adj 'best'

bettan 1pl pret < **betan**

betwēonan prep wd 'between'

betweox prep wd 'between'

beþeaht past ptc < *beþeccan* 'to cover, overwhelm' (irreg wkv); **beþeahton** 3pl pret

beþencan 1pl pres subj w refl object 'to bethink oneself, to reflect' (wkv §95)

beþenede 3s pret < *beþennan* 'to cover' (wkv §524)

beþōhte 3s pret < **beþencan**

bewǣfed past ptc *bewǣfan* 'to clothe' (wkv like *hieran* §94)

beweaxne npl past ptc < *beweaxan* 'to grow over, cover with' (stv VII(*a*) §517)

bewefen past ptc < *bewefan* 'to cover over' (stv V §517)

bewēop 3s pret < *bewēpan* 'to weep for, bewail' (stv VII(*a*) §517)

bewrigen past ptc < *bewrēon* 'to cover' (contr stv I §521)

bewunden past ptc < *bewindan* 'to wind round, clasp, surround' (stv III §518)

bewȳpð = *bewēpð* 3s pres < *bewēpan*. See **bewēop**

bi/bī prep wd/a 'about'

biddan 'to ask, pray' (sometimes w refl object) (stv V §519); **bidde** 1s pres/2s pres subj; **biddende** pres ptc

bifian 'to tremble' (wkv 2 §526); **bifode** 1s pret

bifongen past ptc < *befōn* 'to surround' (stv VII(*b*) §521)

bigange = *bigonge* ds < **bigong**

bigong m 'worship'

bigstandað 3pl pres < *bigstandan* 'to stand by, support' (stv VI §519)

bilecgað 3pl pres < *bilecgan* 'to cover, surround, envelop' (irreg wkv); **bilegde** 3s pret

billgeslihtes gs < *billgesliht* n 'sword-clash, battle'

billum dpl < *bill* n 'sword' (§503)

binnan (1) adv 'within'; (2) prep wd 'inside'

binom = **benam**

bīon = **bēon**

bireþ 3s pres < **beran**

birgenne ds < *birgenn* f 'grave' (§504)

Birino ds 'Birinus'

bisceop m 'bishop' (§502)

biscep = **bisceop**

biscepdōme ds < *biscepdōm* m 'bishopric' (§502)

biscepe ds < **bisce(o)p**

biscepsetl n 'bishop's seat, bishopric'

biscepsuna ds < *biscepsunu* m 'godson (at confirmation)' (*Guide* §61)

biscop = **bisceop**; **biscope** ds; **biscopes** gs

bīsena gpl < *bīsen* f 'example' (§504)

bisgo as < *bisgo* f 'care, toil' (irreg)

bit 3s pres < **biddan**. A contr form of *bideþ*

bite as < *bite* m 'bite, cut' (*Guide* §§45–6)

bitre npl < *biter* adj 'bitter, fierce, grim' (§§505, 507)

bið < **bēon**. See §528

biworpen past ptc < *biweorpan* 'to surround' (stv III §518)

blācað 3s pres < *blācian* 'to grow pale' (wkv 2 §526)

blace st asf < *blæc* 'black' (§§505, 507, *Guide* §70)

blandenfeax adj 'grey-haired'

blǣcern n 'lamp, candle' (§503)

blǣd m 'prosperity, glory, splendour' (§502); **blǣdes** gs

blēdum = *blǣdum* dpl < **blǣd**

blēom contr dpl < *blēo* n 'colour' (§503); **blēos** contr gs

bletsunge as < *bletsung* f 'blessing' (§504)

blīcan 'to shine' (stv I §517)

blinne ds < *blinn* n 'ceasing, cessation' (§503)

blisse oblique case < *bliss* f 'merriment, happiness, grace' (§504)

blissian 'to rejoice, be glad'

blīðe ns/pl < *blīðe* adj 'joyous, cheerful' (*Guide* §73); **blīðum** ds

blōd n 'blood' (§503); **blōde** ds

blōdegesan ds < *blōdegesa* 'bloody terror' (§§500–1)

blōdgyte m 'bloodshed'

blōstman npl < *blōstma* m 'blossom' (§§500–1)

blōtan 'to sacrifice'

blōwende pres ptc < *blōwan* 'to flower, flourish' (stv VII(*a*) §517)

bōc f 'book'. See **bēc**; **bōca** gpl; **bōcum** dpl

bodad past ptc < *bodian*. See **bodigean**

bodigean 'to announce, preach' = *bodian* (wkv 2 §526); **bodude** 3s pret

bōgum dpl < *bōg* m 'arm' (§502)

bolgenmōd adj 'enraged'

bolstrum dpl < *bolster* m 'bolster, cushion' (§502)

booc = **bōc**

borda gpl < *bord* n 'shield' (§503)

bordweall m 'wall of shields'

bordwudu apl < *bordwudu* m 'shield' (*Guide* §61)

bōsme ds < *bōsm* m 'bosom, hold' (§502); **bōsmum** dpl

bōte ds < *bōt* f 'help, remedy' (§504)

brād adj 'broad'; **brāde** st n/apl; **brādost**

super 'broadest'; **brādre** comp nsn 'broader'

bræc 3s pret < *brecan* 'to break' (stv IV §519)

bræcan = bræcon

bræcon pl pret < *brecan*. See **bræc**

brædre = brādre

brægen n 'brain'

brēber m 'bramble'

bregdan 'to draw, drag' (stv III §518)

brēgdon 3pl pret < *brēgan* 'to terrify' (wkv like *hīeran* §94)

brego m 'ruler, lord, king'

brenge 3s pres subj < *brengan* 'to bring' (wkv *Guide* §§122, 123.2)

brēost (gender varies) 'breast'

brēostsefa m 'mind, heart'

brēostum dpl < **brēost**

brerd m 'rim'

brērum dpl < *brēr* f 'briar, bramble' (§504)

Bretene 'Britain', used in various cases

Bretenlond 'Britain'

Bretone = Bretene

Bretta gpl < **Brettas**

Brettas n/apl 'Britons'

Brettisc adj 'British'

Brettum dpl < **Brettas**

Bretwalas apl 'Britons'; **Bretwalum** dpl

brim n 'sea, flood' (§503)

brimclifu apl < *brimclif* n 'sea-cliff' (§503)

brimu apl < **brim**

bringað (1) Text 17 imp pl; (2) Text 29 3pl pres < *bringan* 'to bring' (stv III §518 not found in pret (*Guide* §§122, 123.2)); **bringe** 3s pres subj

Brixonte the name of a river

brōce ds < *brōc* m 'brook'

brogan ds < *broga* m 'terror' (§§500–1)

brōhton 3pl pret < *brengan* (*Guide* §§122, 123.2)

bronda gpl < *brond* m 'burning, fire' (§502)

brosnað 3s pres < *brosnian* 'to decay' (wkv 2 §526)

brōþer = brōþor

brōþor m 'brother'. This form can be n/a/gs or n/apl (*Guide* §60)

brōþur = brōþor

brūcan 'to make use of, enjoy' wg (stv II §517); **brūcað** 3pl pres

brūn adj 'brown, gleaming'; **brūnne** st asm (§§505, 507)

bryhtm m 'twinkling (of an eye)'

bryne m 'burning, flame, heat'

bryttan as < *brytta* m 'distributor, giver' (§§500–1)

bryttigan 'to possess, enjoy'

bū n/apln < **bēgen**

būað 3pl pres < *būan* 'to live, inhabit, cultivate' (wkv §§522–3); **būde** 3s pret

budon 3pl pret < *bēodan* 'to offer' (stv II §517)

bufan prep wd 'above'

būgan (Text 39/18) = *būan*. See **būað**; **būgan** (elsewhere) 'to bow, submit to' (stv II §517); **bugon** 3pl pret

bundenne st asm < *bunden* past ptc < *bindan* 'to bind, join' (stv III §518)

būre ds < *būr* n 'bower, chamber' (§503)

burg f 'dwelling in a fort, enclosure, fort'

Burgrēde ds 'Burgred'

burgsittendan wk dsm < *burgsittende* 'city-dwelling/native'

burgtūnas npl < *burgtūn* m 'city' (§502)

burgum dpl < **burg**

burgware as < *burgwaru* = **burhwaru**

burh = burg

burhstede m 'courtyard (of fort)'

burhwaru m/f collective noun 'the inhabitants of a **burg**, citizens'

burston 3pl pret < *berstan* 'to break, fall, crash' (stv III §518)

būtan (1) prep wd/a 'without, out of, except'; (2) conj with subj 'unless'; (3) conj with ind 'except (that)'

būton = būtan

būtū acc dual 'both two' (*Guide* §84)

byddan = biddan

bȳne adj 'cultivated, inhabited'; **bȳnum** st ds (§§505, 507)

byre m 'time'

byrgenne = birgenne

byrig g/ds or n/apl < **burg**

byrnan gs or apl < **byrne**

byrne f 'corslet, coat of mail' (§§500–1)

byrnende pres ptc < *byrnan* 'to burn'

byrnum dpl < **byrne**

Byrtene as 'Britain'

byrð = birð 3s pres < **beran**

byrþnes gs < *byrþen* m 'child' (§502)

bysmeredon 3pl pret < *bysmerian* 'to mock, revile' (wkv §525)

bȳsne ds < *bȳsen* f 'original, exemplar' (§504)

byð = bið

bȳwan 'to polish'

campe ds < *camp* m 'battle, warfare' (§502)

campstede ds < *campstede* m 'battlefield' (*Guide* §§45–6)

can 3s pres < **cunnan**

cancell scribal abbreviation 'chancellor'

candel f 'candle, lantern'

candelmæssan ds < *candelmæsse* f 'Candlemas, the Feast of the Purification (2 February)' (§§500–1)

canōnes gs < *canōn* m 'canon' (§502)

Cantware 'the people of Kent'; **Cantwarum** dpl

cāseras npl < **cāsere**

cāsere m 'emperor, ruler' (*Guide* §§45–6)

cealf n 'calf'

cēas 3s pret < *cēosan* 'to choose' (stv II §517)

ceasterwaran npl 'citizens'

ceastre a/gs < *ceaster* f 'fort, town' (§504)

cempan apl < *cempa* m 'warrior, champion' (§§500–1)

cende npl past ptc < **cennan**

cēne npl < *cēne* adj 'bold, fierce' (*Guide* §73); **cēnestan** npl super adj

cennan 'to bring forth, bear (offspring)' (wkv like *fyllan* §94); **cenneð** 3s pres

cēol m 'ship'

cēpemannum dpl < *cēpemann* m 'trader, merchant'

Cerdice ds 'Cerdic'

cild n/as or n/apl < *cild* n 'child' (§503); **cilda** gpl; **cilde** ds; **cildes** gs; **cildra** gpl (*Guide* §34); **cildum** dpl

cile m 'chill'

cing m 'king' (§502) = **cyning**; **cinge** ds; **cinges** gs

cining = **cing**

cirde 3s pret < *cirran* 'to turn oneself, submit' (wkv like *fyllan* §94)

ciricean as/npl < *cirice* f 'temple, church' (§§500–1)

clǣnsian 'to cleanse, purify'

Clementes gs 'Clement's'

cliopode = **clipode**

clipode 3s pret < *clipian* 'to speak (out), call, summon' (wkv 2 §526)

clūdig adj 'rocky'

clufon 3pl pret < *clēofan* 'to cleave' (stv II §517)

clypode = **clipode**

clyppað 3pl pres < *clyppan* 'to embrace'

cnapa m 'child, youth, servant' (§§500–1); **cnapan** oblique case

cnear m 'ship'

cnēo apl < *cnēo* n 'knee'

cnēomāgum dpl < *cnēomǣg* 'kinsman' (§502)

cneoris f 'tribe, nation'

cnēowu apl < *cnēo* n 'knee' (*Guide* §40)

cniht m 'young man'

cnysede 3s pret < *cnyssan* 'to beat, defeat' (wkv 1 §524)

collenferhðe st npl < *collenferhð* adj 'proud, elated' (§§505, 507)

cōlodon 3pl pret < *cōlian* 'to be cold' (wkv 2 §526)

cōm 1/3s pret < **cuman**

cōman = **cōmon**

cōme 3s pret subj < **cuman**

comēta m 'comet'

cōmon 3pl pret < **cuman**

compienne w *tō* infl inf < *compian* 'to fight'

compweorod n 'army, host' (§503); **compweorodes** gs

compwige ds < *compwig* 'battle' (§503)

con 1s pres < **cunnan**

consensi in Latin formula 'agreed'

corn n 'corn, seed'

corsias a proper name (no capital in MS)

corðre ds < *corðor* n 'troop, band, retinue' (§503)

cratu apl < *cræt* n 'chariot' (§503, *Guide* §36)

cræft m 'might, courage; art, skill, ability'

Crēacas npl 'Greeks'

crēad 3s pret < *crūdan* 'to press, hasten' (stv II §517)

Crīste ds < *Crīst* 'Christ' (§502); **Crīstes** gs (§502)

Crīstesmǣl n 'Christ's mark, the Cross'

Crīstna = **Crīstne**

Crīstne st npl < *Crīsten* adj 'Christian' (§§505, 507)

crungon 3pl pret < *cringan* 'to fall in battle' (stv III §518)

cū gs < *cū* f 'cow' (irreg noun)

cuæð = **cwæþ**. See **cwǣde**

cuma m 'stranger, guest'

cuman 'to come' (stv IV §519); **cumað** 1pl pres

cumblum dpl < *cumbol* n 'banner, standard' (§503)

cumbolgehnastes gs < *cumbolgehnast* n 'clash of banners, battle' (§503)

Cumbran as 'Cumbra'

cume s pres subj < **cuman**; **cumen**, past ptc; **cumene** pl past ptc; **cumeð** 3pl pres = fut

cunnan 'to know (how)' (§96); **cunne** 3s pres subj; **cunnen** 3pl pres subj; **cunnon** 3pl pres; **cunnun** 3pl pres

cuōm = **cōm**

cuōmon = **cōmon**

cūþ adj 'known'

cūþlice adv 'certainly, to be sure'

cūðe 1s pret < **cunnan**

cūðlicre as of comp adj 'more certain'

cūðon 1/3pl pret < **cunnan**

cwǣde 2s pret < **cweþan**; **cwǣden** 3pl pret subj; **cwǣdon** 3pl pret; **cwǣþ** 1/3s pret

cwealme ds < *cwealm* n 'pain, torment, death' (§503)

cwellendum st dsn past ptc < *cwellan* 'to kill' (cf. the last sentence of Text 25 and fig. 36)

cwēn f 'woman, wife, royal princess'

Cwēna gpl < **Cwēnas**

Cwēnas npl the name of a tribe

cwēnum dpl < **cwēn**

cweþan 'to say, name, order, call' (stv V §§97, 515); **cweþe** 3s pres subj; **cweðe** 1s pres; **cweþenne** w *tō* infl inf

cwic adj 'living'; **cwica** wk nsm (§§505–6); **cwican** = *cwicum* st dsn (§§505–7)

cwidas apl < *cwide* m 'saying, proverb' (*Guide* §§45–6)

cwōm = **cōm**

cwōme = **cōme**

cyle ds < *cyle* m 'chill' (*Guide* §§45–6)

cyme ds < *cyme* m 'coming' (*Guide* §§45–6)

cymeð 3s pres < **cuman**

cȳmlicor comp adv 'more splendidly'

cyn n 'race, lineage'

cynedōme ds < *cynedōm* m 'kingly rule, government' (§502)

cynelicum st dsm < *cynelic* 'royal, public' (§§505, 507)

cynerīce ds < *cynerīce* n 'kingdom' (*Guide* §§45–6)

cynesetle ds < *cynesetl* n 'throne' (§503)

cyng(c) = **cyning**; **cynge** ds; **cynges** gs

cyning m 'king' (§502); **cyninga** gpl; **cyningas** n/apl

cyningc = **cyning**

cyninge ds < **cyning**; **cyninges** gs

cynn n 'family, race, lineage' (§503); **cynna** gpl; **cynnes** gs

cyrce f 'church' (§§500–1); **cyrcean** ds

cyre m 'choice'

cyrican a/ds < *cyrice* = **cyrce**

cyricean = **cyrcean**. See **cyrce**

cyrmdon 3pl pret < *cyrman* 'to cry out' (wkv like *hīeran* §94)

cyssað 3pl pres < *cyssan* 'to kiss' (wkv like *settan* §94)

cyst as < *cyst* f 'best' (§504)

cyste 3s pret < *cyssan*. See **cyssað**

cȳðan 'to proclaim, make known' (wkv like *hīeran* §94); **cȳðe** 1s pres; **cȳðed** past ptc

cȳððe as < *cȳþþ* f 'native land' (§504)

dagas n/apl < **dæg**; **dagum** dpl

dala = *dalu* apl < *dæl* 'valley, abyss' (§503, *Guide* §36)

daroða gpl < *daroð* m 'spear, javelin' (§502); w **lāf** f 'legacy, leavings' = 'survivors of battle'

dǣd f 'deed' (§504); **dǣda** npl; **dǣde** g/ds

dǣdfruman gs < *dǣdfruma* m 'doer of deeds' (§§500–1)

dǣdum dpl < **dǣd**

dæg m 'day' (§502, *Guide* §36); **dæge** ds

dægrēd n 'daybreak, dawn'

dægweorces gs < *dægweorc* n 'day's work, service' (§503)

dǣl m 'portion, share, district' (§502)

dǣlan 'to divide, share' (wkv like *hīeran* §94); **dǣlde** 3s pret

dǣle ds < **dǣl**; **be suman dǣle** 'to some extent, partly'

dēad adj 'dead'; **dēada** wk nsm (§§505–6); **dēadan** wk gsm (§§505–6); **dēade** st apl/ wk nsn (§§505–7)

dearr 1s pres < *durran* 'to dare' (§96)

dēað m 'death' (§502)

dēaðdrepe ds < *dēaðdrepe* m 'death-blow' (*Guide* §§45–6)

dēaðe ds < **dēað**

dēl = **dǣl**

delfan 'to dig' (stv III §518)

dena npl < *denu* f 'valley, dale' (§504)

Dena gpl < *Dene* 'Danes'

Denescan = **Deniscan**. See **denisc**

denisc adj 'Danish'; **Deniscan** wk oblique case (§§505–6); **deniscne** st asm (§§505, 507); **deniscra** gpl

dēofle ds < **dēofol**

dēofol m 'devil' (§502)

dēofolgildum dpl < *dēofolgild* n 'devil-worship, idolatry' (§503)

dēop adj 'deep, awful, severe'; **dēopan** wk apl

dēophycgende ns past ptc used as adj 'deeply thinking, thoughtful'

dēoplice adv 'deeply, profoundly'

dēor as/npl *dēor* n '(wild) animal, beast' (§503)

dēoran wk asm < *dēor* adj 'bold, brave, grievous, violent' (§§505–6)

deorcan wk dpl < *deorc* adj 'dark' (§§505–6)

dēore asn < *dēore* adj 'precious, beloved'; **dēores** gs

dēorum dpl < *dēor*. See **dēoran**

dereð 3s pres < *derian* 'to hurt, injure' wd (wkv §525)

dēð 3s pres < **dōn**

dide = **dyde** < **dōn**

dimme npl < *dimm* adj 'dark, gloomy'

dō < **dōn**

dogode see Text 40/9 note

dōgores gs < *dōgor* f 'day'

dohte 3s pret < *dugan* 'to avail, be of use' (irreg vb *Guide* §130)

dohtor f 'daughter'. This form can be s or pl, and almost any case (*Guide* §60); **dohtra** gpl

dol adj 'foolish'

dolg npl < *dolg* n 'wound' (§503)

dollice adv 'foolishly, rashly'

dōm m 'judgment, law, opinion, power, glory, honour' (§502). See the General Index *sv dom*; **dōme** ds; **dōmes** gs

domne scribal abbreviation 'lord'

dōn 'to do, make, cause' (§89)

dorste 1s pret < *durran* 'to dare' (§96)

doru apl < *dor* n 'door' (*Guide* §61)

dōð 2pl pres < **dōn**

draca m 'dragon, sea-monster, serpent, the

devil' (§§500–1); **dracan** oblique case; **dracena** gpl

drāf 3s pret < **drīfan**

drēam m 'joy, gladness, mirth, melody, music' (§502); **drēamas** n/apl; **drēamum** dpl

drēfde 2s pret subj < **drēfan** 'to stir up, disturb' (wkv like *hīeran* §94)

drēogan 'to experience, endure' (stv II §517); **drēogeð** 3s pres

drēorig adj 'sad, mournful'

drēorsele m 'dreary/desolate hall'

drīfan 'to drive' (stv I §517)

drige adj 'dry' (*Guide* §73); **drigeum** st dsn

drihte npl < *driht* f 'crowd, host'; in pl 'men' (§504)

drihten m 'ruler, king, lord; God, Christ, the Lord' (§502); **drihtne** ds; **drihtnes** gs

drium (1)Text 16 v. 21 dsn 'to dry [land]'; (2) Text 16 v. 29 dpl adj = **drigeum**. See **drige**

druncon 3pl pret < *drincan* 'to drink' (stv III §518)

dryhten = **drihten**

dryhtfolca gpl < *dryhtfolc* n 'people, troop' (§503)

dryhtlicestum super dsm < *dryhtlic* adj 'lordly'

dryhtnes = **drihtnes**. See **drihten**

dryhtscipes gs < *dryhtscipe* m 'heroic deeds, valour' (*Guide* §§45–6)

dryncfæt n 'drinking-vessel, cup'

drȳs gs < *drȳ* m 'magician, sorcerer'

dugeþum dpl < **dugoð**

dugoð m 'army, body of noble retainers, heavenly host' (§502)

duguð = **dugoð**

duguðum = **dugeþum**

dūna npl < *dūn* f 'moor, hill' (§504)

dunnade 3s pret < *dunnian* 'to become dark' (wkv 2 §526)

durron 1pl pres < *durran*. See **dorste**

duru n/as < *duru* f 'door' (*Guide* §61)

dux Latin word = **ealdormann**

dwelode < *dwelian* 'to lead astray, deceive' (wkv 2 §526)

dyde 3s pret < **dōn**; **dydon** 3pl pret

dȳfde 3s pret < *dȳfan* 'to dip' (wkv like *hīeran* §94)

dȳre npl < *dȳre* adj 'costly, expensive' (*Guide* §73)

ēa as/ds < *ēa* f 'river' (here indeclinable)

ēac (1) adv 'also, and, likewise'; (2) prep wd 'together with, besides, in addition to'

ēad n 'riches, happiness'

ēadig adj 'wealthy, happy, blessed, prosperous'; **ēadige** st nplm (§§505, 507)

ēadignesse as/gs < *ēadigness* f 'happiness, prosperity' (§504)

ēadmōdlīce adv 'humbly'

Ēadmundes gs 'Edmund's'

Ēadweardes gs 'Edward's'

eaforan n/apl < *eafora* m 'son' (§§500–1)

ēagan oblique case < *ēage* n 'eye' (§§500–1); **ēagum** dpl

eahta num 'eight'

eahtoþan ds < *eahtoþa* num 'eighth'

eal (1) adj 'all, every, entire'; (2) adv 'fully, wholly, quite'

ēalā interj 'alas!, oh!, lo!'

eald adj 'old, ancient, experienced, tried, honoured'; **ealdan** wk asn (§§505–6)

ealdað 3s pres < *ealdian* 'to grow old' (wkv 2 §526)

ealde wk nsf/st npl < **eald** (§§505–7); **ealdes** st gsn; **ealdne** st asm

ealdor m 'master, lord, prince' (§502)

ealdorbisceop m 'high-priest'

ealdorlangne st asm < *ealdorlang* adj 'life-long' (§§505, 507)

ealdorman(n) = **aldorman(n)**; **ealdormannum** dpl

ealdorspell n 'old story, old saying'

ealdre (1) **tō ealdre** 'for ever' ds < *ealdor* n 'life' (§503); (2) elsewhere ds < **ealdor** m

ealdres gs < **ealdor** m

ealgodon 3pl pret < *ealgian* 'to defend' (wkv §526)

eall adj 'all, every, entire'; **ealla** apl; **eallan** = **eallum** dpl; **ealle** st is or n/apl, or wk nsf/n (§§505–7); **ealles** st gsm/n (§§505, 507)

eallinga adv 'entirely, altogether'

eallon = **eallum** dpl < **eall** adj; **eallra** gpl

eallswā … eallswā adv 'just as' … conj 'as'

eallum st dsm/n or dpl < **eall** (§§505–7)

eallunga = **eallinga**

ealne st asm < **eal** adj

ēalond n 'island' (§503); **ēalonde** ds; **ēalondes** gs

ealra gpl < **eal** adj; **ealre** gsf

ealswā … ealswā conj 'as' … adv 'so'

ēam m 'uncle'; **ēames** gs

ēaran apl < *ēare* 'ear' (§§500–1)

eard m 'native place, country, dwelling-place, land'; **earde** ds

eardian 'to dwell, inhabit' (wkv §526); **eardiað** 3pl pres

earfoþa gpl < *earfoþe* n 'hardship, labour, trouble, suffering' (*Guide* §§45–6)

earfoðnissum dpl < *earfoðniss* f 'hardship, affliction, pain' (§504)

earfoðu apl < *earfoðe*. See **earfoþa**

eargebland n 'wave-blend, surge'

earm adj 'poor, miserable, wretched'; **earme** wk asn (§§505–6)

earmlice adv 'miserably'

earmra gpl < **earm**

earn m 'eagle'

earne = *eargne* st asm < *earg* adj 'sluggish, wretched' (§§505, 507)

eart 2s pres < **bēon/wesan** 'to be' (§528)

ēast (1) adj 'easterly'; (2) adv 'eastwards'

ēastan adv 'from the east'

ĒastEngla gpl 'of the East Angles'; **Ēast-Engle** n/apl 'the East Angles'; **ĒastEnglum** dpl 'the East Angles'

ēasteweard adv 'eastwards'

ēastewearde asn adj in **ealle Cent ēaste-wearde** 'all the east of Kent'

ēastewerd = **ēasteweard**

Ēastor 'Easter'

ēastrīce ds < *ēastrīce* n 'eastern (Frankish) kingdom' (*Guide* §§45–6)

Ēastron 'Easter'

ĒastSeaxe n/apl 'the East Saxons'

ēaþe (1) adj 'easy, smooth'; (2) adv 'easily'

eaxlgespanne ds < *eaxlgespann* n 'cross-beam, intersection' (§503)

eaxlum dpl < *eaxl* f 'shoulder' (§504)

Ebriscgeðiode ds < *Ebriscgeðiode* n 'the Hebrew language' (*Guide* §§45–6)

ēcan wk oblique case < **ēce** (§§505–6); **ēcæ** dsn

ēce adj 'eternal'. This form can appear in various cases, both strong and weak (§§505–7, *Guide* §73); **ēces** st gsm

ecg f 'edge, sword'

Ecgberhte ds 'Ecgberht'

ecghete m 'sword hatred, violence, war'

Ecgrice ds 'Ecgric'

ecgum dpl < **ecg**

ecnisse ds < *ecniss* f 'eternity' (§504)

edisce ds < *edisc* m 'pasture, meadow' (§502)

edlēanes gs < *edlēan* n 'reward' (§503)

Edwines gs 'Edwin's'

ēe ds < *ēg* f 'island' in **in Lindisfarena ēe** = *in insula Lindisfarnensi* 'in the island of Lindisfarne'

efenhlyttan npl < *efenhlytta* m 'sharer, partner' (§§500–1)

efne (1) interj 'behold!'; (2) adv in **efne swylce ... swylce** 'exactly such ... as'

efstan 'to hasten, hurry'

eft adv 'again, then, afterwards, back, likewise, moreover'

ege ds < *ege* m 'fear, terror' (*Guide* §§45–6)

egesan npl < *egesa* 'fear, horror, peril' (§§500–1)

egesfull adj 'inspiring awe, terrible'

egeslic adj 'awful, dreadful'; **egeslice** npl

eglond n 'island'

ego Latin word 'I'

Egypta gpl < **Egypte**

Egypte npl 'Egyptians'

Egyptiscan wk npl < *Egyptisc* adj 'Egyptian' (§§505–6); **Egyptiscra** gpl

Egyptum dpl < **Egypte**

ehtere m 'persecutor'

ehtnysse g/ds < *ehtnyss* f 'persecution' (§504)

ēhton 3pl pret < *ēhtan* 'to pursue, persecute' (wkv like *settan* §94)

ele ds < *ele* m 'oil' (*Guide* §§45–6)

Elenan gs 'Elena's'

elles adv 'else, otherwise, besides'

ellor adv 'elsewhere'

elmessan as < *elmesse* f 'alms' (wk §§500–1)

elmesse ds < *elmess* f 'alms' (st §504)

elne ds < *ellen* n 'zeal, courage'; **elnes** gs

embe prep wa 'about, concerning'

emnlange prep wd 'along'

ende m 'end, conclusion, boundary, direction, part, district'. This form can be n/a/ds or n/apl (*Guide* §§45–6)

endebirdnisse = **endebyrdnesse**

endebyrdnes(s) f 'order, arrangement, method' (§504); **endebyrdnesse** as

endlyftan ds < *endlyfta* num 'eleventh'

engel m 'angel' (§502)

engellicum dpl < *engellic* adj 'angelic, of angels'

engla gpl < **engel**

Engla gpl < **Engle**; **Englan** wk apl

Engle n/apl 'Angles'

Englisc adj 'English'; **engliscan** wk apl (§§505–6)

englum dpl < **engel**

engyl = **engel**

ēode 3s pret < **gān** (§529); **ēodon** 3pl pret

eoferes gs < *eofer* m '(wild) boar' (§502)

Eoforwicceastre ds 'York'

eoletes gs < *eolet* n 'sea-journey, voyage' (§503)

eom 1s pres < **bēon/wesan** 'to be' (§528)

ēoredcystum dpl < *ēoredcyst* f 'troop, company' (§504)

eorl m '(brave) man, warrior, leader, chief, nobleman' (§502); **eorla** gpl; **eorlas** n/apl; **eorlum** dpl

eorþan oblique case < **eorþe**

eorþe f 'earth, ground, country, district, world' (§§500–1)

eorðlice wk asn < *eorðlic* adj 'earthly, worldly' (§§505–6)

eorðscrafu apl < *eorðscræf* n 'cave-dwelling, cavern' (*Guide* §36); **eorðscræfe** ds

eorðsele m 'earth-hall, cave-dwelling'

eorðwelan < *eorðwela* m 'wealth, worldly prosperity' (§§500–1)

eoselas npl < *eosel* m 'ass' (§502); **eoseles** gs

ēow a/dpl < þū 'thou' (§494)
ēower (1) gpl < þū (§494) 'of you'; (2) poss 'your, yours'; ēowre npl
eps scribal abbreviation for *episcopus* 'bishop'
ercebiscop m 'archbishop'
ergende npl pres ptc < erian
erian 'to plough'
ēstum dpl < *ēst* m 'favour, grace', used as adv 'gladly'
Ēstum dpl 'the Ests'
etan 'to eat' (stv V §517)
ettan 'to graze, pasture'
ēþel m 'country, native land'

fadian 'to arrange, dispose'
fadunge ds < *fadung* f 'arrangement, order'
fāgne st asm < *fāg* adj 'decorated, shining' (§§505, 507)
fāh adj (1) Text 46/476 'hostile'; (2) Text 51/13 'guilty, stained'
fāhne = fāgne
fāmgode 3s pret < *fāmgian* 'to foam' (wkv 2 §526)
fāmigbosma adj 'foamy-bosomed'
fāmīhēals adj 'foamy-necked'
fand 3s pret < findan
faran 'to go, travel; (w on) to come' (stv VI §517)
Faraon n/as 'Pharaoh'
farað 3pl pres < faran; fare 1s pres = fut; fareð 3s pres
fæc n 'space of time' (§503); fæce ds
fæder m 'father'. This form can be n/a/g/ds (*Guide* §60); fæderas n/apl; fæderes gs; fæderum dpl
fǣgan = fǣgum st dsn < *fǣge* adj 'fated, doomed (to die), dead' (*Guide* §73)
fǣge < *fǣge* adj. See fǣgan; (1) in Text 48/880 asn; (2) elsewhere nplm
fæger adj 'beautiful, pleasant, agreeable'; fægere npl; fægran wk dsf (§§505–6)
fǣgum st dsm/n or dpl < fǣge (§§505–7)
fǣhþo f 'hostility, violence, vendetta, enmity'
fǣhðu as, a variant of fǣhþo
fǣle adj 'faithful, beloved'
fær Text 8/33 n 'ship, vessel'
fǣr Text 46/453 m 'calamity, peril, sudden attack'
færeð 3s pres < faran
fǣrgripum dpl < *fǣrgripe* m 'sudden grip' (*Guide* §§45–6)
fǣringa adv 'suddenly'
fæst adj 'fast = firm, fixed, secure'
fæste adv 'fast = firmly, securely'
fæstlice adv 'firmly, resolutely, strictly, constantly'
fæt Text 21/4 n 'vat, vessel, jar'
fǣt Text 17 v. 27 adj 'fat'

fǣted past ptc = adj 'decorated with gold'
fætt = fǣt
fǣttum dpl < *fætt* n 'gold plate' (§503)
fǣtum = fǣttum
fæðme ds < *fæðm* m 'breast, embrace' (§502); fæþmum dpl
feaht 3s pret < *feohtan* 'to fight' (stv III §518)
feala = fela
feallan 'to fall, fall in battle' (stv VII(*a*) §517); feallende pres ptc
fealone st asm < *fealu* adj 'fallow = yellow, tawny, (perhaps) shining' (*Guide* §71); fealwa wk nsm
fēam contr dpl < *fēa(wa)* adj 'few'; fēawum dpl
feax n 'hair' (§503); feaxe ds
Febr scribal abbreviation 'February'
fēdað 3pl pres < *fēdan* 'to feed'
fela indeclinable = all cases, often wg 'many'
felalēofan wk gsm < *felalēof* adj 'very dear, beloved' (§§505–6)
feld m 'field (of battle)'
fēng (1) Text 42/355 *fēng* m 'grip, grasp'; (2) elsewhere 1/3s pret < fōn
fenne ds < *fenn* n 'fen, marsh' (§503)
fēo ds < feoh
feoh n 'cattle, property, money, treasure' (*Guide* §38)
feohgehāte ds < *feohgehāt* n 'promise of money' (§503)
feohlēase st npl < *feohlēas* adj 'without money' (§§505, 507)
fēol 3s pret < feallan
fēoldan 3pl pret < *fealdan* 'to fold' (stv VII(*a*) §517)
fēollon 3pl pret < feallan
fēond m 'enemy, foe, adversary, the devil' (§502); fēonda gpl; fēondas n/apl; fēondum dpl
feor adj and adv 'far, distant, remote'
fēore ds < feorh
feorg = feorh
feorh m 'life, soul, spirit' (*Guide* §39)
feorhādle ds < *feorhādl* 'fatal disease' (§504)
feorhbealo n 'life-bale, violent death'
feorhcynna gpl < *feorhcynn* n 'race of men' (§503)
feorlen adj 'far off, distant'
feormie 3s pres subj < *feormian* 'to polish, furbish' (wkv §526); feormynd = feormiend uninfl npl pres ptc 'polishers, furbishers'
feorr adv 'far, far off'
fēorþan dsm < *fēorþa* num 'fourth' (§§505–6)
fēorðe nsf < *fēorða*. See fēorþan
feorwegum dpl < *feorweg* m 'far way'; in pl 'distant parts' (§502)
fēos gs < feoh
fēower num 'four'

fēowertig num 'forty'

fēran 'to go, come, depart, march, act, obtain, suffer' (wkv like *hīeran* §94); fērde 1/3s pret; fērdon 3pl pret

ferhðsefan ds < *ferhðsefa* m 'mind' (§§500–1)

ferlorene asf past ptc < *forlēosan* 'to lose' (stv II §517)

fers uninfl apl < *fers* n 'verse'

fersce st nplm < *fersc* adj 'fresh' (§§505, 507)

ferþe ds < *fer(h)þ* m 'mind, spirit' (§502)

fēt ds or n/apl < *fōt* m 'foot' (§520)

fēðegāst m 'warlike spirit'. Some editors read *fēðegest*; see next entry

fēðegestas npl < *fēðegest* m 'stranger, traveller' (§502)

fierd f 'national levy, Anglo-Saxon army', later used also of the Danes; 'military campaign or expedition' (§504); fierde ds

fīf num 'five', sometimes used without inflexion in oblique cases; fīfe infl n(pl)

fīftan dsm < *fīfta* num 'fifth' (§§505–6)

fīftiges gs < *fīftig* num 'fifty'

fīftȳne num 'fifteen'

fihtling m 'fighter'

findan 'to find' (stv III §518); findest 2s pres

fingras npl < *finger* m 'finger' (§502)

Finnas npl '[Finns], Lapps'

fiorme as < *fiorm* f 'use, benefit, sustenance' (§504)

first m 'time'

firum dpl < *firas* plm 'men, human beings' (§502)

fiscaþe ds < *fiscaþ* m 'fishing' (§502)

fitte ds < *fitt* f 'song, poem' (§504)

flāne gs < *flān* f 'arrow' (§504)

flǣschoma m 'body' (§§500–1)

flēah 3s pret < *flēon* 'to flee (from), escape' (contr stv II §521)

flēame ds < *flēam* m 'flight' (§502)

flēogende npl past ptc < *flēogan* 'to fly' (stv II §517)

flēoð 3pl pres < *flēon*. See flēah

flet n 'floor, dwelling, hall'

flocce ds < *flocc* m 'flock, company, troop' (§502)

flōd m 'mass of water, flood, wave, current' (§502)

flōdblāc adj 'pale as the flood' or 'pale through fear of the flood'

flōdegsa m 'flood-terror'

flōdes gs < flōd

flōdweard m 'the flood-guardian, God'

flōr m 'floor'

flot n 'deep water, sea'

flota m 'ship, vessel, fleet, sailor' (§§500–1); flotan oblique case; flotena gpl

flōweð 3s pres < *flōwan* 'to flow'

fluge 3s pret subj < *flēon*. See flēah; flugon 3pl pret

flyman as < *flyma* m 'outlaw, exile, fugitive' (§§500–1)

folc n 'people, nation, tribe, troop, army' (§503)

folccūðne st asm < *folccūð* adj 'public, well-known' (§§505, 507)

folce ds < folc; folces gs

folcgefeoht npln 'pitched battles' (§503)

folcgesteallan dpl (with -an for -um) < *folcgestealla* m 'comrade in war' (§§500–1)

folcmǣlum = *floccmǣlum* dpl 'in troops/bands'

folcstede ds < *folcstede* 'battle-field' (*Guide* §§45–6)

folcum dpl < folc

foldan oblique case < *folde* f 'earth, ground, land, country, world' (§§500–1)

foldgrǣfe ds < *foldgrǣf* n 'earth-grave' (§503)

folgiende nsm pret ptc < *folgian* 'to follow' (wkv 2 §526); folgode 3s pret

folgoð m 'condition of life, destiny'

folmum dpl < *folm* f 'hand' (§504)

fon Text 29/13 = *fann* f 'fan, winnowing instrument'

fōn 'to undertake'; w on/tō 'to take up, receive, begin'; fōn tō rīce 'to become king' (contr stv VII(*b*) §521)

for adv 'too, very'; prep wd/a (1) place 'before, in the sight/presence of, as far as'; (2) time 'during, before'; (3) cause 'because of'; (4) other 'instead of'; (5) for hwȳ/hwǣm? 'why?'; (6) on its use in prep advs and conjs like *for þǣm* (*þe*), see the textual notes and §§124–6

fōr 1/3s pret < faran

forbærnað 3pl pres < *forbærnan* 'to cause to burn, burn up, be consumed by fire' (wkv like *hīeran* §94); forbærndon 3pl pret; forbærned past ptc; forbærneð 3s pres

ford in Oxena ford 'Oxford'; forda in Oxna forda ds 'Oxford'

fore prep wd/a 'for, on behalf of, on account of, instead of, before'

fōre 3s pret subj < faran

forebecna = *forebecnu* npl < *forebecn* n 'sign, portent' (§503)

foregange 3s pres subj < *foregangan* 'to go before'

foregīslas apl < *foregīsl* m 'preliminary hostage' (§502)

foresǣde wk nsf past ptc 'aforesaid'

forespeca m 'advocate, sponsor' (§§500–1); forespecan npl

foresprecena wk nsm past ptc 'aforesaid'

forgelde 3s pres subj < *forg(i)eldan* 'to indemnify, save' (stv III §518)

forgiefene aplm past ptc < *forgiefan* 'to give' (stv V §517)

forgiemde 1s pret < *forgieman* 'to neglect, transgress' (wkv like *hieran* §94)

forgrunden uninfl asm past ptc < *forgrindan* 'to destroy, consume' (stv III §518)

forhabban 'to hold back, restrain'

forhergedon 3pl pret < *forhergian* 'to plunder, ravage' (wkv §§525 or 526); **forhergod** past ptc

forht adj 'afraid'

forhtigende npl past ptc — adj 'frightened'

forhwan/forhwon interrog adv 'why?'

forhwæga adv 'somewhere, about'

forildan 'to put off, delay'

forlæst contr 2s pres < **forlætan** (*Guide* §112.2)

forlætan 'to lose, abandon, neglect, release, allow' (stv VII(*b*) §517); **forlætað** 2pl pres; **forlæten** past ptc

forlegene st npl past ptc — adj 'adulterous' (§§505, 507)

forlēt 1/3s pret < **forlætan**; **forlēton** 3pl pret

forliden st nsm past ptc — adj 'shipwrecked'; **forlidena** wk nsm (§§505–6); **forlidenan** wk asm

forligru apl < *forliger* n 'immorality' (§503)

forlogene st npl past ptc — adj 'perjured' (§§505, 507)

forma adj 'first, earliest' (§§505–6); **forman** ds

fornam 3s pret < *forniman* 'to carry off, destroy, consume' (stv §519)

fornæh adv 'almost, very nearly'

foroft adv 'very often'

fōron 3pl pret < **faran**

forsāwon 3pl pret < *forsēon* 'to reject, scorn, despise' (contr stv V §521); **forseah** 3s pret; **forsēoð** 2pl pres

forsiðe ds < *forsið* m 'departure, death' (§502)

forslægene st nplm past ptc < *forslēan* 'to kill, destroy' (contr stv VI §521)

forsodene st nplm past ptc < *forsēoðan* 'wither, consume' (stv II w *d* for *ð*; cf. §519)

forspæce ds < *forspæc* f 'advocacy, defence, excuse' (§504)

forspendað 3pl pres < *forspendan* 'to spend, squander'

forspilde 3s pret < *forspillan* 'to waste' (wkv like *fyllan* §94)

forstæl 3s pret < *forstelan* 'to steal (away)' (stv IV §517)

forste ds < *forst* m 'frost' (§502); **forstes** gs

forswelgan 'to consume, taste, swallow' (stv III §518); **forswelge** 3s pres subj

forswige 3s pres subj < *forswigian* 'to pass over in silence, keep secret'

forswiðe adv 'very much, utterly'

forsworene st nsm past ptc — adj 'forsworn, perjured'

forsyngod st nsm past ptc — adj 'deep in sin, corrupt'

forþ adv 'forwards, away, still, continually, henceforward, simultaneously, continuously'

forþām (1) adv (looking back) 'therefore'; (looking forward) 'for this reason'; (2) alone or with *þe* conj 'because'. See §§124–6

forþan — **forþām**

forþfērde 3s pret < *forþfēran* 'to depart, die' (wkv like *hieran* §94)

forðganges gs < *forðgang* m 'advance, escape' (§502)

forðgesceaft f 'eternal decree'

forþon — **forþām**

forðweges gs < *forðweg* m 'journey, departure'

forþȳ — **forþām**

forwearþ 1/3s pret < **forweorðan**

forweorðan 'to perish, pass away, deteriorate' (stv III §§513, 516); **forweorðe** 1s pres

forwierndon 3pl pret < *forwiernan* 'to refuse' (wkv like *hieran* §94)

forwordene st nplm past ptc < **forweorðan**

forwundod past ptc < *forwundian* 'to wound sorely' (wkv 2 §526)

forwyrcan 'to forfeit' (wkv §95)

fōta gpl < *fōt* m 'foot' (§520)

fōtmæla gpl < *fōtmæl* n 'foot-measure, foot' (§503); **fōtmælum** dpl

fōtum dpl < *fōt*. See **fōta**

fracodes st gsm < *fracod* adj 'vile, wicked' — noun (§§505, 507)

fracoðast super < *fracoð* adj 'most offensive'

fram prep wd (place) 'from, by'; (time) 'from, since'; (agent) 'by'

frætwa gpl < **frætwe**

frætwe pl f 'treasures, ornaments, trappings, armour' (§504)

frēa m 'ruler, lord, king; the Lord, Christ, God; husband' (§§500–1); **frēan** oblique case

frēcendlice adv 'dangerously, perilously'

frēcne adj 'dangerous, terrible, wicked'; **frēcnum** st dpl (§§505, 507)

fremdan wk nplm < *fremde* 'foreign, strange' (§§505–6); **fremdum** st dsm (§§505, 507)

fremian 'to serve, benefit' (wkv 2 §526)

fremman 'to do, advance, perfect' (wkv §524)

fremode 3s pret < **fremian**

fremsumnesse as < *fremsumness* f 'benefit' (§504)

fremum dpl < *fremu* f 'advantage, benefit, beneficial deed' (§504)

frēolico — *frēolicu* st npln < *frēolic* 'free, freeborn' (§§505, 507) frēonda gpl < *frēond* 'friend'

frēondliðe adj 'kind to one's friends'

frēondscipe, frēondscype m 'friendship'

frēondum dpl < *frēond*. See frēonda

fretað 3pl pres < *fretan* 'to eat, devour'

frī = *frīo* st asn < *frīo* irreg adj 'free'

fricge 1s pres < *fricgan* 'to ask, enquire' (stv V §517 with wk pres *Guide* §116)

frige Text 31/6 nplm < *frīge* irreg adj 'free'

frige Text 14/26 2s imp < *fricgan*. See fricge

frignan 'to ask, enquire'; frignende nsm pres ptc

frīora gpl < *frīo*. See frī

friþ m/n 'peace, security, refuge'; friþe ds; friþes gs

frōda wk nsm < *frōd* 'old, wise' (§§505–6); frōdran comp nplm

from = fram

Frome place-name 'Frome'

fromesta wk nsm < *fromest* super of adj *from* 'active, bold, strong'

fromsīþ m 'departure'

fromweardum st dsm < *fromweard* adj 'about to depart/die' (§§505, 507)

fruman g/ds < *fruma* m 'beginning, originator, instigator' (§§500–1)

frumbearn npl < *frumbearn* n 'first-born child' (§503)

frumsceaft m 'creation'

frȳnd = *friend* n/apl < *frēond* m 'friend' (§§17–18)

fugeles gs < *fug(e)l* m 'bird'; fugla gpl; fugle ds; fugles gs

fuhton 3pl pret < *feohtan* 'to fight' (stv III §518)

ful (1) adj wg 'full, complete'; (2) adv 'very, fully, thoroughly'

fulborenum st dsn < *fulboren* adj 'fully-born' (§§505, 507)

fūle st npl < *fūl* adj 'foul, unclean, impure' (§§505, 507)

full adv 'very'; be fullan 'fully, perfectly'

fullan See full

fulluht m/f/n(!) 'baptism, Christianity'; fulluhte ds

fullum st dsm < *full* adj 'full' (§§505, 507)

fulne st asm < *ful* adj (§§505, 507)

fultome = fultume. See fultum

fultum m 'help, support, protection, army' (§502); fultume ds

fultumian 'to help' (wkv 2 §526)

fulwihte g/ds < *fulwiht* = fulluht; fulwihtes gs

fulwuht = fulluht

funde irreg 3s pret < *findan* 'to find' (stv III §518); funden past ptc

furðon adv 'even'

furðor adv 'further'

furður = furðor

fūs adj wg 'eager/ready for, brave, noble'; fūse wk asn (§§505–6)

fylgean 'to follow' (irreg wkv); fylgen 1pl pres subj; fyliende nsm pres ptc; fyligde 3s pret

fylstan 'to help' wd (wkv 1 §§522–3)

fȳr n 'fire' (§503)

fȳra gpl < *fȳras* plm 'men, mankind' (§502)

fȳrbendum dpl < *fȳrbend* m 'fire(-forged) band' (§502)

fyrd = fierd; fyrde g/ds

fyre ds < fȳr

fȳrene st nplm < *fȳren* adj 'fiery, of fire' (§§505, 507)

fyres gs < fȳr

fyrhtu ds < *fyrhtu* f 'fear, dread' (not declined)

fyrhōglēaw adj 'wise, prudent'

fyrmest super adv 'in the first place, at first'

fyrst m 'period, space of time, time'

gā various s pres forms < *gān* (§529)

gafol n 'tribute, tax, debt' (§503); gafole ds

galan 'to sing, call, cry' (stv VI §517)

gallia = *Gallia* 'Gaul'

gān 'to go' (§529)

gangan 'to go' = gān; gangað 2 imp pl

gange (1) Text 51/23 ds < *gang* m 'going, flow' (§502); (2) elsewhere 3s pres subj < gangan

garmittinge ds < *garmitting* f 'clash of spears, battle' (§504)

garsecg m 'ocean, sea'

gārum dpl < *gār* m 'spear' (§502)

gāst m 'breath, human being, soul, spirit, angel' (§502); gāsta gpl; gāstas npl; gāste ds; gāstes gs

gāstlēasne st asm < *gāstleas* adj 'lifeless' (§§505, 507)

gāstlice wk asn < *gāstlic* adj 'spiritual' (§§505–6); gāstlicum = *gāstlican* wk dsn

gāð 2 imp pl < gān

gǣlsa adj 'greedy'

gǣlsan ds < *gǣlsa* m 'pride, luxury' (§§500–1)

gǣþ 3s pres < gān

ge conj 'and'; ge ... ge 'both ... and' (§119)

gē npl 'ye/you' (§494)

gēac m 'cuckoo'

geador adv 'together'

geaf 3s pret < *giefan* 'to give' (stv V §517)

geald 3s pret < *gieldan* 'to pay' (stv III §518)

gealga m 'gallows, cross' (§§500–1); gealgan as

gēar m/n 'year' (§§502, 503)

gēara (1) Text 51/28 adv 'of yore, long ago'; (2) elsewhere gpl < gēar

gēardagum dpl < *gēardagas* plm 'days of yore' (§502)

gēare ds < *gēar*; **gēares** gs

gearoþoncolre st dsf < *gearoþoncol* adj 'ready-witted' (§§505, 507)

gearwad past ptc < *gearwian* 'to prepare, form' (wkv 2 §526)

gearwe st npl < *gearu* adj 'ready, prepared' (*Guide* §71)

gearwost super < *gearwe* adv 'well, clearly'

Gēata gpl 'of the Geats'

gēate ds < *gēat* n 'gate'

geatolic adj 'adorned, splendid'

ge-æfnan 'to hold, sustain' (wkv 1 §§522-3)

ge-ærneð 3s pres < *ge-ærnan* 'to gain by riding' (wkv 1 §§522-3)

ge-æðele adj 'natural'

ge-bād 1/3s pret < **(ge-)bīdan**

ge-bæded past ptc < *bædan* 'to compel' (wkv like *hieran* §94)

ge-bǣron 3pl pret < *(ge-)beran* 'to bear' (stv IV §517)

ge-bēorscipe ds < *ge-bēorscipe* m 'feast' (*Guide* §§45-6); **ge-bēorscipes** gs

ge-bīdan 'to wait for, experience' (wa/g (stv I §517)

ge-blanden past ptc < *(ge-)blandan* 'to mix' (stv VII(*b*) §517)

ge-bletsade 3s pret < *(ge-)bletsian* 'to bless' (wkv 2 §526)

ge-blissod past ptc < *(ge-)blissian* 'to make happy, gladden' (wkv 2 §526)

ge-bolgen past ptc < *(ge-)belgan* 'to become angry' (stv III §518); — adj 'angry'

ge-borene st npl past ptc < *(ge-)beran*. See **ge-bǣron**

ge-bræc f 'breaking, destruction'

ge-brocod past ptc < *(ge-)brocian* 'to crush, afflict' (wkv 2 §526)

ge-brōðor m 'brother'. See **brōþor**; **ge-brōðrum** dpl

ge-būgan 'to turn to' (stv II §517)

ge-byrd f 'order'

ge-byrede 3s pret < *(ge-)byrian* 'to befit, belong to' (wkv §525); **ge-byreþ** 3s pret

ge-byrge 3s pres subj < *ge-byrgan* 'to taste, eat' (wkv like *hieran* §94)

ge-byrgenne gs < *(ge-)byrgenn* f 'grave' (§504)

ge-bysgad past ptc < *(ge-)bysgian* 'to trouble, afflict' (wkv 2 §526)

ge-cēosan 'to choose, seek out, test, accept' (stv II §515)

ge-cierdon 3pl pret < *(ge-)cierran* 'to come, go, turn, submit' (wkv like *hieran* §94)

ge-cirdon = **ge-cierdon**

ge-cnāwan 'to know, understand, acknowledge, ascertain' (stv VII(*a*) §517); **ge-**

cnāwað 2pl imp; **ge-cnāwe** 3s pres subj; **ge-cnāwen** past ptc

ge-coran = **ge-coren**

ge-coren past ptc < **(ge-)cēosan**

ge-corene See Text 44/285 note

ge-corenum dpl past ptc < **(ge-)cēosan**

ge-cueden past ptc < **(ge-)cweþan**

ge-curon 3pl pret < **(ge-)cēosan**

ge-cwæð 3s pret < **(ge-)cweþan**

ge-cwemlice adv 'graciously, humbly'

ge-cweþan 'to say, name, order, call' (stv V §§97, 515)

ge-cynda apl < *ge-cynd* f 'birth, offspring' (§504); **ge-cynde** as

ge-cyrde = *ge-cierde* 3s pret < *(ge-)cierran*. See **ge-cierdon**; **ge-cyrred** = *ge-cierred* past ptc

ge-cȳþan 'to make known' (wkv like *hieran* §94); **ge-cȳþed** past ptc

ge-cȳþnis f 'testimony, testament'

ge-cȳðde 3s pret < **(ge-)cȳþan**

ge-dǣlan 'to divide, share, distribute' (wkv like *hieran* §94); **ge-dǣlde** 3s pret ind/subj

ge-dēmed past ptc < *(ge-)dēman* 'to decide, decree' (wkv like *hieran* §94)

ge-dihte 3s pret < *(ge-)dihtan* 'to dictate' (wkv like *settan* §94)

ge-dōn (1) inf (2) past ptc < *(ge-)dōn* 'to do, make, cause' (§89)

ge-drēas 3s pret < *(ge-)drēosan* 'to fall, perish' (stv II §519)

ge-drēfed past ptc < *(ge-)drēfan* 'to trouble, afflict' (wkv like *hieran* §94)

ge-drencte npl past ptc < *drencan* 'to drown' (wkv like *settan* §94)

ge-droren past ptc < *(ge-)drēosan*

ge-drync m 'drink, drinking' (§502); **ge-drynce** ds

ge-dwolsum adj 'misleading'

ge-dyde 3s pret < **(ge-)dōn**; **ge-dyden** 3pl pret subj; **ge-dydon** 3pl pret

ge-dyrstlǣcan 'to dare'

ge-earnian 'to earn, deserve'

ge-earnungum dpl < *(ge-)earnung* f 'merit' (§504)

ge-edcucode 3s pret < *(ge-)edcucian* 'to revive' (wkv 2 §526) = perf 'has revived, is alive'

ge-endebyrd past ptc < *(ge-)endebyrdan* 'to arrange' (wkv like *sendan* §89)

ge-endode 3s pret < *(ge-)endian* 'to end' (wkv 2 §526)

ge-ēodon 3pl pret < *(ge-)gān* 'to go, overrun, win' (§529)

ge-fadian 'to arrange'

ge-faran 'to go, proceed, act' (stv VI §517); **ge-faren** past ptc = adj 'dead' ge-fægene st npl < (*ge-*)*fægen* adj 'glad' wg (§§505, 507)

ge-færenne st asm past ptc < **ge-faran**

ge-fæstnodon 3pl pret < *fæstnian* 'to secure, make firm' (wkv 2 §526)

gefe = *giefe* apl < *giefu* f 'gift' (§504)

ge-feah 3s pret < (*ge-*)*fēon* 'to rejoice' wg (contr stv §521)

ge-feaht 1/3s pret < (*ge-*)*feohtan* 'to fight, gain by fighting' (stv III §518)

ge-fēan a/ds < (*ge-*)*fēa* m 'joy' (§§500–1)

ge-fēlan 'to feel'; ge-fēle 3s pres subj

ge-fēng 3s pret < (*ge-*)*fōn* 'to capture' (contr stv VII(*b*) §521); ge-fēngun 3pl pret

ge-feoht n 'fight, fighting, battle' (§503); ge-feohte ds; ge-feohtum dpl

ge-fēol = ge-fēoll

ge-fēoll 3s pret < (*ge-*)*feallan* 'to fall, die' (stv VII(*a*) §517)

ge-fēran = ge-fērum in our texts. See ge-fērena

ge-fērena gpl < *ge-fēra* 'comrade, man' (§§500–1); ge-fērum dpl

ge-feterod past ptc < *ge-feterian* 'to fetter, bind' (wkv 2 §526)

ge-fillednys f 'fulfilment'

ge-flæscnesse ds < *ge-flæscness* f 'incarnation' (§504)

ge-fliemde 3s pret < (*ge-*)*flīeman* 'to put to flight, banish' (wkv like *hīeran* §94); ge-fliemdon 3pl pret; ge-flȳmed = *ge-flīemed* past ptc

ge-fohten past ptc < (*ge-*)*feohtan* 'to fight' (stv III §518)

ge-fōr 3s pret < (*ge-*)*faran*. See **faran**

ge-frætewod past ptc < (*ge-*)*frætewian* 'to ornament, adorn' (wkv 2 §526)

ge-fremede 1s pret < (*ge-*)*fremman* 'to do, commit' (§524); ge-fremedon 3pl pret

ge-fuhton 3pl pret < (*ge-*)*feohtan* 'to fight, gain by fighting' (stv III §518)

ge-fuhtun = ge-fuhton

ge-fultumade 3s pret < (*ge-*)*fultumian* 'to help' (wkv 2 §526); ge-fultumadon 3pl pret

ge-fulwad past ptc < (*ge-*)*fulwian* 'to baptize' (wkv 2 §526)

ge-fylda st nplf past ptc < (**ge-**)**fyllan** (1)

ge-fyllan (1) Text 17 v. 16 'to fill'; (2) Text 51/38 'to fell, destroy' (wkv §94)

ge-fylled past ptc < (**ge-**)**fyllan** (2)

ge-fyrn adv 'formerly'

ge-fȳsed past ptc < (*ge-*)*fȳsan* 'to send forth, drive' (wkv like *hīeran* §94)

ge-gaderode 3s pret < (*ge-*)*gad(e)rian* 'to gather, assemble'; ge-gadrodon 3pl pret

ge-gangeð 3s pres < (*ge-*)*gangan* 'to happen'

ge-gearwod past ptc < (*ge-*)*gearwian* 'to prepare, equip' (wkv 2 §526)

ge-giredan 3pl pret < (*ge-*)*gir(w)an* 'to make ready, equip' (wkv 1 §§522–3)

ge-girla m 'garment, attire' (§§500–1)

gegnum adv 'straight on, forward'

ge-grāp 3s pret < (*ge-*)*grīpan* 'to grasp, snatch, take (hold of)' (stv I §517); ge-gripene st npl past ptc

ge-gyred = ge-gyrwed. See ge-gyrwan

ge-gyrelan as < (*ge-*)*gyrela* = ge-girla

ge-gyrwan 'to prepare, clothe, adorn' (wkv 1 §§522–3); ge-gyrwed past ptc

ge-hādod past ptc < (*ge-*)*hādian* 'to ordain, consecrate' (wkv 2 §526)

ge-hālgade st nplm past ptc < **ge-hālgian** (§§505, 507)

ge-hālgian 'to hallow, consecrate, dedicate, ordain' (wkv 2 §526); ge-hālgod past ptc; ge-hālgode 3s pret

ge-hāta gpl < (*ge-*)*hāt* n 'promise, vow' (§503)

ge-hātene st npl past ptc < (*ge-*)*hātan* 'to command, promise, name, call' (stv VII(*b*) §517)

ge-hātlandes gs < *ge-hātland* n 'promised land' (§503)

ge-healdsum adj 'provident, safe, virtuous' wg

ge-heht = ge-hēt

ge-hergade 3s pret < (*ge-*)*hergian* 'to ravage, plunder, capture' (wkv 2 §526); ge-hergod past ptc; ge-hergoden 3pl pret

ge-hēt 3s pret < (*ge-*)*hātan*. See ge-hātene; ge-hēton 3pl pret

ge-hīersumade 3s pret subj < (*ge-*)*hīersumian* 'to conquer, make obedient' (wkv 2 §526)

ge-hīersume st apl < (*ge-*)*hīersum* adj 'obedient' (§§505, 507)

ge-hiht imp s < (*ge-*)*hihtan* 'to trust'

ge-hīrde = ge-hȳrde. See ge-hȳr

ge-hīrsumode 3s pret < (*ge-*)*hīrsumian* 'to obey, serve' (wkv 2 §526) wd

ge-hnǣged past ptc < (*ge-*)*hnǣgan* 'to humble, vanquish' (wkv like *hīeran* §94)

ge-horsude st nplm past ptc < (*ge-*)*horsian* 'to provide with horses' (wkv 2 §526) (see §§505, 507)

ge-hrān 3s pret < (*ge-*)*hrīnan* 'to touch, reach' (stv I §517)

ge-hwām ds < *ge-hwā* 'each/any/every one, whoever' (§499)

ge-hwǣde npl < *ge-hwǣde* adj 'small, young' (*Guide* §73)

ge-hwǣne as < *ge-hwā*. See ge-hwām

ge-hwǣs gs < *ge-hwā*. See ge-hwām

ge-hwǣþer 'either, both, each'; ge-hwæþre dsf

ge-hwēr = *ge-hwǣr* 'everywhere, always'

ge-hwerfde 3s pret < (*ge-*)*hwerfan* 'to turn, convert' (wkv like *hieran* §94)

ge-hwilc = **ge-hwylc**

ge-hwilcne = **ge-hwylcne**. See **ge-hwylc**

ge-hwylc 'each, every'; w **ānra** 'each one'; **ge-hwylce** isn; **ge-hwylces** gsm; **ge-hwylcne** asm

ge-hȳd past ptc < (*ge-*)*hȳdan* 'to furnish with skin' (wkv like *sendan* §89)

ge-hȳdde st apl past ptc < (*ge-*)*hȳdan* 'to hide' (wkv like *sendan* §89)

ge-hȳr imp s < (*ge-*)*hȳran* = (*ge-*)*hīeran* 'to hear' (§94); **ge-hȳrde** 2/3s pret; **ge-hȳre** = *ge-hȳraþ* imp pl; **ge-hȳrest** 2s pres

ge-hȳrsumode = **ge-hirsumode**

ge-lamp 3s pret < (*ge-*)*limpan*. See **ge-limpð**

ge-læccað 3pl pres < (*ge-*)*læccan* 'to capture, catch, grasp' (irreg wkv *Guide* §121.3)

ge-læddon 3pl pret< (*ge-*)*lædan* 'to lead, bring' (wkv like *sendan* §89); **ge-læded** past ptc

ge-læhte 3s pret < *ge-læccan*. See **ge-læccað**

ge-læredre st dsf < (*ge-*)*læred* adj 'learned, skilled' (§§505, 507)

ge-læstan 'to do, perform, carry out' (wkv like *settan* §94); **ge-læston** 3pl pret

ge-lēafan ds < (*ge-*)*lēafa* m 'faith, belief' (§§500–1)

ge-leaþade st npl past ptc < *laþian* 'to invite, summon' (wkv 2 §526)

ge-lende 3s pret < *lendan* 'to land, arrive' (wkv like *sendan* §89)

ge-leornad past ptc < (*ge-*)*leornian* 'to learn' (wkv 2 §526); **ge-leornade** 3s pret

ge-lettan 'to hinder, delay'

ge-lēwede st npl < *ge-lēwed* adj 'weak, blemished' (§§505, 507)

ge-līc adj 'alike, similar, like'

ge-līca m 'an equal' (§§500–1); **ge-līcan** as

ge-līcost super < *ge-līc* 'most like' wd

ge-līcum dpl < **ge-līc**

ge-limplicre st dsf < *ge-limplic* adj 'suitable, fitting' (§§505, 507)

ge-limpð 3s pres < (*ge-*)*limpan* 'to happen, occur' (stv III §518)

ge-liornod = **ge-leornad**

ge-liornodon 3pl pret 'learned'. See **ge-leornad**

ge-lōme adv 'often, frequently'

ge-lomp 3s pret < (*ge-*)*limpan*. See **ge-limpð**

ge-long adj 'belonging, dependent'

ge-lumpon 3pl pret < (*ge-*)*limpan*. See **ge-limpð**

ge-lustfullicor comp < adv (*ge-*)*lustfullice* 'gladly, heartily'

ge-lȳfdre gs < *ge-lȳfed* adj 'advanced'

ge-lȳfe 1s pres < (*ge-*)*lȳfan* 'to believe'

ge-man 1s pres < (*ge-*)*munan* 'to remember' (§96)

ge-mānan gs < *ge-māna* m 'fellowship' (§§500–1)

ge-mane adj 'having a mane'

ge-mæccan ds < (*ge-*)*mæcca* m 'husband' (§§500–1)

ge-mægnde 3s pret < (*ge-*)*mægnan* 'to mix, join' (wkv like *hieran* §94)

ge-mænan wk asf < *ge-mæne* adj 'common, public' (§§505–6)

ge-mænelicum st dsm < (*ge-*)*mænelic* adj 'common, universal' (§§505, 507)

ge-mætte 3s pret < (*ge-*)*mætan* 'to dream' wd (impers wkv like *settan* §94)

gēmde 3s pret < *gēman* 'to care, take heed' (wkv like *hieran* §94)

ge-met Text 20/28 n 'measure, metre'

ge-mēt Text 17/vv 24 and 32 past ptc < (*ge-*) *mētan* 'to meet, find' (wkv like *settan* §94); **ge-mēted** alternative past ptc; **ge-mētton** 3pl pret

ge-mon = **ge-man**

ge-mong prep wd 'among'

ge-mōt n 'assembly, council'; **ge-mōtes** gs

ge-munde 1/2s pret < (*ge-*)*munan*. See **ge-man**

ge-mynde ds < (*ge-*)*mynd* f 'memory' (§504)

ge-myndig adj 'mindful' wg

gēn adv 'yet'; **ne ... þā gēn** 'by no means'

ge-nam 3s pret < (*ge-*)*niman* 'to take, capture, receive' (stv IV §519)

ge-naman = **ge-namon**

ge-namon 3pl pret < (*ge-*)*niman*. See **ge-nam**

ge-nāp 3s pret < (*ge-*)*nīpan* 'to grow dark' (stv I §517)

ge-neahhe adv 'often, earnestly'

ge-nēalæhte 3s pret < (*ge-*)*nēalæcan* 'to come near, approach' wd (irreg wkv *Guide* §121.3)

ge-nēatas npl < *ge-nēat* m 'companion, follower' (§502)

ge-nemned past ptc < (*ge-*)*nemnan* 'to name, call' (wkv like *hieran* §94)

ge-nēop See Text 46/476 note

ge-nerede 3s pret < (*ge-*)*nerian* 'to save' (wkv §525)

ge-nime 3s pres subj < (*ge-*)*niman*. See **ge-nam**

ge-niwad past ptc < (*ge-*)*niwian* 'to renew' (wkv 2 §526)

ge-nōge st npl < *ge-nōg/nōh* adj 'enough, many' (§§505, 507); **ge-nōhne** st asm < *ge-nōh*

ge-nom = **ge-nam**

ge-numen past ptc < (*ge-*)*niman*. See **ge-nam**

geofon n 'ocean, sea, flood'

geogoðe ds < *geogoð* f 'youth' (§504)

gēomorne st asm < *gēomor* adj 'troubled, sad' (§§505, 507); **gēomorre** st dsf; **gēomre** st apl

gēomrian 'to be sad, lament, complain'

geond prep wa 'through'

geondbrǣded past ptc < *geondbrǣdan* 'to cover, spread' (wkv like *hīeran* §94)

geondsprengde 3s pret < *geondsprengan* 'to besprinkle' (wkv like *hīeran* §94)

geong adj 'young'; **geongan** wk apl (§§505–6); **geonge** st npl (§§505, 507); **geongne** st asm

geongordōmes gs < *geongordōm* m 'discipleship, allegiance' (§502)

geongra m 'disciple, follower'

georndon 3pl pret < *geornan* 'to ask for' wg (wkv like *hīeran* §94)

georne (1) Text 44/287 st nplm < *georn* adj 'eager' (§§505, 507); (2) elsewhere adv 'eagerly, completely, quickly'

geornlicor comp adv 'more zealously/carefully'

geornost super adv w **swā … (swā)** 'as eagerly as'

ge-rǣdde 3s pret < *(ge-)rǣdan* 'to advise, design' (wkv like *hīeran* §94)

gere Text 48/859 adv 'clearly, exactly'

gēre Text 5/59 = **gēare**

ge-refa m 'high official, reeve, sheriff'

ge-rehte 3s pret < *(ge-)reccan* 'to judge' (irreg wkv *Guide* §121.3)

ge-reno npl < *ge-rene* n 'ornament' (§503)

ge-renode st apl past ptc < *ge-renian* 'to adorn' (wkv 2 §526)

ge-reorde ds < *(ge-)reord* f 'feast' (§504)

ge-restan 'to rest from' wg

ge-ridon 3pl pret < *ge-rīdan* 'to ride over, occupy' (stv I §517)

ge-rihtan 'to amend, correct' (wkv like *settan* §94); **ge-rihte** 3s pres subj

ge-rīpode st npl past ptc < *(ge-)rīpian* 'to ripen' (wkv 2 §526)

ge-risenlicre asn comp < *ge-risenlic* adj 'suitable, honourable'

ge-rȳno apl < *(ge-)rȳne* n 'mystery' (§503)

ge-samnode st nplm past ptc < *ge-samnian* 'to assemble, gather together' (wkv 2 §526)

ge-sāwe 1s pret subj < *(ge-)sēon* 'to see' (contr stv V §521); **ge-sāwon** 3pl pret

ge-sǣlde 3s pret < *(ge-)sǣlan* 'to happen, arise' (wkv like *hīeran* §94); **ge-sǣleð** 3s pres

ge-sǣlig adj 'happy, blessed'; **ge-sǣlige** st npl (§§505, 507); **ge-sǣliglice** adv 'happily, blessedly'

ge-sǣnde 3s pret < *(ge-)sendan* 'to send' (wkv §89)

ge-sǣt 3s pret < *(ge-)sittan* 'to sit, occupy, preside over' (stv V §519); **ge-sǣton** 3pl pret

ge-scēadan 'to judge, decide'

ge-sceaft f 'fate, dispensation, creation, creature' (§504); **ge-sceafta** gpl; **ge-sceafte** ds

ge-sceape ds < *ge-sceap* n 'creation' (§503)

ge-scēod Text 46/489 3s pret < *(ge-)sceððan* 'to harm, destroy' wd (irreg stv)

ge-scēod Text 46/507 past ptc < *(ge-)scēon* 'to happen to, befall' wd (wkv)

ge-scipode st nplm past ptc < *(ge-)scipian* 'to take ship, embark' (wkv 2 §526)

ge-scrīdian 'to clothe, dress'

ge-scȳ apl < *(ge-)scō* m 'shoe' (§§17–18)

ge-seah 1/3s pret < *(ge-)sēon*. See **ge-sāwe**

ge-sealde 3s pret < *(ge-)sellan* 'to give, deliver to' (§95)

ge-secean 'to seek, go to, attain'

ge-sēgon 3pl pret < *(ge-)sēon*. See **ge-sāwe**

ge-seh = **ge-seah**

ge-semede st npl past ptc < *(ge-)sēman* 'to reconcile' (wkv like *hīeran* §94)

ge-sēne adj 'visible, evident'

ge-sēo 2s pres subj < *(ge-)sēon*. See **ge-sāwe**; **ge-seoh** 2s imp; **ge-sēoþ** 3pl pres; **ge-seowene** st nplm past ptc

ge-seted past ptc < *(ge-)settan* 'to establish, compose, arrange, place' (wkv §94); **ge-sett** alternative past ptc; **ge-sette** 3s pret

ge-sewen past ptc < *(ge-)sēon*. See **ge-sāwe**

ge-sibbra gpl < *(ge-)sibb* m/f 'kinsmen, -women' (§§502, 504)

ge-sīene = **ge-sēne**

ge-sīhton 3pl pret < *(ge-)sīcan* 'to suckle' (wkv *Guide* §121.3)

ge-sion = *ge-sēon*. See **ge-sāwe**

ge-sīþas npl < *ge-sīþ* m 'comrade, companion, retainer, warrior' (§502)

ge-slægen past ptc < *(ge-)slēan* 'to strike, gain by fighting, kill', w **wæl** 'to slaughter' (contr stv VI §521); **ge-slegen** alternative past ptc; **ge-slegene** See Text 31/15 note; **ge-slōg** 3s pret; **ge-slōgon** 3pl pret; **ge-slōh** 3s pret

ge-smerod past ptc < *(ge-)smerian* 'to anoint' (wkv 2 §526)

ge-sōhte 3s pret < *(ge-)sēcan* 'to seek, visit, attack' (wkv §95); **ge-sōhton** 3pl pret

ge-somnad past ptc < *(ge-)somnian* 'to assemble, collect, gather together' (wkv 2 §526); **ge-somnodon** 3pl pret

ge-spæc 3s pret < *(ge-)specan* 'to speak' (stv V §519)

ge-sprǣcon 3pl pret < *(ge-)sprecan* 'to speak' (stv V §519); **ge-sprec** = *ge-spræc* 3s pret

ge-stāh 3s pret < *ge-stīgan* 'to go, reach, ascend, mount' (stv I §517)

ge-strēon Text 23/19 npl < (*ge-*)*strēon* n 'property, treasure'; Text 9/3166 as

ge-sunde st npl < *ge-sund* adj 'safe, whole, sound' (§§505, 507); **ge-sundran** comp nplm

ge-sūpe 3s pres subj < (*ge-*)*sūpan* 'to swallow, drink' (stv II §517)

ge-swealh 3s pret < (*ge-*)*swelgan* 'to swallow, devour' (stv III §518)

ge-swearc 3s pret < (*ge-*)*sweorcan* 'to grow dark' (stv III §518)

ge-sweostor plf 'sisters'

ge-swican 'to cease, desert, abandon' (stv I §517); **ge-swicon** 3pl pret

ge-swince ds < (*ge-*)*swinc* n 'toil, hardship' (§503)

ge-swincfull adj 'toilsome, painful'

ge-swutelað 3s pres < (*ge-*)*swutelian* 'to show, reveal, prove' (wkv 2 §526); **ge-swuteliað** 2pl pres

ge-syhðe ds < (*ge-*)*syhð* f 'sight' (§504)

ge-sȳne = **ge-sēne**

ge-synto f 'health, prosperity'

ge-tacnode 3s pret < (*ge-*)*tacnian* 'to mark, betoken' (wkv 2 §526)

ge-tacnung f 'sign, presage, token'

ge-tæht past ptc < (*ge-*)*tǣcan* to teach, show, assign' (wkv *Guide* §121.3)

ge-timbrade 3s pret < (*ge-*)*timbrian* 'to build' (wkv 2 §526)

ge-timbred past ptc < (*ge-*)*timbran* 'to build' (wkv 1 §§522-3)

ge-timbro apl < *ge-timbre* 'building' (*Guide* §§45-6)

ge-trēowþa npl < (*ge-*)*trēowþ* f 'truth, faith, pledge' (§504)

ge-trēowra gpl < (*ge-*)*trēowe* adj 'true, faithful' (*Guide* §73)

ge-trȳwða apl = **ge-trēowþa**

ge-twǣfan 'to prevent from, hinder' wg

ge-twinnas npl < (*ge-*)*twinn* m 'twin' (§502)

ge-tygðedon 3pl pret < (*ge-*)*tygðian* 'to grant' wg (wkv §525)

ge-þafade 3s pret < (**ge-**)*þafian* 'to allow, approve' (wkv 2 §526)

ge-þafunge as < (*ge-*)*þafung* f 'consent' (§504)

ge-þance ds < (*ge-*)*þanc* m 'mind' (§502)

ge-þeaht as < (*ge-*)*þeaht* n 'counsel, advice' (§503)

ge-ðeahteras npl < (*ge-*)*ðeahtere* m 'counsellor' (*Guide* §§45-6)

ge-þencan/ge-þencean 'to think, consider, devise' (wkv §95)

ge-ðēoda gpl < (*ge-*)*ðēod* f 'language' (§504)

ge-ðigð 3s pres < (*ge-*)*ðicgan* 'to accept, receive, taste, partake of'

ge-þinges gs < *ge-þinge* n 'outcome, result' (*Guide* §§45-6)

ge-ðiode ds < (*ge-*)*ðīod* f 'language' (§504)

ge-þrowedon 3pl pret < (*ge-*)*þrowian* 'to suffer' (wkv §525); **ge-þrowode** 3s pret (§526)

ge-þūht past ptc < (*ge-*)*þyncan* 'to seem' (§95); **wæs ge-þūht** 'seemed'

ge-unclǣnsade 3s pret < (*ge-*)*unclǣnsian* 'to pollute, defile' (wkv 2 §526)

ge-ūþe 3s pret < (*ge-*)*unnan* 'to grant' wa/g (like *cunnan* §96); **ge-ūðen** 3pl pret subj

ge-waden past ptc < *wadan* 'to travel, advance, pervade' (stv VI §517)

ge-wald = **ge-weald**

ge-wann 3s pret < **ge-winnan**

ge-wāt 1/3s pret < (**ge-**)*wītan*

ge-wænd past ptc < (*ge-*)*wændan* 'to turn, change, (wg) go on' (wkv like *sendan* §89); **ge-wænde** 3s pret

ge-wealc n 'rolling, tossing'

ge-weald n 'power, control, command, possession' (§503); **ge-wealde** ds

ge-wearð 3s pret < (*ge-*)*weorðan* 'to happen, become' (stv III §§513, 516)

ge-welhwylcan wk dsm < (*ge-*)*welhwylc* 'each, nearly every' (§§505-6)

ge-wēnde Text 29/15 st npl past ptc < (*ge-*)*wēnan* 'to think, believe' (wkv like *hīeran* §94). But see Text 29/15 note

ge-wende = **ge-wǣnde**. See **ge-wænd**

ge-weorc n 'fortification' (§503); **ge-weorce** ds

ge-weorþade 3s pret < (*ge-*)*weorþian* 'to honour, exalt, reward' (wkv 2 §526); **ge-weorðod** past ptc

ge-wilnode 3s pret < *ge-wilnian* 'to desire' (wkv 2 §526)

ge-winn n 'conflict, strife, war' (§503)

ge-winnan 'to conquer, gain, obtain' (stv III §518)

ge-winnes gs < **ge-winn**

ge-wistfullian 'to feast' (wkv 2 §526); **ge-wistfullode** 3s pret subj

ge-wistlǣcan 'to feast, banquet'

ge-witan Text 33/5 npl < (*ge-*)*wita* 'witness' (§§500-1)

ge-witan Text 8/42 'to come, go, depart, die, mount' (stv I §517)

ge-wite Text 31/28 imp s < *ge-witan* 'to get to know, find out' (§96)

ge-wite Text 19/26 3s pres subj < **ge-wītan**; **ge-witen** past ptc; **ge-witene** st nmpl past ptc (§§505, 507); **ge-witenes** st gs past ptc = adj 'dead'; **ge-wīteð** 3s pres

ge-witlocan ds < *ge-witloca* m 'mind' (§§500–1)

ge-witon Text 36/53 3pl pret < **ge-wītan**; ge-wīton Text 33/22 1pl pres subj

ge-wōd 3s pret < (*ge-*)*wadan*. See **ge-waden**

ge-worden past ptc < (*ge-*)*weorþan*, w **bēon** 'to be made, become' (§§513, 516)

ge-worhte Text 44/273 3s pret subj < **ge-wyrcan**; elsewhere 3s pret ind; **ge-worhton** 3pl pret ind

ge-writ n 'writing, scripture, book' (§503); **ge-writes** gs; **ge-writum** dpl

ge-wuna adj wd 'accustomed to'

ge-wunan npl < *ge-wuna* m 'custom, habit' (§§500–1)

ge-wunnen past ptc < **ge-winnan**

ge-wurde 3s pret subj < (*ge-*)*weorðan*. See **ge-wearð**

ge-wyrcan 'to do, perform, bring about, (wg) gain' (wkv §95); **ge-wyrcað** 3pl pres; **ge-wyrce** 3s pres subj; **ge-wyrcean** = **ge-wyrcan**

ge-wyrmed past ptc < (*ge-*)*wyrman* 'to warm' (wkv 1 §§522–3)

ge-wyrðeð 3s pres < (*ge-*)*weorðan*. See **ge-wearð**

giedd n 'song, poem' (§503). See Text 40/19 note; **gieddes** gs

gierede 3s pret < *gier(w)an* 'to deck, adorn' (wkv 1 §§522–3)

gīet adv 'yet, still, hereafter'; **þā gīet**, 'yet, still, also'

gif conj (1) 'if' introducing adv clauses; (2) 'if, whether' introducing noun clauses

gife 3s pres subj < *gi(e)fan* 'to give'

gifernessa apl < *giferness* f 'greed, gluttony' (§504)

gifre adj 'useful'

gihðe ds < *gihðu* f 'care, anxiety, trouble' (§504)

gilpe ds < *gilp* m 'pride, arrogance' (§502)

gimmas npl < *gimm* m 'gem, precious stone' (§502)

gingne st asm < *ging* adj 'young'; **gingra** ns comp 'younger'

giogoðe ds < *giogoð* = **gioguð** f 'youth, young people' (§504)

giond prep wa 'throughout'

git Text 34/14 adv 'yet, also, moreover'

git Text 39/16, 17 n dual 'ye/you two' (§494)

gitsunga apl < *gitsung* f 'greediness, desire' (§504)

gīu adv 'formerly, of old'

glād 3s pret < *glīdan* 'to glide' (stv I §517)

glēaw adj 'wise, prudent'; **glēawe** st asf (§§505, 507)

glēd f 'flame, glowing coal'

glēobēames gs < *glēobēam* m 'musical instrument, harp' (§502)

glisedon 3pl pret < *glisian* 'to shine, glitter' (wkv §525)

gnornað 3s pres < *gnornian* 'to mourn, grieve' (wkv 2 §526)

gnornra comp < *gnorn* adj 'sad, depressed'

god/God m/n 'god/God' (§§502–3); **goda** Text 19/14 gpl

gōd adj 'good'; **gōda** wk nsm (§§505–6)

godcunde st apl < *godcund* adj 'religious, spiritual' (§§505, 507)

godcundnesse gs < *godcundness* f 'divinity, Godhead' (§504)

gōddædan dpl < *gōddæd* f 'good deed' (*-an* for *-um* §504)

gode/Gode ds < god/God

gōde Text 44/291 st isn < **gōd**; Text 4/23 st asf; Text 11/2249 st nplm (§§505, 507)

gōdena wk gpl < **gōd** (§§505–6)

godes/Godes gs < god/God

gōdes st gsm/n < **gōd** (§§505, 507)

gōdlecran asmcomp < *gōdlec* adj 'goodly, excellent'

godo npl < **god**

gōdra st gpl < **gōd** (§§505, 507); **gōdre** st dsf

godspellian 'to preach the gospel, evangelize'

godum dpl < **god**

gold n 'gold'; **golde** ds

goldgiefan npl < *goldgiefa* 'gold-giver, lord' (§§500–1)

goldhilted adj 'golden-hilted'

goldhord apl < *goldhord* n 'treasure of gold' (§503)

goldsele m 'gold-hall, hall in which gold is distributed'

gomelfeax adj 'grey-haired'

gomen n 'sport, joy, mirth'

gongan 'to walk'; **gonge** 1s pres; **gongende** pres ptc

gram adj 'angry, hostile'

grǣdigne st asm < *grǣdig* 'greedy' (§§505, 507)

grǣge wk asn < **grǣg** adj 'grey' (§§505, 506)

grēate st nplm < *grēat* adj 'great, massive' (§§505, 507)

grēotan 'to cry, lament'

grēote ds < *grēot* n 'sand, earth' (§503)

grēt 3s pres < *grētan* 'to greet, salute' (wkv like *settan* §94); **grētte** 3s pret

grimlic adj 'cruel, terrible, severe'

grimme adv 'painfully, bitterly'

grið n 'truce, (temporary) peace' (§503); **griðe** ds

grund m 'ground, bottom (of the sea), abyss, hell, plain, land' (§502); **grundas** apl

gryre ds < *gryre* m 'horror, terror' (*Guide* §§45–6)

guma m 'man, lord, hero' (§§500–1); **guman** Text 51/49 gs, Text 13/215 npl; **gumena** gpl

gūðēað m 'death in battle'

gūðe ds < *gūð* f 'combat, battle, war' (§504)

gūðgewǣdo apl < *gūðgewǣde* n 'armour' (*Guide* §§45–6)

gūðhafoc m 'war-hawk, eagle'

gūðsceorp n 'armour'

gūðsearo n 'armour'

gyf = **gif**

gyllende isn pres ptc = adj 'yelling, shrieking'

gylp m 'boasting, arrogance, pride'

gylpan 'to boast, exult'

gylta gpl < *gylt* m 'sin, fault, offence' (§502)

gȳmð 3s pres < *gȳman* 'to care for, correct'

gyrde as < *gyrd* f 'rod, staff'

gyrwanne w **tō** infl inf < *gyrwan* 'to prepare'

gȳt = **gīet**

gȳta = **gīet**

habban 'to have, hold, possess, experience, look after' (§527); **tō habbanne** infl inf; **habbaþ** 3pl pres
The verb **habban** is also used, like MnE 'to have', as an auxiliary of the (plu)perfect tense

hādbrycas apl < *hādbryce* m 'injury to someone in holy orders' (*Guide* §§45–6)

hāde ds < *hād* m 'rank, office' (§502)

hafast 2s pres < **habban**; **hafað** 3s pres

hafen past ptc < **hebban**

hafoc m 'hawk'

hafu 1s pres < **habban**

Hagustaldes hām 'Hexham'

haldonne w **tō** infl inf < *healdan*. See **heald**

hāle st npl < *hāl* adj 'sound, safe, whole' (§§505, 507)

hālette 3s pret < *hālettan* 'to greet, hail' (wkv like *settan* §94)

hālga Text 3/41 wk nsm < *hālig* (§§505, 506), Text 28/7 irreg gpl; **hālgan** wk oblique case; **hālgum** dpl 'saints'

hālig adj 'holy, godly, saintly', sometimes = noun 'saint'; **hālige** Text 28/9 See §437; Text 46/486 asf; Text 48/840 asn; Text 48/852 aplf; Text 51/11 nplm; **hāligra** gpl

hālne st asm < *hāl* (§§505, 507). See **hāle**

hām Texts 35/717 & 41/117 as < *hām* m 'home' (§502), Text 10/1248 uninfl dat, elsewhere adv 'home'; **hāmas** apl; **hāme** ds

hamora gpl < *hamor* m 'hammer' (§502)

hand f 'hand' (*Guide* §61); **handa** Text 25/6 apl, elsewhere ds; **handan** irreg dpl;

handæ Text 37/21 ds. In Text 37/23 **hand** itself is ds

handplegan gs < *handplega* m 'handplay, battle' (§§500–1)

handum dpl < **hand**

handweorc n 'handiwork'

hangen past ptc < *hōn* (contr stv VII(*b*) §517) 'to hang, crucify'

hār adj 'hoary, grey, old'

Hardacnūdes, -cnūtes gs 'of Hardacnut'

hāre apl < **hār**

hasopādan wk as < *hasopād* adj 'grey-coated' (§§505–6)

hāten past ptc < *hātan* 'to command (§122), promise, call, name' (stv VII(*b*) §517)

hātran comp npl < *hāt* adj 'hot'

hātte s 'is/was called'; **hātton** pl 'are/were called' (§511)

hatunge < *hatung*. See Text 33/11 note

hæbbe 1s pres ind/3s pres subj < **habban**; **hæbben** 3pl pres subj; **hæfde** 1/3s pret; **hæfdon** 1/3pl pret

hæftnīede ds < *hæftnīed* f 'captivity' (§504)

hæfð 3s pres < **habban**

hǣle as < *hǣlo* f 'safety, prosperity, luck'

hǣlend m 'Saviour, Christ'; **hǣlendes** gs

hæleð m 'man, hero, fighter'; in Text 11/2247 & Text 49/1 **hæleð** is npl; **hæleða** gpl; **hæleþas** npl; **hæleþum** dpl

hǣlo = **hǣle**

hǣt = **hēt**

hǣþen adj 'heathen, pagan, Danish'; **hæþene** apl; **hæðenra** gpl; **hæþne** npl; **hæþnum** strong ds

hǣwene wk nsf < *hǣwen* adj 'blue' (§§505–6)

hē 'he' (§495); w masc inanimate antecedents 'it'

hēafde ds < *hēafod* n 'head' (§503); **hēafdon** Text 10/1242 dpl

heafdon Text 7/20 = *hæfdon*. See **hæbbe**

hēafdu n/apl < *hēafod*. See **hēafde**; **hēafdum** dpl

hēage st nplm < *hēah* adj 'tall, lofty' (§§505, 507)

hēahran comp asm < *hēah*. See **hēage**

hēahðungene npl < *hēahðungen* adj 'of high rank, illustrious'

heald 2s imp < *healdan* 'to hold, guard, possess, keep, observe, rule' (stv VII(*a*) §517); **healdaþ** 3pl pres; **tō healdes** corrupt form of infl inf. See Text 7/50 note

healf 'half' f or 'half' adj; **healf** in our texts occurs only with **gēar** 'a half year' or 'half a year' except in Text 4/37, in the note to which the combination of an ordinal numeral and a noun is explained; **healfa** apl < noun; **healfan** wk dsm < adj (§§505–6); **healfe** as < noun; **healfum** st dsm < adj (§§505, 507)

hēalic st apln < *hēalic* 'proud, haughty' (§§505, 507)
heall f 'hall, dwelling, palace'; **healle** as/ds
healua late ds < **healf** f 'behalf'
healðegnas apl < *healðegn* m 'hall-thane' (§502)
hēan wk dsm < *hēah*. See **hēage**
hēanne See Text 51/40 note
hēap m 'band, troop, company'
heard adj 'hard, severe, strong, bold'; **hearda** wk nsm (§§505–6); **heardes** st gsm/n (§§505, 507)
heardlice adv 'boldly, resolutely'
heardmōde st npl < *heardmōd* adj 'brave' (§§505, 507)
heardran comp asf < **heard**; **heardum** st dsm (§§505, 507)
hearpan s oblique case < *hearpe* f 'harp' (§§500–1)
hearra m 'lord, master'; **hearran** a/ds
hēarran = **hēahran**
heaðolinde apl < *heaðolind* f 'shield (of linden-wood)' (§504)
heaþostēapa wk nsm < *heaþostēap* adj 'battle-steep, towering in battle' (§§505–6)
heaðowædum dpl < *heaðowǣd* f 'war-dress, armour' (§504)
hebban 'to lift, raise up' (stv VI w wk pres, *Guide* §116)
hefelic adj 'severe, violent'
hefenum = **heofonum**
hefigtīme adj 'troublesome, tedious'
hēhsta super nsm < *hēah*. See **hēage**
heht = **hēt**
helan apl < *hela* m 'heel' (§§500–1)
helle ds < *hell* f 'hell' (§504)
hellewītes gs < *hellewīte* n 'hell-torment' (*Guide* §§45–6)
helm m 'protection, protector, helmet' (§502); **helmas** apl; **helmum** dpl
helpe f 'help'
helpendra gpl pres ptc < *helpan* 'to help'
helwara gpl < *helware* plm 'dwellers in Hell' (*Guide* §§45–6)
hēo 'she' (§495); w fem inanimate antecedents, 'it'; but sometimes **hēo** = **hīe**
heofenas apl < **heofon**
heofenlicere st dsf < *heofenlic* adj 'heavenly, celestial' (§§505, 507)
heofne ds < **heofon**; **heofnes** gs
heofon m 'sky, firmament, heaven' (§502); **heofona** gpl; **heofonas** apl; **heofones** gs
heofonlecan wk gsm < *heofonlec* adj 'heavenly, celestial' (§§505–6); **heofonlican** wk gsm
heofonrīces gs < *heofonrice* n 'kingdom of heaven' (*Guide* §§45–6)
heofonum dpl < **heofon**

hēold 1/3s pret < *healdan*. See **heald**; **hēolde** 3s pret subj; **hēoldon** 3pl pret
heolfre ds < *heolfor* n 'gore, blood' (§503)
heonan/heonon adv 'hence, from here, away'
heora gpl all genders < **hē** (§495) 'their(s), of them'
heord f 'care, custody'
heortan ds (Text 33/17) < *heorte* f 'heart'. The form **heortan** is sing because each mother has one heart; **heortum** dpl (Text 14/20) is plur because more than one person is involved! Both are good OE
heorufæðmum dpl < *heorufæðm* m 'deadly embrace' (§502)
heorðgenēatas npl < *heorðgenēat* 'hearth-companion, retainer' (§502)
hēowes See Text 29/12 note
hēowon 3pl pret < *hēawan* 'to hew, cleave, strike, kill' (stv VII(a) §517)
her adv 'here, at this place/date, hither, in this world'
here n/a/ds < *here* m 'harrying, plundering, devastation; raiding band, army' (*Guide* §§45–6). See §184 fn 7
hereblēaðe st nplm < *hereblēað* adj 'cowardly' (§§505, 507)
herede 3s pret < *herian* = **herigean**; **heredon** 3pl pret
hereflȳman apl < *hereflȳma* m 'fugitive, deserter' (§§500–1)
herelāfum dpl < *herelāf* f 'remnant of an army' or 'booty' (§504). If the latter in Text 36/47, an ironic use
herenesse ds < *hereness* f 'praise' (§504)
herepād f 'corslet, coat of mail'
hererēaf f 'war spoil, plunder, booty'
heretoga m 'commander, general'
herewōpa gpl < *herewōp* m 'cry of an army' (§502)
herge = ds < **here**
hergen 3s pres subj < *hergan* = **herigean**
herges = gs < **here**
hergiað 3pl pres < *hergian* 'to ravage, plunder, harry, capture' (wkv 2 §526); **hergoden** = **hergodon** 3pl pret
hergung f 'harrying, ravaging' (§504); **hergunga** ds
heriað imp pl < *herian* = **herigean**
herige = ds < **here**
herigean 'to praise, commend, extol' (irreg wkv)
heriges = gs < **here**
hērum dpl < *hēr* n 'hair' (§503)
hēt 1/3s pret < *hātan*. See **hāten**; **hēte** Text 27/17 2s pret
hete Text 44/301 m 'hostility, punishment'
hetelice adv 'violently, horribly, punishingly'

heton 3pl pret < *hātan*. See **hāten**
hettend uninfl npl < *hettend* m 'enemy'
heðenra = **hæðenra**
hī asf or n/apl all genders < **hē** (§495) 'her' or 'they/them'
hīda gpl < *hīd* f 'hide of land' (§504). The size of a hide varied greatly .
hider adv 'hither, on/to this side'
hīe asf or n/apl all genders < **hē** (§495) 'her' or 'they/them'
hiene asm < **hē** (§495) 'him'
hiera gpl all genders < **hē** (§495) 'their(s), of them'
hierde 3s pret < *hieran* 'to hear' (wkv §94); **hierdon** 3pl pret
hiere gsf < **hē** (§495) 'of it'
hierran comp ds < *hēah*. See **hēage**
hig = **hīe**
hige ns/ds < *hige* m 'thought, mind, heart, courage, pride' (*Guide* §§45–6)
higegēomor adj 'sad in mind'
Higelāces gs 'of Higelac'
hiht m 'hope, joy, bliss'
hilde a/ds < *hild* f 'battle, combat' (§504)
hildebordum dpl < *hildebord* n 'battle-shield' (§503)
hilderandas apl < *hilderand* m 'battle-shield' (§502)
hilderinc m 'warrior'
hildewǣpnum dpl < *hildewǣpen* n 'war-weapon' (§503)
him dsm/n or dpl all genders < **hē** (§495) 'him, to/from it' or 'them'
hindan adv 'from behind, in the rear'
hine asm < **hē** (§495) 'him, it'
hīo aplf < **hē** (§495) = **hīe** 'them'
hīofende st nplm pres ptc < *hīofan* 'to lament' (§§505, 507)
hīoldon = **hēoldon**. See **hēold**
hiora gpl all genders < **hē** (§495) 'their(s), of them'
hira = **hiora**
hire g/dsf < **hē** (§495) 'her, its, of/to/from her/it'
his gsm/n < **hē** (§495) 'his, its, of it'
hit n/asn < **hē** (§495) 'it'
hīwnesse ds < *hīwness* f 'hue, colour, appearance, form' (§504)
hīwunge ds < *hīwung* f 'marriage' (§504)
hlade 3s pres subj < *hladan* 'to take, draw' (stv VI §517); **tō hladenne** infl inf
hlāf m 'loaf, bread, food'
hlafdige f 'lady, queen'
hlāford m 'lord, ruler, husband, the Lord, God' (§502); **hlāforde** ds; **hlāfordes** gs
hlǣdre as < *hlǣder* f 'ladder' (§504)
hleahtor m 'laughter'
hlēo m 'protection, mound'. Some editors read *hlǣw* m 'grave-mound, barrow'

hlēobordum dpl < *hlēobord* n 'protecting board' (§503)
hlēoðrode 3s pret < *hlēoðrian* 'to speak' (wkv 2 §526)
hlihhan 'to laugh'
hlin m 'maple'
hliste 3s pres subj < *hlistan* 'to listen'
hlīþes gs < *hliþ* n 'hillside' (§503)
hlyte ds < *hlyte* m 'portion, company' (*Guide* §§45–6)
hneccan ds < *hnecca* m 'neck' (§§500–1)
hōe ds < *hōh* m 'neck of land' (*Guide* §37)
hofe ds < *hof* n 'enclosed space, enclosure, dwelling' (§503)
hogode See Text 40/9 note
holde st nplm < *hold* adj 'loyal' (§§505, 507)
holen m 'holly'
holm m 'sea, water'
holmweall m 'wall of sea water'
holtes gs < *holt* m 'wood, forest' (§502)
hond a/ds < *hond* f 'hand' (*Guide* §61); **honda** ds; **hondum** dpl
hord n 'hoard, treasure' (§503); **horde** ds
hordwearda gpl < *hordweard* m 'guardian of treasure' (§502)
horhgum st/dsm < *horhg* = *horig* adj 'dirty' (§§505, 507)
hōringas npl < *hōring* m 'adulterer, fornicator' (§502)
hornas apl < *horn* m 'horn' (§502)
hornreced n 'gabled hall'
hors n 'horse'. In Text 23, **hors** is apl, as, and then npl; see §503
Horsan as 'Horsa'
horses gs < **hors**; **horsum** dpl
hostes npl, a mythical tribe
hrā n 'corpse, carrion'
hraðe adv 'quickly, immediately'
hrædest super nsn < *hræd* adj 'quick'
hrædlice adv 'quickly'
hræfn m 'raven'
hrægle ds < *hrægl* n 'dress, clothing' (§503)
hrēam m 'noise, alarm, lamentation'
hrēman 'to exult, boast'
hrēmge st nplm < *hrēmig* adj 'vaunting, exulting' (§§505, 507)
hrēowcearig adj 'troubled, sad'
hrinen past ptc < *hrīnan* 'to touch' (stv I §517)
hring m 'ring'; **byrnan hring** 'ring mail'
hringed adj 'made of rings'
hringedstefna m '(ship with) ringed prow'
hrōfe ds < *hrōf* m 'roof'
Hrōþgāres gs 'Hrothgar's'
hrusan ds < *hruse* f 'earth, ground' (§§500–1)
hryre m 'fall'
hrysedon 3pl pret < *hryssan* 'to shake' (wkv §524)

hū adv and conj 'how'

huerf = *hwearf* 3s pret < *hweorfan* 'to go, turn' (stv III §518)

hund num 'hundred'; **hund nigontigon** dpl 'with ninety'; **hunde** apl < **hund** num; **hundred** num 'hundred'; **hundtēontiges** gs < *hundtēontig* num 'hundred'

hundum dpl < *hund* m 'hound, dog' (§502)

hunger/hungor m 'hunger, desire, famine' (§502); **hungre** ds

hunticgan npl < *hunticge* f 'huntress' (§§500–1)

huntoðe ds < *huntoð* m 'hunting' (§502)

hupseax n 'short sword, dagger'

huru adv 'certainly, however'

hūs n 'house' (§503), used metaphorically in Text 48/880; **hūse** ds; **hūsum** dpl

hwā (1) Text 11/2252 'anyone who'; (2) elsewhere 'someone, anyone'. See §499

hwæne asm < *hwā* interrog 'who' (§499)

hwær conj 'where'

hwæt (1) Text 44/278 adv 'why?'; (2) Text 32/7 pron **hwæt lȳtles** 'some/any little thing'; elsewhere either (3) interj 'lo!, behold!' or (4) interrog 'what' (§499)

hwæthwugu pron 'something'

hwætran comp npl < *hwæt* adj 'active, bold, brave'

hwæþer conj 'whether'

hwæþere/hwæþre adv 'however, nevertheless'

hwæðres gs < *hwæðer* pron 'which of two'

hwelc 'what, of what sort'; **hwelce** apl

hwelp m 'whelp, cub'

hwene adv 'somewhat, a little'

hwēop 3s pret < *hwōpan* 'to threaten' (stv VII(*a*) §517)

hweðer pron 'which of two'

hwilc adj 'some, any'; **hwilces** gsm; **hwilcne** asm

hwīle as < *hwīl* f 'while, time' (§504); **þā hwīle þe** conj literally 'during the time in which' and so 'while'; **hwīlum** dpl = adv 'sometimes, once'

hwīt adj 'white'

hwonne conj 'until'

hwȳ interrog 'why'

hwylc interrog 'what, of what sort'

hwylcne Text 29/13 asm < *hwylc* adj 'some, any'; Text 29/18 **swā hwylcne swā** asm 'whichever'

hwylcne Text 48/861 asm < *hwylc* interrog 'which'; **hwylcre** dsf; **hwylcum** dsm

hwȳlum = hwīlum. See **hwīle**

hȳ = hī

hycgan 'to think'

hȳda apl < *hȳd* f 'hide, skin' (§504); **hȳde** ds

hyge ds < *hyge* = hige

hygeblīþran comp nplm < *hygeblīþe* adj 'glad at heart'

hygesceaftum dpl < *hygesceaft* f 'mind, heart' (§504)

hyht = hiht

hyhtgifa m 'giver of joy'

hyldan 'to bow, bend down'

hyldo f 'favour, grace, protection, allegiance'

hylt 3s pres < *healdan*. See **heald**

hyne = hine

hyra = hiera

hyrde Text 48/858 m 'shepherd'

hȳrde 1s pret < *hȳran* 'to hear, obey' (wkv §94); **hȳrdon** 1/3pl pret; **hȳre** Text 47 v. 1 3s pres subj

hyre = hire

hȳrlinga gpl < *hȳrling* m 'hireling' (§502); **hȳrlingum** dpl

hyrnednebban asm < *hyrnednebba* adj 'horn-beaked' (§§505–6)

hyrsta apl < *hyrst* f 'jewel, treasure, armour' (§504)

hyrstedgolde ds < *hyrstedgold* n 'well-wrought/decorated gold' (§503). Some editors print *hyrsted golde* 'decorated with gold'

hyrsumnysse ds < *hyrsumnyss* f 'obedience, humility' (§504)

hys = his

hyt = hit

hȳðe ds < *hȳð* f 'harbour' (§504)

Ianr scribal abbreviation 'January'

ic 'I' (§494)

idesa gpl < *ides* f 'woman, wife, lady, queen' (§504); **idese** a/ds

idus Latin 'Ides'

īege ds < *īeg* f 'island' (§504)

ieldran npl < *ieldra* m 'elder, ancestor' (§§500–1)

iernende npln pres ptc < *iernan* 'to run'

ieð comp adv 'more easily'

īge = īege

īglande ds < *īgland* n 'island' (§503)

ilca 'same' (§§505–6); **ilcan** oblique cases; **ilce** asn

in (1) prep wa/d/i (place) 'in, into, on, to'; (time) 'in, at, about'; (purpose) 'for'; (2) adv 'within'. Often replaced by **on**

inbryrded nsm pres ptc < *inbryrdan* 'to inspire, excite' (wkv 1 §§522–3)

indeum 'India'

indryhto f 'honour, glory'

ingeþanc n 'thought, mind' (§503). This form can be as or apl; see note *sv* **heortan**

ingonge ds < *ingong* m 'entry' (§502)

innan prep wa 'into'

inne adv 'within'; **innor** comp 'further'

þ m 'womb' (§502); **innoðas**

ıl pres ptc < *insittan* 'to sit

instæpe m 'entrance, threshold'
.5–6)
'cause, sake' (§§500–1); **intingan**

.rep wa/d 'into'
ıdhlemmas npl < *inwidhlemm* m 'malicious wound' (§502)
inwitta m 'adversary, evil/deceitful one'
inwrige 2s pret subj < *inwrēon* 'to disclose, reveal' (contr stv I §521)
īow dpl < **þū** (§494) 'to you'
īrena gpl < *īren* n 'sword' (§503)
is 'is' (§528)
Isaace ds 'Isaac'
īsig adj 'icy, covered with ice'
Israhēla gpl < *Israhēlas* plm 'Israelites' (§502)
Israhēlisce wk nsn < *Israhēlisc* adj 'Israelitish' (§§505–6)
iū adv 'of old, formerly'
Iūdēa gpl 'of the Jews'
Iūdithe gs 'of Judith'
iuguðe ds < *iuguð* f 'youth'
iung adj 'young' (§§505–7); **iunga** wk nsm; **iungan** wk gs; **iunge** wk nsf; **iunges** st gsm; **iungra** gpl
Iusto Latin ds 'by Justus'
iūwine apl < *iūwine* m 'old friend, friend of bygone days' (*Guide* §§45–6)
īw m 'yew'

kalendas Latin 'calends'
kincg, king m 'king' (§502); **kinge** ds; **kinges** gs
kyning m 'king' (§502); **kyningas** n/apl; **kyninge** ds

lā interj 'lo! behold! oh! ah!'
lāc See Text 40/1 note
lāce 1s pres < *lācan* 'to play, leap, fly, fight'
lāde ds < *lād* f 'journey' (§504)
lāf f 'what is left, remnant, legacy'; **bronda lāfe** as 'legacy of fires, ashes'; **tō lāfe** ds 'as a remnant, leftover'; **lāfum** dpl
lāgon 3pl pret < *licgan* 'to lie (dead)' (stv V with wk pres §519)
lagu m 'sea, ocean'
lagum dpl < *lagu* f 'law' (§504)
lahbrycas apl < *lahbryce* m 'breach of the law' (*Guide* §§45–6)
lambyrde gs < *lambyrd* f 'imperfect birth' (§504)
land n 'earth, land, territory, district, realm, property, country (not town)' (§503); **lande** ds; **landes** gs; **landum** dpl

lang adj 'long'; **langan** wk dsn (§§505–6); **lange** (1) Text 51/24 st asf (§§505, 507); elsewhere either (2) st n/apl or (3) **lange** adv 'long, a long time'
langoþe ds < *langoþ* m 'longing' (§502)
lār f 'lore, doctrine, learning, advice, teaching' (§504); **lāre** a/ds
lārēow m 'teacher, master, preacher' (§502); **lārēowas** n/apl
lārum dpl < **lār**
lāst m 'footprint' (§502); **on lāst legdon** 'followed'
lāstworda gpl < *lāstword* n 'fame after death' (§503)
late adv 'late'
lāð adj 'hated, hostile' (§§505–7); **lāðan** wk dsf; **lāðe** st npl; **lāðra** st gpl; **lāðum** dpl
lǣdan 'to lead, take, carry, lift' (wkv like *hīeran* §94); **on lyft lǣdan** 'lifted into the air'; **lǣdde** 3s pret; **lǣddon** 3pl pret
Lǣden n 'Latin'
Lǣdenbōcum dpl < *lǣdenbōc* f 'Latin book' (§504)
Lǣdene ds < **Lǣden**; **Lǣdenes** gs
Lǣdengeðīode ds < *Lǣdengeðīode* n 'Latin language' (*Guide* §§45–6)
Lǣdenware plm 'Latin people, Romans'
lǣfdon 3pl pret < *lǣfan* 'to leave, bequeath' (wkv like *hīeran* §94)
lǣg 3s pret < *licgan*. See **lāgon**
lǣn n 'lease'
lǣne adj 'transitory'
lǣran 'to teach, persuade, urge' (wkv like *hīeran* §94); **lǣrde** 3s pret; **lǣre** 3s pres subj; **lǣred** past ptc; **tō lǣrenne** infl inf
lǣs adv 'less'; **nōht þon lǣs** 'nevertheless'; **þī lǣs þe** 'lest'; **þȳ lǣs** Text 43/6 'lest'; **þē lǣs** Text 34/35 'lest'. See also Text 5/65–6 note & Text 15/11 note
lǣssan dsn < *lǣssa* adj 'less, smaller, inferior'; **lǣsse** asn
lǣsste wk nsn < *lǣst* adj 'least, smallest'; **lǣsta** wk nsm; **lǣstan** wk asm (§§505–6)
lǣt imp s < *lǣtan*. See **lēt**
lætbyrde gs < *lætbyrd* f 'slow birth' (§504)
leahtra gpl < *leahtor* m 'sin, vice' (§502)
lēan n 'reward, compensation, retribution'
lēas adj 'false, lax, careless, devoid/bereft of (wg)'; **lēase** st aplm (§§505, 507)
lēg m 'fire, flame'
lēgbysig adj 'busy with/troubled by fire'
legdon 3pl pret < *lecgan* 'to lay, go' (irreg wkv). See **lāst**
leger n 'lying in, couch/bed, death' (§503); **legere** ds
lencg adv 'longer'
lendunum dpl < *lendunu* npl 'loins' (§503)
leng adv 'longer'

lenge ds < *leng* f 'length, height' (§504)
lengest adv 'longest'
lengran apl < *lengra* adj 'longer' (§§505–6)
lēoda gpl < *lēod* m 'man' (*Guide* §46), in pl 'men, mortals, people, nation'; **lēode** npl; **lēodum** dpl
lēof adj 'dear, beloved, pleasant, agreeable'; **lēofan** wk npl (§§505–6)
leofað = **lifað**
lēofe Text 38/34 st npl < *lēof* (§§505, 507), elsewhere st nsf; **lēofes** st gsm; **lēofesta** super nsm 'dearest'; **lēofne** st asm
lēoftæle adj 'kind, dear, agreeable'
lēoht n 'light'; **lēohte** Text 51/5 ds
lēohte Text 22/21 st apln < *lēoht* adj 'light, bright'; Text 29/2 st npln
leomu = *limu* n/apl < **lim**
lēon apl < *lēo* m/f 'lion/lioness' (*Guide* §25); **lēona** gpl
lēoð as/pl < *lēoð* n 'song, poem' (§503)
lēoðwyrhta m 'poet'. In Text 43/3 the form is perhaps best taken as gpl
lertices npl, mythical wild beasts
lēt 3s pret < *lǣtan* 'to let, allow' (stv VII(*b*) §517); **lēton** 3pl pret
libban 'to live' (irreg wkv *Guide* §126); **libbende** st nsm pres ptc
līc n 'body'
licað 3s pres < *lician* 'to please' (wkv 2 §526)
līce ds < **līc**
licgað 3pl pres < *licgan*. See **lāgon**; **licgende** ns pres ptc
lichamlice adv 'bodily, personally'
liden past ptc < *līðan* 'to traverse, cross' (stv I §§517, 513)
lides gs < *lid* n 'vessel, ship' (§503)
līf n 'life, existence, way of life' (§503)
lifað 3s pres < **libban**; **lifdon** 3pl pret
life ds < **līf**; **lifes** gs
lifge 3s pres subj < **libban**; **lifgende** npl pres ptc; **lifgendne** st asm (§§505, 507); **lifgendra** gpl
ligge ds < *ligg* = *līg* m 'flame, fire' (§502)
ligræscas npl < *ligræsc* m 'lightning, flash of light' (§502)
lim n 'limb' (§503); **lima** apl; **limum** dpl
liornunga ds < *liornung* f 'learning, study' (§504)
lissum dpl < *liss* f 'kindness, grace, joy' (§504)
list m 'skill'
litel adv 'little, shortly'
lītles gs < *lītel* adj 'little'
līð 3s pres < *licgan*. See **lāgon**
līðende npl < *līðend* m 'seafarer, voyager' (§502)
līðost ns super < *līðe* 'gentle, kind'

liðsmen npl < *liðsman* m 'seaman, sailor' (§§17–18)
lōcað 3s pres < *lōcian* 'to look'; **lōcað ... fram** 'regards with disfavour' (wkv 2 §526)
lōchwā 'whoever, anyone who'
lof n 'praise, glory, repute'. See *lof* in General Index
lofgeornost adj 'most eager for praise'. See §413
lofsangum dpl < *lofsang* m 'song of praise, hymn, psalm' (§502)
lond = **land**; **londe** ds
longaþes gs < *longaþ* m 'longing'
longe st asf < *long* adj 'long' (§§505, 507)
losað 3s pres < *losian* 'to fail, perish, depart from' (wkv 2 §526)
loxas apl < *lox* m 'lynx' (§502)
lufan a/ds < *lufe* f 'love' (§§500–1)
lufian 'to love' (§526); **lufiað** 2pl pres; **lufiend** pres ptc = noun 'lover'; **lufige** 1s pres; **lufodon** 3pl pret
lunnon 3pl pret < *linnan* 'to part from' wd (stv III §518)
lust m 'desire, pleasure, joy' (§502); **lustum** dpl
luuelice adv 'willingly, gladly'
lȳfde 3s pret < *lȳfan* 'to agree, grant, concede' (wkv like *hīeran* §94)
lyft f 'air, sky' (§504); **lyfte** ds; **on lyfte** 'aloft, in the air'
lȳsan 'to release, redeem, ransom'
lȳt indeclinable noun 'little'
lȳtle st oblique case < *lȳtel* adj 'little, small' (§§505, 507)
lȳtlingum dpl < *lȳtling* m/f 'little one, infant, child'

mā 'more' (1) adj; (2) indeclinable noun; (3) adv
mādma gpl < *mādm* m 'treasure' (§502)
mǣga Text 36/40 gpl < *mǣg* m 'kinsman, son' (§502); Text 37/26 uncertain – see note; **mǣgan** Text 42/372, 385 as
magan Text 25/16 ds < *maga* m 'stomach' (§§500–1)
magan Text 34/35 1pl pres < *magan*. See **mæg**; **magon** 1/3pl pres
magorinca gpl < *magorinc* m 'young warrior' (§502)
mǣgum dpl < **mǣg**
man m (1) 'human being, person male or female'; (2) '(brave) man'; (3) in impers constructions 'one, people, they'
māna gpl < *mān* n 'evil deed, crime' (§503)
mancyn n 'mankind' (§503); **mancynnes** gs
mandryhtne ds < *mandryhten* m 'lord' (§502)
māndæda apl < *māndæd* f 'evil deed, sin, crime' (§504)

See **māna**

... < *manig* adj 'many, many a,
..., 507); **manegum** dpl
... nsm < *mānfull* adj 'wicked'

...pl = **manege**
... ds < *manigeo* f 'multitude'
...eald adj 'complicated'
...gra gpl < *manig*. See **manege**
...nn = man; **manna** gpl; **mannes** gs
mannslagan npl < *mannslaga* m 'manslayer,
murderer' (§§500–1)
mannsylena apl < *mannsylenu* f 'traffic in
men, selling of people (as slaves)' (§504)
mannum dpl < **mann**
mānscaða m 'evil-doer, wicked ravager'
mansleht m 'manslaughter, homicide'
(§502); **manslyhtas** apl
mānsworan npl < *mānswora* m 'perjurer'
(§§500–1)
mānweorcum dpl < *mānweore* adj 'sinful'
(§§505, 507)
māra adj 'more, greater' (§§505–6); **māran**
as/pl; **māre** n/asn
marmorstānes gs < *marmorstān* m '(piece
of) marble' (§502)
martyra gpl < *martyr* m/f 'martyr' (§§502,
504)
martyrdōme ds < *martyrdōm* m 'martyrdom'
(§502)
maþelode 3s pret < *maþelian* 'to speak, make
a speech' (wkv 2 §526)
māðm m 'treasure' (§502); **māðma** gpl
mǣden n 'maiden'
mǣg Text 35/737 m 'kinsman' (§502); **mǣge**
Text 15/2 ds
mǣg 1/3s pret < *magan* 'to be able' (§96);
mǣge 3s pret subj; **mǣgen** Text 24 (3
times) 3pl pres subj
mǣgen (other than in Text 24) n 'might,
power, valour, force, host, army' (§503);
mǣgena gpl; **mǣgenes** gs
mǣgenþrēatas apl < *mǣgenþrēat* m 'mighty
host' (§502)
mǣgn n 'might, power'
mǣgrǣsas apl < *mǣgrǣs* m 'attack on a
kinsman/relative' (§502)
mǣgslagan npl < *mǣgslaga* m 'slayer of a
kinsman, killer of a relative' (§502)
mǣgwinum dpl < *mǣgwine* m 'friend and
relative' (*Guide* §§45–6)
mǣgð uninfl gs < *mǣgð* f 'maiden'
mǣgða gpl < *mǣgð* f 'tribe' (§504)
mǣla gpl < *mǣl* n 'time, occasion' (§503)
mænego uninfl ds < **mænigo**
mænige st nsm < *manig*. See **manege**
mænigfealde st aplf < *mænigfeald* adj 'mani-

fold, numerous, varied' (§§505, 507);
mænigfealdre nsn comp
mænigo f 'company, host, multitude';
mænio uninfl ds
mǣran wk oblique case < *mǣre* adj 'famous,
great, excellent, splendid, sublime'. This
form can be ns/npl all genders (*Guide* §73);
mǣrne st asm; **mǣrost** nsn super; **mǣrra**
gpl comp. See Text 12/329 note
mǣrða a/gpl < *mǣrð* f 'glory, fame, famous
deed' (§504); **mǣrðum** dpl
mæssan ds < **mæsse**
mæsse f 'mass, mass-day, feast, festival'
(§§500–1), often in compounds
mæssedæg m 'mass-day, festival' (§502);
mæssedæge ds
mæsseprēost m '(mass-)priest'
mæsserbanan npl < *mæsserbana* m 'slayer of
a priest' (§§500–1)
mæst m 'ship's mast' (§502); **mæste** Text
8/36 ds
mǣst ealle adv + npl adj 'almost all'
mǣst super adj 'most, greatest'; **mǣstan** wk
oblique cases (§§505–6); **mǣste** wkn/asn
mǣwes gs < *mǣw* m 'sea-gull'
me occasionally = **man** (3)
mē a/ds < **ic** (§494) 'me'
meaht 2s pres < *magan* 'to be able' (§96)
meahte Text 20/19 as < *meaht* f 'might,
power' (§504)
meahte elsewhere 1/3s pret < *magan*. See
meaht; **meahton** 3pl pret
mearh m 'horse, steed'
mec = **mē**
mēca gpl < *mēce* m 'sword, blade' (*Guide*
§§45–6); **mēce** Text 46/495 ds; **mēcum** dpl
mēde Text 49/15 See note
mēde Text 12/334 ds < *mēd* f 'reward' (§504)
medmiclum st dsn < *medmicel* adj 'short'
(§§505, 507)
mehten 3pl pret subj < *magan*. See **meaht**;
mehton 3pl pret ind
meldode 3s pret < *meldian* 'to proclaim,
reveal' (wkv 2 §526)
men *i*-mutation ds or n/apl (§§17–18) < **man**
mengeo/menigo = **mænigo**
menn = **men**
menniscnesse/menniscnisse ds < *mennisc-
ness* f 'incarnation' (§504)
meodoburgum dpl < *meodoburg* f 'mead-
city, happy city' (§504)
meolc/meoluc f 'milk'
meotodes gs < *meotod* m 'creator, God,
Christ' (§502)
meras n/apl < **mere**
Mercna gpl 'of the Mercians'
mere m 'ocean, sea, lake' (§502). This form
can be n/a/ds (*Guide* §§45–6)

meredēaŏ m 'sea-death' (§502); **meredēaŏa** gpl

mereflōdes gs < *mereflōd* n 'sea-flood, surging sea' (§503)

merelāde ds < *merelād* f 'ocean track, sea path' (§504)

merestrēam m 'ocean current' (§502); **mere-strēames** gs

meretorras npl < *meretorr* m 'sea-tower, tower of sea-water' (§504)

mete m 'meat, food' (*Guide* §§45–6)

metelīste ds < *metelīst* f 'lack of food, starvation' (§504)

metes gs < **mete**

metod = *meotod*. See **meotodes**

metsunga as < *metsung* f 'feeding, provisioning' (§504)

mētte 3s pret < *mētan* 'to meet, find, encounter' (wkv like *settan* §94); **mētton** 3pl pret

metud = *meotod*. See **meotodes**

mēŏum st dsm < *mēŏe* adj 'sad, tired, troublesome' (§§505, 507)

micclum dpln = adv 'greatly' < *micel* adj 'great, intense, much, many, (of time) long' (§§505–7); **micelne** st asm

micelnesse ds < *micelness* f 'multitude, abundance' (§504)

micelre st dsf < *micel*. See **micclum**; *micla* wk nsm; **miclan** wk asm; **micle** oblique case s/pl; **miclum** dpln, sometimes as adv 'greatly' (§§505–7)

mid (1) adv 'at the same time, together'; (2) prep wa/d (place) '(in company) with, in the presence of'; (time) 'at'; (manner) 'through, by means of'; (3) on its use in prep advs and conjs like *mid þǣm* (*þe*), see the textual notes and §§124–6

middan wintra dsn 'at midwinter' (*Guide* §40)

middangeard m 'the world, earth, mankind' (§502); **middangeardes** gs

middel n 'middle, centre'

middeweard (1) adv 'in the middle'; (2) adj 'middle'; **middeweardan** wk dsm (§§505–6)

midne st asm < *mid* adj 'mid' (§§505, 507); **midre** st dsf

Miercna gpl 'of the Mercians'

mihta gpl < *miht* f 'might, power' (§504); **mihte** Text 19/17 as

mihte elsewhere 1/3s pret < *magan*. See **meaht**

mihtig adj 'mighty, important' (§§505–7); **mihtiga** wk nsm; **mihtigra** comp nsm; **mihtigum** st dsm

mihton 3pl pret < *magan*. See **meaht**

mīl f 'mile' (§504); **mīla** gpl

milde adj 'mild, merciful, gracious, gentle' (*Guide* §73)

mildelice adv 'graciously'

mildheortnesse ds < *mildheortness* f 'pity, mercy' (§504)

mildne st asm < **milde**; **mildust** nsm super

mile ds < **mīl**

miltestrum dpl < *miltestre* f 'prostitute'

miltse ds < *milts* f 'favour, mercy, reverent joy' (§504)

mīlum dpl < **mīl**

mīn (1) gs < **ic** (§494) 'of me'; (2) poss 'my, mine'; **mīne** st oblique case s/pl (§§505, 507); **mīnes** st gsm/n; **mīnne** st asm; **mīnra** st gpl; **mīnre** st g/dsf; **mīnum** st dsm/n or dpl; **mīre** = **mīnre**

misdǣda gpl < *misdǣd* f 'evil deed, sin' (§504); **misdǣdan** wk apl

mislice st aplm < *mislic* adj 'various, manifold' (§§505, 507)

mislimpe 3s pres subj < *mislimpan* 'to go wrong' (stv III §518)

misthleoþum dpl < *misthleoþ* n 'misty slope' (§503)

mistlice st apln = **mislice**

mōd n 'heart, mind, spirit, courage, pride, power, violence' (§503)

mōdceare a/ds < *mōdcearu* f 'sorrow, grief' (§504)

mōddra gpl < *mōddor* f 'mother' (*Guide* §60); **mōddru** npl

mōde ds < **mōd**

mōder n/gs < *mōder* f 'mother' (*Guide* §60)

mōderlicum st dpl < *mōderlic* adj 'maternal' (§§505, 507)

mōdewǣga See Text 46/499–500a note

mōdge st aplm < **mōdig**

mōdgemynd n 'mind, thought'

mōdgeþanc m 'mind, thought, purpose'

mōdgode 3s pret < *mōdgian* 'to rage' (wkv 2 §526)

mōdig adj 'valiant, brave, raging, violent'; **mōdige** st nplm (§§505, 507); **mōdigre** st gsf

mōdor f 'mother' (*Guide* §60)

mōdsefan ds < *mōdsefa* m 'heart, mind, spirit' (§§500–1)

Moise ds 'Moses'

moldan as < *molde* f 'earth' (§§500–1)

mon = **man**

mōna m 'moon' (§§500–1); **mōnan** as

mōnaþ m 'month'. This form is either as or uninfl apl in our texts

mondryhtne ds < *mondryhten* m 'lord' (§502)

monegum dpl < *monig* adj 'many, many a, much'; **monige** st n/apl (§§505, 507)

monn = **man**; **monna** gpl; **monnan** wk asm

ᵹs < *moncynn* n 'mankind'

< **monn**

mōnaþ; **mōnŏes** gs

st super < *monŏwǣre* adj 'gentle,

moor, swamp, hill' (§502); **mōras**
pl; **mōre** ds; **mōres** gs
gentīd f 'morning'
orþorwyrhtan npl < *morþorwyrhta* m
'murderer' (§§500–1)

morŏdǣda apl < *morŏdǣd* f 'murder, deadly
sin' (§504)

mōrŏra gpl < *mōrŏor* n 'mortal sin, torment,
punishment' (§503)

mōrum dpl < **mōr**

mōstan 3pl pret < *mōtan* 'to be allowed, may'
(§96); **mōste** 3s pret; **mōsten** 3pl pret subj;
mōston 2/3pl pret; **mōt** 1s pres; **mōtan**
3pl pres; **mōte** 2s pres subj; **mōten** 1pl
pres subj; **mōton** 1pl pres

Moyse ds 'Moses'; **Moyses** n/gs 'Moses/of
Moses'

multon 3pl pret < *meltan* 'to melt, dissolve'
(stv III §518)

munecum dpl < *munuc* m 'monk' (§502)

munuchāde ds < *munuchād* m 'monastic
orders' (§502)

murnende nsn pres ptc < *murnan* 'to worry,
care, mourn, sorrow'

mūŏ m 'mouth' (§502)

mūþan a/ds < *mūþa* m 'mouth (of river),
estuary, entrance to house, door' (§§500–1)

mūþe ds < **mūþ**

mycclan wk dsm < *micel*. See **micclum**;
mycclum st dsn; **mycel** = *micel*; **myclum**
dplm/n, sometimes = adv 'greatly'

mylenscearpum dplm < *mylenscearp* adj
'sharp'

myltestran npl < *myltestre* f 'prostitute'
(§§500–1)

mynster n 'monastery, cathedral'

mynsterhatan npl < *mynsterhata* m 'persecutor of monasteries' (§§500–1)

mynstre ds < **mynster**

mynte 3s pret < *myntan* 'to intend' (wkv like
settan §94)

myrgen f 'joy, pleasure'

myrhŏa apl < *myrhŏ* f 'joy'

myslicere st dsf < *mislic*. See **mislice**

nā (1) adv 'not (at all), no', negating clauses,
phrases, and words other than verbs; (2)
conj **nā . . . nā** 'neither . . . nor', **nā þæt ān**
'not only'

nabbaŏ = **ne** + *habbaŏ* 3pl pres < **habban**
(§§108–9)

nacan gs < *naca* m 'ship' (§§500–1)

nacodne st asm < *nacud* adj 'naked' (§§505,
507)

nāh = **ne** + *āh* 1/3s pres < *āgan* 'to have'
(§§96, 108–9)

nāht pron 'nothing' (§§108–9)

nalǣs/nales/nalles adv 'no, by no means,
not at all'

nam 1/3s pret < **niman**

nama m 'name, reputation' (§§500–1);
naman oblique case

namon 3pl pret < **niman**

nān pron and adj 'not, no one, no'; **nāne** st
asf (§§505, 507); **nānre** st dsf; **nānum** st
dsn/dplm (§§108–9)

nānwuht = **nāht**

nāt = **ne** + *wāt* 1s pres < *witan* 'to know'
(§96)

nāwiht = **nāht**

nāŏelǣs 'nevertheless'

nāŏor ne . . . ne 'neither . . . nor'

nǣdran n/apl < *nǣdre* f 'adder, snake'
(§§500–1); **nǣdrena** gpl

nǣfde = **ne** + *hæfde* 3s pret < **habban** 'to
have' (§§108–9)

nǣfre adv 'never' (§§108–9)

nægledcnearrum dpl < *nægledcnearr* m
'nailed ship' (§502)

næglum dpl < *nægl* m 'nail' (§502)

nǣnig pron and adj 'no one, none, not any,
no' (§§108–9)

nǣnne st asm < **nān**

nǣre = **ne** + *wǣre* 3s pret subj < **wesan** 'to
be (§§528, 108–9); **nǣron** 3pl pret; **næs** 3s
pret

næsse ds < *næss* m 'pit' (§502)

nе (1) adv 'not, no'; (2) conj (**ne . . .**) **ne**
'(neither . . .) nor' (§§108–10, 119)

nēade ds < *nēad* f 'necessity' (§504)

nēah (1) adv 'near'; (2) prep wd 'near'

neahte = **nihte**. See **niht**

nēalescan 'to approach' wd

nēalice adv 'nearly, about'

nēalæcŏ 3s pres < **nēalecan**

nearolice adv 'densely, cryptically'

nearon 3pl pres 'are not' (§§108–9)

nēata gpl < *nēat* n 'animal, beast, (pl) cattle'
(§503)

nēaweste ds < *nēawest* f 'neighbourhood,
presence' (§504)

neb(b) n 'nose'. This form can be as/pl

nefa m 'nephew'

nele/nelle 3s pres = **ne** + *wil(l)e* < **willan** 'to
wish to, will' (§89)

nemnan 'to call, name' (wkv like *hīeran* §94);
nemde st nplf past ptc (§§505, 507);
nemnde 3s pret

nemne (1) prep wa 'except'; (2) conj 'except
(that)'

nemned past ptc < nemnan; nemneþ 3s pres

nēod f 'need, duty'

nēodlicor comp adv 'more zealously'

nēolum dpl < *nēol* adj 'deep'

neom = ne + *eom* 'am not' (§§528, 108–9)

neoþor comp adv 'inferior'

nēosan 'to seek out'

nēowne st asm < *nēowe* adj 'new' (*Guide* §73)

nīedbeðearfosta st nplf super < *nīedbeðearf* adj 'necessary' (§§505, 507)

nigontigon in þrim 7 hund nigontigon dpl num 'ninety-three'

nigoþan wk dsm/asf < *nigoðe* num 'ninth' (§§505–6)

niht f 'night, darkness' (§504); nihta gpl; nihte ds; nihtes gsm = adv 'by night'; nihtum dpl

niman 'to take, capture, occupy' (stv §519); niman tō + d 'to take to/as'; niman friþ/ griþ 'to make peace'; nimað 3pl pres; nime 3s pres subj; nimð 3s pres

nis = ne + *is* 'is not' (§§528, 108–9)

nīð m 'strife, enmity, malice'

niðer adv 'below, beneath'

nīðhēdige st npl < *nīðhēdig* adj 'hostile' (§§505, 507)

nīðum dpl < *niðas* plm 'men, mankind' (§502)

niwan adv 'newly, lately'

nīwe adj 'new' (*Guide* §73); nīwes st gsn

nō = nā

nōht = nāht; nōht þon lǣs 'nevertheless'

nolde 3s pret = ne + *wolde* < *willan* 'to wish to, will' (§89); noldon 1/3pl pret

nom = nam

noman ds < nama

norþ adv 'north(wards)'

Norþanhymbra gpl 'of the Northumbrians'

norðerna wk nsm < *norðerne* adj 'northern' (*Guide* §73)

norðeweard adj 'north(ward)'; norðeweardum st dsn (§§505, 507)

Norþhymbra gpl < Norþhymbre 'the Northumbrians'; Norþhymbrum dpl

Norðmanna gpl < *Norðman* 'Norseman'; Norðmen(n) n/apl (§§17–18)

norþmest super adv 'furthest north'

Norðmonna = Norðmanna

norþor comp adv 'further north'

Norðwalas n/apl 'the Welsh, Wales' (§502)

norðweardum st dsn < norðeweard

nosa npl < *nosu* f 'nose' (§504)

note ds < *notu* f 'employment, office' (§504)

Nouembris 'November'

nū (1) adv 'now'; (2) conj 'now (that)'; nū . . . nū 'now that'

Numetores gs 'Numetor's'

nydboda m 'messenger of evil, distress'

nȳde adv 'needs, necessarily'

nȳdinga adv 'by force'

nȳhst super adj 'nearest' wd; nȳhstan w æt 'at last'

nyste 3s pret = ne + *wiste* < *witan* 'to know' (§§96, 108–9)

nyt adj 'useful'

nytte ds < *nytt* f 'use, advantage'

nyttnesse gs < *nyttness* f 'advantage'

nytwurðe adj 'useful, profitable'

nȳxstan w æt 'at last'

nyðer = niðer

Octobris 'October'

of (1) adv 'off, away'; (2) prep wd 'of, out of, from; by; about, concerning'

ofēode 3s pret < *ofgān* 'to go out' (§529)

ofer (1) adv 'above, on high, across'; (2)prep wa/d 'over, across, through; on, upon; after; contrary to'

ofercōmon 3pl pret < *ofercuman* 'to overcome' (stv IV §519)

oferēode 3s pret < ofergān

oferferan 'to traverse, cross'

ofergān past ptc < *ofergān* 'to overrun' (§529)

ofergenga m 'traveller'

oferhergeada 3s pret < *oferhergean* 'to overrun, ravage' (wkv 2 §526); oferhergeade 3s pret; *oferhergeadon* 3pl pret

ofermēdan wk asm < *ofermēde* adj 'proud, arrogant' (*Guide* §73)

ofermēde n 'pride'

ofermōdes gs = adv < *ofermōd* n 'pride' (§503)

oferswīþde 3s pret < *oferswiþan* 'to overpower, conquer' (wkv like *hieran* §94)

Offan gs 'Offa's'

ofgeaf 3s pret < *ofgiefan* 'to give up, leave' (stv V §519)

oflongad past ptc < *oflongian* 'to seize with longing' (wkv 2 §526)

ofslagen/ofslægen past ptc < *ofslēan* 'to strike off, destroy, kill, slay' (contr stv VI §521); ofslægene st nplm past ptc (§§505, 507); ofslēað imp pl; ofslegen past ptc; ofslōg 1/3s pret; ofslōge 2s pret subj; ofslōgon 3pl pret; ofslōh 3s pret

ofstang 3s pret < *ofstingan* 'to stab to death' (stv III §518)

ofste ds < *ofst* f 'haste' (§504)

ofostlice adv 'quickly, hastily'

oft adv 'often, frequently'; oftor comp; oftost super

oleccan 'to flatter, propitiate'

oifendan gs < *olfenda* m 'camel' (§§500–1)

on prep w a/d (place) 'in, into, on, to, among'; (time) 'in, at, about'; (other uses)

(in exchange) for'. Often
... OE; it is over six times more
... r texts
... < *onirnan* 'to spring open' (stv

... ptc < *onǣlan* 'to burn' (wkv like
... 94)
... 3s pret < *onbregdan* 'to swing open'
... III §518)
... nēow 3s pret < *oncnāwan* 'to perceive' (stv
VII(*a*) §517)

oncyrde st nplm past ptc < *oncyrran* 'to turn'
(wkv like *fyllan* §94)

ond conj 'and'

ondetnesse gs < *ondetness* f 'confession, vow'
(§504)

ondette 3s pret < *ondettan* 'to confess, vow'
(wkv like *settan* §94)

ondrēdon 3pl pret < *ondrǣdan* 'to fear' w refl
pron (stv VII(*b*) §517); **ondrǣt** imp s

ondsware as < *ondswaru* f 'answer, solution'
(§504)

ondswarede 3s pret < *ondswarian* 'to answer'
(wkv like *werian* §525); **ondswarigende**
pres ptc

ondweardan wk asm < *ondweard* adj 'present' (§§505–6)

onfangenre (see Text 21/11 note) st dsf past
ptc < *onfōn* 'to take, receive, accept' wa/
g/d (contr stv VII(*b*) §521); **onfeng** 3s pret;
onfengon 3pl pret; **onfengun** 3pl pret;
onfōn (1) inf; (2) Text 19/19 1pl pres subj

onfond 3s pret < *onfindan* 'to find out' (stv III
§518)

onfongen past ptc < *onfōn*. See **onfangenre**

ongan(n) 3s pret < *onginnan* 'to begin' (stv III
§518)

ongēan (1) adv 'back'; (2) prep wa/d 'towards, opposite to'

ongeat 3s pret < *ongietan*. See **ongēton**

ongēn = **ongēan**

ongēton 3pl pret < *ongietan* 'to perceive,
realize, recognize, distinguish, hear' (stv V
§519)

ongin imp s < *onginnan*. See **ongan(n)**;
onginneð 3s pres

ongitað 3pl pres < *ongietan*. See **ongēton**

ongon 3s pret < *onginnan*. See **ongan(n)**;
ongunne 3s pret subj; **ongunnon** 3pl pret

ongyldan 'to atone for, pay (the penalty) for'

ongynneð 3s pret < *onginnan*. See **ongan(n)**

ongyrede 3s pret < *ongyr(w)an* 'to unclothe,
strip' (wkv 1 §§522–3)

ongytan = *ongietan*. See **ongēton**

onhnīgaþ 3pl pres < *onhnigan* 'to bow, worship'

onhrēran 'to move, disturb' (wkv like *hīeran*
§94); **onhrēred** past ptc

onhworfen past ptc < *onhweorfan* 'to change,
reverse' (stv III §518)

onhyrded past ptc < *onhyrdan* 'to harden'
(wkv like *sendan* §89)

onhæbbe 1s pres < *onhebban* 'to lift up'. See
hebban

onlīðigan 'to yield'

onlong prep wg 'along, by the side of'

onlūtan 'to bow, bend down'

onmedlan ds/npl < *onmēdla* m 'pomp, mag-
nificence' (§§500–1)

ono hwæt interj 'behold!'

onsǣge adj 'assailing, attacking'

onsended past ptc < *onsendan* 'to send out/
forth, yield up' (wkv §89)

onsit 3s pres < *onsittan* 'to oppress, be seated
in, occupy'; **onsite** imp s

onslēpte 3s pret < *onslēpan* 'to go to sleep'
(wkv like *settan* §94)

onspecendan dpl < *onspecenda*, -*e* m/f
'accuser, plaintiff' (§§500–1)

onstealde 3s pret < *onstellan* 'to create,
establish' (wkv *Guide* §122)

onsȳn f 'countenance, face'

onufan prep wa 'in addition to'

onwalde ds < *onwald* m 'authority, rule'
(§502)

onȳtan See Text 7/4 note

open adj 'open'; **opene** npl

openlice adv 'openly, publicly, plainly'

ōr n 'beginning'

ōran ds < *ōra* m 'bank, shore, edge' (§§500–1)

orlegstunde as < *orlegstund* f 'time of adversi-
ty' (§504), expressing duration of time

ormēte st nplm < *ormēte* 'huge, intense'
(*Guide* §73)

ormōd adj 'despondent, despairing'

Ottanforda ds 'Otford'

oþ (1) prep wa/d 'up to, as far as, until'; (2)
conj 'until'

ōþer 'one of two, second, another'; **ōþer ...
ōþer** 'the one ... the other, other than';
ōþere st npln (§§505, 507); **ōþerne** st asm;
ōþerre st dsf

oðfæste st npl past ptc < *oðfæstan* 'to set to'
(wkv like *settan* §94)

oðfeallan 'to fall off, decline'

oðflitan 'to take by litigation'

oþīewde 3s pret < *oþīewan* 'to appear, (w refl
pron) to show itself' (wkv like *hīeran* §94)

ōðra st nplf < *ōþer* (§§505, 507); **ōðran** =
ōðrum dpl; **ōþre** st oblique case s/pl;
ōþres st gsm; **ōþru** st apln; **ōþrum** dsm/n
or dpl

oððan conj 'or'

oððæt conj 'until'

oþþe (1) occasionally = *oþ þe* conj 'until'; (2)
conj 'or'; **oþþe ... oþþe** 'either ... or'

oðþringeð 3s pres < *oðþringan* 'to take'
owiht 'anything'
oxan gs or n/apl < *oxa* m 'ox' (§§500–1)
Oxnaforda ds 'Oxford'

pallium See Text 3/6 note
papa m 'pope'
paŏ m 'path'. See Text 46/488 note
Petre ds 'Peter'
Pharaones gs 'Pharaoh's'
plega m 'play, festivity, gear for sport'
plegade 3s pret < *plegian* 'to play, fight' (wkv 2 §526). See Text 48/804–5 note
plegan Text 31/12 'to play'
plegan elsewhere a/ds < **plega**
plegendan wk dsm pres ptc < *plegian* (§§505–6). See **plegade**; **plegodon** 3pl pret
pleoh n 'danger, responsibility'
plēolic adj 'dangerous'
prēostas npl < *prēost* m 'priest' (§502)
punda gpl < *pund* n 'pound' (§503)

rād 3s pret < *rīdan* 'to ride' (stv I §517)
radorum dpl < *rador* m 'sky, heaven' (§502)
randbyrig npl < *randburg* f 'shield-wall (of waves)' (*i*-mutation pl §§17–18)
raþe adv 'quickly'
rǣd m 'advice, plan'
rǣdan 'to advise, suggest, read, rule, control'; **tō rǣdenne** infl inf; **rǣdeð** 3s pres
rǣdlice adv 'quickly'
rǣdnesse ds < *rǣdness* f 'speed' (§504)
rǣdþeahtende npl pres ptc as adj 'deliberating, wise'
rǣpton 3pl pret < *rǣpan* 'to bind, capture, enslave' (wkv like *settan* §94)
rǣrde 3s pret < *rǣran* 'to raise up' (wkv like *hieran* §94)
rēad adj 'red'; **rēada** wk nsm (§§505–6); **rēade** wk apln; **rēaden** = *rēadan* wk dsm; **rēadum** st dsn (§§505, 507)
rēaferas npl < *rēafere* m 'robber, plunderer' (*Guide* §§45–6)
rēaflāc n 'robbery, rapine'
reahte 3s pret < *reccan* 'to tell, narrate' (irreg wkv *Guide* §122)
rēc m 'smoke'
reccelēase st npl < *reccelēas* adj 'careless, negligent' (§§505, 507)
reced n 'hall' (§503); **recede** ds; **recedes** gs
rehte = **reahte**
Remuse ds 'Remus'
rēnig adj 'rainy'
rēoman ds < *rēoma* m 'membrane' (§§500–1)
rēonian wk dsn < *rēoni(g)* adj 'sorrowful' (§§505–6)

reordberend uninfl npl 'speech-bearers, humans'
rēotugu st nsf < *rēotug* adj 'sad' (§§505, 507)
reste a/ds < *rest* f 'rest, repose, bed' (§504)
rēðan wk g/dsf < *rēðe* adj 'fierce, cruel, terrible, violent'; **rēðe** st npln (§§505–7)
ribb npl < *ribb* n 'rib' (§503)
Ricarde ds 'Richard'
rīce n 'kingdom'. This form can be n/a/ds (*Guide* §§45–6); **fōn tō rīce** 'to become king'; **rīces** gs
rīcne st asm < *rīce* adj 'powerful, of high rank'
ricsian 'to rule' (wkv 2 §526); **ricsode** 3s pret; **ricsodon** 3pl pret
rīdeð 3s pres < *rīdan*. See **rād**
riht adj 'right'
rihte ds < *riht* n '(what is) right' (§503); **rihtes** gs
rihtlice adv 'rightly, righteously'
rihtwis adj 'righteous, just'
rīmtale ds < *rīmtalu* f 'number' (§504)
rinc m 'man, warrior, hero'; **rinca** gpl; **rincas** npl
rīne 3s pres subj < *rīnan* 'to rain'
rixade 3s pret < *rixian* = **ricsian**; **rixsade** 3s pret
rōd f 'rood, cross, gallows' (§504); **rōda** a/gpl; **rōde** g/ds
roderum dpl < *rodor* m 'sky, heaven' (§502)
rodorcyninges gs < *rodorcyning* m 'king of heaven' (§502)
rōfe st nplm < *rōf* adj 'strong, valiant, noble' (§§505, 507)
rofene st nplf past ptc < *rēofan* 'to rend, break' (stv II §517)
rōhtan 3pl pret < *reccan*/*rēcan* 'to care' (wkv like *sēcan* §95)
Romana gpl < **Romane** 'the Romans'
Romuluse ds 'Romulus'; **Romuluses** gs
ryhtes See Text 27/7 note
ryhtfædrencyn n 'direct paternal descent/pedigree'
ryhtrace ds < *ryhtracu* f 'correct account' (§504)
rȳmde 3s pret < *rȳman* 'to sweep away' (wkv like *hieran* §94)
ryne ds < *ryne* m 'running' (*Guide* §§45–6)
rȳperas npl < *rȳpere* m 'robber, plunderer' (*Guide* §§45–6)

saga imp s < **secgan**
sāh 3s pret < *sigan* 'to sink, set' (stv I §517)
saka See Text 28/3–4 note
salde = **sealde**
salowīgpadan wk asm < *salowīgpad* adj 'dark-coloured' (§§505–6)
same w swǣ adv 'likewise, similarly'

e same time, together'

…aint'; **Sanctes** gs; **Sanctus** ns

…**sande** ds

…singing, psalm' (§502)

…uffering, sorrow' (§503); **sāre** ds

…rely, grievously'

… st dsm < *sārlic* adj 'sorrowful'

…5, 507)

… a/ds < *sāwl* f soul (§504); *sāwle* ds

wllēasne st as < *sāwllēas* adj 'soulless, lifeless' (§§505, 507)

sāwlum dpl < *sāwl*. See **sāule**

sǣ m/f 'sea'. This form can be all cases and both numbers except g/dpl

Sǣbyrhte ds 'Sǣbyrht'

sǣcce ds < *sǣcc* f 'strife, contest' (§504)

sǣd adj 'sated/satiated with' wg

sǣde 1/3s pret < **secgan**

sǣl n 'hall'

sǣldon 3pl pret < *sǣlan* 'to fasten, moor' (wkv like *hīeran* §94)

sǣlða as < *sǣlð* f 'happiness' (§504)

sǣmanna gpl < *sǣmann* m 'seaman' (§502)

sǣnacan as < *sǣnaca* m 'ship' (§§500–1)

sǣndest 2s pres < **sendan**

sǣnæssas apl < *sǣnæss* m 'sea-ness, headland' (§502)

sǣriman ds < *sǣrima* m 'sea-shore, coast' (§§500–1)

sǣs gs < **sǣ**

sæt 1/3s pret < *sittan*. See **sit**; **sǣton** 3pl pret; **sǣtun** 3pl pret

sǣwudu m 'sea-wood, ship'

scamað 3s pres < *scamian* impers vb wd (person) and wg (thing) (wkv 2 §526)

scame ds < *scamu* f 'shame' (§504)

sceadu apl < *scead* n 'shade, shadow' (§503)

sceadugenga m 'shadow-goer, walker in darkness'

sceal(l) 1/3s pres < **sculan**

sceandlican wk asf < *sceandlic* adj 'shameful, disgraceful' (§§505–6)

scēap n 'sheep' (§503)

sceapen past ptc < *scieppan* 'to shape, create, form, arrange, destine' (stv *Guide* §103.1)

scēapes gs < **scēap**

sceard adj 'deprived of' wg

sceare as < *scearu* f 'tonsure' (§504)

scēatas apl < *scēat* m 'surface, region' (§502); **scēatum** dpl

sceaða m 'criminal, robber, assassin'

scēoc 3s pret < *scacan* 'to depart' (stv VI §517)

sceolde 1/3s pret < **sculan**; **sceolden** 3pl pret subj; **sceoldon** 3pl pret; **sceolon** 3pl pres

sceolu f 'troop, host'

scēop 3s pret < *scieppan*. See **sceapen**

scēotend uninfl nplm 'shooters, warriors'

sceððan 'to hurt, injure' wd

scicelse/scicilse ds < *scicels* m 'cloak' (§502)

scīnan 'to shine' (stv I §517); **scīnað** 3pl pres; **scinon** 3pl pret

scip n 'ship' (§503); **scipa** gpl

scipene ds < *scipen* f 'cattle-shed'

scipes gs < **scip**

scipflotan npl < *scipflota* m 'sailor, pirate' (§§500–1)

sciphere m 'naval force, ship-borne army, crew of warship'

sciphlæsta gpl < *sciphlæst* m 'ship's crew' (§502); **sciphlæstas** apl

scipu n/apl < **scip**; **scipum** dpl

scītan ds < *scīte* f 'sheet, linen cloth' (§§500–1)

scoldon 3pl pret < **sculan**

scome = **scame**

sconcan apl < *sconca* m 'shank, leg' (§§500–1)

scoten past ptc < *scēotan* 'to shoot' (stv II §517)

Scotta gpl < **Scottas** apl 'Scots'; **Scottum** dpl (§502)

scrīðan See §465 and Text 35/703 note

scrūde ds < *scrūd* n 'clothing, garments' (§503)

scrýdað imp pl < *scrýdan* 'to clothe, dress'

scs scribal abbreviation *Sanctus* 'Saint'

scufon 3pl pret < *scūfan* 'to shove, push' (stv II §517)

sculan 'to be obliged to' (§96); **sculon** 1/3 pl pres

scyld m 'shield'

scyle 3s pres subj < **sculan**

scynscaþa m 'demon foe'

scypa = **scypu**

scyppend m 'creator' (§502)

scyppende pres ptc < *scieppan*. See **sceapen**

scyppendes gs < **scyppend**

scypu apl < **scip**

scyrtran apl < *scyrtra* adj 'shorter' (§§505–6)

scyte as < *scyte* m 'shooting, flight' expressing distance (*Guide* §§45–6)

Scyttisc adj 'Scottish'

se (1) dem (a) w noun 'the/that' (b) alone 'that/he/it'; (2) rel 'who'. See §§496, 498, 65

seah 1s pret < *sēon* 'to see' (contr stv V §521)

sealde 3s pret < *sellan* 'to give, betray, deliver to' (wkv §95); **sealdest** 2s pret

sealtum dpl < *sealt* adj 'salt'

searacræftas apl < *searacræft* m 'fraud' (§502)

searað 3s pres < *searian* 'to grow sere, fade' (wkv 2 §526)

searobunden past ptc = adj 'cunningly fastened'

searoþoncelra gpl < *searoponcel* adj 'wise'

searwum dpl < *searo* n 'skill' = adv 'skilfully' (*Guide* §40)

seaxses gs < *seaxs* n 'knife' (§503)

sēcan 'to seek, ask/look for, pursue, visit' (wkv §95)

secg m 'man, hero, warrior' (§502); *secga* gpl

secgan 'to say, explain, tell of, speak, signify' (wkv §97)

secgas npl < **secg**

secgaŏ 3pl pres < **secgan**; **secge** 1s pres

secgean = **secgan**

sefan as < *sefa* m 'mind, spirit, heart' (§§500–1)

sege imp s < **secgan**

seldcymas npl < *seldcyme* m 'seldom/infrequent coming' (*Guide* §§45–6)

sele (1) Text 17 v 12 imp s < *sellan*. See **sealde**; (2) Text 35/713 ds < *sele* m 'hall' (§502)

seledrēam m 'joy of the hall'

selesta super adj 'best'; **selestan** asm (§§505–6)

self 'self'

selflicne st asm < *selflic* adj 'vain' (§§505, 507)

selfum st ds/plm < **self** (§§505, 507)

sellaŏ imp pl < *sellan*. See **sealde**

selran dsn < *selra* adj 'better' (§§505–6)

sendan 'to send (forth), impel, throw, put' (wkv §89); **sendaŏ** 3pl pres; **sende** 3s pret

sēo (1) Text 7/32 = **sǣ**; (2) Text 37/7 = **sīe**; (3) Text 28/9 = **sīen**. See **sīe**; (4) elsewhere = nsf < **se**

sēoc adj 'sick, ill'; **sēoce** st asf (§§505, 507)

seofon num 'seven'; **seofone** nplm (§§505, 507)

seofoþan dsm < *seofoþa* adj 'seventh' (§§505–6); **seofoþe** asn

seolf = **self**; **seolfre** st dsf (§§505, 507)

seolfres gs < *seolfor* n 'silver' (§503)

seondon = **sindon**

seoŏe See Text 33/4 note

set past ptc < *settan* 'to set, put, fix' (wkv §94)

setle ds < *setl* n 'seat, setting (of sun)' (§503)

setlgonge ds < *setlgong* m 'setting, sinking' (§502)

sette 3s pret < *settan*. See **set**; **setton** 3pl pret

sī = **sīe**

sibbegedriht f 'band of retainers/kinsmen'

siblegeru apl < *sibleger* n 'incest' (§503)

sīdan (1) Text 42/370 wk dsf < *sīd* adj 'broad, vast' (§§505–6); (2) ds/apl < *sīde* f 'side' (§§500–1)

sīde (1) Text 34/26 adv 'wide(ly)'; (2) st aplm/f < *sīd* adj 'broad, vast' (§§505, 507)

sīe s pres subj < **bēon/wesan** (§528); **sīen** pl pres subj; **sīg** = **sīe**

sige m 'victory'

sigebēacen n 'emblem of victory, cross'

sigebēam m 'tree of victory, cross' (§502); **sigebēamas** apl; **sigebēame** ds

sigebearn n 'victorious son, Christ'

sigefæstran comp nplm < *sigefæst* adj 'victorious'

sigerōfe st nplm < *sigerōf* adj 'triumphant' (§§505, 507)

sigeþēode ds < *sigeþēod* f 'victorious/powerful nation' (§504)

siglu apl < *sigle* n 'jewel, brooch, necklace' (*Guide* §§45–6)

sigorfæst adj 'victorious'

silf = **self**

silst 2s pres < *sellan*. See **sealde**

sim(b)le adv 'always'

sinc n 'treasure'

sincalda wk nsm < *sincald* adj 'perpetually cold' (§§505–6)

since ds < **sinc**; **sinces** gs

sinchroden ptc = adj 'treasure/jewel-adorned'

sind(on) pl pres < **bēon/wesan** (§528)

sindrum dpl < *sinder* n 'cinder, impurity' (§503)

sing imp s < **singan** 'to sing' (stv III §518)

sīnne asm < *sīn* refl poss 'his own'

sint = **sind(on)**

sio = **sēo** nsf < **se**

sit 3s pres < *sittan* 'to sit, remain, occupy' (§519); **sitte** 2s pres subj

sīþ m 'journey, voyage, occasion, time, experience, departure, death' (§502)

sīþade 3s pret < **sīþian**

sīþes gs < **sīþ**

siŏŏfate ds < *siŏŏfat* m 'journey, expedition' (§502)

sīþian 'to go, travel, wander' (wkv 2 §526)

siþþan (1) adv 'after(wards), hereafter, since, thereupon'; (2) conj 'when, since, after, from the time that, inasmuch as'; (3) prep 'after'

sīŏum dpl < **sīþ**

slǣpe ds < *slǣp* m 'sleep' (§502)

slǣpende pres ptc < *slǣpan* 'to sleep'

slēap 3s pret < *slūpan* 'to glide, slip' (stv II §517)

slēaŏ 3pl pres < *slēan* 'to strike, kill, dash, rush' (contr stv VI §521)

slege ds < *slege* m 'slaying, slaughter' (*Guide* §§45–6)

slīdeŏ 3s pres < *slīdan* 'to lapse, go astray'

slīŏan wk asf < *slīŏe* adj 'dire, cruel' (*Guide* §73)

slōgon 3pl pret < *slēan*. See **slēaŏ**; **slōh** 3s pret

smalost super < *smæl* adj 'narrow, slender, thin, fine'; **smælre** comp nsn

smiþa gpl < *smiþ* m 'smith, craftsman' (§502)

...ãðan 'to cut' (stv I §517)
...*snelness* f 'agility' (§504)
...ubj < *snīwan* 'to snow'
...s < *snoternyss* f 'wisdom' (§504)
...dom'
...Text 28/3–4 note
...pret < **sēcan**; **sōhton** 3pl pret
...d adv 'together'
...a adv 'at once, immediately'; **sōna swā**
conj 'when, as soon as'
song 3s pret < *singan*. See **sing**
songes gs < **sang**
sorge g/ds < *sorg* f 'sorrow, pain, grief' (§504)
sorgfullne st asm < *sorgfull* adj 'sorrowful'
(§§505, 507)
sorgum dpl < *sorg*. See **sorge**
sōð (1) m 'truth' (§502); (2) adj 'true, genuine'
sōðan wk asm < *sōd* adj (§§505–6)
sōðlice adv 'truly, indeed, really, certainly'
sōþra gpl < **sōð** adj
spāw 3s pret < *spīwan* 'to spew, spit' (stv I §517)
spæc 1s pret < **specan**; **spǣcan** 3s pret
spearwa m 'sparrow'
specan 'to speak, say' (stv V §519)
spēd f 'power, riches, wealth' (§504); **spēda** a/gpl
spēddropum dpl < *spēddropa* m 'useful drop, ink' (§§500–1)
spēde apl < **spēd**
spēdig adj 'powerful'
spelbodan apl < *spelboda* m 'messenger' (§§500–1)
spellode 3s pret subj < *spellian* 'to announce, proclaim' (wkv 2 §526)
spellum dpl < *spell* n 'narrative' (§503)
spēone 3s pret subj < *spanan* 'to incite, urge' (stv VII(*a*) §517)
speremon m 'spoorman, tracker'
spīwe 3s pres subj < *spīwan*. See **spāw**
spore ds < *spor* n 'spoor, track' (§503)
sporwreclas See Text 27/11 note
spræc 3s pret < *sprecan*. See **sprǣcon**; **sprǣcan** 3pl pret
sprǣce g/ds < *sprǣc* f 'language, statement, speech, narrative' (§504)
sprǣcon 1pl pret < *sprecan* 'to speak, converse, say, declare' (stv V §519); **sprecende** pres ptc
spycð 3s pres < **specan**
spyrede 3s pret < *spyrian* 'to travel, make a track' (wkv §525)
spyrigean 'to follow (in the footsteps of)'
stala apl < *stalu* f 'stealing, theft' (§504)
standan 'to stand' (stv VI §519)
stāngreopum dpl < *stāngreope* m 'handful of stones' (*Guide* §§45–6)

staþe ds < *staþ* n 'shore, river-bank' (§503)
staþolfæst adj 'fixed, firm'
staþolfæstlice adv 'firmly'
staðulas apl < *staðul* m 'foundation' (§502)
stæfne ds < *stæfn* f 'voice' (§504); **stæfnum** dpl
stænene st nplm < *stænen* adj '(made of) stone' (§§505, 507)
stæppe (1) 3s pres subj; (2) 1s pres < *stæppan* 'to step, go'
stǣr n 'history, narrative'
stēam m 'steam, vapour'
stēape as aplm < *stēap* adj 'steep, high' (§§505, 507)
stede m 'place'
stedefest adj 'steady, firm'
stefn Text 13/212 m 'prow' (§502); Text 36/34 **stefne** ds
stefne Text 51/30 ds < *stefn* m 'stem, trunk, root' (§502)
stellende pres ptc < *stellan* 'to place, set'
steorra m 'star'
stigon 3pl pret < *stīgan* 'to go (up), step' (stv I §517)
stilnesse as < *stilness* f 'stillness, peace' (§504)
stiðmōd adj 'resolute, brave'
stōd 1/3s pret < **standan**; **stōdon** 3pl pret
stōl m 'seat, throne' (§502); **stōle** ds
stondað 3pl pres < **standan**
stōp 3s pret < *steppan* 'to step, go' (stv VI w wk pres §§517, 519)
storm m 'storm, tempest' (§502); **storme** ds
stōw f 'place' (§504); **stōwa** apl; **stōwe** ds; **stōwum** dpl
strang adj 'strong'; **strange** st nplm (§§505, 507); **strangran** apln comp 'stronger'
strǣt f 'street' (§504); **strǣte** a/gs
strēam m 'stream, river, current, flood' (§502); **strēamas** npl; **strēames** gs
strenglicran asm < *strenglicra* adj 'stronger' (§§505–6)
strīðe ds < *strīð* m 'strife, contest' (§502)
strūdunga apl < *strūdung* f 'spoliation, robbery' (§504)
styccemǣlum adv 'here and there'
styric n 'calf'
styrme 3s pres subj < *styrman* 'to storm'
sum 'someone, something, one, a certain'; **suman** dsm; **sume** n/apl; **sume . . . sume** 'some . . . others'
sumera ds < *sumer* m 'summer' (*Guide* §61)
sumere dsf < **sum**; **sumne** asm; **sumon** dsn
sumorlangne st asm < *sumorlang* adj 'summer-long' (§§505, 507)
sumorlida m 'summer army/expedition'
sumre dsf < **sum**; **sumum** dsm/dpl
Sumursǣtum dpl 'the people of Somerset'
suna ds/apl < *sunu*. See **suno**

sund n 'sea, ocean, water'
sundoryrfes gs < *sundoryrfe* m 'private inheritance' (*Guide* §§45–6)
sunnan g/ds < **sunne** f 'sun'
suno npl < *sunu* m 'son' (Guide §61)
sūþ (1) adj 'south'; (2) adv 'south'
sūþan adv 'in/on/from the south'
sūðeweardum st dsn < *sūðeweard* adj 'south(ward), southern' (§§505, 507)
swā (1) adv 'so, thus'; (2) conj (**swā**) **swā** '(just) as', often correl with **swā** adv; Texts 22/10 & 34/2 **swā . . . swā** 'the . . . the'; **swā (. . .) þæt** 'so (. . .) that'; (**swylc**) **swā** w subj 'as if'; **sōna swā** 'as soon as'; **swā þēah** 'however'. I have tried to explain other uses in the Textual Notes
swāf 3pl pret < *swīfan. . . on* 'to intervene' (stv I §517)
swān m 'swineherd, peasant'
swang 3s pret < *swingan* 'to strike' (stv III §518)
swāþēah adv 'however'
swāse st nplf < *swās* adj 'dear, intimate, gentle' (§§505, 507)
swāte ds < *swāt* m 'blood'; **swātes** gs
swātigne st asm < *swātig* adj 'gory, blood-covered' (§§505, 507)
swǣ = **swā**; **swǣ same** adv 'likewise, similarly'
swǣfon 3pl pret < **swefan**
swǣran wk gsf < *swǣr* adj 'sad, grievous, sluggish' (§§505–6)
swǣrbyrde gs < *swǣrbyrd* f 'difficult birth' (§504)
swǣs adj 'dear, intimate, gentle'; **swǣsra** gpl
swǣsendum dpl < *swǣsende* n usually pl 'feast, banquet' (*Guide* §§45–6)
swǣtan 'to bleed, sweat'; **swǣtað** 3pl pres
swæð n 'track'
swealg 3s pret < *swelgan* 'to swallow, devour' (stv III §518)
sweart adj 'black, dark'; **sweartan** wk asm/f (§§505–6)
sweartlast adj 'with black tracks'
swefan 'to slumber, sleep (in death), die' (stv V §517); **swefað** 3pl pres
swefn n 'sleep, dream' (§503); **swefna** gpl
swēg m 'sound'
swelce (1) conj w subj 'as if'; (2) **ēac swelce** 'likewise, moreover'
swelces gs < *swelc* 'such'
swelteð 3s pres < *sweltan*. See **swulton**
swēop 3s pret < *swāpan* 'to sweep, rush' (stv VII(a) §517)
swēor m 'father-in-law' (§502); **swēora** gpl
sweord n 'sword' (§503); **sweorda** gpl; **sweordes** gs; **sweordum** dpl
swēot n 'band, troop'

sweotole adv 'clearly, openly'
swēras npl < *swēr* m 'pillar, column' (§502)
swerige 1s pres < *swerigan* 'to swear'
swēte adj 'sweet' = noun
swētnesse ds < *swētness* f 'sweetness' (§504)
swicdōmas apl < *swicdōm* m 'fraud, deceit, treason' (§502); **swicdōme** ds
swiceð 3s pres < *swīcan* 'to wander, be wanting'
swifta wk nsm < *swift* adj 'swift' (§§505–6); **swiftan** wk npln
swiftnesse ds < *swiftness* f 'speed' (§504)
swiftoste wk asn super < *swift*. See **swifta**; **swiftre** st dsf (§§505, 507); **swiftum** st dsm
swilce (1) conj alone/w subj 'as if'; (2) **swilce . . . ēac** 'likewise, moreover'
swilces gs < *swilc* 'such'; **swilcum** dpl
swin n 'swine'
swingeð 3s pres < *swingan* 'to fly'
swioðole ds < *swioðol* m 'fire, flame' (§502)
swipode 3s pret < *swipian* 'to lash, scourge' (wkv 2 §526)
swīþe adv 'very, much, greatly'
swiðmōd adj 'brave, arrogant'
swiðost adv 'most, especially'
swīðran wk asf comp < *swīð* adj 'powerful'; **on þā swīþran healfe** 'on the right hand'
swiðrode 3s pret < *swiðrian* 'to diminish, abase, subside' (wkv 2 §526)
swōgende pres ptc < *swōgan* 'to resound, roar'
swulton 3pl pret < *sweltan* 'to die, perish' (stv III §518)
swurd = **sweord**
swutol adj 'clear, evident, manifest'
swyftoste wk apln super < *swift* adj 'swift'
swylc swā conj w subj 'as if' Text 19/23
swylce (1) < **swylc** 'such (as)' Text 33/15 apl, Text 41/83 nplm; **swylce . . . swylce** 'such . . . as' Text 10/1249 isn, Text 9/3164 aplf; (2) conj 'as if' w subj Text 40/1; 'as if, like' alone Texts 16 v 22 & 48/803; (3) elsewhere 'also, likewise, moreover'; **swylce ēac** 'likewise, moreover'; **ge swylce** 'and also'
swylteð = **swelteð**
swȳþe adv 'very, much, greatly'; **swȳþor** adv 'more'
sȳ = **sīe**
sylf 'self' (§§505–7); **sylfa** wk nsm; **sylfne** st asm; **sylfre** st g/df; **sylfum** st dsm/dpl
syllic adj 'marvellous, wondrous'; **syllicre** See Text 51/4 note
syluan wk gsf < **sylf**
symble ds < *symbel* n 'feast' (§503)
symle adv 'ever, always'
synd/syndan/syndon pl pres < **bēon/ wesan** (§528)
syndriglice adv 'separately, individually'

203

...sinful' (§§505–7)

...'to sin' (wkv 2 §526)

...f 'injury caused by

...sin' (§504); **synnan** wk apl
...**num** dpl
...*rce* f 'shirt of mail' (§§500–1)

...< *syxta* num 'sixth'
...im 'sixty'
...n = **siþþan**

...n n 'token, sign, portent, evidence, proof'
(§503); **tācne** ds; **tācnum** dpl
tān npl < *tā* f 'toe' (§§500–1)
tǣcð 3s pres < *tǣcan* 'to teach'
tægl m 'tail'
tēah 3s pret < *tēon* 'to pull, drag, lead' (contr
stv II §521)
tēaras apl < *tēar* m 'tear' (§502)
tefore prep 'before'
telg m 'dye, colour'
tellan 'to assign, attribute'
Temes(e) R. Thames
tēode 3s pret < *tēon* 'to create, prepare,
adorn' (wkv like *hīeran* §94)
tēonan ds < *tēona* m 'hurt, reproach, insult'
(§§500–1)
tēoþan dsm < *tēoþa* num 'tenth' (§§505–6);
tēoþe asn
tēð apl < *tōð* m 'teeth' (§§17–18)
ticcen n 'kid, young of goat'
tīd f 'time, period, hour, festal tide' (§504)
tīddege ds < *tīddæg* m 'span of life, lifetime,
final hour' (§502)
tīde a/ds < **tīd**
tigras apl < *tiger* m 'tiger' (§502)
tiid = **tīd**
tilgende pres ptc < *tilian* 'to cultivate, till'
wg; to endeavour, try'; **tilien** 1pl pres subj
tilra gpl < *til* adj 'good'; **tilu** st nsf (§§505,
507)
tīma n 'time, lifetime' (§§500–1); **tō tīman** ds
'on time'
tintreglican wk gsn < *tintreglic* adj 'torment-
ing' (§§505–6)
tīr m 'fame, glory, honour'
tīðienne w **tō** infl inf < *tīðian* 'to grant' wg of
thing, wd of person
tīwes niht 'Monday night'
tō (1) adv 'thither, thereto'; 'too'; 'also,
besides, in addition'; (2) prep wd (place)
'at, alongside, to, towards'; (time) 'at'; (purpose) w infl inf 'to'; (defining) 'for, as'; (3)
prep wg (motion) 'to'; (time) 'at'; (4) on its
use in prep advs and conjs like *tō þǣm* (*þe*),
see the textual notes and §§124–6

tōbrocene st npln past ptc < *tōbrecan* 'to
shatter, violate' (stv IV §517)
tōcyme m 'coming'
tōdæg 'today'
tōdǣlað 3pl pres < *tōdǣlan* 'to divide' (wkv
like *hīeran* §94); **tōdǣled** past ptc;
tōdǣlede st nplf past ptc
tōemnes prep wd 'alongside'
tōfōr 3s pret < *tōfaran* 'to disperse, separate'
(stv VI §517)
tōforan prep wd 'before, in front of'
tōgædere adv 'together'
tōgēanes prep wd 'towards, against' (following the word it governs)
tōgeþēodde 3s pret < *tōgeþēodan* 'to add'
(wkv like *hīeran* §94)
tōmiddes adv 'in the midst'
top m 'ball'
tōrȳpte 3s pret < *tōrȳpan* 'to scratch' (wkv
like *settan* §94)
tōslītað 3pl pres < *tōslītan* 'to tear asunder,
destroy'; **tōslīteð** 3s pres
tōsomne adv 'together'
tōweard prep wd 'towards'
tōweardan wk gsm < *tōweard* adj 'impending, to come, future' (§§505–7); **tōwearde**
st apln; **tōweardra** gpl
treddode 3s pret < *treddian* 'to step, go' (wkv
2 §526)
trēo a/ds < *trēo* n 'tree'
trēow n 'tree'
trymede 3s pret subj < *trymman* 'to prepare,
strengthen, fortify, arm, encourage' (wkv 1
§524); **tō trymmanne** infl inf
tū Text 27/17 = **þū** 'thou'
tū Text 5/45 an < *twēgen*. See **twā**
tuā = **twā**
tuelftan asf < *tuelfta* num 'twelfth' (§§505–6)
tugon 3pl pret < *tēon*. See **tēah**
tūne ds < *tūn* m 'field, farm, village, town,
homestead' (§502)
tungol n 'star'
tūnæ ds < *tūn*. See **tūne**
turfhagan ds < *turfhaga* m 'grassy plot'
(§§500–1)
tuun = *tūn*. See **tūne**
tuxas apl < *tūx/tūsc* m 'tusk' (§502)
twā n/a f/n < *twēgen* num 'two'; **twām** d all
genders; **twēgen** n/am; **twēgra** g all
genders
twēo m 'doubt, uncertainty' (§§500–1);
twēon ds
twēonige 3s pres subj < *twēonigan* 'to be
doubtful' (impers vb wg of thing, wd of person)
tyhð 3s pres < *tēon*. See **tēah**
tȳn num 'ten'
tȳr = **tīr**

tysliað 3s pres < *tyslian* 'to attire' (wkv 2 §526)
tyslunge as < *tyslung* f '(way of) dressing' (§504)

Þ = þæt
þā (1) dem asf or n/apl all genders < **se** (see §64); (2) used as rel, alone or with **þe** (see §65); (3) adv 'then'; (4) conj 'when', of a single completed act in the past. See Text 20/2–10 note. On *þā . . . þā* 'then/when . . . when/then', see §137; **þā gīet** 'yet still also'
þām dsm/n or dpl all genders < **se** (see §§124–6)
þan variant spelling of **þām** or **þon** (see §§124–6)
þanan = þanon
þanc m 'thanks, gratitude'
þancedon 3pl pret < *þancian* 'to thank' (wkv 2 §526)
þanon adv 'thence, from there'
þār = þ̣ær
þāra gpl < **se**
þāre = þ̣ære
þās asf or n/apl all genders < **þes** (see §64)
þæ = þe
þ̣æm variant spelling of **þām** (see §§124–6)
þæne = þone
þænne = þonne
þ̣ær (1) adv 'there, thither, then'; (2) conj 'where, whither, when, (rarely) if'. On correl *þ̣ær . . . þ̣ær*, see §137
þ̣æra = þāra
ð̣æræt adv 'thereat'
þ̣ære g/dsf < **se**
þ̣ærrihte adv 'instantly, immediately'
þ̣ærtō adv 'thereto, thither'
þæs (1) dem gsm/n < **se**; (2) adv 'afterwards, thither, then'; **tō þæs** 'to that point, so'; (3) conj **þæs** (. . .) **þe/þæt** 'when, after, because, since, as, so (. . .) that'
þæt n/asn < **se**. A word of many functions. (1) It is most likely to be dem 'that' w/wo a noun; (2) rel 'that, which, what'; (3) conj '(so) that'. If these do not fit, look for the combination **swā/þæs** (. . .) **þæt** 'so (. . .) that' (§§121, 123) or for one of the prep advs or conjs described in §§124–6
þætte (1) Text 40/18 'that which'; (2) Text 46/510 A disputed idiom; translate 'who'; (3) elsewhere conj = **þæt** 'that'
þæt þe = þætte (3)
þē a/ds < **þū** 'thee'
þē = þȳ
þe (1) indecl rel alone representing all cases & numbers 'who, (to) whom, whose'; (2) rel in combination w **se**. On (1) & (2) see §65; (3) = **þȳ**; (4) in prep conjs (§§124–6); (5) (**þe** . . .) **þe** '(either . . .) or'

þēah (1) adv 'yet, however, nevertheless, moreover' alone and w **swā/hwæþre**; (2) **þēah (þe)** conj 'although'
þearf f 'need'
ðearle adv 'violently, sorely'
þēaw m 'custom' (§502); **þēawas** apl
þec = þē 'thee'
þegenas npl < *þeg(e)n* m 'thane' (§502); **þegna** gpl; **þegnum** dpl
þencan 'to think' (wkv §95)
þenden conj 'while'
ðenode 3s pret < *ðenian* 'to serve' wd (wkv 2 §526)
þēnunge a/ds < *þēnung* f 'service' (§504)
þēod f 'people' (§504)
þēodde 1s pret < *þēodan* 'to subject oneself to' wd (wkv like *hīeran* §94)
þēode Text 46/487 npl < **þēod**. Elsewhere a/g/ds
þēoden m 'ruler, prince, king'
ðēodguman npl < *ðēodguma* m 'man, retainer, warrior' (§§500–1)
þēodscipe m 'people, nation'
ðēodum dpl < **þēod**
þēof m 'thief, robber'
þēos nsf < **þes**
þeossum dsm/dpl < **þes**
þeostorcofan ds < *þeostorcofa* m 'dark chamber' (§§500–1)
þēow m 'servant' (§502); **ðēowe** Text 16 v 31 ds
þēowe Text 31/8 st npl < *þēow* adj 'slave, servile' (§§505, 507)
ðēowian 'to serve, be subject to' (wkv 2 §526); **þēowie** 3s pres subj; **þēowode** 1s pret
þēowum dpl < **þēow**
þes nsm 'this' (§497)
þet = þæt
þī = þȳ
ðicgean 'to eat, consume'
þider adv 'thither'
þihtan See Text 37/24–5 note
þīn gs < **þū** 'thy, thine, of thee' (§494)
þincan 'to seem' (wkv §95); **þinceð** 3s pres; **þincð** 3s pres
þīne asf/npl < **þīn**; **þīnes** gsn
þing n 'thing, possession, circumstance, event' (§503). In our texts this form is n/apl; **þinga** gpl
ðingade 1s pret < **þingian**
þinge ds < **þing**, **mid nānum þinge** 'in no way, not at all'; **þinges** gs; **æniges þinges** 'at all'
þingian 'to intercede (for)' wd (wkv 2 §526)
þingon/þingum dpl < **þing**
þingð = þincð. See **þincan**
ðīnra gpl < **þīn**; **þīnre** gsf; **þīnum** dpl
ðīoda npl < **þēod**

(§497); **þise** = **þisum**
... **ðison** dsn; **ðisse** dsf;
... **es** gsn; **þissum** dsm/n or
...; **þisum** = **þissum**
... **þencan**
... pret < *þolian* 'to suffer, endure'
... 26)
... n < **se** (see §§124–6)
... adv 'thence, from there'
... = **þanc**; **þonces** gs, **Godes þonces**
... by the grace of God'
... **one** asm < **se**
þonne (1) adv 'then'; (2) conj 'when(ever), if'.
See Text 20/2–10 note
þonon = **þonan**
þorfte 1/3s pret < *þurfan* 'to need, have occasion to' (irreg vb *Guide* §130); **þorfton** 3pl
pret
ðoðor m 'ball' (§502); **þoðere** ds
þreanedum dpl < *þreaned* f 'cruel compul-
sion, misery' (§504)
þreat m 'troop, band, oppression, calamity'
(§502); **on þreat** see Text 40/2 note;
þreate ds
þrecwudu m 'spear'
þreo num an/f 'three'; **þreora** gpl
þridda num 'third' (§§505–6); **þriddan** asm;
þridde nsf; **þriddum** dsm
þrim d < *þrie* num 'three'
þritig num 'thirty'
þriwa adv 'thrice'
þrowere m 'sufferer, martyr'
þrowian 'to suffer, die' (wkv 2 §526);
þrowodon 3pl pret
þrowunge ds < *þrowung* f 'suffering, martyrdom, passion' (§504)
þrym(m) m 'glory, majesty, power, troop'
(§502)
þrymlic adj 'mighty, magnificent'
þrymme ds < **þrymm**; **þrymmes** gs
þrymsittendum st dsm < *þrymsittende* adj
'dwelling in glory/heaven' (§§505, 507)
þryttyne num 'thirteen'
þryðswyð adj 'strong, mighty'
þu 'thou' (§494)
þuhte 3s pret < *þyncan* 'to seem' (§95)
þurfe 1s pres < *þurfan*. See **þorfte**
þurh (1) prep wa/g/d 'through' expressing
place, time, cause, instrument, and agent;
(2) adv 'throughout'
þurharn 3s pret < *þurhirnan* 'to run through,
pierce' (stv III §518)
þurhdrifan 3pl pret < *þurhdrifan* 'to drive
through, pierce' (stv I §517)
þurhfleo 3s pres subj < *þurhfleon* 'to fly
through' (contr stv II §521)

þus(s) adv 'thus, in this way'
þusend num 'thousand'; **þusendu** apl
þweale ds < *þweal* n 'bath, bathing-place'
(§503)
þy (1) ism/n < **se**; (2) adv 'then, therefore, for
that reason, (w comp) the/by that'; (3) conj
'since, because'; in prep advs & conjs
§§124–6; **þy . . . þy** 'for that reason/
because . . . because/therefore'; **þy . . . þy**
w comp 'the . . . the'
þy læs (þe) conj 'lest'
þynceð 3s pres < *þyncan*. See **þuhte**; **ðyncð**
3s pres
ðys isn < **þes**; **þysan** dsn; **þyses** gsn
þyslic adj 'such, of this sort'
þyssa gpl < **þes**; **þysse** Text 37/27 perhaps
= **þissum** dsm, elsewhere g/dsf; **þyssere**
dsf; **ðyssum** dsn; **þysum** dsn

Ualentines n 'Valentine'
uhtan ds < *uhte* f 'dawn'
unarimedlico st apln < *unarimedlic* adj
'immeasurable, uncountable' (§§505, 507)
unæþele npl < *unæþele* adj 'not noble'
(*Guide* §73)
unc acc dual < **we** 'us two' (§494); **uncer** g 'of
us two, our', **uncerne** asm 'our'
uncræftan dpl < *uncræft* m 'evil practice'
(§502; *-an* for *-um*)
uncuð adj 'unknown'
undæde as < *undæd* f 'wicked deed, crime'
(§504)
under (1) prep wa/d 'under, among, before,
during'; (2) adv 'beneath, below'
underbeginnenne w **to** infl inf 'to undertake'
underfengan 1pl pret < *underfon* 'to receive,
undergo' (contr stv VII(*a*) §521)
underþeodde 3s pret < *underþeodan* 'to sub-
jugate, subject' (wkv like *hieran* §94)
understandan 'to understand, take note of';
understandað 3pl pres; **Understandað**
imp pl; **understande** 3s pres subj
unearg adj 'bold'
unfæger adj 'ugly, hideous'
unforbærned adj 'unburnt'
unforhtre nsn comp < *unforht* adj 'fearless,
bold'
unfrið m 'breach of peace, enmity, war'
ungefoge adv 'excessively'
ungehirsum adj 'disobedient, rebellious'
ungelæredan wk nplm < *ungelæred* adj 'ig-
norant' (§§505–6)
ungeleaffulnysse gs < *ungeleaffulnyss* f
'unbelief' (§504)
ungelic adj 'unlike, different'; **ungelice** See
Text 40/3 note
ungelymp n 'mishap, misfortune'

ungemetlic adj 'immense, immeasurable'

ungerim m 'countless number'

ungesǣlða npl < *ungesǣlð* f 'trouble, misfortune' (§504)

ungeþuǣrnes f 'discord, disturbance'

ungewittige st npl < *ungewittig* adj 'witless, without understanding' (§§505, 507)

ungewunelic adj 'unusual, strange'

ungrundes gs < *ungrund* adj 'vast'

unhāl adj 'ill, weak'

unhlēowan See Text 46/495 note

unlǣdan wk dsm/wk aplm < *unlǣde* adj 'poor, wretched, miserable, accursed'

unlifgendes gs < *unlifgende* adj 'lifeless' (*Guide* §73)

unlȳtel adj 'great'

unmǣtan wk dsn < *unmǣte* adj 'great, vast' (*Guide* §73)

unnon 3pl pres < *unnan* 'to grant, give' wd (person) wg (thing) (irreg v as *cunnan* §96)

unrǣdes = *unrǣdas* apl < *unrǣd* m 'lack of plan, folly' (§502)

unriht n 'wrong, sin, wickedness' (§503); **unrihta** gpl

unrihtlice adv 'wrongly, wickedly'

unrīm n 'countless number, large host'

unryhtum dpl < *unryht* adj 'wrong, unlawful'

unscrīdde 3s pret < *unscrīdan* 'to undress, strip' (wkv like *hīeran* §94)

unsida apl < *unsidu* m 'bad custom, vice' (*Guide* §61)

unþances gs < *unþanc* m 'displeasure' (§502); **heora unþances** 'against their will'

unþēawum dpl < *unþēaw* m 'vice, sin, fault' (§502)

unwāclīcne st asm < *unwāclīc* adj 'not mean, splendid' (§§505, 507)

unwǣrlice adv 'carelessly'

unwrītere m 'careless scribe'

unwurþað 3s pres < *unwurþian* 'to treat with contempt, dishonour' (wkv 2 §526)

ūp adv 'up, upwards, up stream, inland'

ūpāspringende st nplm pres ptc < *ūpā-springan* 'to spring up, rise' (*Guide* §73)

ūpāstignesse ds < *ūpāstigness* f 'ascension' (§504)

ūpcyme m 'rising, origin, source'

ūphēa nplf < *ūphēah* adj 'lofty' (*Guide* §72)

upp = **ūp**

uppan prep wa/d 'on, upon, above, up to'

uppe adv 'up, above, aloft'

uppon = **uppan**

ūpweard adv 'upwards'

ūra apln < *ūre* 'our' g < *wē* 'our, of us' (§494)

ūs d/a < *wē* 'us' (§494)

ūsic = **ūs**

ūt adv 'out, outside'

utan Text 34 *passim* = **uton**

ūtan Text 25/3 adv 'from outside'

ūte adv 'outside'

ūtfūs adj 'ready/eager to set out'

ūtgonge ds < *ūtgong* m 'departure, exodus' (§502)

uton = *wuton* 1pl pres subj used with inf 'let us'

ūðwitan npl < *ūðwita* m 'scholar, sage' (§§500–1)

uuiþ = **wiþ** prep wa/d 'against'

uuoldon 3pl pret < *willan*. See **woldan**

wā interj wd 'woe to'

wāce wk asn < *wāc* 'weak, frail' (§§505–6); **wācran** wk npl comp

wadan 'to go, stride, advance' (stv VI §517)

wāgon 3pl pret < *wegan* 'to bear, carry' (stv V §517)

Wālas n/aplm 'the Welsh, British' (§502)

waldend = **wealdend**

Wālum dpl < **Wālas**

wambe as < *wamb* f 'belly, stomach'

wang m 'land, plain'

wann 3s pret < **winnan**

wānre st dsf < *wān* adj 'dark, black' (§§505, 507)

was = **wæs**. See **wǣron**

wāst 2s pres < *witan* 'to know' (§96); **wāt** 1/3s pres

waðema gpl < *waðem* m 'wave' (§502)

wæccende pres ptc < *wæccan* 'to be awake, watch'

wǣdla m 'a poor man, beggar'

wǣdum dpl < *wǣd* f 'garment, apparel'

wǣfersȳne ds < *wǣfersȳn* f 'spectacle' (§504)

wǣg m 'wave' (§502); **wǣgas** npl; **wǣge** Text 46/458 ds

wǣge Text 11/2253 n 'cup, flagon'

wǣgholm m 'billowy sea'

wǣglīðendum dpl < *wǣglīðende* m 'seafarer' (*Guide* §§45–6)

wæl n 'slaughter, carnage, battlefield, the slain'

wælbenna Text 46/492 npl < *wælbenn* f explained by editors as meaning either 'deadly wound' or 'deadly bond (of the sea)'

wælcyrian npl < *wælcyrie* f 'sorceress' (§§500–1)

wælfæðmum dpl < *wælfæðm* m 'deadly embrace' (§502)

wælfelda ds < *wælfeld* m 'battlefield' (*Guide* §61)

wælmist m 'deadly mist, mist of death'

wælrēowe npl < *wælrēow* adj 'cruel, savage'

wælstōwe g/ds < *wælstōw* f 'slaughter-place, battlefield' (§504); **āgan wælstōwe geweald** 'to conquer, gain the victory'

wǣnde 3s pret < **wendan**

wǣpen n 'weapon' (§503)

wǣpengewrixles gs < *wǣpengewrixl* n 'hostile encounter' (§503)

wǣpna gpl < **wǣpen**; **wǣpnum** dpl

wǣran = **wǣron**

wǣre Text 48/822 as < *wǣr* f 'covenant' (§504)

wǣre elsewhere 3s pret subj < **wesan** (§528)

wǣrlice adv 'carefully'

wǣron/wǣrun pl pret < **wesan** (§528); **wǣs** 1/3s pret

wǣstme ds < *wǣstm* m 'form, stature' (§502)

wǣtan ds < *wǣta* m 'moisture, blood' (§§500-1)

wǣter n 'water, sea' (§503); **wǣtere** ds; **wǣteres** gs; **wǣtre** ds

wǣtte 3s pret < *wǣtan* 'to wet, moisten' (wkv like *settan* §94)

wǣ̆ōde 3s pret < *wǣ̆ōan* 'to hunt' (wkv like *hīeran* §94)

wē 'we' (§494)

Wēalas = **Wālas**

wealda ds < *weald* m 'forest' (*Guide* §61)

wealdend m 'ruler, lord, king' (§502); **wealdendes** gs. In our Texts, refers to God or Christ

wealhstodas apl < *wealhstod* m 'translator' (§502)

weall m 'wall' (§502); **weallas** npl

weallendan wk asm pres ptc < *weallan* 'to surge, boil' (§§505-6)

weallfæsten n 'rampart, fortress' (§503). In Text 46/484 npl

weard m 'guardian, protector'

weardaō 3s pres < *weardian* 'to guard, possess, occupy, remain in, keep to' (wkv 2 §526); **weardiaō** 3pl pres; **weardigan** inf; **weardode** 3s pret

wearp 3s pret < *weorpan* 'to throw' (stv III §518)

wearþ 1/3s pret < **weorþan**

weaxende pres ptc < *weaxan* 'to grow'; **weaxeō** 3s pres

weccan 'to kindle'

wed(d) n/apl < *wed(d)* n 'pledge, vow' (§503)

wēdde 3s pret < *wēdan* 'to rage, become mad' (wkv like *hīeran* §94)

weder n 'weather, wind, storm' (§503)

Wedera, Wedra gpl 'of the Weders/Geats'

wedre ds < **weder**

weg m 'way, path, journey' (§502); **wegas** npl

wege 3s pres subj < *wegan*. See **wāgon**

weges gs < **weg**; **wegum** dpl

wel adv 'well, very, fully'

welan as < *wela* m 'wealth' (§§500-1)

welig adj 'wealthy, prosperous'

wēmend m 'herald, one who declares'

wēn f 'expectation' (§504); **wēna** npl. See Text 40/13 note

wendan 'to turn, go, change, translate' (wkv like *sendan* §89); **wende** 3s pret; **wenden** 1pl pres subj; **wendon** Text 24/19, 21, 23 3pl pret

wēndon Text 24/14 & Text 15/10 3pl pret < *wēnan* 'to think' (wkv like *hīeran* §94)

wēnum dpl < **wēn**

weofode ds < *weofod* n 'altar' (§503)

wēollon 3pl pret < *weallan* 'to gush, seethe' (stv VII(*a*) §517)

weorc n 'work, task, deed, affliction, pain' (§503). This form can be n/as or pl; **weorce** ds; **weorces** gs

weorod n 'army, company, band, host' (§503); **weoroda** gpl; **weorode** ds; **weorodum** dpl

weorō adj 'worthy, honoured, dear'

weorþan 'to become, be, happen, come to pass' (stv III §§513, 516); **weorōe** Text 42/373 3s pres subj

weorþe Text 19/31 adj 'worth, worthy, deserving of'

weorþe Text 34/12 ds < *weorþ* n 'money, price' (§503)

weorþeō 3s pres < **weorþan**

weorōgeornra gpl < *weorōgeorn* adj 'high-souled, worthy, of good intentions' (§§505-7)

weorōiaō imp pl < *weorōian* 'to worship, honour, praise' (wkv 2 §526)

weorōlice adv 'worthily, honourably'

weorōodon 3pl pret < *weorōian*. See **weorōiaō**

weorþunge ds < *weorþung* f 'repute, honour' (§504)

weorude ds < **weorod**

weoruldhāde ds < *weoruldhād* m 'secular life' (§502)

wēpan 'to weep'

wer m 'man, husband, warrior' (§502); **wera** gpl; **weras** n/apl

werbēamas apl < *werbēam* m 'protecting barrier' (§502)

weres gs < **wer**

wergas apl < *werg* m 'criminal' (§502)

wērig adj 'weary'

werod = *weorod*. In Text 17 v. 25 translates Lat *chorus* 'choral dance, band of dancers and singers'

werode 3s pret < *werian* 'to defend' (wkv 2 §526)

wes Text 7/2 = **wǣs** 3s pret. See **wǣron**

wesan 'to be' (§528)

Wesseaxe 'the West Saxons' (*Guide* §§45-6); **Wesseaxna** gpl; **Wesseaxnum** dpl

west adv 'west, westwards'

wēste adj 'waste, uninhabited'

wēstne ds < *wēsten* f 'desert, wilderness' (§504)

Westseaxne 'the West Saxons' (*Guide* §§45– 6); Westseaxna gpl; Westseaxum dpl; Westsex(e)na gpl

Westwālas 'the West Welsh, the Cornish, Cornwall'

westweard adv 'westwards'

wexende = weaxende

weðeras npl < *weðer* m 'ram' (§502)

wīc n 'dwelling-place, habitation' (§503). This form can be n/as or pl

wiccan npl < *wicce* f 'witch' (§§500–1)

wīciað 3pl pres < *wīcian* 'to dwell, encamp' (wkv 2 §526)

wicon 3pl pret < *wīcan* 'to give way, collapse' (stv I §517)

wīctūnum dpl < *wīctūn* m 'court' (§502)

wicum dpl < wīc. In pl, 'fortress, entrenchments'

wide adv 'wide, widely'

widlāstum See Text 40/9 note

widsīð m 'long journey'

wīf n 'woman, lady, wife' (§503). This form can be n/as or pl

wifman, wifmon m 'woman, female servant'

wīfum dpl < wīf

wīg n 'war, battle' (§503)

wigbord npl < *wīgbord* n 'shield' (§503)

wigend indecl npl < *wigend* m 'warrior'

wiges gs < wīg

wīgfruman ds < *wīgfruma* m 'war-chief' (§§500–1)

wigges gs < wīg

wīgsmiðas npl < *wīgsmið* m 'warrior' (§502)

wihtæ adv 'at all'

Wihte ēalond 'the Isle of Wight'

Wihtlande ds 'the Isle of Wight'

wiites gs < *wiite/wīte* n 'punishment, torment' (*Guide* §§45–6)

wilde st nplm/asn < *wilde* adj 'wild, untamed, uncultivated' (*Guide* §73)

wildēor npl < *wil(d)dēor* n 'wild beast' (§503)

wile 3s pres < *willan*. See willað

wilfægen adj 'joyful'

Wilisce st aplm < *Wilisc* adj 'Welsh' (§§505, 507)

willan a/ds < *willa* m 'will, wish, joy' (§§500– 1)

willað 3pl pres < *willan* 'to wish, desire' (§89); willæ 3s pres subj; wille 1s pres/3s pres subj

willgifa m 'gracious giver, ruler'

wilna gpl < *willa*. See willan

wilnunga ds < *wilnung* f 'desire' (§504)

wilsīð m 'wished-for journey'

wind m 'wind' (§502); winde ds

wine Text 38/50 m 'friend, lord'

wine Text 45/1 ds < *wīn* n 'wine' (§503)

winnan 'to trouble oneself, toil, suffer, fight, contend, conquer' (stv III §518); winnende pres ptc

winreced n 'wine-hall'

winter n 'winter' (§503). This form can be n/as or pl; in the latter it can often be translated 'years'

wintersetl n 'winter-quarters'

wintertīde ds < *wintertīd* f 'winter-time' (§504)

wintra ds/gpl < winter (*Guide* §61); wintre Text 6/7 gpl; wintres gs

wiotan npl < *wiota* m 'wise man, councillor' (§§500–1); wiotena gpl

wiotonne w tō infl inf < *witan* 'to know' (§96)

wīre ds < *wīr* m '(ornamental) wire' (§502)

wisan as < *wīse* f 'way, custom, manner' (§§500–1)

wīsdōm m 'wisdom'

wīse st aplm < *wīs* adj 'wise, learned' (§§505, 507)

wislic adj 'wise, prudent'

wislice adv 'certainly, for sure'

wisse = wiste

wiste 3s pret < *witan* 'to know' (§96)

wistfylle gs < *wistfyllu* f 'fill of feasting' (§504)

wiston 3pl pret < *witan* 'to know' (§96)

wit 'we two' (§494)

wita m 'wise man, councillor' (§§500–1)

wītan Text 28/4 See note

witan Text 34/11, 18 1pl pres < *witan* 'to know' (§96); elsewhere npl < wita

wīte Text 14/17 3s pres subj < *wītan* 'to blame'; elsewhere n 'punishment'

witena gpl < wita

witlēas adj 'witless, foolish'

witodlice adv 'verily, undoubtedly, indeed, for sure'

witodre See Text 46/472 note

witrod See Text 46/492 note

witum dpl < wita

wiþ prep (1) wa/d 'towards, against, in return for, from, near, by, at, besides'; (2) wg 'towards, to, at, against'; (3) Text 7/19 wið þām þe 'on condition that'

wiðcwæð 3s pres < *wiðcweþan* 'to refuse' (stv V §§97, 515)

wiðmetenesse ds < *wiðmeteness* f 'comparison' (§504)

wiðsacan 'to abandon, renounce'

wlanc adj 'proud, stately, arrogant'; wlance st npl (§§505, 507)

wlitig adj 'radiant, comely'

wlonce st npl < wlanc (§§505, 507)

wōd 3s pret < wadan

wōge ds < wōh

wōh n 'error, mistake' (§503)

wolcnum dpl < *wolcen* n 'cloud' (§503). In pl 'sky'

woldan 3pl pret < *willan* 'to wish, desire' (§89); **wolde** 3s pret; **woldon** 3pl pret

wommum dpl < *womm* m 'sin, iniquity' (§502)

won 3s pret < **winnan; wonn** 1s pret

wōp m 'weeping, lamentation' (§502); **wōpe** ds

worc = weorc

word n 'word, speech, command, report' (§503). This form can be n/as or pl; **worda** gpl

wordbēotunga as < *wordbēotung* f 'promise' (§504)

wordes gs < **word; wordum** dpl

worhtan 3pl pret < **wyrcan; worhte** 3s pret

world, worold f 'world' (§504); **worolde** ds

woroldrīce ds < *woroldrīce* n 'earthly kingdom' (*Guide* §§45–6)

woroldstrūderas npl < *woruldstrūdere* m 'robber, spoliator' (*Guide* §§45–6)

worpod past ptc < *worpian* 'to pelt, stone' (wkv 2 §526)

woruld = world; worulde ds

woruldstrenga gpl < *woruldstrengu* f 'world-strength, physical strength' (§504)

wrāh 3s pret < *wrēon* 'to cover, hide' (contr stv I §521)

wrāþe adv 'fiercely'

wrāþum st dsm < *wrāþ* adj 'hostile', as noun (§§505, 507)

wræc 3s pret < *wrecan* 'to avenge, utter' (stv V §517)

wræcfullum st dsn < *wræcfull* adj 'wretched, miserable' (§§505, 507)

wræclice adv 'abroad', "into a far country"'

wræcsīþa gpl < *wræcsīþ* m 'journey of exile or peril' (§502); **wræcsīþas** apl

wrætlic adj 'artistic, elegant, splendid, wondrous'

wrece 1s pres < *wrecan*. See **wræc**

wrīteras apl < *wrītere* m 'writer, scribe, author' (*Guide* §§45–6); **wrītere** ds

wrȳ 3s pres subj < *wrēon*. See **wrāh**

wucan ds/apl < *wuce* f 'week' (§§500–1); **wucena** gpl; **wucum** dpl

wuda ds < *wudu* m 'wood' (*Guide* §61)

wudurēc m 'wood-smoke'

wudutrēow n 'forest tree'

wuldor n 'glory, honour, praise, thanks' (§503)

Wuldorfæder m 'Father of Glory, God'

wuldorgesteald npln 'splendid treasures' (§503)

wuldre ds < **wuldor; wuldres** gs

wulf m 'wolf'

Wulfes gs 'of Wulf, Wulf's'

wulfheafedtrēo n 'gallows, cross'

wulle a/ds < *wull* f 'wool' (§504)

wunade 3s pret < *wunian*. See **wunedon**

wunden past ptc < *windan* 'to twist, curl, eddy' (stv III §518)

wundenlocc adj 'with braided locks'

wundenstefna m '(ship with) curved prow'

wundon 3pl pret < *windan*. See **wunden**

wundor n 'wonder, miracle, marvel' (§503). This form can be n/as or pl

wundorlic adj 'wonderful, glorious'

wundra gpl < **wundor**

wundrade 1s pret < *wundrian* 'to wonder'

wundrunge ds < *wundrung* f 'wonder, astonishment' (§504)

wundum dpl < *wund* f 'wound'

wunedon 3pl pret < *wunian* 'to inhabit, dwell (in), remain, occupy' (wkv §§525–6); **wuniaðˇ** 3pl pres; **wunigan** inf

wunnon 3pl pret < **winnan**

wunode 3s pret < *wunian*. See **wunedon**

wurdon 3pl pret < **weorþan; wurþan** inf

wurðfull adj 'worthy, honoured, good'; **wurðfullan** wk dsn (-*an* probably = -*um* §§505–7)

wurðlicum st dsn < *wurðlic* adj 'honoured, exalted' (§§505, 507)

wurðscipe ds < *wurðscipe* m 'honour, dignity' (*Guide* §§45–6)

wyllað 3pl pres < *willan*. See **willað; wylle** Text 51/1 1s pres, Text 32/26 3s pres subj

wyn f 'joy, delight, rapture'

wynbēam m 'tree of gladness, holy cross'

wynlicran comp apln < *wynlic* adj 'pleasant, beautiful, joyful' (§§505–6)

wynna gpl < **wyn; wynnum** dpl

wynsum adj 'pleasant, delightful, joyful'

wyrcan, wyrcean 'to do, perform, build, construct' (wkv §95)

wyrd f 'fate' (§504). See General Index *sv wyrd;* **wyrda** gpl

wyrndon 3pl pret < *wyrnan* 'to refuse' wd (person) wg (thing) (wkv like *hīeran* §94)

wyrsa comp adj 'worse' (§§505–6); **wyrse** nsn

Wyrtgeorne ds 'Wyrtgeorn'

wyrð 3s pres < **weorþan**

wyrþe adj 'worthy, capable, fit' (*Guide* §73); **wyrðes** gs

wyruldcyninga gpl < *woruldcyning* m 'earthly king' (§502)

wyste 3s pret < *witan* 'to know' (§96)

wytum dpl < *wita* 'wise man, councillor' (§§500–1)

ȳcan 'to increase, cause to grow'; **ȳcað** 3pl pres

ȳfel n 'evil, harm' (§503)

ȳfelan wk nplm < *ȳfel* adj 'evil, wicked' (§§505–6)

ȳfele ds < **ȳfel** n

ȳfelian 'to grow worse'

ȳfle st npln < *ȳfel* adj 'evil, wicked' (§§505, 507)

ylcan oblique case < *ylca* adj 'same' (§§505–6)

yld f 'age, old age' (§504); **ylde** g/ds; **yldo** alternative ns

yldra comp adj 'elder' (§§505–6); **yldran** apl

yldum dpl < *ylde* npl 'men' (*Guide* §§45–6)

ylcan = **ylcan**

ymb prep wa (1) place 'at, around, near'; (2) time 'at, after', *not* 'about'; (3) 'concerning, about'

ymban prep wa 'after'

ymbclypte 3s pret < *ymbclyppan* 'to embrace, clasp' (wkv like *settan* §94)

ymbe = **ymb**

ymbhæfd past ptc < *ymbhabban* 'to surround' (§527)

ymbsittendan apl < *ymbsittenda* m 'one sitting near, by-sitter (!)' (§§500–1)

yppinge npl < *ypping* f 'accumulation, mass' (§504)

yrfe n 'property'

yrmð f 'crime, reproach, misery' (§504); **yrmþa** gpl

yrn imp s < *yrnan* 'to run, hasten'; **yrnende** nsm pres ptc; **yrnendum** dsn pres ptc

yrre (1) Text 46/506 adj 'angry'; (2) elsewhere n 'anger'

yrremōd adj 'angry, wrathful'

ys = **is**

Ysrahela gpl 'of the Israelites'

ȳð f 'wave, water' (§504); **ȳða** gpl

ȳþelice adv 'easily'

ȳþgesēne adj 'easily seen, in abundance'

ȳþlāde npl < *ȳþlād* f 'way across the waves, voyage' (§504)

ȳðum dpl < **ȳð**

ȳwe 3s pres subj < *ȳwan* 'to reveal, disclose'

Grammatical and Lexical Index

Entries in roman or arabic figures refer to sections unless preceded by p(p).

Alphabetization: æ is alphabetized separately, following *a*; þ and ð will be found together under þ, following *t*.

This Index does not include references to merely passing mentions.

All Old English (OE) phenomena will be found under the entry 'Old English', with cross-references only when they seem necessary.

General Index

Entries in roman or arabic figures refer to sections unless preceded by p(p).

Alphabetization: æ is alphabetized separately, following *a*; þ follows *t*.

This Index does not include references to merely passing mentions of persons, places, or things. Only the most important names in §§181–8 are indexed.

For entries concerned with poetry and prose, see initially 'poetry, Old English' and 'prose, Old English', respectively.

An attempt to index all references to individual poems and prose texts had to be abandoned for reasons of space.